HANDBOOKS

CHARLESTON & SAVANNAH

JIM MOREKIS

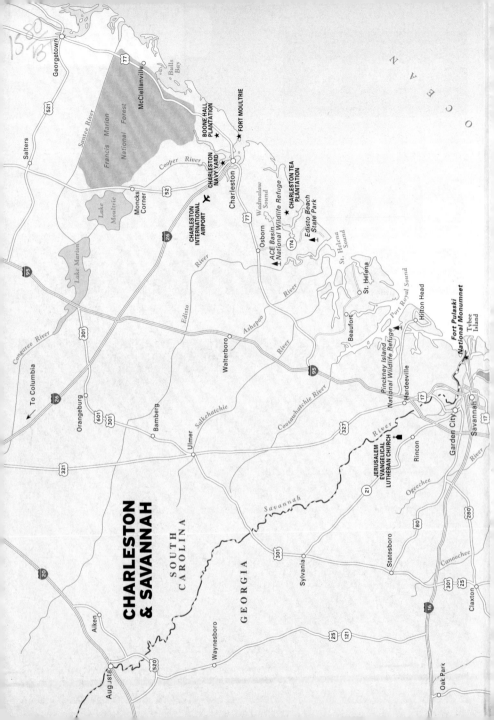

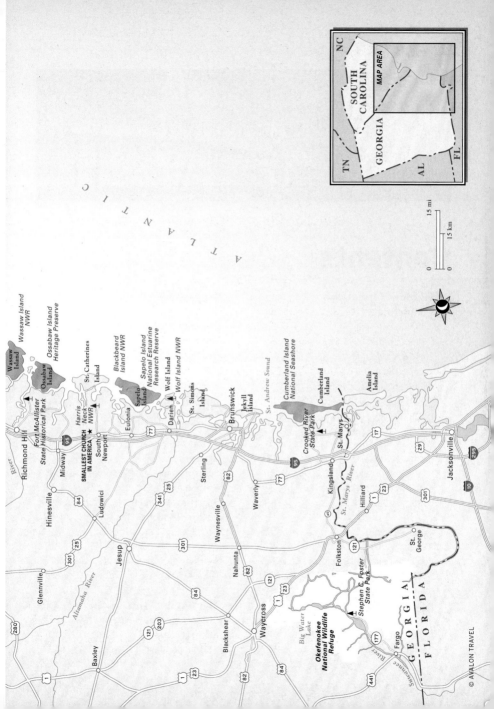

Contents

Discover Charleston & Savannah

As more and more people discover the subtle, compelling charms of these two Southern gems, the inevitable comparisons begin. Stereotypes abound, such as the famous adage "In Charleston they ask what your mother's maiden name is, and in Savannah they ask what you're drinking." But the truth is that Savannah can be just as obsessed with arcane genealogy, and anyone who's ever spent a weekend night in downtown Charleston knows that city is no stranger to a carousing good time.

The key difference between the two is actually physical. Charleston's charms are more serendipitous, its architecture more Caribbean. The compact, winding downtown means a new surprise awaits you around every corner. That's the magic of Charleston. Savannah, with its more spacious downtown, has more room to breathe, to walk, and to stretch out. And there are those matchless, tidy squares, still studied as marvels of urban design. Savannah's classically Anglophilic architecture tends more toward the stately.

While both cities love a good time, Charleston—with its vast selection of nationally renowned restaurants—is definitely more of a foodie's paradise. Savannah, on the other hand—with its unusual "to-go cup" law allowing open containers of alcoholic beverages on the street—loves nothing more than a boisterous party.

Perhaps we should be talking instead about the things that tie the two together. Charleston and Savannah share a parallel history; stubborn individuality and defiance against the norm have been constants, as evidenced by their key roles in the American Revolution and the Civil War.

The entire area shares in common a rare natural beauty, with the South Carolina Lowcountry and the Georgia coast together comprising the largest contiguous salt marsh in the world and one of the most unique ecosystems on the planet. Kayakers are at home paddling in the blackwater of the ACE Basin or the vast Okefenokee Swamp. Beachgoers are often amazed at the underrated quality of the area's serene strands.

Most of all, however, the greatest treasure of this region is its people. The folks down here love a good story, a good conversation, and a good laugh. Indeed, it's one of America's enduring ironies that deep in the heart of our most conservative region lie some of our most fun-loving cities. New Orleans heads the list, of course, but Charleston and Savannah are hard on its heels. It's not just the fabled Southern hospitality; it's a joie de vivre born out of great weather and proximity to the ever-invigorating water of the rivers, marshes, and ocean.

Planning Your Trip

▶ WHERE TO GO

Charleston

One of America's oldest cities and an early national center of arts and culture, Charleston's legendary taste for the high life is matched by its forward-thinking outlook. The birthplace of the Civil War is not just a city of museums resting on its historic laurels. Situated on a hallowed spit of land known as "the peninsula," the Holy City is now a vibrant, creative hub of the New South.

Beaufort and the Lowcountry

The Lowcountry's mossy, laid-back pace belies its former status as the heart of American plantation culture and the original cradle of secession. Today it is a mix of history (Beaufort and Bluffton), natural beauty (the ACE Basin), resort development (Hilton Head), military bases (Parris Island), and relaxed beaches (Edisto and Hunting Islands).

Savannah

Surprisingly cosmopolitan for a Deep South city, Savannah's quirky hedonism permeates any visit. The brainchild of General James Oglethorpe, the city's layout is studied even today as a masterpiece of urban design. Whether you're admiring an antebellum home from the cotton era or enjoying the sea breeze and a cocktail out on Tybee Island, a sense of fun imbues all parts of life here.

The Golden Isles

Georgia's Golden Isles are home to one-third of the East Coast's salt marsh, and their natural beauty is a testament to the Gilded Age millionaires who kept the area largely undeveloped over the years. Even today, this region evokes a timeless mystique redolent of Spanish missions, Native American shell ring ceremonies, insular but friendly shrimping communities, and lonely English outposts.

IF YOU HAVE...

"Gracie" sculpture in Bonaventure Cemetery, Savannah

- **THREE DAYS:** Charleston, Beaufort, and Savannah.
- **FIVE DAYS:** Add Edisto Island, Hunting Island, Bluffton, and Hilton Head Island.
- **ONE WEEK:** Add the ACE Basin, Jekyll Island, and St. Simons Island.
- **TEN DAYS:** Add Cumberland Island and the Okefenokee Swamp.

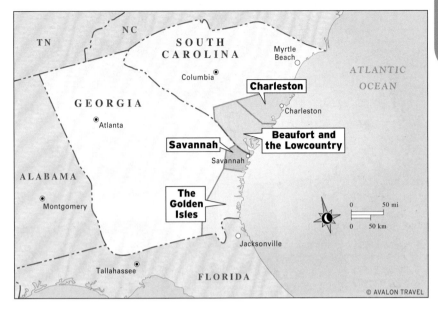

▶ WHEN TO GO

Springtime is for lovers, and it's no coincidence that springtime is when most love affairs with the region begin. Unless you have severe pollen allergies—not a trivial concern given the literal explosion of plant life at this time—you should try to experience this area at its peak of natural beauty during the magical period from mid-March to mid-May. Not surprisingly, lodging is the most expensive and most difficult to secure at that time.

The hardest time to get a room in Charleston is during Spoleto from Memorial Day through mid-June. Hilton Head's busiest time is during the RBC Heritage golf tournament in mid-April. Savannah's tricky time of year is the St. Patrick's Day celebration, a multiday event clustering around March 17. While last-minute cancellations are always possible, the only real guarantee is to secure reservations as far in advance as possible (a full year in advance is not unusual for these peak times).

Activity here slows down noticeably in July and August. But overall, summertime in the South gets a bad rap and is often not appreciably worse than summers north of the Mason–Dixon Line—though it's certainly more humid.

My favorite time of year on the southeastern coast is the middle of November, when the tourist crush noticeably subsides. Not only are the days delightful and the nights crisp (but not frigid), you can get a room at a good price.

What to Take

Unless you're coming in the winter to take advantage of lower rates or to enjoy the copious seasonal cheer, there's not much need

Charleston's Rainbow Row

for a heavy jacket. A sweater or windbreaker will do fine for chillier days. Also note that the ocean and the larger rivers can generate some surprisingly crisp breezes, even on what otherwise might be a warm day.

Because of the area's temperate climate, perspiration is likely to be a constant travel companion; pack accordingly. Whatever you wear, stay with natural fabrics such as cotton.

The humidity and generally warm weather combine for a miserable experience with polyester and other synthetic fabrics.

Unless you're coming in the hottest days of summer or the coldest part of winter—both unlikely scenarios—plan on a trip to a drugstore or supermarket to buy some bug spray or Skin So Soft, an Avon product that also keeps away the gnats.

Explore Charleston & Savannah

► THE BEST OF CHARLESTON AND SAVANNAH

Both cities share an abiding respect for social manners and mores, for history, for making money, and for good food and strong drink. They differ in outlook: Charleston has one well-shod foot firmly in the global future, whereas Savannah tends to be more insular. The difference is also one of scale: Savannah's downtown is bigger and has more room to breathe and stretch out, whereas Charleston's charms are more compact and serendipitous. This "Best of" tour will allow you to come to your own conclusions.

Day 1

Begin your journey in Charleston, the Holy City, named not for its piety but for the steeples in its skyline. First, feel the pulse of the city by going to its bustling heart, Marion Square. Maybe do a little shopping on King Street and at Old City Market afterward. Take a sunset stroll around the Battery and admire Rainbow Row before diving right into a great meal at one of the city's fine restaurants.

Day 2

Today you put your historian's hat on and visit one of Charleston's great house museums, such as the Aiken-Rhett House or the Edmondston-Alston House. Have a hearty Southern-style lunch, then take an afternoon trip to Fort

Bonaventure Cemetery

scenic garden at the Owens-Thomas House

the Ernest F. Hollings ACE Basin National Wildlife Refuge

Sumter. After another fantastic Charleston dinner, take a stroll or carriage ride through the French Quarter to close the evening.

Day 3

After a hearty breakfast, head over the Ashley River to gorgeous Middleton Place, where you'll tour the gardens. Then stop at nearby Drayton Hall and see one of the oldest and best-preserved plantation homes in the nation. Head on into Beaufort and spend the afternoon walking around the beautifully preserved historic district.

Day 4

Go over the bridge to St. Helena Island and visit historic Penn Center. From there, drive on to nearby Hunting Island State Park, where you can climb the lighthouse and enjoy the beach. On the way to Savannah, make a late afternoon stop in Old Bluffton to shop for art, see the beautiful Church of the Cross on the May

River, and have a light dinner. Check into a cute B&B in Savannah and relax for the night, maybe stopping in a pub for a pint or two.

Day 5

Hit downtown Savannah hard today, starting with a walk down River Street. Then enjoy the aesthetic charms of the two adjacent museums, one traditional and one modern, comprising the Telfair Museums. Tour the exquisite Owens-Thomas House Museum and then take a walk through the squares, visiting the Cathedral of St. John the Baptist in Lafayette Square and the Mercer-Williams House on Monterey Square.

Day 6

On your way out to Tybee Island, stop for a walk through amazing Bonaventure Cemetery and pay your respects to native son Johnny Mercer. Then hit scenic and historically important Fort Pulaski National

SOUTHERN COOKING: HIGH-STYLE AND HOME-STYLE

FRESH SEAFOOD

The best seafood places put a premium on freshly harvested fish and shellfish.

- **Bowens Island Restaurant,** Charleston–Gloriously unpretentious.
- **Desposito's,** Savannah–Shrimp and oysters dockside.
- **Red Fish,** Hilton Head Island–Stylish but always fresh.
- **Saltus River Grill,** Beaufort–Meeting and eating place.
- **Speed's Kitchen,** Shellman Bluff–Delicacies right off the boat.
- **Old School Diner,** Harris Neck–Simple seafood in an eccentric environment.

NEW SOUTHERN

The area is home to some adventurous chefs offering an updated take on Lowcountry classics.

- **Elizabeth on 37th,** Savannah–Still Savannah's premier fine dining spot.
- **FIG,** Charleston–Three words: tomato tarte tatin.
- **McCrady's,** Charleston–Chef Sean Brock's creations are almost too good to be true.
- **Sapphire Grill,** Savannah–Closest thing to a Charleston restaurant in Savannah.
- **Tristan,** Charleston–Traditional favorites in a nontraditional interior.

CLASSIC SOUTHERN

Your best bets for fine old-school Southern cooking:

- **Gullah Grub,** St. Helena Island–Lowcountry home-cooking at its most real.
- **Hominy Grill,** Charleston–Comfort-food hit with locals and visitors alike.
- **See Wee Restaurant,** Charleston–Possibly the best she-crab soup on the planet.
- **Dixie Supply Cafe and Bakery,** Charleston–Diner-style brunch faves.

- **Mrs. Wilkes' Dining Room,** Savannah–Old-school "pass the plate" community seating in a historic home.

BARBECUE

The pleasures of the pig are never far away in this region. Here are the best coastal 'cue joints:

- **Angel's BBQ,** Savannah–Hipsters do 'cue too.
- **Fiery Ron's Home Team BBQ,** Charleston–My favorite barbecue spot in the world, believe it or not.
- **JB's Smokeshack,** Charleston–Lowcountry classic on James Island.
- **Georgia Pig,** Brunswick–Going old school off U.S. 17.
- **Po Pigs Bo-B-Q,** Edisto Island–Great 'cue on a friendly island.

Fiery Ron's Home Team BBQ in Charleston

Fort Sumter, where the Civil War began

the Altamaha River

Monument. Scoot on into Tybee and take a climb to the top of the Tybee Lighthouse before dinner.

Day 7

Drive down scenic U.S. 17 through the Altamaha River estuary and stop by historic Hofwyl-Broadfield Plantation, near Brunswick, for an authentic glimpse at an old rice plantation. Go over the causeway and enjoy the afternoon at The Village on St. Simons Island, with a visit to historic Fort Frederica National Monument.

Day 8

This morning, head to the Jekyll Island Historic District. Tour the grounds and have lunch at any of the great restaurants on-site. Rent a bike and pedal up to the Clam Creek Picnic Area, checking out the Horton House Tabby Ruins along the way. Ride on the sand to Driftwood Beach and relax awhile.

Day 9

This morning, drive to St. Marys and have a walk around the cute little downtown area before heading out on the ferry to Cumberland Island National Seashore for a full day of biking or hiking the many trails among the ruins and dunes.

Day 10

Make the drive into Folkston on to the Suwannee Canal Recreation Area at Okefenokee National Wildlife Refuge. Take a guided tour up and down the blackwater canal, or walk the trails out to the swamp's prairie vistas and drink in this unique natural beauty.

COASTAL CRUISING ON U.S. 17

Fans of retro Americana and roadside kitsch will find a treasure trove of down-home sites along the old Coastal Highway, now known as U.S. 17. Before the arrival of the interstate highway system, U.S. 17 was by far the most-traveled route in the region. While now just a shadow of its former self, it is still a vital roadway and contains a lot of interesting, little-known history. Here's a look at some of the highlights, beginning just north of Charleston and ending at Brunswick, Georgia.

- **Sweetgrass Baskets:** A stretch of U.S. 17 in Mt. Pleasant north of Charleston has been dubbed the "Sweetgrass Basket Makers Highway" in honor of the many wooden stalls along its length hosting local African American artisans selling their homemade sweetgrass baskets, a centuries-old tradition with African roots.

- **Arthur Ravenel Jr. Bridge:** The longest cable-stayed bridge in the western hemisphere joins Mt. Pleasant with Charleston proper. It has a pedestrian and bike lane too.

- **Coburg Cow:** This nearly century-old dairy advertisement—a slowly rotating milk cow—was once near pastureland outside city limits. Find it in West Ashley on the portion of U.S. 17 known as the "Savannah Highway," just west of Charleston.

- **Old Sheldon Church:** A very short drive off U.S. 17, the ruins of the Old Sheldon Church—burned by both the British during the Revolution and the Yankees during the Civil War—are huge, stark, and poignant. Going south on U.S. 17, take a right onto Old Sheldon Church Road.

- **Firework Stands:** At the intersection of U.S. 17 and I-95 at Hardeeville you'll find many garish, colorful stores selling enough fireworks to blow you to the moon and back.

- **Keller's Flea Market:** South of Savannah on U.S. 17, at the intersection with Highway 204 (Abercorn Extension), find this classic rambling and friendly Southern flea market. Look for the statue of the hat-wearing cow out front.

- **Midway Church:** In the Liberty County town of Midway is this beautiful 1792 church, whose congregation once boasted two of Georgia's signers of the Declaration of Independence. Don't miss the historic cemetery across the street.

- **Smallest Church in North America:** On the side of the road near South Newport find the miniscule and charming Memory Park Christ Chapel, erected in 1950.

- **Butler Island Plantation Ruins:** Just south of Darien, Georgia, on the west side of U.S. 17, find this tall chimney—the only surviving remnant of the Butler plantation. English actress Fanny Kemble, who married a Butler heir, wrote the first influential abolitionist work *Journal of a Residence on a Georgian Plantation* after witnessing the miserable life of the slaves who worked here. (Strangely, the nearby historical marker makes no mention of this.)

- **Brunswick Stewpot:** Allegedly the container in which the first batch of Brunswick Stew was cooked up, you can find this cast iron pot in Brunswick, Georgia, at the corner of U.S. 17 and the Torras Causeway to St. Simons Island.

Keller's Flea Market, south of Savannah

► AFRICAN AMERICAN HERITAGE

The cities and Sea Islands of the Lowcountry and Georgia coast are integral to a full understanding of the experience of African Americans in the South. More than that, they are living legacies, with a thriving culture—called Gullah in South Carolina and Geechee in Georgia—whose roots can be traced directly back to West Africa.

Day 1

Begin your trip in Charleston with a busy day on foot. Shop in Old City Market; it never hosted a slave auction, but during its heyday, it was home to a number of African American entrepreneurs and vendors. Don't forget to walk by Cabbage Row, inspiration for "Catfish Row" of the African American–themed George Gershwin opera *Porgy and Bess*. Visit the newly opened Old Slave Mart and learn more about the Middle Passage and how Charleston's black population overcame the legacy of slavery. Spend the rest of the afternoon browsing through the research library at the Avery Research Center, one of the main repositories of Gullah culture and history.

Day 2

Early this morning, take the ferry out to Fort Sumter, where the Civil War began. From the fort you can see nearby undeveloped Morris Island, scene of the 1863 Battle of Battery Wagner, featuring the first all-black regiment in the U.S. Army, the 54th Massachusetts, whose tale was recounted in the film *Glory*. Visit the wrought-iron garden of the noted black Charleston artisan Philip Simmons. After lunch take a guided African American history tour of downtown Charleston or tour the Aiken-Rhett House, with its excellently and respectfully preserved aspects of the African American servants who made the historic property run.

Vestiges of days gone by are everywhere in Charleston.

stained glass inside First African Baptist Church in Savannah

CIVIL WAR HISTORY

This area is well known for its role in the Civil War. Throughout the region there are plenty of military history sights that highlight the Civil War era.

· In Charleston, take the ferry out to **Fort Sumter,** where the Civil War began, as well as **Fort Moultrie,** which hosted a young Edgar Allan Poe in the years prior to the war.

· See the newly raised **CSS *Hunley*** at the decommissioned Navy Yard (only open Friday–Saturday).

· Visit historic **Drayton Hall,** the country's oldest standing plantation home, saved from the torch only because Union troops thought it might have been used to quarantine smallpox victims.

· Beaufort served as a medical center for Union occupation troops, who even used **St. Helena's Episcopal Church** as a hospital.

· In Savannah, stop at the **Green-Meldrim House** where General Sherman made his headquarters.

· Visit **Fort Pulaski,** which a young Lieutenant Robert E. Lee helped build. It was later defeated by the first use of rifled artillery in warfare.

· In Richmond Hill, stop by **Fort McAllister,** overrun by Union troops in 1864.

You can still see battle damage at Fort Pulaski.

Day 3

Leave Charleston and cross the Ashley River for a trip to the National Trust–owned Drayton Hall; take the guided tour and pay respects at the African American cemetery. Then make the hour drive down to Beaufort. While walking around the scenic historic district, visit the Smalls House, home of the African American Civil War hero Robert Smalls, as well as his burial site at the Tabernacle Baptist Church. Drive by the Barners Barnwell Sams House to see where

SEASIDE ROMANCE

Spanish moss, friendly beaches, sunsets over the water, sultry weather, moonlit carriage rides–what more could you ask for? The Lowcountry and Georgia coast pretty much wrote the book on romantic getaways for couples. Here's a starter list of the most romantic spots.

CHARLESTON

- Romantic B&Bs include the **John Rutledge House** and **Two Meeting Street.**

- Enjoy a quiet Italian dinner at **Il Cortile del Re** or a fantastic French dinner at **La Fourchette.**

- Don't forget a carriage ride or art gallery stroll through the **French Quarter.**

- And as women can tell you, shopping can be sexy! Visit the great stores on **King Street.**

BEAUFORT AND THE LOWCOUNTRY

- Stroll through the walkable, picturesque **Beaufort Historic District.**

- Visit the driftwood beach on nearby **Hunting Island State Park** and enjoy the stunning views from the top of the lighthouse.

- **Edisto Island** is a wonderful place for a relaxing, no-hassle beach getaway.

SAVANNAH

- Relax on the grass at vast, scenic **Forsyth Park,** surrounded by Victorian architecture.

- Yes, cemeteries can be romantic, especially gorgeous **Bonaventure Cemetery.**

- Avoid the lines at The Lady & Sons and instead have a quiet French dinner at **Brasserie 529.** Share a coffee, sweet treat, or perhaps a signature martini at **Lulu's Chocolate Bar.**

- Have a nightcap at **Rocks on the Roof** on top of the Bohemian Hotel Savannah and watch the big cargo ships roll in and out on the river.

- Up for a crazy night of dancing? **Club One**'s the ticket.

THE GOLDEN ISLES

- Stay at the **Jekyll Island Club Hotel,** former stomping ground of the world's richest people. Rent a bike and crisscross the whole island in the late afternoon, coming back to the Club to enjoy a romantic dinner by the fireplace at the **Courtyard at Crane.**

- Take the ferry to **Cumberland Island National Seashore,** surely one of the most romantic locations on earth. Rent a bike on arrival and take your time pedaling among the ruins of the old mansions, making sure to visit the chapel at **First African Baptist Church,** site of the wedding of John F. Kennedy Jr. and Carolyn Bessette. Before you board the ferry to conclude your journey, maybe you'll get lucky and encounter some of the island's famous wild horses, a fitting symbol of passion and romance.

Many Charleston hotels provide complimentary bikes.

the Old Slave Mart Museum

Harriet Tubman worked as a nurse and helped ferry slaves to freedom on the Underground Railroad. Visit Beaufort National Cemetery and see the memorial to the African American troops of the 54th and 55th Regiments of the U.S. Army in the Civil War.

Day 4

Make the short drive over the Beaufort River to St. Helena Island and spend the morning on the scenic campus of the Penn Center, a key clearinghouse for study and celebration of Gullah culture and the site of activism by Martin Luther King Jr. in the 1960s. Head on into Hilton Head, stop by the Coastal Discovery Museum, and take an African American heritage tour, visiting the site of Mitchelville, the first community of freed slaves in the United States. An alternate plan for today is to make the trip inland to Walterboro to visit the Tuskegee Airmen Memorial at the regional airport.

Day 5

Drive an hour into Savannah and check out the African American Monument statue on River Street. Head over to the former center of black life in Savannah, Martin Luther King Jr. Boulevard (once West Broad Street), and see the Ralph Mark Gilbert Civil Rights Museum and then tour the First African Baptist Church in City Market, the oldest black congregation in North America. Nearby is the new Haitian Memorial, a nod to the volunteers who helped the cause of independence in the Revolutionary War.

Day 6

Today you visit the Second African Baptist Church, where Sherman announced the famous "40 acres and a mule" field order. Close by is the Beach Institute, a repository of African American art, culture, and history. Then check out the restored schoolroom at Massie School, Savannah's first African American school, and the Carnegie Library, Savannah's first black library, where future Supreme Court Justice Clarence Thomas once studied.

Day 7

On the way out of Savannah, visit Laurel Grove South, a historic African American cemetery with stirring memorials to some of Savannah's most notable black figures. Jump on U.S. 17 and head down to Harris Neck National Wildlife Refuge, once the site of an African American community, displaced for a World War II airfield. Be sure to visit the vernacular Gould Cemetery near the landing within the refuge. An alternate plan is to drive all the way down to little Meridian near Darien and take the ferry out to Sapelo Island, taking a guided day tour of the island and its rich Gullah/Geechee history, including the community of Hog Hammock.

live oaks and colorful azaleas on Magnolia Plantation in Charleston

LIFE'S A BEACH

There are plenty of beaches to enjoy on the Georgia and South Carolina coast, many of them made even more enjoyable by the fact that they tend to get much less traffic than more touristy areas. Here's a quick guide to match the beach to the trip:

FAMILY FRIENDLY

- **Hilton Head Island**'s beaches are roomy and spotlessly maintained. And because no alcohol is allowed on them, they're more geared to families with children.

- **Isle of Palms** outside Charleston is home to the Wild Dunes Resort, which caters to beach-loving families.

- Quiet **Edisto Island** has absolutely none of the flash that young people tend to gravitate to, but it is extraordinarily safe and friendly.

- Popular state park **Hunting Island** is a great place to enjoy family time on the beach. Don't miss the hike to the top of the lighthouse!

- A playground for the people of Georgia by order of the state legislature, **Jekyll Island** is a safe, roomy, and friendly getaway.

SPORTIN' LIFE

- You can ride your bike for 12 miles on the expansive, hard-packed sand all around **Hilton Head Island,** as well as enjoy a number of more strenuous adventures such as parasailing.

- **Sullivan's Island** offers a long stretch of easy beach bicycling just outside Charleston.

- Charleston's **Folly Beach** offers some of the East Coast's best surfing.

- **Tybee Island** offers a number of kayak adventures, parasailing, and boogie boarding. Enjoy a nice bike ride on a converted rail bed that takes you into the grounds of historic Fort Pulaski.

PEACE AND QUIET

- Evocative, romantic, and isolated, **Cumberland Island** is virtually the mossy picture of the old Sea Island South.

- The total lack of chain hotels and high-rises on **Edisto Island** means a very laid-back and thoroughly noncommercial beach experience.

- Low-traffic **Sapelo Island** offers friendly folks and a really beautiful beach.

- Even lower-traffic **Daufuskie Island** is where you want to go when only the most laid-back will do.

DOG-FRIENDLY

- Easily the two most dog-friendly beaches in the area covered by this book are **Hunting Island State Park,** South Carolina, and **Jekyll Island,** Georgia. Just keep 'em on a leash and you're fine year-round.

- For a Charleston-area dog beach, go straight to **Isle of Palms.**

- **Hilton Head** doesn't allow canines at all Memorial Day–Labor Day, but you can take them on a leash 10 A.M.–5 P.M. from April 1 until the day before Memorial Day.

- On **Edisto Island,** your pup must be on a leash May 1–October 31, under voice command or on a leash all other times.

- Sorry, Rover can't come over to Tybee Island, Georgia, at all.

a yoga class on the beach at Hilton Head

▶ ON THE WATER, IN THE AIR

The Charleston and Savannah area isn't just about old homes and Civil War memories. It's also framed by the largest contiguous salt marsh in the world, not only a kayaker's paradise but an amazing natural habitat for birds, both indigenous and migratory. Here's a weeklong trip hitting the green highlights.

Day 1

Begin at the Cape Romain National Wildlife Refuge north of Charleston. Bull Island and Capers Island are highlights of this largely maritime preserve, which comprises 66,000 acres of kayaking opportunities. If you're in town October–March, bird-watchers can visit the 22-acre Crab Bank Heritage Preserve in Charleston Harbor. Tonight relax over a world-class dinner in Charleston's Historic District.

Day 2

Today's a full day for kayaking in the ACE Basin, comprising the estuaries of the Ashepoo, Combahee, and Edisto Rivers (the latter being the largest and most traveled). Public landings and guided tours abound for trips on these nearly pristine blackwater runs. Serious bird-watchers can visit the Bear Island and Donnelly Wildlife Management Areas within the ACE Basin, as well as at the impounded old paddy fields at the Ernest Hollings ACE Basin National Wildlife Refuge.

Day 3

Now you head down to Tybee Island outside Savannah for either a day trip across the Back River to undeveloped Little Tybee Island, where wilderness camping is allowed, or a kayak run at Skidaway Narrows, where bird-watchers will enjoy seeing the osprey nests on the channel markers near Skidaway Island State Park, another great bird-watching spot.

Either way, treat yourself tonight to a great dinner in Savannah's Historic District.

Day 4

Another day in the Savannah area, this time west of town on the undeveloped blackwater Ebenezer Creek. Bird-watching opportunities abound amid the cypress swamps, crisscrossed by old paddy field dikes. Later today visit the nearby Savannah National Wildlife Refuge, with parts in both South Carolina and Georgia and an excellent bird- (and gator!) watching area.

Day 5

Bird-watchers mustn't miss a trip to Harris Neck National Wildlife Refuge, world-renowned for its colonies of wood storks and other waterfowl. Make sure to have a meal at nearby Shellman Bluff, a picturesque little shrimping village with a couple of excellent, authentic down-home seafood restaurants.

Day 6

This morning, make a run down the hybrid blackwater Altamaha River, Georgia's largest. Amid the remnants of what were once some of America's largest rice and cotton plantations, you'll see a stunning display of waterfowl and migratory birds. Tonight have a nice dinner on relaxing St. Simons Island, or make it onto Jekyll Island in time to see the birds on the north-side beaches.

Day 7

This is a full day at Okefenokee National Wildlife Refuge, a vast natural wonderland that belies the name "swamp." On its broad "prairies" bird-watchers will see a nearly unmatched variety of species for this region, and kayakers can paddle down several blackwater runs amid the cypress.

LITERARY LARKS

The area from Charleston down to Glynn County, Georgia, has hosted some of America's most beloved literary figures, each indelibly influenced in some way by the charms and mystique of the area itself. Here are some literary highlights of the area, with an eye toward soaking in the aspects of the South Carolina and Georgia coast that had such an impact on these authors' work.

- **Dorothea Benton Frank:** Fans can have a seafood lunch in Mount Pleasant outside Charleston on Shem Creek, namesake for her novel of the same title. Afterwards you can head over to the beach on nearby Sullivan's Island, namesake of Frank's novel *Sullivan's Island* and the place of her birth. Edgar Allan Poe was inspired to write *The Gold Bug* by his stay on Sullivan's Island during a stint in the Army.

- **Fanny Kemble:** A couple of miles south is Butler Island Plantation, where English actress Fanny Kemble, married to the owner, was moved to write *Journal of Residence on a Georgia Plantation*, one of the first anti-slavery books.

- **Flannery O'Connor:** In Savannah, visit the Flannery O'Connor Childhood Home and tour her church, the Cathedral of St. John the Baptist.

- **John Berendt:** Devotees of *Midnight in the Garden of Good and Evil* will enjoy the Mercer-Williams House, Club One, and Bonaventure Cemetery, which is also the final resting place of two of Savannah's most beloved native writers, Oscar-winning lyricist Johnny Mercer and Pulitzer-winning author Conrad Aiken.

- **Melissa Faye Green:** Darien, Georgia, is where Melissa Faye Green set her best-seller *Praying for Sheetrock*.

- **Pat Conroy:** Connoisseurs can visit Charleston's The Citadel, setting for *The Lords of Discipline*; Daufuskie Island, setting of *The Water is Wide*; and Beaufort, where he grew up. Conroy's dad Donald, the "Great Santini" himself, is buried in Beaufort National Cemetery.

- **Walt Kelly:** For fans of the classic comic strip "Pogo," there's Okefenokee Swamp!

the Mercer-Williams House on Monterey Square

CHARLESTON

Charleston made news in 2011 when it unseated San Francisco for the first time ever in the annual *Condé Nast Traveler* Reader's Choice award for "Top U.S. City." That giant-killing win was quite a coup for this smallish, old-fashioned city in the Deep South. But the most revealing Charleston award is its perennial ranking at the top of the late Marjabelle Young Stewart's annual list for "Most Mannerly City in America." (Charleston has won the award so many times that Stewart's successor at the Charleston School of Protocol and Etiquette, Cindy Grosso, has retired the city from the competition.) This is a city that takes civic harmony so seriously that it boasts the country's only "Livability Court," a binding legal proceeding which meets regularly to enforce local quality-of-life ordinances.

Everyone who spends time in Charleston comes away with a story to tell about the locals' courtesy and hospitality. Mine came while walking through the French Quarter admiring a handsome old single house on Church Street, one of the few that survived the fire of 1775. To my surprise, the woman chatting with a friend nearby turned out to be the homeowner. Noticing my interest, she invited me, a total stranger, inside to check out the progress of her renovation.

To some eyes, Charleston's hospitable nature has bordered on licentiousness. From its earliest days, the city gained a reputation for vice.

HIGHLIGHTS

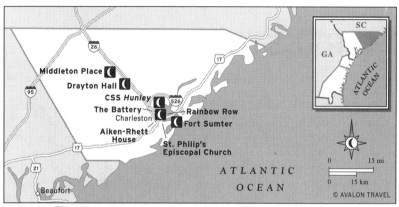

LOOK FOR **◖** TO FIND RECOMMENDED SIGHTS, ACTIVITIES, DINING, AND LODGING.

◖ The Battery: Tranquil surroundings combine with beautiful views of Charleston Harbor, key historical points in the Civil War, and amazing mansions (page 32).

◖ Rainbow Row: Painted in warm pastels, these old merchant homes near the cobblestoned waterfront take you on a journey to Charleston's antebellum heyday (page 35).

◖ Fort Sumter: Take the ferry to this historic place where the Civil War began, and take in the gorgeous views along the way (page 42).

◖ St. Philip's Episcopal Church: A sublimely beautiful sanctuary and two historic graveyards await you in the heart of the evocative French Quarter (page 44).

◖ Aiken-Rhett House: There are certainly more ostentatious house museums in Charleston, but none that provide such a virtually intact glimpse into real antebellum life (page 54).

◖ Drayton Hall: Don't miss Charleston's oldest surviving plantation home and one of the country's best examples of professional historic preservation (page 60).

◖ Middleton Place: Wander in and marvel at one of the world's most beautifully landscaped gardens—and the first in North America (page 63).

◖ CSS Hunley: Newly ensconced for public viewing in its special preservation tank, the first submarine to sink a ship in battle is a moving example of bravery and sacrifice (page 66).

(The city's nickname, "The Holy City," derives from the skyline's abundance of church steeples rather than any excess of piety among its citizens.) The old drinking clubs are gone, and the yearly bacchanal of Race Week—in which personal fortunes were won or lost in seconds—is but a distant memory. But that hedonistic legacy is alive and well today in Charleston;

the city is full of lovers of strong drink and serious foodies, with every weekend night finding downtown packed with partiers, diners, and show-goers.

Don't mistake the Holy City's charm and joie de vivre for weakness, however. That would be a mistake, for within Charleston's velvet glove has always been an iron fist. This is where the colonists scored their first clear victory over the British during the Revolution (another Charleston first). This is the place where the Civil War began, and which stoically endured one of the longest sieges in modern warfare during that conflict. This is the city that survived the East Coast's worst earthquake in 1886 and one of its worst hurricanes a century later.

Despite its fun-loving reputation, a martial spirit is never far from the surface in Charleston, from The Citadel military college along the Ashley River, to the aircraft carrier *Yorktown* moored at Patriots Point, to the cannonballs and mortars that children climb on at the Battery, and even to the occasional tour guide in Confederate garb.

Some of the nation's most progressive urban activity is going on in Charleston despite its reputation for conservatism, from the renovation of the old Navy Yard in North Charleston, to impressive green start-ups, to any number of sustainable residential developments. Charleston is a leader in conservation as well, with groups like the Lowcountry Open Land Trust and the Coastal Conservation League setting an example for the entire Southeast in how to bring environmental organizations and the business community together to preserve the area's beauty and ecosystem.

While many visitors come to see the Charleston of Rhett Butler and Pat Conroy— finding it and then some, of course—they leave impressed by the diversity of Charlestonian life. It's a surprisingly cosmopolitan mix of students, professionals, and longtime inhabitants—who discuss the finer points of Civil War history as if it were last year, party on Saturday night like there's no tomorrow, and go to church on Sunday morning dressed in their finest.

But don't be deceived by these history-minded people. Under the carefully honed tradition and the ever-present ancestor worship, Charleston possesses a vitality of vision that is irrepressibly practical and forward-looking.

HISTORY

Unlike so many of England's colonies in America that were based on freedom from religious persecution, Carolina was strictly a commercial venture from the beginning. The tenure of the Lords Proprietors—the eight English aristocrats who literally owned the colony— began in 1670 when the *Carolina* finished its journey to Albemarle Creek on the west bank of the Ashley River.

Those first colonists would set up a small fortification called Charles Towne, named for Charles II, the first monarch of the Restoration. In a year they'd be joined by colonists from the prosperous but overcrowded British colony of Barbados, who brought a Caribbean sensibility that exists in Charleston to this day.

Finding the first Charles Towne not very fertile and vulnerable to attack from Native Americans and the Spanish, they moved to the peninsula and down to "Oyster Point," what Charlestonians now call White Point Gardens. Just above Oyster Point they set up a walled town, bounded by modern-day Water Street to the south (then a marshy creek, as the name indicates), Meeting Street to the west, Cumberland Street to the north, and the Cooper River on the east.

Growing prosperous as a trading center for deerskin from the great American interior, Charles Towne came into its own after two nearly concurrent events in the early 1700s: the decisive victory of a combined force of Carolinians and Native American allies against the fierce Yamasee people, and the final eradication of the pirate threat in the deaths of Blackbeard and Stede Bonnet.

Flushed with a new spirit of independence, Charles Towne threw off the control of the anemic, disengaged Lords Proprietors, tore down the old defensive walls, and was reborn as an outward-looking, expansive, and increasingly cosmopolitan city that came to be called Charleston. With safety from hostile incursion

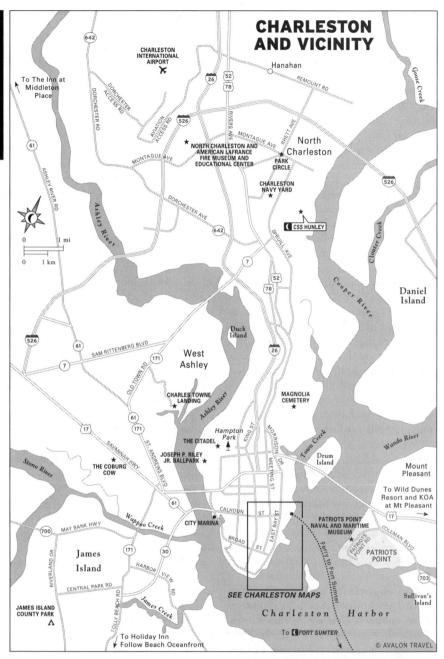

CHARLESTON AND VICINITY

© JIM MOREKIS

Charleston's nickname is "The Holy City" because of its numerous church steeples.

came the time of the great rice and indigo plantations. Springing up all along the Ashley River soon after the introduction of the crops, they turned the labor and expertise of imported Africans into enormous profit for their owners. However, the planters preferred the pleasures and sea breezes of Charleston, and gradually summer homes became year-round residences.

It was during this colonial era that the indelible Charlestonian character was stamped: a hedonistic aristocracy combining a love of carousing with a love of the arts; a code of chivalry meant both to reflect a genteel spirit and reinforce the social order; and, ominously, an ever-increasing reliance on slave labor.

As the storm clouds of civil war gathered in the early 1800s, the majority of Charleston's population was of African descent, and the city was the main importation point for the transatlantic slave trade. The worst fears of white Charlestonians seemed confirmed during the alleged plot by slave leader Denmark

Vesey in the early 1820s to start a rebellion. The Lowcountry's reliance on slave labor put it front and center in the coming national confrontation over abolition, which came to a head literally and figuratively in the bombardment of Fort Sumter in Charleston Harbor in April 1861.

By war's end, not only did the city lay in ruins—mostly from a disastrous fire in 1861, as well as from a 545-day Union siege—so did its way of life. Pillaged by Northern troops and freed slaves, the great plantations along the Ashley became the sites of the first strip mining in the United States, as poverty-stricken owners scraped away the layer of phosphate under the topsoil to sell—perhaps with a certain poetic justice—as fertilizer.

The Holy City didn't really wake up until the great "Charleston Renaissance" of the 1920s and 1930s, when the city rediscovered art, literature, and music in the form of jazz and the world-famous Charleston dance. This was also the time that the world rediscovered

NOT JUST A MATTER OF BLUE AND GRAY

While this area is best known for its role in the Civil War–Charleston's as the instigator of the conflict, and Savannah's as the terminus of Sherman's notorious "March to the Sea"–this is a drastic oversimplification. Although South Carolina was the "cradle of secession," it also lost more men in the fight for American independence than any other colony, including Massachusetts. Here are some military history highlights from other eras:

In Charleston, go to **The Citadel** and enjoy the colorful weekly parade of cadets, the fabled "Thin Grey Line," most Fridays at 3 P.M. In Mount Pleasant, eat lunch in the mess hall of the **USS Yorktown** at the **Patriot's Point Naval Museum.** Visit historic **Middleton Place,** home of one of the signers of the Declaration of Independence and where some scenes from Mel Gibson's *The Patriot* were filmed.

On Parris Island, tour the **Marine Recruit Depot Parris Island** and see one of the oldest European archaeological sites in the United States, **Charlesfort.**

In Savannah, head to **Battlefield Park** and see the replicated British redoubt marking the failed Siege of Savannah. Visit **Old Fort Jackson,** an 1812-era installation on the Savannah River. Tour the **Mighty Eighth Air Force Museum,** which honors the contributions of the Eighth Air Force, founded in Savannah in 1942.

In Darien, Georgia, is **Fort King George,** the first English outpost in Georgia. Nearby is **Harris Neck National Wildlife Refuge,** formerly a World War II airfield.

On St. Simons Island is **Fort Frederica,** a tabby fort built by General James Oglethorpe, and the nearby **Battle of Bloody Marsh** site, where Oglethorpe ended the Spanish threat to Georgia.

While the big U.S. Navy Trident sub base at Kings Bay, Georgia, is not open to the public, check out the **St. Marys Submarine Museum** in St. Marys, which pays tribute to the "Silent Service."

Charleston. In the 1920s George Gershwin read local author DuBose Heyward's novel *Porgy* and decided to write a score around the story. Along with lyrics by Ira Gershwin, the three men's collaboration became the first American opera, *Porgy and Bess,* which debuted in New York in 1935. It was also during this time that a new appreciation for Charleston's history sprang up, as the local Preservation Society spearheaded the nation's first historic preservation ordinance.

World War II brought the same economic boom that came to much of the South then, most notably with an expansion of the Navy Yard and the addition of a military air base. By the 1950s, the automobile suburb and a thirst for "progress" claimed so many historic buildings that the inevitable backlash came with the formation of the Historic Charleston Foundation, which continues to lead the fight to keep intact the Holy City's architectural legacy.

Civil rights came to Charleston in earnest with a landmark suit to integrate the Charleston Municipal Golf Course in 1960. The biggest battle, however, would be the 100-day strike in 1969 against the Medical University of South Carolina, then, as now, a large employer of African Americans.

Charleston's next great renaissance—still ongoing today—came with the redevelopment of downtown and the fostering of the tourism industry under the nearly 40-year tenure of Mayor Joe Riley, during which so much of the current visitor-friendly infrastructure became part of daily life here. Today, Charleston is completing the transition away from a military and manufacturing base and attracting professionals and artists to town.

PLANNING YOUR TIME

Even if you're just going to confine yourself to the peninsula, I can't imagine spending less than two nights. You'll want half a day for shopping on King Street and a full day for seeing various attractions and museums. Keep in mind that one of Charleston's key sights, Fort Sumter, will take almost half a day to see once you factor in ticketing and boarding time for the ferry out to the fort and back; plan accordingly.

If you have a car, there are several great places to visit off the peninsula—especially the plantations along the Ashley. None are very far away, and navigation in Charleston is a snap. The farthest site from downtown should take no more than 30 minutes, and because the plantations are roughly adjacent, you can visit all of them in a single day if you get an early start.

While a good time is never far away in Charleston, keep in mind that this is the South, and Sundays can get pretty slow. While the finely honed tourist infrastructure here means that there will always be something to do, the selection of open shops and restaurants dwindles on Sundays, though most other attractions keep working hours.

But for those of us who love the old city, there's nothing like a Sunday morning in Charleston—church bells ringing, families on their way to worship, a beguiling slowness in the air, perhaps spiced with the anticipation of a particular Charleston specialty—a hearty and delicious Sunday brunch.

The real issue for most visitors boils down to two questions: How much do you want to spend on accommodations, and in which part of town do you want to stay? Lodging is generally not cheap in Charleston, but because the price differential is not that much between staying on the peninsula and staying on the outskirts, I recommend the peninsula. You'll pay more, but not *that* much more, with the bonus of probably being able to walk to most places you want to see—which, after all, is the best way to enjoy the city.

ORIENTATION

Charleston occupies a peninsula bordered by the Ashley River to the west and the Cooper River to the east, which "come together to form the Atlantic Ocean," according to the haughty phrase once taught to generations of Charleston schoolchildren.

Although the lower tip of the peninsula actually points closer to southeast, that direction is regarded locally as due south, and anything toward the top of the peninsula is considered due north.

The peninsula is ringed by islands, many of which have become heavily populated suburbs. Clockwise from the top of the peninsula they are: Daniel Island, Mount Pleasant, Isle of Palms, Sullivan's Island, Morris Island, Folly Island, and James Island. The resort island of Kiawah and the much less-developed Edisto Island are farther south down the coast.

North Charleston is not only a separate municipality; it's also a different state of mind. A sprawling combination of malls, light industry, and low-income housing, it also boasts some of the more cutting-edge urban redesign activity in the area.

While Charlestonians would scoff, the truth is that Charleston proper has a surprising amount in common with Manhattan. Both are on long spits of land situated roughly north–south. Both were settled originally at the lower end in walled fortifications—Charleston's walls came down in 1718, while Manhattan still has its Wall Street as a reminder. Both cityscapes rely on age-old north–south streets that run nearly the whole length—Charleston's King and Meeting Streets, with only a block between them, and Manhattan's Broadway and Fifth Avenue. And like Manhattan, Charleston also has its own "Museum Mile" just off of a major green space, in Charleston's case up near

Marion Square—though certainly its offerings are not as expansive as those a short walk from New York's Central Park.

Unfortunately, also like Manhattan, parking is at a premium in downtown Charleston. Luckily the city has many reasonably priced parking garages, which I recommend that you use. But cars should only be used when you have to. Charleston is best enjoyed on foot, both because of its small size and the cozy, meandering nature of its old streets, designed not for cars and tour buses but for boots, horseshoes, and carriage wheels.

Charleston is made up of many small neighborhoods, many of them quite old. The boundaries are confusing, so your best bet is to simply look at the street signs (signage in general is excellent in Charleston). If you're in a historic neighborhood, such as the French Quarter or Ansonborough, a smaller sign above the street name will indicate that.

Other key terms you'll hear are "the Crosstown," the portion of U.S. 17 that goes across the peninsula; "Savannah Highway," the portion of U.S. 17 that traverses "West Ashley," which is the suburb across the Ashley River; "East Cooper," the area across the Cooper River that includes Mount Pleasant, Isle of Palms, and Daniel and Sullivan's Islands; and "the Neck," up where the peninsula narrows. These are the terms that locals use, and hence what you'll see in this guide.

Sights

Though most key sights in Charleston do indeed have some tie to the city's rich history, house museums are only a subset of the attractions here. Charleston's sights are excellently integrated into its built environment, and often the enjoyment of nearby gardens or a lapping river is part of the fun.

SOUTH OF BROAD

As one of the oldest streets in Charleston, the east-west thoroughfare of Broad Street is not only a physical landmark, it's a mental one as well. The first area of the Charleston peninsula to be settled, the area south of Broad Street—often shortened to the mischievous acronym "SOB" by local wags—features older homes, meandering streets (many of them built on "made land" filling in former wharfs), and a distinctly genteel, laid-back feel.

As you'd expect, it also features more affluent residents, sometimes irreverently referred to as "SOB Snobs." This heavily residential area has no nightlife to speak of and gets almost eerily quiet after hours, but rest assured that plenty of people live here.

While I highly recommend just wandering among these narrow streets and marveling at the lovingly restored old homes, keep in mind that almost everything down here is in private hands. Don't wander into a garden or take photos inside a window unless you're invited to do so (and given Charleston's legendary hospitality, that can happen).

◖ The Battery

For many, the Battery (E. Battery St. and Murray Blvd., 843/724-7321, daily 24 hours, free) is the single most iconic Charleston spot, drenched in history and boasting dramatic views in all directions. A look to the south gives you the sweeping expanse of the Cooper River, with views of Fort Sumter, Castle Pinckney, Sullivan's Island, and, off to the north, the old carrier *Yorktown* moored at Mount Pleasant. A landward look gives you a view of the adjoining, peaceful **White Point Gardens,** the sumptuous mansions of the Battery, and a beguiling peek behind them into some of the oldest neighborhoods in Charleston.

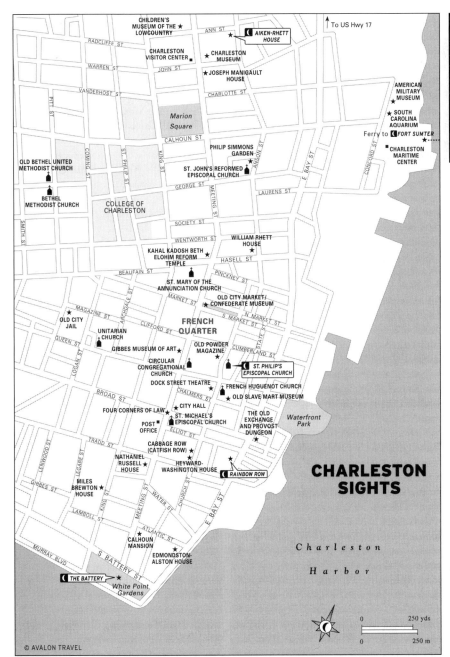

To US Hwy 17

CHILDREN'S
MUSEUM OF THE ★
LOWCOUNTRY

ANN ST

RADCLIFFE ST

AIKEN-RHETT
HOUSE

CHARLESTON
VISITOR CENTER

CHARLESTON
MUSEUM

WARREN ST

JOHN ST

★ JOSEPH MANIGAULT
HOUSE

VANDERHOST ST

AMERICAN
MILITARY
MUSEUM

CHARLOTTE ST

★ SOUTH
CAROLINA
AQUARIUM

PITT ST

Marion
Square

Ferry to ◖ FORT SUMTER

COMING ST

CALHOUN ST

CHARLESTON
MARITIME
CENTER

PHILIP SIMMONS
GARDEN

ANSON ST

E BAY ST

OLD BETHEL UNITED
METHODIST CHURCH

ST. PHILIP'S ST

KING ST

ST. JOHN'S REFORMED
EPISCOPAL CHURCH

CONCORD ST

BETHEL
METHODIST CHURCH

GEORGE ST

MEETING ST

LAURENS ST

COLLEGE OF
CHARLESTON

SMITH ST

SOCIETY ST

WENTWORTH ST

WILLIAM RHETT
HOUSE

KAHAL KADOSH BETH
ELOHIM REFORM ★
TEMPLE

HASELL ST

BEAUFAIN ST

PINCKNEY ST

ST. MARY OF THE
ANNUNCIATION CHURCH

MAGAZINE ST

MARKET ST

OLD CITY MARKET/
★ CONFEDERATE MUSEUM

ARCHDALE ST

OLD CITY ★
JAIL

FRENCH
QUARTER

S MARKET ST

N MARKET ST

CLIFFORD ST

UNITARIAN
CHURCH

QUEEN ST

OLD POWDER
MAGAZINE

CUMBERLAND ST

LOGAN ST

GIBBES MUSEUM OF ART ★

STATE ST

CIRCULAR
CONGREGATIONAL
CHURCH

◖ ST. PHILIP'S
EPISCOPAL CHURCH

BROAD ST

DOCK STREET THEATRE

CHALMERS ST

★ FRENCH HUGUENOT CHURCH

★ OLD SLAVE MART MUSEUM

FOUR CORNERS OF LAW ★ ★ CITY HALL

ST. MICHAEL'S ★
EPISCOPAL CHURCH

THE OLD
EXCHANGE
AND PROVOST
DUNGEON

Waterfront
Park

POST
OFFICE

ELLIOT ST

LENWOOD ST

LEGARE ST

TRADD ST

CABBAGE ROW
(CATFISH ROW) ★

NATHANIEL
RUSSELL ★
HOUSE

KING ST

MEETING ST

HEYWARD-
WASHINGTON HOUSE

WATER ST

CHURCH ST

◖ RAINBOW ROW

**CHARLESTON
SIGHTS**

GIBBES ST

MILES
BREWTON ★
HOUSE

LAMBOLL ST

E BAY ST

ATLANTIC ST

MURRAY BLVD

CALHOUN
MANSION

Charleston

S BATTERY ST

EDMONDSTON-
ALSTON HOUSE

Harbor

◖ THE BATTERY ★

White Point
Gardens

0   250 yds

0   250 m

© AVALON TRAVEL

But if you had been one of the first European visitors to this tip of the peninsula about 400 years ago, you'd have seen how it got its first name, Oyster Point: This entire area was once home to an enormous outcropping of oysters. Their shells glistened bright white in the harsh Southern sun as a ship approached from sea, hence its subsequent name, White Point. Although the oysters are long gone and much of the area you're walking on is actually reclaimed marsh, the Battery and White Point Gardens are still a balm for the soul.

Once the bustling (and sometimes seedy) heart of Charleston's maritime activity, the Battery was where pirate Stede Bonnet and 21 of his men were hanged in 1718. As you might imagine, the area got its name for hosting cannons during the War of 1812, with the current distinctive seawall structure built in the 1850s.

Contrary to popular belief, no guns fired from here on Fort Sumter, as they would have been out of range. However, many thankfully inoperable cannons, mortars, and piles of shot still reside here, much to the delight of kids of all ages. This is where Charlestonians gathered in a giddy, party-like atmosphere to watch the shelling of Fort Sumter in 1861, blissfully ignorant of the horrors to come. A short time later the North would return the favor, as the Battery and all of Charleston up to Broad Street would bear the brunt of shelling during the long siege of the city (the rest was out of reach of Union guns).

But now, the Battery is a place to relax, not fight. The relaxation starts with the fact that there's usually plenty of free parking all along Battery Street. A promenade all around the periphery is a great place to stroll or jog. Add the calming, almost constant sea breeze and the meditative influence of the wide, blue Cooper River and you'll see why this land's end—once so martial in nature—is now a favorite place for after-church family gatherings, travelers, lovestruck couples, and weddings (about 200 a year at the gazebo in White Point Gardens).

Still, military history is never far away in Charleston, and one of the chief landmarks at the Battery is the USS *Hobson* Memorial, remembering the sacrifice of the men of that vessel when it sank after a collision with the carrier USS *Wasp* in 1952.

Look for the three-story private residence where East Battery curves northward. You won't be taking any tours of it, but you should be aware that it's the **DeSaussure House** (1 E. Battery St.), best known in Charleston history for hosting rowdy, celebratory crowds on the roof and the piazzas to watch the 34-hour shelling of Fort Sumter in 1861.

Edmondston-Alston House

The most noteworthy single attraction on the Battery is the 1825 Edmondston-Alston House (21 E. Battery St., 843/722-7171, www.middletonplace.org, Mon. 1–4:30 p.m., Tues.–Sat. 10 a.m.–4:30 p.m., Sun. 1:30–4:30 p.m., $10 adults, $8 students), the only Battery home open to the public for tours. This is one of the most unique and well-preserved historic homes in the United States, thanks to the ongoing efforts of the Alston family, who acquired the house from shipping merchant Charles Edmondston for $15,500 after the Panic of 1837 and still live on the third floor (tours only visit the first two stories).

Over 90 percent of the home's furnishings are original items from the Alston era, a percentage that's almost unheard of in the world of house museums. (Currently the House is owned and administered by the Middleton Place Foundation, best known for its stewardship of Middleton Place along the Ashley River.) You can still see the original paper bag used to store the house's deeds and mortgages. There's also a copy of the Ordinance of Secession and some interesting memorabilia from the golden days of Race Week, that time in February when all of Charleston society came out to bet on horses, carouse, and show off their finery. The

Edmondston-Alston House has withstood storms, fires, earthquakes, and Yankee shelling, due in no small part to its sturdy construction; its masonry walls are two bricks thick, and it features both interior and exterior shutters. Originally built in the Federal style, second owner Charles Alston added several Greek Revival elements, notably the parapet, balcony, and piazza, where General Beauregard watched the attack on Fort Sumter.

◖ Rainbow Row

At 79–107 East Bay Street, between Tradd and Elliot Streets, is one of the most photographed sights in the United States: colorful Rainbow Row. The reason for its name becomes obvious when you see the array of pastel-colored mansions, all facing the Cooper River. The bright, historically accurate colors—nine of them, to be exact—are one of the many vestiges you'll see around town of Charleston's Caribbean heritage, a legacy of the English settlers from the colony of Barbados who were among the city's first citizens.

The homes are unusually old for this fire-, hurricane-, and earthquake-ravaged city, with most dating from 1730 to 1750. As you admire Rainbow Row from across East Battery, keep in mind you're actually walking on what used to be water. These houses were originally right on the Cooper River, their lower stories serving as storefronts on the wharf. The street was created later on top of landfill, or "made land" as it's called locally. Besides its grace and beauty, Rainbow Row is of vital importance to American historic preservation. These were the first Charleston homes to be renovated and brought back from early-20th-century seediness. The restoration projects on Rainbow Row directly inspired the creation of the Charleston Preservation Society, the first such group in the United States.

© JIM MOREKIS

Rainbow Row

Continue walking up the High Battery past Rainbow Row and find Water Street. This aptly named little avenue was in fact a creek in the early days, acting as the southern border of the original walled city. The large brick building on the seaward side housing the Historic Charleston Foundation sits on the site of the old Granville bastion, a key defensive point in the wall.

Nathaniel Russell House

Considered one of Charleston's grandest homes despite being built by an outsider from Rhode Island, the Nathaniel Russell House (51 Meeting St., 843/724-8481, www.historiccharleston.org, Mon.–Sat. 10 A.M.–5 P.M., Sun. 2–5 P.M., last tour begins 4:30 P.M., $10 adults, $5 children) is now a National Historic Landmark and one of the country's best examples of neoclassicism. Built in 1808 for the then-princely sum of $80,000 by Nathaniel Russell, a.k.a. "King of the Yankees," the home is furnished as accurately as possible to represent not only the lifestyle of the Russell family but the 18 African American servants who shared the premises. The house was eventually bought by the Allson family, who amid the poverty of Civil War and Reconstruction decided in 1870 to sell it to the Sisters of Charity of Our Lady of Mercy as a school for young Catholic women.

Restorationists have identified 22 layers of paint within the home, which barely survived a tornado in 1811, got away with only minimal damage in the 1886 earthquake, but was damaged extensively by Hurricane Hugo in 1989 (and was since repaired). As with fine antebellum homes throughout coastal South Carolina and Georgia, the use of faux finishing is prevalent throughout, mimicking surfaces such as marble, wood, and lapis lazuli. Visitors are often most impressed by the Nathaniel Russell House's magnificent "flying" spiral staircase, a work of such sublime carpentry and engineering that it needs no external support, twisting upward of its own volition.

When you visit, keep in mind that you're in the epicenter of not only Charleston's historic preservation movement but perhaps the nation's as well. In 1955, the Nathaniel Russell House was the first major project of the Historic Charleston Foundation, which raised $65,000 to purchase it. Two years later, admission fees from the house would support Historic Charleston's groundbreaking revolving fund for preservation, the prototype for many such successful programs. For an extra $6, you can gain admission to the Aiken-Rhett House farther uptown, also administered by the Historic Charleston Foundation.

Calhoun Mansion

The single largest of Charleston's surviving grand homes, the 1876 Calhoun Mansion (16 Meeting St., 843/722-8205, www.calhounmansion.net, tours daily 11 A.M.–5 P.M., $15) boasts 35 opulent rooms (with 23 fireplaces!) in a striking Italianate design taking up a whopping 24,000 square feet. The grounds feature some charming garden spaces. A new 90-minute "grand tour" is available for $50 pp; call for an appointment. Though the interiors at this privately run house are packed with antiques and furnishings, be aware that not all of them are accurate or period.

Miles Brewton House

A short distance from the Nathaniel Russell House but much less viewed by visitors, the circa-1769 Miles Brewton House (27 King St.), now a private residence, is maybe the best example of Georgian-Palladian architecture in the world. The almost medieval wrought-iron fencing, or chevaux-de-frise, was added in 1822 after rumors of a slave uprising spread through town. This imposing double house was the site of not one but two headquarters of occupying armies, British General Clinton in the Revolution and the federal garrison after the end of the Civil War. The great Susan Pringle

KNOW YOUR CHARLESTON HOUSES

Charleston's homes boast not only a long pedigree but an interesting and unique one as well. Here are the basics of local architecture:

Single House: A legacy of the early Barbadians among the first settlers here, the Charleston single house is named for the fact that it's a single room wide. The phrase refers to layout, not style, which can range from Georgian to Federal to Greek Revival, or a combination. Furnished with full-length piazzas, or long verandas, on the south side to take advantage of southerly breezes, the single house is perhaps the nation's first sustainable house design. The house is lengthwise on the lot, with the entrance on the side of the house. This means the "backyard" is actually the side yard. They're everywhere in Charleston, but Church Street has great examples, including 90, 92, and 94 Church Street, and the oldest single house in town, the 1730 Robert Brewton House (71 Church St.).

Double House: This layout is two rooms wide with a central hallway and a porched facade facing the street. Double houses often had separate carriage houses. The Aiken-Rhett and Heyward-Washington houses are good examples.

Charleston Green: This uniquely Charlestonian color—extremely dark green that looks pitch black in low light—has its roots in the aftermath of the Civil War. The federal government distributed surplus black paint to contribute to reconstruction of the ravaged peninsula, but Charlestonians were too proud (and tasteful) to use as-is. So they added a tiny bit of yellow to each gallon, producing Charleston green.

Earthquake Bolt: Structural damage after the 1886 earthquake was so extensive that many buildings were retrofitted with one or more long iron rods running wall to wall to keep the house stable. The rod was capped at both ends by a "gib plate," often disguised with a decorative element such as a lion's head, an S or

X shape, or other design. Earthquake bolts can be seen all over town, but notable examples are at 235 Meeting Street, 198 East Bay Street, 407 King Street, and 51 East Battery (a rare star design); 190 East Bay Street is unusual for having both an X and an S plate on the same building.

Joggling Board: This long (10-15 feet) flexible plank of cypress, palm, or pine with a handle at each end served various recreational purposes for early Charlestonians. As babies, they might be bounced to sleep. As small children, they might use it as a trampoline. Later it was a method of courtship, whereby a couple would start out at opposite ends and bounce until they met in the middle.

Carolopolis Award: For over 50 years, the Preservation Society of Charleston has handed out these little black badges, to be mounted near the doorway of the winning home, to local homeowners who have renovated historic properties downtown. On the award you'll see "Carolopolis," the Latinized name of the city; "Condita A.D. 1670," the Latin word for founding with the date of Charleston's inception; and another date referring to when the award was given.

Ironwork: Before the mid-19th century, wrought iron was a widely used ornament. Charleston's best-known blacksmith, the late Philip Simmons, made a life's work of continuing the ancient craft of working in wrought iron, and his masterpieces are visible throughout the city, most notably at the Philip Simmons Garden (91 Anson St.), a gate for the Visitors Center (375 Meeting St.), and the Philip Simmons Children's Garden at Josiah Smith Tennent House (Blake St. and East Bay St.). *Chevaux-de-frise* are iron bars on top of a wall through which project some particularly menacing spikes. They became popular after the Denmark Vesey slave revolt conspiracy of 1822. The best example is on the wall of the Miles Brewton House (27 King St.).

© JIM MOREKIS

the Miles Brewton House, host to two occupying army headquarters

Frost, principal founder of the Charleston Preservation Society and a Brewton descendant, grew up here.

Heyward-Washington House

The Heyward-Washington House (87 Church St., 843/722-0354, www.charlestonmuseum. org, Mon.–Sat. 10 A.M.–5 P.M., Sun. 1–5 P.M., $10 adults, $5 children, combo tickets to Charleston Museum and Manigault House available) takes the regional practice of naming a historic home for the two most significant names in its pedigree to its logical extreme. Built in 1772 by the father of Declaration of Independence signer Thomas Heyward Jr., the house also hosted George Washington during the president's visit to Charleston in 1791. It's now owned and operated by the Charleston Museum. The main attraction at the Heyward-Washington House is its masterful woodwork, exemplified by the cabinetry of legendary

Charleston carpenter Thomas Elfe. You'll see his work all over the house, from the mantles to a Chippendale chair. Look for his signature, a figure eight with four diamonds.

Cabbage Row

You know these addresses, 89–91 Church Street, better as "Catfish Row" in Gershwin's opera *Porgy and Bess* (itself based on the book *Porgy* by the great Charleston author DuBose Heyward, who lived at 76 Church St.). Today this complex—which once housed 10 families—next to the Heyward-Washington House is certainly upgraded from years past, but the row still has the humble appeal of the tenement housing it once was, primarily for freed African American slaves after the Civil War. The house nearby at 94 Church Street was where John C. Calhoun and others drew up the infamous Nullification Acts that eventually led to the South's secession.

St. Michael's Episcopal Church

The oldest church in South Carolina, St. Michael's Episcopal Church (71 Broad St., 843/723-0603, services Sun. 8 A.M. and 10:30 A.M., tours available after services) is actually the second sanctuary on this spot. The first church here was made out of black cypress and was called St. Philip's, or "the English Church," which was later rebuilt on Church Street. Although the designer is not known, we do know that work on this sanctuary in the style of Christopher Wren began in 1752 as a response to the overflowing congregation at the rebuilt St. Philips, and it didn't finish until 1761. Other than a small addition on the southeast corner in 1883, the St. Michael's you see today is virtually unchanged, including the massive pulpit, outsized in the style of the time. Services here over the years hosted such luminaries as Marquis de Lafayette, George Washington, and Robert E. Lee, the latter two of whom are known to have sat in the "governor's pew." Two signers of the U.S. Constitution, John Rutledge and Charles Cotesworth Pinckney, are buried in the sanctuary. The 186-foot steeple, painted black during the Revolution in a futile effort to disguise it from British guns, actually sank eight inches after the earthquake of 1886. Inside the tower, the famous "bells of St. Michael's" have an interesting story to tell, having made seven transatlantic voyages for a variety of reasons. They were forged in London's Whitechapel Foundry and sent over in 1764, only to be brought back as a war prize during the Revolution, after which they were returned to the church. Damaged during the Civil War, they were sent back to the foundry of their birth to be recast and returned to Charleston. In 1989 they were damaged by Hurricane Hugo, sent back to Whitechapel yet again, and returned to St. Michael's in 1993. Throughout the lifespan of the bells, the clock tower has continued to tell time, although the minute hand wasn't added until 1849.

St. Michael's offers informal, free guided tours to visitors after Sunday services; contact the greeter for more information.

Four Corners of Law

No guidebook is complete without a mention of the famous intersection of Broad and Meeting Streets, named Four Corners of Law for its confluence of federal law (the Post Office building), state law (the state courthouse), municipal law (City Hall), and God's law (St. Michael's Episcopal Church). That's all well and good, but no matter what the tour guides may tell you, the phrase "Four Corners of Law" was actually popularized by *Ripley's Believe It or Not!* Still, there's no doubt that this intersection has been key to Charleston from the beginning. Meeting Street was laid out around 1672 and takes its name from the White Meeting House of early Dissenters, meaning non-Anglicans. Broad Street was also referred to as Cooper Street in the early days. Right in the middle of the street once stood the very first statue in the United States, a figure of William Pitt erected in 1766.

WATERFRONT

Charleston's waterfront is a place where tourism, history, and industry coexist in a largely seamless fashion. Another of the successful—if at one time controversial—developments spearheaded by Mayor Joe Riley, the centerpiece of the harbor area as far as visitors are concerned is Waterfront Park up toward the High Battery. Farther up the Cooper River is Aquarium Wharf, where you'll find the South Carolina Aquarium, the American Military Museum, the Fort Sumter Visitor Education Exhibit, and the dock where you take the various harbor ferries, whether to Fort Sumter or just a calming ride on the Cooper River.

The Old Exchange and Provost Dungeon

It's far from glamorous, but nonetheless the Old Exchange and Provost Dungeon (122 E. Bay St., 843/727-2165, www.oldexchange.com, daily 9 A.M.–5 P.M., $7 adults, $3.50 children

THE GREAT CHARLESTON EARTHQUAKE

The Charleston peninsula is bordered by three faults, almost like a picture frame: the Woodstock Fault above North Charleston, the Charleston Fault running along the east bank of the Cooper River, and the Ashley Fault to the west of the Ashley River. On August 31, 1886, one of them buckled, causing one of the most damaging earthquakes ever to hit the United States.

The earthquake of 1886 was actually signaled by several foreshocks earlier that week. Residents of the nearby town of Summerville, South Carolina, 20 miles up the Ashley River, felt a small earthquake after midnight on Friday, August 27. Most slept through it. But soon after dawn a larger shock came, complete with a loud bang, causing many to run outside their houses. That Saturday afternoon another tremor hit Summerville, breaking windows and throwing a bed against a wall in one home. Still, Charlestonians remained unconcerned. Then, that Tuesday at 9:50 P.M. came the big one. With an epicenter somewhere near the Middleton Place plantation, the Charleston earthquake is estimated to have measured about 7 on the Richter scale. Tremors were felt across half the country, with the ground shaking in Chicago and a church damaged in Indianapolis. A dam 120 miles away in Aiken, South Carolina, immediately gave way, washing a train right off the tracks. Cracks opened up parallel to the Ashley River, with part of the riverbank falling into the water. Thousands of chimneys all over the state either fell or were rendered useless. A Charleston minister at his summer home in Asheville, North Carolina, described a noise like the sound of wheels driving straight up the mountain, followed by the sound of many railroad cars going by. A moment later, one corner of his house lifted off the ground and slammed back down again. The quake brought a series of "sand blows," a particularly disturbing phenomenon whereby craters open up and spew sand and water up into the air like a small volcano. In Charleston's case, some of the craters were 20 feet wide, shooting debris another 20 feet into the air. The whole event lasted less than a minute.

In crowded Charleston, the damage was horrific; over 2,000 buildings destroyed, a quarter of the city's value gone, 27 killed immediately and almost 100 more to die from injuries and disease. Because of the large numbers of newly homeless, tent cities sprang up in every available park and green space. The American Red Cross's first field mission soon brought some relief, but the scarcity of food, and especially fresh water, made life difficult for everyone.

Almost every surviving building had experienced structural damage, in some cases severe, so a way had to be found to stabilize them. This led to the widespread use of the "earthquake bolt" now seen throughout older Charleston homes. Essentially acting as very long screws with a washer on each end, the idea of the earthquake bolt is simple: Poke a long iron rod through two walls that need stabilizing, and cap the ends. Charleston being Charleston, of course, the end caps were often decorated with a pattern or symbol.

The seismic activity of Charleston's earthquake was so intense that more than 300 aftershocks occurred in the 35 years after the event. In fact, geologists think that most seismic events measured in the region today—including a large event in December 2008—also centering near Summerville—are probably also aftershocks.

Earthquake bolts are a common sight in Charleston.

the Pineapple Fountain at Waterfront Park

and students) at the intersection of East Bay and Meeting Streets is brimming with history. It is known as one of the three most historically significant colonial buildings in the United States, along with Philadelphia's Independence Hall and Boston's Faneuil Hall. This is actually the old Royal Exchange and Custom House, with the cellar serving as a British prison, all built in 1771 over a portion of the old 1698 fortification wall, some of which you can see today. Three of Charleston's four signers of the Declaration of Independence did time downstairs for sedition against the crown. Later, happier times were experienced upstairs in the Exchange, as it was here that the state selected its delegates to the Continental Congress and ratified the U.S. Constitution, and it's where George Washington took a spin on the dance floor. Nearly a victim of early 20th-century shortsightedness—it was almost demolished for a gas station in 1913—the building now belongs to the Daughters of the American Revolution.

Fans of kitsch will get a hoot out of the animatronic Hall of the Presidents–style figures. Kids might especially get a scary kick out of the basement dungeon, where the infamous pirate Stede Bonnet was imprisoned in 1718 before being hanged with his crew on the Battery.

Waterfront Park

Dubbing it "this generation's gift to the future," Mayor Joe Riley made this eight-acre project another part of his downtown renovation. Situated on Concord Street roughly between Exchange Street and Vendue Range, Waterfront Park (843/724-7327, daily dawn–dusk, free) was, like many waterfront locales in Charleston, built on what used to be marsh and water. This particularly massive chunk of "made land" juts about a football field's length farther out than the old waterline. Visitors and locals alike enjoy the relaxing vista of Charleston Harbor, often from the many swinging benches arranged in an unusual front-to-back, single-file pattern all down the pier. On the end you can find viewing binoculars to see the various sights out on the Cooper River, chief among them the USS *Yorktown* at Patriot's Point and the big bridge to Mount Pleasant. Children will enjoy the large "Vendue" wading fountain at the Park's entrance off Vendue Range, while a bit farther south is the large and quite artful Pineapple Fountain with its surrounding wading pool. Contemporary art lovers of all ages will appreciate the nearby **Waterfront Park City Gallery** (34 Prioleau St., Mon.–Fri. noon–5 p.m., free).

South Carolina Aquarium

Honestly, if you've been to the more expansive aquariums in Monterey or Boston, you might be disappointed at the breadth of offerings at the South Carolina Aquarium (100 Aquarium Wharf, 843/720-1990, www.scaquarium.org, March–Aug. daily 9 a.m.–5 p.m., Sept.–Feb. daily 9 a.m.–4 p.m., $20 adults, $13 children, combo tickets with Fort Sumter tour available). But nonetheless, it's clean and well done and is a great place for the whole family to have some fun while getting educated about the rich aquatic life off the coast and throughout this small but ecologically diverse state.

When you enter you're greeted with the 15,000-gallon Carolina Seas tank, with placid nurse sharks and vicious-looking moray eels. Other exhibits highlight the five key South Carolina ecosystems: beach, salt marsh, coastal plain, piedmont, and mountain forest. Another neat display is the Touch Tank, a hands-on collection of invertebrates found along the coast, such as sea urchins and horseshoe crabs. The pièce de résistance, however, is certainly the three-story Great Ocean Tank with literally hundreds of deeper-water marine creatures, including sharks, puffer fish, and sea turtles. Speaking of sea turtles: A key part of the aquarium's research and outreach efforts is the Turtle Hospital, which attempts to rehabilitate

and save sick and injured specimens. The hospital has so far saved 20 sea turtles, the first one being a 270-pound female affectionately known as "Edisto Mama."

American Military Museum

Slightly out of place thematically with the Aquarium, the American Military Museum (360 Concord St., 843/577-7000, www. americanmilitarymuseum.org, Mon.–Sat. 10 a.m.–6 p.m., Sun. 1–5 p.m., $9 adults, $6 students) is one of those under-the-radar types of small museums that can be unexpectedly enriching. Certainly its location near the embarkation point for the Fort Sumter ferry hasn't hurt its profile. It's heavy on uniforms, with a wide range all the way from the Revolution to the modern day. My favorite is the 1907 naval uniform from the cruiser USS *Charleston,* part of Teddy Roosevelt's Great White Fleet. There's also a good collection of rare military miniatures.

◖ Fort Sumter

This is it: the place that brought about the beginning of the Civil War, a Troy for modern times. Though many historians insist the war would have happened regardless of President Lincoln's decision to keep Fort Sumter (843/883-3123, www.nps.gov/fosu, hours seasonal, free) in federal hands, nonetheless the stated *casus belli* was Major Robert Anderson's refusal to surrender the fort when requested to do so in the early morning hours of April 12, 1861. A few hours later came the first shot of the war, fired from Fort Johnson by Confederate Captain George James. That 10-inch mortar shell, a signal for the general bombardment to begin, exploded above Fort Sumter, and nothing in Charleston, or the South, or the United States, would ever be the same again. Notorious secessionist Edmund Ruffin gets credit for firing the first shot in anger, only moments after James's signal shell,

MARY CHESNUT'S DIARY

I have always kept a journal after a fashion of my own, with dates and a line of poetry or prose, mere quotations, which I understood and no one else, and I have kept letters and extracts from the papers. From today forward I will tell the story in my own way.

Mary Boykin Chesnut

She was born in the middle of the state, but Mary Boykin Chesnut's seminal Civil War diary—originally titled *A Diary From Dixie* and first published in 1905—provides one of the most extraordinary eyewitness accounts of antebellum life in Charleston you'll ever read. By turns wise and witty, fiery and flirtatious, Chesnut's writing is a gripping, politically savvy, and dryly humorous chronicle of a life lived close to the innermost circles of Confederate decision-makers. Her husband, James Chesnut Jr., was a U.S. Senator until South Carolina seceded from the Union, whereupon he became a key aide to Confederate President Jefferson Davis and a general in the Confederate Army.

The diary runs from February 1861—three months before the firing on Fort Sumter, which she witnessed—to August 1865, after the Confederate surrender. Along the way the diary shifts to and from various locales, including Montgomery, Alabama; Richmond, Virginia; Columbia, South Carolina; and, of course, Charleston. A sample excerpt is typical of her high regard for the Holy City:

On the Battery with the Rutledges, Captain Hartstein was introduced to me. He has done some heroic things—brought home some ships and is a man of mark. Afterward he sent me a beautiful bouquet, not half so beautiful, however, as Mr. Robert Gourdin's, which already occupied the place of honor on my center table. What a dear, delightful place is Charleston!

Chesnut was a Southern patriot, and as you might imagine some of her observations are wildly politically incorrect by today's standards. But while supportive of slavery and suspicious of the motives of abolitionists—"People in those places expect more virtue from a plantation African than they can insure in practise among themselves with all their own high moral surroundings," she says of white Northern abolitionists—she does allow for a few nuanced looks at the lives of African Americans in the South, as in this observation about her own house servants after the fall of Fort Sumter:

You could not tell that they even heard the awful roar going on in the bay, though it has been dinning in their ears night and day. People talk before them as if they were chairs and tables. They make no sign. Are they stolidly stupid? or wiser than we are; silent and strong, biding their time?

While the diary begins on a confident note regarding the South's chances in the war, as the news from the battlefield gets worse we see how Southerners cope with the sure knowledge that they will lose:

I know how it feels to die. I have felt it again and again. For instance, some one calls out, "Albert Sidney Johnston is killed." My heart stands still. I feel no more. I am, for so many seconds, so many minutes, I know not how long, utterly without sensation of any kind—dead; and then, there is that great throb, that keen agony of physical pain, and the works are wound up again. The ticking of the clock begins, and I take up the burden of life once more.

Southern historian C. Vann Woodward compiled an annotated edition of the Chesnut diary in 1981, *Mary Chesnut's Civil War*, which won a Pulitzer Prize the following year. Her words came to even wider national exposure due to extensive quotations from her diary in Ken Burns's PBS miniseries *The Civil War*.

from a battery at Cummings Point. Ruffin's 64-pound projectile scored a direct hit, smashing into the fort's southwest corner. The first return shot from Fort Sumter was fired by none other than Captain Abner Doubleday, the father of baseball. The first death of the Civil War also happened at Fort Sumter, not from the Confederate bombardment but on the day after. U.S. Army Private Daniel Hough died when the cannon he was loading, to be fired as part of a 100-gun surrender salute to the Stars and Stripes, exploded prematurely. Today the battered but still-standing Fort Sumter remains astride the entrance to Charleston Harbor on an artificial 70,000-ton sandbar. Sumter was part of the so-called Third System of fortifications ordered after the War of 1812. Interestingly, the fort was still not quite finished when the Confederate guns opened up on it 50 years later, and it never enjoyed its intended full complement of 135 big guns.

As you might expect, you can only visit by boat, specifically the approved concessionaire **Fort Sumter Tours** (843/881-7337, www. fortsumtertours.com, $17 adults, $10 ages 6–11, $15 seniors). Once at the fort, there's no charge for admission. Ferries leave from Liberty Square at Aquarium Wharf on the peninsula three times a day during the high season (Apr.–Oct.); call or check the website for times. Make sure to arrive about 30 minutes before the ferry departs. You can also get to Fort Sumter by ferry from Patriot's Point at Mount Pleasant through the same concessionaire.

Budget at least 2.5 hours for the whole trip, including an hour at Fort Sumter. At Liberty Square on the peninsula is the **Fort Sumter Visitor Education Center** (340 Concord St., daily 8:30 A.M.–5 P.M., free), so you can learn more about where you're about to go. Once there, you can be enlightened by the regular ranger's talks on the fort's history and construction (generally at 11 A.M. and 2:30 P.M.), take in the interpretive exhibits throughout

the site, and enjoy the view of the spires of the Holy City from afar. For many, though, the highlight is the boat trip itself, with beautiful views of Charleston Harbor and the islands of the Cooper River estuary. If you want to skip Sumter, you can still take an enjoyable 90-minute ferry ride around the harbor and past the fort on the affiliated **Spiritline Cruises** (800/789-3678, www.spiritlinecruises. com, $17 adults, $10 ages 6–11).

Some visitors are disappointed to find many of the fort's gun embrasures bricked over. This was done during the Spanish-American War, when the old fort was turned into an earthwork and the newer Battery Huger (pronounced "Huge-E") was built on top of it.

FRENCH QUARTER

Unlike the New Orleans version, Charleston's French Quarter is Protestant in origin and flavor. Though not actually given the name until a preservation effort in the 1970s, historically this area was indeed the main place of commerce for the city's population of French Huguenots, primarily a merchant class who fled religious persecution in their native country. Today the five-block area—roughly bounded by East Bay, Market Street, Meeting Street, and Broad Street—contains some of Charleston's most historic buildings, its most evocative old churches and graveyards, its most charming narrow streets, and its most tasteful art galleries.

◖ St. Philip's Episcopal Church

With a pedigree dating back to the colony's fledgling years, St. Philip's Episcopal Church (142 Church St., 843/722-7734, www.stphilipschurchsc.org, sanctuary Mon.–Fri. 10 A.M.–noon and 2–4 P.M., services Sun. 8:15 A.M.) is the oldest Anglican congregation south of Virginia. That pedigree gets a little complicated and downright tragic at times, but any connoisseur of Charleston history needs to be clear on the fine points: The first St. Philip's was built in 1680 at the corner of Meeting Street and Broad Street, the present site of St. Michael's Episcopal Church. That first St. Philip's was badly damaged by a hurricane in 1710, and the city fathers approved the building of a new sanctuary dedicated to the saint on Church Street. However, that building was nearly destroyed by yet another hurricane during construction. Fighting with local Native Americans further delayed rebuilding in 1721. Alas, that St. Philip's burned to the ground in 1835—a distressingly common fate for so many old buildings in this area. Construction immediately began on a replacement, and it's that building you see today. Heavily damaged by Hurricane Hugo in 1989, a $4.5 million renovation kept the church usable. So, to recap: St. Philip's was originally on the site of the present St. Michael's. And while St. Philip's is the oldest congregation in South Carolina, St. Michael's has the oldest physical church building in the state. Are we clear?

South Carolina's great statesman John C. Calhoun—who ironically despised Charlestonians for what he saw as their loose morals—was originally buried across Church Street in the former "stranger's churchyard," or West Cemetery, after his death in 1850. (Charles Pinckney and Edward Rutledge are two other notable South Carolinians buried here.) But near the end of the Civil War, Calhoun's body was moved to an unmarked grave closer to the sanctuary in an attempt to hide its location from Union troops, who it was feared would go out of their way to wreak vengeance on the tomb of one of slavery's staunchest advocates and the man who invented the doctrine of nullification. In 1880, with Reconstruction in full swing, the state legislature directed and funded the building of the current large memorial in the West Cemetery.

French Huguenot Church

One of the oldest congregations in town, the French Huguenot Church (44 Queen St., 843/722-4385, www.frenchhuguenotchurch.org,

liturgy Sun. 10:30 A.M.) also has the distinction of being the only remaining independent Huguenot Church in the country. Founded around 1681 by French Calvinists, the church had about 450 congregants by 1700. While refugees from religious persecution, they weren't destitute, as they had to pay for their passage to America. As is the case with so many historic churches in the area, the building you see isn't the original sanctuary. The first church was built on this site in 1687, and became known as the "Church of Tides" because at that time the Cooper River lapped at its property line. This sanctuary was deliberately destroyed as a firebreak during the great conflagration of 1796. The church was replaced in 1800, but that building was in turn demolished in favor of the picturesque, stucco-coated Gothic Revival sanctuary you see today, which was completed in 1845 and subsequently survived Union shelling and the 1886 earthquake. Does the church look kind of Dutch to you? There's a good reason for that. In their diaspora, French Huguenots spent a lot of time in Holland and became influenced by the tidy sensibilities of the Dutch people. The history of the circa-1845 organ is interesting as well. A rare "tracker" organ, so named for its ultra-fast linkage between the keys and the pipe valves, it was built by famed organ builder Henry Erben. After the fall of Charleston in 1865, Union troops had begun dismantling the instrument for shipment to New York when the church organist, T. P. O'Neale, successfully pleaded with them to let it stay.

Sunday services are conducted in English now, but a single annual service in French is still celebrated in April. The unique Huguenot Cross of Languedoc, which you'll occasionally see ornamenting the church, is essentially a Maltese Cross, its eight points representing the eight beatitudes. Between the four arms of the cross are four fleurs-de-lis, the age-old French symbol of purity.

Dock Street Theatre

Fresh from an extensive multiyear renovation

FRENCH HUGUENOTS

A visitor can't spend a few hours in Charleston without coming across the many French-sounding names so prevalent in the region. Some are common surnames, such as Ravenel, Manigault ("MAN-i-go"), Gaillard, Laurens, or Huger ("huge-EE"). Some are street or place names, such as Mazyck or Legare ("Le-GREE"). Unlike the predominantly French Catholic presence in Louisiana and coastal Alabama, the Gallic influence in Charleston was strictly of the Calvinist Protestant variety. Known as Huguenots, these French immigrants—refugees from an increasingly intolerant Catholic regime in their mother country—were numerous enough in the settlement by the 1690s that they were granted full citizenship and property rights if they swore allegiance to the British crown.

The Huguenot's quick rise in Charleston was due to two factors. Unlike other colonies, Carolina never put much of a premium on religious conformity, a trait that exists to this day despite the area's overall conservatism. And unlike many who fled European monarchies to come to the New World, the French Huguenots were far from poverty-stricken. Most had to buy their own journeys across the Atlantic and arrived already well educated and skilled in one or more useful trades. In Charleston's early days, they were mostly farmers or tar burners (makers of tar and pitch for maritime use). In later times their pragmatism and work ethic would lead them to higher positions in local society, such

as lawyers, judges, and politicians. One of the wealthiest Charlestonians of all, the merchant Gabriel Manigault, was by some accounts the richest person in the American colonies during the early 1700s. South Carolina's most famous French Huguenot of all was Francis Marion, the "Swamp Fox" of Revolutionary War fame. Born on the Santee River, Marion grew up in Georgetown and is now interred near Moncks Corner.

During the 18th century a number of charitable aid organizations sprang up to serve various local groups, mostly along ethnoreligious lines. The wealthiest and most influential of them all was the South Carolina Society, founded in 1737 and first called "The Two Bit Club" because of the original weekly dues. The society still meets today at its building at 72 Meeting Street, designed in 1804 by none other than Manigault's grandson, also named Gabriel, who was Charleston's most celebrated amateur architect. Another aid organization, the **Huguenot Society of Carolina** (138 Logan St., 843/723-3235, www.huguenotsociety.org, Mon.-Fri. 9 A.M.-2 P.M.), was established in 1885. Their library is a great research tool for anyone interested in French Protestant history and genealogy.

To this day, the spiritual home of Charleston's Huguenots is the same as always: the French Huguenot Church on Church Street, one of the earliest congregations in the city. Though many of the old ways have gone, the church still holds one liturgy a year (in April) in French.

project, the Dock Street Theatre (135 Church St., 843/720-3968), right down the street from the Huguenot Church, is where any thespian or lover of the stage must pay homage to this incarnation of the first theater built in the Western Hemisphere. In a distressingly familiar Charleston story, the original 1736 Dock Street Theatre burned down. A second theater opened on the same site in 1754. That building was in turn demolished for a grander edifice in 1773, which, you guessed it, also burned down. The current building dates from 1809, when the Planter's Hotel was built near the site of the

original Dock Street Theatre. To mark the theater's centennial, the hotel added a stage facility in 1835, and it's that building you see today. For the theater's second centennial, the Works Progress Administration completely refurbished Dock Street back into a working theater in time to distract Charlestonians from the pains of the Great Depression. In addition to a very active and well-regarded annual season from the resident Charleston Stage Company, the 464-seat venue has hosted umpteen events of the Spoleto Festival over the past three decades and since its renovation continues to do so.

© JIM MOREKIS

the newly restored Dock Street Theatre, one of America's oldest playhouses

Old Powder Magazine

The Old Powder Magazine (79 Cumberland St., 843/722-9350, www.powdermag.org, Mon.–Sat. 10 A.M.–4 P.M., Sun. 1–4 P.M., $2 adults, $1 children) may be small, but the building is quite historically significant. The 1713 edifice is the oldest public building in South Carolina and also the only one remaining from the days of the Lords Proprietors. As the name indicates, this was where the city's gunpowder was stored during the Revolution. The magazine is designed to implode rather than explode in the event of a direct hit. This is another labor of love of the Historic Charleston Foundation, which has leased the building—which from a distance looks curiously like an ancient Byzantine church—from The Colonial Dames since 1993. It was opened to the public as an attraction in 1997. Now directly across the street from a huge parking garage, the site has continuing funding issues, so occasionally the hours for tours can be erratic. Inside, you'll see displays, a section of the original brick, and an exposed earthquake rod. Right next door is the privately owned, circa-1709 **Trott's Cottage,** the first brick dwelling in Charleston.

Old Slave Mart Museum

Slave auctions became big business in the South after 1808, when the United States banned the importation of slaves, thus increasing both price and demand. The auctions, with slaves forced to stand on display on long tables, generally took place in public buildings where everyone could watch the wrenching spectacle of families being torn apart and lives ruined. But in the 1850s, public auctions in Charleston were put to a stop when city leaders discovered that visitors from European nations—all of which had banned slavery outright years before—were horrified at the practice. The slave trade was moved indoors to "marts" near the Cooper River waterfront where the sales could be conducted out of the public eye. The

© JIM MOREKIS

Circular Congregational Church

last remaining such structure is the Old Slave Mart Museum (6 Chalmers St., 843/958-6467, www.charlestoncity.info, Mon.–Sat. 9 A.M.–5 P.M., $7 adults, $5 children, free under age 6). Built in 1859, and originally known as Ryan's Mart after the builder, it was only in service a short time before the outbreak of the Civil War. The last auction was held in November 1863. After the war, the Slave Mart became a tenement, and then in 1938 an African American history museum. The city of Charleston acquired the building in the 1980s and reopened it as a museum in late 2007. There are two main areas: the orientation area, where visitors learn about the transatlantic slave trade and the architectural history of the building itself; and the main exhibit area, where visitors can see documents, tools, and displays recreating what happened inside during this sordid chapter in local history and celebrating the resilience of the area's African American population.

NORTH OF BROAD

This tourist-heavy part of town is sometimes called the Market area because of its proximity to the Old City Market. We'll start east at the border of the French Quarter on Meeting Street and work our way west and north toward Francis Marion Square.

Circular Congregational Church

The historic Circular Congregational Church (150 Meeting St., 843/577-6400, www.circularchurch.org, services fall–spring Sun. 11 A.M., summer Sun. 10:15 A.M., tours Mon.–Fri. 10:30 A.M.) has one of the most interesting pedigrees of any house of worship in Charleston, which is saying a lot. Originally held on the site of the "White Meeting House," for which Meeting Street is named, services were held here beginning in 1681 for a polyglot mix of Congregationalists, Presbyterians, and Huguenots. For that reason it was often called the Church of Dissenters (*Dissenter* being the common term at the time for anyone not an Anglican). As with many structures in town, the 1886 earthquake necessitated a rebuild, and the current edifice dates from 1891. Ironically, in this municipality called "the Holy City" for its many high spires, the Circular Church has no steeple, and instead stays low to the ground in an almost medieval fashion. Look for the adjacent meeting house, which gave the street its name; a green-friendly addition houses the congregation's Christian outreach, has geothermal heating and cooling, and boasts Charleston's only vegetative roof.

Gibbes Museum of Art

The Gibbes Museum of Art (135 Meeting St., 843/722-2706, www.gibbesmuseum.org, Tues.–Sat. 10 A.M.–5 P.M., Sun. 1–5 P.M., $9 adults, $7 students, $5 ages 6–12) is one of those rare Southern museums that manages a good blend of the modern and the traditional, the local and the international. Beginning in 1905 as the Gibbes Art Gallery—the final wish of James Shoolbred Gibbes, who willed $100,000 for its construction—the complex has grown through the years in size and influence. The key addition to the original beaux arts building came in 1978 with the addition of the modern wing in the rear, which effectively doubled the museum's display space. Shortly thereafter the permanent collection and temporary exhibit space was also expanded. Serendipitously, these renovations enabled the Gibbes to become the key visual arts venue for the Spoleto Festival, begun about the same time. The influential Gibbes Art School in the early 20th century formed a close association with the Woodstock School in New York, bringing important ties and prestige to the fledgling institution. Georgia O'Keeffe, who taught college for a time in Columbia, South Carolina, brought an exhibit here in 1955. The first solo show by an African American artist came here in 1974 with an exhibit of the work of William H. Johnson. Don't miss the nice little garden and its centerpiece, the 1972 fountain and sculpture of Persephone by Marshall Fredericks.

Unitarian Church

In a town filled with cool old church cemeteries, the coolest belongs to the Unitarian Church (4 Archdale St., 843/723-4617, www.charlestonuu.org, services Sun. 11 A.M., free tours Fri.–Sat. 10 A.M.–1 P.M.). As a nod to the beauty and power of nature, vegetation and shrubbery in the cemetery have been allowed to take their natural course (walkways excepted). Virginia creeper wraps around 200-year-old grave markers, honeybees feed on wildflowers, and tree roots threaten to engulf entire headstones. The whole effect is oddly relaxing, making it one of my favorite places in Charleston. The church itself—the second-oldest such edifice in Charleston and the oldest Unitarian sanctuary in the South—is pretty nice too. Begun in 1776 because of overcrowding at the Circular Congregational Church, the brand-new building saw rough usage by British troops during the Revolution. In 1787 the church was repaired, though it was not officially chartered as a Unitarian church until 1839. An extensive modernization happened in 1852, during which the current English Perpendicular Gothic Revival walls were installed, along with the beautiful stained-glass windows. The church was spared in the fire of 1861, which destroyed the old Circular Church but stopped at the Unitarian Church's property line. Sadly, it was not so lucky during the 1886 earthquake, which toppled the original tower. The version you see today is a subsequent and less grand design.

Directly next door is **St. John's Lutheran Church** (5 Clifford St., 843/723-2426, www.stjohnscharleston.org, worship Sun. 8:30 A.M. and 11 A.M.), which had its origin in 1742 when Dr. Henry Melchior Muhlenberg stopped in town for a couple of days on his way to minister to the burgeoning Salzburger colony in

THE NEW CHARLESTON GREEN

Most people know "Charleston green" as a unique local color, the result of adding a few drops of yellow to post–Civil War surplus black paint. But these days the phrase might refer to all the environmentally friendly development in Charleston, which you might find surprising considering the city's location in one of the most conservative states in the country's most conservative region.

The most obvious example is the ambitious Navy Yard redevelopment, which seeks to repurpose the closed-down facility. That project is part of a larger civic vision to reimagine the entire 3,000-acre historic Noisette community of North Charleston, with an accompanying wetlands protection conservancy. From its inception in 1902 at the command of President Theodore Roosevelt through the end of the Cold War, the Charleston Navy Yard was one of the city's biggest employers. Closed down in 1995 as part of a national base realignment plan, locals feared the worst. But a 340-acre section, the **Navy Yard at Noisette** (www. navyyardsc.com), now hosts an intriguing mix of green-friendly design firms, small nonprofits, and commercial maritime companies. The activity centers on the restoration of three huge former naval warehouses at 7, 10, and 11 Storehouse Row. Nearby, on the way to where the CSS *Hunley* is currently being restored, is the big Powerhouse, once the electrical station for the whole yard and now envisioned as the center of a future entertainment and retail district. In the meantime, the Navy Yard's no-frills retro look is so realistic that it has played host to scenes of the Lifetime TV series *Army Wives*. But the largest Navy Yard development is still to come. Clemson University—with the help of a massive federal grant, largest in the school's history—will oversee one of the world's largest wind turbine research facilities, to be built in Building 69. The project is expected to create hundreds of local jobs.

Also in North Charleston, local retail chain Half Moon Outfitters has a green-friendly warehouse facility in an old Piggly Wiggly grocery store. The first LEED (Leadership in Energy and Environmental Design) Platinum-certified building in South Carolina, the warehouse features solar panels, rainwater reservoirs, and locally harvested or salvaged interiors. There's also the LEED-certified North Charleston Elementary School as well as North Charleston's adoption of a "dark skies" ordinance to cut down on light pollution. On the peninsula, the historic meeting house of the Circular Congregation Church, which gave Meeting Street its name, has a green addition with geothermal heating and cooling, rainwater cisterns, and Charleston's first vegetative roof.

In addition to walking the historic byways of the Old Village of Mount Pleasant, architecture and design buffs might also want to check out the 243-acre **I'On** (www.ionvillage.com) "neo-traditional" planned community, a successful model for this type of pedestrian-friendly New Urbanist development. On adjacent Daniel Island, the developers of that island's 4,000-acre planned residential community have been certified as an "Audubon Cooperative Sanctuary" for using wildlife-friendly techniques on its golf and recreational grounds. Even ultra-upscale Kiawah Island has gone green in something other than golf—the fabled Kiawah bobcats are making a comeback, thanks to the efforts of the Kiawah Conservancy.

Why has Charleston proven so adept at moving forward? Locals chalk it up to two things: affluent, well-connected Charlestonians who want to maintain the area's quality of life, and the forward-thinking leadership of Mayor Joe Riley in Charleston and Mayor Keith Summey in North Charleston. For many Charlestonians, however, the green movement manifests in simpler things: the pedestrian and bike lanes in the new Ravenel Bridge over the Cooper River, the thriving city recycling program, or the Sustainable Seafood Initiative, a partnership of local restaurants, universities, and conservation groups that brings the freshest, most environmentally responsible dishes to your table when you dine out in Charleston.

© JIM MOREKIS
the restored Old City Market

Ebenezer, Georgia. He would later be known as the father of the Lutheran Church in America. To see the sanctuary at times other than Sunday mornings, go by the office next door Monday–Friday 9 A.M.–2 P.M. and they'll let you take a walk through the interior.

Old City Market

Part kitschy tourist trap, part glimpse into the old South, part community gathering place, Old City Market (Meeting St. and Market St., 843/973-7236, daily 6 A.M.–11:30 P.M.) remains Charleston's most reliable, if perhaps least flashy, attraction. It is certainly the practical center of the city's tourist trade, not least because so many tours originate nearby. Originally built on Daniel's Creek—claimed from the marsh in the early 1800s after the city's first marketplace at Broad and Meeting Streets burned in 1796—one of City Market's early features was a colony of vultures who hung around for scraps of meat from the many butcher stalls. Sensing that the carrion eaters would keep the area cleaner than any human could, city officials not only allowed the buzzards to hang around, they were protected by law, becoming known as "Charleston eagles" in tongue-in-cheek local jargon. No matter what anyone tries to tell you, Charleston's City Market never hosted a single slave auction. Indeed, when the Pinckney family donated this land to the city for a "Publick Market," one stipulation was that no slaves were ever to be sold here—or else the property would immediately revert to the family's descendants. And judging by the prevalence of the Pinckney name in these parts to this day, there has never been a shortage of potential claimants should that stipulation have been violated. A recent multi-million-dollar renovation has prettified the bulk of City Market into a more big-city air-conditioned pedestrian shopping mall. It's not as shabbily charming as it once was, but certainly offers a more comfortable stroll during the warmer months.

Confederate Museum

Located on the second floor of City Market's iconic main building, Market Hall on Meeting Street, the small but spirited Confederate Museum (188 Meeting St., 843/723-1541, Tues.–Sat. 11 A.M.–3:30 P.M., $5 adults, $3 children, cash only) hosts an interesting collection of Civil War memorabilia, with an emphasis on the military side, and is also the local headquarters of the United Daughters of the Confederacy. Perhaps its best contribution, however, is its research library.

William Rhett House

The oldest standing residence in Charleston is the circa-1713 William Rhett House (54 Hasell St.), which once belonged to the colonel who captured the pirate Stede Bonnet. It's now a private residence, but you can admire this excellent prototypical example of a Charleston single house easily from the street and read the nearby historical marker.

St. Mary of the Annunciation Church

The oldest Roman Catholic church in the Carolinas and Georgia, St. Mary of the Annunciation (89 Hasell St., 843/722-7696, www.catholic-doc.org/saintmarys, mass Sun. 9:30 A.M.) traces its roots to 1789, when the Irish priest Father Matthew Ryan was sent to begin the first Catholic parish in the colony. The original church was destroyed in the great Charleston fire of 1838, and the present sanctuary dates from immediately thereafter. While it did receive a direct hit from a Union shell during the siege of Charleston in the Civil War—taking out the organ—the handsome Greek Revival edifice has survived in fine form the 1886 earthquake, the great hurricane of 1893, and 1989's Hurricane Hugo. You can tour the interior most weekdays 9:30 A.M.–3:30 P.M.

Kahal Kadosh Beth Elohim Reform Temple

The birthplace of Reform Judaism in the United States and the oldest continuously active synagogue in the nation is Kahal Kadosh Beth Elohim Reform Temple (90 Hasell St., 843/723-1090, www.kkbe.org, services Sat. 11 A.M., tours Mon.–Fri. 10 A.M.–noon, Sun. 10 A.M.–4 P.M.). The congregation—Kahal Kadosh means "holy community" in Hebrew—was founded in 1749, with the current temple dating from 1840 and built in the Greek Revival style so popular at the time. The temple's Reform roots came about indirectly because of the great fire of 1838. In rebuilding, some congregants wanted to introduce musical instruments into the temple—previously a no-no—in the form of an organ. The Orthodox contingent lost the debate, and so the new building became the first home of Reform Judaism in the country, a fitting testament to Charleston's longstanding ecumenical spirit of religious tolerance and inclusiveness. Technically speaking, because the Holocaust destroyed all Reform temples in Europe, this is actually the oldest existing Reform synagogue in the world.

Old City Jail

If you made a movie called *Dracula Meets the Lord of the Rings,* the Old City Jail (21 Magazine St., 843/577-5245) might make a great set. Built in 1802 on a lot set aside for public use since 1680, the edifice was the indeed the Charleston County lockup until 1939. It was once even more imposing, but the top story and a large octagonal tower fell victim to the 1886 earthquake. Its history is also the stuff from which movies are made. Some of the last pirates were jailed here in 1822 while awaiting hanging, as was slave rebellion leader Denmark Vesey. (As a response to the aborted Vesey uprising, Charleston for a while required that all black sailors in port be detained at the jail.) During the Civil War, prisoners of both armies were held here at various times.

The Old City Jail currently houses the American College of the Building Arts. Unless you're a student there, the only way to tour the Old Jail is through **Bulldog Tours** (40 N. Market St., 843/722-8687, www.bulldogtours. com). Their Haunted Jail Tour ($18 adults, $10 children) starts daily at 7 P.M., 8 P.M., 9 P.M., and 10 P.M.; meet at the jail.

UPPER KING AREA

For many visitors, the area around King Street north of Calhoun Street is the most happening area of Charleston, and not only because its proximity to the Visitors Center makes it the first part of town many see up close. On some days—Saturdays when the Farmers Market is open, for instance—this bustling, active area of town seems a galaxy away from the quiet grace of the older South of the Broad area. Its closeness to the beautiful College of Charleston campus means there's never a shortage of young people around to patronize the area's restaurants and bars and to add a youthful feel. And its closeness to the city's main shopping district, King Street, means there's never a shortage of happy shoppers toting bags of new merchandise.

Marion Square

While The Citadel moved lock, stock, and barrel almost a century ago, the college's old home, the South Carolina State Arsenal, still overlooks 6.5-acre Francis Marion Square (between King St. and Meeting St. at Calhoun St., 843/965-4104), a reminder of the former glory days when this was the institute's parade ground, the "Citadel Green" (the old Citadel is now a hotel). Interestingly, Marion Square can still be used as a parade ground, under agreement with the Washington Light Infantry and the Sumter Guard, which lease the square to the city. Seemingly refusing to give up on tradition—or perhaps just attracted by the many female College of Charleston students—uniformed cadets from The Citadel are still chockablock in Marion Square on any given weekend, a bit of local flavor that reminds you that you're definitely in Charleston. Marion Square is named for the "Swamp Fox" himself, Revolutionary War hero and father of modern guerrilla warfare Francis Marion, for whom the hotel at the square's southwest corner is also named. The newest feature of Marion Square is the Holocaust Memorial on Calhoun Street. However, the dominant monument is the towering memorial to John C. Calhoun. Its 1858 cornerstone includes one of the more interesting time capsules you'll encounter: $100 in Continental money, a lock of John Calhoun's hair, and a cannonball from the Fort Moultrie battle. Marion Square hosts many events, including the Farmers Market every Saturday mid-April–late December, the Food and Wine Festival, and, of course, some Spoleto events.

College of Charleston

The oldest college in South Carolina and the first municipal college in the country, the College of Charleston (66 George St., 843/805-5507, www.cofc.edu) boasts a fair share of history in addition to the way its 12,000-plus students bring a modern, youthful touch to so much of the city's public activities. While its services are no longer free, despite its historic moniker the College is now a full-blown state-supported university in its own right. Though the college has its share of modernistic buildings, a stroll around the campus will uncover some historic gems. The oldest building on this gorgeous campus, the Bishop Robert Smith House, dates from the year of the College's founding, 1770, and is now the president's house; find it on Glebe Street between Wentworth and George. The large Greek Revival building dominating the College's old quad off George and St. Philip's Streets is the magnificent Randolph Hall (1828), the oldest functioning college classroom in the country and now host to the president's office. The huge circular feature directly in front of it is "The Cistern," a historic reservoir that's a popular place for students to sit in the grass and enjoy the sun filtering through the live oaks. The cistern is also where then-candidate Barack Obama spoke at a rally in January 2008. Movies that have included scenes shot on campus include *Cold Mountain, The Patriot,* and *The Notebook.* If you have an iPhone or iPod Touch, you can download a neat self-guided tour, complete with video, from the Apple iTunes App Store (www.apple.com).

The College's main claims to academic fame are its outstanding Art History and Marine Biology departments and its performing arts program. The **Halsey Institute of Contemporary Art** (54 St. Philip St., 843/953-5680, www.halsey.cofc.edu, Mon.–Sat. 11 A.M.–4 P.M.) focuses on modern visual art and also offers film screenings and lectures.

The groundbreaking **Avery Research Center for African American History and Culture** (843/953-7609, www.cofc.edu/avery, Mon.–Fri. 10 A.M.–5 P.M., Sat. noon–5 P.M.) features rotating exhibits from its permanent archive collection.

Charleston Museum

During its long history, the Charleston Museum (360 Meeting St., 843/722-2996, www.charlestonmuseum.org, Mon.–Sat. 9 A.M.–5 P.M., Sun. 1–5 P.M., $10 adults, $5 children, combo tickets to Heyward-Washington and Manigault Houses available) has moved literally all over town. It's currently housed in a noticeably modern building, but make no mistake: This is the nation's oldest museum, founded in 1773. It strives to stay as fresh and relevant as any new museum, with a rotating schedule of special exhibits in addition to its very eclectic permanent collection. For a long time this was the only place to get a glimpse of the CSS *Hunley,* albeit just a fanciful replica in front of the main entrance. (Now you can see the real thing at its conservation site in North Charleston, and it's even smaller than the replica would indicate.) Much of the Charleston Museum's collection focuses on aspects of everyday life of Charlestonians, from the aristocracy to slaves, including items such as utensils, clothing, and furniture. There are quirks as well, such as the Egyptian mummy and the fine lady's fan made out of turkey feathers. A particular and possibly surprising specialty includes work and research by noted regional naturalists like John James Audubon, André Michaux, and Mark Catesby. There are also numerous exhibits chronicling the local history of Native Americans and African Americans. There's something for children too in the hands-on interactive "Kidstory." The location is particularly convenient, being close not only to the excellent Charleston Visitors Center and its equally excellent parking garage but also to the Joseph Manigault House (which the museum runs), the Children's Museum of the Lowcountry, and the Gibbes Museum of Art.

Joseph Manigault House

Owned and operated by the nearby Charleston Museum, the Joseph Manigault House (350 Meeting St., 843/723-2926, www.charlestonmuseum.org, Mon.–Sat. 10 A.M.–5 P.M., Sun. 1–5 P.M., last tour 4:30 P.M., $10 adults, $5 children, combo tickets to Charleston Museum and Heyward-Washington House available) is sometimes called the "Huguenot House." Its splendor is a good reminder of the fact that the French Protestants were far from poverty-stricken, unlike so many groups who came to America fleeing persecution. This circa-1803 National Historic Landmark was designed by wealthy merchant and investor Gabriel Manigault for his brother, Joseph, a rice planter of local repute and fortune. (Gabriel, quite the crackerjack dilettante architect, also designed Charleston City Hall.) The three-story brick town house is a great example of Adams, or Federal, architecture. The furnishings are top-notch examples of 19th-century handiwork, and the rooms have been restored as accurately as possible, down to the historically correct paint colors. The foundations of various outbuildings, including a privy and slaves' quarters, are clustered around the picturesque little Gate Temple to the rear of the main house in the large enclosed garden. Each December, the Manigault House offers visitors a special treat, as the Garden Club of Charleston decorates it in period seasonal fashion, using only flowers that would have been used in the 19th century.

◖ Aiken-Rhett House

One of my favorite spots in all of Charleston and a comparatively recent acquisition of the Historic Charleston Foundation, the poignant Aiken-Rhett House (48 Elizabeth St., 843/723-1159, www.historiccharleston.org, Mon.–Sat.

© JIM MOREKIS

the Aiken-Rhett House

10 A.M.–5 P.M., Sun 2–5 P.M., last tour 4:15 P.M., $10 adults, $5 children) shows another side of that organization's mission. Whereas the Historic Charleston–run Nathaniel Russell House seeks to recreate a specific point in time, work at the Aiken-Rhett House emphasizes conservation and research. Built in 1818 and expanded by South Carolina Governor William Aiken Jr., after whom we know the house today, parts of this huge, rambling, almost Dickensian house remained sealed from 1918 until 1975 when the family relinquished the property to the Charleston Museum, providing historians with a unique opportunity to study original documents from that period. As you walk the halls, staircases, and rooms—seeing the remains of original wallpaper and the various fixtures added through the years—you can really feel the impact of the people who lived within these walls and get a great sense of the full sweep of Charleston history. While the docents are very friendly and helpful, the main way to enjoy the Aiken-Rhett House is by way of a self-guided MP3 player audio tour—unique in Charleston. While you might think this isolates you from the others in your party, it's actually part of the fun—you can synchronize your players and move as a unit if you'd like.

Children's Museum of the Lowcountry

Yet another example of Charleston's savvy regarding the tourist industry is the Children's Museum of the Lowcountry (25 Ann St., 843/853-8962, www.explorecml.org, Tues.–Sat. 9 A.M.–5 P.M., Sun. 1–5 P.M., $7, free under age 12 months). Recognizing that historic homes and Civil War memorabilia aren't enough to keep a family with young children in town for long, the city established this museum in 2005 specifically to give families with kids aged 3 months to 12 years a reason to spend more time (and money) downtown. A wide variety of hands-on activities—such as a 30-foot

© JIM MOREKIS

ironwork at the Philip Simmons Garden

shrimp boat replica and a medieval castle—stretch the definition of *museum* to its limit. In truth, this is just as much an indoor playground as a museum, but no need to quibble. The Children's Museum has been getting rave reviews since it opened, and visiting parents and their children seem happy with the city's investment.

Philip Simmons Garden

Charleston's most beloved artisan is the late Philip Simmons. Born on nearby Daniel Island in 1912, Simmons went through an apprenticeship to become one of the most sought-after decorative ironworkers in the United States. In 1982 the National Endowment for the Arts awarded him its National Heritage Fellowship. His work is on display at the National Museum of American History, the Smithsonian Institution, and the Museum of International Folk Art in Santa Fe, New Mexico, among many other places. In 1989, the congregation

at Simmons's **St. John's Reformed Episcopal Church** (91 Anson St., 843/722-4241, www.st-johnsre.org) voted to make the church garden a commemoration of the life and work of this legendary African American artisan, who died in 2009 at age 97. Completed in two phases, the Bell Garden and the Heart Garden, the project is a delightful blend of Simmons's signature graceful, sinuous style and fragrant flowers.

Old Bethel United Methodist Church

The history of the Old Bethel United Methodist Church (222 Calhoun St., 843/722-3470), the third-oldest church building in Charleston, is a little confusing. Completed in 1807, the church once stood across Calhoun Street, until a schism formed in the black community over whether they should be limited to sitting in the galleries (in those days in the South, blacks and whites attended church together far more frequently than during the

© JIM MOREKIS

a peek inside the Citadel barracks

Jim Crow era). The entire black congregation wanted out, so in 1852 it was moved aside for the construction of a new church for whites, and then entirely across the street in 1880. Look across the street and sure enough you'll see the circa-1853 **Bethel Methodist Church** (57 Pitt St., 843/723-4587, worship Sun. 9 A.M. and 11:15 A.M.).

HAMPTON PARK AREA

Expansive Hampton Park is a favorite recreation spot for Charlestonians. The surrounding area near the east bank of the Ashley River has some of the earliest suburbs of Charleston, now in various states of restoration and hosting a diverse range of residents. Hampton Park is bordered by streets all around, which can be fairly heavily trafficked because this is the main way to get to The Citadel. But the park streets are closed to traffic Saturday mornings in the spring 8 A.M.–noon so neighborhood people, especially those with young children, can enjoy

themselves without worrying about the traffic. This is also where the Charleston Police stable their Horse Patrol steeds.

The Citadel

Although for many its spiritual and historic center will always be at the old state Arsenal in Marion Square, The Citadel (171 Moultrie St., 843/953-3294, www.citadel.edu, grounds daily 8 A.M.–6 P.M.) has been at this 300-acre site farther up the peninsula along the Ashley River since 1922 and shows no signs of leaving. Getting there is a little tricky, in that the entrance to the college is situated behind beautiful Hampton Park off Rutledge Avenue, a main north–south artery on the western portion of the peninsula. The Citadel (technically its full name is The Citadel, The Military College of South Carolina) has entered popular consciousness through the works of graduate Pat Conroy, especially his novel *Lords of Discipline,* starring a thinly disguised "Carolina Military

Institute." Other famous Bulldog alumni include construction magnate Charles Daniel (for whom the school library is named); Ernest "Fritz" Hollings, South Carolina governor and longtime U.S. senator; and current Charleston Mayor Joe Riley. You'll see The Citadel's living legacy all over Charleston in the person of the ubiquitous cadet, whose gray-and-white uniform, ramrod posture, and impeccable manners all hark back to the days of the Confederacy. But to best experience The Citadel, you should go to the campus itself.

There's lots for visitors to see, including **The Citadel Museum** (843/953-6779, daily noon–5 P.M., free), on your right just as you enter campus; the "Citadel Murals" in the Daniel Library; "Indian Hill," the highest point in Charleston and former site of an Indian trader's home; and the grave of U.S. General Mark Clark of World War II fame, who was Citadel president from 1954 to 1966. Ringing vast Summerall Field—the huge open space where you enter campus—are the many castle-like cadet barracks. If you peek inside their gates, you'll see the distinctive checkerboard pattern on which the cadets line up. All around the field itself are various military items, such as a Sherman tank and an F-4 Phantom jet. The most interesting single experience for visitors to The Citadel is the colorful Friday afternoon dress parade on Summerall Field, in which cadets pass for review in full dress uniform (the fabled "long gray line") accompanied by a marching band and pipers. Often called "the best free show in Charleston," the parade happens almost every Friday at 3:45 P.M. during the school year; you might want to consult the website before your visit to confirm. Arrive well in advance to avoid parking problems.

The institute was born out of panic over the threat of a slave rebellion organized in 1822 by Denmark Vesey. The state legislature passed an act establishing the school to educate the strapping young men picked to protect Charleston from a slave revolt. Citadel folks will proudly tell you they actually fired the first shots of the Civil War, when on January 9, 1861, two cadets fired from a battery on Morris Island at the U.S. steamer *Star of the West* to keep it from supplying Fort Sumter. After slavery ended—and with it the school's original raison d'être—The Citadel continued, taking its current name in 1910 and moving to the Ashley River in 1922. While The Citadel is rightly famous for its pomp and circumstance—as well as its now-defunct no-lock "honor system," done away with after the Virginia Tech shootings—the little-known truth is that to be one of the 2,000 or so currently enrolled Citadel Bulldogs, you don't have to go through all that, or the infamous "Hell Week" either. You can just sign up for one of their many evening graduate school programs.

Joseph P. Riley Jr. Ballpark

When you hear Charlestonians talk about "The Joe" (360 Fishburne St., 843/577-3647, www.riverdogs.com), they're referring to this charming minor-league baseball stadium, home of the Charleston River Dogs, a New York Yankees affiliate playing April–August in the venerable South Atlantic League. It's also another part of the civic legacy of longtime Mayor Joe Riley, in this case in partnership with the adjacent Citadel. Inspired by the retro design of Baltimore's Camden Yards, The Joe opened in 1997 to rave reviews from locals and baseball connoisseurs all over the nation. From downtown, get there by taking Broad Street west until it turns into Lockwood Drive. Follow that north until you get to Brittlebank Park and The Joe, right next to the Citadel.

WEST ASHLEY

Ironically, Charleston's first postwar automobile suburb also has roots back to the first days of the colony's settlement and was the site of some of the antebellum era's grandest plantations. As the cost of housing on the peninsula continues to rise, this area on the west bank of the Ashley River is experiencing a newfound cachet today for hipsters and young families alike. For most visitors, though, the biggest draws are the ancient plantations and historic sites along the west bank of the river: Charles Towne Landing, Drayton Hall, Magnolia Plantation, and Middleton Place, farthest north. Getting to this area from Charleston proper is easy. Take U.S. 17 ("the Crosstown") west across the Ashley River to the junction with Highway 61 and take a right (north) onto Highway 61; veer right to get on Highway 7 for Charles Towne Landing, or stay left on Highway 61 for the plantations.

Charles Towne Landing

Any look at West Ashley must begin where everything began, with the 600-acre historic site Charles Towne Landing (1500 Old Towne Rd., 843/852-4200, www.charlestowne.org, daily 9 A.M.–5 P.M., $7.50 adults, $3.50 students, free under age 6). This is where Charleston's original settlers first arrived from Barbados and camped in 1670, remaining only a few years before eventually moving to the more defensible peninsula where the Holy City now resides. For many years the site was in disrepair and borderline neglect, useful mainly as a place to ship busloads of local schoolchildren on field trips. However, a recent long-overdue upgrade came to fruition with a grand "reopening" of sorts in 2006, which has been very well received and has given the Landing a newfound sheen of respect. A beautiful and fully seaworthy replica of a settlers' ship is the main highlight, docked creek-side on the far side of the long and well-done exploration trail through the site. You can get on board, and a helpful ranger will explain aspects of the ship as well as the original settlement. Another highlight is the archaeological

© JIM MOREKIS

Put yourself into the shoes of explorers at Charles Towne Landing.

© JIM MOREKIS

Drayton Hall

remnant of the original palisade wall (there's a reconstructed palisade to show what it looked like). Ranger-guided programs are available Wednesday–Friday at 10 A.M.; call ahead for reservations.

Not just a historic site, this is also a great place to bring the family. It has Charleston's only zoo, the "Animal Forest," featuring otters, bears, cougars, and buffalo, and 80 acres of beautiful gardens to relax in, many featuring fabulously ancient live oaks and highlighting other indigenous flora the settlers would have been familiar with. A new audio tour has been instituted, where you can rent an MP3 player ($5), but the self-guided approach works just fine, and you can get a nice map from the front desk to help you around. The outdoor highlights of Charles Towne Landing are obvious, but don't miss the fantastic exhibits inside the visitors center, which are particularly well done and give a comprehensive and informative look back at the time of the original settlers.

Drayton Hall

A mecca for historic preservationists all over the country, Drayton Hall (3380 Ashley River Rd., 843/769-2600, www.draytonhall.org, daily 9 A.M.–4 P.M., $18 adults, $8 ages 12–18, $6 ages 6–11, grounds only $8) is remarkable not only for its pedigree but for the way in which it has been preserved. This stately redbrick Georgian-Palladian building, the oldest plantation home in the country that is open to the public, has been literally historically preserved—as in no electricity, heat, or running water. Since its construction in 1738 by John Drayton, son of Magnolia Plantation founder Thomas, Drayton Hall has survived almost completely intact through the ups and downs of Lowcountry history. Drayton died while fleeing the British in 1779; subsequently his house served as the headquarters of British General Clinton and later General Cornwallis. In 1782, however, American General "Mad Anthony" Wayne claimed the house as his own headquarters. During the Civil War, Drayton Hall escaped the depredations of the conquering Union Army, one of only three area plantation homes to survive. Three schools of thought have emerged to explain why it was spared the fate of so many other plantation homes: (1) A slave told the troops it was owned by "a Union Man," Drayton cousin Percival, who served alongside Admiral David Farragut of "damn the torpedoes" fame; (2) General William Sherman was in love with one of the Drayton women; and (3) one of the Draytons, a doctor, craftily posted smallpox warning flags at the outskirts of the property. Of the three scenarios, the last is considered most likely.

Visitors expecting the more typical approach to house museums, i.e. subjective renovation with period furnishings that may or may not have any connection with the actual house, might be disappointed. But for others the experience at Drayton Hall is quietly exhilarating, almost in a Zen-like way. Planes are routed around the house so that no rattles will endanger its structural integrity. There's no furniture to speak of, only bare rooms, decorated with original paint, no matter how little remains. It can be jarring at first, but after you get into it you might wonder why anyone does things any differently.

Another way the experience is different is in the almost military professionalism of the National Trust for Historic Preservation, which has owned and administered Drayton Hall since 1974. The guides hold degrees in the field, and a tour of the house—offered punctually at the top of the hour, except for the last tour of the day, which starts on the half-hour—takes every bit of 50 minutes, about twice as long as most house tours. A separate 45-minute program is "Connections: From Africa to America," which chronicles the diaspora of the slaves who originally worked this plantation, from their capture to their eventual freedom. "Connections" is given at 11:15 A.M., 1:15 P.M., and 3:15 P.M.

The site comprises not only the main house but two self-guided walking trails, one along the peaceful Ashley River and another along the marsh. Note also the foundations of the two "flankers," or guest wings, at each side of the main house. They survived the Yankees only for one to fall victim to the 1886 earthquake and the other to the 1893 hurricane. Also on-site is an African American cemetery with at least 33 known graves. It's kept deliberately untended and unlandscaped to honor the final wish of Richmond Bowens (1908–1998), the seventh-generation descendant of some of Drayton Hall's original slaves.

Magnolia Plantation and Gardens

A different legacy of the Drayton family is Magnolia Plantation and Gardens (3550 Ashley Rd., 843/571-1266, www.magnoliaplantation. com, Mar.–Oct. daily 9 A.M.–4:30 P.M., call for winter hours, $15 adults, $10 children, free under age 6). It claims not only the first garden in the United States, dating back to the 1680s, but also the first public garden, dating to 1872. Magnolia's history spans back two full centuries before that, however, when Thomas Drayton Jr.—scion of Norman aristocracy, son of a wealthy Barbadian planter—came from the Caribbean to build his own fortune. He immediately married the daughter of Stephen Fox, who began this plantation in 1676. Through wars, fevers, depressions, earthquakes, and hurricanes, Magnolia has stayed in the possession of an unbroken line of Drayton descendants to this very day.

As a privately run attraction, Magnolia has little of the academic veneer of other plantation sites in the area, most of which have long passed out of private hands. There's a slightly kitschy feel here, the opposite of the quiet dignity of Drayton Hall. And unlike Middleton Place a few miles down the road, the gardens here are anything but manicured, with a wild, almost playful feel. That said, Magnolia can

the maze at Magnolia Plantation and Gardens

© JIM MOREKIS

claim fame to being one of the earliest bona fide tourist attractions in the United States and the beginning of Charleston's now-booming tourist industry. It happened after the Civil War, when John Grimke Drayton, reduced to near-poverty, sold off most of his property, including the original Magnolia Plantation, just to stay afloat. (In a common practice at the time, as a condition of inheriting the plantation, Mr. Grimke, who married into the family, was required to legally change his name to Drayton.) The original plantation home was burned during the war—either by Union troops or freed slaves—so Drayton barged a colonial-era summer house in Summerville, South Carolina, down the Ashley River to this site and built the modern Magnolia Plantation around it specifically as an attraction. Before long, tourists regularly came here by crowded boat from Charleston (a wreck of one such ferry is still on-site). Magnolia's reputation became so exalted that at one point Baedecker's listed it as

one of the three main attractions in America, alongside the Grand Canyon and Niagara Falls. The family took things to the next level in the 1970s, when John Drayton Hastie bought out his brother and set about marketing Magnolia Plantation and Gardens as a modern tourist destination, adding more varieties of flowers so that something would always be blooming nearly year-round. While spring remains the best—and also the most crowded—time to come, a huge variety of camellias blooms in early winter, a time marked by a yearly Winter Camellia Festival.

Today Magnolia is a place to bring the whole family, picnic under the massive old live oaks, and wander the lush, almost overgrown grounds. Children will enjoy finding their way through "The Maze" of manicured camellia and holly bushes, complete with a viewing stand to look within the giant puzzle. Plant lovers will enjoy the themed gardens such as the Biblical Garden, the Barbados Tropical Garden, and the

Audubon Swamp Garden, complete with alligators and named after John James Audubon, who visited here in 1851. Hundreds of varieties of camellias, clearly labeled, line the narrow walkways. House tours, the 45-minute Nature Train tour, the 45-minute Nature Boat tour, and a visit to the Audubon Swamp Garden run about $8 pp extra for each offering.

Of particular interest is the poignant old Drayton Tomb, along the Ashley River, which housed many members of the family until being heavily damaged in the 1886 earthquake. Look closely at the nose of one of the cherubs on the tomb; it was shot off by a vengeful Union soldier. Nearby you'll find a nice walking and biking trail along the Ashley among the old paddy fields.

Middleton Place

Not only the first landscaped garden in America but still one of the most magnificent in the world, Middleton Place (4300 Ashley River Rd., 843/556-6020, www.middletonplace.org, daily 9 A.M.–5 P.M., $25 adults, $15 students, $10 children, guided house tour $12 extra) is a sublime, unforgettable combination of history and sheer natural beauty. Nestled along a quiet bend in the Ashley River, the grounds contain a historic restored home, working stables, and 60 acres of breathtaking gardens, all manicured to perfection. A stunning piece of modern architecture, the Inn at Middleton Place completes the package in surprisingly harmonic fashion. First granted in 1675, Middleton Place is the culmination of the Lowcountry rice plantation aesthetic. That sensibility is most immediate in the graceful Butterfly Lakes at the foot of the green landscaped terrace leading up to the Middleton Place House itself, the only surviving remnant of the vengeful Union occupation. The two wing-shaped lakes, 10 years in construction, seem to echo the low paddy

© JIM MOREKIS

Middleton Place

fields that once dotted this entire landscape. In 1741 the plantation became the family seat of the Middletons, one of the most notable surnames in U.S. history. The first head of the household was Henry Middleton, president of the First Continental Congress, who began work on the meticulously planned and maintained gardens. The plantation passed to his son Arthur, a signer of the Declaration of Independence; then on to Arthur's son Henry, governor of South Carolina; and then down to Henry's son Williams Middleton, a signer of the Ordinance of Secession. It was then that things turned sour, both for the family and for the grounds themselves. As the Civil War wound down, on February 22, 1865, the 56th New York Volunteers burned the main house and destroyed the gardens, leaving only the circa-1755 guest wing, which today is the Middleton Place House Museum. The great earthquake of 1886 added insult to injury by wrecking the Butterfly Lakes. It wasn't until 1916 that renovation began, when heir J. J. Pringle Smith took on the project as his own. No one can say he wasn't successful. At the garden's bicentennial in 1941, the Garden Club of America awarded its prestigious Bulkley Medal to Middleton Place. In 1971 Middleton Place was named a National Historic Landmark, and 20 years later the International Committee on Monuments and Sites named Middleton Place one of six U.S. gardens of international importance. In 1974, Smith's heirs established the nonprofit Middleton Place Foundation, which now owns and operates the entire site.

All that's left of the great house are the remains of the foundation, still majestic in ruin. Today visitors can tour the excellently restored **Middleton Place House Museum** (4300 Ashley River Rd., 843/556-6020, www.middleton-place.org, guided tours Mon. 1:30–4:30 P.M., Tues.–Sun. 10 A.M.–4:30 P.M., $12)—actually the only remaining "flanker" building—and see furniture, silverware, china, and books belonging to the Middletons as well as family portraits by Thomas Sully and Benjamin West.

A short walk takes you to the Plantation Stableyards, where costumed craftspeople still work using historically authentic tools and methods, surrounded by a happy family of domestic animals. The newest addition to the Stableyards is a pair of magnificent male water buffalo. Henry Middleton originally brought a pair in to work the rice fields—the first in North America—but today they're just there to relax and add atmosphere. They bear the Turkish names of Adem (the brown one) and Berk (the white one), or "Earth" and "Solid." Meet the fellas daily 9 A.M.–5 P.M. If you're like most folks, however, you'll best enjoy simply wandering and marveling at the gardens. "Meandering" is not the right word to describe them, since they're systematically laid out. "Intricate" is the word I prefer, and that sums up the attention to detail that characterizes all the garden's portions, each with a distinct personality and landscape design template. To get a real feel for how things used to be here, for an extra $15 pp you can take a 45-minute carriage ride through the bamboo forest to an abandoned rice field. Rides start around 10 A.M. and run every hour or so, weather permitting.

The 53-room **Inn at Middleton Place,** besides being a wholly gratifying lodging experience, is also a quite self-conscious and largely successful experiment. Its bold Frank Lloyd Wright–influenced modern design, comprising four units joined by walkways, is modern. But both inside and outside it manages to blend quite well with the surrounding fields, trees, and riverbanks. The Inn also offers kayak tours and instruction—a particularly nice way to enjoy the grounds from the waters of the Ashley—and features its own organic garden and labyrinth, intriguing modern counterpoints to the formal gardens of the plantation itself.

They still grow the exquisite Carolina Gold rice in a field at Middleton Place, harvested in the old style each September. You can sample some of it in many dishes at the **Middleton Place Restaurant** (843/556-6020, www.middletonplace.org, lunch daily 11 A.M.–3 P.M., dinner Tues.–Thurs. 6–8 P.M., Fri.–Sat. 6–9 P.M., Sun. 6–8 P.M., $15–25). Hint: You can tour the gardens for free if you arrive for a dinner reservation at 5:30 P.M. or later.

The Coburg Cow

The entire stretch of U.S. 17 (Savannah Highway) heading into Charleston from the west is redolent of a particularly Southern brand of retro Americana. The chief example is the famous Coburg Cow, a large, rotating dairy cow accompanied by a bottle of chocolate milk. The current installation dates from 1959, though a version of it was on this site as far back as the early 1930s when this area was open countryside. During Hurricane Hugo the Coburg Cow was moved to a safe location. In 2001 the attached dairy closed down, and the city threatened to have the cow moved or demolished. But community outcry preserved the delightful landmark, which is visible today on the south side of U.S. 17 in the 900 block. You can't miss it—it's a big cow on the side of the road!

NORTH CHARLESTON

For years synonymous with crime, blight, and sprawl, North Charleston—actually a separate municipality—was for the longest time considered a necessary evil by most Charlestonians, who generally ventured there only to shop at a mall or see a show at its concert venue, the Coliseum. But as the cost of real estate continues to rise on the peninsula in Charleston proper, more and more artists and young professionals are choosing to live here. Make no mistake: North Charleston still has its share of crime and squalor, but some of the most exciting things going on in the metro area are taking place right here. While many insisted that the closing of the U.S. Navy Yard in the 1990s

would be the economic death of the whole city, the free market stepped in and is transforming the former military facility into a hip mixed-use shopping and residential area. This is also where to go if you want to see the raised submarine CSS *Hunley*, now in a research area on the grounds of the old Navy Yard. In short, North Charleston offers a lot for the more adventurous traveler and will no doubt only become more and more important to the local tourist industry as the years go by. And as they're fond of pointing out up here, there aren't any parking meters.

Magnolia Cemetery

Although not technically in North Charleston, historic Magnolia Cemetery (70 Cunnington Ave., 843/722-8638, Sept.–May daily 8 A.M.–5 P.M., Jun.–Aug. daily 8 A.M.–6 P.M.) is on the way, well north of the downtown tourist district in the area called "The Neck." This historic burial ground, while not quite the aesthetic equal of Savannah's Bonaventure, is still a stirring site for its natural beauty and ornate memorials as well as for its historic aspects. Here are buried the crewmen who died aboard the CSS *Hunley*, reinterred after their retrieval from Charleston Harbor. In all, over 2,000 Civil War dead are buried here, including five Confederate generals and 84 rebels who fell at Gettysburg and were moved here.

Charleston Navy Yard

A vast postindustrial wasteland to some and a fascinating outdoor museum to others, the Charleston Navy Yard is in the baby steps of rehabilitation from one of the Cold War era's major military centers to the largest single urban redevelopment project in the United States. The Navy's gone now, forced off the site during a phase of base realignment in the mid-1990s. But a 340-acre section, the **Navy Yard at Noisette** (1360 Truxtun Ave., 843/302-2100, www.navyyardsc.com, daily 24 hours), now hosts an intriguing mix of homes, green design firms, nonprofits, and commercial maritime companies and was named the country's sixth-greenest neighborhood by *Natural Home* magazine in 2008. It has even played host to some scenes of the Lifetime TV series *Army Wives*. Enter on Spruill Avenue and you'll find yourself on wide streets lined with huge, boarded-up warehouse facilities, old machine shops, and dormant power stations. A notable project is the restoration of **10 Storehouse Row** (2120 Noisette Blvd., 843/302-2100, Mon.–Fri. 9 A.M.–5 P.M.), which now hosts the American College of Building Arts along with design firms, galleries, and a small café. Nearby, Clemson University will soon be administering one of the world's largest wind turbine research facilities. At the north end lies the new **Riverfront Park** (843/745-1087, daily dawn–dusk) in the old Chicora Gardens military residential area. There's a nifty little fishing pier on the Cooper River, an excellent naval-themed band shell, and many sleekly designed modernist sculptures paying tribute to the sailors and ships that made history here. From Charleston you get to the Navy Yard by taking I-26 north to exit 216B (you can reach the I-26 junction by just going north on Meeting Street). After exiting, take a left onto Spruill Avenue and a right onto McMillan Avenue, which takes you straight in.

◖ CSS *Hunley*

For the longest time, the only glimpse of the ill-fated Confederate submarine was a not-quite-accurate replica outside the Charleston Museum. But after maritime novelist and adventurer Clive Cussler and his team finally found the *Hunley* in 1995 off Sullivan's Island, the tantalizing dream became a reality: We'd finally find out what it looked like, and perhaps even be lucky enough to bring it to the surface. That moment came on August 8, 2000,

© JIM MOREKIS

replica of the CSS *Hunley* outside the Charleston Museum

when a team comprising the nonprofit **Friends of the Hunley** (Warren Lasch Conservation Center, 1250 Supply St., Bldg. 255, 866/866-9938, www.hunley.org, Sat. 10 A.M.–5 P.M., Sun. noon–5 P.M., $12, free under age 5), the federal government, and private partners successfully implemented a plan to safely raise the vessel. It was recently moved to its new home in the old Navy Yard, named after Warren Lasch, chairman of the Friends of the Hunley. You can now view the sub in a 90,000-gallon conservation tank on the grounds of the old Navy Yard, see the life-size model from the TNT movie *The Hunley,* and look at artifacts such as the "lucky" gold piece of the commander. You can even see facial reconstructions of some of the eight sailors who died on board the sub that fateful February day in 1864, when it mysteriously sank right after successfully destroying the USS *Housatonic* with the torpedo attached to its bow. So that research and conservation can be performed during the week, tours only happen on Saturday–Sunday. Because of this limited window of opportunity and the popularity of the site, I strongly recommend reserving tickets ahead of time. The sub itself is completely submerged in an electrolyte formula to better preserve it, and photography is strictly forbidden. (The remains of the crew lie in Magnolia Cemetery, where they were buried in 2004 with full military honors.) To get to the Warren Lasch Center from Charleston, take I-26 north to exit 216B. Take a left onto Spruill Avenue and a right onto McMillan Avenue. Once in the Navy Yard, take a right on Hobson Avenue, and after about one mile take a left onto Supply Street. The Lasch Center is the low white building on the left.

Park Circle

The focus of restoration in North Charleston is the old Park Circle neighborhood (intersection of Rhett Ave. and Montague Ave., www.parkcircle.net). The adjacent **Olde North Charleston** development has a number of quality shops, bars, and restaurants.

Fire Museum

It's got a mouthful of a name, but the **North Charleston and American LaFrance Fire Museum and Educational Center** (4975 Centre Pointe Dr., 843/740-5550, www.legacyofheroes.org, Mon.–Sat. 10 A.M.–5 P.M., Sun. 1–5 P.M., last ticket 4 P.M., $6 adults, free under age 14), right next to the huge Tanger Outlet Mall, does what it does with a lot of chutzpah—which is fitting considering that it pays tribute to firefighters and the tools of their dangerous trade. The museum, which opened in 2007 and shares a huge 25,000-square-foot space with the North Charleston Convention and Visitors Bureau, is primarily dedicated to maintaining and increasing its collection of antique American LaFrance firefighting vehicles and equipment. The 18 fire engines here date from 1857 to 1969. The museum's exhibits have taken on greater poignancy in the wake of the tragic loss of nine Charleston firefighters killed trying to extinguish a warehouse blaze on U.S. 17 in summer 2007—second only to the 9/11 attacks as the largest single loss of life for a U.S. firefighting department.

EAST COOPER

The main destination in this area on the east bank of the Cooper River is the island of Mount Pleasant, primarily known as a peaceful, fairly affluent suburb of Charleston—a role it has played for about 300 years now. Although few old-timers (called "hungry necks" in local lingo) remain, Mount Pleasant does have several key attractions well worth visiting—the old words of former Charleston mayor John Grace notwithstanding: "Mount Pleasant is neither a mount, nor is it pleasant." Through Mount Pleasant is also the only land route to access Sullivan's Island, Isle of Palms, and historic Fort Moultrie. Shem Creek, which

RAISING THE *HUNLEY*

The amazing, unlikely raising of the Confederate submarine CSS *Hunley* from the muck of Charleston harbor sounds like the plot of an adventure novel—which makes sense considering that the major player is an adventure novelist. For 15 years, the undersea diver and best-selling author Clive Cussler looked for the final resting place of the *Hunley*. The sub was mysteriously lost at sea after sinking the USS *Housatonic* on February 17, 1864, with the high-explosive "torpedo" mounted on a long spar on its bow. It marked the first time a sub ever sank a ship in battle.

For over a century before Cussler, treasure-seekers had searched for the sub, with P. T. Barnum even offering $100,000 to the first person to find it. But on May 3, 1995, a magnetometer operated by Cussler and his group, the National Underwater Marine Agency, discovered the *Hunley*'s final resting place—in 30 feet of water and under three feet of sediment about four miles off Sullivan's Island at the mouth of the harbor. Using a specially designed truss to lift the entire sub, a 19-person dive crew and a team of archaeologists began a process that would result in raising the vessel on August 8, 2000. But before the sub could be brought up, a dilemma had to be solved: For 136 years the saltwater of the Atlantic had permeated its metallic skin. Exposure to air would rapidly disintegrate the entire thing. So the conservation team, with input from the U.S. Navy, came up with a plan to keep the vessel submerged in a special solution indefinitely at the specially constructed **Warren Lasch Conservation Center** (1250 Supply St., Bldg. 255, 866/866-9938, www.hunley.org, Sat. 10 A.M.-5 P.M., Sun.

noon-5 P.M., $12, free under age 5) in the old Navy Yard while research and conservation was performed on it piece by piece.

And that's how you see the *Hunley* today, submerged in its special conservation tank, still largely covered in sediment. Upon seeing the almost unbelievably tiny, cramped vessel—much smaller than most experts imagined it would be—visitors are often visibly moved at the bravery and sacrifice of the nine-man Confederate crew, who no doubt would have known that the *Hunley*'s two previous crews had drowned at sea in training accidents. Theirs was, in effect, a suicide mission. That the crew surely realized this only makes the modern visitor's experience even more poignant.

The Warren Lasch Center, operated under the auspices of Clemson University, is only open to the public on weekends. Archaeology continues apace during the week—inch by painstaking inch, muck and tiny artifacts removed millimeter by millimeter. The process is so thorough that archaeologists have even identified an individual eyelash from one of the crewmembers. Other interesting artifacts include a three-fold wallet with a leather strap, owner unknown; seven canteens; and a wooden cask in one of the ballast tanks, maybe used to hold water or liquor or even used as a chamber pot.

The very first order of business once the sub was brought up, however, was properly burying those brave sailors. In 2004, Charleston came to a stop as a ceremonial funeral procession took the remains of the nine to historic Magnolia Cemetery, where they were buried with full military honors.

bisects Mount Pleasant, was once the center of the local shrimping industry, and while there aren't near as many shrimp boats as there once were, you can still see them docked or on their way to and from a trawling run. (Needless to say, there are a lot of good seafood restaurants around here as well.) The most common route for visitors is by way of U.S. 17 over the massive Arthur Ravenel Jr. Bridge.

Patriots Point Naval and Maritime Museum

Directly across Charleston Harbor from the old city lies the Patriots Point Naval and Maritime Museum complex (40 Patriots Point Rd., 843/884-2727, www.patriotspoint.org, daily 9 A.M.–6:30 P.M., $18 adults, $11 ages 6–11, free for active-duty military), one of the first chapters in Charleston's tourism renaissance.

COURTESY OF CHARLESTONCVB.COM

the USS *Yorktown* at Patriots Point

The project began in 1975 with what is still its main attraction, the World War II aircraft carrier **USS Yorktown,** named in honor of the carrier lost at the Battle of Midway. Much of "The Fighting Lady" is open to the public, and kids and nautical buffs will thrill to walk the decks and explore the many stations below deck on this massive 900-foot vessel, a veritable floating city. You can even have a full meal in the CPO Mess Hall just like the crew once did (except you'll have to pay $8.50 pp). And if you really want to get up close and personal, try the Navy Flight Simulator for a small additional fee. Speaking of planes, aviation buffs will be overjoyed to see that the *Yorktown* flight deck (the top of the ship) and the hangar deck (right below) are packed with authentic warplanes, not only from World War II but from subsequent conflicts the ship participated in. You'll see an F6F Hellcat, an FG-1D Corsair, and an SBD Dauntless like those that fought the Japanese, on up to an F-4F Phantom and an F-14 Tomcat from the jet era.

Patriots Point's newest exhibit is also on the *Yorktown:* the **Medal of Honor Memorial Museum,** which opened in 2007 by hosting a live broadcast of the *NBC Nightly News.* Included in the cost of admission, the Medal of Honor museum is an interactive experience documenting the exploits of the medal's honorees from the Civil War through today. Other ships moored beside the *Yorktown* and open for tours are the Coast Guard cutter USCG *Ingham,* the submarine USS *Clamagore,* and the destroyer USS *Laffey,* which survived being hit by three Japanese bombs and five kamikaze attacks—all within an hour. The Vietnam era is represented by a replica of an entire Naval Support Base Camp, featuring a river patrol boat and several helicopters.

A big plus is the free 90-minute guided tour. If you really want to make a family history day out of it, you can also hop on the ferry from Patriots Point to Fort Sumter and back.

Old Village

It won't blow you away if you've seen Charleston, Savannah, or Beaufort, but Mount Pleasant's old town has its share of fine colonial and antebellum homes and historic churches. Indeed, Mount Pleasant's history is almost as old as Charleston's. First settled for farming in 1680, it soon acquired cachet as a great place for planters to spend the hot summers away from the mosquitoes inland. The main drag is Pitt Street, where you can shop and meander among plenty of shops and restaurants (try an ice cream soda at the historic Pitt Street Pharmacy). The huge meeting hall on the waterfront, Alhambra Hall, was the old ferry terminal.

Boone Hall Plantation

Visitors who've also been to Savannah's Wormsloe Plantation will see the similarity in the majestic, live oak–lined entrance avenue to Boone Hall Plantation (1235 Long Point Rd., 843/884-4371, www.boonehallplantation.com, mid-Mar.–Labor Day Mon.–Sat. 8:30 A.M.–6:30 P.M., Sun. noon–5 P.M., Labor Day–Nov. Mon.–Sat. 9 A.M.–5 P.M., Sun. 1–4 P.M., Dec.–mid-Mar. Mon.–Sat. 9 A.M.–5 P.M., Sun. noon–5 P.M., $19.50 adults, $9.50 children). But this site is about half a century older, dating back to a grant to Major John Boone in the 1680s (the oaks of the entranceway were planted in 1743). Unusually in this area, where fortunes were originally made mostly on rice, Boone Hall's main claim to fame was as a cotton plantation as well as a noted brick-making plant. Boone Hall takes the phrase "living history" to its extreme, as it's not only an active agricultural facility but lets visitors go on "u-pick" walks through its fields, which boast succulent strawberries, peaches, tomatoes, and even pumpkins in October—as well as free hayrides. Currently owned by the McRae family, which

first opened it to the public in 1959, Boone Hall is called "the most photographed plantation in America." And photogenic it certainly is, with natural beauty to spare in its scenic location on the Wando River and its adorable Butterfly Garden. But as you're clicking away with your camera, do keep in mind that the plantation's "big house" is not original; it's a 1935 reconstruction. While Boone Hall's most genuine historic buildings include the big Cotton Gin House (1853) and the 1750 Smokehouse, to me the most poignant and educational structures by far are the nine humble brick slave cabins from the 1790s, expertly restored and most fitted with interpretive displays. The cabins are the center of Boone Hall's educational programs, including an exploration of Gullah culture at the outdoor "Gullah Theatre" on the unfortunately named Slave Street. Summers see some serious Civil War reenacting going on. In all, three different tours are available: a 30-minute house tour, a tour of Slave Street, and a garden tour.

Charles Pinckney National Historic Site

This is one of my favorite sights in Charleston, for its uplifting, well-explored subject matter as well as its tastefully maintained house and grounds. Though "Constitution Charlie's" old Snee Farm is down to only 28 acres from its original magnificent 700, the Charles Pinckney National Historic Site (1240 Long Point Rd., 843/881-5516, www.nps.gov/chpi, daily 9 A.M.–5 P.M., free) that encompasses it is still an important repository of local and national history. Sometimes called "the forgotten Founder," Charles Pinckney was not only a hero of the American Revolution and a notable early abolitionist but one of the main authors of the U.S. Constitution. His great aunt Eliza Lucas Pinckney was the first woman agriculturalist in the United States, responsible for opening up the indigo trade. Her son

Charles Cotesworth Pinckney was one of the signers of the Constitution. The current main house, doubling as the visitors center, dates from 1828, 11 years after Pinckney sold Snee Farm to pay off debts. That said, it's still a great example of Lowcountry architecture, replacing Pinckney's original home, where President George Washington slept and had breakfast under a nearby oak tree in 1791 while touring the south. Another highlight at this National Park Service–administered site is the 0.5-mile self-guided walk around the site, some of it on boardwalks over the marsh. No matter what anyone tells you, no one is buried underneath the tombstone in the grove of oak trees bearing the name of Constitution Charlie's father, Colonel Charles Pinckney. The marker incorrectly states the elder Pinckney's age, so it was put here only as a monument. A memorial to the colonel is in the churchyard of the 1840s-era Christ Church about one mile down Long Point Road.

Isle of Palms

This primarily residential area of about 5,000 people received the state's first "Blue Wave" designation from the Clean Beaches Council for its well-managed and preserved beaches. Like adjacent Sullivan's Island, there are pockets of great wealth here, but also a laid-back, windswept beach-town vibe. You get here from Mount Pleasant by taking the Isle of Palms Connector off U.S. 17 (Johnnie Dodds/Chuck Dawley Blvd.). Aside from just enjoying the whole scene, the main self-contained attraction here is **Isle of Palms County Park** (14th Ave., 843/886-3863, www.ccprc.com, May–Labor Day daily 9 A.M.–7 P.M., Mar.–Apr. and Sept.–Oct. daily 10 A.M.–6 P.M., Nov.–Feb. daily 10 A.M.–5 P.M., $7 per vehicle, free for pedestrians and cyclists), with its oceanfront beach, complete with umbrella rental, a volleyball court, a playground, and lifeguards. Get here by taking the Isle of Palms Connector

(Hwy. 517) from Mount Pleasant, going through the light at Palm Boulevard, and taking the next left at the gate. The island's other claim to fame is the excellent (and surprisingly affordable) **Wild Dunes Resort** (5757 Palm Blvd., 888/778-1876, www.wilddunes.com), with its two Fazio golf courses and 17 clay tennis courts. Breach Inlet, between Isle of Palms and Sullivan's Island, is where the Confederate sub *Hunley* sortied to do battle with the USS *Housatonic*. During 1989's Hurricane Hugo, the entire island was submerged.

Sullivan's Island

Part funky beach town, part ritzy getaway, Sullivan's Island has a certain timeless quality. While much of it was rebuilt after Hurricane Hugo's devastation, plenty of local character remains, as evidenced by some cool little bars in its tiny "business district" on the main drag of Middle Street. There's a ton of history on Sullivan's, but you can also just while the day away on the quiet, windswept beach on the Atlantic, or ride a bike all over the island and back. Unless you have a boat, you can only get here from Mount Pleasant. From U.S. 17, follow the signs for Highway 703 and Sullivan's Island. Cross the Ben Sawyer Bridge, and then turn right onto Middle Street; continue for about 1.5 miles.

FORT MOULTRIE

While Fort Sumter gets the vast bulk of the media, the older Fort Moultrie (1214 Middle St., 843/883-3123, www.nps.gov/fosu, daily 9 A.M.–5 P.M., $3 adults, free under age 16) on Sullivan's Island actually has a much more sweeping history. Furthering the irony, Major Robert Anderson's detachment at Fort Sumter at the opening of the Civil War was actually the Fort Moultrie garrison, reassigned to Sumter because Moultrie was thought too vulnerable from the landward side. Indeed, Moultrie's first incarnation, a perimeter of felled palm trees,

© JIM MOREKIS

Fort Moultrie on Sullivan's Island

didn't even have a name when it was unsuccessfully attacked by the British in the summer of 1776, the first victory by the colonists in the Revolution. The redcoat cannonballs bounced off those soft, flexible trunks, and thus was born South Carolina's nickname, "The Palmetto State." The hero of the battle, Sergeant William Jasper, would gain immortality for putting the blue and white regimental banner—forerunner to the modern blue and white state flag—on a makeshift staff after the first one was shot away. Subsequently named for the commander at the time, William Moultrie, the fort was captured by the British in a later engagement. That first fort fell into decay and a new one was built over it in 1798 but was soon destroyed by a hurricane. In 1809 a brick fort was built here; it soon gained notoriety as the place where the great chief Osceola was detained soon after his capture, posing for the famous portrait by George Catlin. His captors got more than they bargained for when they

jokingly asked the old guerrilla soldier for a rendition of the Seminole battle cry. According to accounts, Osceola's realistic performance scared some bystanders half to death. The chief died here in 1838, and his modest grave site is still on-site, in front of the fort on the landward side. Other famous people to have trod on Sullivan's Island include Edgar Allan Poe, who was inspired by Sullivan's lonely, evocative environment to write *The Gold Bug* and other works. There's a Gold Bug Avenue and a Poe Avenue here today, and the local library is named after him as well. A young Lieutenant William Tecumseh Sherman was also stationed here during his Charleston stint in the 1830s before his encounter with history in the Civil War. Moultrie's main Civil War role was as a target for Union shot during the long siege of Charleston. It was pounded so hard and for so long that its walls fell below a nearby sand hill and were finally unable to be hit anymore. A full military upgrade happened in the late

1800s, extending over most of Sullivan's Island (some private owners have even bought some of the old batteries and converted them into homes). It's the series of later forts that you'll visit on your trip to the Moultrie site, which is technically part of the Fort Sumter National Monument and administered by the National Park Service.

Most of the outdoor tours are self-guided, but ranger programs typically happen Memorial Day–Labor Day daily at 11 A.M. and 2:30 P.M. There's a bookstore and visitors center across the street, offering a 20-minute video on the hour and half-hour 9 A.M.–4:30 P.M. Keep in mind there's no regular ferry to Fort Sumter from Fort Moultrie; the closest ferry to Sumter leaves from Patriots Point on Mount Pleasant.

BENCH BY THE ROAD

Scholars say that about half of all African Americans alive today had an ancestor who once set foot on Sullivan's Island. As the first point of entry for at least half of all slaves imported to the United States, the island's "pest houses" acted as quarantine areas so slaves could be checked for communicable diseases before going to auction in Charleston proper. But few people seem to know this. In a 1989 magazine interview, African American author and Nobel laureate Toni Morrison said about historic sites concerning slavery, "There is no suitable memorial, or plaque, or wreath or wall, or park or skyscraper lobby. There's no 300-foot tower, there's no small bench by the road." In 2008, that last item became a reality, as the first of several planned "benches by the road" was installed on Sullivan's Island to mark the sacrifice of enslaved African Americans. It's a simple black steel bench, with an attached marker and a nearby plaque. The Bench by the Road is at the Fort Moultrie visitors center.

FOLLY BEACH

A large percentage of the town of Folly Beach was destroyed by Hurricane Hugo in 1989, and erosion since then has increased and hit the beach itself pretty hard. All that said, enough of Folly's funky charm is left to make it worth visiting. Called "The Edge of America" during its heyday from the 1930s through the 1950s as a swinging resort getaway, Folly Beach is now a slightly beaten but enjoyable little getaway on this barrier island. As with all areas of Charleston, the cost of living here is rapidly increasing, but Folly Beach still reminds locals of a time that once was: a time of soda fountains, poodle skirts, stylish one-piece bathing suits, and growling hot rods. Folly's main claim to larger historic fame is playing host to George Gershwin, who stayed at a cottage on West Arctic Avenue to write the score for *Porgy and Bess,* set across the harbor in downtown Charleston. (Ironically, Gershwin's opera couldn't be performed in its original setting until 1970 because of segregationist Jim Crow laws.) Original *Porgy* author DuBose Heyward stayed around the corner at a summer cottage on West Ashley Avenue that he dubbed "Follywood."

Called Folly Road until it gets to the beach, Center Street is the main drag here, dividing the beach into east and west. In this area you'll find the **Folly Beach Fishing Pier** (101 E. Arctic Ave., 843/588-3474, Apr.–Oct. daily 6 A.M.–11 P.M., Nov. and Mar. daily 7 A.M.–7 P.M., Dec.–Feb. daily 8 A.M.–5 P.M., $7 parking, $8 fishing fee), which replaced the grand old wooden pier-and-pavilion structure that tragically burned down in 1960.

Back in the day, restaurants, bars, and amusement areas with rides lined the way up to the old pavilion. As the premier musical venue in the region, the pavilion hosted legends like Tommy and Jimmy Dorsey, Benny Goodman, and Count Basie. The new fishing pier, while not as grand as the old one, is worth visiting—a massive, well-built edifice jutting over 1,000 feet into the Atlantic with a large diamond-shaped pavilion at the end. Fishing-rod holders

a view of Folly Beach from the pier

© JIM MOREKIS

and cleaning stations line the entire thing. Out on the "front beach," daytime activities once included boxing matches and extralegal drag races. In the old days, the "Washout" section on the far west end was where you went to go crabbing or fly-fishing or maybe even steal a kiss from your sweetie. Today, though, the Washout is known as the prime surfing area in the Carolinas, with a dedicated group of diehards.

To get to Folly Beach from Charleston, go west on Calhoun Street and take the James Island Connector. Take a left on Folly Road (Hwy. 171), which becomes Center Street on into Folly Beach.

At the far east end of Folly Island, about 300 yards offshore, you'll see the **Morris Island Lighthouse,** an 1876 beacon that was once surrounded by lush green landscape, now completely surrounded by water as the land has eroded around it. Now privately owned, there's an extensive effort to save and preserve the lighthouse (www.savethelight.org). There's also an effort to keep high-dollar condo development off of beautiful bird-friendly Morris Island itself (www.morrisisland.org). To get there while there's still something left to enjoy, take East Ashley Street until it dead-ends. Park in the lot and take a 0.25-mile walk to the beach.

TOURS

Because of the city's small, fairly centralized layout, the best way to experience Charleston is on foot—either yours or via hooves of equine nature. Thankfully, there's a wide variety of walking and carriage tours for you to choose from. The sheer number and breadth of tour options in Charleston is beyond the scope of this section. For a full selection of available tours, visit the **Charleston Visitor Reception and Transportation Center** (375 Meeting St., 800/774-0006, www.charlestoncvb.com, Mon.–Fri. 8:30 A.M.–5 P.M.), where they have entire walls of brochures for all the latest tours,

DOIN' THE CHARLESTON

It has been called the biggest song and dance craze of the 20th century. It first entered the American public consciousness via New York City in a 1923 Harlem musical called *Runnin' Wild*, but the roots of the dance soon to be known as the Charleston were indeed in the Holy City. No one is quite sure of the day and date, but local lore assures us that members of Charleston's legendary Jenkins Orphanage Band were the first to start dancing that crazy "Geechie step," a development that soon became part of the band's act. The Jenkins Orphanage was started in 1891 by the African American Baptist minister Reverend D. J. Jenkins and was originally housed in the Old Marine Hospital at 20 Franklin Street (which you can see today, although it's not open to the public). To raise money, Reverend Jenkins acquired donated instruments and started a band comprising talented orphans from the house. The orphans traveled as far away as London, where they were a hit with the locals but not with the constabulary, who unceremoniously fined them for stopping traffic. A Charleston attorney who happened to be in London at the time, Augustine Smyth, paid their way back home, becoming a lifelong supporter of the orphanage in the process.

From then on, playing in donated old Citadel uniforms, the Jenkins Orphanage Band frequently took its act on the road. They played at the St. Louis and Buffalo expositions, and even at President Taft's inauguration. They also frequently played in New York, and it was there that African American pianist and composer James P. Johnson heard the Charlestonians play and dance to their Gullah rhythms, considered exotic at the time. Johnson would incorporate what he heard into the tune "Charleston," one of many songs in the revue *Runnin' Wild*. The catchy song and its accompanying loose-limbed dance seemed tailor-made for the Roaring '20s and its liberated, hedonistic spirit. Before long the Charleston had swept the nation, becoming a staple of jazz clubs and speakeasies across the country, and indeed, the world.

with local tourism experts on-site. Here are some notable highlights.

Walking Tours

If you find yourself walking around downtown soon after dark, you'll almost invariably come across a walking tour in progress, with a small cluster of people gathered around a tour guide. There are too many walking tours to list them all, but here are the best.

For more than 10 years, **Ed Grimball's Walking Tours** (306 Yates Ave., 843/762-0056, www.edgrimballtours.com, $16 adults, $8 children) has run two-hour tours on Friday–Saturday mornings, courtesy of the knowledgeable and still-sprightly Ed himself, a native Charlestonian. All of Ed's walks start from the big Pineapple Fountain in Waterfront Park, and reservations are a must. **Original Charleston Walks** (45 Broad St., 800/729-3420, www.

charlestonwalks.com, daily 8:30 A.M.–9:30 P.M., $18.50 adults, $10.50 children) has received much national TV exposure. They leave from the corner of Market and State Streets and have a full slate of tours, including a popular adults-only pub crawl. **Charleston Strolls Walk with History** (843/766-2080, www.charlestonstrolls.com, $18 adults, $10 children) is another popular tour good for a historical overview and tidbits. They have three daily embarkation points: Charleston Place (9:30 A.M.), the Days Inn (9:40 A.M.), and the Mills House (10 A.M.). **Architectural Walking Tours** (173 Meeting St., 800/931-7761, www.architecturalwalkingtoursofcharleston.com, $20) offers an 18th-century tour Monday and Wednesday–Saturday at 10 A.M. and a 19th-century tour at 2 P.M., which are geared more toward historic preservation. They leave from the Meeting Street Inn (173 Meeting

St.). A relatively new special interest tour is **Charleston Art Tours** (53 Broad St., 843/860-3327, www.charlestonarttours.com, $49). The brainchild of local artists Karen Hagan and Martha Sharp, this tour is led by a professional artist guide and includes refreshments and a gift bag from one of the featured galleries. The Fine Art Tour ($50) runs 2–4 P.M. and leaves from 27½ State Street. They also run a Charleston Renaissance tour ($55), which includes a visit to the Gibbes Museum of Art (Tues.–Sat. 10 A.M.) and a "Gibbes Museum Plus" tour (Thurs. and Sat. 1:30 P.M.)

Ghost tours are very popular in Charleston. **Bulldog Tours** (40 N. Market St., 843/722-8687, www.bulldogtours.com) has exclusive access to the Old City Jail, which features prominently in most of their tours. Their most popular tour, the Haunted Jail Tour ($18 adults, $10 children) leaves daily at 7 P.M., 8 P.M., 9 P.M., and 10 P.M.; meet at the Old City Jail (21 Magazine St.). The Ghosts and Dungeons tour ($18) leaves March–November Tuesday–Saturday at 7 P.M. and 9 P.M. from 40 North Market Street. Other tours include the Ghosts and Graveyard Tour (7:30 P.M. and 9:30 P.M., $18) and the adults-only Dark Side of Charleston (daily 8 P.M. and 10 P.M., $18). **Tour Charleston** (184 E. Bay St., 843/723-1670, www.tourcharleston.com, $18) offers two paranormal tours, Ghosts of Charleston I, which leaves daily at 5:30 P.M., 7:30 P.M., and 9:30 P.M. from Waterfront Park, and Ghosts of Charleston II, which leaves at 7 P.M. and 9 P.M. from Marion Square.

Carriage Tours

The city strictly regulates the treatment and upkeep of carriage horses and mules, so there's not a heck of a lot of difference in service or price among the various tour companies. Typically, rides take 1–1.5 hours and hover around $20 per adult, about half that per child. Tours sometimes book up early, so call ahead. The oldest service in town is **Palmetto Carriage Works** (40 N. Market St., 843/723-8145, www.carriagetour.com), which offers free parking at its "red barn" base near City Market. Another popular tour is **Old South Carriage Company** (14 Anson St., 843/723-9712, www.oldsouthcarriage.com) with its Confederate-clad drivers. **Carolina Polo & Carriage Company** (16 Hayne St., 843/577-6767, www.cpcc.com) leaves from several spots, including the Doubletree Hotel and their Hayne Street stables.

Motorized Tours

Leaving from Charleston Visitor Reception and Transportation Center (375 Meeting St.), **Adventure Sightseeing** (843/762-0088, www.touringcharleston.com, $20 adults, $11 children) offers several comfortable 1.5–2 hour rides, including the only motorized tour to the Citadel area. Tour times are daily at 9:30 A.M., 10 A.M., 10:30 A.M., 10:45 A.M., 11:30 A.M., 12:20 P.M., 1:30 P.M., and 2:45 P.M. You can make a day of it with **Charleston's Finest Historic Tours** (843/577-3311, www.historictoursofcharleston.com, $19 adults, $9.50 children), which has a basic two-hour city tour each day at 10:30 A.M. and offers some much longer tours to outlying plantations. They offer free downtown pickup from most lodgings. The old faithful **Gray Line of Charleston** (843/722-4444, www.graylineofcharleston.com, $20 adults, $12 children) offers a 90-minute tour departing from the Visitors Center March–November daily every 30 minutes 9:30 A.M.–3 P.M. (hotel pickup by reservation). The last tour leaves at 2 P.M. during the off-season.

African American History Tours

Charleston is rich in African American history, and a couple of operators specializing in this area are worth mentioning: Al Miller's **Sites & Insights Tours** (843/762-0051, www.sitesandinsightstours.com, $13–18) has several packages, including a Black History and Porgy & Bess Tour as well as a good combo city and island tour, all departing from the Visitors Center. Alphonso Brown's **Gullah Tours** (843/763-7551, www.gullahtours.com, $18), featuring stories told in the Gullah dialect, all leave from the African American Art Gallery (43 John St.) near the Visitors Center Monday–Friday at 11 A.M. and 1 P.M. and Saturday at 11 A.M., 1 P.M., and 3 P.M.

Water Tours

The best all-around tour of Charleston Harbor is the 90-minute ride offered by **Spiritline Cruises** (800/789-3678, www.spiritlinecruises.com, $17 adults, $10 ages 6–11), which leaves from either Aquarium Wharf or Patriots Point. Allow about 30 minutes for ticketing and boarding. They also have a three-hour dinner cruise in the evening leaving from Patriots Point (about $50 pp) and a cruise to Fort Sumter. **Sandlapper Water Tours** (843/849-8687, www.sandlappertours.com, $20–27)

offers many types of evening and dolphin cruises on a 45-foot catamaran. They also offer Charleston's only waterborne ghost tour. Most of their tours leave from the Maritime Center near East Bay and Calhoun Streets.

Ecotours

This aspect of Charleston's tourism scene is very well represented. The best operators include: **Barrier Island Eco Tours** (50 41st Ave., 843/886-5000, www.nature-tours.com, from $38), taking you up to the Cape Romain Refuge out of Isle of Palms; **Coastal Expeditions** (514-B Mill St., 843/884-7684, www.coastalexpeditions.com, prices vary), with a base on Shem Creek in Mount Pleasant, offering several different-length sea kayak adventures; and **PaddleFish Kayaking** (843/330-9777, www.paddlefish-kayaking.com, from $45), offering several kinds of kayaking tours (no experience necessary) from downtown, Kiawah Island, and Seabrook Island.

Entertainment and Events

Charleston practically invented the idea of diversion and culture in the United States, so it's no surprise that there's plenty to do here, from museums to festivals and a brisk nightlife scene.

NIGHTLIFE

Unlike the locals-versus-tourists divide you find so often in other destination cities, in Charleston it's nothing for a couple of visitors to find themselves at a table next to four or five college students enjoying themselves in true Charlestonian fashion: loudly and with lots of good food and strong drink nearby. Indeed, the Holy City is downright ecumenical in its partying. The smokiest dives also have some of the best brunches. The toniest restaurants also have

some of the most hopping bar scenes. Tourist hot spots written up in all the guidebooks also have their share of local regulars. But through it all, one constant remains: Charleston's finely honed ability to seek out and enjoy the good life. It's a trait that comes naturally and traditionally, going back to the days of the earliest Charleston drinking and gambling clubs, like the Fancy Society, the Meddlers Laughing Club, and the Fort Jolly Volunteers. Bars close in Charleston at 2 A.M. The old days of the "mini-bottle"—in which no free pour was allowed and all drinks had to be made from the little airline bottles—are gone, and it seems that local bartenders have finally figured out how to mix a decent cocktail. At the retail level, all hard-liquor sales stop at 7 P.M., with none at all on Sundays. You can buy beer and wine in grocery stores 24-7.

Pubs and Bars

In a nod to the city's perpetual focus on well-prepared food, it's difficult to find a Charleston watering hole that *doesn't* offer really good food in addition to a well-stocked bar. One of Charleston's favorite neighborhood spots is **Moe's Crosstown Tavern** (714 Rutledge Ave., 843/722-3287, daily 11 A.M.–2 A.M.) at Rutledge and Francis in the Wagener Terrace/Hampton Square area. A newer location, **Moe's Downtown Tavern** (5 Cumberland St., 843/577-8500, daily 11 A.M.–2 A.M.) offers a similar vibe and menu, but the original, and best, Moe's experience is at the Crosstown.

Nipping on Moe's heels for best pub food in town is **A.C.'s Bar and Grill** (467 King St., 843/577-6742, daily 11 A.M.–2 A.M.). Though this dark, quirky watering hole might seem out of place in the increasingly tony Upper King area, this only adds to its appeal. A.C.'s at its best is all things to all people: Charleston's favorite late-night bar, a great place to get a burger basket, and also one of the best (and certainly most unlikely) Sunday brunches in town, featuring chicken and waffles.

The action gets going late at **Social Wine Bar** (188 E. Bay St., 843/577-5665, daily 4 P.M.–2 A.M.), a hopping hangout near the French Quarter. While the hot and cold tapas are tasty—I like the special sashimi—the real action here, as you'd expect, is the wine. They offer at least 50 wines by the glass and literally hundreds by the bottle. My favorite thing to do here is partake of the popular "flights," triple tastes of kindred spirits, as it were. If the pricing on the menu seems confusing, ask your server to help you out.

Johnson's Pub (12 Cumberland St., 843/958-0662, daily noon–2 A.M.), a quirky but popular downtown spot, offers seven varieties of burger, all incredible, plus great pizza; it's

also well known for its Caesar salad. Oh, yeah, and they keep the drinks coming too.

The Guinness flows freely at **Tommy Condon's Irish Pub** (160 Church St., 843/577-3818, www.tommycondons.com, Sun.–Thurs. 11 A.M.–2 A.M., dinner until 10 P.M., Fri.–Sat. 11 A.M.–2 A.M., dinner until 11 P.M.)—after the obligatory and traditional slow-pour, that is—as do the patriotic Irish songs performed live most nights. You have three sections to choose from in this large, low building right near City Market: the big outdoor deck, the cozy pub itself, and the back dining room with classic wainscoting.

If it's a nice day out, a good place to relax and enjoy happy hour outside is **Vickery's Bar and Grill** (15 Beaufain St., 843/577-5300, www.vickerysbarandgrill.com, Mon.–Sat. 11:30 A.M.–2 A.M., Sun. 11 A.M.–1 A.M., kitchen closes 1 A.M.), actually part of a small regional chain based in Atlanta. Start with the oyster bisque, and maybe try the turkey and brie sandwich or crab cakes for your entrée.

Because of its commercial nature, Broad Street can get quiet when the sun goes down and the office workers disperse back to the burbs. But a warm little oasis can be found a few steps off Broad Street in the **Blind Tiger** (36–38 Broad St., 843/577-0088, daily 11:30 A.M.–2 A.M., kitchen closes Mon.–Thurs. 10 P.M., Fri.–Sun. 9 P.M.), which takes its name from the local Prohibition-era nickname for a speakeasy. Wood panels, Guinness and Bass on tap, and some good bar-food items make this a good stop off the beaten path if you find yourself in the area. A patio out back often features live music.

Located not too far over the Ashley River on U.S. 17, Charleston institution **Gene's Haufbrau** (17 Savannah Hwy., 843/225-4363, www.geneshaufbrau.com, daily 11:30 A.M.–2 A.M.) is worth making a special trip into West Ashley. Boasting the largest beer selection in Charleston—from the Butte Creek

Poe's Tavern is a great hangout on Sullivan's Island.

Organic Ale from California to a can of PBR—Gene's also claims to be the oldest bar in town, established in 1952.

Though Sullivan's Island has a lot of high-dollar homes, it still has friendly watering holes like **Dunleavy's Pub** (2213-B Middle St., 843/883-9646, Sun.–Thurs. 11:30 A.M.–1 A.M., Fri.–Sat. 11:30 A.M.–2 A.M.). Inside is a great bar festooned with memorabilia, or you can enjoy a patio table. The other Sullivan's watering hole of note is **Poe's Tavern** (2210 Middle St., 843/883-0083, daily 11 A.M.–2 A.M., kitchen closes 10 P.M.) across the street, a nod to Edgar Allan Poe and his service on the island as a clerk in the U.S. Army. It's a lively, mostly-locals scene, set within a fun but suitably dark interior (though you might opt for one of the outdoor tables on the raised patio). Simply put, no trip to Sullivan's is complete without a stop at one (or possibly both) of these two local landmarks, each within a stone's throw of the other.

If you're in Folly Beach, enjoy the great views and the great cocktails at **Blu Restaurant and Bar** (1 Center St., 843/588-6658, www.blu-follybeach.com, $10–20) inside the Holiday Inn Folly Beach Oceanfront. There's nothing like a Spiked Lemonade on a hot Charleston day at the beach. Another notable Folly Beach watering hole is the **Sand Dollar Social Club** (7 Center St., 843/588-9498, Sun.–Fri. noon–1 A.M., Sat. noon–2 A.M.), the kind of cash-only, mostly local, and thoroughly enjoyable dive you often find in little beach towns. You have to pony up for a "membership" to this private club, but it's only a buck. There's a catch, though: You can't get in until your 24-hour "waiting period" is over.

If you find yourself up in North Charleston, by all means stop by **Madra Rua Irish Pub** (1034 E. Montague Ave., 843/554-2522, daily 11 A.M.–1 A.M.), an authentic watering hole with a better-than-average pub food menu that's also a great place to watch a soccer game.

© JIM MOREKIS

Live Music

Charleston's music scene is best described as hit-and-miss. There's no distinct "Charleston sound" to speak of (especially now that the heyday of Hootie and the Blowfish is long past), and there's no one place where you're assured of finding a great band any night of the week. The scene is currently in even more of a state of flux because the city's best-regarded live rock club, Cumberland's on King Street, closed in 2007 after 15 years in business. The best place to find up-to-date music listings is the local free weekly *Charleston City Paper* (www.charleston-citypaper.com).

These days the hippest music spot in town is out on James Island at **The Pour House** (1977 Maybank Hwy., 843/571-4343, www.charles-tonpourhouse.com, 9 P.M.–2 A.M. on nights with music scheduled, call for info), where the local characters are sometimes just as entertaining as the acts onstage. The venerable **Music Farm** (32 Ann St., 843/722-8904, www.musicfarm.com) on Upper King isn't much to look at from the outside, but inside the cavernous space has played host to all sorts of bands over the past two decades. Recent concerts have included G. Love and Special Sauce, Third Eye Blind, Galactic, Modest Mouse, and Drive-By Truckers.

For jazz, check out **Mistral** (99 S. Market St., 843/722-5708, Sun.–Thurs. 11 A.M.–11 P.M., Fri.–Sat. 11 A.M.–midnight). There's a constant stream of great performers from a variety of traditions, including Dixieland, every night of the week—not to mention some awesome food. Another great jazz place—and, like Mistral, a very good restaurant to boot—is **Mercato** (102 N. Market St., 843/722-6393, www.mercato-charleston.com, bar 4 P.M.–2 A.M., late-night food menu until 1 A.M.). Italian in menu and feel, the live jazz and R&B (Wed.–Sat.) at this establishment—owned by the same company that owns the five-star Peninsula Grill—is definitely all-American. The late kitchen hours are a great bonus.

Lounges

Across the street from Gene's Haufbrau, the retro-chic **Voodoo Lounge** (15 Magnolia Lane, 843/769-0228, Mon.–Fri. 4 P.M.–2 A.M., Sat.–Sun. 5:30 P.M.–2 A.M., kitchen until 1 A.M.) is another very popular West Ashley hangout. It has a wide selection of trendy cocktails and killer gourmet tacos.

The aptly named **Rooftop Bar and Restaurant** (23 Vendue Range, 843/723-0485, Tues.–Sat. 6 P.M.–2 A.M.) at the Library Restaurant in the Vendue Inn is a very popular waterfront happy-hour spot from which to enjoy the sunset over the Charleston skyline. It's also a hot late-night hangout with a respectable menu.

Located in a 200-year-old building and suitably right above a cigar store, **Club Habana** (177 Meeting St., 843/853-5900, Mon.–Sat. 5 P.M.–1 A.M., Sun. 6 P.M.–midnight) is the perfect place to sink down into a big couch, warm yourself by the fireplace, sip a martini (or port, or single-malt scotch), and enjoy a good smoke in the dim light. Probably the last, best vestige of the cigar-bar trend in Charleston, Club Habana remains popular. You get your cigars downstairs in Tinderbox Internationale, which features a range of rare "Legal Cuban" smokes, rolled from preembargo tobacco that has been warehoused for decades in Tampa, Florida.

Dance Clubs

The **Trio Club** (139 Calhoun St., 843/965-5333, Thurs.–Sat. 9 P.M.–2 A.M.), right off Marion Square, is a favorite place to make the scene. There's a relaxing outdoor area with piped-in music, an intimate sofa-filled upstairs bar for dancing and chilling, and the dark candlelit downstairs with frequent live music. Without a doubt Charleston's best dance club is **Club Pantheon** (28 Ann St., 843/577-2582, Fri.–Sun. 10 P.M.–2 A.M.).

Gay and Lesbian

Charleston is very tolerant by typical Deep

CHARLESTON NATIVES

In addition to the long list of historic figures, some notable modern personalities born in Charleston or closely associated with the city include:

- Counterculture artist Shepard Fairey, who designed the iconic "Hope" campaign poster for Barack Obama
- Actress Mabel King (*The Wiz*)
- Actress-model Lauren Hutton
- Author Nancy Friday
- Actor Thomas Gibson (*Criminal Minds*)
- Author-lyricist DuBose Heyward
- Author Josephine Humphreys
- Author Sue Monk Kidd (*The Secret Life of Bees*)
- Actress Vanessa Minnillo (attended high school)
- Actor Will Patton (*Remember the Titans*)
- Author Alexandra Ripley
- Musician Darius Rucker (singer for Hootie & the Blowfish, now a solo country artist)
- Comedian Andy Dick
- Comedian Stephen Colbert

South standards, and this tolerance extends to gays and lesbians as well. Most gay- and lesbian-oriented nightlife centers in the Upper King area. Charleston's hottest and hippest dance spot of any type, gay or straight, is **Club Pantheon** (28 Ann St., 843/577-2582, Fri.–Sun. 10 P.M.–2 A.M.) on Upper King on the lower level of the parking garage across from the Visitors Center (375 Meeting St.). Pantheon is not cheap—cover charges are routinely well over $10—but it's worth it for the great DJs, the dancing, and the people-watching, not to mention the drag cabaret on Friday and Sunday nights. Just down the street from Club

Pantheon—and owned by the same people—is a totally different kind of gay bar, **Dudley's** (42 Ann St., 843/577-6779, daily 4 P.M.–2 A.M.). Mellower and more appropriate for conversation or a friendly game of pool, Dudley is a nice contrast to the thumping Pantheon a few doors down.

Though **Vickery's Bar and Grill** (15 Beaufain St., 843/577-5300, www.vickerysbarandgrill.com, Mon.–Sat. 11:30 A.M.–2 A.M., Sun. 11 A.M.–1 A.M., kitchen closes 1 A.M.) does not market itself as a gay and lesbian establishment, it has nonetheless become quite popular with that population—not least because of the good reputation its parent tavern in Atlanta has with that city's large and influential gay community.

PERFORMING ARTS
Theater

Unlike the more puritanical (literally) colonies farther up the American coast, Charleston was from the beginning an arts-friendly settlement. The first theatrical production in the western hemisphere happened in Charleston in January 1735, when a nomadic troupe rented a space at Church and Broad Streets to perform Thomas Otway's *The Orphan*. The play's success led to the building of the Dock Street Theatre on what is now Queen Street. On February 12, 1736, it hosted its first production, *The Recruiting Officer,* a popular play for actresses of the time because it calls for some female characters to wear tight-fitting British army uniforms. Live theater became a staple of Charleston social life, with notable thespians including both Edwin and Junius Booth (brothers of Lincoln's assassin John Wilkes) and Edgar Allan Poe's mother Eliza performing here. Several high-quality troupes continue to keep that proud old tradition alive, chief among them being **Charleston Stage** (843/577-7183, www.charlestonstage.com), the resident company of the Dock Street Theatre. In addition to its well-received regular season of classics and

STEPHEN COLBERT, NATIVE SON

A purist would insist that Charlestonians are born, not made. While it's true that Comedy Central star Stephen Colbert was actually born in Washington DC, he did spend most of his young life in the Charleston suburb of James Island, attending the Porter-Gaud School. And regardless of his literal birthplace, few would dispute that Colbert is the best-known Charlestonian in American pop culture today.

While it's commonly assumed that Colbert's surname is a link to Charleston's French Huguenot heritage, the truth is that it's really an Irish name. To further burst the bubble, Colbert's father, a vice president at Charleston's Medical University of South Carolina, adopted the current French pronunciation himself—historically his family pronounced the *t* at the end. That being said, Colbert returns quite often to Charleston, as he did in a December 2007 performance at the Sottile Theater, *I am Charleston—and So Can You!*, a play on the title of his recent book.

In 2007, Colbert cooperated with Ben & Jerry's Ice Cream to create a new flavor, "Americone Dream" (vanilla with fudge-covered waffle cone pieces and caramel swirl), proceeds from which went to the Coastal Community Foundation of South Carolina. To unveil the flavor, Colbert appeared at "The Joe" and threw out the first pitch at a Charleston River Dogs minor league game. Soon after, Colbert told *Charleston* magazine that he and wife Evelyn "went to the Pig and bought eight pints"—a reference to the ubiquitous Southern grocery chain Piggly Wiggly, a.k.a. "the Pig."

Later that year, Colbert embarked on an ill-fated tongue-in-cheek bid to get on the South Carolina presidential primary ballot, which never materialized. In a video message to the South Carolina Agricultural Summit in November he cried mock tears and said, "I wanted to be president of South Carolina so bad. I was going to be sworn in on a sack of pork ribs and I was going to institute the death penalty for eating Chinese shrimp."

---

modern staples, Charleston Stage has debuted more than 30 original scripts over the years, most recently *Gershwin at Folly,* recounting the composer's time at Folly Beach working on *Porgy and Bess.*

The city's most unusual players are **The Have Nots!** (843/853-6687, www.thehavenots.com), with a total ensemble of 35 comedians who typically perform their brand of edgy improv every Friday night at Theatre 99 (280 Meeting St.). The players of **PURE Theatre** (843/723-4444, www.puretheatre.org) perform at the Circular Congregation Church's Lance Hall (150 Meeting St.). Their shows emphasize compelling, mature drama, beautifully performed. This is where to catch less-glitzy, more-gritty productions like *Rabbit Hole, American Buffalo,* and *Cold Tectonics,* a hit at Piccolo Spoleto. **The Footlight Players** (843/722-4487, www.footlightplayers.net) are the oldest continuously

active company in town (since 1931). This community-based amateur company performs a mix of crowd-pleasers (*The Full Monty*) and cutting-edge drama (*This War is Live*) at their space at 20 Queen Street.

Music

The forerunner to the **Charleston Symphony Orchestra** (CSO, 843/554-6060, www.charlestonsymphony.com) performed for the first time on December 28, 1936, at the Hibernian Hall on Meeting Street. During that first season the CSO accompanied *The Recruiting Officer,* the inaugural show at the renovated Dock Street Theatre. For seven decades, the CSO continued to provide world-class orchestral music, gaining "Metropolitan" status in the 1970s, when they accompanied the first-ever local performance of *Porgy and Bess,* which despite its Charleston setting couldn't be performed locally before then due to segregation laws. Due to financial difficulty, the CSO cancelled its 2010–2011 season. They are making quite the comeback of late, however, and I suggest checking the website for upcoming concerts.

The separate group **Chamber Music Charleston** (843/763-4941, www.chambermusiccharleston.org), which relies on many core CSO musicians, continues to perform around town, including at Piccolo Spoleto. They play a wide variety of picturesque historic venues, including the Old Exchange (120 E. Bay St.), the Calhoun Mansion (16 Meeting St.), and the Footlight Players Theatre (20 Queen St.). They can also be found at private house concerts, which sell out quickly.

The excellent music department at the College of Charleston sponsors the annual **Charleston Music Fest** (www.charlestonmusicfest.com), a series of chamber music concerts at various venues around the beautiful campus, featuring many faculty members of the college as well as visiting guest artists. Other college musical offerings include: The **College of Charleston Concert Choir** (www.cofc.edu/music), which performs at various venues, usually churches, around town during the fall; the **College of Charleston Opera,** which performs at least one full-length production during the school year and often performs at Piccolo Spoleto; and the popular **Yuletide Madrigal Singers,** who sing in early December at a series of concerts in historic Randolph Hall.

Dance

The premier company in town is the 20-year-old **Charleston Ballet Theatre** (477 King St., 843/723-7334, www.charlestonballet.org). Its 18 full-time dancers perform a great mix of classics, modern pieces, and, of course, a yuletide *Nutcracker* at the Gaillard Municipal Auditorium. Most performances are at the Sottile Theatre (44 George St., just off King St.) and in the Black Box Theatre at their home office on Upper King Street.

CINEMA

The most interesting art house and indie venue in town is currently **The Terrace** (1956 Maybank Hwy., 843/762-9494, www.terrace-theater.com), and not only because they offer beer and wine, which you can enjoy at your seat. Shows before 5 P.M. are $7. It's west of Charleston on James Island; get there by taking U.S. 17 west from Charleston and go south on Highway 171, then take a right on Maybank Highway (Hwy. 700).

For a generic but good multiplex experience, go over to Mount Pleasant to the **Palmetto Grande** (1319 Theater Dr., 843/216-8696).

FESTIVALS AND EVENTS

Charleston is a festival-mad city, especially in the spring and early fall. And new festivals are being added every year, further enhancing the hedonistic flavor of this city that has also mastered the art of hospitality. Here's a look through the calendar at all the key festivals in the area.

January

Held on a Sunday in late January at historic Boone Hall Plantation on Mount Pleasant, the **Lowcountry Oyster Festival** (www.charlestonlowcountry.com, 11 A.M.–5 P.M., $8, food additional) features literally truckloads of the sweet shellfish for your enjoyment. Gates open at 10:30 A.M., and there's plenty of parking. Oysters are sold by the bucket and served with crackers and cocktail sauce. Bring your own shucking knife or glove, or buy them on-site.

February

One of the more unique events in town is the **Southeastern Wildlife Exposition** (various venues, 843/723-1748, www.sewe.com, $12.50 per day, $30 for 3 days, free under age 13). For the last quarter century, the Wildlife Expo has brought together hundreds of artists and exhibitors to showcase just about any kind of naturally themed art you can think of, in over a dozen galleries and venues all over downtown. Kids will enjoy the live animals on hand as well.

March

Generally straddling late February and the first days of March, the four-day **Charleston Food & Wine Festival** (www.charlestonfoodandwine. com, various venues and admission) is a glorious celebration of one of the Holy City's premier draws: its amazing culinary community. While the emphasis is on Lowcountry gurus like Donald Barickman of Magnolia's and Robert Carter of the Peninsula Grill, guest chefs from as far away as New York, New Orleans, and Los Angeles routinely come to show off their skills. Oenophiles, especially of domestic wines, will be in heaven as well. Tickets aren't cheap—an all-event pass is over $500 pp—but then again, this is one of the nation's great food cities, so you might find it worth every penny.

Immediately before the Festival of Houses and Gardens is the **Charleston International Antiques Show** (40 E. Bay St., 843/722-3405, www.historiccharleston.org, admission varies), held at Historic Charleston's headquarters at the Missroon House on the High Battery. It features over 30 of the nation's best-regarded dealers and offers lectures and tours.

Mid-March–April, the perennial favorite **Festival of Houses and Gardens** (843/722-3405, www.historiccharleston.org, admission varies) is sponsored by the Historic Charleston Foundation and is held at the very peak of the spring blooming season for maximum effect. In all, the Festival goes into a dozen historic neighborhoods to see about 150 homes. Each day sees a different three-hour tour of a different area, at about $45 pp. This is a fantastic opportunity to peek inside some amazing old privately owned properties that are inaccessible to visitors at all other times. A highlight is a big oyster roast and picnic at Drayton Hall.

Not to be confused with the above festival, the **Garden Club of Charleston House and Garden Tours** (843/530-5164, www.thegardenclubofcharleston.com, $35) are held over a weekend in late March. Highlights include the Heyward-Washington House and the private garden of the late great Charleston horticulturalist Emily Whaley.

One of Charleston's newest and most fun events, the five-night **Charleston Fashion Week** (www.fashionweek.charlestonmag.com, admission varies) is sponsored by *Charleston* magazine and benefits a local women's charity. Mimicking New York's Fashion Week events under tenting in Bryant Park, Charleston's version features runway action under big tents in Marion Square—and, yes, past guests have included former contestants on *Project Runway.*

April

The annual **Cooper River Bridge Run** (www. bridgerun.com) happens the first Saturday in April (unless that's Easter weekend, in which case it runs the week before) and features a six-mile jaunt across the massive new Arthur Ravenel Bridge over the Cooper River, the longest cable span in the western hemisphere. It's not for those with a fear of heights, but it's still one of Charleston's best-attended events—with well over 30,000 participants. The whole crazy idea started when Dr. Marcus Newberry of the Medical University of South Carolina in Charleston was inspired by an office fitness trail in his native state of Ohio to do something similar in Charleston to promote fitness. Participants can walk the course if they choose, and many do. Signaled with the traditional cannon shot, the race still begins in Mount Pleasant and ends downtown, but over the years the course has changed to accommodate growth—not only in the event itself but in the city. Auto traffic, of course, is rerouted from the night before the race. The Bridge Run remains the only elite-level track and field event in South Carolina, with runners from Kenya typically dominating year after year. Each participant in the Bridge Run now must wear a transponder chip; new "Bones in Motion" technology allows you to track a favorite runner's exact position in real time during the race. The 2006 Run had wheelchair participants for the first time. There's now a Kid's Run in Hampton Square the Friday before, which also allows strollers.

From 1973 to 2000—except for 1976, when it was in Florida—the **Family Circle Cup** (161 Seven Farms Dr., Daniel Island, 843/856-7900, www.familycirclecup.com, admission varies) was held at Sea Pines Plantation on Hilton Head Island. But the popular Tier 1 Women's tennis tournament in 2001 moved to Daniel Island's brand-new Family Circle Tennis Center, specifically built for the event through a partnership of *Family Circle* magazine and the city of Charleston. (The Tennis Center is also open to the public and hosts many community events as well.)

Mount Pleasant is the home of Charleston's shrimping fleet, and each April sees all the boats parade by the Alhambra Hall and Park for the **Blessing of the Fleet** (843/884-8517, www.townofmountpleasant.com). Family events and lots and lots of seafood are also on tap.

May

Free admission and free parking are not the only draws at the outdoor **North Charleston Arts Festival** (5000 Coliseum Dr., www.northcharleston.org), but let's face it, that's important. Held beside North Charleston's Performing Arts Center and Convention Center, the festival features music, dance, theater, multicultural performers, and storytellers. There are a lot of kids' events as well.

Held over three days at the Holy Trinity Greek Orthodox Church up toward the Neck, the **Charleston Greek Festival** (30 Race St., 843/577-2063, www.greekorthodoxchs.org, $3)

offers a plethora of live entertainment, dancing, Greek wares, and, of course, fantastic Greek cuisine cooked by the congregation. Parking is not a problem, and there's even a shuttle to the church from the lot.

One of Charleston's newest annual events is the **Charleston International Film Festival** (843/817-1617, www.charlestoniff.com, various venues and prices). Despite being a relative latecomer to the film-festival circuit, the event is pulled off with Charleston's usual aplomb.

Indisputably Charleston's single biggest and most important event, **Spoleto Festival USA** (843/579-3100, www.spoletousa.org, admission varies) has come a long way since it was a sparkle in the eye of the late Gian Carlo Menotti three decades ago. Though Spoleto long ago broke ties with its founder, his vision remains indelibly stamped on the event from start to finish. There's plenty of music, to be sure, in genres that include orchestral, opera, jazz, and avant-garde, but you'll find something in every other performing art, such as dance, drama, and spoken word, in traditions from Western to African to Southeast Asian. For 17 days from Memorial Day weekend through early June, Charleston hops and hums nearly 24 hours a day to the energy of this vibrant, cutting-edge, yet accessible artistic celebration, which dominates everything and every conversation for those three weeks. Events happen in historic venues and churches all over downtown and as far as Middleton Place, which hosts the grand finale under the stars. If you want to come to Charleston during Spoleto—and everyone should, at least once—book your accommodations and your tickets far in advance. Tickets usually go on sale in early January for that summer's festival.

As if all the hubbub around Spoleto didn't give you enough to do, there's also **Piccolo Spoleto** (843/724-7305, www.piccolospoleto.com, various venues and admission), literally "little Spoleto," running concurrently.

A MAN, A PLAN: SPOLETO!

Sadly, Gian Carlo Menotti is no longer with us, having died in 2007 at the age of 95. But the overwhelming success of the composer's brainchild and labor of love, **Spoleto Festival USA,** lives on, enriching the cultural and social life of Charleston and serving as the city's chief calling card to the world at large.

Menotti began writing music at age seven in his native Italy. As a young man he moved to Philadelphia to study music, where he shared classes—and lifelong connections—with Leonard Bernstein and Samuel Barber. His first full-length opera, *The Consul,* would garner him the Pulitzer Prize, as would 1955's *The Saint of Bleecker Street.* But by far Menotti's best-known work is the beloved Christmas opera *Amahl and the Night Visitors,* composed especially for NBC television in 1951. At the height of his fame in 1958, the charismatic and mercurial genius—fluent and witty in five languages—founded the "Festival of Two Worlds" in Spoleto, Italy, specifically as a forum for young American artists in Europe. But it wasn't until nearly two decades later, in 1977, that Menotti was able to make his long-imagined dream of an American counterpart a reality.

Attracted to Charleston because of its longstanding support of the arts, its undeniable good taste, and its small size—ensuring that his festival would always be the number-one activity in town while it was going on—Menotti worked closely with the man who was to become the other key part of the equation: Charleston Mayor Joe Riley, then in his first term in office. Since then, the city has built

on Spoleto's success by founding its own local version, **Piccolo Spoleto**—literally, "little Spoleto"—which focuses exclusively on local and regional talent.

Things haven't always gone smoothly. Menotti and the stateside festival parted ways in 1993, when he took over the Rome Opera. Making matters more uneasy, the Italian festival—run by Menotti's longtime partner (and later adopted son) Chip—also became estranged from what was intended to be its soul mate in South Carolina. (Chip was later replaced by the Italian Culture Ministry.) But perhaps this kind of creative tension is what Menotti intended all along. Indeed, each spring brings a Spoleto USA that seems to thrive on the inherent conflict between the festival's often cutting-edge offerings and the very traditional city that hosts it. Unlike so many of the increasingly generic arts "festivals" across the nation, Spoleto still challenges its audiences, just as Menotti intended it to. Depending on the critic and the audience member, that modern opera debut you see may be groundbreaking or gratuitous. The drama you check out may be exhilarating or tiresome.

Still, the crowds keep coming, attracted just as much to Charleston's many charms as to the art itself. Each year, a total of about 500,000 people attend both Spoleto and Piccolo Spoleto. (Despite the weak economy, the 2009 edition actually broke a five-day ticket sales record.) Nearly one-third of the attendees are Charleston residents—the final proof that when it comes to supporting the arts, Charleston puts its money where its mouth is.

The intent of Piccolo Spoleto—begun just a couple of years after the larger festival came to town and run by the city's Office of Cultural Affairs—is to give local and regional performers a time to shine, sharing some of that larger spotlight on the national and international performers at the main event. Of particular interest to visiting families will be Piccolo's children's events, a good counter to some of the decidedly more adult fare at Spoleto USA.

June

Technically part of Piccolo Spoleto but gathering its own following, the **Sweetgrass Cultural Arts Festival** (www.sweetgrassfestival.org) is held the first week in June in Mount Pleasant at the Laing Middle School (2213 U.S. 17 N.). The event celebrates the traditional sweetgrass basket-making skills of African Americans in the historical Christ Church Parish area of Mount Pleasant. If you want to buy some

sweetgrass baskets, celebrated at June's Sweetgrass Cultural Arts Festival

sweetgrass baskets made by the world's foremost experts in the field, this would be the time.

The free, weekend-long, outdoor **Charleston Harbor Fest** (www.charleston-harborfest.org, free) at the Maritime Center on the waterfront is without a doubt one of the coolest events in town for the whole family. You can see and tour working tall ships, and watch master boatbuilders at work building new ones. There are free sailboat rides into the harbor, and the U.S. Navy provides displays. As if all that weren't enough, you get to witness the start of the 777-mile annual Charleston-to-Bermuda race.

July

Each year over 30,000 people come to see the **Patriots Point Fourth of July Blast** (866/831-1720), featuring a hefty barrage of fireworks shot off the deck of the USS *Yorktown* moored on the Cooper River in the Patriots Point complex. Food, live entertainment, and kids' activities are also featured.

September

From late September into the first week of October, the city-sponsored **MOJA Arts Festival** (843/724-7305, www.mojafestival.com, various venues and admission) highlights the cultural contributions of African Americans and people from the Caribbean with dance, visual art, poetry, cuisine, crafts, and music in genres that include gospel, jazz, reggae, and classical. In existence since 1984, MOJA's name comes from the Swahili word for "one," and its incredibly diverse range of offerings in so many media have made it one of the Southeast's premier events. Highlights include a Reggae Block Party and the always-fun Caribbean Parade. Some events are ticketed, while others, such as the kids' activities and many of the dance and film events, are free.

For five weeks from the last week of September into October, the Preservation Society of Charleston hosts the much-anticipated **Fall Tours of Homes & Gardens** (843/722-4630, www.preservationsociety.org, $45). The tour takes you into over a dozen local residences and is the nearly 90-year-old organization's biggest fund-raiser. Tickets typically go on sale the previous June, and they tend to sell out very quickly.

October

Another great food event in this great food city, on a weekend in October, the **Taste of Charleston** (1235 Long Point Rd., 843/577-4030, www.charlestonrestaurantassociation.com, 11 A.M.–5 P.M., $12) is held at Boone Hall Plantation in Mount Pleasant and sponsored by the Greater Charleston Restaurant Association. Over 50 area chefs and restaurants come together so you can sample their wares, including a wine and food pairing, with proceeds going to charity.

November

Plantation Days at Middleton Place (4300 Ashley River Rd., 843/556-6020, www.middletonplace.org, daily 9 A.M.–5 P.M., last tour 4:30 P.M., guided tour $10) happen each Saturday in November, giving visitors a chance to wander the grounds and see artisans at work practicing authentic crafts, as they would have done in antebellum days, with a special emphasis on the contributions of African Americans. A special treat comes on Thanksgiving, when a full meal is offered on the grounds at the Middleton Place restaurant (843/556-6020, www.middletonplace.org, reservations strongly recommended).

Though the **Battle of Secessionville** actually took place in June 1862 much farther south, November is the time the battle is reenacted at Boone Plantation (1235 Long Point Rd., 843/884-4371, www.boonehallplantation.com, $17.50 adults, $7.50 children) on Mount Pleasant. Call for specific dates and times.

December

A yuletide in the Holy City is an experience you'll never forget, as the **Christmas in Charleston** (843/724-3705, www.charlestoncity.info) events clustered around the first week of the month prove. For some reason—whether it's the old architecture, the friendly people, the churches, the carriages, or all of the above—Charleston feels right at home during Christmas. The festivities begin with Mayor Joe Riley lighting the city's 60-foot Tree of Lights in Marion Square, followed by a parade of brightly lit boats from Mount Pleasant all the way around Charleston up the Ashley River. The key event is the Sunday Christmas Parade through downtown, featuring bands, floats, and performers in the holiday spirit. The Saturday Farmers Market in the square continues through the middle of the month with a focus on holiday items.

Shopping

For a relatively small city, Charleston has an impressive amount of big-name, big-city stores to go along with its charming one-of-a-kind locally owned shops. I've never known anyone to leave Charleston without bundles of good stuff.

KING STREET

Without a doubt, King Street is by far the main shopping thoroughfare in the area. It's unique not only for the fact that so many national name stores are lined up so close to each other but because there are so many great restaurants of so many different types scattered in and among the retail outlets, ideally positioned for when you need to take a break to rest and refuel. Though I don't necessarily recommend doing so—Charleston has so much more to offer—a visitor could easily spend an entire weekend doing nothing but shopping, eating, and carousing up and down King Street from early morning to the wee hours of the following morning. King Street has three distinct areas with three distinct types of merchandise: Lower King is primarily top-of-the-line antiques stores (most are closed Sundays, so plan your trip accordingly); Middle King is where you'll find upscale name-brand outlets such as Banana Republic and American Apparel as well as some excellent shoe stores; and Upper King, north of Calhoun Street, is where you'll find funky housewares shops, generally locally owned.

Antiques

A relatively new addition to Lower King's cluster of antique shops, **Alexandra AD** (156 King St., 843/722-4897, Mon.–Sat. 10 A.M.–5 P.M.) features great chandeliers, lamps, and fabrics. As the name implies, **English Patina** (179 King

King Street is the center of shopping in Charleston.

St., 843/853-0380, Mon.–Sat. 10 A.M.–5 P.M.) specializes in European furniture, brought to its big James Island warehouse three times a year in shipping containers. Since 1929, **George C. Birlant & Co.** (191 King St., 843/722-3842, Mon.–Sat. 9 A.M.–5:30 P.M.) has been importing 18th- and 19th-century furniture, silver, china, and crystal, and also deals in the famous "Charleston Battery Bench." On the 200 block, **A'riga IV** (204 King St., 843/577-3075, Mon.–Sat. 10:30 A.M.–4:30 P.M.) deals in a quirky mix of 19th-century decorative arts, including rare apothecary items. **Carlton Daily Antiques** (208 King St., 843/853-2299, Mon.–Sat. 10 A.M.–5:30 P.M.) intrigues with its unusual focus on art deco and modernist pieces and furnishings.

Art Galleries

Ever since native son Joseph Allen Smith began one of the country's first art collections in Charleston in the late 1700s, the Holy City has been fertile ground for visual artists. For most visitors, the center of visual arts activity is in the French Quarter between South Market and Tradd Streets. Thirty galleries reside here within short walking distance, including: **Charleston Renaissance Gallery** (103 Church St., 843/723-0025, www.fineart-south.com, Mon.–Sat. 10 A.M.–5 P.M.), specializing in 19th- and 20th-century oils and sculpture, featuring artists from the American South, including some splendid pieces from the Charleston Renaissance; the city-funded **City Gallery at Waterfront** (34 Prioleau St., 843/958-6484, Tues.–Fri. 11 A.M.–6 P.M., Sat.–Sun. noon–5 P.M.); the **Pink House Gallery** (17 Chalmers St., 843/723-3608, http://pinkhouse-gallery.tripod.com, Mon.–Sat. 10 A.M.–5 P.M.), in the oldest tavern building in the South, circa 1694; **Helena Fox Fine Art** (106-A Church St., 843/723-0073, www.helenafox-fineart.com, Mon.–Sat. 10 A.M.–5 P.M.), dealing in 20th-century representational art; the **Anne Worsham Richardson Birds Eye View**

MAYOR JOE'S LEGACY

Few cities anywhere have been as greatly influenced by one mayor as Charleston has by Joseph P. "Joe" Riley, reelected in November 2011 to his 10th four-year term (he swears this will be his last). "Mayor Joe," or just "Joe," as he's usually called, is not only responsible for instigating the vast majority of redevelopment in the city, he continues to set the bar for its award-winning tourism industry—always a key component in his long-term plans.

Riley won his first mayoral race at the age of 32, the second Irish American mayor of the city. The first was John Grace, elected in 1911 and eventually defeated by the allegedly anti-Catholic Thomas P. Stoney. Legend has it that soon after winning his first mayoral election in 1975, Riley was handed an old envelope written decades before by the Bishop of Charleston, addressed to "The Next Irish Mayor." Inside was a note with a simple message: "Get the Stoneys."

The well-regarded lawyer, Citadel grad, and former member of the state legislature had a clear vision for his administration: It would bring unprecedented numbers of women and minorities into city government, rejuvenate then-seedy King Street, and enlarge the city's tax base by annexing surrounding areas (during Riley's tenure the city has grown from 16.7 square miles to over 100). But in order to make any of that happen, one thing had to happen first—Charleston's epidemic street crime had to be brought under control. Enter a vital partner in Riley's effort to remake Charleston: Chief of Police Reuben Greenberg. From 1982 to 2005, Greenberg—who intrigued locals and the national media not only for his dominant personality but because he was that comparative rarity, an African American Jew—turned old ideas of law enforcement in Charleston upside down through his introduction of "community policing." Charleston cops would have to have a college degree. Graffiti would not be tolerated. And for the first time in recent memory, they would have to walk beats instead of stay in their cars. With Greenberg's help, Riley was able to keep together the unusual coalition of predominantly white business and corporate interests and African American voters that brought him into office in the first place.

It hasn't all been rosy. Riley was put on the spot in 2007 after the tragic deaths of the "Charleston 9" firefighters, an episode which seemed to expose serious policy and equipment flaws in the city's fire department. And he's often been accused of being too easily infatuated with high-dollar development projects instead of paying attention to the needs of regular Charlestonians, such as perennial flooding problems.

Here's only a partial list of the major projects and events Mayor Joe has made happen in Charleston that visitors are likely to enjoy:

- Charleston Maritime Center
- Charleston Place
- Children's Museum of the Lowcountry
- Hampton Park rehabilitation
- King Street-Market Street retail district
- Mayor Joseph P. Riley Ballpark (named after the mayor at the insistence of city council, over his objections)
- MOJA Arts Festival
- Piccolo Spoleto
- The South Carolina Aquarium
- Spoleto USA
- Waterfront Park
- West Ashley Bikeway & Greenway

Gallery (119-A Church St., 843/723-1276, www.anneworshamrichardson.com, Mon.–Sat. 10 A.M.–5 P.M.), home of South Carolina's official painter of the state flower and state bird; and the more modern-oriented **Robert Lange Studios** (2 Queen St., 843/805-8052, www. robertlangestudios.com, daily 11 A.M.–5 P.M.). The best way to experience the area is to go on one of the popular and free **French Quarter ArtWalks** (843/724-3424, www.frenchquarter-arts.com), held the first Friday of March, May, October, and December 5–8 P.M. and featuring lots of wine, food, and, of course, art. You can download a map at the website.

One of the most important single venues, the nonprofit **Redux Contemporary Art Center** (136 St. Philip St., 843/722-0697, www.reduxstudios.org, Tues.–Thurs. noon–8 P.M., Fri.–Sat. noon–5 P.M.) features modernistic work in a variety of media, including illustration, video installation, blueprints, performance art, and graffiti. Outreach is hugely important to this venture and includes lecture series, classes, workshops, and internships. For a more modern take from local artists, check out the **Sylvan Gallery** (171 King St., 843/722-2172, www.thesylvangallery.com, Mon.–Fri. 9 A.M.–5 P.M., Sat. 10 A.M.–5 P.M., Sun. 11 A.M.–4 P.M.), which specializes in 20th- and 21st-century art and sculpture. Right up the street and incorporating works from the estate of Charleston legend Elizabeth O'Neill Verner is **Ann Long Fine Art** (177 King St., 843/577-0447, www.annlongfineart.com, Mon.–Sat. 11 A.M.–5 P.M.), which seeks to combine the painterly aesthetic of the Old World with the edgy vision of the New. Farther up King and specializing in original Audubon prints and antique botanical prints is **The Audubon Gallery** (190 King St., 843/853-1100, www.audubonart.com, Mon.–Sat. 10 A.M.–5 P.M.), the sister store of the Joel Oppenheimer Gallery in Chicago. In the Upper King area is **Gallery Chuma** (43 John St., 843/722-7568, www.gallerychuma.com, Mon.–Sat. 10 A.M.–6 P.M.), which specializes in the art of the Gullah people of the South Carolina coast. They do lots of cultural and educational events about Gullah culture as well as display art on the subject.

Charleston's favorite art supply store is **Artist & Craftsman Supply** (434 King St., 843/579-0077, www.artistcraftsman.com, Mon.–Sat. 10 A.M.–7 P.M., Sun. noon–5 P.M.), part of a well-regarded Maine-based chain. They cater to the pro as well as the dabbler and have a fun children's art section as well.

Books and Music

It's easy to overlook at the far southern end of retail development on King, but the excellent **Preservation Society of Charleston Book and Gift Shop** (147 King St., 843/722-4630, Mon.–Sat. 10 A.M.–5 P.M.) is perhaps the best place in town to pick up books on Charleston lore and history as well as locally themed gift items. The charming **Pauline Books and Media** (243 King St., 843/577-0175, Mon.–Sat. 10 A.M.–6 P.M.) is run by the Daughters of Saint Paul and carries Christian books, Bibles, rosaries, and images from a Roman Catholic perspective. Housed in an extremely long and narrow storefront on Upper King, Jonathan Sanchez's funky and friendly **Blue Bicycle Books** (420 King St., 843/722-2666, www.bluebicyclebooks.com, Mon.–Sat. 10 A.M.–6 P.M., Sun. 1–6 P.M.) deals primarily in used books and has a particularly nice stock of local and regional books, art books, and fiction.

Clothes

Cynics may scoff at the proliferation of high-end national retail chains on Middle King, but rarely will a shopper find so many so conveniently located, and in such a pleasant environment. The biggies are: **The Gap** (269 King St., 843/577-2498, Mon.–Thurs. 10 A.M.–7 P.M., Fri.–Sat. 10 A.M.–8 P.M., Sun. 11 A.M.–7 P.M.); **Banana Republic** (247 King St., 843/722-6681, Mon.–Fri. 10 A.M.–7 P.M., Sat. 10 A.M.–8 P.M., Sun. noon–6 P.M.); **J.Crew** (264 King St., 843/534-1640, Mon.–Thurs. 10 A.M.–6 P.M., Fri.–Sat. 10 A.M.–8 P.M., Sun. noon–6 P.M.); and **American Apparel** (348 King St., 843/853-7220, Mon.–Sat. 10 A.M.–8 P.M., Sun. noon–7 P.M.). Of particular note is the massive **Forever 21** (211 King St., 843/937-5087, www.forever21.com, Sun.–Wed. 10 A.M.–8 P.M., Thurs.–Sat. 10 A.M.–9 P.M.), housed in what was formerly Saks Fifth Avenue. This edition of the well-known tween mecca goes well beyond what you're probably

Blue Bicycle Books on Upper King Street

used to in other markets and features clothes for (slightly) older women as well as a small men's section.

For a locally owned clothing shop, try the innovative **Worthwhile** (268 King St., 843/723-4418, www.shopworthwhile. com, Mon.–Sat. 10 A.M.–6 P.M., Sun. noon–5 P.M.), which has lots of organic fashion. Big companies' losses are your gain at **Oops!** (326 King St., 843/722-7768, Mon.–Fri. 10 A.M.–6 P.M., Sat. 10 A.M.–7 P.M., Sun. noon–6 P.M.), which buys factory mistakes and discontinued lines from major brands at a discount, passing along the savings to you. The range here tends toward colorful and preppy. If hats are your thing, make sure you visit **Magar Hatworks** (57 Cannon St., 843/577-7740, leighmagar@aol.com, www.magarhatworks.com), where Leigh Magar makes and sells her whimsical, all-natural hats, some of which she designs for

Barneys New York. Another notable locally owned clothing store on King Street is the classy **Berlins Men's and Women's** (114–120 King St., 843/722-1665, Mon.–Sat. 9:30 A.M.–6 P.M.), dating from 1883.

Health and Beauty

The Euro-style window display of **Stella Nova** (292 King St., 843/722-9797, Mon.–Sat. 10 A.M.–7 P.M., Sun. 1–5 P.M.) beckons at the corner of King and Society. Inside this locally owned cosmetics store and studio you'll find a wide selection of high-end makeup and beauty products. There's also a Stella Nova day spa (78 Society St., 843/723-0909, Mon.–Sat. 9 A.M.–6 P.M., Sun. noon–5 P.M.).

Inside the Francis Marion Hotel near Marion Square is **Spa Adagio** (387 King St., 843/577-2444, Mon.–Sat. 10 A.M.–7 P.M., Sun. by appointment only), offering massage, waxing, and skin and nail care. On Upper King you'll find

Allure Salon (415 King St., 843/722-8689, Tues. and Thurs. 10 A.M.–7 P.M., Wed. and Fri. 9 A.M.–5 P.M., Sat. 10 A.M.–3 P.M.) for stylish haircuts.

Home, Garden, and Sporting Goods

With retail locations in Charleston and Savannah and a new cutting-edge, green-friendly warehouse in North Charleston, **Half Moon Outfitters** (280 King St., 843/853-0990, www.halfmoonoutfitters.com, Mon.–Sat. 10 A.M.–7 P.M., Sun. noon–6 P.M.) is something of a local legend. Here you can find not only top-of-the-line camping and outdoor gear and good tips on local recreation but some really stylish outdoorsy apparel as well. A couple of good home and garden stores are worth mentioning on Upper King: **Charleston Gardens** (650 King St., 866/469-0118, www.charlestongardens.com, Mon.–Sat. 9 A.M.–5 P.M.) for furniture and accessories; and **Haute Design Studio** (489 King St., 843/577-9886, www.hautedesign. com, Mon.–Fri. 9 A.M.–5:30 P.M.) for upper-end furnishings with an edgy feel.

Jewelry

Joint Venture Estate Jewelers (185 King St., 843/722-6730, www.jventure.com, Mon.–Sat. 10 A.M.–5:30 P.M.) specializes in antique, vintage, and modern estate jewelry as well as pre-owned watches, including Rolex, Patek Philippe, and Cartier. Since 1919, **Croghan's Jewel Box** (308 King St., 843/723-3594, www.croghansjewelbox.com, Mon.–Fri. 9:30 A.M.–5:30 P.M., Sat. 10 A.M.–5 P.M.) has offered amazing locally crafted diamonds, silver, and designer pieces to generations of Charlestonians. An expansion in the late 1990s tripled the size of the historic location. **Art Jewelry by Mikhail Smolkin** (312 King St., 843/722-3634, www.fineartjewelry.com, Mon.–Sat. 10 A.M.–5 P.M.) features one-of-a-kind pieces by this St. Petersburg, Russia, native.

Shoes

Rangoni of Florence (270 King St., 843/577-9554, Mon.–Sat. 9:30 A.M.–6 P.M., Sun. 12:30–5:30 P.M.) imports the best women's shoes from Italy, with a few men's designs as well. **Copper Penny Shooz** (317 King St., 843/723-3838, Mon.–Sat. 10 A.M.–7 P.M., Sun. noon–6 P.M.) combines hip and upscale fashion. Funky and fun **Phillips Shoes** (320 King St., 843/965-5270, Mon.–Sat. 10 A.M.–6 P.M.) deals in Dansko for men, women, and kids (don't miss the awesome painting above the register of Elvis fitting a customer). **Mephisto** (322 King St., 843/722-4666, www.mepcomfort.com, Mon.–Sat. 10 A.M.–6 P.M.) deals in that incredibly comfortable, durable brand. A famous locally owed place for footwear is **Bob Ellis Shoe Store** (332 King St., 843/722-2515, www.bobellisshoes.com, Mon.–Sat. 10 A.M.–6 P.M.), which has served Charleston's elite with high-end shoes since 1950.

CHARLESTON PLACE

Charleston Place (130 Market St., 843/722-4900, www.charlestonplaceshops.com, Mon.–Wed. 10 A.M.–6 P.M., Thurs.–Sat. 10 A.M.–8 P.M., Sun. noon–5 P.M.), a combined retail-hotel development begun to much controversy in the late 1970s, was the first big downtown redevelopment project of Mayor Riley's tenure. While naysayers said people would never come downtown to shop for boutique items, Riley proved them wrong, and 30 years later The Shops at Charleston Place and the Riviera (the entire complex has itself been renovated through the years) remains a big shopping draw for locals and visitors alike. Highlights inside the large, stylish space include Gucci, Talbots, Louis Vuitton, Yves Delorme, Everything But Water, and Godiva.

NORTH OF BROAD

In addition to the myriad of tourist-oriented shops in the Old City Market itself, there are a few gems in the surrounding area that also appeal to locals. For years dominated by a flea market vibe, **Old City Market** (Meeting St. and Market St., 843/973-7236, daily 6 A.M.– 11:30 P.M.) was recently upgraded and is now chockablock with boutique retail all along its lengthy interior. The more humble crafts tables are toward the back. If you must have one of the handcrafted sweetgrass baskets, try out your haggling skills—the prices have wiggle room built in.

Women come from throughout the region to shop at the incredible consignment store **The Trunk Show** (281 Meeting St., 843/722-0442, Mon.–Sat. 10 A.M.–6 P.M.). You can find one-of-a-kind vintage and designer wear and accessories. Some finds are bargains, some not so much, but there's no denying the quality and breadth of the offerings. For a more budget-conscious and countercultural vintage shop, walk a few feet next door to **Factor Five** (283 Meeting St., 843/965-5559), which has retro clothes, rare CDs, and assorted paraphernalia. **Indigo** (4 Vendue Range, 800/549-2513, Sun.–Thurs. 10 A.M.–6 P.M., Fri.–Sat. 10 A.M.–7 P.M.), a favorite home accessories store, has plenty of one-of-a-kind pieces, many of them by regional artists and rustic in flavor, almost like outsider art. Affiliated with the hip local restaurant chain Maverick Kitchens, **Charleston Cooks!** (194 East Bay St., 843/722-1212, www.charlestoncooks.com, Mon.–Sat. 10 A.M.–9 P.M., Sun. 11 A.M.–6 P.M.) has an almost overwhelming array of gourmet items and kitchenware, and even offers cooking classes.

OFF THE PENINSULA

Though the best shopping is in Charleston proper, there are some noteworthy independent

The Trunk Show on Meeting Street

© JIM MOREKIS

stores in the surrounding areas. Mount Pleasant boasts a fun antiques and auction spot, **Page's Thieves Market** (1460 Ben Sawyer Blvd., 843/884-9672, www.pagesthievesmarket.com, Mon.–Fri. 9 A.M.–5:30 P.M., Sat. 9 A.M.–5 P.M.). The biggest music store in the region is **The Guitar Center** (7620 Rivers Ave., 843/572-9063, Mon.–Fri. 11 A.M.–7 P.M., Sat. 10 A.M.–7 P.M., Sun. noon–6 P.M.) in North Charleston across from Northwood Mall. With just about everything a musician might want or need, it's part of a chain that has been around since the late 1950s, but the Charleston location is relatively new. Probably Charleston's best-regarded home goods store is the nationally recognized **ESD, Elizabeth Stuart Design** (422 Savannah Hwy./U.S. 17, 843/225-6282, www.esdcharleston.com, Mon.–Sat. 10 A.M.–6 P.M.), with a wide range of antique and new furnishings, art, lighting, jewelry, and more.

SHOPPING CENTERS

The newest and most pleasant mall in the area is the retro-themed, pedestrian-friendly **Mount Pleasant Towne Center** (1600 Palmetto Grande Dr., 843/216-9900, www.mtpleasanttownecentre.com, Mon.–Sat. 10 A.M.–9 P.M., Sun. noon–6 P.M.), which opened in 1999 to serve the growing population of East Cooper residents tired of having to cross a bridge to get to a big mall. In addition to national chains you'll find a few cool local stores in here, like Stella Nova spa and day salon, Shooz by Copper Penny, and the men's store Jos. A. Banks.

You'll find the **Northwoods Mall** (2150 Northwoods Blvd., North Charleston, 843/797-3060, www.shopnorthwoodsmall.com, Mon.–Sat. 10 A.M.–9 P.M., Sun. noon–6 P.M.) up in North Charleston. Anchor stores include Dillard's, Belk, Sears, and J. C. Penney. North Charleston also hosts the **Tanger Outlet** (4840 Tanger Outlet Blvd., 843/529-3095, www.tangeroutlet.com, Mon.–Sat. 10 A.M.–9 P.M., Sun. 11 A.M.–6 P.M.). Get factory-priced bargains from stores such as Adidas, Banana Republic, Brooks Brothers, CorningWare, Old Navy, Timberland, and more.

Citadel Mall (2070 Sam Rittenberg Blvd., 843/766-8511, www.shopcitadel-mall.com, Mon.–Sat. 10 A.M.–9 P.M., Sun. noon–6 P.M.) is in West Ashley (and curiously not at all close to the actual Citadel college). Anchors here are Dillard's, Parisian, Target, Belk, and Sears.

Sports and Recreation

Because of the generally great weather in Charleston, helped immensely by the steady, soft sea breeze, outdoor activities are always popular and available. Though it's not much of a spectator sports town, there are plenty of things to do on your own, such as golf, tennis, walking, hiking, boating, and fishing.

ON THE WATER
Beaches
In addition to the charming town of Folly Beach itself, there's the modest county-run **Folly Beach County Park** (1100 W. Ashley Ave., Folly Beach, 843/588-2426, www.ccprc.com, May–Feb. daily 10 A.M.–dark, Mar.–Apr. daily 9 A.M.–dark, $7 per vehicle, free for pedestrians and cyclists) at the far west end of Folly Island. It has a picnic area, restrooms, outdoor showers, and beach chair and umbrella rentals. Get here by taking Highway 171 (Folly Rd.) until it turns into Center Street, and then take a right on West Ashley Avenue.

On Isle of Palms you'll find **Isle of Palms County Park** (14th Ave., Isle of Palms, 843/886-3863, www.ccprc.com, fall–spring daily 10 A.M.–dark, summer daily 9 A.M.–dark, $5 per

© DAVEALLENPHOTO/123RF.COM

Folly Beach County Park

vehicle, free for pedestrians and cyclists), which has restrooms, showers, a picnic area, a beach volleyball area, and beach chair and umbrella rentals. Get there by taking the Isle of Palms Connector (Hwy. 517) to the island, go through the light at Palm Boulevard, and take the next left at the park gate. There's good public beach access near the Pavilion Shoppes on Ocean Boulevard, accessed via J C Long Boulevard.

On the west end of Kiawah Island to the south of Charleston is **Kiawah Island Beachwalker Park** (843/768-2395, www. ccprc.com, Mar.–Apr. and Oct. Sat.–Sun. only 10 A.M.–6 P.M., May–Aug. daily 9 A.M.–7 P.M., Sept. daily 10 A.M.–6 P.M., Nov.–Feb. closed, $7 per vehicle, free for pedestrians and cyclists), the only public facility on this mostly private resort island. It has restrooms, showers, a picnic area with grills, and beach chair and umbrella rentals. Get there from downtown by taking Lockwood Avenue onto the Highway 30 Connector bridge over the Ashley

River. Turn right onto Folly Road, then take a left onto Maybank Highway. After about 20 minutes you'll take another left onto Bohicket Road, which leads you to Kiawah in 14 miles. Turn left from Bohicket Road onto the Kiawah Island Parkway. Just before the security gate, turn right on Beachwalker Drive and follow the signs to the park.

For a totally go-it-alone type of beach day, go to the three-mile-long beach on the Atlantic Ocean at **Sullivan's Island.** There are no facilities, no lifeguards, strong offshore currents, and no parking lots on this residential island (park on the side of the street). There's also a lot of dog-walking on this beach, since no leash is required November–February. Get there from downtown by crossing the Ravenel Bridge over the Cooper River and bearing right onto Coleman Boulevard, which turns into Ben Sawyer Boulevard. Take the Ben Sawyer Bridge onto Sullivan's Island. Beach access is plentiful and marked.

Kayaking

An excellent outfit for guided kayak tours is **Coastal Expeditions** (654 Serotina Court, 843/881-4582, www.coastalexpeditions.com), which also runs the only approved ferry service to the Cape Romain National Wildlife Refuge. They'll rent you a kayak for roughly $50 per day. Coastal Expeditions also sells an outstanding kayaking, boating, and fishing map of the area (about $12). **Barrier Island Eco Tours** (50 41st Ave., 843/886-5000, www.nature-tours.com) takes you up to the Cape Romain refuge out of Isle of Palms. **PaddleFish Kayaking** (843/330-9777, www.paddlefishkayaking.com) offers several kinds of kayaking tours (no experience necessary) and is quite accommodating in terms of scheduling them. Another good tour operator is **Nature Adventures Outfitters** (1900 Iron Swamp Rd., McClellanville, 800/673-0679) out of Awendaw Island. Closer to town, many kayakers put in at the **Shem Creek Marina** (526 Mill St., 843/884-3211, www.shemcreekmarina.com) or the public **Shem Creek Landing** in Mount Pleasant. From here it's a safe, easy paddle—sometimes with appearances by dolphins or manatee—to the Intracoastal Waterway. Some kayakers like to go from Shem Creek straight out into Charleston Harbor to **Crab Bank Heritage Preserve,** a prime birding island. Another good place to put in is at **Isle of Palms Marina** (50 41st Ave., 843/886-0209) behind the Wild Dunes Resort on Morgan Creek, which empties into the Intracoastal Waterway. Local company **Half Moon Outfitters** (280 King St., 843/853-0990; 425 Coleman Blvd., 843/881-9472, www.halfmoonoutfitters.com, Mon.–Sat. 10 A.M.–7 P.M., Sun. noon–6 P.M.) sponsors an annual six-mile Giant Kayak Race at Isle of Palms Marina in late October, benefiting the Coastal Conservation League.

Behind Folly Beach is an extensive network of waterways, including lots of areas that are great for camping and fishing. The Folly River Landing is just over the bridge to the island. On Folly Island, a good tour operator and rental house is **OceanAir Sea Kayak** (520 Folly Rd., 800/698-8718, www.seakayaksc.com).

Fishing and Boating

For casual fishing off a pier, try the well-equipped new **Folly Beach Fishing Pier** (101 E. Arctic Ave., Folly Beach, 843/588-3474, $5 parking, $8 fishing fee, rod rentals available) on Folly Beach or the **North Charleston Riverfront Park** (843/745-1087, www.north-charleston.org, daily dawn–dusk) along the Cooper River on the grounds of the old Navy Yard. Get onto the Navy Yard grounds by taking I-26 north to exit 216B. Take a left onto Spruill Avenue and a right onto McMillan Avenue.

Key local marinas include **Shem Creek Marina** (526 Mill St., 843/884-3211, www.shemcreekmarina.com), **Charleston Harbor Marina** (24 Patriots Point Rd., 843/284-7062, www.charlestonharbormarina.com), **Charleston City Marina** (17 Lockwood Dr., 843/722-4968), **Charleston Maritime Center** (10 Wharfside St., 843/853-3625, www.cmcevents.com), and the **Cooper River Marina** (1010 Juneau Ave., 843/554-0790, www.ccprc.com).

Good fishing charter outfits include **Barrier Island Eco Tours** (50 41st Ave., 843/886-5000, www.nature-tours.com, about $80) out of Isle of Palms; **Bohicket Boat Adventure & Tour Co.** (2789 Cherry Point Rd., 843/559-3525, www.bohicketboat.com) out of the Edisto River; and **Reel Fish Finder Charters** (315 Yellow Jasmine Court, Moncks Corner, 843/697-2081). Captain James picks up clients at many different marinas in the area. For a list of all public landings in Charleston County, go to www.ccprc.com.

Diving

Diving here can be challenging because of the fast currents, and visibility can be low. But as you'd expect in this historic area, there are plenty of wrecks, fossils, and artifacts. In fact, there's an entire Cooper River Underwater Heritage Trail with the key sites marked for divers. Offshore diving centers on the network of offshore artificial reefs (see www.dnr. sc.gov for a list and locations), particularly the "Charleston 60" sunken barge and the new and very popular "Train Wreck," comprising 50 deliberately sunk New York City subway cars. The longtime popular dive spot known as the "Anchor Wreck" was recently identified as the Norwegian steamer *Leif Erikkson,* which sank in 1905 after a collision with another vessel. In addition to being fun dive sites, these artificial reefs have proven to be important feeding and spawning grounds for marine life.

Probably Charleston's best-regarded outfitter and charter operator is **Charleston Scuba** (335 Savannah Hwy., 843/763-3483, www. charlestonscuba.com) in West Ashley. You also might want to check out **Cooper River Scuba** (843/572-0459, www.cooperriverdiving.com) and **Atlantic Coast Dive Center** (209 Scott St., 843/884-1500).

Surfing and Boarding

The surfing at the famous **Washout** area on the eastside of Folly Beach isn't what it used to be due to storm activity and beach erosion. But the diehards still gather at this area when the swell hits—generally about 3–5 feet (occasionally with dolphins). Check out the conditions yourself from the three views of the Folly Surfcam (www.follysurfcam.com).

The best local surf shop is undoubtedly the historic **McKevlin's Surf Shop** (8 Center St., Folly Beach, 843/588-2247, www.mckevlins. com) on Folly Beach, one of the first surf shops on the East Coast, dating to 1965 (check out an employee's "No Pop-Outs" blog at http:// mckevlins.blogspot.com). Other shops include **Barrier Island Surf Shop** (2013 Folly Rd., Folly Beach, 843/795-4545) and **The Point Break** (369 King St., 843/722-4161) on the

peninsula. For lessons, **Folly Beach Shaka Surf School** (843/607-9911, www.shakasurfschool. com) offers private and group sessions at Folly; you might also try **Sol Surfers Surf Camp** (843/881-6700, www.solsurfers.net) in Mount Pleasant. Kiteboarders might want to contact **Air** (1313 Long Grove Dr., Mount Pleasant, 843/388-9300, www.catchsomeair.us), which offers several levels of lessons.

Water Parks

During the summer months, Charleston County operates three water parks, though none are on the peninsula: **Splash Island Waterpark** (444 Needlerush Pkwy., Mount Pleasant, 843/884-0832); **Whirlin' Waters Adventure Waterpark** (University Blvd., North Charleston, 843/572-7275); and **Splash Zone Waterpark at James Island County Park** (871 Riverland Dr., 843/795-7275), on James Island west of town. Admission runs about $10 pp. Go to www.ccprc.com for more information.

ON LAND
Golf

The country's first golf course was constructed in Charleston in 1786. The term "green fee" is alleged to have evolved from the maintenance fees charged to members of the South Carolina Golf Club and Harleston Green in what's now downtown Charleston. So, as you'd expect, there's some great golfing in the area, generally on the outlying islands. Here are some of the highlights; fees are averages and subject to season and time of day.

The folks at the nonprofit **Charleston Golf, Inc.** (423 King St., 843/958-3629, www. charlestongolfguide.com) are your best one-stop resource for tee times and packages. The main public course is the 18-hole **Charleston Municipal Golf Course** (2110 Maybank Hwy., 843/795-6517, www.charlestoncity.info, $40). To get here from the peninsula, take U.S. 17

south over the Ashley River, take Highway 171 (Folly Rd.) south, and then take a right onto Maybank Highway. Probably the most renowned area facilities are at the acclaimed **Kiawah Island Golf Resort** (12 Kiawah Beach Dr., Kiawah Island, 800/654-2924, www.kiawahgolf.com), about 20 miles from Charleston. The resort has five courses in all, the best-known of which is the **Kiawah Island Ocean Course,** site of the famous "War by the Shore" 1991 Ryder Cup. This 2.5-mile course, which is walking-only until noon each day, hosted the Senior PGA Championship in 2007 and will host the 2012 PGA Championship. The Resort offers a golf academy and private lessons galore. These are public courses, but be aware that tee times are limited for golfers who aren't guests at the resort.

Two excellent resort-style public courses are at **Wild Dunes Resort Golf** (5757 Palm Blvd., Isle of Palms, 888/845-8932, www.wilddunes. com, $165) on Isle of Palms. The 18-hole **Patriots Point Links** (1 Patriots Point Rd., Mount Pleasant, 843/881-0042, www.patriotspointlinks.com, $100) on the Charleston Harbor right over the Ravenel Bridge is one of the most convenient courses in the area, and it boasts some phenomenal views. Also on Mount Pleasant is perhaps the best course in the area for the money, the award-winning **Rivertowne Golf Course** (1700 Rivertowne Country Club Dr., Mount Pleasant, 843/856-9808, www. rivertownecountryclub.com, $150) at the Rivertowne Country Club. Opened in 2002, the course was designed by Arnold Palmer.

Tennis

Tennis fans are in for a treat at the new **Family Circle Tennis Center** (161 Seven Farms Dr., 800/677-2293, www.familycirclecup.com, Mon.–Thurs. 8 A.M.–8 P.M., Fri. 8 A.M.–7 P.M., Sat. 8 A.M.–5 P.M., Sun. 9 A.M.–5 P.M., $15 per hour) on Daniel Island. This multimillion-dollar facility is owned by the city of Charleston and

was built in 2001 specifically to host the annual Family Circle Cup women's competition, which was previously held in Hilton Head for many years. But it's also open to the public year-round (except when the Cup is on) with 17 courts.

The best resort tennis activity is at the **Kiawah Island Golf Resort** (12 Kiawah Beach Dr., Kiawah Island, 800/654-2924, www.kiawahgolf.com), with a total of 28 courts. There are four free, public, city-funded facilities on the peninsula: **Moultrie Playground** (Broad St. and Ashley Ave., 843/769-8258, www.charlestoncity.info, six lighted hard courts), **Jack Adams Tennis Center** (290 Congress St., six lighted hard courts), **Hazel Parker Playground** (70 East Bay St., on the Cooper River, one hard court), and **Corrine Jones Playground** (Marlowe St. and Peachtree St., two hard courts). Over in West Ashley, the city also runs the public **Charleston Tennis Center** (19 Farmfield Rd., 843/769-8258, www.charlestoncity.info, 15 lighted courts).

Hiking and Biking

If you're like me, you'll walk your legs off just making your way around the sights on the peninsula. Early risers will especially enjoy the beauty of dawn breaking over the Cooper River as they walk or jog along the Battery or a little farther north at Waterfront Park. Charleston-area beaches are perfect for a leisurely bike ride on the sand. Sullivan's Island is a particular favorite, and you might be surprised at how long you can ride in one direction on these beaches. Those desiring a more demanding use of their legs can walk or ride their bike in the dedicated pedestrian and bike lane on the massive **Arthur Ravenel Jr. Bridge** over the Cooper River, the longest cable-stayed bridge in the western hemisphere. The extra lanes are a huge advantage over the old span on the same site, and a real example for other cities to follow in sustainable transportation solutions. There's public parking on both sides of the bridge, on the Charleston side off Meeting Street and on the Mount Pleasant side on the road to Patriots Point. **Bike the Bridge Rentals** (360 Concord St., 843/853-2453, www.bikethebridgerentals. com) offers self-guided tours over the Ravenel Bridge and back on a Raleigh Comfort bike, and also rents road bikes for lengthier excursions. In West Ashley, there's an urban walking and biking trail, the **West Ashley Greenway,** built on a former rail bed. The 10-mile trail runs parallel to U.S. 17 and passes parks, schools, and the Clemson Experimental Farm, ending near John Island. To get to the trailhead from downtown, drive west on U.S. 17. About 0.5 miles after you cross the bridge, turn left onto Folly Road (Hwy. 171). At the second light, turn right into South Windermere Shopping Center; the trail is behind the center on the right.

The most ambitious trail in South Carolina is the **Palmetto Trail** (www.palmettoconservation.org), begun in 1997 and eventually covering 425 miles from the Atlantic to the Appalachians. The coastal terminus near Charleston, the seven-mile Awendaw Passage through the Francis Marion National Forest, begins at the trailhead at the Buck Hall Recreational Area (843/887-3257, $5 vehicle fee), which has parking and restroom facilities. Get there by taking U.S. 17 north from Charleston about 20 miles and through the Francis Marion National Forest and then Awendaw. Take a right onto Buck Hall Landing Road.

Another good nature hike outside town is on the eight miles of scenic and educational trails at **Caw Caw Interpretive Center** (5200 Savannah Hwy., Ravenel, 843/889-8898, www. ccprc.com, Wed.–Fri. 9 A.M.–3 P.M., Sat.–Sun. 9 A.M.–5 P.M., $1) on an old rice plantation.

One of the best outfitters in town is **Half Moon Outfitters** (280 King St., 843/853-0990, www.halfmoonoutfitters.com, Mon.–Sat. 10 A.M.–7 P.M., Sun. noon–6 P.M.). They

have a Mount Pleasant location (425 Coleman Blvd., 843/881-9472) as well, and it has better parking.

Bird-Watching

Right in Charleston Harbor is the little **Crab Bank Heritage Preserve** (803/734-3886), where thousands of migratory birds can be seen, depending on the season. October–April you can either kayak there yourself or take a charter with **Nature Adventures Outfitters** (1900 Iron Swamp Rd., Awendaw Island, 800/673-0679). On James Island southwest of Charleston is **Legare Farms** (2620 Hanscombe Point Rd., 843/559-0763, www.legarefarms. com), which holds migratory bird walks ($6 adults, $3 children) in the fall each Saturday at 8:30 A.M.

Ice-Skating

Ice-skating in South Carolina? Yep, 100,000 square feet of it, year-round at the two NHL-size rinks of the **Carolina Ice Palace** (7665 Northwoods Blvd., North Charleston, 843/572-2717, www.carolinaicepalace.com, $7 adults, $6 children). This is also the practice facility for the local hockey team, the Stingrays, as well as where the Citadel hockey team plays.

SPECTATOR SPORTS
Charleston River Dogs

A New York Yankees farm team playing in the South Atlantic League, the Charleston River Dogs (www.riverdogs.com, $5 general admission) play April–August at Joseph P. Riley Jr. Park, a.k.a. "The Joe" (360 Fishburne St.). The park is great, and there are a lot of fun promotions to keep things interesting should the play on the field be less than stimulating (as minor league ball often can be). Because of the intimate, retro design of the park, there are no bad seats, so you might as well save a few bucks and go for the general admission ticket. From downtown, get to The Joe by taking Broad

Street west until it turns into Lockwood Drive. Follow that north until you get to Brittlebank Park and The Joe, next to the Citadel. Expect to pay $3–5 for parking.

Family Circle Cup

Moved to Daniel Island in 2001 from its longtime home in Hilton Head, the prestigious Family Circle Cup women's tennis tournament is held each April at the **Family Circle Tennis Center** (161 Seven Farms Dr., Daniel Island, 843/856-7900, www.familycirclecup.com, admission varies). Almost 100,000 people attend the multiple-week event. Individual session tickets go on sale the preceding January.

Charleston Battery

The professional A-League soccer team Charleston Battery (843/971-4625, www.charlestonbattery.com, about $10) play April–July at Blackbaud Stadium (1990 Daniel Island Dr.) on Daniel Island, north of Charleston. To get here from downtown, take I-26 north and then I-526 to Mount Pleasant. Take exit 23A, Clements Ferry Road, and then a left on St. Thomas Island Drive. Blackbaud Stadium is about one mile along on the left.

South Carolina Stingrays

The ECHL professional hockey team the South Carolina Stingrays (843/744-2248, www.stingrayshockey.com, $15) get a good crowd out to their rink at the North Charleston Coliseum (5001 Coliseum Dr., North Charleston), playing October–April.

Citadel Bulldogs

The Citadel (171 Moultrie St., 843/953-3294, www.citadelsports.com) plays Southern Conference football home games at Johnson-Hagood Stadium, next to the campus on the Ashley River near Hampton Park. The basketball team plays home games at McAlister Field House on campus. The school's hockey team skates home games at the Carolina Ice Palace (7665 Northwoods Blvd., North Charleston).

Accommodations

As one of the country's key national and international destination cities, Charleston has a very well-developed infrastructure for housing visitors—a task made much easier by the city's longstanding tradition of hospitality. Because the bar is set so high, few visitors experience a truly bad stay in town. Hotels and bed-and-breakfasts are generally well maintained and have a high level of service, ranging from very good to excellent. There's a 12.5 percent tax on hotel rooms in Charleston.

SOUTH OF BROAD
$150-300

On the south side of Broad Street is a great old Charleston lodging, **◖ Governor's House Inn** (117 Broad St., 843/720-2070, www.governorshouse.com, $285–585). This circa-1760 building, a National Historic Landmark, is associated with Edward Rutledge, signer of the Declaration of Independence. Though most of its 11 guest rooms—all with four-poster beds, period furnishings, and high ceilings—go for around $300, some of the smaller guest rooms can be had for closer to $200 in the off-season.

The nine guest rooms of **◖ Two Meeting Street Inn** (2 Meeting St., 843/723-7322, www.twomeetingstreet.com, $220–435) down by the Battery are individually appointed, with themes like "The Music Room" and the "The Spell Room." The decor in this 1892 Queen Anne bed-and-breakfast is very traditional, with lots of floral patterns and hunt club–style

CHARLESTON

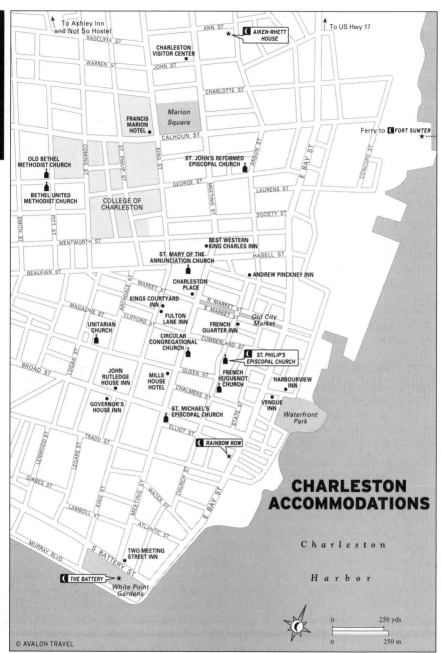

To Ashley Inn and Not So Hostel

RADCLIFFE ST

WARREN ST

ANN ST

To US Hwy 17

★ ☾ *AIKEN-RHETT HOUSE*

CHARLESTON VISITOR CENTER

JOHN ST

CHARLOTTE ST

Marion Square

Ferry to ☾ *FORT SUMTER* ★

FRANCIS MARION HOTEL

CALHOUN ST

OLD BETHEL METHODIST CHURCH

COMING ST

ST. PHILIP ST

KING ST

MEETING ST

ANSON ST

E. BAY ST

CONCORD ST

ST. JOHN'S REFORMED EPISCOPAL CHURCH

GEORGE ST

LAURENS ST

BETHEL UNITED METHODIST CHURCH

COLLEGE OF CHARLESTON

SOCIETY ST

SMITH ST

PITT ST

WENTWORTH ST

BEST WESTERN KING CHARLES INN

HASELL ST

BEAUFAIN ST

ST. MARY OF THE ANNUNCIATION CHURCH

● ANDREW PINCKNEY INN

MAGAZINE ST

ARCHDALE ST

MARKET ST

CHARLESTON PLACE

KINGS COURTYARD INN

CLIFFORD ST

FULTON LANE INN

N. MARKET ST

S. MARKET ST

Old City Market

UNITARIAN CHURCH

FRENCH QUARTER INN

CIRCULAR CONGREGATIONAL CHURCH

CUMBERLAND ST

☾ *ST. PHILIP'S EPISCOPAL CHURCH*

BROAD ST

LOGAN ST

JOHN RUTLEDGE HOUSE INN

MILLS HOUSE HOTEL

QUEEN ST

FRENCH HUGUENOT CHURCH

HARBOURVIEW INN

CHALMERS ST

STATE ST

CHURCH ST

VENDUE INN

GOVERNOR'S HOUSE INN

ST. MICHAEL'S EPISCOPAL CHURCH

Waterfront Park

ELLIOT ST

TRADD ST

☾ *RAINBOW ROW* ★

LENWOOD ST

LEGARE ST

KING ST

MEETING ST

WATER ST

E. BAY ST

CHARLESTON ACCOMMODATIONS

GIBBES ST

LAMBOLL ST

ATLANTIC ST

C h a r l e s t o n

MURRAY BLVD

S. BATTERY ST

TWO MEETING STREET INN

H a r b o r

☾ *THE BATTERY* ★

White Point Gardens

0   250 yds

0   250 m

© AVALON TRAVEL

pieces and artwork. It's considered by many to be the most romantic lodging in town, and you won't soon forget the experience of sitting on the veranda enjoying the sights, sounds, and breezes. Three of the guest rooms—the Canton, Granite, and Roberts—can be had for not much over $200.

WATERFRONT AND FRENCH QUARTER $150-300

About as close to the Cooper River as a hotel gets, the **Harbourview Inn** (2 Vendue Range, 843/853-8439, www.harbourviewcharleston. com, $259) comprises a "historic wing" and a larger, newer, but still tastefully done main building. For the best of those eponymous harbor views, try to get a room on the third floor or you might have some obstructions. It's the little touches that keep guests happy here, with wine, cheese, coffee, tea, and cookies galore and an emphasis on smiling, personalized service. The guest rooms are quite spacious, with big baths and 14-foot ceilings. You can take your complimentary breakfast—good but not great—in your room or eat it on the nice rooftop terrace.

Over $300

The guest rooms and the thoroughly hospitable service are the focus at the nearby **◖ Vendue Inn** (19 Vendue Range, 843/577-7970, www. vendueinn.com, $359). With a range of decor from colonial to French Provincial, all guest rooms are sumptuously appointed in that boutique style, with lots of warm, rich fabrics, unique pieces, and high-end bath amenities. That said, the public spaces are cool as well, with a cozy den area with chess and checkers and a nice area in which to enjoy your excellent, made-to-order hot breakfast (complimentary!). They have a row of bikes out front for guests to use, free of charge, to roam around the city. The inn gets a lot of traffic in the evenings because

of the popular Library restaurant and its hopping Rooftop Bar, which has amazing views.

Another great place in this part of town is the **French Quarter Inn** (166 Church St., 843/722-1900, www.fqicharleston.com, $359). The decor in the 50 surprisingly spacious guest rooms is suitably high-period French, with low-style noncanopied beds and crisp fresh linens. Many guest rooms feature fireplaces, whirlpool baths, and private balconies. One of Charleston's hottest restaurants, Tristan, is on the ground floor. You're treated to champagne on your arrival, and goodies are available all day, with wine and cheese served every night at 5 P.M.

NORTH OF BROAD $150-300

It calls itself a boutique hotel, perhaps because each room is totally different and sumptuously appointed. But the charming **◖ Andrew Pinckney Inn** (199 Church St., 843/937-8800, www.andrewpinckneyinn.com, $200–290) is very nearly in a class by itself in Charleston not only for its great rates but for its casual West Indies–style decor, charming courtyard, gorgeous three-story atrium, and rooftop terrace on which you can enjoy your complimentary (and delicious) breakfast. For the money and the amenities, it's possibly the single best lodging package in town.

Free parking, a great location, friendly staff, and reasonable prices are the highlights of the **Best Western King Charles Inn** (237 Meeting St., 843/723-7451, www.kingcharlesinn.com, $200–250). It's not where you'd want to spend your honeymoon, but it's plenty nice enough, and frequent visitors to town swear by it.

If you plan on some serious shopping, you might want to stay right on the city's main shopping thoroughfare at the **Kings Courtyard Inn** (198 King St., 866/720-2949, www.kingscourtyardinn.com, $240–270). This 1853 Greek Revival building houses a lot more guest rooms—more than 40—than meets the eye,

© JIM MOREKIS

Charleston Place is considered Charleston's premier hotel.

and it can get a little crowded at times. Still, its charming courtyard and awesome location on King Street are big bonuses, as is the convenient but cramped parking lot right next door (about $12 per day, a bargain for this part of town), with free in-and-out privileges.

Although it is a newer building by Charleston standards, the **Mills House Hotel** (115 Meeting St., 843/577-2400, www.ichotelsgroup.com, $285–380) boasts an important pedigree and still tries hard to maintain the old tradition of impeccable Southern service at this historic location. An extensive round of renovations completed in 2007 has been well received. Dating to 1853, the first incarnation was a grand edifice that hosted luminaries such as Robert E. Lee. Through the years, fire and restoration wrought their changes, and the modern version basically dates from an extensive renovation in the 1970s. Because of its healthy banquet and event schedule—much of it centering on the

very good restaurant and lounge inside—the Mills House isn't the place to go for peace and quiet. Rather, this Holiday Inn–affiliated property is where you go to feel the bustle of downtown Charleston and to be conveniently close to its main sightseeing and shopping attractions. Some of the upper floors of this seven-story building offer spectacular views.

Over $300

Considered Charleston's premier hotel, **Charleston Place** (205 Meeting St., 843/722-4900, www.charlestonplace.com, $419–590) maintains a surprisingly high level of service and decor considering its massive 440-room size. Now owned by the London-based Orient-Express Hotels, Charleston Place is routinely rated as one of the best hotels in North America by *Condé Nast Traveler* and other publications. The guest rooms aren't especially large, but they are well appointed, featuring Italian marble baths, high-speed Internet, and voice messaging—and, of course, there's a pool available. A series of suite offerings—Junior, Junior Executive, Parlor, and the 800-square-foot Senior—feature enlarged living areas and multiple TVs and phones. A Manager's Suite on the Private Club level up top comprises 1,200 square feet of total luxury that will set you back at least $1,600 per night. It's the additional offerings that make Charleston Place closer to a lifestyle decision than a lodging decision. The on-site spa (843/937-8522) offers all kinds of massages, including couples and "mommy to be" sessions. Diners and tipplers have three fine options to choose from: the famous **Charleston Grill** (843/577-4522, dinner daily from 6 P.M.) for fine dining; the breakfast, lunch, and brunch hot spot **Palmetto Cafe** (843/722-4900, breakfast daily 6:30–11 A.M., lunch daily 11:30 A.M.–3 P.M.); and the **Thoroughbred Club** (daily 11 A.M.–midnight) for cocktails and afternoon tea.

On the north side of Broad Street, the magnificent 🌙 **John Rutledge House Inn** (116 Broad St., 843/723-7999, www.johnrutledgehouseinn.com, $300–442) is very close to the old South of Broad neighborhood not only in geography but in feel. Known as "America's most historic inn," the Rutledge House boasts a fine old pedigree indeed: Built for Constitution signer John Rutledge in 1763, it's one of only 15 homes belonging to the original signers to survive. George Washington breakfasted here with Mrs. Rutledge in 1791. The interior is stunning: Italian marble fireplaces, original plaster moldings, and masterful ironwork abound in the public spaces. The inn's 19 guest rooms are divided among the original mansion and two carriage houses. All have antique furnishings and canopy beds, and some suites have fireplaces and whirlpool baths. A friendly and knowledgeable concierge will give you all kinds of tips and make reservations for you.

Affiliated with the Kings Courtyard—and right next door, in fact—is the smaller, cozier **Fulton Lane Inn** (202 King St., 866/720-2940, www.fultonlaneinn.com, $300), with its lobby entrance on tiny Fulton Lane between the two inns. Small, simple guest rooms—some with fireplaces—have comfortable beds and spacious baths. This is the kind of place for active people who plan to spend most of their days out and about but want a cozy place to come back to at night. You mark down your continental breakfast order at night, leave it on your doorknob, and it shows up at the *exact* time you requested the next morning. Then when you're ready to shop and walk, just go down the stairs and take the exit right out onto busy King Street. Also nice is the $12-per-day parking with free in-and-out privileges.

UPPER KING AREA
Under $150
Stretching the bounds of the "Upper King" definition, we come to the **Ashley Inn** (201 Ashley Ave., 843/723-1848, www.charleston-sc-inns.com, $100–125) well northwest of Marion Square, almost in the Citadel area. Although it's too far to walk from here to most any historic attraction in Charleston, the Ashley Inn does provide free bikes to its guests as well as free off-street parking, a particularly nice touch. It also deserves a special mention not only because of the romantic, well-appointed nature of its six guest rooms, suite, and carriage house but for its outstanding breakfasts. You get to pick a main dish, such as Carolina sausage pie, stuffed waffles, or cheese blintzes.

$150-300
In a renovated 1924 building overlooking beautiful Marion Square, the **Francis Marion Hotel** (387 King St., 843/722-0600, www.francismarioncharleston.com, $200–300) offers quality accommodation in the hippest, most bustling area of the peninsula—but be aware that it's quite a walk down to the Battery from here. The guest rooms are plush and big, though the baths can be cramped. The hotel's parking garage costs a reasonable $12 per day, with valet parking available until about 8 P.M. A Starbucks in the lobby pleases many a guest on their way out or in. Most rooms hover around $300, but some are a real steal.

HAMPTON PARK AREA
Under $150
Charleston's least-expensive lodging is also its most unique, the 🌙 **Not So Hostel** (156 Spring St., 843/722-8383, www.notsohostel.com, $21 dorm, $60 private). The already-reasonable prices also include a make-your-own bagel breakfast, off-street parking, bikes, high-speed Internet access in the common room, and even an airport, train, and bus shuttle. The inn actually comprises three 1840s Charleston single houses, all with the obligatory piazzas to catch the breeze. (However, unlike some hostels,

there's air-conditioning in all the rooms.) Because the free bike usage makes up for its off-the-beaten-path location, a stay at the Not So Hostel is a fantastic way to enjoy the Holy City on a budget, while having the opportunity to meet cool people from all over the world who are also staying here. One caveat: While they offer private rooms in addition to dorm-style accommodation, keep in mind this is still a hostel, despite the Charleston-style hospitality and perks. In other words, if there's a problem at 3 A.M., you may not be able to get anyone to help you in a hurry.

WEST ASHLEY
$150-300

Looking like Frank Lloyd Wright parachuted into a 300-year-old plantation and got to work, **(The Inn at Middleton Place** (4290 Ashley River Rd., 843/556-0500, www.theinnatmiddletonplace.com, $215–285) is one of Charleston's most unique lodgings—and not only because it's on the grounds of the historic and beautiful Middleton Place Plantation. The four connected buildings, comprising over 50 guest rooms, are modern yet deliberately blend in with the forested, neutral-colored surroundings. The spacious guest rooms have that same woody minimalism, with excellent fireplaces, spacious Euro-style baths, and huge floor-to-ceiling windows overlooking the grounds and the river. Guests also have full access to the rest of the gorgeous Middleton grounds. The only downside is that you're a lengthy drive from the peninsula and all its attractions, restaurants, and nightlife. While those who need constant stimulation will be disappointed in the deep quietude here, nature-lovers and those in search of peace and quiet will find this almost paradise. And don't worry about food—the excellent Middleton Place Restaurant is open for lunch and dinner.

ISLE OF PALMS
$150-300

One of the more accessible and enjoyable resort-type stays in the Charleston area is on the Isle of Palms at **Wild Dunes Resort** (5757 Palm Blvd., 888/778-1876, www.wilddunes.com, $254–320). This is the place to go for relaxing, beach-oriented vacation fun, either in a traditional hotel room, a house, or a villa. Bustling Mount Pleasant is only a couple of minutes away, and Charleston proper not much farther.

FOLLY BEACH
$150-300

The upbeat but still cozy renovation of the **Holiday Inn Folly Beach Oceanfront** (1 Center St., 843/588-6464, $250–270) has locals raving. If you're going to stay on Folly Beach, this hotel—with its combination of attentive staff and great oceanfront views—is the place to be.

CAMPING

Charleston County runs a family-friendly, fairly boisterous campground at **James Island County Park** (871 Riverland Dr., 843/795-7275, www.ccprc.com, $31 tent site, $37 pull-through site). A neat feature here is the $5-pp round-trip shuttle to the Visitors Center downtown, Folly Beach Pier, and Folly Beach County Park. The Park also has 10 furnished cottages (843/795-4386, $138) for rental, sleeping up to eight people. Reservations are recommended. For more commercial camping in Mount Pleasant, try the **KOA of Mt. Pleasant** (3157 U.S. 17 N., 843/849-5177, www.koa.com, from $30 tent sites, from $50 pull-through sites).

Food

If you count the premier food cities in the United States on one hand, Charleston has to be one of the fingers. Its long history of good taste and livability combines with an affluent and sophisticated population to attract some of the brightest chefs and restaurateurs in the country. Kitchens here eschew fickle trends, instead emphasizing quality, professionalism, and most of all, freshness of ingredients. In a sort of Southern Zen, the typical Charleston chef seems to take pride in making a melt-in-your-mouth masterpiece out of the culinary commonplace—in not fixing what ain't broke, as they say down here. (I've heard Charleston's cuisine described as "competent classics," which also isn't far off the mark.) Unlike Savannah, its more drink-oriented neighbor to the south, even Charleston's bars have great food. So don't assume you have to make reservations at a formal restaurant to fully enjoy the cuisine here. An entire volume could easily be written about Charleston restaurants, but here's a baseline from which to start your epicurean odyssey. You'll note a high percentage of 【 recommendations in the list; there's a good reason for that.

SOUTH OF BROAD
Classic Southern

The only bona fide restaurant in the quiet old South of Broad area is also one of Charleston's best and oldest: 【 **Carolina's** (10 Exchange St., 843/724-3800, Sun.–Thurs. 5–10 P.M., Fri.–Sat. 5–11 P.M., $18–30). There's a new chef in town, Jeremiah Bacon, a Charleston native who spent the last seven years honing his craft in New York City. His Lowcountry take on European classics includes grilled salmon with potato gnocchi, tagliatelle with Lowcountry prosciutto, and pan-roasted diver scallops, with as many fresh ingredients as possible from the nearby Kensington Plantation.

A tried-and-true favorite that predates Bacon's tenure, however, is Perdita's *fruit de mer*—a recipe that goes back to the restaurant's 1950s predecessor, Perdita's, which is commonly regarded as Charleston's first fine-dining restaurant. If you can get the whole table to agree, try the $49-pp Perdita's four-course tasting menu (wine flights extra). A recent renovation of this Revolutionary War–era building—once the legendary Sailor's Tavern—hasn't negatively affected the romantic ambience of the three themed areas: Perdita's Room (the oldest dining area), the Sidewalk Room, and the Bar Room. Free valet parking is a nice plus.

French

If you find yourself in lodging near the Broad Street area—or if you just love crepes—you will want to acquaint yourself with the **Queen Street Grocery** (133 Queen St., 843/723-4121, www.queenstreetgrocerycafe.com, Mon.–Sat. 8 A.M.–8:30 P.M., kitchen Mon.–Sat. 10 A.M.–5 P.M., Sun. 11 A.M.–3 P.M., $7–10). The kind of place frequented almost exclusively by locals, this corner store is where you can load up on light groceries, beer, wine, and cigarettes—as well as some of the tastiest made-to-order crepes this side of France.

WATERFRONT
New Southern

Few restaurants in Charleston inspire such impassioned vocal advocates as 【 **McCrady's** (2 Unity Alley, 843/577-0025, www.mccradys-restaurant.com, Sun.–Thurs. 5:30–10 P.M., Fri.–Sat. 5:30–11 P.M., $28–40). Housed in Charleston's oldest tavern building (circa 1788), McCrady's is also known as Charleston's best-kept secret, since despite its high quality it has managed to avoid the siege of tourists common at many local fine-dining spots. But their loss

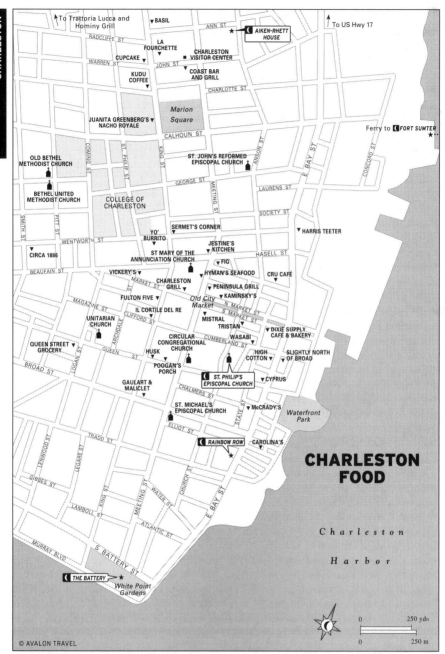

To Trattoria Lucca and Hominy Grill

BASIL

RADCLIFFE ST

ANN ST

AIKEN-RHETT HOUSE

To US Hwy 17

LA FOURCHETTE

CHARLESTON VISITOR CENTER

CUPCAKE

WARREN ST

JOHN ST

KUDU COFFEE

COAST BAR AND GRILL

CHARLOTTE ST

Marion Square

JUANITA GREENBERG'S NACHO ROYALE

CALHOUN ST

Ferry to FORT SUMTER

CONCORD ST

E BAY ST

OLD BETHEL METHODIST CHURCH

COMING ST

ST PHILIP ST

KING ST

ST. JOHN'S REFORMED EPISCOPAL CHURCH

ANSON ST

BETHEL UNITED METHODIST CHURCH

GEORGE ST

MEETING ST

LAURENS ST

COLLEGE OF CHARLESTON

SMITH ST

PITT ST

WENTWORTH ST

SOCIETY ST

HARRIS TEETER

CIRCA 1886

YO' BURRITO

SERMET'S CORNER

BEAUFAIN ST

ST MARY OF THE ANNUNCIATION CHURCH

JESTINE'S KITCHEN

HASELL ST

VICKERY'S

FIG

MARKET ST

HYMAN'S SEAFOOD

CRU CAFÉ

CHARLESTON GRILL

PENINSULA GRILL

FULTON FIVE

IL CORTILE DEL RE

Old City Market

KAMINSKY'S

MAGAZINE ST

N MARKET ST

CLIFFORD ST

ARCHDALE

S MARKET ST

UNITARIAN CHURCH

MISTRAL

DIXIE SUPPLY CAFE & BAKERY

TRISTAN

QUEEN STREET GROCERY

LOGAN ST

QUEEN ST

HUSK

CIRCULAR CONGREGATIONAL CHURCH

CUMBERLAND ST

WASABI

HIGH COTTON

SLIGHTLY NORTH OF BROAD

BROAD ST

POOGAN'S PORCH

ST. PHILIP'S EPISCOPAL CHURCH

CYPRUS

GAULART & MALICLET

CHALMERS ST

ST. MICHAEL'S EPISCOPAL CHURCH

STATE ST

McCRADY'S

Waterfront Park

ELLIOT ST

LENWOOD ST

TRADD ST

LEGARE ST

RAINBOW ROW

CAROLINA'S

CHARLESTON FOOD

KING ST

MEETING ST

WATER ST

CHURCH ST

GIBBES ST

LAMBOLL ST

E BAY ST

ATLANTIC ST

Charleston

MURRAY BLVD

S BATTERY ST

Harbor

THE BATTERY

White Point Gardens

0   250 yds

0   250 m

© AVALON TRAVEL

© JIM MOREKIS

Get a great crepe at the Queen Street Grocery.

can be your gain as you enjoy the prodigious talents of Chef Sean Brock, whose *sous vide,* or vacuum cooking, is spoken of in hushed tones by his clientele. McCrady's is not the place to gorge on usual Lowcountry fare. Portions here are small and dynamic, based on a rotating seasonal menu. Many diners find the seven-course Chef's Tasting ($90), in which you get whatever floats Chef Brock's boat that night, a near-religious experience. For an extra $75, master sommelier Clint Sloan provides paired wine selections. Or you can just go with a three-course ($45) or four-course ($60) dinner where you pick your courses. You may read complaints in online reviews about the prices at McCrady's. Let me set the record straight: (a) They're not really that high at all when you break them down per item, and (b) the perfect blending of flavors you will enjoy with any dish on the menu is worth every penny and then some. Quite simply, McCrady's is a world-class restaurant that, were it in just about any other city

in the world, would actually set you back quite a bit more. Just go.

While not as flashy as some other local chefs, Craig Deihl has, over the past decade, brought **Cypress** (167 E. Bay St., 843/727-0111, www. magnolias-blossom-cypress.com, Sun.–Thurs. 5:30–10 P.M., Fri.–Sat. 5:30–11 P.M., $20–40) to the forefront of the local foodie movement. From aged beef from a local farm to sustainably caught wreckfish, the menu reflects a deep commitment to locavore sensibilities. Any meat or seafood entrée is a can't-lose proposition here. They also offer table-side service of chateaubriand or rack of lamb for two.

FRENCH QUARTER
New Southern

With an art deco–style vibe that's a refreshing change from the usual Charleston restaurant decor, **Tristan** (55 Market St., 843/534-2155, www.tristandining.com, Mon.–Thurs. 11:30 A.M.–10 P.M., Fri.–Sat.

11:30 A.M.–11 P.M., Sun. 11 A.M.–10 P.M., $18–32) inside the French Quarter Inn draws raves for its globally influenced cuisine. At last count, the copious wine list boasted over 400 labels. The real scene here is for the à la carte Sunday brunch, with crab cake benedicts, corned beef hash, frittatas, live jazz, and Bloody Marys galore. Save room for the ridiculously good fried chocolate doughnut dessert.

NORTH OF BROAD
Asian

For whatever reason, the Asian influence is not prevalent in Charleston cuisine. But **Wasabi** (61 State St., 843/577-5222, Mon.–Thurs. 11 A.M.–9:30 P.M., Fri.–Sat. 11 A.M.–11 P.M., Sun. noon–9 P.M., $10–15) has made quite a name for itself as a great place for sushi downtown, though its hibachi work is impressive as well. The bar gets hopping after dinner.

Breakfast and Brunch

You can sit inside the crowded, noisy diner, or outside literally in the parking lot of a strip mall; either way you're doing the right thing at ◖**Dixie Supply Cafe and Bakery** (62 State St., 843/722-5650, www.dixiecafecharleston.com, daily 8 A.M.–2:30 P.M., $8–10), certainly one of the humblest but no doubt tastiest places in Charleston and perhaps the entire South. Dixie Supply has gained a certain amount of cachet lately with the filming of a *Diners, Drive-ins and Dives* episode, but don't let the trendiness keep you away. What you get at this simple old-school eatery is some of the best comfort food you'll ever taste, with a focus on breakfast and brunch items. A case could be made that their signature Tomato Pie—melted cheese over a perfect tomato slice with a delicious crust on the bottom, served with a hunk of sweet potato cornbread—is the single best dish in Charleston. However, you could make the same case for their Shrimp 'n' Grits or, for that matter their "stuffed" french toast. You place your order at the front counter, the cooks a few feet away. When your plate is ready, they call you, and you just come up and get your food and take it back to your table. It can get crowded, but just brave the lines and go. And while they do take plastic, they appreciate cash.

Classic Southern

Walk through the gaslit courtyard of the Planter's Inn at Market and Meeting Streets into the stately yet surprisingly intimate dining room of the ◖ **Peninsula Grill** (112 N. Market St., 843/723-0700, www.peninsula-grill.com, daily from 5:30 P.M., $28–35) and begin an epicurean journey you'll not soon forget. Known far and wide for impeccable service as well as the mastery of Chef Robert Carter, Peninsula Grill is perhaps Charleston's quintessential purveyor of high-style Lowcountry cuisine and the odds-on favorite as best restaurant in town. From the lobster skillet cake and crab cake appetizer to the bourbon-grilled jumbo shrimp to the benne-crusted rack of lamb to sides like wild mushroom grits and hoppin' John, the menu reads like a "greatest hits" of regional cooking. You'll almost certainly want to start with the sampler trio of soups and finish with Carter's legendary coconut cake, a family recipe. Whatever you choose in between those bookends is almost guaranteed to be excellent. Choose from 20 wines by the glass or from over 300 bottles. Four stars from the Mobil Travel Club, four diamonds from AAA, and countless other accolades have come this restaurant's way. Needless to say, reservations are strongly recommended.

Named for a now-deceased beloved dog who once greeted guests, **Poogan's Porch** (72 Queen St., 843/577-2337, www.poogansporch.com, lunch Mon.–Fri. 11:30 A.M.–2:30 P.M., dinner daily 5–9:30 P.M., brunch Sat.–Sun. 9 A.M.–3 P.M., $12–20) is the prototype of a classic Charleston restaurant: lovingly restored old home, professional but unpretentious service, great fried green tomatoes, and rich, calorie-laden Lowcountry classics. I can't decide which entrée I like best, the crab cakes or the shrimp and grits. Some swear that even the biscuits at Poogan's—flaky, fresh-baked, and moist—are better than some entrées around town, although that's a stretch. Brunch is the big thing here, a bustling affair with big portions, Bloody Marys, mimosas, and soft sunlight bathing what were, after all, living and dining rooms where people once lived.

Executive chef Sean Brock of McCrady's fame already has a healthy reputation as one of Charleston's—indeed, the country's—leading purveyors of the farm-to-table fine dining aesthetic, and one with a particularly Southern panache. He cements that reputation with the opening of ◖ Husk (76 Queen St., 843/577-2500, www.huskrestaurant.com, lunch Mon.–Sat. 11:30 A.M.–2 P.M., dinner Sun.–Thurs. 5:30–10 P.M., Fri.–Sat. 5:30–11 P.M., brunch Sun. 10 A.M.–2:30 P.M., $25), voted "Best New Restaurant in the U.S." by *Bon Appétit* magazine soon after its 2011 opening. While the hype is a little overdone, Husk is still firmly in the top tier of local restaurants. Upon entering the cleanly restored interior of the multistory historic home this once was, you'll see a blackboard with the origins of the day's ingredients—the farms and their location, never more than a day's drive away. Understandably, the spare, focused menu—"If it doesn't come from the South, it's not coming through the door," Brock says of his ingredients—is constantly changing with the seasons. On a recent lunch visit my party enjoyed two types of catfish (a fried catfish BLT on Texas toast and a lightly cornmeal-dusted broiled catfish with local vegetables), Husk's signature cheeseburger, and—wait for it—lamb barbecue. We finished with a sweet potato pie dessert to die for. The emphasis on the freshest of ingredients means a subtle, unpretentious palette of flavors. Unlike many of today's trendy chefs,

Brock doesn't overseason the food, so you taste it the way nature intended. Husk is literally right next door to Poogan's Porch, and as with Poogan's, reservations are recommended.

For many visitors to Charleston, there comes a point when they just get tired of stuffing themselves with seafood. If you find yourself in that situation, the perfect antidote is ◖ **High Cotton** (199 E. Bay St., 843/724-3815, www.mavericksouthernkitchens.com, Mon.–Thurs. 5:30–10 P.M., Fri. 5:30–11 P.M., Sat. 11:30 A.M.–2:30 P.M. and 5:30–11 P.M., Sun. 10 A.M.–2 P.M. and 5:30–10 P.M., $20–44), a meat-lovers paradise offering some of the best steaks in town as well as a creative menu of assorted lamb and pork dishes. Chef Anthony Gray places heavy emphasis on using fresh local ingredients, both veggies or game, and the rotating menu always reflects that. None of this comes particularly cheap, but splurges rarely do. In the woody (and popular) bar area there's usually a solo live pianist or sax player after 6 P.M.

The long lines at Wentworth and Meeting Streets across from the fire station are waiting to follow Rachael Ray's lead and get into **Jestine's Kitchen** (251 Meeting St., 843/722-7224, Tues.–Thurs. 11 A.M.–9:30 P.M., Fri.–Sat. 11 A.M.–10 P.M., $8–15) to enjoy a simple, Southern take on such meat-and-three comfort food classics as meatloaf, pecan-fried fish, and fried green tomatoes. Most of the recipes are handed down from the restaurant's namesake, Jestine Matthews, the African American woman who raised owner Dana Berlin.

French

On the north side of Broad Street itself you'll find **Gaulart & Maliclet** (98 Broad St., 843/577-9797, www.fastandfrench.org, Mon. 8 A.M.–4 P.M., Tues.–Thurs. 8 A.M.–10 P.M., Fri.–Sat. 8 A.M.–10:30 P.M., $12–15), subtitled "Fast and French." This is a gourmet bistro with a strong takeout component. Prices are especially

© JIM MOREKIS

Il Cortile del Re

reasonable for this area of town, with great lunch specials under $10 and Thursday-night "fondue for two" coming in at just over $20.

Mediterranean

One of the most romantic restaurants in Charleston—which is saying a lot—**Il Cortile del Re** (193A King St., 843/853-1888, Mon.–Sat. 5–10:30 P.M., $18–30) is amid the antiques stores on Lower King. Thankfully the Italian owners don't overdo the old country sentimentality, either in atmosphere or in menu. Sure, the tablecloths are white and the interior is warm, dark, and decorated with opera prints. But the piped-in music is long on cool jazz and short on over-the-top tenors, and the skinny wine bar in the front room is a favorite destination all its own. Portions here manage to be simultaneously large and light, as in the overtopped mussel plate in a delightfully thin and spicy tomato sauce, or the big spinach salad with goat cheese croutons sprinkled

with a subtle vinaigrette. The entrées emphasize the Tuscan countryside, focusing both on slow-roasted meats and sublime takes on traditional pasta dishes. My favorite is the perfect roasted lamb in a dark juniper and rosemary sauce, served on a bed of what are likely to be the best mashed potatoes in the world. Save room for the gelato dessert, served swimming in a pool of dark espresso.

Literally right around the corner from Il Cortile del Re is the other in Charleston's one-two Italian punch, **Fulton Five** (5 Fulton St., 843/853-5555, Mon.–Sat. from 5:30 P.M., $15–32). The cuisine of northern Italy comes alive in this bustling, dimly lit room, from the *bresaola* salad of spinach and thin dried beef to the caper-encrusted tuna on a bed of sweet pea risotto. It's not cheap, and the portions aren't necessarily the largest, but with these tasty, non-tomato-based dishes and this romantic, gusto-filled atmosphere, you'll be satiated with life itself.

One of Charleston's original hip people-watching spots and still a personal favorite is **Sermet's Corner** (276 King St., 843/853-7775, lunch daily 11 A.M.–3 P.M., dinner Sun.–Thurs. 4–10 P.M., Fri.–Sat. 4–11 P.M., $9–16), at the bustling intersection of King and Wentworth Streets. Charismatic chef and owner Sermet Aslan—who also painted most of the artwork on the walls of this charming, high-ceilinged space—dishes up large, inexpensive portions of Mediterranean-style goodies like panini, pastas, pestos, calamari, and inventive meat dishes.

Mexican

If you find yourself craving Mexican while shopping on King Street, duck about a block down Wentworth Street to find the cavernous, delightful **Yo' Burrito** (86 Wentworth St., 843/853-3287, www.yoburrito.com, Sun.–Thurs. 11 A.M.–10 P.M., Fri.–Sat. 11 A.M.–11 P.M., $5–8), a local legend in its own right. Order at the counter from a variety of overstuffed specialty burritos, tasty quesadillas, and stacked nachos, and take a seat at one of the large communal-style tables, perhaps enjoying a freshly squeezed lemonade while you wait. But the real kicker is the condiment bar of homemade salsas.

New Southern

Don't be put off by the initials of **Slightly North of Broad** (192 East Bay St., 843/723-3424, www.mavericksouthernkitchens.com, lunch Mon.–Fri. 11:30 A.M.–3 P.M., dinner daily 5:30–11 P.M., $15–35). Its acronym, "SNOB," is an ironic play on the often pejorative reference to the insular South of Broad neighborhood. This hot spot, routinely voted best restaurant in town in such contests, is anything but snobby. Hopping with happy foodies for lunch and dinner, the fun is enhanced by the long open kitchen with its own counter area. The dynamic but comforting menu here is practically a bible of the new wave of Lowcountry cuisine, with dishes like beef tenderloin, jumbo lump crab cakes, grilled barbecue tuna—and of course the sinful Wednesday night dinner special: deviled crab-stuffed flounder. An interesting twist at SNOB is the selection of "medium plates," i.e., dishes a little more generous than an appetizer but with the same adventurous spirit.

Just across the street from Hyman's Seafood is that establishment's diametrical opposite, the intimate bistro and stylish bar **◖FIG** (232 Meeting St., 843/805-5900, www.eatatfig.com, Mon.–Thurs. 6–11 P.M., Fri.–Sat. 6 P.M.–midnight, $20–25)—but the two do share one key thing: a passion for fresh, simple ingredients. While Hyman's packs in the tourists, FIG—short for "Food Is Good"—attracts young professional scenesters as well as the diehard foodies. Chef Mike Lata won James Beard's Best Chef of the Southeast award in 2009. FIG is one of Charleston's great champions of the Sustainable Seafood Initiative, and the kitchen

staff strives to work as closely as possible with local farmers and anglers in determining its seasonal menu.

Inside the plush Charleston Place Hotel you'll find **◖Charleston Grill** (224 King St., 843/577-4522, www.charlestongrill.com, dinner daily from 6 P.M., $27–50), one of the city's favorite (and priciest) fine-dining spots for locals and visitors alike. Veteran executive chef Bob Waggoner was recently replaced by his longtime sous chef Michelle Weaver, but the menu still specializes in French-influenced Lowcountry cuisine like a niçoise vegetable tart. There are a lot of great fusion dishes as well, such as the tuna and *hamachi* sashimi topped with pomegranate molasses and lemongrass oil. Reservations are a must.

A new hit with local foodies, **Cru Café** (18 Pinckney St., 843/534-2434, lunch Tues.–Sat. 11 A.M.–3 P.M., dinner Tues.–Thurs. 5–10 P.M., Fri.–Sat. 5–11 P.M., $20–24) boasts an adventurous menu within a traditional-looking Charleston single house, with a choice of interior or exterior seating. Sample entrées include Poblano and Mozzarella Fried Chicken and Seared Maple Leaf Duck Breast.

The hard-to-define **Mistral** (99 S. Market St., 843/722-5708, Sun.–Thurs. 11 A.M.–11 P.M., Fri.–Sat. 11 A.M.–midnight, $10–25) is part seafood restaurant, part sexy French bistro, part Lowcountry living. With live, serious jazz blowing it hot Monday–Saturday nights and some of the best mussels and shrimp in the area served up fresh, all you really need to do is enjoy. If you're not a shellfish fan, try the sweetbreads or their excellent veal.

Seafood

Hyman's Seafood (215 Meeting St., 843/723-6000, www.hymanseafood.com, Mon.–Thurs. 11 A.M.–9 P.M., Fri.–Sun. 11 A.M.–11 P.M., $14–25) is thought by many locals to border on a tourist trap. That said, this is a genuine tradition—rest assured

© JIM MOREKIS

the oyster bar at Hyman's Seafood

that some member of the same family that began Hyman's in 1890 will be on the premises any time it's open for business. To keep things manageable, Hyman's offers the same menu and prices for both lunch and dinner. After asking for some complimentary fresh boiled peanuts in lieu of bread, start with the Carolina Delight, a delicious appetizer (also available as an entrée) involving a lightly fried cake of grits topped with your choice of delectable seafood, or maybe a half dozen oysters from the Half Shell oyster bar. In any case, definitely try the she-crab soup, some of the best you'll find anywhere. As for entrées, the ubiquitous Lowcountry crispy scored flounder is always a good bet. Alas, this establishment, popular with locals and visitors as well as the occasional movie star, doesn't take reservations, so budget your time accordingly. Lunch crowds are generally lighter, although that's a relative term.

UPPER KING AREA
Asian

There's usually a long wait to get a table at the great Thai place **Basil** (460 King St., 843/724-3490, www.basilthairestaurant.com, lunch Mon.–Thurs. 11:30 A.M.–2:30 P.M., dinner Mon.–Thurs. 5–10:30 P.M., Fri.–Sat. 5–11 P.M., Sun. 5–10 P.M., $15–23) on Upper King, since they don't take reservations. But Basil also has one of the hippest, most happening bar scenes in the area, so you won't necessarily mind. (Tip: Basil calls your cell phone when your table is ready, so a lot of people go across the street to Chai's to have a drink while they wait.) Basil is a long, loud room with big open windows for people-watching. But most of the action takes place inside, as revelers down cosmos and diners enjoy fresh, succulent takes on Thai classics like cashew chicken and pad thai, all cooked by Asian chefs. The signature dish, as you might imagine, is the basil duck.

LOWCOUNTRY LOCAVORES

It might seem strange that a Deep South city founded in 1670 would be on the country's cutting edge of the sustainable food movement, but that's the case with Charleston. Perhaps more seamlessly than any other community in the United States, Charleston has managed to merge its own indigenous and abiding culinary tradition with the "new" idea that you should grow your food as naturally as possible and purchase it as close to home as you can. From bacon to snapper to sweet potatoes, the typical Charleston dish of today is much like it was before the days of processed factory food and back to its soulful Southern roots.

Spurred in part by an influx of trained chefs after the establishment of the Spoleto Festival in the 1970s, the locavore movement in Charleston came about less from market demand than from the efforts of a diehard cadre of epicureans committed to sustainability and the principles of community-supported agriculture (CSA). Spearheaded by visionaries like the James Beard Award-winning Mike Lata of the bistro FIG and McCrady's Sean Brock, a multitude of sustainable food initiatives have sprung up in Charleston and the Lowcountry, such as the South Carolina Aquarium's Sustainable Seafood Initiative (http://scaquarium.org), partnering with local restaurants to assure a sustainable wild-caught harvest; Certified South Carolina (www.certifiedsc.com), guaranteeing that the food you eat was grown in the Palmetto State; a local chapter of the Slow Food Movement (http://slowfoodcharleston.org); and Cypress Artisan Meat Share (www.magnolias-blossom-cypress.com), in which a group of highly regarded restaurants makes their fine locally sourced meats available to the public.

The list of Holy City restaurants relying almost exclusively on local and sustainable sources is too long to replicate in this space, but here are a few notable examples:

- Husk (76 Queen St., 843/577-2500, www.huskrestaurant.com)
- McCrady's (2 Unity Alley, 843/577-0025, www.mccradysrestaurant.com)
- Cypress (167 E. Bay St., 843/727-0111, www.magnolias-blossom-cypress.com)
- Charleston Grill (224 King St., 843/577-4522, www.charlestongrill.com)
- High Cotton (199 E. Bay St., 843/724-3815, www.mavericksouthernkitchens.com)
- FIG (232 Meeting St., 843/805-5900, www.eatatfig.com)
- Al Di La (25 Magnolia Rd., 843/571-2321)
- Queen Street Grocery (133 Queen St., 843/723-4121)
- Carolina's (10 Exchange St., 843/724-3800)
- Middleton Place Restaurant (4300 Ashley River Rd., 843/556-6020, www.middletonplace.org)
- Circa 1886 (149 Wentworth St., 843/853-7828, www.circa1886.com)
- COAST Bar and Grill (39D John St., 843/722-8838, www.coastbarandgrill.com)
- Cru Café (18 Pinckney St., 843/534-2434)
- Hominy Grill (207 Rutledge Ave., 912/937-0930)
- Il Cortile del Re (193A King St., 843/853-1888)
- Peninsula Grill (112 N. Market St., 843/723-0700, www.peninsulagrill.com)
- Tristan (55 Market St., 843/534-2155, www.tristandining.com)

French

A taste of the Left Bank on Upper King, the intimate bistro ◖ **La Fourchette** (432 King St., 843/722-6261, Mon.–Sat. from 6 P.M., $15–20) is regarded as the best French restaurant in town and, *naturellement,* one of the most romantic. You'll be pleasantly surprised by the reasonable prices as well. Cassoulet, the French national dish, is front and center among Chef Perig Goulet's concoctions, arriving in its own casserole dish on a trivet. Whatever you do, make sure you start with the *pommes frites* double-fried in duck fat. Your arteries may not thank you, but your taste buds will.

Mexican

The best quesadilla I've ever had was at **Juanita Greenberg's Nacho Royale** (439 King St., 843/723-6224, www.juanitagreenbergs.com, daily 11 A.M.–11 P.M., $6–8)—perfectly packed with jack cheese but not overly so, full of spicy sausage, and finished with a delightful *pico de gallo*. This modest Mexican joint on Upper King caters primarily to a college crowd, as you can tell from the reasonable prices, the large patio out back, the extensive tequila list, and the bar that stays open until 2 A.M. on weekends.

Seafood

Many say the cashew-encrusted seared rare tuna on a bed of crabmeat and buckwheat noodles at **COAST Bar and Grill** (39D John St., 843/722-8838, www.coastbarandgrill.com, daily from 5:30 P.M., $18–30) is the single best dish in Charleston. I wouldn't go that far, but it's certainly up there. COAST makes the most of its loud, hip former warehouse setting. Beautifully textured Lowcountry-themed paintings and kitschy faux-Polynesian items ring the walls, as the clanging silverware competes with the boisterous conversation. While the fun-loving decor in the dining room will suck you in, what keeps you happy is what goes on in the kitchen—specifically on its one-of-a-kind hickory-and-oak grill, which cooks up some of the freshest seafood in town. The raw bar is also satisfying, with a particularly nice take on and selection of seviche. COAST is a strong local advocate of the Sustainable Seafood Initiative, whereby restaurants work directly with the local fishing industry to make the most of the area's stock while making sure it thrives for future generations. Getting here is a little tricky: find Rue de Jean on John Street and then duck about 100 feet down the alley beside it.

COLLEGE OF CHARLESTON AREA
New Southern

Focusing on purely seasonal offerings that never stay on the menu longer than three months, **◖ Circa 1886** (149 Wentworth St., 843/853-7828, www.circa1886.com, Mon.–Sat. 5:30–9:30 P.M., $23–32) combines the best Old World tradition of Charleston with the vibrancy of its more adventurous kitchens. The restaurant—surprisingly little-known despite its four-star Mobil rating—is located in the former carriage house of the grand Wentworth Mansion B&B just west of the main College of Charleston campus. It is now the playground of Chef Marc Collins, who delivers entrées like a robust beef au poivre and a shrimp-and-crab stuffed flounder, to name two recent offerings. The service here is impeccable and friendly, the ambience classy and warm, and the wine list impressive. Be sure to check the daily prix fixe offerings; those can be some great deals.

HAMPTON PARK AREA
Classic Southern

Moe's Crosstown Tavern (714 Rutledge Ave., 843/722-3287, Mon.–Sat. 11 A.M.–midnight, bar until 2 A.M., $10–15) is not only one of the classic Southern dives but has one of the best kitchens on this side of town, known for hand-cut fries, great wings, and, most of all, excellent burgers. On Tuesdays, the burgers are half price at happy hour—one of Charleston's best deals.

With a motto like "Grits are good for you," you know what you're in store for at **Hominy Grill** (207 Rutledge Ave., 912/937-0930, breakfast Mon.–Fri. 7:30–11:30 A.M., lunch and dinner daily 11:30 A.M.–8:30 P.M., brunch Sat.–Sun. 9 A.M.–3 P.M., $10–20), set in a renovated barbershop at Rutledge Avenue and Cannon Street near the Medical University of South Carolina. Primarily revered for his Sunday brunch, Chef Robert Stehling has fun—almost mischievously so—breathing new life into American and Southern classics. Because this is largely a locals' place, you can impress your friends back home by saying you had the rare pleasure of the Hominy's sautéed shad roe with bacon and mushrooms—when the shad are running, that is.

Italian

A new rave of Charleston foodies is the Tuscan-inspired fare of Chef Ken Vedrinski at ◖ **Trattoria Lucca** (41 Bogard St., 843/973-3323, www.trattorialuccadining.com, Tues.–Thurs. 6–10 P.M., Fri.–Sat. 6–11 P.M., Sun. 5–8 P.M., $20–23). The menu is simple but perfectly focused, featuring handmade pasta and signature items like the pork chop or the fresh cheese plate. You'll be surprised at how much food your money gets you here. Sunday evenings see a family-style prix fixe communal dinner.

WEST ASHLEY
American

The kitchen at **Gene's Haufbrau** (17 Savannah Hwy., 843/225-4363, www.geneshaufbrau. com, daily 11:30 A.M.–1 A.M., $6–10) complements its fairly typical bar-food menu with some good wraps. Start with the "Drunken Trio" (beer-battered cheese sticks, mushrooms, and onion rings) and follow with a portobello wrap or a good old-fashioned crawfish po'boy. One of the best meals for the money in town is Gene's rotating $6.95 blue plate special, offered Monday–Friday 11:30 A.M.–4:30 P.M. The late-night kitchen hours, until 1 A.M., are a big plus.

Barbecue

For connoisseurs, **Bessinger's** (1602 Savannah Hwy., 843/556-1354, www.bessingersbbq. com) is worth the trip over to West Ashley for its Carolina-style mustard-based wizardry. There are two scenes at Bessinger's, the

Make sure you try Fiery Ron's ribs and pulled pork.

© JIM MOREKIS

sit-down Southern buffet (Thurs. 5–8 P.M., Fri.–Sat. 5–9 P.M., Sun. noon–8 P.M., $11.50 adults, $6 children)—Friday is fried catfish night—and the Sandwich Shop (Mon.–Sat. 10:30 A.M.–9:30 P.M., $6.35 for a "Big Joe" basket) for quick takeout. In old-school tradition, Bessinger's is a dry joint that doesn't sell alcohol. (To clarify: Bessinger's in Charleston was founded by the brother of Maurice Bessinger, who started the Columbia-based "Maurice's Gourmet BBQ" chain, famous for its ultra-right-wing neo-Confederate sensibilities. You may safely patronize Bessinger's in Charleston without worrying that you are supporting anything you may have objections to.)

However, another West Ashley joint, **(Fiery Ron's Home Team BBQ** (1205 Ashley River Rd., 843/225-7427, www.hometeambbq.com, Mon.–Sat. 11 A.M.–9 P.M., Sun. 11:30 A.M.–9 P.M., $7–20) is even better than Bessinger's. I cannot say enough about both the pulled pork and the ribs, which rank with the best I've had anywhere in the country. Even the sides are amazing here, including perfect collards and tasty mac-and-cheese. Chef Madison Ruckel provides an array of table-side sauces, including hot sauce, indigenous South Carolina mustard sauce, and his own "Alabama white," a light and delicious mayonnaise-based sauce. As if that weren't enough, the owners' close ties to the regional jam-band community means there's great live blues and indie rock after 10 P.M. most nights (Thursday is bluegrass night) to spice up the bar action, which goes until 2 A.M.

Classic Southern

Tucked away on the grounds of the Middleton Place Plantation is the romantic **Middleton Place Restaurant** (843/556-6020, www.middletonplace.org, lunch daily 11 A.M.–3 P.M., dinner Tues.–Thurs. 6–8 P.M., Fri.–Sat. 6–9 P.M., Sun. 6–8 P.M., $15–25). Theirs is a respectful take on traditional plantation fare like hoppin'

John, gumbo, she-crab soup, and collards. The special annual Thanksgiving buffet is a real treat. Reservations are required for dinner. A nice plus is being able to wander the gorgeous landscaped gardens before dusk if you arrive at 5:30 P.M. or later with a dinner reservation.

Mediterranean

Anything on this northern Italian–themed menu is good, but the risotto—a legacy of original chef John Marshall—is the specialty dish at **Al Di La** (25 Magnolia Rd., 843/571-2321, www.aldilarestaurant.com, Tues.–Sat. 6–10 P.M., $13–20), a very popular West Ashley fine dining spot. Reservations are recommended.

New Southern

One of the more unassuming advocates of farm-to-table dining, **(Glass Onion** (1219 Savannah Hwy., 843/225-1717, www.ilovetheglassonion.com, Mon.–Thurs. 11 A.M.–9 P.M., Fri. 11 A.M.–10 P.M., Sat. 4–10 P.M., brunch Sat. 10 A.M.–3 P.M., $15) is also in an unassuming location, on U.S. 17 (Savannah Hwy.) on the western approaches to town. That said, their food is right in the thick of the sustainable food movement, and is also incredibly tasty to boot (not to mention more parking than downtown). The interior says "diner," and indeed the emphasis here is on Southern soul and comfort food classics. A recent trip saw a duck leg with pork belly as a special entrée, and a chicken and andouille gumbo that was zesty without being overspiced, thick without being pasty. There are occasional "all-you-can-eat quail" nights, and every Tuesday is Fried Chicken Dinner night, offering what many insist is the best fried chicken in Charleston. The Glass Onion also boasts a good variety of specialty craft brews to wash it all down with. Another plus: In this town full of Sunday brunches, Glass Onion's specialty is a Saturday brunch!

MOUNT PLEASANT

Most restaurant action in Mount Pleasant centers on the picturesque shrimping village of Shem Creek, which is dotted on both banks with bars and restaurants, most dealing in fresh local seafood. As with Murrells Inlet up the coast, some spots on Shem Creek border on tourist traps. Don't be afraid to go where the lines aren't.

Seafood

A well-regarded spot on Shem Creek is **Water's Edge** (1407 Shrimp Boat Lane, 843/884-4074, daily 11 A.M.–11 P.M., $20–30), which consistently takes home a *Wine Spectator* Award of Excellence for its great selection of vintages. Native Charlestonian Jimmy Purcell concentrates on fresh seafood with a slightly more upscale flair than many Shem Creek places.

Right down the road from Water's Edge is another popular spot, especially for a younger crowd: **Vickery's Shem Creek Bar and Grill** (1313 Shrimp Boat Lane, 843/884-4440, daily 11:30 A.M.–1 A.M., $11–16). With a similar menu to its partner location on the peninsula, this Vickery's has the pleasant added bonus of a beautiful view overlooking the Creek. You'll get more of the Vickery's Cuban flair here, with a great black bean soup and an awesome Cuban sandwich.

If you find yourself thirsty and hungry in Mount Pleasant after dark, you might want to stop in the **Reddrum Gastropub** (803 Coleman Blvd., 843/849-0313, www.reddrumpub.com, Mon.–Tues. 5:30–9 P.M., Wed.–Sat. 5:30–10 P.M.), so named because the food here is just as important as the drink. While you're likely to need reservations for the dining room, where you can enjoy Lowcountry–Tex-Mex fusion-style cuisine with a typically Mount Pleasant–like emphasis on seafood, the bar scene is very hopping and fun, with live music every Wednesday–Thursday night.

Vegetarian

For a vegetarian-friendly change of pace from seafood, go to the **Mustard Seed** (1026 Chuck Dawley Blvd., 843/849-0050, Mon.–Sat. 11 A.M.–2:30 P.M. and 5–9:30 P.M., $14–18). The pad thai is probably the best thing on New York–trained chef Sal Parco's creative and dynamic menu, but you might also get a kick out of the sweet potato ravioli.

For a real change of pace, try **The Sprout Cafe** (629 Johnnie Dodds Blvd., 843/849-8554, www.thehealthysprout.com, Mon.–Fri. 6 A.M.–8 P.M., Sat. 9 A.M.–3 P.M., Sun. 11 A.M.–3 P.M., $3–10) on U.S. 17. Dealing totally in raw foods, the obvious emphasis here is on health and freshness of ingredients. You might be surprised at the inventiveness of their breakfast-through-dinner seasonal menu—memorably described by the staff as "grab and go"—which might include a tasty crepe topped with a pear-and-nut puree and maple syrup, or a raw squash and zucchini "pasta" dish topped with walnut "meatballs."

SULLIVAN'S ISLAND

A new location of **◖ Fiery Ron's Home Team** (2209 Middle St., 843/883-3131, www.hometeambbq.com, kitchen Mon.–Sat. 11 A.M.–11 P.M., Sun. 11:30 A.M.–11 P.M., $8–14) provides the same incredible melt-in-your-mouth pork and ribs made famous by the original West Ashley location. For a friendly bite and an adult beverage or two, go straight to **Poe's Tavern** (2210 Middle St., 843/883-0083, daily 11 A.M.–2 A.M., kitchen until 10 P.M.), a nod to Edgar Allan Poe's stint at nearby Fort Moultrie. **Atlanticville** (2063 Middle St., 843/883-9452, www.atlanticville.net, daily 5:30–10 P.M., brunch Sun. 10 A.M.–2 P.M., $25) is where to go for classic fine dining on Sullivan's. If you just want to pick up some healthy goodies for picnicking on the beach, head to the little **Green Heron Grocery** (2019 Middle St., 843/883-0751).

FOLLY BEACH
Breakfast and Brunch

The closest thing to a taste of old Folly is the **Lost Dog Café** (106 W. Huron St., 843/588-9669, daily 6:30 A.M.–3 P.M., $5–7), so named for its bulletin board stacked with alerts about lost pets, pets for adoption, and newborns for sale or giveaway. They open early, the better to offer a tasty, healthy breakfast to the surfing crowd. It's a great place to pick up a quick, inexpensive, and tasty meal while you're near the beach.

Mexican

Taco Boy (15 Center St., 843/588-9761, Sun.–Thurs. 11 A.M.–10 P.M., Fri.–Sat. 11 A.M.–11 P.M., $5–15) is a fun place to get a fish taco, have a margarita, and take a walk on the nearby beach afterward. Though no one is under any illusions that this is an authentic Mexican restaurant, the fresh guacamole is particularly rave-worthy, and there's a good selection of tequilas and beers *hecho en México,* with the bar staying open until 2 A.M. on weekends.

Seafood

Fans of the legendary **◖ Bowens Island Restaurant** (1870 Bowens Island Rd., 843/795-2757, Tues.–Sat. 5–10 P.M., $5–15, cash only), on James Island just before you get to Folly, went into mourning when it burned to the ground in 2006. But you can't keep a good oysterman down, and owner Robert Barber rebuilt. Regulars insist that this institution, which began in the 1940s as a fishing camp, remains as old-school as ever. A universe removed from the Lexus-and-khaki scene downtown, Bowens Island isn't the place for the uptight. This is the place to go when you want shovels of oysters literally thrown onto your table, freshly steamed and delicious and all-you-can-eat. The fried shrimp, flounder, and hush puppies are incredible too. The understated setting—a nondescript building with little to no signage—only adds to the authenticity of the whole experience. To get there from the peninsula, take Calhoun Street west onto the James Island Connector (Hwy. 30). Take exit 3 onto Highway 171 south and look for Bowens Island Road on the right. The restaurant will be on the left in a short while, after passing by several ritzy McMansions that in no way resemble the restaurant you're about to experience.

NORTH CHARLESTON

If you have a hankering for pizza in North Charleston, don't miss **EVO Pizzeria** (1075 E. Montague Ave., 843/225-1796, www.evopizza.com, lunch Tues.–Fri. 11 A.M.–2:30 P.M., dinner Tues.–Fri. 5–10 P.M., Sat. 6–10 P.M., $10–15) in the Olde North Charleston area at Park Circle. They specialize in a small but rich menu of unusual gourmet pizza toppings, like pistachio pesto.

COFFEE, TEA, AND SWEETS

By common consensus, the best java joint in Charleston is **Kudu Coffee** (4 Vanderhorst Ave., 843/853-7186, Mon.–Sat. 6:30 A.M.–7 P.M., Sun. 9 A.M.–6 P.M.) in the Upper King area. A kudu is an African antelope, and the Africa theme extends to the beans, which all have an African pedigree. Poetry readings and occasional live music add to the mix. A lot of green-friendly, left-of-center community activism goes on here as well; a recent discussion group was titled "How to Survive the Bible Belt but Still Find God." The adjacent African art store is owned by the coffeehouse.

If you find yourself needing a quick pick-me-up while shopping on King Street, avoid the lines at the two Starbucks on the avenue and instead turn east on Market Street and duck inside **City Lights Coffeehouse** (141 Market St., 843/853-7067, Mon.–Thurs. 7 A.M.–9 P.M., Fri.–Sat. 7 A.M.–10 P.M., Sun. 8 A.M.–6 P.M.). The sweet goodies are delectable in this cozy little Euro-style place, and the Counter Culture organic coffee is to die for. If you're really lucky, they'll have some of their Ethiopian Sidamo brewed.

A unique Charleston phenomenon on Upper King by Marion Square is the aptly named **Cupcake** (433 King St., 843/853-8181, www.freshcupcakes.com, Mon.–Sat. 10 A.M.–7 P.M.). Their eponymous specialty compels Charlestonians to form lines onto the sidewalk, waiting to enjoy one or more of the 30 flavors of little cakes. Routinely voted as having the best desserts in the city, the cakes alone at **Kaminsky's** (78 N. Market St., 843/853-8270, daily noon–2 A.M.) are worth the trip to the City Market area. The fresh fruit torte, the red velvet, and the "Mountain of Chocolate" are the three best sellers. There's also a Mount Pleasant location (1028 Johnnie Dodds Blvd., 843/971-7437).

MARKETS AND GROCERIES

A fun and favorite local fixture April–mid-December, the **Charleston Farmers Market** (843/724-7309, www.charlestoncity.info, Sat. 8 A.M.–2 P.M.) rings beautiful Marion Square with stalls of local produce, street eats, local arts and crafts, and kids' activities. Running April–October, East Cooper has its own version in the

Mount Pleasant Farmers Market (843/884-8517, http://townofmountpleasant.com, Tues. 3 P.M.–dark) at the Moultrie Middle School on Coleman Boulevard.

For organic groceries or a quick healthy bite while you're in Mount Pleasant, check out **Whole Foods** (923 Houston Northcutt Blvd., 843/971-7240, daily 8 A.M.–9 P.M.). The biggest and best supermarket near the downtown area is the regional chain **Harris Teeter** (290 E. Bay St., 843/722-6821, daily 24 hours). There are other Harris Teeter stores in Mount Pleasant (920 Houston Northcutt Blvd. and 620 Long Point Rd., 843/881-4448) and Folly Beach (675 Folly Rd., 843/406-8977). For a charming grocery shopping experience, try **King Street Grocery** (435 King St., 843/958-8004, daily 8 A.M.–midnight) on Upper King. If you're down closer to the Battery, go to the delightful **Queen Street Grocery** (133 Queen St., 843/723-4121, Mon.–Sat. 8 A.M.–8:30 P.M., kitchen Mon.–Sat. 10 A.M.–5 P.M., Sun. 11 A.M.–3 P.M.). Need groceries at 4 A.M. on Folly Beach? Go to **Bert's Market** (202 E. Ashley Ave., 843/588-9449, daily 24 hours).

Information and Services

VISITORS CENTERS

I highly recommend a stop at the **Charleston Visitor Reception and Transportation Center** (375 Meeting St., 800/774-0006, www.charlestoncvb.com, Mon.–Fri. 8:30 A.M.–5 P.M.). Housed in a modern building with an inviting, open design, the Center has several high-tech interactive exhibits, including an amazing model of the city under glass. Wall after wall of well-stocked, well-organized brochures will keep you informed on everything a visitor would ever want to know about or see in the city. A particularly welcoming touch is the inclusion of the work of local artists all around the center. I recommend using the attached

parking garage not only for your stop at the Center but also anytime you want to see the many sights this part of town has to offer, such as the Charleston Museum, the Manigault and Aiken-Rhett Houses, and the Children's Museum. The big selling point at the center is the friendliness of the smiling and courteous staff, who welcome you in true Charleston fashion and are there to book rooms and tours and find tickets for shows and attractions. If for no other reason, you should go to the center to take advantage of the great deal offered by the **Charleston Heritage Passport** (www.heritagefederation.org), which gives you 40 percent off admission to all of Charleston's key historic homes, the Charleston Museum, and the two awesome plantation sites on the Ashley River: Drayton Hall and Middleton Place. You can get the Heritage Passport *only* at the Charleston Visitor Reception and Transportation Center on Meeting Street.

Other area visitors centers include the **Mt. Pleasant-Isle of Palms Visitors Center** (Johnnie Dodds Blvd., 843/853-8000, daily 9 A.M.–5 P.M.) and the new **North Charleston Visitors Center** (4975B Centre Pointe Dr., 843/853-8000, Mon.–Sat. 10 A.M.–5 P.M.).

HOSPITALS

If there's a silver lining in getting sick or injured in Charleston, it's that there are plenty of high-quality medical facilities available. The premier institution is the **Medical University of South Carolina** (171 Ashley Ave., 843/792-2300, www.muschealth.com) in the northwest part of the peninsula. Two notable facilities are near each other downtown: **Roper Hospital** (316 Calhoun St., 843/402-2273, www.roperhospital.com) and **Charleston Memorial Hospital** (326 Calhoun St., 843/792-2300). In Mount Pleasant there's **East Cooper Regional Medical Center** (1200 Johnnie Dodds Blvd., www.eastcoopermedctr.com). In West Ashley there's **Bon Secours St. Francis Hospital** (2095 Henry Tecklenburg Ave., 843/402-2273, www.ropersaintfrancis.com).

POLICE

For nonemergencies in Charleston, West Ashley, and James Island, contact the **Charleston Police Department** (843/577-7434, www.charlestoncity.info). You can also contact the police department in Mount Pleasant (843/884-4176). North Charleston is a separate municipality with its own police department (843/308-4718, www.northcharleston.org). Of course, for emergencies always call **911.**

MEDIA
Newspapers

The daily newspaper of record is the *Post and Courier* (www.charleston.net). Its entertainment insert, *Preview,* comes out on Thursdays. The free alternative weekly is the *Charleston City Paper* (www.charlestoncitypaper.com), which comes out on Wednesdays and is the best place to find local music and arts listings. A particularly well-done and lively metro glossy is *Charleston* magazine (www.charlestonmag.com), which comes out once a month.

Radio and Television

The National Public Radio affiliate is the South Carolina ETV radio station WSCI at 89.3 FM. South Carolina ETV is on television at WITV. The local NBC affiliate is WCBD, the CBS affiliate is WCSC, the ABC affiliate is WCIV, and the Fox affiliate is WTAT.

LIBRARIES

The main branch of the **Charleston County Public Library** (68 Calhoun St., 843/805-6801, www.ccpl.org, Mon.–Thurs. 9 A.M.–9 P.M., Fri.–Sat. 9 A.M.–6 P.M., Sun. 2–5 P.M.) has been at its current site since 1998. Named for Sullivan's Island's most famous visitor, the **Edgar Allan Poe** (1921 I'on Ave., 843/883-3914, www.ccpl.org, Mon. and Fri. 2–6 P.M., Tues., Thurs., and Sat. 10 A.M.–2 P.M.) has been housed in Battery Gadsden, a former Spanish-American War gun emplacement, since 1977.

The College of Charleston's main library is the **Marlene and Nathan Addlestone Library** (205 Calhoun St., 843/953-5530, www.cofc.edu), home to special collections, the Center for Student Learning, the main computer lab, the media collection, and even a café. The college's **Avery Research Center for African American History and Culture** (125 Bull St., 843/953-7609, www.cofc.edu/avery, Mon.–Fri. 10 A.M.–5 P.M., Sat. noon–5 P.M.) houses documents relating to the history and culture of African Americans in the Lowcountry.

For other historical research on the area,

check out the collections of the **South Carolina Historical Society** (100 Meeting St., 843/723-3225, www.southcarolinahistoricalsociety.org, Mon.–Fri. 9 A.M.–4 P.M., Sat. 9 A.M.–2 P.M.). There's a $5 research fee for nonmembers.

GAY AND LESBIAN RESOURCES

Contrary to many media portrayals of the region, Charleston is quite open to gays and lesbians, who play a major role in arts, culture, and business. As with any other place in the South, however, it's generally expected that people—straights as well—will keep personal matters and politics to themselves in public settings. A key local advocacy group is the **Alliance for Full Acceptance** (29 Leinbach Dr., Suite D-3, 843/883-0343, www.affa-sc.org). The **Lowcountry Gay and Lesbian Alliance** (843/720-8088) holds a potluck the last Sunday of each month. For the most up-to-date happenings, try the Gay Charleston blog (http://gaycharleston.ccpblogs.com), part of the *Charleston City Paper.*

Getting There and Around

BY AIR

Way up in North Charleston is **Charleston International Airport** (CHS, 5500 International Blvd., 843/767-1100, www.chs-airport.com), served by AirTran (www.airtran.com), American Airlines (www.aa.com), Continental Airlines (www.continental.com), Delta (www.delta.com), United Airlines (www.ual.com), and US Airways (www.usairways.com). As in most cities, taxi service from the airport is regulated. This translates to about $30 for two people from the airport to Charleston Place downtown.

BY CAR

There are two main routes into Charleston, I-26 from the west-northwest (which dead-ends downtown) and U.S. 17 from the west (called Savannah Highway when it gets close to Charleston proper), which continues on over the Ravenel Bridge into Mount Pleasant and beyond. There's a fairly new perimeter highway, I-526 (Mark Clark Expressway), which loops around the city from West Ashley to North Charleston to Daniel Island and into Mount Pleasant. It's accessible both from I-26 and U.S. 17. Keep in mind that I-95, while certainly a gateway to the region, is actually a good ways out of Charleston, about 30 miles west of the city.

Car Rentals

Charleston International Airport has rental kiosks for **Avis** (843/767-7031), **Budget** (843/767-7051), **Dollar** (843/767-1130), **Enterprise** (843/767-1109), **Hertz** (843/767-4550), **National** (843/767-3078), and **Thrifty** (843/647-4389). There are a couple of rental locations downtown: **Budget** (390 Meeting St., 843/577-5195) and **Enterprise** (398 Meeting St., 843/723-6215). **Hertz** has a location in West Ashley (3025 Ashley Town Center Dr., 843/573-2147), as does **Enterprise** (2004 Savannah Hwy., 843/556-7889).

BY BUS

Public transportation by **Charleston Area Regional Transit Authority** (CARTA, 843/724-7420, www.ridecarta.com) is a convenient and inexpensive way to enjoy Charleston without the more structured nature of an organized tour. There's a wide variety of routes, but most visitors will limit their acquaintance to the tidy, trolley-like **DASH** (Downtown Area Shuttle) buses run by CARTA primarily for visitors. Each ride is $1.75 pp ($0.85 seniors). The best deal is the $6 one-day pass, which you get at the Charleston Visitors Center (375 Meeting St.). Keep in mind that DASH only stops at designated places. DASH has three routes: the 210, which runs a northerly circuit from the Aquarium to the College of Charleston; the 211, running up and down the parallel Meeting and King Streets from Marion Square down to the Battery; and the 212 Market/Waterfront shuttle from the Aquarium area down to Waterfront Park.

BY TAXI

The South is generally not big on taxis, and Charleston is no exception. The best bet is simply to call rather than try to flag one down. Charleston's most fun service is **Charleston Black Cabs** (843/216-2627, www.charleston-blackcabcompany.com), using Americanized versions of the classic British taxi. A one-way ride anywhere on the peninsula below the bridges is about $10 pp, and rates go up from there. They're very popular, so call as far ahead as you can or try to get one at their stand at Charleston Place. Two other good services are **Safety Cab** (843/722-4066) and **Yellow Cab** (843/577-6565).

You can also try a human-powered taxi service from **Charleston Rickshaw** (843/723-5685). A cheerful (and energetic) young cyclist will pull you and a friend to most points on the lower peninsula for about $10–15. Call 'em or find one by City Market. They work late on Friday and Saturday nights too.

PARKING

As you'll quickly see, parking is at a premium in downtown Charleston. An exception seems to be the large number of free spaces all along the Battery, but unless you're an exceptionally strong walker, that's too far south to use as a reliable base from which to explore the whole peninsula. Most metered parking downtown is on and around Calhoun Street, Meeting Street, King Street, Market Street, and East Bay Street. That may not sound like a lot, but it constitutes the bulk of the area that most visitors visit. Most meters have three-hour limits, but you'll come across some as short as 30 minutes. Technically you're not supposed to "feed the meter" in Charleston, as city personnel put little chalk marks on your tires to make sure people aren't overstaying their welcome. Metered parking is free 6 P.M.–6 A.M. and all day Sunday. On Saturdays, expect to pay.

The city has several conveniently located and comparatively inexpensive parking garages. I strongly suggest that you make use of them. They're located at: The Aquarium, Camden and Exchange Streets, Charleston Place, Concord and Cumberland Streets, East Bay and Prioleau Streets, Marion Square, Gaillard Auditorium, Liberty and St. Philip Streets, Majestic Square, the Charleston Visitor Reception and Transportation Center, and Wentworth Street. There are several private parking garages as well, primarily clustered in the City Market area. They're convenient, but many have parking spaces that are often too small for some vehicles. The city's website (www.charlestoncity.info) has a good interactive map of parking.

Greater Charleston

Although one could easily spend a lifetime enjoying the history and attractions of Charleston itself, there are many unique experiences to be had in the less-developed areas surrounding the city. Generally there are two types of vibes: isolated close-knit communities with little overt development (although that's changing), or private resort-style communities amid stunning natural beauty.

SUMMERVILLE AND VICINITY

The Dorchester County town of Summerville, population 30,000, is gaining a reputation as a friendly, scenic, and upscale suburb north of Charleston. That's funny, since that's basically what Summerville has always been. Founded as Pineland Village in 1785, Summerville made its reputation as a place for plantation owners and their families to escape the insects and heat of the swampier areas of the Lowcountry. While the plantation system disintegrated with the South's loss in the Civil War, Summerville got a second wind at the turn of the 20th century, when it was recommended by doctors all over the world as a great place to recover from tuberculosis (supposedly all the turpentine fumes in the air from the pine trees were a big help). Summerville is about 30 minutes from downtown Charleston; take I-26 north.

Sights

Due to its longstanding popularity as a getaway for wealthy planters and then as a spa town, Summerville boasts a whopping 700 buildings on the National Register of Historic Places. For a walking tour of the historic district, download the map at www.visitsummerville.com or pick up a hard copy at the **Summerville Visitors Center** (402 N. Main St., 843/873-8535). Alas, the grand old Pine Forest Inn, perhaps the greatest of all Summerville landmarks, Winter

White House for presidents William Taft and Theodore Roosevelt, was torn down after World War II, a victim of the Florida vacation craze. Much visitor activity in Summerville centers on **Azalea Park** (S. Main St. and W. 5th St. S., daily dusk–dawn, free), rather obviously named for its most scenic inhabitants. Several fun yearly events take place here, most notably the **Flowertown Festival** (www.flowertownfestival.com, free) each April, a three-day affair heralding the coming of spring and the blooming of the flowers. One of the biggest festivals in South Carolina, 250,000 people usually attend. Another event, **Sculpture in the South** (www.sculptureinthesouth.com) in May, takes advantage of the extensive public sculpture in the park.

To learn more about Summerville's interesting history, go just off Main Street to the **Summerville-Dorchester Museum** (100 E. Doty Ave., 843/875-9666, www.summervilledorchestermuseum.org, Mon.–Sat. 9 A.M.–2 P.M., donation). Located in the former town police station, the museum has a wealth of good exhibits and boasts a new curator, Chris Ohm, with wide local experience, including at Middleton Place and with the CSS *Hunley* project in North Charleston.

Just south of Summerville on the way back to Charleston is the interesting **Colonial Dorchester State Historic Site** (300 State Park Rd., 843/873-1740, www.southcarolinaparks.com, daily 9 A.M.–6 P.M., $2 adults, free under age 16), chronicling a virtually unknown segment of Carolina history. Turns out a contingent of Massachusetts Puritans ("Congregationalists" in the parlance of the time) were given special dispensation in 1697 to form a settlement of their own specifically to enhance commercial activity on the Ashley River, which they did in fine form. Today

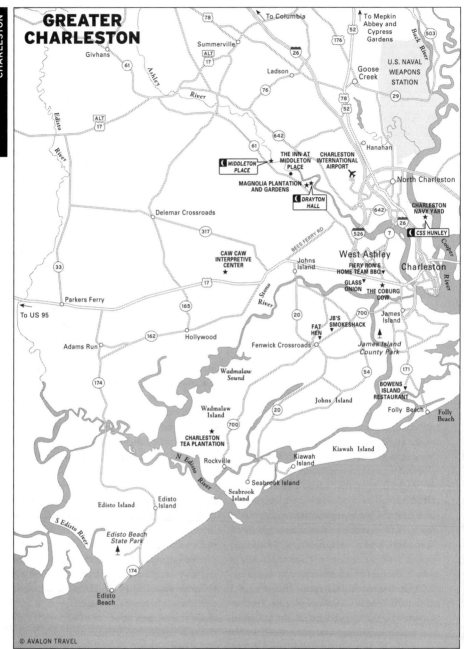

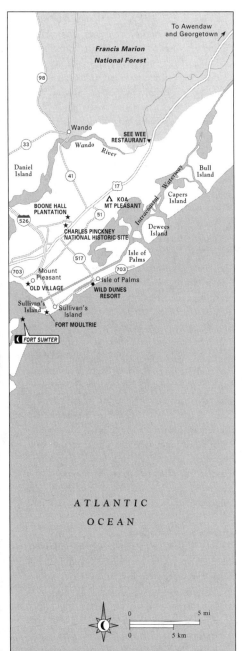

little is left of old Dorchester but the tabby walls of the 1757 fort overlooking the Ashley. Don't miss the unspectacular but still historically vital remains of the wooden wharf on the walking trail along the river, once the epicenter of a thriving port. Other sites include restorations of the palisade wall and a community house–turned–butterfly garden. The most-photographed thing on-site is the bell tower of the Anglican church of St. George—which actually wasn't where the original settlers worshipped and was in fact quite resented by them since they were forced to pay for its construction. The dispute with the Anglican Church became tense enough to cause many Congregationalists to leave and settle little Midway, Georgia, where many became key figures in the movement for American independence. The resulting Revolutionary War would be the downfall of Dorchester itself, abandoned during the upheaval.

Accommodations and Food

The renowned **Woodlands Resort & Inn** (125 Parsons Rd., 843/875-2600, $325–650) is one of a handful of inns in United States with a five-star rating both for lodging and dining. Its 18 guest rooms within the 1906 great house are decorated in a mix of old-fashioned plantation high-style and contemporary designer aesthetics, with modern, luxurious baths. There's also a freestanding guest cottage ($850) that seeks to replicate a hunting-lodge type of vibe. As you'd expect, there's a full day spa on the premises; a one-hour massage, the most basic offering, will run you $110. The pool is outside, but it's heated for year-round enjoyment, at least theoretically. Woodlands is making a big play for the growing pet-friendly market and eagerly pampers your dog or cat while you stay. You might not want to leave the grounds, but you should take advantage of their complimentary bikes to tour around historic Summerville. Within Woodlands is its award-winning world-class restaurant, simply called **The Dining Room** (Mon.–Sat. 11 A.M.–2 P.M. and 6–9 P.M., brunch Sun. 11:30 A.M.–2 P.M., $25–40). It will come as no surprise to find out that the 900-entry wine list and sommelier are collectively awesome, as are the desserts. Jackets are required, and reservations are strongly advised.

In Summerville proper, try **Mustard Seed** (101 N. Main St., 843/821-7101, lunch Mon.–Sat. 11 A.M.–2:30 P.M., dinner Mon.–Thurs. 5–9 P.M., Fri.–Sat. 5–10 P.M., $8–10), a health-food restaurant that doesn't skimp on the taste. For a more down-home-style pancakes-and-sandwich place that's popular with the locals at all hours of the day, try **Flowertown Restaurant** (120 E. 5th N. St., 843/871-3202, daily 24 hours, $8).

Another popular local landmark is **Guerin's Pharmacy** (140 S. Main St., 843/873-2531, Mon.–Fri. 9 A.M.–6 P.M., Sat. 9 A.M.–5 P.M.), which claims to be the State's oldest pharmacy. Complete with an old-fashioned soda fountain, they offer malted milkshakes and lemonade.

Moncks Corner
MEPKIN ABBEY

The little Berkeley County burg of Moncks Corner is actually named for a person, not a vocation. But nonetheless that's where you'll find a fully active, practicing Trappist monastery, Mepkin Abbey (1098 Mepkin Abbey Rd., 843/761-8509, www.mepkinabbey.org, Tues.–Fri. 9 A.M.–4:30 P.M., Sat. 9 A.M.–4 P.M., Sun. 1–4 P.M., closed Mon., free), notable for the fact that it's not only open to visitors but welcomes them. The beautiful Abbey and grounds on the Cooper River are on what was once the plantation of the great Carolina statesman Henry Laurens (whose ashes are buried here), and later the home of famous publisher Henry Luce and his wife Clare Boothe Luce. The focal point of natural beauty is the Luce-commissioned **Mepkin Abbey Botanical Garden,** a 3,200-acre

tract with a camellia garden designed by noted landscape architect Loutrel Briggs, a native New Yorker who made Charleston his adopted home.

When they're not in prayer, the monks generally observe silence. In accordance with the emphasis the order puts on the spiritual value of manual labor, farming is the main physical occupation, with the monks' efforts producing eggs, honey, preserves, soap, and even compost from the gardens, all of which you can purchase in the Abbey gift shop in the reception center, which will always be your first stop. Tours of the Abbey itself are usually given Tuesday–Saturday at 11:30 A.M. and Sunday at 3 P.M.

The majority of visitors to the Abbey are casual day visitors, eager to enjoy the relaxing quiet, the kiss of the river's breeze, and the humming of the honeybees. But for those wanting a contemplative, quiet retreat of a distinctly Christian nature, the Abbey lets you stay up to six nights in one of their guesthouses (married couples can also take advantage of this). As you'd imagine, the accommodations are Spartan—a bed, a desk, and a reading chair, with a private bath. Linens, towels, and soap are provided, but other than access to the library, there's no other modern stimulation. Retreatants eat with the monks, enjoying the same strict vegetarian diet and the same strict mealtime silence (though at lunch, a single monk reads aloud from a book). Monks will assist retreat guests in the protocols of the Abbey's prayer schedule.

CYPRESS GARDENS

Nature lovers can also enjoy Cypress Gardens (3030 Cypress Gardens Rd., 843/553-0515, www.cypressgardens.info, daily 9 A.M.–5 P.M., last admission 4 P.M., $10 adults, $5 ages 6–12), which carries with it a lot of the same quiet, meditative nature of the Abbey, although it's entirely secular. One of the first nature preserves in the Lowcountry, Cypress Garden is

THE MONKS OF MONCKS CORNER

Near Moncks Corner, South Carolina, the old Mepkin Plantation is now the home of the monks of Mepkin Abbey. How and why a monastery came to be in this semirural corner of the Deep South is worth a closer look. Originally the plantation of the great South Carolina statesman and Revolutionary War hero Henry Laurens, by 1936 the grounds had come into the hands of famed *Time* magazine publisher Henry Luce. In 1949, Henry and his wife Clare Boothe—a renowned congresswoman and playwright—donated a large portion of Mepkin to the Roman Catholic Church to be used as a monastery. In response, 29 monks from the Abbey of Gethsemane in Kentucky answered the call and moved to the Lowcountry to begin Mepkin Abbey. (Although it is home to actual monks, the little town of Moncks Corner north of Charleston was actually named for Thomas Monck, a merchant in the area.)

Mepkin Abbey's monks are of the Order of Cistercians of the Strict Observance, more commonly known simply as Trappists. With the credo "pray and work," the Trappists believe manual labor provides worshippers with the best opportunity to share and experience creation and restoration. They also view manual labor as following in the footsteps of the "Poor Christ"—since their work enriches and provides for the surrounding community, especially the disadvantaged.

Much of the monks' labor centers on various farm activities. Until recently the harvesting of chicken eggs—almost 10 million annually—was the main source of revenue to maintain the Abbey. In the wake of a controversy surrounding those eggs—which began when a member of the animal rights group PETA masqueraded as a retreat guest and secretly filmed the abbey's chicken coops—the abbey has decided to phase out egg production and sale and turn to other products to raise money.

As part of their vows, Mepkin Abbey's monks remain silent during the early and late parts of the day. Their daily schedule is very strict, as follows (Sundays are slightly different):

- 3 A.M.: Rise

- 3:20 A.M.: Vigils, followed by 30 minutes of meditation, then a reading or private prayer

- 5:30 A.M.: Lauds, followed by breakfast

- 7:30 A.M.: Eucharist, followed by 15 minutes thanksgiving and Terce

- 8:30-11:30 A.M.: Silence ends, and morning work period begins

- Noon: Midday prayer, followed by dinner

- 1-1:40 P.M.: "Siesta" (optional)

- 1:45-3:30 P.M.: Afternoon work period

- 5 P.M.: Supper

- 6 P.M.: Vespers

- 7:35 P.M.: Compline

- Silence begins as monks retire for the day.

the life's work of Benjamin R. Kittredge and his son Benjamin Jr. Together they brought back the former glory of the old Dean Hall plantation, which the elder Kittredge, a New Yorker who married into a wealthy Charleston family, had bought in 1909. Instead of rice, the main crop was to be flowers—*millions* of flowers, including azaleas, daffodils, camellias, wisteria, dogwoods, roses, lotuses, and then some. The old paddy system was made navigable for small boats—today they're glass-bottomed—to meander among the tall cypress trees. The

city of Charleston acquired the tract from the family, and later Berkeley County would come into possession of it. The current 170-acre park was heavily damaged during Hurricane Hugo in 1989 but has made quite a comeback, and its inspiring and calming natural beauty remains true to the vision of the Kittredges. The founders would certainly approve of a particularly modern addition, the Butterfly House, a 2,500-square-foot building packed full of butterflies, caterpillars, turtles, and birds. Just go in quietly, remain as quiet as you can, and the

COURTESY OF MEPKIN ABBEY

the church at Mepkin Abbey

butterflies will find you, an unforgettable experience for child and adult alike.

You can also walk two nature trails and enjoy the flora and fauna of this area untouched by modern development. There's a new "Crocodile Isle" exhibit with several rare species of the reptile. A freshwater aquarium has 30 species of fish as well as about 20 species of reptiles and amphibians. Out on the water, you can enjoy one of those glass-bottomed boat rides on the blackwater or—and this is what I recommend—paddle yourself in a canoe (included in the admission price) among the gorgeous cypress trees.

AWENDAW AND POINTS NORTH

This area just north of Charleston along U.S. 17—named for the Sewee Indian village originally located here, and known to the world chiefly as the place where Hurricane Hugo made landfall in 1989—is seeing some new growth, but still hews to its primarily rural, nature-loving roots.

Sewee Visitor and Environmental Education Center

Twenty miles north of Charleston you'll find the Sewee Visitor and Environmental Education Center (5821 U.S. 17, 843/928-3368, www.fws.gov/seweecenter, Tues.–Sat. 9 A.M.–5 P.M., free). Besides being a gateway of sorts for the almost entirely aquatic Cape Romain National Wildlife Refuge, Sewee is primarily known for its population of rare red wolves, who were part of a unique release program on nearby Bull Island begun in the late 1970s.

Cape Romain National Wildlife Refuge

One of the best natural experiences in the area is north of Charleston at Cape Romain National Wildlife Refuge (5801 U.S. 17 N., 843/928-3264, www.fws.gov/caperomain, year-round daily dawn–dusk). Essentially comprising four barrier islands, the 66,000-acre refuge—almost all of which is marsh—provides a lot of great paddling opportunities, chief among them **Bull Island** (no overnight camping). A fairly lengthy trek from where you put in lies famous Boneyard Beach, where hundreds of downed trees lie on the sand, bleached by sun and salt. Slightly to the south within the refuge, **Capers Island Heritage Preserve** (843/953-9300, www.dnr.sc.gov, daily dawn–dusk, free) is still a popular camping locale despite heavy damage from 1989's Hurricane Hugo. Get permits in advance by calling the South Carolina Department of Natural Resources. You can kayak to the refuge yourself or take the only approved ferry service from **Coastal Expeditions** (514B Mill St., Mount Pleasant, 843/881-4582, www.coastalexpeditions.com). **Barrier Island Eco Tours** (50 41st Ave., Isle of Palms, 843/886-5000, www.nature-tours.com) on Isle of Palms also runs trips to the area.

I'on Swamp Trail

Once part of a rice plantation, the I'on Swamp Trail (843/928-3368, www.fs.fed.us, daily dawn–dusk, free) is one of the premier bird-watching sites in South Carolina, particularly during spring and fall migrations. The rare Bachman's warbler, commonly considered one of the most elusive birds in North America, has been seen here. To get here, head about 15 miles north of Mount Pleasant and take a left onto I'on Swamp Road (Forest Service Rd. 228). The parking area is 2.5 miles ahead on the left.

Food

A must-stop roadside diner in the Awendaw area is ◖ **See Wee Restaurant** (4808 U.S. 17 N., 843/928-3609, Mon.–Thurs. 11 A.M.–8:30 P.M., Fri.–Sat. 11 A.M.–9:30 P.M., Sun. 11 A.M.–8 P.M., $10–23), located about 20 minutes' drive north of Charleston in a humble

former general store on the west side of U.S. 17 (the restrooms are still outside). Folks come from Charleston and as far away as Myrtle Beach to enjoy signature menu items like the grouper and the unreal she-crab soup, considered by some epicures to be the best in the world; you can't miss with any of their seafood entrées. Occasionally the crowds can get thick, but rest assured it's worth any wait.

POINTS WEST AND SOUTHWEST
Caw Caw Interpretive Center

Just west of Charleston on U.S. 17 you'll find the unique Caw Caw Interpretive Center (5200 Savannah Hwy., Ravenel, 843/889-8898, www.ccprc.com, Wed.–Sun. 9 A.M.–5 P.M., $1), a treasure trove for history buffs and naturalists wanting to learn more about the old rice culture of the South. With a particular emphasis on the expertise of those who worked on the rice plantations using techniques they brought with them from Africa, the county-run facility comprises 650 acres of land on an actual former rice plantation built on a cypress swamp, eight miles of interpretive trails, an educational center with exhibits, and a wildlife sanctuary with seven different habitats. Most Wednesday and Saturday mornings, guided bird walks are held at 8:30 A.M. ($5 pp). You can put in your own canoe for $10 October–April on Saturdays and Sundays. Bikes and dogs aren't allowed on the grounds.

Johns Island

The outlying community of Johns Island is where you'll find **Angel Oak Park** (3688 Angel Oak Rd., Mon.–Sat. 9 A.M.–5 P.M., Sun. 1–5 P.M.), home of a massive live oak, 65 feet in circumference, that's well over 1,000 years old and commonly considered the oldest tree east of the Mississippi River. The tree and the park are owned by the city of Charleston, and the grounds are often used for weddings and special events. Get here from Charleston by taking U.S. 17 over the Ashley River, then Highway 171 to Maybank Highway. Take a left onto Bohicket Road near the Piggly Wiggly, and then look for signs on the right.

Here is also where you'll find **Legare Farms** (2620 Hanscombe Point Rd., 843/559-0763, www.legarefarms.com), open to the public for various activities, including its annual pumpkin patch in October, its "sweet corn" festival in June, and bird walks (Sat. 8:30 A.M., $6 adults, $3 children) in fall.

If you find your tummy growling on Johns Island, don't miss **Fat Hen** (3140 Maybank Hwy., 843/559-9090, Tues.–Sat. 11:30 A.M.–3 P.M. and 5:30–10 P.M., Sun. 10 A.M.–3 P.M., $15–20), a self-styled "country French bistro" begun by a couple of old Charleston restaurant hands. The fried oysters are a particular specialty. There's also a bar menu for late-night hours (10 P.M.–2 A.M.).

If barbecue is more your thing, head straight to **JB's Smokeshack** (3406 Maybank Hwy., 843/557-0426, www.jbssmokeshack. com, Wed.–Sat. 11 A.M.–8:30 P.M., $8), one of the best 'cue joints in the Lowcountry. They offer a buffet for $8.88 pp ($5 under age 11), or you can opt for a barbecue plate, including hash, rice, and two sides. In a nice twist, the plates include a three-meat option: pork, chicken, ribs, or brisket.

Wadmalaw Island

Like Johns Island, Wadmalaw Island is one of those lazy, scenic areas gradually becoming subsumed within Charleston's growth. That said, there's plenty of meandering, laid-back beauty to enjoy, and a couple of interesting sights.

Currently owned by the R. C. Bigelow Tea corporation, the **Charleston Tea Plantation** (6617 Maybank Hwy., 843/559-0383, www. charlestonteaplantation.com, Mon.–Sat. 10 A.M.–4 P.M., Sun. noon–4 P.M., free) is no cute living history exhibit: It's a big, working tea plantation—the only one in the U.S.—with acre after acre of *Camellia sinensis* being worked by modern farm machinery. Visitors get to see a sample of how the tea is made, "from the field to the cup." Factory tours are free, and a trolley tour of the "Back 40" is $10. And, of course, there's a gift shop where you can sample and buy all types of teas and tea-related products. Unlike many agricultural sites in the area, the 127-acre Charleston Tea Plantation was never actually a plantation. It was first planted at the relatively late date of 1960, when the Lipton tea company moved some plants from Summerville, South Carolina, to its research facility on Wadmalaw Island. Lipton decided the climate and high labor costs of the American South weren't conducive to making money, so they sold the land to two employees, Mack Fleming and Bill Hall, in 1987. The two held onto the plantation until 2003, when R. C. Bigelow won it at auction for $1.28 million. Growing season is from April through October. The tea bushes, direct descendants of plants brought over in the 1800s from India and China, "flush up" 2–3 inches every few weeks during growing season. To get here from Charleston, take the Ashley River Bridge, stay left to Folly Road (Hwy. 171), turn right onto Maybank Highway for 18 miles, and look for the sign on the left.

The muscadine grape is the only varietal that dependably grows in South Carolina. That said, the state has several good wineries, among them Wadmalaw's own **Irvin House Vineyard** (6775 Bears Bluff Rd., 843/559-6867, www.charlestonwine.com, Thurs.–Sat. 10 A.M.–5 P.M.), the Charleston area's only vineyard. Jim Irvin, a Kentucky boy, and his wife, Anne, a Johns Island native, make several varieties of muscadine wine here, with tastings and a gift shop. They also give free tours of the 50-acre grounds every Saturday at 2 P.M. There's a Grape-stomping Festival at the end of each August ($5 per car). Also on the Irvin

Vineyard grounds you'll find **Firefly Distillery** (6775 Bears Bluff Rd., 843/559-6867, www.fireflyvodka.com), home of their signature Firefly Sweet Tea Vodka. They offer tastings (Feb.–Dec. Wed.–Sat. 11 A.M.–5 P.M., $6 per tasting). To get here from Charleston, go west on Maybank Highway about 10 miles to Bears Bluff Road, veering right. The vineyard entrance is on the left after about eight miles.

Kiawah Island

Only one facility for the general public exists on beautiful Kiawah Island, the **Kiawah Island Beachwalker Park** (843/768-2395, www.ccprc.com, Mar.–Apr. and Sept. daily 10 A.M.–6 P.M., May–Labor Day daily 9 A.M.–7 P.M., Oct. Mon.–Fri. 9 A.M.–5 P.M., Sat.–Sun. 10 A.M.–6 P.M., Nov.–Feb. daily 10 A.M.–5 P.M., $7 per vehicle, free for pedestrians and cyclists). Get here from downtown Charleston by taking Lockwood Drive onto the Highway 30 Connector bridge over the Ashley River. Turn right onto Folly Road, then a left onto Maybank Highway. After about 20 minutes, take a left onto Bohicket Road, which leads to Kiawah in 14 miles. Turn left from Bohicket Road onto the Kiawah Island Parkway. Just before the security gate, turn right on Beachwalker Drive and follow the signs to the park.

The island's other main attraction is the **Kiawah Island Golf Resort** (12 Kiawah Beach Dr., 800/654-2924, www.kiawahgolf.com), which is a key location for PGA tournaments. Several smaller private, family-friendly resorts exist on Kiawah, with fully furnished homes

and villas and every amenity you could ask for and then some, giving you full access to the island's 10 miles of beautiful beach. Go to www.explorekiawah.com for a full range of options or call 800/877-0837.

Through the efforts of the **Kiawah Island Conservancy** (23 Beachwalker Dr., 843/768-2029, www.kiawahconservancy.org), over 300 acres of the island have been kept as an undeveloped nature preserve. The island's famous bobcat population has made quite a comeback, with somewhere between 24 and 36 animals currently active. The bobcats are vital to the island ecosystem, since as top predator they help cull what would otherwise become untenably large populations of deer and rabbit. As a side note, while you're enjoying the beautiful scenery of the islands on the Carolina coast, it's always important to remember that most, including Kiawah, were logged or farmed extensively in the past. While they're certainly gorgeous now, it would be incorrect to call them "pristine."

Seabrook Island

Like its neighbor Kiawah, Seabrook Island is also a private resort–dominated island. In addition to offering miles of beautiful beaches, on its 2,200 acres are a wide variety of golfing, tennis, equestrian, and swimming facilities as well as extensive dining and shopping options. There are also a lot of kids' activities as well. For information on lodging options and packages, go to www.seabrook.com or call 866/249-9934.

BEAUFORT AND THE LOWCOUNTRY

For many people around the world, the Lowcountry is the first image that comes to mind when they think of the American South. For the people that live here, the Lowcountry is altogether unique, but it does embody many of the region's most noteworthy qualities: an emphasis on manners, a constant look back into the past, and a slow and leisurely pace (embodied in the joking but largely accurate nickname "Slowcountry").

History hangs in the humid air where first the Spanish came to interrupt the native tribes' ancient reverie, then the French, followed by the English. Although time, erosion, and development have erased most traces of these various occupants, you can almost hear their ghosts in the rustle of the branches in a sudden sea breeze, or in the piercing call of a heron over the marsh.

Artists and arts lovers the world over are drawn here to paint, photograph, or otherwise be inspired by some of the most gorgeous wetlands in the United States, so vast that human habitation appears fleeting and intermittent. Sprawling between Beaufort and Charleston is the huge ACE (Ashley, Combahee, Edisto) Basin, a beautiful and important estuary and a national model for good conservation practices. In all, the defining characteristic of the Lowcountry is its liquid nature—not only literally, in the creeks and waterway that dominate every vista and the seafood cooked in all manner of ways, but figuratively too, in the

© JIM MOREKIS

BEAUFORT

HIGHLIGHTS

◖ **Henry C. Chambers Waterfront Park:** Walk the dog or while away the time on a porch swing at this clean and inviting gathering place on the serene Beaufort River (page 140).

◖ **St. Helena's Episcopal Church:** To walk through this Beaufort sanctuary and its walled graveyard is to walk through Lowcountry history (page 142).

◖ **Penn Center:** Not only the center of modern Gullah culture and education, this is a key site in the history of the civil rights movement as well (page 152).

◖ **Hunting Island State Park:** One of the most peaceful natural getaways on the East Coast but only minutes away from the more civilized temptations of Beaufort (page 158).

◖ **ACE Basin:** It can take a lifetime to learn your way around this massive, marshy estuary—or just a few hours soaking in its lush beauty (page 159).

◖ **Edisto Beach State Park:** Relax at this quiet, friendly, and relatively undeveloped Sea Island, a mecca for shell collectors (page 164).

◖ **Pinckney Island National Wildlife Refuge:** This well-maintained sanctuary is a major birding location and a great getaway from nearby Hilton Head (page 169).

◖ **Coastal Discovery Museum at Honey Horn:** This beautifully repurposed plantation house and spacious grounds near the island's entrance are a great way to learn about Hilton Head history, both human and natural (page 170).

◖ **Old Bluffton:** Gossipy and gorgeous by turns, this charming village on the May River centers on a thriving artists colony (page 186).

◖ **South Carolina Artisans Center:** Visual artists and fine craftspeople from all over the state contribute work to this high-quality collective in Walterboro (page 192).

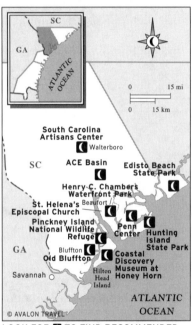

LOOK FOR ◖ TO FIND RECOMMENDED SIGHTS, ACTIVITIES, DINING, AND LODGING.

slow but deep quality of life here. Once outside what passes for urban areas, you'll find yourself taking a look back through the decades to a time of roadside produce stands, shade-tree mechanics, and men fishing and crabbing on tidal creeks—not for sport but for the family dinner. Indeed, not so very long ago, before the influx of resort development, retirement subdivisions,

and tourism, much of the Lowcountry was like a flatter, more humid Appalachia—poverty-stricken and desperately underserved. While the archetypal South has been marketed in any number of ways to the rest of the world, here you get a sense that this is the real thing—timeless, endlessly alluring, but somehow very familiar.

South of Beaufort is the historically

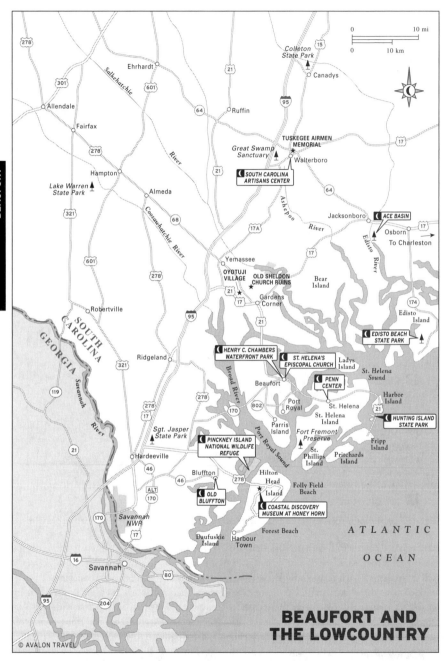

BEAUFORT AND THE LOWCOUNTRY

© AVALON TRAVEL

significant Port Royal area and the East Coast Marine Recruit Depot of Parris Island. East of Beaufort is the center of Gullah culture, St. Helena Island, and the scenic gem of Hunting Island. To the south is the scenic but entirely developed golf and tennis mecca, Hilton Head Island, and Hilton Head's close neighbor but diametrical opposite in every other way, Daufuskie Island, another important Gullah center. Nestled between is the close-knit and gossipy little village of Bluffton on the gossamer May River.

PLANNING YOUR TIME

The small scale and comparative lack of traffic in most of the Lowcountry are its more charming aspects. Don't let that fool you into thinking you can knock everything out in a day, though. That would defeat the purpose, which is not only to see the sights but to fully enjoy its laid-back, slow, and leisurely pace.

A common-sense game plan is to use the centrally located Beaufort as a home base. Take at least half a day of leisure to walk all over Beaufort. Another full day should go to

St. Helena's Penn Center and on to Hunting Island. If you're in the mood for a road trip, dedicate a full day to tour the surrounding area to the north and northeast, with perhaps a jaunt to the ACE Basin National Wildlife Refuge, and a stop at the Old Sheldon Church Ruins in the late afternoon on your way back to Beaufort. If you have extra time, split it between Port Royal and a tour of the historic and military sites of interest on Parris Island.

While the New York accents fly fast and furious on Hilton Head Island, that's no reason for you to rush. Certainly a casual visitor can do Hilton Head in a day, but its natural attractions beg for a more considered sort of enjoyment. Plan on at least half a day just to enjoy the fine, broad beaches alone. I recommend another half day to tour the island itself, maybe including a stop in Sea Pines for a late lunch or dinner.

While most of the marketing materials make scant mention of it, nature lovers shouldn't miss the Pinckney Island National Wildlife Refuge, gorgeous enough to be a must-see but small and convenient enough to fully enjoy in a few hours.

Beaufort

Sandwiched halfway between the prouder, louder cities of Charleston and Savannah, Beaufort is in many ways a more authentic slice of life from the past than either of those two. Long a staple of movie crews seeking to portray some archetypal aspect of the old South (*The Prince of Tides, The Great Santini, Forrest Gump*) or just to film beautiful scenery for its own sake (*Jungle Book, Last Dance*), Beaufort— pronounced "BYOO-fert," by the way, not "BO-fort"—features many well-preserved examples of Southern architecture, most all of them in idyllic, family-friendly neighborhoods.

The pace in Beaufort is languid, slower even than the waving Spanish moss in the massive

old live oak trees. The line between business and pleasure is a blurry one here. As you can tell from the signs you see on storefront doors saying things like "Back in an hour or so," time is an entirely negotiable commodity. The architecture combines the relaxed Caribbean flavor of Charleston with the Anglophilic dignity of Savannah. In fact, plenty of people prefer the individualistic old homes of Beaufort, seemingly tailor-made for the exact spot on which they sit, to the historic districts of either Charleston or Savannah in terms of sheer architectural delight.

While you'll run into plenty of charming and gracious locals during your time here, you

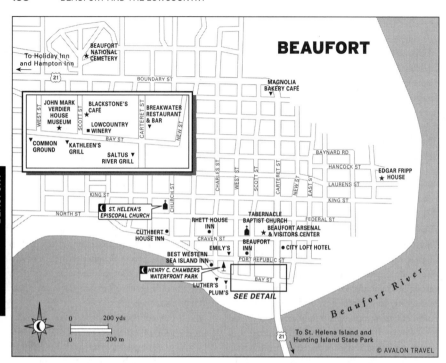

might be surprised at the number of transplanted Northerners. That's due not only to the high volume of retirees who've moved to the area but the active presence of three major U.S. Navy facilities: the Marine Corps Air Station Beaufort, the Marine Corps Recruit Depot on nearby Parris Island, and the Beaufort Naval Hospital. Many is the time a former sailor or Marine has decided to put down roots in the area after being stationed here, the most famous example being author Pat Conroy's father, a.k.a. "The Great Santini."

HISTORY

Though little known to most Americans, the Port Royal Sound area is not only one of the largest natural harbors on the East Coast, it's one of the nation's most historic places, a fact made all the more maddening in how little of that history remains.

This was the site of the second landing by the Spanish on the North American continent, the expedition of Captain Pedro de Salazar in 1514 (Ponce de León's more famous landing at St. Augustine was but a year earlier). A Spanish slaver made a brief stop in 1521, long enough to name the area Santa Elena—one of the oldest European place-names in the United States. Port Royal Sound didn't get its modern name until the first serious attempt at a permanent settlement, Jean Ribault's exploration in 1562. Though ultimately disastrous, Ribault's base of Charlesfort was the first French settlement in America. Ribault returned to France for reinforcements to find his country in an all-out religious civil war. He sought safety in England only to be clapped in the Tower of London. Meanwhile his soldiers at Charlesfort became restive and revolted against their absentee commander, with most moving to the French settlement Fort Caroline near present-day Jacksonville, Florida. In a twist straight out of Hollywood, in 1565 Fort Caroline bought food and a ship to return to France from a passing vessel, which turned out to be commanded by the infamous English privateer John Hawkins. While the French waited for a favorable wind for the trip home, who should arrive but Jean Ribault himself, fresh out of prison and at the head of 600 French soldiers and settlers sent to rescue his colony. In yet another unlikely development, a Spanish fleet soon appeared, intent on driving the French out for good. Ribault went on the offensive, intending to mount a preemptive attack on the Spanish base at St. Augustine. However, a storm wrecked the French ships, and Ribault was washed ashore near St. Augustine and killed by waiting Spanish troops. As if the whole story couldn't get any stranger, back at Charlesfort things had become so desperate for the 27 original colonists who stayed behind that they decided to build a ship to sail back home to France—technically the first ship built in America for a transatlantic crossing. The vessel made it across the Atlantic, but not without paying a price; running out of food, the French soldiers began eating shoe leather before moving on, so the accounts say, to eating each other. Twenty survivors were rescued in the English Channel.

After the French faded from the scene, Spaniards came to garrison Santa Elena. But steady Indian attacks and Francis Drake's attack on St. Augustine forced the Spanish to abandon the area in 1587. Within the next generation, British indigo planters had established a firm presence in the Port Royal area, chief among them John "Tuscarora Jack" Barnwell of Port Royal Island and Thomas Nairn of St. Helena. These men would go on to found the town of Beaufort, named for Henry Somerset, Duke of Beaufort, and it was chartered in 1711 as part of the original Carolina colony. In 1776, Beaufort planter Thomas Heyward Jr. signed the Declaration of Independence. After independence was gained, Lowcountry planters turned to cotton as the main cash crop, since England had been their prime customer for indigo. The gambit paid off, and Beaufort soon became one of the wealthiest towns in the new nation. The so-called "golden age" of Sea Island cotton saw storm clouds gather on the horizon as the Lowcountry became the hotbed of secession, with the very first Ordinance of Secession being drawn up in Beaufort's Milton Maxey House. Only seven months after secessionists fired on Fort Sumter in nearby Charleston in 1861, a huge Union fleet sailed into Port Royal and occupied Hilton Head, Beaufort, and the rest of the Lowcountry for the duration of the war—a relatively uneventful occupation that ensured that many of the classic homes would survive.

Gradually developing their own distinct dialect and culture, much of it linked to their West African roots, isolated Lowcountry African Americans became known as the Gullah. Evolving from an effort by abolitionist missionaries early in the Civil War, in 1864 the Penn School was formed on St. Helena Island specifically to teach the children of the Gullah communities. Now known as the Penn Center, the facility has been a beacon for the study of this aspect of African American culture ever since.

The 20th century ushered in a time of increased dependence on military spending, with the opening of a training facility on Parris Island in the 1880s (the Marines didn't begin training recruits there until 1915). The Lowcountry got a further boost from wartime spending in the 1940s. Parris Island, already thriving as a Marine hub, was joined by the Marine Corps Naval Air Station in nearby Beaufort in 1942. In 1949, the Naval Hospital opened.

Today, the tourism industry has joined the military as a major economic driver in the Lowcountry. Hollywood discovered its charms as well, in a series of critical and box-office hits like *The Big Chill, The Prince of Tides,* and *Forrest Gump.*

ORIENTATION

Don't be discouraged by the big-box sprawl that assaults you on the approaches to Beaufort on Boundary Street, lined with the usual discount megastores, fast food outlets, and budget motels. This is a popular area for relocation as well as for visitors, and when you add to the mix the presence of several bustling military facilities, you have a recipe for gridlock and architectural ugliness. But after you make the big 90-degree bend where Boundary turns into Carteret Street—known locally as the "Bellamy Curve"—it's like entering a whole new world of slow-paced, Spanish moss–lined avenues, friendly people, gentle breezes, and inviting storefronts. While you can make your way to downtown by taking Carteret Street all the way to Bay Street—don't continue over the big bridge unless you want to go straight to Lady's Island and St. Helena Island—I suggest availing yourself of one of the "Downtown Access" signs before you get that far. Because Carteret Street is the only way to that bridge, it can get backed up at rush hour. By taking a quick right and then a left all the way to Bay Street, you can come into town from the other, quieter end, with your first glimpse of downtown proper being its timelessly beguiling views of the Beaufort River.

Once there, try to park your car slightly outside the town center and simply walk everywhere you want to go. Conversely, you can park in the long-term metered spaces at the marina. Unlike Charleston or Savannah, any visitor in reasonably good shape can walk the entire length and breadth of Beaufort's 300-acre downtown with little trouble. In fact, that's by far the best way to experience it.

SIGHTS
◖ Henry C. Chambers Waterfront Park

Before you get busy shopping, dining, and admiring Beaufort's fine old homes, go straight to the town's pride and joy since 1980, the Henry C. Chambers Waterfront Park (843/525-7054, www.cityofbeaufort. org, daily 24 hours), stretching for hundreds of feet directly on the Beaufort River. A tastefully designed, well-maintained, and user-friendly mix of walkways, bandstands, and patios, Waterfront Park is a favorite gathering place for locals and visitors alike, beckoning one and all with its open green space and wonderful marsh-front views. My favorite part is the long row of swinging benches on which to peacefully sit and while away the time looking out over the marsh. Kids will especially enjoy the park not only because there's so much room to run around but for the charming playground at the east end near the bridge, complete with a jungle gym in the form of a Victorian home. The clean, well-appointed public restrooms are a particularly welcome feature.

John Mark Verdier House Museum

A smallish but stately Federalist building on the busiest downtown corner, the Verdier House Museum (801 Bay St., 843/379-6335, www.historicbeaufort.org, Mon.–Sat. 10 a.m.–4 p.m., $5) is the only historic Beaufort home open to regular tours. Built in 1805 for the wealthy planter John Mark Verdier, its main claim to fame was acting as the Union headquarters during the long occupation of Beaufort during the Civil War. However, perhaps its most intriguing link to history—a link it shares with Savannah's Owens-Thomas House—is its connection to the Revolutionary War hero the Marquis de Lafayette, who stayed at the Verdier House on the Beaufort leg of his 1825 U.S. tour. Despite the late hour of his arrival, a crowd gathered at the corner of Bay and Scott Streets, and Lafayette finally had to come to the entranceway to satisfy their desire for a

PAT CONROY'S LOWCOUNTRY

I was always your best subject, son.
Your career took a nose dive after
The Great Santini came out.

Colonel Donald Conroy, to his son Pat

Although born in Georgia, no other person is as closely associated with the South Carolina Lowcountry as author Pat Conroy. After moving around as a child in a military family, he began high school in Beaufort. His painful teen years there formed the basis of his first novel, a brutal portrait of his domineering Marine pilot father, Colonel Donald Conroy, a.k.a. Colonel Bull Meecham of *The Great Santini* (1976). Many scenes from the 1979 film adaptation were filmed at the famous Tidalholm, the Edgar Fripp House (1 Laurens St.) in Beaufort. (The house was also front and center in *The Big Chill*.)

Conroy's pattern of thinly veiled autobiography actually began with his first book, the self-published *The Boo*, a tribute to a teacher at The Citadel in Charleston while Conroy was still a student there. His second work, *The Water is Wide* (1972), is a chronicle of his experiences teaching in a one-room African American school on Daufuskie Island. Though ostensibly a straightforward first-person journalistic effort, Conroy changed the location to the fictional Yamacraw Island, supposedly to protect Daufuskie's fragile culture from curious outsiders. The 1974 film adaptation starring Jon Voight was titled *Conrack* after the way his students mispronounced his name. You can visit that same two-room school today on Daufuskie. Known as the Mary Field School, the building is now a local community center.

Conroy also wrote the foreword to the cookbook *Gullah Home Cooking the Daufuskie Way: Smokin' Joe Butter Beans, Ol' 'Fuskie Fried Crab Rice, Sticky-Bush Blackberry Dumpling,* and Other Sea Island Favorites by Daufuskie native and current Savannah resident Sallie Ann Robinson. Conroy would go on to publish in 1980 *The Lords of Discipline*, a reading of his real-life experience with the often-savage environment faced by cadets at The Citadel—though Conroy would change the name, calling it the Carolina Military Institute. Still, when it came time to make a film adaptation in 1983, The Citadel refused to allow it to be shot there, so the "Carolina Military Institute" was filmed in England instead.

For many of his fans, Conroy's *The Prince of Tides* is his ultimate homage to the Lowcountry. Surely, the 1991 film version starring Barbra Streisand and Nick Nolte—shot on location and awash in gorgeous shots of the Beaufort River marsh—did much to implant an idyllic image of the area with audiences around the world. According to local legend, Streisand originally didn't intend to make the film in Beaufort, but a behind-the-scenes lobbying effort allegedly coordinated by Conroy himself, and including a stay at the Rhett House Inn, convinced her.

The Bay Street Inn (601 Bay St.) in Beaufort was seen in the film, as was the football field at the old Beaufort High School. The beach scenes were shot on nearby Fripp Island. Interestingly, some scenes set in a Manhattan apartment were actually shot within the old Beaufort Arsenal (713 Craven St.), now a visitors center. Similarly, the Beaufort Naval Hospital doubled as New York's Bellevue.

Despite the many personal tribulations he faced in the area, Conroy has never given up on the Lowcountry and still makes his home here with his family on Fripp Island. As for the "Great Santini" himself, you can visit the final resting place of Colonel Conroy in the Beaufort National Cemetery—Section 62, Grave 182.

---

speech. When the Verdier House was faced with demolition in the 1940s, the Historic Beaufort Foundation purchased the house and renovated it to its current state, reflective of the early 1800s.

Beaufort Arsenal and Visitors Center

The imposing yellow-gray tabby facade of the 1852 Beaufort Arsenal (713 Craven St.) once housed the Beaufort Museum, which sadly closed due to financial issues. The historic

BEAUFORT

© JIM MOREKIS

Henry C. Chambers Waterfront Park

building currently houses the relocated offices of the Beaufort Chamber of Commerce and Convention and Visitors Bureau (843/986-5400, www.beaufortsc.org, daily 9 A.M.–5:30 P.M.), and you can find plenty of visitor information and gifts inside; there are also public restrooms.

◖ St. Helena's Episcopal Church

Nestled within the confines of a low brick wall surrounding this historic church and cemetery, St. Helena's Episcopal Church (505 Church St., 843/522-1712, Tues.–Fri. 10 A.M.–4 P.M., Sat. 10 A.M.–1 P.M.) has witnessed some of Beaufort's most compelling tales. Built in 1724, this was the parish church of Thomas Heyward, one of South Carolina's signers of the Declaration of Independence. John "Tuscarora Jack" Barnwell, an early Indian fighter and one of Beaufort's founders, is buried on the grounds.

The balcony upstairs in the sanctuary was intended for black parishioners; as was typical throughout the region before the Civil War, both races attended the same church services. After the entire congregation fled with the Union occupation, Federal troops decked over the second floor and used St. Helena's as a hospital—with surgeons using tombstones as operating tables. The wooden altar was carved by the crew of the USS *New Hampshire* while the warship was docked in the harbor during Reconstruction.

While the cemetery and sanctuary interior are likely to be your focus, take a close look at the church exterior—many of the bricks are actually ships' ballast stones. Also be aware that you're not looking at the church's original footprint; the building has been expanded several times since its construction (a hurricane in 1896 destroyed the entire east end). A nearly $3 million restoration, mostly for structural repairs, was completed in 2000.

© JIM MOREKIS

The Beaufort visitors center is in the old Beaufort Arsenal.

Tabernacle Baptist Church

Built in 1845, this handsome sanctuary (911 Craven St., 843/524-0376) had a congregation of over 3,000 before the Civil War. Slaves made up most of the congregation, though the vast majority of slaves generally worshipped separately on plantation ground. During the war, freed slaves purchased the church for their own use. A congregant was the war hero Robert Smalls, who kidnapped the Confederate steamer he was forced to serve on and delivered it to Union forces. He is buried in the church cemetery and has a nice memorial dedicated to him there, proudly facing the street.

Beaufort National Cemetery

It's not nearly as poignantly ornate as Savannah's Victorian cemeteries, but Beaufort National Cemetery (1601 Boundary St., daily 8 A.M.–sunset) is worth a stop, as you enter or leave Beaufort, for its history. Begun by order of Abraham Lincoln in 1863, this is one of the few cemeteries containing the graves of both Union and Confederate troops, mostly the former. National Cemetery is where 19 soldiers of the all-black Massachusetts 54th and 55th Infantries were reinterred with full military honors after being found on Folly Island near Charleston. Sergeant Joseph Simmons, Buffalo Soldier and veteran of both world wars, is buried here, as is none other than "The Great Santini" himself, novelist Pat Conroy's father, Donald.

A Walking Tour of Beaufort Homes

One of the more unique aspects of the Lowcountry is the large number of historic homes in private hands. When buyers purchase one of these fine old homes, they generally know what's in store: a historical marker of some sort might be nearby, organized tours will periodically swing by their home, and production companies will sometimes approach them about using the home as a film set. It's a trade-off most homeowners are only too glad to accept.

Here's a walking tour of some of Beaufort's fine historic homes in private hands. You won't be taking any tours of the interiors, but these homes are part of the legacy of the area and are locally valued as such. Be sure to respect the privacy of the inhabitants by keeping the noise level down and not trespassing on private property to take photos. And be amazed at the fine old live oaks all around.

- **Thomas Fuller House:** Begin at the corner of Harrington and Bay Streets and view the 1796 Thomas Fuller House (1211 Bay St.), one of the oldest in Beaufort and even more unique in that much of the building material is tabby (hence the home's other name, the Tabby Manse).

- **Milton Maxcy House:** Walk east on Bay Street one block and take a left on Church Street; walk up to the corner of Church and Craven Streets. Otherwise known as the Secession House (113 Craven St.), this 1813 home was built on a tabby foundation dating from 1743. In 1860, when it was the residence of attorney Edmund Rhett, the first Ordinance of Secession was signed here, and the rest, as they say, is history.

- **Lewis Reeve Sams House:** Pick up the walking tour on the other side of the historic district, at the foot of the bridge in the old neighborhood simply called "The Point." The beautiful Lewis Reeve Sams House (601 Bay St.) at the corner of Bay and New Streets, with its double-decker veranda, dates from 1852 and like many Beaufort mansions served as a Union hospital during the Civil War.

- **Berners Barnwell Sams House:** Continue up New Street, where shortly ahead on the left you'll find the 1818 Berners Barnwell Sams House (310 New St.), which served as the African American hospital during the Union occupation. Harriet Tubman of Underground Railroad fame worked here for a time as a nurse.

- **Joseph Johnson House:** Continue up New Street and take a right on Craven Street. Cross East Street to find the 1850 Joseph Johnson House (411 Craven St.), with the massive live oak in the front yard. Legend has it that when the Yankees occupied Hilton Head, Mr. Johnson buried his valuables under an outhouse. After the war he returned to find his home for sale due to unpaid back taxes. He dug up his valuables, paid the taxes, and resumed living in the home. You might recognize the home from the film *Forces of Nature*.

- **Marshlands:** Backtrack to East Street, walk north to Federal Street, and go to the end. Built by James R. Verdier, Marshlands (501 Pinckney St.) was used as a hospital during the Civil War, as many Beaufort homes were, and is now a National Historic Landmark. It was the setting of Francis Griswold's 1931 novel *A Sea Island Lady*.

- **The Oaks:** Walk up to King Street and take a right. Soon after you pass a large open park on the left, King Street dead-ends at the Short Street. The Oaks (100 Laurens St.) at this corner was owned by the Hamilton family, who lost a son who served with General Wade Hampton's cavalry in the Civil War. After the conflict, the family couldn't afford the back taxes, and neighbors paid the debts and returned the deed to the Hamiltons.

- **Edgar Fripp House:** Continue east on Laurens Street toward the water to find this handsome Lowcountry mansion, sometimes called Tidalholm (1 Laurens St.). Built in 1856 by the wealthy planter for whom nearby Fripp Island is named, this house was a key setting in *The Big Chill* and *The Great Santini*.

- **Francis Hext House:** Go back to Short Street, walk north to Hancock Street, and take a left. A short way ahead on the right, the handsome red-roofed estate known as Riverview (207 Hancock St.) is one of the oldest structures in Beaufort; it was built in 1720.

- **Robert Smalls House:** Continue west on Hancock Street, take a short left on East Street, and then a quick right on Prince Street. The 1834 Robert Smalls House (511

Prince St.) was the birthplace of Robert Smalls, a former slave and Beaufort native who stole the Confederate ship *Planter* from Charleston Harbor while serving as helmsman and delivered it to Union troops in Hilton Head. Smalls and a few compatriots commandeered the ship while the officers were at a party at Fort Sumter. Smalls used the bounty for the act of bravery to buy his boyhood home. After the war, Smalls was a longtime U.S. congressman.

Organized Tours

Colorful character Jon Sharp runs the popular **Jon Sharp's Walking History Tour** (843/575-5775, www.jonswalkinghistory.com, Tues.–Sat. 11 A.M., $20), taking a break during the summer months. The two-hour jaunt begins and ends at the Downtown Marina and takes you all through the downtown area. **The Spirit of Old Beaufort** (103 West St. Extension, 843/525-0459, www.thespiritofoldbeaufort.com, Mon.–Sat. 10:30 A.M., 2 P.M., and 7 P.M., $13 adults, $8 children) runs a year-round series of good walking tours, roughly two hours long, with guides usually in period dress. If you don't want to walk, you can hire one of their guides to join you in your own vehicle (from $50).

As you might expect, few things could be more Lowcountry than an easygoing carriage ride through the historic neighborhoods. **Southurn Rose Buggy Tours** (843/524-2900, www.southurnrose.com, daily 10 A.M.–5 P.M., $18 adults, $7 children)—yes, that's how they spell it—offers 50-minute narrated carriage rides of the entire Old Point, including movie locations, embarking and disembarking near the Downtown Marina about every 40 minutes.

An important specialty bus tour in the area is **Gullah-N-Geechie Man Tours** (843/838-7516, www.gullahngeechietours.net, $20 adults, $18 children), focusing on the rich Gullah history and culture of the St. Helena Island area, including the historic Penn Center. Call for pickup information.

ENTERTAINMENT AND EVENTS
Nightlife

Those looking for a rowdy time will be happier seeking it in the notorious party towns of Charleston or Savannah. However, a few notable places in downtown Beaufort do double duty as dining havens and neighborhood watering holes. Sadly, the well-regarded restaurant within the Beaufort Inn on Port Republic Street closed for good in 2007. But several establishments tucked together on Bay Street, all with café seating out back facing the waterfront, can also show you a good time.

The convivial **Kathleen's Grill** (822 Bay St., 843/524-2500, daily 11 A.M.–2 A.M.) features live music by a variety of regional artists. Weekend tunes crank up about 10 P.M. **Plum's** (904½ Bay St., 843/525-1946, daily 5 P.M.–2 A.M.) offers not only a tasty menu but some fun at 10 P.M. when the kitchen closes down and the focus turns to its great beer selection. Close by is **Luther's Rare & Well Done** (910 Bay St., 843/521-1888, daily 5 P.M.–midnight, $15), which offers a late-night appetizer menu to go with its rock-oriented live music on weekends.

Performing Arts

Beaufort's fine arts scene is small but professional in outlook. Most performances are based in the nice new Performing Arts Center on the oak-lined campus of the University of South Carolina Beaufort (USCB, 801 Carteret St., 843/521-4100). A prime mover of the local performing arts scene is **Beaufort Performing Arts Inc.** (www.uscb.edu), formed by a mayoral task force in 2003 specifically to encourage arts and cultural development within the area. The most recent season, with performances at USCB's Performing Arts Center, included performances by Celtic fiddler Natalie MacMaster, the Claremont Trio, and the Bee Gees. Ticket prices typically range $12–40.

Perhaps surprisingly for such a small place,

Beaufort boasts its own full orchestra, the **Beaufort Orchestra** (1106 Carteret St., 843/986-5400, www.beaufortorchestra.org), which plays in the Performing Arts Center. A recent season included Paganini's Violin Concerto in D, Tchaikovsky's "Pathétique" Symphony No. 6, and *Beaufort Goes to Broadway.*

Cinema

One of only two functional drive-ins in the state, the **Highway 21 Drive In** (55 Parker Dr., 843/846-4500, www.hwy21drivein.com) has two screens, great sound, and awesome concessions that include Angus beef hamburgers. All you need to provide is the car and the company. The best multiplex in the area is the cool **Sea Turtle Cinemas** (106 Buckwalter Pkwy., 843/706-2888, www.seaturtlecinemas.com) in the Berkeley Place shopping center.

Festivals and Events

Surprisingly for a town so prominent in so many films, Beaufort didn't have its own film festival until 2007. The **Beaufort Film Festival** (843/986-5400, www.beaufortfilmfestival. com) is held in February. It's small in scale—the inaugural festival was only two days, at a now-defunct theater—but boasts a diverse range of high-quality, cutting-edge entries, including shorts and animation.

Foodies will also enjoy **A Taste of Beaufort** (www.downtownbeaufort.com), usually held the first Saturday in May, which features the offerings of two dozen or so local restaurants with live music, all along historic Bay Street.

Now over 20 years old, the **Gullah Festival of South Carolina** celebrates Gullah history and culture on Memorial Day weekend at various locations throughout town, mostly focusing on Waterfront Park.

By far the biggest single event on the local festival calendar is the over 50-year-old **Beaufort Water Festival** (www.bftwaterfestival.com), held over two weeks in June or July

each year, centering on the Waterfront Park area. One of the most eclectic and idiosyncratic events of its kind in a region already known for quirky hyperlocal festivals, the Beaufort Water Festival features events as diverse as a raft race, badminton, boccie, billiards, croquet, and golf tournaments, a children's toad fishing tournament, a ski show, a bed race, a street dance, and all sorts of live music and local art exhibits. The signature events are the Saturday-morning two-hour Grand Parade and a blessing and parade of the shrimp fleet on the closing Sunday.

Fall in the Lowcountry means shrimping season, and early October brings the **Beaufort Shrimp Festival** (www.beaufortsc.org). Highlights include an evening concert with specially lighted shrimp boats docked along the river, a 5K run over the Woods Memorial Bridge, and a more laid-back 5K walk through the historic district. Various cooking competitions are held, obviously centering around the versatile crustaceans that are the raison d'être of the shrimp fleet.

St. Helena Island hosts the three-day **Penn Center Heritage Days** (www.penncenter. com) each November, without a doubt the Beaufort area's second-biggest celebration after the Water Festival. Focusing on Gullah culture, history, and delicious food, Heritage Days does a great job of combining fun with education. The event culminates in a colorful Saturday-morning parade, featuring lots of traditional Gullah garb, from St. Helena Elementary School to the Penn Center Historic District.

SHOPPING

The Beaufort area's shopping allure comes from the rich variety of independently owned shops, most of which keep a pretty high standard and don't deal too much in touristy schlock. The main drag in town, Bay Street, is also the shopping hub. Note that in Beaufort's shops as well as most everything else in town, hours of operation are loose guidelines and not rigidly observed.

My favorite shop in Beaufort is **The Bay Street Trading Company** (808 Bay St., 843/524-2000, www.baystreettrading.com, Mon.–Fri. 10 A.M.–5:30 P.M., Sat. 10 A.M.–5 P.M., Sun. noon–5 P.M.), sometimes known simply as "The Book Shop," which has a very friendly staff and the best collection of Lowcountry-themed books I've seen in one place.

Across the street, the recently renovated Old Bay Marketplace, with a facade so bright red you can't miss it, hosts a few cute shops, most notably the stylish **Lulu Burgess** (917 Bay St., 843/524-5858, Mon.–Sat. 10 A.M.–6 P.M., Sun. noon–5 P.M.), an eclectic store that brings a rich, quirky sense of humor to its otherwise tasteful assortment of gift items for the whole family.

A unique gift item, as well as something you can enjoy on your own travels, can be found at **Lowcountry Winery** (705 Bay St., 843/379-3010, Mon.–Sat. 10 A.M.–5 P.M.). Not only can you purchase bottles of their various red and white offerings, they host tastings daily in the tasting room (because of state law, they must charge a fee for the tasting, but it's only $1 pp).

Just off the Waterfront Park and right across the walk from Common Grounds coffee shop is the delightful **Lollipop Shop** (103 West St. Extension, 843/379-POPS—843/379-7677, www.thelollipopshop.net, Mon.–Thurs. 10 A.M.–5 P.M., Fri.–Sat. 10 A.M.–9 P.M., Sun. 1–5 P.M.). Part of a regional franchise chain, the Lollipop Shop offers a wide range of treats from jelly beans to M&Ms in custom colors as well as wind-up toys and stuff-them-yourself teddy bears.

Art Galleries

As you'd expect in such a visually stirring locale, there's a plethora of great art galleries in the Beaufort–St. Helena area. While most are clustered on Bay Street, there are gems scattered all over. Almost all are worth a look, but here are a few highlights.

My favorite gallery in town is the simply named **The Gallery** (802 Bay St., 843/470-9994, www.thegallery-beaufort.com, Mon.–Sat. 11 A.M.–5 P.M.). Deanna Bowdish brings in the most cutting-edge regional contemporary artists in a large, friendly, loftlike space. The **Beaufort Art Association Gallery** (1001 Bay St., 843/379-2222, www.beaufortartassociation.com, Mon.–Sat. 10 A.M.–5 P.M.) hosts rotating exhibits by member artists in the stately and historic Elliott House. A complete art experience blending the traditional with the cutting-edge is at the **I. Pinckney Simons Art Gallery** (711 Bay St., 843/379-4774, www.ipinckneysimonsgallery.com, Tues.–Fri. 11 A.M.–5 P.M., Sat. 11 A.M.–3 P.M.), which is pronounced "Simmons" despite the spelling. There you will find not only paintings but compelling photography, sculpture, and jewelry as well, all by local and regional artists of renown.

Right on the water is a fun local favorite, the **Longo Gallery** (103 Charles St., 843/522-8933, Mon.–Sat. 11 A.M.–5 P.M.). Owners Suzanne and Eric Longo provide a whimsical assortment of less traditional art than you might find in the more touristy waterfront area. Take Charles Street as it works its way toward the waterfront, and the gallery is right behind a storefront on the corner of Charles and Bay Streets.

You'll find perhaps the area's best-known gallery over the bridge on St. Helena Island. Known regionally as one of the best places to find Gullah folk art, **Red Piano Too** (870 Sea Island Parkway, 843/838-2241, www.redpianotoo.com, Mon.–Sat. 10 A.M.–5 P.M.) is on the corner before you turn onto the road to the historic Penn Center. Over 150 artists from a diverse range of traditions and styles are represented in this charming little 1940 building with the red tin awning, historically significant in its own right because it once hosted a produce cooperative that was the first store in the area to pay African Americans with cash rather than barter for goods.

SPORTS AND RECREATION

Beaufort County comprises over 60 islands, so it's no surprise that nearly all recreation in the area revolves around the water, which dominates so many aspects of life in the Lowcountry. The closer to the ocean you get, the more it's a salt marsh environment. But as you explore more inland, in the sprawling ACE Basin, you'll encounter primarily blackwater.

Kayaking

The Lowcountry is tailor-made for kayaking. Most kayakers put in at the public landings in nearby Port Royal (1 Port Royal Landing Dr., 843/525-6664) or Lady's Island (73 Sea Island Pkwy., 843/522-0430), across the river from downtown Beaufort. The catch here, as with all of the Lowcountry, is to know your way around if you choose to leave the main waterways. It's easy to get lost because of the sheer number of creeks, and they all seem to look the same once you get into them a good ways. If you don't feel comfortable with your navigation skills, it's a good idea to contact Kim and David at **Beaufort Kayak Tours** (843/525-0810, www.beaufortkayaktours.com), who rent kayaks and can guide you on a number of excellent tours of all three key areas. They charge about $40 for adults and $30 for children for a two-hour trip. A tour with Beaufort Kayak Tours is also the best (and nearly the only) way to access the historically significant ruins of the early British tabby Fort Frederick, now located on the grounds of the Beaufort Naval Hospital and inaccessible by car.

Fishing and Boating

Key marinas in the area are the **Downtown Marina** (1006 Bay St., 843/524-4422) in Beaufort, the **Lady's Island Marina** (73 Sea Island Pkwy., 843/522-0430), and the **Port Royal Landing Marina** (1 Port Royal Landing Dr., 843/525-6664). Hunting Island has a popular 1,000-foot fishing pier at the south end.

A good local fishing charter service is Captain Josh Utsey's **Lowcountry Guide Service** (843/812-4919, www.beaufortscfishing.com). Captain Ed Hardee (843/441-6880) offers good inshore charters.

The ACE Basin is a very popular fishing, crabbing, and shrimping area. It has about two dozen public boat ramps, with colorful names like Cuckold's Creek and Steamboat Landing. There's a useful map of them all at www.acebasin.net, or look for the brown signs along the highway.

Hiking and Biking

Despite the Lowcountry's, well, lowness, biking opportunities abound. It might not get your heart rate up like a ride in the Rockies, but the area lends itself to laid-back two-wheeled enjoyment. Many local B&Bs provide bikes free for guests, and you can rent your own just across the river from Beaufort in Lady's Island at **Lowcountry Bikes** (102 Sea Island Pkwy., 843/524-9585, Mon.–Tues. and Thurs.–Fri. 10 A.M.–6 P.M., Wed. 10 A.M.–1 P.M., Sat. 10 A.M.–3 P.M., about $5 per hour). They can also hook you up with some good routes around the area.

Bicycling around Beaufort is a delight for its paucity of traffic as well as its beauty. Port Royal is close enough that you can easily make a circuit to that little town. To get to Port Royal from Beaufort, take Bay Street west to Ribaut Road (U.S. 21) and veer left onto Paris Avenue into downtown Port Royal, where the biking is easy, breezy, and fun.

For a visually delightful ride, the bridge over the Beaufort River also features a pedestrian and bike lane with some awesome views. You can either turn back at the base of the bridge and go back into Beaufort or push on to Lady's Island and St. Helena Island, although the traffic on U.S. 21 can get daunting.

ACCOMMODATIONS

Beaufort's historic district is blessed with an abundance of high-quality accommodations that blend well with their surroundings. There are plenty of budget-minded chain places, some of them acceptable, in the sprawl of Boundary Street outside of downtown, but here are some suggestions within bicycling distance of the Historic District. (That's not a hypothetical, as most inns offer free bicycles to use as you please during your stay.)

Under $150

The **Best Western Sea Island Inn** (1015 Bay St., 843/522-2090, www.bestwestern.com, $135–170) is a good value for those for whom the B&B experience is not paramount. Anchoring the southern end of the historic district in a tasteful low brick building, the Best Western offers decent service, basic amenities, and surprisingly attractive rates for the location on Beaufort's busiest street.

$150-300

Any list of upscale Beaufort lodging must highlight the ◖ **Beaufort Inn** (809 Port Republic St., 843/379-4667, www.beaufortinn.com, $152–425), consistently voted one of the best B&Bs in the nation. It's sort of a hybrid in that it comprises not only the 1897 historic central home but also a cluster of freestanding historical cottages, each with a charming little porch and rocking chairs. With everything connected by gardens and pathways, you could almost call it a campus. Still, for its sprawling nature—44 guest rooms in total—the Beaufort Inn experience is intimate, with attentive service and top-flight amenities such as wet bars, large baths, and sumptuous king beds. Within or outside the main building, each suite has a character all its own, whether it's the 1,500-square-foot Loft Apartment (complete with a guest bedroom and a full kitchen) or one of the cozier (and more affordable) Choice Rooms with a queen-sized bed.

The 18-room, circa-1820 **Rhett House Inn** (1009 Craven St., 843/524-9030, www.

rhetthouseinn.com, $175–320) is the local vacation getaway for the stars. Such arts and entertainment luminaries as Robert Redford, Julia Roberts, Ben Affleck, Barbra Streisand, Dennis Quaid, and Demi Moore have all stayed here at one time or another. Owner Steve Harrison is also a local realtor and no doubt has helped many a guest relocate to town after they've fallen in love with it while staying at his inn. As if Beaufort's great restaurants weren't caloric enough, you can put on a few pounds just staying at the Rhett House. Of course you get the requisite full Southern breakfast, but you'll also be treated to afternoon tea and pastries, more munchies at cocktail hour, and homemade late-night desserts.

There's nothing like enjoying the view of the Beaufort River from the expansive porches of the ◖ **Cuthbert House Inn** (1203 Bay St., 843/521-1315, www.cuthberthouseinn.com, $205–250), possibly the most romantic place to stay in Beaufort. This grand old circa-1790 Federal mansion was once the home of the wealthy Cuthbert family of rice and indigo planters and is now on the National Register of Historic Places. General Sherman spent a night here in 1865. Some of the king rooms have fireplaces and claw-foot tubs. Of course you get a full Southern breakfast, in addition to sunset hors d'oeuvres on the veranda.

While a stay at a B&B is the classic way to enjoy Beaufort, many travelers swear by the new **City Loft Hotel** (301 Carteret St., 843/379-5638, www.citylofthotel.com, $200). Housed in a former motel, City Loft is a total modernist makeover, gleaming from stem to stern with chrome and various art deco touches. While the stay is definitely "boutique," the prices aren't.

FOOD
Breakfast and Brunch

One of the best breakfasts I've had anywhere was a humble two-egg plate for five bucks

BEAUFORT

LOWCOUNTRY BOIL OR FROGMORE STEW?

Near Beaufort it's called Frogmore stew after the township (now named St. Helena) just over the river. Closer to Savannah it's simply called Lowcountry boil. Supposedly the first pot of this delectable, hearty concoction was made by Richard Gay of the Gay Fish Company. As with any vernacular dish, dozens of local and family variants abound. The key ingredient that makes Lowcountry boil/Frogmore stew what it is—a well-blended mélange with a character all its own rather than just a bunch of stuff thrown together in a pot of boiling water—is some type of crab-boil seasoning. You'll find Zatarain's seasoning suggested on a lot of websites, but Old Bay is far more common in the eponymous Lowcountry where the dish originated.

In any case, here's a simple six-serving recipe to get you started. The only downside is that it's pretty much impossible to make it for just a few people. The dish is intended for large gatherings, whether a football tailgate party on a Saturday or a family afternoon after church on Sunday. Note the typical ratio of one ear of corn and 0.5 pounds each of meat and shrimp per person.

- 6 ears fresh corn on the cob, cut into 3-inch sections
- 3 pounds smoked pork sausage, cut into 3-inch sections
- 3 pounds fresh shrimp, shells on
- 5 pounds new potatoes
- 6 ounces Old Bay Seasoning

Put the sausage and potato pieces, along with half of the Old Bay, in two gallons of boiling water. When the potatoes are about halfway done, about 15 minutes in, add the corn and boil for about half that time, seven minutes. Add the shrimp and boil for another three minutes, until they just turn pink. Do not overcook the shrimp. Take the pot off the heat and drain; serve immediately. If you cook the shrimp just right, the oil from the sausage will cause those shells to slip right off.

This is but one of dozens of recipes. Some cooks add some lemon juice and beer in the water as it's coming to a boil; others add onion, garlic, or green peppers.

at Beaufort's most popular morning hangout, **C Blackstone's Café** (205 Scott St., 843/524-4330, Mon.–Sat. 7:30 A.M.–2:30 P.M., Sun. 7:30 A.M.–2 P.M., under $10), complete with tasty hash browns, a comparative rarity in this part of the country, where grits rule as the breakfast starch of choice. Tucked on a side street just off busy Bay Street, Blackstone's roomy but inviting interior—festooned with various collegiate, nautical, and military motifs and a checkerboard floor—has more than enough room for you to spread out and relax before continuing on with your travels (there's even free Wi-Fi).

Burgers and Sandwiches

Another longtime lunch favorite is **Magnolia Bakery Café** (703 Congress St., 843/524-1961,

Mon.–Sat. 9 A.M.–5 P.M., under $10). It's a little ways north of the usual tourist area but well worth going out of your way for (Beaufort is pretty small, after all). Lump crab cakes are a particular specialty item, but you can't go wrong with any of the lunch sandwiches. They even offer a serviceable crepe. Vegetarian diners are particularly well taken care of with a large selection of black-bean burger plates. As the name indicates, the range of desserts here is tantalizing, to say the least, with the added bonus of a serious espresso bar.

Coffeehouses

The charming and popular **Common Ground** (102 West St., 843/524-2326, daily 7:30 A.M.– 10 P.M.) coffeehouse in the Waterfront Park area is not only a great place for a light sandwich or sweet treat; the java is a cut above most such places, featuring a wide selection of excellent fair-trade "Dancing Goat" brews.

New Southern

The stylishly appointed **Wren Bistro, Bar and Market** (210 Carteret St., 843/524-9463, $15–25) is known for any of its chicken dishes. While the food is great, the interior is particularly well-done, simultaneously warm and classy. As seems to be typical of Beaufort, the lunches are as good as the dinners.

Seafood

The hottest dinner table in town is at the **Saltus River Grill** (802 Bay St., 843/379-3474, Sun.–Thurs. 5–9 P.M., Fri.–Sat. 5–10 P.M., $10–39). Executive chef Jim Spratling has made this fairly new restaurant, housed in a historic tabby building on the waterfront, famous throughout the state for its raw bar menu featuring oysters from Nova Scotia, Chesapeake Bay, Oregon, and British Columbia. Sushi lovers can also get a fix here, whether it's a basic California roll or great sashimi. Other specialties include she-crab bisque, lump crab cakes, flounder fillet, and, of course, the ubiquitous shrimp and grits. The Saltus River Grill is more upscale in feel and in price than most Lowcountry places, with a very see-and-be-seen attitude and a hopping bar. Reservations are recommended.

Sharing an owner with the Saltus River Grill is **Plum's** (904½ Bay St., 843/525-1946, lunch daily 11 A.M.–4 P.M., dinner daily 5–10 P.M., $15–25). The short and focused menu keys in on entrées highlighting local ingredients, such as the shrimp penne *al'amatriciana* and fresh black mussel pasta. Because of the outstanding microbrew selection, Plum's is a big nightlife hangout as well; be aware that after 10 P.M., when food service ends but the bar remains open until 2 A.M., it's no longer smoke-free, although there's a friendly porch where you can get some fresh air and feed the resident cat.

An up-and-comer downtown is **Breakwater Restaurant & Bar** (203 Carteret St., 843/379-0052, www.breakwater-restaurant.com, dinner Thurs.–Sat. 6–9:30 P.M., bar until 2 A.M., $10–20). The concise menu makes up in good taste what it lacks in comprehensiveness, with an emphasis on seafood, of course. An especially enticing marine-oriented tapas plate is the diver scallops in a vanilla cognac sauce. (This restaurant recently moved from a West Street location.)

Steaks

Luther's Rare & Well Done (910 Bay St., 843/521-1888, daily 10 A.M.–midnight, from $8) on the waterfront is the kind of meat-lover's place where even the french onion soup has a morsel of rib eye in it. While the patented succulent rubbed steaks are a no-brainer here, the handcrafted specialty pizzas are also quite popular. If a steak is too rich for your blood but you still crave some protein, their hamburgers are awesome too. Housed in a historic pharmacy building, Luther's is also a great place for late eats after many other places in this quiet town have rolled up the sidewalk. A limited menu of appetizers and bar food to nosh on at the inviting and popular bar is available after 10 P.M.

Tapas

Right around the corner from Breakwater is **Emily's** (906 Port Republic St., 843/522-1866, www.emilysrestaurantandtapasbar.com, dinner Mon.–Sat. 4–10 P.M., bar until 2 A.M., $10–20), a very popular fine dining spot that specializes in a more traditional brand of rich, tasty tapas (available 4–5 P.M.) and is known for its active bar scene.

INFORMATION AND SERVICES

The **Beaufort Visitors Information Center** (713 Craven St., 843/986-5400, www.beaufortsc.org, daily 9 A.M.–5:30 P.M.), the headquarters of the Beaufort Chamber of Commerce and Convention and Visitors Bureau, has relocated from its old Carteret Street location and can now be found within the Beaufort Arsenal, once home to the now-closed Beaufort Museum.

The U.S. Postal Service has a **post office** (501 Charles St., 843/525-9085) in downtown Beaufort.

The daily newspaper of record in Beaufort is the *Beaufort Gazette* (www.beaufortgazette. com). An alternative weekly focusing mostly on the arts is *Lowcountry Weekly* (www.lcweekly. com), published every Wednesday.

GETTING THERE AND AROUND

While the Marines can fly their F-18s directly into Beaufort Naval Air Station, you won't have that luxury. The closest major airport to Beaufort is the **Savannah/Hilton Head International Airport** (SAV, 400 Airways Ave., 912/964-0514, www.savannahairport.com) off I-95 outside Savannah. If you're not going into Savannah for any reason, the easiest route to the Beaufort area from the airport is to take I-95's exit 8, and from there to take U.S. 278 east to Highway 170.

Alternately, you could fly into the **Charleston International Airport** (CHS, 5500 International Blvd., www.chs-airport.com), but because that facility is on the far north side of Charleston, it actually might take you longer to get to Beaufort. From the Charleston Airport the best route south to Beaufort is U.S. 17 south, exiting onto U.S. 21 at Gardens Corner and then into Beaufort.

If you're coming into the region by car, I-95 will be your likely primary route, with your main point of entry being exit 8 off I-95 connecting to U.S. 278.

There's no public transportation to speak of in Beaufort, but that's OK—the historic section is quite small and can be traversed in an afternoon. A favorite mode of transport is by bicycle, often complimentary to bed-and-breakfast guests. Rent one at **Lowcountry Bikes** (102 Sea Island Pkwy., 843/524-9585, Mon.–Tues. and Thurs.–Fri. 10 A.M.–6 P.M., Wed. 10 A.M.–1 P.M., Sat. 10 A.M.–3 P.M., about $5 per hour) in Lady's Island just over the bridge.

OUTSIDE BEAUFORT

The areas outside tourist-traveled Beaufort can take you even further back into sepia-toned Americana, into a time of sharecropper homesteads, sturdy oystermen, and an altogether variable and subjective sense of time.

Lady's Island

Directly across the Beaufort River is Lady's Island, now a predominantly residential area with a bigger variety of national shopping and grocery outlets than you'll find in Beaufort proper. However, there are a few places to eat here that are worth mentioning. Cuisine options include the casual **Steamer Oyster and Steak House** (168 Sea Island Pkwy., 843/522-0210, daily 11 A.M.–9:30 P.M., $15–20). The big hit here is the Frogmore stew, a.k.a. Lowcountry boil. For vegan and vegetarian soups, salads, and sandwiches, try **It's Only Natural** (45 Factory Creek Court, 843/986-9595, Mon.–Fri. 8 A.M.–6 P.M., Sat. 9 A.M.–4:30 P.M., $5), which also offers a range of health-food items and produce. It's visible right off the main road, the Sea Island Parkway (U.S. 21). For excellent seafood in the Southern tradition try **Factory Creek Fish Company** (71 Sea Island Pkwy., 843/379-3288, www.factorycreekfishcompany.com, Mon.–Sat. 11 A.M.–10 P.M., Sun. 11 A.M.–9 P.M., $15–20). The shrimp and grits as well as fried catfish are particular favorites.

◖ Penn Center

By going across the Richard V. Woods Memorial Bridge over the Beaufort River on the Sea Island Parkway (which turns into U.S. 21), you'll pass through Lady's Island

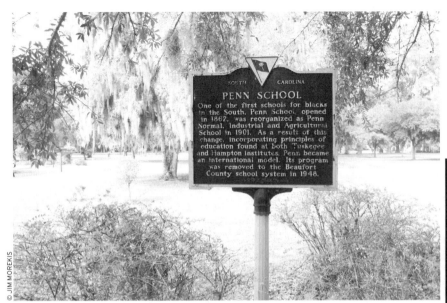

© JIM MOREKIS

the Penn Center on St. Helena Island

and reach St. Helena Island. Known to old-timers as Frogmore, the area took back its old Spanish-derived place name in the 1980s. Today St. Helena Island is most famous for the Penn Center (16 Martin Luther King Jr. Dr., 843/838-2474, www.penncenter.com, Mon.–Sat. 11 A.M.–4 P.M., $4 adults, $2 seniors and children), the spiritual home of Gullah culture and history. When you visit here among the live oaks and humble but well-preserved buildings, you'll instantly see why Martin Luther King Jr. chose this as one of his major retreat and planning sites during the civil rights era. The dream began as early as 1862, when a group of abolitionist Quakers from Philadelphia came during the Union occupation with the goal of teaching recently freed slave children. They were soon joined by African American educator Charlotte Forten. After Reconstruction, the Penn School continued its mission by offering teaching as well as agricultural and industrial trade curricula. In the late 1960s, the Southern Christian

Leadership Conference used the school as a retreat and planning site, with both the Peace Corps and the Conscientious Objector Programs training here. The Penn Center continues to serve an important civil rights role by providing legal counsel to African American homeowners in St. Helena. Because clear title is difficult to acquire in the area due to the fact that so much of the land has stayed in the families of former slaves, developers are constantly making shady offers so that ancestral land can be opened up to upscale development.

The beautiful 50-acre campus of the Penn Center is part of the Penn School Historic District, a National Historic Landmark comprising 19 buildings, most of key historical significance, including Darrah Hall, the oldest building on the campus; the old "Brick Church" right across MLK Jr. Drive; and Gantt Cottage, where Dr. King himself stayed periodically in the 1963–1967 period. Another building, the Retreat House, was intended for Dr.

King to continue his strategy meetings, but he was assassinated before being able to stay there. The museum and bookshop are housed in the Cope Building, now called the York W. Bailey Museum, situated right along MLK Jr. Drive. A self-guided nature trail takes you all around the campus. The key public event here happens each November with the Penn Center Heritage Days, in which the entire St. Helena community comes together to celebrate and enjoy entertainment such as the world-famous, locally based Hallelujah Singers.

To get to the Penn Center from Beaufort, proceed over the bridge until you get to St. Helena Island. Take a right onto MLK Jr. Drive when you see the Red Piano Too Art Gallery. The Penn Center is a few hundred yards down on your right. If you drive past the Penn Center and continue a few hundred yards down MLK Jr. Drive, look for the ancient tabby ruins on the left side of the road. This is the **Chapel of Ease,** the remnant of a 1740 church destroyed by forest fire in the late 1800s.

If you get hungry, just before you take a right to get to the Penn Center on St. Helena Island is **Gullah Grub** (877 Sea Island Pkwy., 843/838-3841, Mon.–Thurs. 11:30 A.M.–7 P.M., under $20), an unpretentious, one-room lunch spot focusing on down-home Southern specialties with a Lowcountry touch, such as hushpuppies, collard greens, and shrimp-'n'-shark.

Fort Fremont Preserve

Military historians and sightseers of a particularly adventurous type will want to drive several miles past the Penn Center on St. Helena Island to visit **Fort Fremont** (Lands End Rd., www.fortfremont.org), daily 9 A.M.–dusk, free). Two artillery batteries remain of this Spanish-American War-era coastal defense fort (an adjacent private residence is actually the old army hospital.) The big guns defending Port Royal Sound are long gone, but the concrete emplacements—along with many very dark tunnels

and small rooms—are still here. I enjoy touring the labyrinthine bowels of the fort, but bring a flashlight and be aware that there is graffiti and evidence of frequent visitation by young partiers. Also be warned that, fascinating as this county-maintained site is, there are no facilities of any kind, including lights and safety guardrails. It's fun to climb all over the gun emplacements, but a fall would be disastrous. When at Fort Fremont, don't miss the opportunity to go down to the small "beach" area on the sound and enjoy the scintillating view.

Old Sheldon Church Ruins

A short ways north of Beaufort are the poignantly desolate ruins of the once-magnificent Old Sheldon Church (Old Sheldon Church Rd., off U.S. 17 just past Gardens Corner, daily dawn–dusk, free). Set a couple of miles off the highway on a narrow road, the serene, oak-lined grounds containing this massive empty edifice give little hint of the violence so intrinsic to its history. One of the first Greek Revival structures in the United States, the house of worship held its first service in 1757 as Prince William's Parish Church. The sanctuary was first burned by the British in 1779, mainly because of reports that the Patriots were using it to store gunpowder captured from a British ship. After being rebuilt in 1826, the sanctuary survived until General Sherman's arrival in 1865, whereupon Union troops razed it once more. Nothing remains now but these towering walls and columns, made of red brick instead of the tabby often seen in similar ruins on the coast. It's now owned by the nearby St. Helena's Episcopal Church in Beaufort, which holds outdoor services here the second Sunday after Easter. In all, it's an almost painfully compelling bit of history set amid stunning natural beauty, and well worth the short drive.

Oyotunji Village

Continuing north of the Sheldon Church a short way, the more adventurous can find

THE LOST ART OF TABBY

Let's clear up a couple of misconceptions about tabby, that unique construction technique combining oyster shells, lime, water, and sand found along the South Carolina and Georgia coast.

First, it did not originate with Native Americans. The confusion is due to the fact that the native population left behind many middens, or trash heaps, of oyster shells. While these middens indeed provided the bulk of the shells for tabby buildings to come, Native Americans had little else to do with it.

Second, although the Spanish were responsible for the first use of tabby in the Americas, contrary to lore almost all remaining tabby in the area dates from later English settlement. The British first fell in love with tabby after the siege of Spanish-held St. Augustine, Florida, and quickly began building with it in their colonies to the north.

Scholars are divided as to whether tabby was invented by West Africans or its use spread to Africa from Spain and Portugal, circuitously coming to the United States through the knowledge of imported slaves. The origin of the word itself is also unclear, as similar words exist in Spanish, Portuguese, Gullah, and Arabic to describe various types of wall.

We do know for sure how tabby is made: The primary technique was to burn alternating layers of oyster shells and logs in a deep hole in the ground, thus creating lime. The lime was then mixed with oyster shells, sand, and freshwater and poured into wooden molds, or "forms," to dry and then be used as building blocks, much like large bricks. Tabby walls were usually plastered with stucco. Tabby is remarkably strong and resilient, able to survive the hurricanes that often batter the area. It also stays cool in the summer and is insect-resistant, two enormous advantages down here.

Following are some great examples of true tabby you can see today on the South Carolina and Georgia coasts, from north to south:

- **Dorchester State Historic Site** in Summerville, north of Charleston, contains a well-preserved tabby fort.

- Several younger tabby buildings still exist in downtown Beaufort: the **Barnwell-Gough House** (705 Washington St.); the Thomas Fuller House, or **"Tabby Manse"** (1211 Bay St.); and the **Saltus House** (800 block of Bay St.), perhaps the tallest surviving tabby structure.

- The **Chapel of Ease** on St. Helena Island dates from the 1740s. If someone tells you Sherman burned it down, don't believe it; the culprit was a forest fire.

- The **Stoney-Baynard Ruins** in Sea Pines Plantation on Hilton Head are all that's left of the home of the old Braddock's Point Plantation. Foundations of a slave quarters are nearby.

- **Wormsloe Plantation** near Savannah has the remains of Noble Jones's fortification of the Skidaway Narrows.

- **St. Cyprian's Episcopal Church** in Darien is one of the largest tabby structures still in use.

- **Fort Frederica** on St. Simons Island has not only the remains of a tabby fort but many foundations of tabby houses in the surrounding settlement.

- The remarkably intact walls of the **Horton-DuBignon House** on Jekyll Island, Georgia, date from 1738, and the house was occupied into the 1850s.

a quirky Lowcountry attraction, Oyotunji Village (56 Bryant Lane, 843/846-8900, www.oyotunjiafricanvillage.org, daily 10 A.M.–dusk, $10). Built in 1970 by self-proclaimed "King" Ofuntola Oseijeman Adelabu Adefunmi I, a former used car dealer with an interesting past, Oyotunji claims to be North America's only authentic African village, with 5–10 families residing on its 30 acres. It also claims to be a separate kingdom and not a part of the United States—though I'm sure the State Department begs to differ.

BEAUFORT

© JIM MOREKIS

Old Sheldon Church ruins

With a mission to preserve the religious and cultural aspects of the Yoruba Orisa culture of West Africa, each spring the village hosts an annual Warrior's Festival, celebrating traditional male rites of passage. Truth is, there's not much to see here but a few poorly built "monuments." But connoisseurs of roadside Americana will be pleased.

Yemassee

Going still farther north on U.S. 17 you'll come to the small, friendly town of Yemassee. Its main claim to fame is nearby **Auldbrass,** designed by Frank Lloyd Wright in 1939. The home is privately owned by Hollywood producer Joel Silver, but rare, much-sought-after tours happen every other year in November through the auspices of the Beaufort County Open Land Trust. To find out about the next tour and to get on the list, email your mailing address to bcolt2@islc.net or call 843/521-2175 to receive ticket information the summer before.

The Amtrak train depot in downtown Yemassee actually is historically important as one of the oldest continuously used train stations in the region. From 1914 to 1964 it was the point of embarkation for Marine recruits headed for boot camp at Parris Island. Under the auspices of the Yemassee Revitalization Corporation, plans are afoot to restore the historic depot to a nostalgic 1940s ambience.

Port Royal

This sleepy hamlet between Beaufort and Parris Island touts itself as a leader in "small-town New Urbanism," with an emphasis on livability, retro-themed shopping areas, and relaxing walking trails. However, Port Royal is still pretty sleepy—but not without very real charms, not the least of which is the fact that everything is within easy walking distance of everything else. The highlight of the year is the annual Soft Shell Crab Festival, held each April to mark the short-lived harvesting season for that favorite crustacean.

While much of the tiny historic district has a scrubbed, tidy feel, the main historic structure is the charming little **Union Church** (11th St., 843/524-4333, Mon.–Fri. 10 A.M.–4 P.M., donation), one of the oldest buildings in town, with guided docent tours.

Don't miss the new boardwalk and observation tower at **The Sands** municipal beach and boat ramp. The 50-foot-tall structure provides a commanding view of Battery Creek. To get to The Sands, go to 7th Street and then turn onto Sands Beach Road.

Another environmentally oriented point of pride is the **Lowcountry Estuarium** (1402 Paris Ave., 843/524-6600, www.lowcountryestuarium.org, Wed.–Sat. 10 A.M.–5 P.M., feedings 11:30 A.M. and 3 P.M., $5 adults, $3 children). The point of the facility is to give hands-on opportunities to learn more about the flora and fauna of the various ecosystems of the Lowcountry, such as salt marshes, beaches, and estuaries.

If you get hungry in Port Royal, try the waterfront seafood haven **11th Street Dockside** (1699 11th St., 843/524-7433, daily 4:30–10 P.M., $17–27). The Dockside Dinner is a great sampler plate with lobster tail, scallops, crab legs, and shrimp. The views of the waterfront and the adjoining shrimp-boat docks are relaxing and beautiful.

Parris Island

Though more commonly known as the home of the legendary **Marine Corps Recruit Depot Parris Island** (283 Blvd. de France, 843/228-3650, www.mcrdpi.usmc.mil, free), the island is also of historic significance as the site of some of the earliest European presence in the New World. The U.S. Marine Corps began its association with Parris Island in 1891, though the

BEAUFORT

© JIM MOREKIS

You don't have to be a U.S. Marine to get something out of a trip to Parris Island.

island's naval roots actually go back to its use as a coaling station during the long Union occupation. By the outbreak of World War I, a full-blown military town had sprung up, now with its own presence on the National Register of Historic Places. In November 1915, Parris Island went into business as a recruit depot, and today it's where all female Marine recruits and all male recruits east of the Mississippi River go through the grueling 13-week boot camp. Almost every Friday during the year marks the graduation of a company of newly minted Marines. That's why you might notice an influx of visitors to the area each Thursday, a.k.a. "Family Day," with the requisite amount of celebration on Fridays after that morning's ceremony.

Unlike many military facilities in the post-9/11 era, Parris Island still hosts plenty of visitors, about 120,000 a year. It's easy to get onto the Depot. Just check in with the friendly sentry at the gate and show your valid driver's license, registration, and proof of insurance. Rental car drivers must show a copy of the rental agreement. On your way to the Depot proper, there are a couple of beautiful picnic areas. Because this is a military base and therefore immune to the rampant residential development that has come to the Lowcountry, you will see some incredible ancient live oak trees in this part of the facility. Once inside, stop first at the **Douglas Visitor Center** (Bldg. 283, Blvd. de France, 843/228-3650, Mon. 7:30 A.M.–noon, Tues.–Wed. 7:30 A.M.–4:30 P.M., Thurs. 6:30 A.M.–7 P.M., Fri. 7:30 A.M.–3 P.M.), a great place to find maps and touring information. As you go by the big parade ground, or "deck," be sure to check out the beautiful sculpture recreating the famous photo of Marines raising the flag on Iwo Jima. A short ways ahead is the **Parris Island Museum** (Bldg. 111, 111 Panama St., 843/228-2951, daily 8:30 A.M.–4:30 P.M., free) a little ways in from the museum, which not only lovingly details the entire U.S. military experience in the area but also features a

good exhibit on the area's earliest colonial history. Be sure to check out the second floor for a particularly detailed and well-done series of exhibits on Marine campaigns through the centuries.

The Spanish built Santa Elena directly on top of the original French settlement, Charlesfort. They then built two other settlements, San Felipe and San Marcos. The Santa Elena–Charlesfort site (http://santaelena.us), now on the circa-1950s depot golf course, is now a National Historic Landmark. Many artifacts are viewable at the nearby **clubhouse-interpretive center** (daily 7 A.M.–5 P.M., free). You can take a self-guided tour; to get to the site from the museum, continue on Panama Street and take a right on Cuba Street. Follow the signs to the golf course and continue through the main parking lot of the course.

Do not use your cell phone while driving. While Parris Island kindly welcomes visitors, be aware that all traffic rules within the camp are strictly enforced, and your vehicle is subject to inspection at any time.

◖ Hunting Island State Park

Rumored to be a hideaway for Blackbeard himself, the aptly named Hunting Island was indeed for many years a notable hunting preserve, and its abundance of wildlife remains to this day. The island is one of the East Coast's best birding spots and also hosts dolphins, loggerheads, alligators, and deer. Thanks to preservation efforts by President Franklin Roosevelt and the Civilian Conservation Corps, however, the island is no longer for hunting but for sheer enjoyment. And enjoy it people do, to the tune of one million visitors per year. A true family-friendly outdoor adventure spot, Hunting Island State Park (2555 Sea Island Pkwy., 866/345-7275, www.huntingisland.com, winter daily 6 A.M.–6 P.M., during daylight saving time daily 6 A.M.–9 P.M., $5 adults, $3 children) has something for everyone—kids, parents, and newlyweds. Yet it still retains a certain sense of lush wildness—so much so that it doubled as Vietnam in the movie *Forrest Gump.*

At the north end past the campground is the island's main landmark, the historic **Hunting Island Light,** which dates from 1875. Although the lighthouse ceased operations in 1933, a rotating light—not strong enough to serve as an actual navigational aid—is turned on at night. While the 167-step trek to the top (donation $2 pp) is quite strenuous, the view from the little observation area at the top of the lighthouse is stunning, a complete panorama of Hunting Island and much of the Lowcountry coast.

At the south end of the island is a marsh walk, nature trail, and a fishing pier complete with a cute little nature center. Hunting Island's three miles of beautiful beaches also serve as a major center of loggerhead turtle nesting and hatching, a process that begins around June as the mothers lay their eggs and culminates in late summer and early fall, when the hatchlings make their daring dash to the sea. At all phases the turtles are strictly protected, and while there are organized events to witness the hatching of the eggs, it is strictly forbidden to touch or otherwise disturb the turtles or their nests. Contact the park ranger for more detailed information. The tropical-looking inlet running through the park is a great place to kayak or canoe.

Getting to Hunting Island couldn't be easier—just take the Sea Island Parkway (U.S. 21) about 20 minutes beyond Beaufort and you'll run right into it.

Fripp Island

If you keep driving past Hunting Island, you'll reach Fripp Island, one of South Carolina's private developed barrier islands. Unlike its more egalitarian neighbor, Fripp only welcomes visitors who are guests of the **Fripp Island Golf and Beach Resort** (800/845-4100, www.frippislandresort.com), which offers a range of lodging

from oceanfront homes to villas to golf cottages. Family-friendly recreation abounds, not only in 36 holes of high-caliber golf but in over three miles of uncrowded beach. A major allure is Camp Fripp, providing activities for kids.

◖ ACE Basin

Occupying pretty much the entire area between Beaufort and Charleston, the ACE Basin—the acronym signifies its role as the collective estuary of the Ashepoo, Combahee, and Edisto Rivers—is one of the most enriching natural experiences the country has to offer. The Basin's three core rivers, the Edisto being the largest, are the framework for a matrix of waterways crisscrossing its approximately 350,000 acres of salt marsh. It's this intimate relationship with the tides that makes the area so enjoyable, and also what attracted so many plantations throughout its history (canals and dikes from the old paddy fields are still visible throughout). Other uses have included tobacco, corn, and lumbering. While the ACE Basin can in no way be called "pristine," it's a testament to the power of nature that after 6,000 years of human presence and often intense cultivation, the Basin manages to retain much of its untamed feel.

The ACE Basin is so big that it is actually divided into several parts for management purposes under the umbrella of the ACE Basin Project (www.acebasin.net), a task force begun in 1988 by the state of South Carolina, the U.S. Fish and Wildlife Service, and various private firms and conservation groups. The project is now considered a model for responsible watershed preservation techniques in a time of often rampant coastal development. A host of species, both common and endangered, thrive in the area, including wood storks, alligators, sturgeon, loggerheads, teals, and bald eagles.

About 12,000 acres of the ACE Basin Project comprise the **Ernest F. Hollings ACE Basin National Wildlife Refuge** (8675 Willtown

© JIM MOREKIS

the Grove Plantation House at the Ernest F. Hollings ACE Basin National Wildlife Refuge

Rd., 843/889-3084, www.fws.gov/acebasin, grounds year-round daily dawn–dusk, office Mon.–Fri. 7:30 A.M.–4 P.M., free), run by the U.S. Fish and Wildlife Service. The historic 1828 **Grove Plantation House** is in this portion of the Basin and houses the refuge's headquarters. Sometimes featured on local tours of homes, it's one of only three antebellum homes left in the ACE Basin. Surrounded by lush, ancient oak trees, it's really a sight in and of itself.

This section of the Refuge, the **Edisto Unit,** is almost entirely composed of impounded paddy fields from the area's role as a rice plantation before the Civil War. Restored rice trunks—the tidal gates used to manage water flow into the paddies—are still used to maintain the amount of water in the impounded areas, which are now rife with birds since the refuge is along the Atlantic Flyway. You may not always see them, but you'll definitely hear their calls echoing over the miles of marsh. (Speaking of miles, there are literally miles

of walking and biking trails throughout the Edisto Unit, through both wetlands and forest.) To get to the Edisto Unit of the Hollings/ACE Basin National Wildlife Refuge, take U.S. 17 to Highway 174 (going all the way down this route takes you to Edisto Island) and turn right onto Willtown Road. The unpaved entrance road is about two miles ahead on the left. There are restrooms and a few picnic tables, but no other facilities of note.

You can also visit the two parts of the **Combahee Unit** of the refuge, which offers a similar scene of trails among impounded wetlands along the Combahee River, with parking; it's farther west near Yemassee. Get here by taking a left off U.S. 17 onto Highway 33. The larger portion of the Combahee Unit is very soon after the turnoff, and the smaller, more northerly portion is about five miles up the road.

About 135,000 acres of the entire ACE Basin falls under the protection of the South Carolina Department of Natural Resources (DNR) as part of the **National Estuarine Research Reserve System** (www.nerrs.noaa.gov/acebasin). The DNR also runs two Wildlife Management Areas (WMAs), **Donnelly WMA** (843/844-8957, www.dnr.sc.gov, year-round Mon.–Sat. 8 A.M.–5 P.M.) and **Bear Island WMA** (843/844-8957, www.dnr.sc.gov, Feb. 1–Oct. 14 Mon.–Sat. dawn–dusk), both of which provide rich opportunities for birding and wildlife observation.

Over 128,000 acres of the ACE Basin Project are permanently protected through conservation easements, management agreements, and fee title purchases. While traditional uses such as farming, fishing, and hunting do indeed continue in the ACE Basin, the area is off-limits to the gated communities, which are sprouting like mildew all along the Carolina coast. Because it is so well defended, the ACE Basin also functions like a huge outdoor laboratory for the coastal scientific community, with constant research going on in botany, zoology, microbiology, and marine science.

Recreation
KAYAKING

A 10-minute drive away from Beaufort in little Port Royal is **The Sands** public boat ramp into Battery Creek. You can also put in at the ramp at the **Lady's Island Marina** (73 Sea Island Pkwy., 843/522-0430) just across the bridge from Beaufort. **Hunting Island State Park** (2555 Sea Island Pkwy., 866/345-7275, www.huntingisland.com, winter daily 6 A.M.–6 P.M., during daylight saving time daily 6 A.M.–9 P.M., $5 adults, $3 children) has a wonderful inlet that is very popular with kayakers.

North and northeast of Beaufort lies the ACE Basin region, with about two dozen public ramps indicated by brown signs. Comprising hundreds of miles of creeks and tributaries in addition to its three rivers, the ACE Basin also features a fun paddling bonus: canals from the old rice plantations. A good service for rental and knowledgeable guided tours of the Basin is **Outpost Moe's** (843/844-2514, www.geocities.ws/outpostmoe), where the basic 2.5-hour tour costs $40 pp, and an all-day extravaganza through the Basin is $80. Moe's provides lunch for most of its tours. Another premier local outfitter for ACE Basin tours is **Carolina Heritage Outfitters** (U.S. 15 in Canadys, 843/563-5051, www.canoesc.com), which focuses on the Edisto River trail. In addition to guided tours ($30) and rentals, you can camp overnight in their cute tree houses ($125) along the kayak routes. They load you up with your gear and drive you 22 miles upriver; then you paddle downriver to the tree house for the evening. The next day, you paddle yourself the rest of the way downriver back to home base.

To have a drier experience of the ACE Basin from the deck of a larger vessel, try **ACE Basin Tours** (1 Coosaw River Dr., Beaufort, 843/521-3099, www.acebasintours.com, Mar.–Nov. Wed. and Sat. 10 A.M., $35 adults, $15 children), which will take you on a three-hour tour in the 40-passenger *Dixie Lady*. To get to their dock, take Carteret Street over the bridge to St. Helena Island, and then take a left on Highway 802 east (Sam's Point Rd.). Continue until you cross Lucy Point Creek; the ACE Basin Tours marina is on your immediate left after you cross the bridge.

If you prefer self-guided paddling, keep in mind that you can spend a lifetime learning your way around the ACE Basin. The state of South Carolina has conveniently gathered some of the best self-guided kayak trips at www.acebasin.net/canoe.html.

BIRD-WATCHING

Because of its abundance of both saltwater and freshwater environments and its relatively low human density, the Lowcountry offers a stunning glimpse into the diversity and majesty of the Southeast's bird population, both regional and migratory. Serious birders swear by **Hunting Island State Park** (2555 Sea Island Pkwy., 866/345-7275, www.hunting-island.com, winter daily 6 A.M.–6 P.M., during daylight saving time daily 6 A.M.–9 P.M., $5 adults, $3 children), which—thanks to its undeveloped state and its spot on key migratory routes—is a great place to see brown pelicans, loons, herons, falcons, plovers, and egrets of all types. Park naturalists conduct frequent guided walks.

The tall observation tower at Port Royal's The Sands, where Battery Creek joins the Beaufort River, is a convenient vantage point from which to see any number of local bird species. The **ACE Basin** (8675 Willtown Rd., 843/889-3084, www.fws.gov/acebasin, grounds year-round dawn–dusk, office Mon.–Fri. 7:30 A.M.–4 P.M.) hosts at least 19 species of waterfowl and 13 species of wading birds.

At the northeast corner of the ACE Basin is the **Bear Island Wildlife Management Area** (843/844-8957, www.dnr.sc.gov, Feb.–Oct. Mon.–Sat. dawn–dusk), considered one of the best birding spots in South Carolina. To get here, take U.S. 21 north of Beaufort to U.S. 17 north. Take a right on Bennett's Point Road and continue south about 13 miles. The entrance is about one mile along, on the left, after crossing the Ashepoo River.

BIKING

Bikes can be rented in Lady's Island at **Lowcountry Bikes** (102 Sea Island Pkwy., 843/524-9585, Mon.–Tues. and Thurs.–Fri. 10 A.M.–6 P.M., Wed. 10 A.M.–1 P.M., Sat. 10 A.M.–3 P.M., about $5 per hour).

GOLF

Golf is much bigger in Hilton Head than in the Beaufort area, but here are some local highlights. The best-regarded public course in the area, and indeed one of the best military courses in the world, is **Legends at Parris Island** (Bldg. 299, Parris Island, 843/228-2240, www.mccssc.com, $30). You have to call in advance for a tee time before you can come on Parris Island to golf.

Another popular public course is **South Carolina National Golf Club** (8 Waveland Ave., Cat Island, 843/524-0300, www.scnational.com, $70). Get to secluded Cat Island by taking the Sea Island Parkway onto Lady's Island and continuing south as it turns into Lady's Island Drive. Turn onto Island Causeway and continue for about three miles.

CAMPING

Hunting Island State Park (2555 Sea Island Pkwy., 866/345-7275, www.huntingisland. com, winter daily 6 A.M.–6 P.M., during daylight saving time daily 6 A.M.–9 P.M., $5 adults, $3 children, $25 campsites, $87–172 cabins) has 200 campsites on the north end of the island, with individual water and electric hookups. Most are available by reservation only, but 20 are available on a first-come, first-served basis. (There used to be plenty of cabins for rent, but beach erosion has sadly made the ones near the water uninhabitable. One cabin near the lighthouse is still available for rent.)

Another neat place to camp is **Tuck in De Wood** (22 Tuc In De Wood Lane, St. Helena, 843/838-2267, $25), a very well-maintained 74-site private campground just past the Penn Center on St. Helena Island.

Edisto Island

One of the last truly unspoiled places in the Lowcountry, Edisto Island has been highly regarded as a getaway spot since the Edisto people first started coming here for shellfish. (Proof of their patronage is in the huge shell midden, or debris pile, at the state park.) In fact, locals here swear that the island was settled by English-speaking colonists even before Charleston was settled in 1670. In any case, we do know that the Spanish established a short-lived mission on St. Pierre's Creek. Then, in 1674, the island was purchased from the Edistos for a few trinkets by the perhaps appropriately named Earl of Shaftesbury. For most of its modern history, cotton plantations specializing in the top-of-the-line Sea Island strain were Edisto Island's main claim to fame—it was called McConkey's Island for most of that time—and after the Civil War fishing became the primary

occupation. Because of several hurricanes in the mid-20th century, little remains from previous eras. Now this barrier island, for the moment unthreatened by the encroachment of planned communities and private resorts so endemic to the Carolina coast, is a nice getaway for area residents in addition to being a great—if a little isolated—place to live for its 800 or so full-time residents. The beaches are quiet and beautiful, the shells are plentiful, the walks are romantic, the people are friendly, and the food is good but casual. The residents operate on "Edisto Time," with a *mañana* philosophy (i.e., it'll get done when it gets done) that results in a mellow pace of life out in these parts.

ORIENTATION

Edisto Island is basically halfway between Beaufort and Charleston. There's one main

© SOPHIA MOREKIS

The beach at Edisto Island is remarkably free of overdevelopment.

BEAUFORT

land route here, south on Highway 174 off U.S. 17. It's a long way down to Edisto, but the 20–30-minute drive is scenic and enjoyable. Most activity on the island centers on the township of Edisto Beach, which voted to align itself with Colleton County for its lower taxes (the rest of Edisto Island is part of Charleston County). Once in town, there are two main routes to keep in mind. Palmetto Boulevard runs parallel to the beach and is noteworthy for the lack of high-rise development so common in other beach areas of South Carolina. Jungle Road runs parallel to Palmetto Boulevard several blocks inland and contains the tiny business district.

◖ EDISTO BEACH STATE PARK

Edisto Beach State Park (8377 State Cabin Rd., 843/869-2156, www.southcarolinaparks. com, Nov.–mid-Mar. daily 8 A.M.–6 P.M., mid-Mar.–Oct. daily 6 A.M.–10 P.M., $4 adults, $1.50 children, free under age 6) is one of the world's foremost destinations for shell collectors. Largely because of fresh loads of silt from the adjacent ACE Basin, there are always new specimens, many of them fossils, washing ashore. The park stretches almost three miles and features the state's longest system of fully accessible hiking and biking trails, including one leading to the 4,000-year-old shell midden, now much eroded from past millennia. The new and particularly well-done **interpretive center** (Tues.–Sat. 9 A.M.–4 P.M.) has plenty of interesting exhibits about the nature and history of the park as well as the surrounding ACE Basin. Don't let the kids miss it.

Like many state recreational facilities in the South, Edisto Beach State Park was developed by the Civilian Conservation Corps (CCC), one of President Franklin D. Roosevelt's New Deal programs during the Great Depression, which had the doubly beneficial effect of employing large numbers of people while establishing much of the conservation infrastructure we enjoy today.

OTHER SIGHTS

The charming **Edisto Museum** (8123 Chisolm Plantation Rd., 843/869-1954, www.edistomuseum.org, Tues.–Sat. 1–4 P.M., $4 adults, $2 children, free under age 10), a project of the Edisto Island Historic Preservation Society, is in the middle of a major expansion that will incorporate a nearby slave cabin. Its well-done exhibits of local lore and history are complemented by a good gift shop. The Edisto Museum is before you get to the main part of the island, off Highway 174.

The **Botany Bay Wildlife Management Area** (www.preserveedisto.org, Wed.–Mon. dawn–dusk, closed on hunt days, free) is a great way to enjoy the unspoiled nature of Edisto Island. On the grounds of two former rice and indigo plantations comprising 4,000 acres, Botany Bay features several historic remains of the old plantations and a small, wonderful beach. There are no facilities to speak of, so pack and plan accordingly.

Opened in 1999 by local snake-hunters the Clamp brothers, the **Edisto Island Serpentarium** (1374 Hwy. 174, 843/869-1171, www.edistoserpentarium.com, hours vary, $13 adults, $10 ages 6–12, $6 ages 4–5, free under ages 3) is educational and fun, taking you up close and personal with a variety of reptilian creatures native to the area. The Serpentarium is on the main route into Edisto before you get to the beach area. Keep in mind they usually close Labor Day–April 30.

TOURS

Edisto has many beautiful plantation homes, relics of the island's longtime role as host to cotton plantations. While all are in private hands and therefore off limits to the public, an exception is offered through **Edisto Island Tours & T'ings** (843/869-9092, $20 adults, $10 under age 13). You'll take a van tour around Edisto's beautiful churches and old plantations. The only other way to see the homes is during the annual **Tour of Homes** (843/869-1954, www.edistomuseum.org) the second weekend in October, run by the Edisto Island Historic Preservation Society. Tickets sell out very early.

SHOPPING

Not only a convenient place to pick up odds and ends, the **Edistonian Gift Shop & Gallery** (406 Hwy. 174, 843/869-4466, daily 9 A.M.–7 P.M.) is also an important landmark, as the main supply point before you get into the main part of town. Think of a really nice convenience store with an attached gift shop and you'll get the picture. For various ocean gear, try the **Edisto Surf Shop** (145 Jungle Rd., 843/869-9283, daily 9 A.M.–5 P.M.). You can find whimsical Lowcountry-themed art for enjoyment or purchase at **Fish or Cut Bait Gallery** (142 Jungle Rd., 843/869-2511, www.fishorcutbaitgallery.com, Tues.–Sat. 10 A.M.–5 P.M.).

If you need some groceries, there's always the **Piggly Wiggly** (104 Jungle Rd., 843/869-0055, Sun.–Thurs. 7 A.M.–9 P.M., Fri.–Sat. 7 A.M.–10 P.M.) grocery store, a.k.a. "The Pig." For fresh seafood, try **Flowers Seafood Company** (1914 Hwy. 174, 843/869-0033, Mon.–Sat. 9 A.M.–7 P.M., Sun. 9 A.M.–5 P.M.).

SPORTS AND RECREATION

As the largest river of the ACE (Ashepoo, Combahee, Edisto) Basin complex, the Edisto River figures large in the lifestyle of residents and visitors. A good public landing is at Steamboat Creek off Highway 174 on the way down to the island. Take Steamboat Landing Road (Hwy. 968) from Highway 174 near the James Edwards School. Live Oak Landing is farther up Big Bay Creek near the Interpretive Center at the State Park. The **Edisto Marina** (3702 Docksite Rd., 843/869-3504) is on the far west side of the island.

Captain Ron Elliott of **Edisto Island Tours** (843/869-1937) offers various ecotours and fishing trips as well as canoe and kayak rentals

for about $25 per day. A typical kayak tour runs about $35 pp for a 1.5–2-hour trip, and he offers a "beachcombing" trip for $15 pp. **Ugly Ducklin'** (843/869-1580) offers creek and inshore fishing charters. You can get gear as well as reserve boat and kayak tours of the entire area, including into the ACE Basin, at **Edisto Watersports & Tackle** (3731 Docksite Rd., 843/869-0663, www.edistowatersports.com). Their guided tours run about $30 pp, with a two-hour rental running about $20.

Riding a bike on Edisto Beach and all around the island is a great relaxing way to get some exercise and enjoy its scenic, laidback beauty. The best place to rent a bike—or a kayak or canoe, for that matter—is **Island Bikes and Outfitters** (140 Jungle Rd., 843/869-4444, Mon.–Sat. 9 A.M.–4 P.M.). Bike rentals run about $16 per day; single kayaks are about $60 per day.

There's one golf course on the island, the 18-hole **Plantation Course at Edisto** (21 Fairway Dr., 843/869-1111, $60), finished in 2006.

ACCOMMODATIONS

A great thing about Edisto Island is the total absence of ugly chain lodging or beachfront condo development. My recommended option is staying at the **Edisto Beach State Park** (843/869-2156, www.southcarolinaparks.com, $25 tent sites, $75–100 cabins) itself, either at a campsite on the Atlantic side or in a marsh-front cabin on the northern edge. During high season (Apr.–Nov.), there's a minimum weeklong stay in the cabins; during the off-season, the minimum stay is two days. You can book cabins up to 11 months in advance, and I strongly recommend doing so as they go very quickly.

If you want something a little more plush, there are rental homes galore on Edisto Island. Because of the aforementioned lack of hotels, this is the most popular option for most vacationers here—indeed, it's just about the only option. Contact **Edisto Sales and Rentals**

Realty (1405 Palmetto Blvd., 800/868-5398, www.edistorealty.com).

FOOD

One of the all-time great barbecue places in South Carolina is on Edisto, **⊆ Po Pigs Bo-B-Q** (2410 Hwy. 174, 843/869-9003, Wed.–Sat. 11:30 A.M.–9 P.M., $4–10) on the way into town. This is the real thing, the full pig cooked in all its many ways: white meat, dark meat, cracklin's, and hash, served in the local style of "all you care to eat." Unlike many BBQ spots, they do serve beer and wine.

Another popular joint on the island is **Whaley's** (2801 Myrtle St., 843/869-2161, Tues.–Sat. 11:30 A.M.–2 P.M. and 5–9 P.M., bar daily 5 P.M.–2 A.M., $5–15), a down-home place in an old gas station a few blocks off the beach. This is a good place for casual seafood

like boiled shrimp, washed down with a lot of beer. The bar is open seven days a week.

Although it was closed in recent years, the legendary **⊆ Old Post Office** (1442 Hwy. 174, 843/869-2339, www.theoldpostofficeres-taurant.com, Tues.–Sun. 5:30–10 P.M., $20), a Lowcountry-style fine-dining spot, kept a devoted clientele for 20 years. It recently reopened with a bang and thankfully kept its old-school mystique intact. Specialties include fine crab cakes drizzled with mousseline sauce, the pecan-encrusted Veal Edistonian, and a Carolina rib eye topped with a pimiento cheese sauce, something of a state culinary tradition.

McConkey's Jungle Shack (108 Jungle Rd., 843/869-0097, Mon.–Fri. 11 A.M.–8 P.M., Sat.–Sun. 8 A.M.–8 P.M., $4–10) on the eastern end of the beach is known for its fish-and-chips basket and great burgers.

Hilton Head Island

Literally the prototype of the modern planned resort community, Hilton Head Island is also a case study in how utterly a landscape can change when enough money is introduced. From Reconstruction until the post–World War II era, the island consisted almost entirely of African Americans with deep historic roots in the area. In the mid-1950s Hilton Head began its transformation into an almost all-white, upscale golf, tennis, and shopping mecca populated largely by Northern transplants and retirees. As you can imagine, the flavor here is now quite different from surrounding areas of the Lowcountry, to say the least, with an emphasis on material excellence, top prices, get-it-done-yesterday punctuality, and the attendant aggressive traffic. Giving credit where it's due, however, Hilton Head knows what its target audience is and delivers the goods in a thoroughly professional manner. While it's easy to dismiss it as a sort of Disney World for the elite—a

disjointed collection of gated communities that take up 70 percent of its land—the truth is that millions of visitors, not all of them elite by any stretch, not only enjoy what Hilton Head has to offer, they swear by it. The attraction is quality, whether in the stunning beaches, outstanding cultural offerings, plush accommodations, attentive service, or copious merchandise. You won't see any litter, and you're unlikely to experience any crime. Certainly that's to Hilton Head's credit and no small reason for its continued success.

One of the unsung positive aspects of modern Hilton Head is its dedication to sustainable living. With the support of voters, the town routinely buys large tracts of land to preserve as open space. Hilton Head was the first municipality in the country to mandate the burying of all power lines, and one of the first to regularly use covenants and deed restrictions. All new development must conform to rigid guidelines

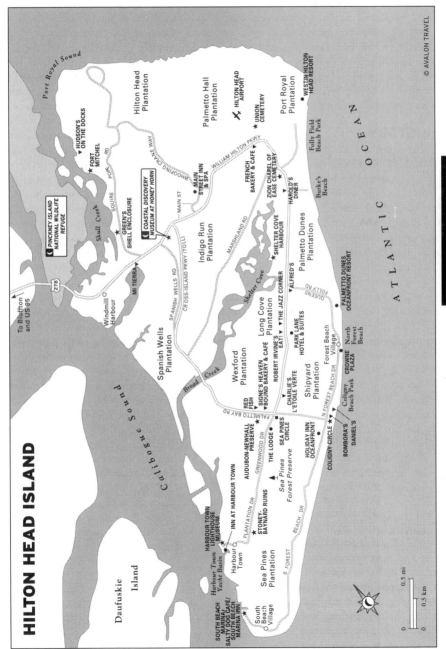

HILTON HEAD ISLAND

© AVALON TRAVEL

on setbacks and tree canopy. It has one of the most comprehensive signage ordinances in the country as well, which means no garish commercial displays will disrupt your views of the night sky. If those are "elite" values, then certainly we might do well in making them more mainstream.

HISTORY

The second-largest barrier island on the East Coast, Hilton Head Island was inhabited by Native Americans at least 10,000 years ago. It was named in 1663 by adventurer Sir William Hilton, who thoughtfully named the island—with its notable headland or "Head"—after himself. Hilton, who was from the British colony of Barbados, like many of Charleston's original settlers, was purposely trying to drum up interest in the island as a commercial venture, famously describing his new namesake as having "sweet water" and "clear sweet air." Though Hilton Head wasn't the first foothold of English colonization in Carolina, it did acquire commercial status first as the home of rice and indigo plantations. Later it gained fame as the first location of the legendary "Sea Island Cotton," a long-grain variety which, following its introduction in 1790 by William Elliott II of the Myrtle Bank Plantation, would soon be the dominant version of the cash crop.

Hilton Head planters were outspoken in the cause of American independence. The chief pattern in the Lowcountry during that conflict involved the British raiding Hilton Head and surrounding areas from their stronghold on Daufuskie Island, burning plantations and capturing slaves to be resold in Caribbean colonies. As a reminder of the savage guerrilla nature of the conflict in the South, British hit-and-run raids on Hilton Head continued for weeks after Cornwallis surrendered.

Nearby Bluffton was settled by planters from Hilton Head Island and the surrounding area in the early 1800s as a summer retreat. Though Charleston likes to claim the label today, Bluffton was actually the genuine "cradle of secession." Indeed, locals still joke that the town motto is "Divided We Stand." Fort Walker, a Confederate installation on the site of the modern Port Royal Plantation development on Hilton Head, was the target of the largest fleet ever assembled in North America at the time, when a massive Union force sailed into Port Royal Sound in October 1861. A month later, the fort—and effectively the entire area—had fallen, though by that time most white residents had long since fled. During the Civil War, Bluffton was also evacuated and, like Hilton Head, escaped serious action. However, in June 1863, Union troops destroyed most of the town except for about a dozen homes and two churches.

Though it seems unlikely given the island's modern demographics, Hilton Head was almost entirely African American through much of the 20th century. When Union troops occupied the island at the outbreak of the Civil War, freed and escaped slaves flocked to the island, and most of the dwindling number of African Americans on the island today are descendants of this original Gullah population.

For the first half of the 20th century, logging was Hilton Head's main commercial pursuit. Things didn't take their modern shape until the 1950s, when the Fraser family bought 19,000 of the island's 25,000 acres with the intent to continue forestry on them. But in 1956—not at all coincidentally the same year the first bridge to the island was built—Charles Fraser convinced his father to sell him the southern tip of Hilton Head. Fraser's brainchild and decades-long labor of love—some said his obsession—Sea Pines Plantation was the prototype of the golf-oriented resort community so common today on both U.S. coasts. Fraser himself was killed in a boating accident in 2002, but he survived to see Sea Pines encompass much of Hilton Head's economic activity, including Harbour

Town, and to see the Town of Hilton Head incorporated in 1983. Fraser is buried under the famous Liberty Oak in Harbour Town, which he personally made sure wasn't harmed during the development of the area.

ORIENTATION

Hilton Head Islanders have long referred to their island as the "shoe" and speak of driving to the toe or going to the heel. If you take a look at a map, you'll see why: Hilton Head bears an uncanny resemblance to a running shoe pointed toward the southeast, with the aptly named Broad Creek forming a near facsimile of the Nike "swoosh" symbol. Running the length and circumference of the shoe is the undisputed main drag, U.S. 278 Business (William Hilton Parkway), which crosses onto Hilton Head right at the "tongue" of the shoe, a relatively undeveloped area where there are still a few old African American communities. The new Cross Island Parkway toll route (U.S. 278), beginning up toward the ankle as you first get on the island, is a quicker, more convenient route straight to the toe near Sea Pines. While it is technically the business spur, when locals say "278" they're talking about the William Hilton Parkway. It takes you along the entire sole of the shoe, including the beaches, and on down to the toe, where you'll find a confusing, crazy British-style roundabout called Sea Pines Circle. It's also the site of the Harbour Town Marina and the island's oldest planned development, Sea Pines Plantation.

There's no "town center" per se, but activity here tends to revolve around just a few places: the Shelter Cove shopping and residential development near the entrance to the island; Coligny Plaza, an older, more casual shopping center near the main beach entrance; Sea Pines Circle, a center of nightlife; and two spots within Sea Pines itself, Harbour Town and South Beach—the former a blend of upscale and family attractions, and the latter catering a bit more to the beach crowd.

While making your way around the island, always keep in mind that the bulk of it consists of private developments, and local law enforcement frowns on people who aimlessly wander among the condos and villas.

SIGHTS

Contrary to what many think, there are quite a few things to do on Hilton Head that don't involve swinging a club at a little white ball or shopping for designer labels but instead celebrate the area's rich history and natural setting. The following are some of those attractions, arranged in geographical order from where you first access the island.

◖ Pinckney Island National Wildlife Refuge

Actually consisting of many islands and hammocks, Pinckney Island National Wildlife Refuge (912/652-4415, daily dawn–dusk, free) is the only part of this small but very well-managed 4,000-acre refuge that's open to the public. Almost 70 percent of the former rice plantation is salt marsh and tidal creeks, making it a perfect microcosm for the Lowcountry as a whole, as well as a great place to kayak or canoe. Native Americans liked the area as well, with a 10,000-year presence and over 100 archaeological sites being identified to date. Like many coastal refuges, it was a private game preserve for much of the 20th century. Some of the state's richest birding opportunities abound here, with observers able to spot gorgeous white ibis, rare wood storks, herons, egrets, eagles, and ospreys with little trouble from its miles of trails. Getting here is easy: On U.S. 278 east to Hilton Head, the refuge entrance is right between the two bridges onto the island.

Green's Shell Enclosure

Less known than the larger Native American shell ring farther south at Sea Pines, the Green's Shell Enclosure (803/734-3886, daily

© JIM MOREKIS

Pinckney Island National Wildlife Refuge

dawn–dusk) is certainly easier to find, and you don't have to pay $5 to enter the area, as with Sea Pines. This three-acre Heritage Preserve dates back to at least the 1300s.

The heart of the site comprises a low embankment, part of the original fortified village. Don't expect to be wowed—shell rings are a subtle pleasure. As is the case with most shell rings, the shells themselves are underneath a layer of dirt; don't disturb them.

To get here, take a left at the intersection of U.S. 278 and Squire Pope Road. Turn left into Greens Park, pass the office on the left, and park. The entrance to the shell enclosure is on the left behind a fence. You'll see a small community cemetery that has nothing to do with the shell ring; veer to your right to get to the short trail entrance. Camping is not allowed.

◖ Coastal Discovery Museum at Honey Horn

With the acquisition of Honey Horn's 70-acre spread of historic plantation land, Hilton Head finally has a full-fledged museum worthy of the name, and the magnificent Coastal Discovery Museum (70 Honey Horn Dr., 843/689-6767, www.coastaldiscovery.org, Mon.–Sat. 9 A.M.–4:30 P.M., Sun. 11 A.M.–3 P.M., free) is an absolute must-see, even for those who came to the island mostly to golf and soak up sun. (The name "Honey Horn" is supposedly based on a mispronunciation by field hands of one of the plantation's owning families, the Hannahans.)

The facility centers on the expertly restored Discovery House, the only antebellum house still existing on Hilton Head. But instead of being a Charleston- or Savannah-style house museum, the Discovery House now hosts a real museum, with exhibits and displays devoted to the history of the island, from the early Spanish explorers to the Sea Island cotton plantations to the modern day. The Museum is also a great one-stop place to sign up for a variety of specialty on-site and off-site guided tours, such as birding and Gullah history tours. The cost for most on-site tours is a very reasonable $10 adults and $5 children. The museum is also a partner with the state of South Carolina in a sea turtle protection program, which you can learn a lot more about once you're here.

But the real draw here is the 0.5-mile trail through the Honey Horn grounds, including several boardwalk viewpoints over the marsh, a neat little butterfly habitat, a few gardens, and a stable and pasture that host Honey Horn May and Tadpole, the museum's two Marsh Tackies—short, tough little ponies descended from Spanish horses and used to great effect by Francis "Swamp Fox" Marion and his freedom fighters in the American Revolution. The trail even features a replica of an ancient Native American shell ring of oyster shells, but do be aware that it is not a genuine shell ring (you can find the real thing at Green's Shell Enclosure a bit farther west on Highway 278 and in Sea Pines at the south end of the island).

While a glance at a map and area signage might convince you that you must pay the $1.25 toll on the Cross Island Parkway to get to Honey Horn, that isn't so. The exit to Honey Horn on the Parkway is actually before you get to the toll plaza, therefore access is free.

Union Cemetery

A modest but key aspect of African American history on Hilton Head is at Union Cemetery (Union Cemetery Rd.), a small burial ground featuring several graves of black Union Army troops (you can tell by the designation "USCI" on the tombstone, for "United States Colored Infantry"). Also of interest are the charming, hand-carved cement tombstones of nonveterans. To get here, turn north off of William Hilton Parkway onto Union Cemetery Road. The cemetery is a short way ahead on the left. There is no signage or site interpretation.

Fort Mitchel and Mitchelville

There's not much left of the old Union encampment at Fort Mitchel, nor of the freedman community, Mitchelville, which grew up alongside it. You can see the earthworks, a couple of cannons, and a historical marker on the grounds of the Hilton Head Plantation, a gated development. Tell the security guard you'd like to see Fort Mitchel. Once inside Hilton Head Plantation, take a left onto Seabrook Drive and then a right onto Skull Creek Drive. Fort Mitchel is a short way ahead on the left. It's not a well-maintained site, but it's an important part of local history.

At the intersection of Bay Gall and Beach City Roads is a marker for the site of Mitchelville, founded in 1862 as the first freedman settlement in the United States. Also on Beach City Road is a fenced-in area with what's left of Fort Howell, a Union encampment built by African American troops.

Zion Chapel of Ease Cemetery

More like one of the gloriously desolate scenes common to the rest of the Lowcountry, this little cemetery in full view of the William Hilton Parkway at Folly Field Road is all that remains of one of the "Chapels of Ease," a string of chapels set up in the 1700s. The Zion Chapel of Ease Cemetery (daily dawn–dusk, free) is said to be haunted by the ghost of William Baynard, whose final resting place is in a mausoleum on the site (the remains of his ancestral home are farther south at Sea Pines Plantation).

Audubon-Newhall Preserve

Plant lovers shouldn't miss this small but very well-maintained 50-acre wooded tract in the south-central part of the island on Palmetto Bay Road between the Cross Island Parkway and Sea Pines circle. Almost all plant life, even that in the water, is helpfully marked and identified. But if all you want to do is just enjoy, that's fine too, because the preserve has two miles of nature trails. Unusually, there's a well-preserved bog environment (*pocosin* to the

Audubon-Newhall Preserve

indigenous people here). The preserve (year-round dawn–dusk, free) is open to the public, but you can't camp here. For more information, call the Hilton Head Audubon Society (843/842-9246).

Sea Pines Plantation

This private residential resort development at the extreme west end of the island—first on Hilton Head and the prototype of every other such development in the country—hosts several attractions that collectively are well worth the $5 per vehicle "road use" fee, which you pay at the main entrance gate.

HARBOUR TOWN

It's not particularly historic and not all that natural, but Harbour Town is still pretty cool. The dominant element is the squat, colorful **Harbour Town Lighthouse Museum** (149 Lighthouse Rd., 843/671-2810, www.harbourtownlighthouse.com, daily 10 A.M.–dusk, $3),

which has never really helped a ship navigate its way near the island. The 90-foot structure was built in 1970 purely to give visitors a little atmosphere, and that it does, as kids especially love climbing the stairs to the top ($2 pp) and looking out over the island's expanse. This being Hilton Head, of course, there's a gift shop too. The other attractions here are the boisterous café and shopping scene around the marina and the nearby park area.

STONEY-BAYNARD RUINS

These tabby ruins (Plantation Dr., dawn–dusk, free) in a residential neighborhood are what remains of the circa-1790 central building of the old Braddock's Point Plantation, first owned by Patriot and raconteur Captain "Saucy Jack" Stoney and then the Baynard family. Active during the island's heyday as a cotton center, the plantation was destroyed after the Civil War. Site interpretation here is barebones, but suffice it to say that this is a great remaining example of colonial tabby architecture. Two other foundations are nearby, one for slave quarters and one whose use is still unknown. Note that there is a $5 fee to enter Sea Pines.

SEA PINES FOREST PRESERVE

The Sea Pines Forest Preserve (175 Greenwood Dr., 843/363-4530, free) is set amid the Sea Pines Plantation golf resort development, but you don't need a bag of clubs to enjoy this 600-acre preserve, which is built on the site of an old rice plantation (dikes and logging trails are still visible). Here you can ride a horse, fish, or just take a walk on the eight miles of trails (dawn–dusk) and enjoy the natural beauty around you. No bike riding is allowed on the trails, however.

In addition to the Native American shell ring farther north off Squire Pope Road, the Sea Pines Forest Preserve also boasts a shell ring set within a canopy of tall pines, forming a natural cathedral of sorts. A combination ceremonial area and communal common space, the shell ring today is actually a series of low rings made of discarded oyster shells covered with earth. The rewards here are contemplative in nature, since the vast bulk of the actual oyster shells are beneath layers of soil. Scientists date the ring itself to about 1450 B.C., although human habitation on the island goes as far back as 8000 B.C.

Tours and Cruises

Most guided tours on Hilton Head focus on the water. **Harbour Town Cruises** (843/363-9023, www.vagabondcruise.com) offers several sightseeing tours as well as excursions to Daufuskie and Savannah. They also offer a tour on a former America's Cup racing yacht.

"Dolphin tours" are extremely popular on Hilton Head, and there is no shortage of operators. **Dolphin Watch Nature Cruises** (843/785-4558, $25 adults, $10 children) departs from Shelter Cove, as does **Lowcountry Nature Tours** (843/683-0187, www.lowcountrynaturetours.com, $40 adults, $35 children, free under age 3). The *Gypsy* (843/363-2900, www.bitemybait.com, $15 adults, $7 children) sails out of South Beach Marina, taking you all around peaceful Calibogue Sound. Two dolphin tours are based on Broad Creek, the large body of water which almost bisects the island through the middle. "Captain Jim" runs **Island Explorer Tours** (843/785-2100, www.dolphintourshiltonhead.com, two-hour tour $45 pp) from a dock behind the old Oyster Factory on Marshland Road. Not to be outdone, "Captain Dave" leads tours at **Dolphin Discoveries** (843/681-1911, two-hour tour $40 adults, $30 under age 13), leaving out of Simmons Landing next to the Broad Creek Marina on Marshland Road. **Outside Hilton Head** (843/686-6996, www.outsidehiltonhead.com) runs a variety of water ecotours and dolphin tours as well as a guided day-trip excursion to Daufuskie, complete with golf cart rental.

There is a notable land-based tour by **Gullah**

Heritage Trail Tours (leaves from Coastal Discovery Museum at Honey Horn, 843/681-7066, www.gullahheritage.com, $32 adults, $15 children) delving into the island's rich, if poorly preserved, African American history, from slavery through the time of the freedmen.

ENTERTAINMENT AND EVENTS
Nightlife

The most high-quality live entertainment on the island is at **The Jazz Corner** (1000 William Hilton Pkwy., 843/842-8620, www.thejazzcorner.com, dinner daily 6–9 P.M., late-night menu after 9 P.M.), which brings in the best names in the country—and outstanding regulars like Bob Masteller and Howard Paul—to perform in this space in the somewhat unlikely setting of a boutique mall, the Village at Wexford. The dinners are actually quite good, but the attraction is definitely the music. Reservations are recommended. Live music starts around 7 P.M.

For years islanders have jokingly referred to the "Barmuda Triangle," an area named for the preponderance of bars within walking distance of Sea Pines Circle. While some of the names have changed over the years, the longtime anchor of the Barmuda Triangle is the **Tiki Hut** (1 S. Forest Beach Dr., 843/785-5126, Sun.–Thurs. 11 A.M.–8 P.M., Fri.–Sat. 11 A.M.–10 P.M., bar until 2 A.M.), actually part of the Holiday Inn Oceanfront Hotel at the entrance to Sea Pines. This popular watering hole is the only beachfront bar on the island, which technically makes it the only place you can legally drink alcohol on a Hilton Head beach. Another Barmuda Triangle staple is **Hilton Head Brewing Company** (7 Greenwood Dr., 843/785-3900, daily 11 A.M.–2 A.M.), the only brewpub on the island and indeed South Carolina's first microbrewery since Prohibition. They offer a wide range of handcrafted brews, from a Blueberry Wheat to a Mocha Porter. Another longtime Triangle fave is **The Lodge**

(7 Greenwood Dr., 843/842-8966, www.hiltonheadlodge.com). After the martini and cigar craze waned, this popular spot successfully remade itself into a beer-centric place with 36 rotating taps. They still mix a mean martini, though. Also nearby is **Murphy's Irish Pub** (81 Pope Ave., 843/842-3448, Mon. 5–10 P.M., Tues.–Thurs. 3 P.M.–midnight, Fri.–Sat. noon–4 A.M., Sun. 11 A.M.–10 P.M.), where the name pretty much says it all (unlike most pubs with made-up Irish names, this one's actually run by a guy named Murphy). There is great bangers and mash in this frequent rugby players' hangout.

Despite its location in the upscale strip mall of the Village at Wexford, the **British Open Pub** (1000 William Hilton Pkwy./Hwy. 278, 843/686-6736) offers a fairly convincing English vibe with, as the name suggests, a heavy golf theme. The fish-and-chips and shepherd's pie are both magnificent.

Inside Sea Pines is the **Quarterdeck Lounge and Patio** (843/842-1999, www.seapines.com, Sun.–Thurs. 5:30–10 P.M., Fri.–Sat. 5:30 P.M.–midnight) at the base of the Harbour Town Lighthouse. This is where the party's at after a long day on the fairways during the Heritage golf tournament. Within Sea Pines at the South Beach marina is also where you'll find **The Salty Dog Cafe** (232 S. Sea Pines Dr., 843/671-2233, www.saltydog.com, lunch daily 11 A.M.–3 P.M., dinner daily 5–10 P.M., bar daily until 2 A.M.), one of the area's most popular institutions (some might even call it a tourist trap) and something akin to an island empire, with popular T-shirts, a gift shop, books, and an ice cream shop, all overlooking the marina. My suggestion, however, is to make the short walk to the affiliated **Wreck of the Salty Dog** (843/671-7327, daily until 2 A.M.) where the marsh views are better and the atmosphere not quite so tacky.

There's only one bona fide gay club on Hilton Head, **Vibe** (32 Palmetto Bay Rd., 843/341-6933, www.vibehhi.com, Mon.–Fri. 8 P.M.–3 A.M., Sat. 8 P.M.–2 A.M.). Wednesday is karaoke night, and Thursdays bring an amateur drag revue.

Performing Arts

Because so many residents migrated here from art-savvy metropolitan areas in the Northeast, Hilton Head maintains a very high standard of top-quality entertainment. Much of the activity centers on the multimillion-dollar **Arts Center of Coastal Carolina** (14 Shelter Cove Lane, 843/842-2787, www.artshhi.com), which hosts touring shows, resident companies, musical concerts, dance performances, and visual arts exhibits.

Now over a quarter-century old and under the direction of maestro John Morris Russell, the **Hilton Head Symphony Orchestra** (843/842-2055, www.hhso.org) performs a year-round season of masterworks and pops programs at various venues, primarily the First Presbyterian Church (540 William Hilton Pkwy./Hwy. 278). They also take their show on the road with several concerts in Bluffton and even perform several "Symphony Under the Stars" programs at Shelter Cove. **Chamber Music Hilton Head** (www.cmhh.org) performs throughout the year with selections ranging from Brahms to Smetana at All Saints Episcopal Church (3001 Meeting St.).

The **South Carolina Repertory Company** (136 Beach City Rd., 843/342-2057, www.hiltonheadtheatre.com) performs an eclectic, challenging season, including musicals, cutting-edge drama, and the avant-garde.

Cinema

There's an art house on Hilton Head, the charming **Coligny Theatre** (843/686-3500, www.colignytheatre.com) in the Coligny Plaza shopping center before you get to Sea Pines. For years this was the only movie theater for miles around, but it has reincarnated as a primarily

© JIM MOREKIS

the Coligny Theatre

indie film venue. Look for the entertaining murals by local artist Ralph Sutton. Showtimes are Monday 11:30 A.M. and 4 P.M., Tuesday and Friday 11:30 A.M., 4 P.M., and 7 P.M., Wednesday–Thursday and Saturday–Sunday 4 P.M. and 7 P.M.

The main multiplex on Hilton Head is **Northridge Cinema 10** (Hwy. 278 and Mathews Dr., 843/342-3800, www.southeastcinemas.com) in the Northridge Plaza shopping center. Off the island is the way-cool new **Sea Turtle Cinemas** (106 Buckwalter Pkwy., 843/706-2888, www.seaturtlecinemas.com) in the Berkeley Place shopping center. To get here, take the William Hilton Parkway (U.S. 278) west off Hilton Head for about 10 miles. Turn left at Buckwalter Parkway. Sea Turtle Cinemas is 0.5 miles farther on the right.

Festivals and Events

Late February–early March brings the **Hilton Head Wine and Food Festival** (www.hiltonheadhospitality.org), culminating in what they call "The East Coast's Largest Outdoor Public Tasting and Auction," which is generally held at the Coastal Discovery Museum at Honey Horn. Some events charge admission.

Hilton Head's premier event is the **RBC Heritage Classic Golf Tournament** (843/671-2248, http://theheritagegolfsc.com), held each April (usually the week after the Master's) at the Harbour Town Golf Links on Sea Pines Plantation. Formerly known as the Verizon Heritage Classic, the event is South Carolina's only PGA Tour event and brings thousands of visitors to town yearly.

A fun and fondly anticipated yearly event is the **Kiwanis Club Chili Cookoff** (www.hiltonheadkiwanis.org), held each October at Honey Horn on the south end. A low admission price gets you all the chili you can eat plus free antacids. All funds go to charity, and all excess chili goes to a local food bank.

Every November brings Hilton Head's

second-largest event, the **Hilton Head Concours d'Elegance & Motoring Festival** (www.hhiconcours.com), a multiday event bringing together vintage car clubs from throughout the nation and culminating in a prestigious "Best of Show" competition. It started as a fund-raiser for the Hilton Head Symphony, but now people come from all over the country to see these fine vintage cars in a beautiful setting.

SHOPPING

As you'd expect, Hilton Head is a shopper's delight, with an emphasis on upscale stores and prices to match. Keep in mind that hours may be shortened in the off-season (Nov.–Mar.). Here's a rundown of the main island shopping areas in the order you'll encounter them as you enter the island.

Shelter Cove

As of this writing, the Mall at Shelter Cove is being completely repurposed, with plans for boutique retail centered around a Belk anchor store. The other two shopping entities at this shopping area on Broad Creek right off the William Hilton Parkway are the **Plaza at Shelter Cove** and the dockside **Shelter Cove Harbour**. The most interesting store at the Plaza is the flagship location of **Outside Hilton Head** (843/686-6996, www. outsidehiltonhead.com, Mon.–Sat. 10 A.M.–5:30 P.M., Sun. 11 A.M.–5:30 P.M.), a complete outdoor outfitter with a thoroughly knowledgeable staff. Whatever outdoor gear you need and whatever tour you want to take, they can most likely hook you up. Shelter Cove Harbour hosts a few cute shops hewing to its overall nautical-vacation theme, such as the clothing stores **Camp Hilton Head** (843/842-3666, Mon.–Sat. 10 A.M.–9 P.M., Sun. noon–5 P.M.) and the marine supplier **Ship's Store** (843/842-7001, Mon.–Sat. 7:30 A.M.–5 P.M., Sun. 7:30 A.M.–4 P.M.).

Village at Wexford

Easily my favorite place to shop on Hilton Head, this well-shaded shopping center on William Hilton Parkway (Hwy. 278) hosts plenty of well-tended shops, including the foodie equipment store **Le Cookery** (843/785-7171, Mon.–Sat. 10 A.M.–6 P.M.), the Lily Pulitzer signature women's store **S.M. Bradford Co.** (843/686-6161, Mon.–Sat. 10 A.M.–6 P.M.) and the aromatic **Scents of Hilton Head** (843/842-7866, Mon.–Fri. 10 A.M.–6 P.M., Sat. 10 A.M.–5 P.M.).

My favorite shop on all Hilton Head is at Wexford, **The Oilerie** (843/681-2722, www. oilerie.com, Mon.–Sat. 10 A.M.–7 P.M., Sun. noon–5 P.M.). This franchise provides free samples of all its high-quality Italian olive oils and vinegars. After you taste around awhile, you pick what you want and the friendly staff bottles it for you in souvenir-quality glassware. They also have a selection of spices, soaps, and other goodies.

Coligny Circle

This is the closest Hilton Head comes to funkier beach towns like Tybee Island or Folly Beach, although it doesn't really come that close. You'll find dozens of delightful and somewhat quirky stores here, many keeping long hours in the summer, like the self-explanatory **Coligny Kite & Flag Co.** (843/785-5483, Mon.–Sat. 10 A.M.–9 P.M., Sun. 11 A.M.–6 P.M.), the hippie-fashion **Loose Lucy's** (843/785-8093, Mon.–Sat. 10 A.M.–6 P.M., Sun. 11 A.M.–5 P.M.), and the Caribbean-flavored **Jamaican Me Crazy** (843/785-9006, daily 10 A.M.–10 P.M.). Kids will love both **The Shell Shop** (843/785-4900, Mon.–Sat. 10 A.M.–9 P.M., Sun. noon–9 P.M.) and **Black Market Minerals** (843/785-7090, Mon.–Sat. 10 A.M.–10 P.M., Sun. 11 A.M.–8 P.M.).

Harbour Town

The Shoppes at Harbour Town (www.seapines.com) are a collection of about 20 mostly boutique stores along Lighthouse Road in

Sea Pines Plantation. At **Planet Hilton Head** (843/363-5177, www.planethiltonhead.com, daily 10 A.M.–9 P.M.) you'll find some cute, eclectic gifts and home goods. Other clothing highlights include **Knickers Men's Store** (843/671-2291, daily 10 A.M.–9 P.M.) and **Radiance** (843/363-5176), a very cute and fashion-forward women's store.

The **Top of the Lighthouse Shoppe** (843/671-2810, www.harbourtownlighthouse. com, daily 10 A.M.–9 P.M.) is where many a climbing visitor has been coaxed to part with some of their disposable income. And, of course, as you'd expect being near the legendary Harbour Town links, there's the **Harbour Town Pro Shop** (843/671-4485), routinely voted one of the best pro shops in the nation.

South Beach Marina

On South Sea Pines Drive at the Marina you'll find several worthwhile shops, including a good ship's store and all-around grocery dealer **South Beach General Store** (843/671-6784, daily 8 A.M.–10 P.M.). I like to stop in the **Blue Water Bait and Tackle** (843/671-3060, daily 7 A.M.–8 P.M.) and check out the cool nautical stuff. They can also hook you up with a variety of kayak trips and fishing charters. And, of course, right on the water there's the ever-popular **Salty Dog Cafe** (843/671-2233, www. saltydog.com, lunch daily 11 A.M.–3 P.M., dinner daily 5–10 P.M.), whose ubiquitous T-shirts seem to adorn every other person on the island.

Thrift Shops

Don't scoff: Every thrift store connoisseur knows the best place to shop secondhand is in an affluent area like Hilton Head, where the locals try hard to stay in style and their castoffs are first-class. Key stops here are **The Bargain Box** (546 William Hilton Pkwy., 843/681-4305, Mon., Wed., and Fri. 1–4 P.M., Thurs. 2–5 P.M., Sat. 9:15 A.M.–12:15 P.M.) and **St. Francis Thrift Store** (2 Southwood Dr.,

843/689-6563, Wed.–Sat. 10 A.M.–3 P.M.) right off the William Hilton Parkway.

Art Galleries

Despite the abundant wealth apparent in some quarters here, there's no freestanding art museum in the area, that role being filled by independent galleries. A good representative example is **Morris & Whiteside Galleries** (220 Cordillo Pkwy., 843/842-4433, www.morris-whiteside.com, Mon.–Fri. 9 A.M.–5 P.M., Sat. 10 A.M.–4 P.M.), located in the historic Red Piano Art Gallery building, which features a variety of paintings and sculpture, heavy on landscapes but also showing some fine figurative work. The nonprofit **Art League of Hilton Head** (14 Shelter Cove Lane, 843/681-5060, Mon.–Sat. 10 A.M.–6 P.M.) is located in the Walter Greer Art Gallery within the Arts Center of Coastal Carolina and displays work by member artists in all media. The **Nash Gallery** (13 Harbourside Lane, 843/785-6424, Mon.–Fri. 10 A.M.–9 P.M., Sat. 10 A.M.–8 P.M., Sun. 11 A.M.–5 P.M.) in Shelter Cove Harbour deals more in North American craft styles. Hilton Head art isn't exactly known for its avant-garde nature, but you can find some whimsical stuff at **Picture This** (78D Arrow Rd., 843/842-5299, Mon.–Fri. 9:30 A.M.–5:30 P.M., Sat. 9:30 A.M.–12:30 P.M.), including a selection of Gullah craft items. A wide range of regional painters, sculptors, and glass artists is featured at **Endangered Arts** (841 William Hilton Pkwy., 843/785-5075, www. endangeredarts.com).

SPORTS AND RECREATION
Beaches

First, the good news: Hilton Head Island has 12 miles of some of the most beautiful safe beaches you'll find anywhere. The bad news is that there are only a few ways to gain access, generally at locations referred to as "beach parks." Don't just drive into a residential

© JIM MOREKIS

The beach at Hilton Head is particularly well-suited for bicycles.

neighborhood and think you'll be able to park and find your way to the beach; for better or worse, Hilton Head is not set up for that kind of casual access.

Driessen Beach Park has 207 long-term parking spaces, costing $0.25 for 30 minutes. There's free parking but fewer spaces at the Coligny Beach Park entrance and at Fish Haul Creek Park. Also, there are 22 metered spaces at Alder Lane Beach Access, 51 at Folly Field Beach Park, and 13 at Burkes Beach Road. Most other beach parks are for permit parking only. Clean, well-maintained public restrooms are available at all the beach parks. You can find beach information at 843/342-4580 and www.hiltonheadislandsc.gov. Beach Park hours vary: Coligny Beach Park is open daily 24 hours; all other beach parks are open March–September daily 6 A.M.–8 P.M. and October–February daily 6 A.M.–5 P.M.

Alcohol is strictly prohibited on Hilton Head's beaches. This may cut down on your vacation fun, but the plus side is the ban makes the beaches very friendly for families. There are lifeguards on all the beaches during the summer, but be aware that the worst undertow is on the northern stretches. Also remember to leave the sand dollars where they are; their population is dwindling due to souvenir hunting.

Kayaking

Kayakers will enjoy Hilton Head Island, which offers several gorgeous routes, including Calibogue Sound to the south and west and Port Royal Sound to the north. For particularly good views of life on the salt marsh, try Broad Creek, which nearly bisects Hilton Head Island, and Skull Creek, which separates Hilton Head from the natural beauty of Pinckney Island. Broad Creek Marina is a good place to put in. There are also two public landings, Haigh Landing and Buckingham Landing, on Mackay Creek at the entrance to the island, one on either side of the bridge.

If you want a guided tour, there are plenty of great kayak tour outfits to choose from in the area. Chief among them is certainly **Outside Hilton Head** (32 Shelter Cove Lane, 800/686-6996, www.outsidehiltonhead.com). They offer a wide range of guided trips, including "The Outback," in which you're first boated to a private island and then taken on a tour of tidal creeks, and five- or seven-hour "Ultimate Lowcountry Day" trips to Daufuskie, Bluffton, or Bull Creek. Other good places to book a tour or just rent a kayak are **Water-Dog Outfitters** (Broad Creek Marina, 843/686-3554) and **Kayak Hilton Head** (Broad Creek Marina, 843/684-1910). Leaving out of the Harbour Town Yacht Basin is **H2O Sports** (843/671-4386, www.h2osportsonline.com), which offers 90-minute guided kayak tours ($30) and rents kayaks for about $20 per hour. Within Palmetto Dunes Oceanfront Resort (4 Queens Folly Rd., 800/827-3006, www.palmetto-dunes.com) is **Palmetto Dunes Outfitters** (843/785-2449, www.pdoutfitters.com, daily 9 A.M.–5 P.M.), which rents kayaks and canoes and offers lessons on the resort's 11-mile lagoon.

Fishing and Boating

As you'd expect, anglers and boaters love the Hilton Head–Bluffton area, which offers all kinds of saltwater, freshwater, and fly-fishing opportunities. Captain Brian Vaughn runs **Off the Hook Charters** (68 Helmsman Way, 843/298-4376, www.offthehookcharters.com), which offers fully licensed half-day trips ($400). **Miss Carolina Sportfishing** (168 Palmetto Bay Rd., 843/298-2628, www.misscarolinafishing.com) offers deep-sea action at a little over $100 per hour. Captain Dave Fleming of **Mighty Mako Sport Fishing Charters** (164 Palmetto Bay Rd., 843/785-6028, www.mightymako.com) can take you saltwater fishing, both back-water and near-shore, on the 25-foot *Mighty Mako* for about $400 for a half-day. If you're at the South Beach Marina area of Sea Pines

Plantation, head into **Blue Water Bait and Tackle** (843/671-3060) and see if they can hook you up with a trip.

Public landings in the Hilton Head area include the Marshland Road Boat Landing and the Broad Creek Boat Ramp under the Charles Fraser Bridge, and the Haigh Landing on Mackay Creek.

Hiking and Biking

Although the very flat terrain is not challenging, Hilton Head provides some scenic and relaxing cycling opportunities. Thanks to wise planning and foresight, the island has an extensive award-winning 50-mile network of biking trails that does a great job of keeping cyclists out of traffic. A big plus is the long bike path paralleling the William Hilton Parkway, enabling cyclists to use that key artery without braving its traffic. There is even an underground bike path beneath the Parkway to facilitate crossing that busy road. In addition, there are also routes along Pope Avenue as well as North and South Forest Beach Drive. Go to www.hiltonheadisland.org/biking to download a map of the entire island bike path network.

For biking purposes, be aware that on some private resort developments, access technically is limited to residents, and you may be challenged and asked where you're residing. Also, pay attention to the miniature stop signs on the bike paths, ignorance of which can lead to some nasty scrapes or worse.

Palmetto Dunes Oceanfront Resort (4 Queens Folly Rd., 800/827-3006, www.pal-mettodunes.com) has a particularly nice 25-mile network of bike paths that all link up to the island's larger framework. Within the resort is **Palmetto Dunes Outfitters** (843/785-2449, www.pdoutfitters.com, daily 9 A.M.–5 P.M.), which will rent you any type of bike you might need. Sea Pines Plantation also has an extensive 17-mile network of bike trails; you can pick up a map at most information kiosks within the plantation.

BEAUFORT

But the best bike path on Hilton Head is the simplest of all, where no one will ask you where you're staying that night: the beach. For a few hours before and after low tide, the beach effectively becomes a 12-mile bike path around most of the island, and a pleasant morning or afternoon ride may well prove to be the highlight of your trip.

There's a plethora of bike rental facilities on Hilton Head with competitive rates. Be sure to ask if they offer free pickup and delivery. Try **Hilton Head Bicycle Company** (112 Arrow Rd., 843/686-6888, Mon.–Sat. 9 A.M.–5 P.M., Sun. noon–5 P.M.).

Hikers will particularly enjoy Pinckney Island National Wildlife Refuge, which takes you through several key Lowcountry ecosystems, from maritime forest to salt marsh. Other peaceful, if nonchallenging, trails are at the Audubon-Newhall Preserve.

Horseback Riding

Within the Sea Pines Forest Preserve is **Lawton Stables** (190 Greenwood Dr., 843/671-2586, www.lawtonstableshhi.com), which features pony rides, a small animal farm, and guided horseback rides through the preserve. You don't need any riding experience, but you do need reservations.

Bird-Watching

The premier birding locale in the area is the **Pinckney Island National Wildlife Refuge** (U.S. 278 east, just before Hilton Head, 912/652-4415, www.fws.gov, free). You can see bald eagles, ibis, wood storks, painted buntings, and many more species. Birding is best in spring and fall. The refuge has several freshwater ponds that serve as wading bird rookeries. During migratory season, so many beautiful birds make such a ruckus that you'll think you've wandered onto an Animal Planet shoot. Another good bird-watching locale is **Victoria Bluff Heritage Preserve**

(803/734-3886, daily dawn–dusk, free), a 1,100-acre pine-and-palmetto habitat. Get here from Hilton Head by taking U.S. 278 off the island. Take a right onto Sawmill Creek Road heading north. The parking area is shortly ahead on the right. Note that there are no facilities here.

Golf

Hilton Head is one of the world's great golf centers, with no less than 23 courses, and one could easily write a book about nothing but that. This, however, is not that book. Perhaps contrary to what you might expect, most courses on the island are public, and some are downright affordable. All courses are 18 holes unless otherwise described; green fees are averages and vary with season and tee time.

The best-regarded course, with prices to match, is **Harbour Town Golf Links** (Sea Pines Plantation, 843/363-4485, www.seapines.com, $239). It's on the island's south end at Sea Pines and is the home of the annual RBC Heritage Classic, far and away the island's number-one tourist draw.

There are two Arthur Hills–designed courses on the island, **Arthur Hills at Palmetto Dunes Resort** (843/785-1140, www.palmettodunes.com, $125) and **Arthur Hills at Palmetto Hall** (Palmetto Hall Plantation, 843/689-4100, www.palmettohallgolf.com, $130), both of which now offer the use of Segway vehicles on the fairways. The reasonably priced **Barony Course** at Port Royal Plantation (843/686-8801, www.portroyalgolfclub.com, $98) also boasts some of the toughest greens on the island. Another challenging and affordable course is the **George Fazio** at Palmetto Dunes Resort (843/785-1130, www.palmettodunes.com, $105).

Hilton Head National Golf Club (60 Hilton Head National Dr., 843/842-5900, www.golf-hiltonheadnational.com), which is actually on the mainland just before you cross the bridge to

Hilton Head, not only boasts a total of 27 challenging holes but is consistently rated among the best golf locales in the world for both condition and service. *Golf Week* has named it one of the country's best golf courses. All three courses are public and green fees at each are below $100.

It's a good idea to book tee times through the **Golf Island Call Center** (888/465-3475, www.golfisland.com), which can also hook you up with good packages.

Tennis

One of the top tennis destinations in the country, Hilton Head has over 20 tennis clubs, some of which offer court time to the public (walk-on rates vary; call for information). They are: **Palmetto Dunes Tennis Center** (Palmetto Dunes Resort, 843/785-1152, www.palmettodunes.com, $30 per hour), **Port Royal Racquet Club** (Port Royal Plantation, 843/686-8803, www.portroyalgolfclub.com, $25 per hour), **Sea Pines Racquet Club** (Sea Pines Plantation, 843/363-4495, www.seapines.com, $25 per hour), **South Beach Racquet Club** (Sea Pines Plantation, 843/671-2215, www.seapines.com, $25 per hour), and **Shipyard Racquet Club** (Shipyard Plantation, 843/686-8804, $25 per hour).

Free, first-come-first-served play is available at the following public courts, maintained by the Island Recreation Association (www.islandreccenter.org): **Chaplin Community Park** (Singleton Beach Rd., four courts, lighted), **Cordillo Courts** (Cordillo Pkwy., four courts, lighted), **Fairfield Square** (Adrianna Lane, two courts), **Hilton Head High School** (School Rd., six courts), and **Hilton Head Middle School** (Wilborn Rd., four courts).

ACCOMMODATIONS

Generally speaking, accommodations on Hilton Head are often surprisingly affordable given their overall high quality and the breadth of their amenities.

Under $150

You can't beat the price at **Park Lane Hotel and Suites** (12 Park Lane, 843/686-5700, www.hiltonheadparklanehotel.com, $130). This is your basic suite-type hotel (formerly a Residence Inn) with kitchens, laundry, a pool, and a tennis court. The allure here is the price, hard to find anywhere these days at a resort location. For a nonrefundable fee, you can bring your pet. The one drawback is that the beach is a good distance away. The hotel does offer a free shuttle, however, so it would be wise to take advantage of that and avoid the usual beach parking hassles. As you'd expect given the price, rooms here tend to go quickly; reserve early.

$150-300

By Hilton Head standards, the **◖Main Street Inn & Spa** (2200 Main St., 800/471-3001, www.mainstreetinn.com, $160–210) can be considered a bargain stay, and with high quality to boot. With its Old World touches, sumptuous appointments, charming atmosphere, and attentive service, this 33-room inn and attached spa on the grounds of Hilton Head Plantation seem like they would be more at home in Charleston than Hilton Head. The inn serves a great full breakfast—not continental—daily 7:30–10:30 A.M. As a bonus, most of the less-expensive guest rooms have a great view of the formal garden, another part of that old Lowcountry appeal that's hard to come by on the island. If you want to upgrade, there are larger guest rooms with a fireplace and a smallish private courtyard for not much more. Overall, it's one of Hilton Head's best values.

Another good place for the price is the **South Beach Marina Inn** (232 S. Sea Pines Dr., 843/671-6498, www.sbinn.com, $186) in Sea Pines. Located near the famous Salty Dog Cafe and outfitted in a similar nautical theme, the inn not only has some pretty large guest rooms for the price, it offers a great view of the marina and has a very friendly feel, great for families

BEAUFORT

with kids and romantic couples alike (especially with a beach on calm Calibogue Sound only a few minutes' walk away). As with all Sea Pines accommodations, staying on the plantation means you don't have to wait in line with other visitors to pay the $5-per-day "road fee." Sea Pines also offers a free trolley to get around the plantation.

One of Hilton Head's favorite hotels for beach lovers is the **Holiday Inn Oceanfront** (1 South Forest Beach Dr., 843/785-5126, www.hihiltonhead.com, $200), home of the famed Tiki Hut bar on the beach. Staff turnover is less frequent here than at other local accommodations, and while it's no Ritz-Carlton and occasionally shows signs of wear, it's a good value on a bustling area of the island. Parking has always been a problem here, but at least there's free valet service.

One of the better resort-type places for those who prefer the putter and the racquet to the Frisbee and the surfboard is the **Inn at Harbour Town** (7 Lighthouse Lane, 843/363-8100, www.seapines.com, $199) in Sea Pines. The big draw here is the impeccable service, delivered by a staff of "butlers" in kilts, mostly Europeans who take the venerable trade quite seriously. While it's not on the beach, you can take advantage of the free Sea Pines Trolley every 20 minutes.

Recently rated the number-one family resort in the U.S. by *Travel + Leisure,* the well-run ◖ **Palmetto Dunes Oceanfront Resort** (4 Queens Folly Rd., 800/827-3006, www.palmettodunes.com, $150–300) offers something for everybody in terms of lodging. There are small, cozy condos by the beach or larger villas overlooking the golf course and pretty much everything in between. The prices are perhaps disarmingly affordable considering the relative luxury and copious recreational amenities, which include 25 miles of very well-done bike trails, 11 miles of kayak and canoe trails, and, of course, three signature links. As with most developments of this type on Hilton Head, most of the condos are privately owned, and therefore each has its particular set of guidelines and cleaning schedules.

A little farther down the island you'll find the **Crowne Plaza Hilton Head Island** (130 Shipyard Dr., 877/620-1682, www.cphiltonhead.com, $160–200), which styles itself as Hilton Head's only green-certified accommodations. The guest rooms are indeed state-of-the-art, and the expansive shaded grounds near the beach are great for relaxation. No on-site golf here, but immediately adjacent is a well-regarded tennis facility with 20 courts.

Another good resort-style experience heavy on the golf is on the grounds of the Port Royal Plantation on the island's north side, **The Westin Resort Hilton Head Island** (2 Grasslawn Ave., 843/681-4000, www.westin.com/hiltonhead, from $200), which hosts three PGA-caliber links. The beach is also but a short walk away. This AAA four diamond–winning Westin offers a mix of suites and larger villas.

Vacation Rentals

Many visitors to Hilton Head choose to rent a home or villa for an extended stay, and there is no scarcity of availability. Try **Resort Rentals of Hilton Head** (www.hhivacations.com) or **Destination Vacation** (www.destinationvacationhhi.com).

FOOD

You'll have no problem finding good restaurants in and around Hilton Head, with a great combination of taste and a comparatively casual atmosphere. Because of the cosmopolitan nature of the population, with so many transplants from the northeastern United States and Europe, there is uniformly high quality. Because of another demographic quirk of the area, its large percentage of senior citizens, you can also find some great deals by looking for some of the common "early bird" dinner specials, usually starting around 5 P.M.

The Crowne Plaza has expansive, relaxing grounds.

Breakfast and Brunch

There are a couple of great diner-style places on the island. Though known more for its hamburgers and Philly cheesesteaks, **❰ Harold's Diner** (641 William Hilton Pkwy., 843/842-9292, Mon.–Sat. 7 A.M.–3 P.M., $4–6) has great pancakes as well as its trademark brand of sarcastic service. Unpretentious and authentic in a place where those two adjectives are rarely used, it has been said of Harold's that "the lack of atmosphere *is* the atmosphere." Be aware that the place is small, popular, and reservations are not taken.

If you need a bite in the Coligny Plaza area, go to **Skillets** (1 N. Forest Beach Dr., 843/785-3131, www.skilletscafe.com, breakfast daily 7 A.M.–5 P.M., dinner daily 5–9 P.M., $5–23) in Coligny Plaza. Their eponymous stock-in-trade is a layered breakfast dish of sautéed ingredients served in a porcelain skillet, like the "Kitchen Sink" (pancakes ringed with potatoes, sausage, and bacon, topped with two poached eggs).

A great all-day breakfast place with a twist is **❰ Signe's Heaven Bound Bakery & Café** (93 Arrow Rd., 843/785-9118, www.signesbakery.com, Mon.–Fri. 8 A.M.–4 P.M., Sat. 9 A.M.–2 P.M., $5–10). Breakfast is tasty dishes like frittatas and breakfast polenta, while the twist is the extensive artisanal bakery, with delicious specialties like the signature key lime pound cake. You'll be surprised at the quality of the food for the low prices. Expect a wait in line at the counter during peak periods.

A fairly well-kept local secret is the **French Bakery and Courtyard Cafe** (430 William Hilton Pkwy./U.S. 278, 843/342-5420, www.frenchbakeryhiltonhead.com, Mon.–Sat. 8:30 A.M.–4 P.M., $5). Set inside the Pineland Station shopping center and with nice open-air seating, French Bakery offers a full range of fresh-baked goods like quiches, croissants, paninis, artisanal breads, cakes, and gourmet pastries.

German

I'm pretty sure you didn't come all the way

to South Carolina to eat traditional German food, but while you're here...check out **◖Alfred's** (807 William Hilton Pkwy./Hwy. 278, 843/341-3117, wwww.alfredsofhiltonhead.com, $20–30), one of the more unique spots on Hilton Head and a big favorite with the locals. Expect a wait. Bratwurst, veal cordon bleu, and of course wiener schnitzel are all standouts. I recommend the German Mix Platter ($25), which features a brat, some sauerbraten, and a schnitzel. That said, owner-chef Alfred Kettering actually offers a lot more than just German food, with a killer veal scaloppine and great grilled salmon, among others. Interestingly, the extensive wine list is overwhelmingly Californian, with only a single German entry, a riesling.

Mediterranean

For upscale Italian, try **Bistro Mezzaluna** (55 New Orleans Rd., 843/842-5011, daily 5–9:30 P.M.). Known far and wide for its osso buco as well as its impeccable service, there's also a great little bar for cocktails before or after dinner.

Mexican

There are a couple of excellent and authentic Mexican restaurants on the island. Just off the William Hilton Parkway near the island's entrance is **◖Mi Tierra** (160 Fairfield Square, 843/342-3409, lunch daily 11 A.M.–4 P.M., dinner Mon.–Fri. 4–9 P.M., Sat.–Sun. 4–10 P.M., $3–15). You'll find lots of traditional seafood dishes, like seviche, octopus, shrimp, and oysters. On Mondays there is often a real mariachi band.

Another great Mexican place—also with a Bluffton location—is **Amigo's Café Y Cantina** (70 Pope Ave., 843/785-8226, Mon.–Sat. 11 A.M.–9 P.M., $8). While its strip-mall locale is not great, the food is fresh, simple, excellent, fast, and inexpensive.

Middle Eastern

Hard to describe but well worth the visit,

◖ Daniel's Restaurant and Lounge (2 N. Forest Beach Dr., 843/341-9379, http://danielshhi.com, daily 4 P.M.–2 A.M., tapas $10–12) combines elements of a traditional Middle Eastern eatery, an upscale tapas place, a beach spot, and a swank bar scene to create one of the more memorable food-and-beverage experiences on the island. Add in the fact that the prices are actually quite accessible and you've got a must-visit. Their "big small plates," meaning larger-portion tapas, run about $10–12 per plate. While they market their Middle Eastern flavor with plates like the cinnamon lamb kebab, their tapas have a cosmopolitan feel and range from a Caribbean salmon steak to chicken pesto sliders.

New Southern

A fairly new addition to the island's foodie scene, **Robert Irvine's Eat!** (1000 William Hilton Pkwy./Hwy. 278, 843/785-4850, www.eathhi.com, dinner Mon.–Sat. from 5 P.M., $15–30), in the Village at Wexford shopping center, is of course a creation of the eponymous Food Channel celebrity chef, who is often seen in the restaurant. The menu tends toward Charleston-esque upgrades of traditional classics, such as the fennel-brined pork chop, blackened snapper and grits, and an extensive tapas menu that includes a she-crab bisque and, yes, fried green tomatoes. Reservations are strongly recommended.

For a casual but tasty sandwich in Coligny Plaza, go straight to **◖ Bombora's Grille and Chill Bar** (101 Pope Ave., 843/689-2662, www.bomborasgrille.com, Mon.–Tues. 1 P.M.–midnight, Wed.–Fri. 11 A.M.–midnight, Sat.–Sun. noon–midnight, $10–15) and order the pulled pork sandwich. Though technically the lack of sauce means it's not barbecue—hence the name—this is an excellent and hearty dish that can stand alongside the 'cue at more "authentic" places. Even the fries are delicious. Wash it all down with a selection from their wide range of handcrafted beers in regular or large growler size.

Seafood

Not to be confused with Charley's Crab House next door to Hudson's, seafood lovers will enjoy the experience down near Sea Pines at ◖ **Charlie's L'Etoile Verte** (8 New Orleans Rd., 843/785-9277, http://charliesgreenstar. com, lunch Tues.–Sat. 11:30 A.M.–2 P.M., dinner Mon.–Sat. 5:30–10 P.M., $25–40), which is considered by many connoisseurs to be Hilton Head's single best restaurant. The emphasis here is on "French country kitchen" cuisine—think Provence, not Paris. In keeping, each day's menu is concocted from scratch and handwritten. Listen to these recent entrées and feel your mouth water: flounder sauté meunière, grilled wild coho salmon with basil pesto, and breast of duck in a raspberry demi-glace. Get the picture? Of course, you'll want to start with the escargot and leeks vol-au-vent, the house pâté, or even some pan-roasted Bluffton oysters. As you'd expect, the wine selection is celestial. Reservations are essential.

A longtime Hilton Head favorite is ◖ **Red Fish** (8 Archer Rd., 843/686-3388, www. redfishofhiltonhead.com, lunch Mon.–Sat. 11:30 A.M.–2 P.M., dinner daily beginning with early-bird specials at 5 P.M., $20–37). Strongly Caribbean in decor as well as the menu, with romanticism and panache to match, this is a great place for couples. The creative but accessible menu by executive chef Sean Walsh incorporates unique spices, fruits, and vegetables for a fresh, zesty palette. The recommended course of action is to pick your own wine from the vast, 1,000-plus-bottle award-winning selection in the attached wine shop and cellar to go with your dinner. Recent highlights from the rotating seasonal menu include the grilled sea bass, the Latin ribs, and yes, the vegetable strudel. Reservations are essential.

Fresh seafood lovers will enjoy one of Hilton Head's staples, the huge **Hudson's on the Docks** (1 Hudson Rd., 843/681-2772, www.hudsonsonthedocks.com, lunch daily 11 A.M.–4 P.M., dinner daily from 5 P.M., $14–23) on Skull Creek just off Squire Pope Road on the less-developed north side. Much of the catch—though not all of it, by any means—comes directly off the boats you'll see dockside. Built on the old family oyster factory, Hudson's is now owned by transplants from, of all places, Long Island, New York. Try the stuffed shrimp filled with crabmeat, or just go for a combination platter. Leave room for one of the homemade desserts crafted by Ms. Bessie, a 30-year veteran employee of Hudson's.

INFORMATION AND SERVICES

The best place to get information on Hilton Head, book a room, or secure a tee time is just as you come onto the island at the **Hilton Head Island Chamber of Commerce Welcome Center** (100 William Hilton Pkwy., 843/785-3673, www.hiltonheadisland.org, daily 9 A.M.–6 P.M.).

Hilton Head's newspaper of record is the *Island Packet* (www.islandpacket.com).

Hilton Head's main **post office** (213 William Hilton Pkwy., 843/893-3490) is in an easy-to-find location.

GETTING THERE AND AROUND

A few years back, the **Savannah International Airport** (SAV, 400 Airways Ave., Savannah, 912/964-0514, www.savannahairport.com) added Hilton Head to its name specifically to identify itself with that lucrative market. It has been a success, and this facility remains the closest large airport to Hilton Head Island and Bluffton. From the airport, go north on I-95 into South Carolina, and take exit 8 onto U.S. 278 east. There is a local regional airport as well, the **Hilton Head Island Airport** (HXD, 120 Beach City Rd., 843/689-5400, www. bcgov.net). While very attractive and convenient, keep in mind that it only hosts propeller-driven commuter planes because of the runway length and concerns about noise.

If you're entering the area by car, the best route is exit 8 off I-95 onto U.S. 278, which takes you by Bluffton and right into Hilton Head. Near Bluffton, U.S. 278 is called Fording Island Road, and on Hilton Head proper it becomes the William Hilton Parkway business route. Technically, U.S. 278 turns into the new Cross Island Parkway, but when most locals say "278"

they're almost always referring to the William Hilton Parkway.

Other than taxi services, there is no public transportation to speak of in the Lowcountry, unless you want to count the free shuttle around Sea Pines Plantation. Taxi services include **Yellow Cab** (843/686-6666), **Island Taxi** (843/683-6363), and **Ferguson Transportation** (843/842-8088).

Bluffton and Daufuskie Island

Just outside Hilton Head are two of the Lowcountry's true gems, Bluffton and Daufuskie Island. While Bluffton's outskirts have been taken over by the same gated community and upscale strip-mall sprawl spreading throughout the coast, at its core is a delightfully charming little community on the quiet May River, now called Old Bluffton, where you'd swear you just entered a time warp.

Daufuskie Island still maintains much of its age-old isolated, timeless personality, and the island—still accessible only by boat—is still one of the spiritual centers of the Gullah culture and lifestyle.

◖ OLD BLUFFTON

Similar to Beaufort, but even quieter and smaller, historic Bluffton is an idyllic village on the banks of the hypnotically serene and well-preserved May River. Bluffton was the original hotbed of secession, with Charleston diarist Mary Chesnut famously referring to the town as "the center spot of the fire eaters." While its outskirts (so-called "Greater Bluffton") are now a haven for planned communities hoping to mimic some aspect of Bluffton's historic patina, the town center itself remains an authentic look at old South Carolina. Retro cuts both ways, however, and Bluffton has been a notorious speed trap for generations. Always obey the speed limit. During their Civil War

occupation, Union troops repaid the favor of those original Bluffton secessionists, which is why only nine homes in Bluffton are of antebellum vintage; the rest were torched in a search for Confederate guerrillas.

The center of tourist activity focuses on the **Old Bluffton Historic District,** several blocks of 1800s-vintage buildings clustered between the parallel Boundary and Calhoun Streets (old-timers sometimes call this "the original square mile"). Many of the buildings are private residences, but most have been converted into art studios and antiques stores. The wares feature a whimsical folk-art quality very much in tune with Bluffton's whole Southern Shangri-la feel. While the artists and shopkeepers are serious about their work, they make it a point to warmly invite everyone in, even when they're busy at work on the latest project.

Heyward House Historic Center

The Heyward House Historic Center (70 Boundary St., 843/757-6293, www.heywardhouse.org, Mon.–Fri. 10 A.M.–4 P.M., Sat. 11 A.M.–2 P.M., tours $5 adults, $2 students) is not only open to tours but serves as Bluffton's visitors center. Built in 1840 as a summer home for the owner of Moreland Plantation, John Cole, the house was later owned by George Cuthbert Heyward, grandson of Declaration of Independence signer Thomas Heyward.

(Remarkably, it stayed in the family until the 1990s.) Of note are the intact slave quarters on the grounds.

The Heyward House also sponsors walking tours of the historic district (843/757-6293, $15, by appointment only). Download your own walking-tour map at www.heywardhouse.org.

Church of the Cross

Don't fail to go all the way to the end of Calhoun Street, as it dead-ends on a high bluff on the May River at the Bluffton Public Dock. Overlooking this peaceful marsh-front vista is the sublimely photogenic Church of the Cross (110 Calhoun St., 843/757-2661, www. thechurchofthecross.net, free tours Mon.– Sat. 10 A.M.–2 P.M.). The current sanctuary was built in 1854 and is one of only two local churches not burned in the Civil War, but the parish itself began in 1767, with the first services on this spot held in the late 1830s. Standing here on the bluff, with the steady south breeze blowing the bugs away and relieving you of the Lowcountry heat, you can see why affluent South Carolinians began building summer homes here in the 1800s. While the church looks as if it were made of cypress, interestingly it's actually constructed of heart pine.

Bluffton Oyster Company

You might want to get a gander at the state's last remaining working oyster house, the Bluffton Oyster Company (63 Wharf St., 843/757-4010, Mon.–Sat. 9 A.M.–5:30 P.M.), and possibly purchase some of their maritime bounty. The adjoining five acres were recently purchased by the Beaufort County Open Land Trust with the intention of evolving the area into a community green space celebrating a key aspect of local heritage, the celebrated May River oyster. Meanwhile, Larry and Tina Toomer continue to oversee the oyster harvesting-and-shucking family enterprise, which has roots going back to the early 1900s.

Waddell Mariculture Center

While the oysters are growing scarce on the May River, get a close-up look at an interesting state-funded seafood farm on the Colleton River estuary, the Waddell Mariculture Center (Sawmill Creek Rd., 843/837-3795). Free tours are available Monday–Wednesday and Friday mornings. Shrimp, fish, and shellfish are some of the "product" raised and harvested here. Get to Waddell by taking U.S. 278 east from Bluffton and then taking a left on Sawmill Creek Road.

SHOPPING

Bluffton's eccentric little art studios, most clustered in a two-block stretch on Calhoun Street, are by far its main shopping draw. Named for the Lowcountry phenomenon you find in the marsh at low tide among the fiddler crabs, Bluffton's **Pluff Mudd Art** (27 Calhoun St., 843/757-5551, Mon.–Sat. 10 A.M.–5:30 P.M.) is a cooperative of 16 great young painters and photographers from throughout the area. The **Guild of Bluffton Artists** (20 Calhoun St., 843/757-5590, Mon.–Sat. 10 A.M.–4:30 P.M.) features works from many local artists, as does the outstanding **Society of Bluffton Artists** (48 Boundary St., 843/757-6586). For cool, custom handcrafted pottery, try **Preston Pottery and Gallery** (10 Church St., 843/757-3084). Another great Bluffton place is the hard-to-define **Eggs'n'tricities** (71 Calhoun St., 843/757-3446). The name pretty much says it all for this fun and eclectic vintage, junk, jewelry, and folk art store.

If you want to score some fresh local seafood for your own culinary adventure, the no-brainer choice is the **Bluffton Oyster Company** (63 Wharf St., 843/757-4010, Mon.–Sat. 9 A.M.–5:30 P.M.), the state's only active oyster facility. They also have shrimp, crab, clams, and fish, nearly all of it from the nearly pristine May River on whose banks it sits.

For a much more commercially intense

BEAUFORT

© JIM MOREKIS

Bluffton's Calhoun Street hosts many offbeat galleries.

experience, head just outside of town on U.S. 278 on the way to Hilton Head to find the dual **Tanger Outlet Centers** (1414 Fording Island Rd., 843/837-4339, Mon.–Sat. 10 A.M.–9 P.M., Sun. 11 A.M.–6 P.M.), an outlet-shopper's paradise with virtually every major brand represented, including Nine West, Ralph Lauren, Abercrombie & Fitch, and dozens more, along with new additions Skechers and the Limited Too. A serious shopper can easily spend most of a day here between its two sprawling malls, Tanger I and Tanger II, so be forewarned.

SPORTS AND RECREATION

A key kayaking outfitter in Bluffton is **Native Guide Kayak Tours** (8 2nd St., 843/757-5411, www.nativeguidetours.com), which features tours of the May and New Rivers led by native Ben Turner. Another good outfit is **Swamp Girls Kayak Tours** (843/784-2249, www.swampgirls.com), the labor of love of Sue Chapman and Linda Etchells.

To put in your own kayak or canoe on the scenic, well-preserved May River, go to the **Alljoy Landing** at the eastern terminus of Alljoy Road along the river. Or try the dock at the end of Calhoun Street near the Church of the Holy Cross. There's also a rough put-in area at the Bluffton Oyster Company (63 Wharf St.), which has a public park adjacent to it. For fishing, public landings include the dock on Calhoun Street, Alljoy Landing, and Bluffton Oyster Company.

For a much more wild hiking and birdwatching experience, go north of Bluffton to **Victoria Bluff Heritage Preserve** (803/734-3886, daily dawn–dusk, free), a 1,100-acre flat-woods habitat notable for featuring all four native species of palmetto tree. There are no facilities, and a lot of hunting goes on in November–December. Get here from Bluffton by taking Burnt Church Road to U.S. 278. Take a right onto U.S. 278 and then a left onto Sawmill Creek Road heading north. The parking area is shortly ahead on the right.

The closest public golf courses to Bluffton are the Arnold Palmer–designed **Crescent Pointe Golf Club** (1 Crescent Pointe Dr., 888/292-7778, www.crescentpointegolf.com, $90) and the nine-hole **Old Carolina Golf Club** (89 Old Carolina Rd., 888/785-7274, www.oldcarolinagolf.com, $26), certainly one of the best golf deals in the region.

ACCOMMODATIONS
Under $150

A quality bargain stay right between Bluffton and Hilton Head is the **Holiday Inn Express Bluffton** (35 Bluffton Rd., 843/757-2002, www.ichotelsgroup.com, $120), on U.S. 278 as you make the run onto Hilton Head proper. It's not close to the beach or to Old Town Bluffton, so you'll definitely be using your car, but its central location will appeal to those who want to keep their options open.

Over $300

For an ultra-upscale spa and golf resort environment near Bluffton, the clear pick is the **Inn at Palmetto Bluff** (476 Mt. Pelia Rd., 843/706-6500, www.palmettobluffresort.com, $650–900) just across the May River. This Auberge property was picked recently as the number-two U.S. resort by *Condé Nast Traveler* magazine. Despite its glitzy pedigree and extremely upper-end prices, it's more Tara than Trump Tower. The main building is modeled after a Lowcountry plantation home, and the idyllic views of the May River are blissful. Lodging is dispersed among a series of cottages and "village home" rentals. Needless to say, virtually your every need is provided for here, though the nearest off-site restaurant of any quality is quite a drive away. That will likely make little difference to you, however, since there are three top-flight dining options on the grounds: the fine dining **River House Restaurant** (843/706-6542, breakfast daily 7–11 A.M., lunch or "porch" menu daily 11 A.M.–10 P.M., dinner

daily 6–10 P.M., $30–40); the **May River Grill** (Tues.–Sat. 11 A.M.–4 P.M., $9–13) at the golf clubhouse; and the casual **Buffalo's** (843/706-6630, Sun.–Tues. 11:30 A.M.–5 P.M., Wed.–Sat. 11:30 A.M.–9 P.M., $10–15).

FOOD
Breakfast and Brunch

No discussion of Bluffton cuisine is complete without the famous **Squat 'n' Gobble** (1231 May River Rd., 843/757-4242, daily 24 hours), a wholly local phenomenon not to be confused with a similarly named chain of eateries in California. Long a site of gossiping and politicking as well as, um, squatting and gobbling, this humble diner on the May River Road in town is an indelible part of the local consciousness. Believe it or not, despite the totally unpretentious greasy-spoon ambience—or because of it—the food's actually quite good. They specialize in the usual "American" menu of eggs, bacon, hamburgers, hot dogs, and fries. There's a tie for best thing on the menu—I can't decide whether the Greek pizza or the barbecue is better, so I'll go with both.

Classic Southern

Another beloved Bluffton institution (and Blufftonians love their institutions) is **Pepper's Porch** (1255 May River Rd., 843/757-2295, Tues.–Sun. 11:30 A.M.–9 P.M., $12–20). Housed in an old barn for drying a local herb called deer tongue, this is the kind of distinctly Southern place where they bring out a basket of little corn muffins instead of bread. Entrées include a great stuffed grouper and delicious, fresh-fried shrimp. Don't miss the fried strawberry dessert, which tastes a million times better than it sounds. Weekends see live music and karaoke in the aptly named Back Bar, a favorite local hangout.

Prime rib is the house specialty at **Myrtle's Bar & Grill** (32 Bruin Rd., 843/757-6300, lunch Tues.–Fri. 11:30 A.M.–2:30 P.M.,

BEAUFORT

dinner Tues.–Sat. 5–9:30 P.M., brunch Sun. 10 A.M.–2 P.M.), generally served on Tuesday nights. They also do a mean flounder. Housed in the old post office, Myrtle's is a favorite local hangout and has recently begun hosting an interactive murder-mystery dinner theater show.

French

Most dining in Bluffton is pretty casual, but you'll get the white tablecloth treatment at **Claude & Uli's Signature Bistro** (1533 Fording Island Rd., 843/837-3336, lunch Mon.–Fri. 11:30 A.M.–2:30 P.M., dinner Mon.–Sat. from 5 P.M., $18–25) just outside of town in Moss Village. Chef Claude has brought his extensive European training and background (which includes Maxim's in Paris) to this romantic little spot. Claude does a great veal cordon bleu as well as a number of fine seafood entrées, such as an almond-crusted tilapia and an excellent seafood pasta. Don't miss their specialty soufflé for dessert, which you should order with dinner as it takes almost half an hour to bake.

Mexican

My favorite restaurant in Bluffton by far is a near-copy of an equally fine Mexican restaurant in Hilton Head, **◖ Mi Tierra** (101 Mellichamp Center, 843/757-7200, lunch daily 11 A.M.–4 P.M., dinner Mon.–Fri. 4–9 P.M., Sat.–Sun. 4–10 P.M., $3–15). They have very high-quality Tex-Mex-style food in a fun atmosphere at great prices. Another highly regarded Mexican place in Bluffton is **Amigo's Café Y Cantina** (133 Towne Dr., 843/815-8226, Mon.–Sat. 11 A.M.–9 P.M., $8).

INFORMATION AND SERVICES

You'll find Bluffton's visitors center in the **Heyward House Historic Center** (70 Boundary St., 843/757-6293, www.heyward-house.org).

A good Bluffton publication is *Bluffton Today* (www.blufftontoday.com).

If you need postal services, Bluffton also has its own **post office** (32 Bruin Rd., 843/757-3588).

DAUFUSKIE ISLAND

Sitting between Savannah and Hilton Head Island and accessible only by water, Daufuskie Island has about 500 full-time residents, most of whom ride around on golf carts or bikes (there's only one paved road, Haig Point Road, and cars are a rare sight). Once the home of rice and indigo plantations and rich oyster beds—the latter destroyed by pollution and overharvesting—the two upscale residential resort communities on the island, begun in the 1980s, give a clue as to where the future lies, although the recent global economic downturn slowed development to a standstill.

The area of prime interest to visitors is the unincorporated western portion, or **Historic District,** the old stomping grounds of Pat Conroy during his stint as a teacher of resident African American children. His old two-room schoolhouse of *The Water is Wide* fame, the **Mary Field School,** is still here, as is the adjacent 140-year-old **Union Baptist Church,** but Daufuskie students now have a surprisingly modern new facility (middle school students are still ferried to mainland schools every day). Farther north on Haig Point Road is the new **Billie Burn Museum,** housed in the old Mt. Carmel Church and named after the island's resident historian. On the southern end you'll find the **Bloody Point Lighthouse,** named for the vicious battle fought nearby during the Yamasee War of 1815 (the light was actually moved a 0.5 miles inland in the early 1900s). Other areas of interest throughout the island include Native American sites, tabby ruins, the old Baptist Church, and a couple of cemeteries. Otherwise there's really not much to do on Daufuskie. It's a place where you go to see a slice of Sea Island and Gullah history and relax, relax, relax. While at one time there was

WHO ARE THE GULLAH?

A language, a culture, and a people with a shared history, Gullah is more than that–it's also a state of mind. Simply put, the Gullah are African Americans of the Sea Islands of South Carolina and Georgia. (In Georgia, the term *Geechee,* from the nearby Ogeechee River, is more or less interchangeable.) Protected from outside influence by the isolation of this coastal region after the Civil War, Gullah culture is the closest living cousin to the West African traditions of their ancestors imported as slaves.

While you might hear that *Gullah* is a corruption of "Angola," some linguists think it simply means "people" in a West African language. In any case, the Gullah speak what is known as a creole language, meaning one derived from several sources. Gullah combines elements of Elizabethan English, Jamaican patois, and several West African dialects; for example "goober" (peanut) comes from the Congo *n'guba.* Another creole element is a word with multiple uses, for example Gullah's *shum* could mean "see them," "see him," "see her," or "see it" in either past or present tense, depending on context. Several white writers in the 1900s published collections of Gullah folk tales, but for the most part the Gullah tongue was simply considered broken English. That changed with the publication of Lorenzo Dow Turner's groundbreaking *Africanisms in the Gullah Dialect* in 1949. Turner traced elements of the language to Sierra Leone in West Africa and more than 300 Gullah words directly to Africa.

Gullah is typically spoken very rapidly, which of course only adds to its impenetrability to the outsider. Gullah also relies on colorful turns of phrase. *"E tru mout"* ("He true mouth") means the speaker is referring to someone who doesn't lie. *"Ie een crack muh teet"* ("I didn't even crack my teeth") means "I kept quiet." A forgetful Gullah speaker might say, *"Mah head leab me"* ("My head left me").

Gullah music, as practiced by the world-famous Hallelujah Singers of St. Helena Island, also uses many distinctly African techniques, such as call and response (the folk hymn "Michael Row the Boat Ashore" is a good example). The most famous Americans with Gullah roots are boxer Joe Frazier (Beaufort), hip-hop star Jazzy Jay (Beaufort), NFL great Jim Brown (St. Simons Island, Georgia), and Supreme Court Justice Clarence Thomas (Pin Point, Georgia, near Savannah).

Upscale development continues to claim more and more traditional Gullah areas, generally by pricing them out through rapidly increasing property values. Today, the major pockets of living Gullah culture in South Carolina are in Beaufort, St. Helena Island, Daufuskie Island, Edisto Island, and a northern section of Hilton Head Island.

The old ways are not as prevalent as they were, but several key institutions are keeping alive the spirit of Gullah: the **Penn Center** (16 Martin Luther King Dr., St. Helena, 843/838-2474, www.penncenter.com, Mon.-Sat. 11 A.M.-4 P.M., $4 adults, $2 seniors and children) on St. Helena Island near Beaufort; the **Avery Research Center** (66 George St., Charleston, 843/953-7609, www.cofc.edu/avery, Mon.-Fri. 10 A.M.-5 P.M., Sat. noon-5 P.M.) at the College of Charleston; and **Geechee Kunda** (622 Ways Temple Rd., Riceboro, Georgia, 912/884-4440, www.geecheekunda.net) near Midway off U.S. 17.

BEAUFORT

an operating resort and spa on the island, as of this writing it was bankrupt and closed, with no clear plans to reopen.

For overnight stays, you can rent a humble cabin at **Freeport Marina** (843/785-8242, rates vary). For the freshest island seafood, check out the **Old Daufuskie Crab Company** (Freeport Marina, 843/785-6652, daily 11:30 A.M.–9 P.M., $7–22).

A public ferry between Daufuskie and Hilton Head is **Calibogue Cruises** (843/342-8687). It brings you in on the landward side of the island, and from there you can take shuttles or rent golf carts or bikes.

Points Inland

It's very likely that at some point you'll find yourself traveling inland from Beaufort, given that area's proximity to I-95. While generally more known for offering interstate drivers a bite to eat and a place to rest their heads, there are several spots worth checking out in their own right, especially Walterboro and the Savannah National Wildlife Refuge.

WALTERBORO

The very picture of the slow, moss-drenched Lowcountry town—indeed, the municipal logo is the silhouette of a live oak tree—Walterboro is a delightful, artsy oasis. Right off I-95, Walterboro serves as a gateway of sorts to the Lowcountry, and the cheap commercial sprawl on the interstate shows it. But don't be put off by this ugliness—once you get into town it's

as charming as they come, with roots dating back to 1783 and offering the added bonus of being one of the best antiquing locales in South Carolina. Convenient and eminently walkable, the two-block Arts and Antiques District on Washington Street centers on over a dozen antiques and collectible stores on the town's main drag, interspersed with gift shops and eateries.

Sights

☾ SOUTH CAROLINA ARTISANS CENTER

If you're in town, don't miss the South Carolina Artisans Center (334 Wichman St., 843/549-0011, www.scartisanscenter.com, Mon.–Sat. 10 A.M.–6 P.M., Sun. 1–6 P.M., free), an expansive and vibrant collection of the best work of local and regional painters, sculptors, jewelers, and other craftspeople, for sale and for

the South Carolina Artisans Center in Walterboro

© JIM MOREKIS

enjoyment. Imagine a big-city folk art gallery, except without the pretension, and you get the idea. It's not on the main drag, but it's only about a block around the corner, so there's no excuse not to drop in. You can find most any genre represented here, including jewelry, watercolors, shawls, photography, and sweetgrass baskets. The Artisans Center hosts numerous receptions, and every third Saturday of the month they hold live artist demonstrations 11 A.M.–3 P.M.

MUSEUMS

Walterboro boasts three museums. The newly relocated and upgraded **Colleton Museum** (506 E. Washington St., 843/549-2303, www.colletonmuseum.com, Tues. noon–6 P.M., Wed.–Fri. 10 A.M.–5 P.M., Sat. 10 A.M.–noon, free) is one of the best examples of a small town museum you're likely to find anywhere. In aesthetically pleasing fashion, it houses some perhaps surprisingly lively exhibits exploring area history and culture from prehistory to the present day, all packed with charmingly unique and interesting artifacts of everyday life in this historic community.

The **Bedon-Lucas House Museum** (205 Church St., 843/549-9633, Thurs.–Sat. 1–4 P.M., $3 adults, free under age 8) was built by a local planter in 1820. An example of the local style of "high house," built off the ground to escape mosquitoes and catch the breeze, the house today is a nice mix of period furnishings and unadorned simplicity.

The **Slave Relic Museum** (208 Carn St., 843/549-9130, www.slaverelics.org, Mon.–Thurs. 9:30 A.M.–5 P.M., Sat. 10 A.M.–3 P.M., $6 adults, $5 children) houses the area Center for Research and Preservation of the African American Culture. It features artifacts, photos, and documents detailing the Atlantic passage, slave life, and the Underground Railroad.

TUSKEGEE AIRMEN MEMORIAL

Yes, the Tuskegee Airmen of World War II fame were from Alabama, not South Carolina. But a contingent trained in Walterboro, at the site of the present-day Lowcountry Regional Airport (537 Aviation Way, 843/549-2549) a short ways south of downtown on U.S. 17. Today, on a publicly accessible, low-security area of the airport stands the Tuskegee Airmen Memorial, an outdoor monument to these brave flyers. There's a bronze statue and several interpretive exhibits.

GREAT SWAMP SANCTUARY

A short ways out of town in the other direction is the Great Swamp Sanctuary (www.thegreatswamp.org, daily dawn–dusk, free), a still-developing ecotourism project focusing on the Lowcountry environment. Located in one of the few braided-creek habitats accessible to the public, the 842-acre Sanctuary has three miles of walking and biking trails, some along the path of the old Charleston-Savannah stagecoach route. Kayakers and canoeists can paddle along over two miles of winding creeks. A 10,000-square-foot interpretive center is in the works. There are three entry points to the Great Swamp Sanctuary, all off Jefferies Boulevard. In west-to-east order from I-95: north onto Beach Road, north onto Detreville Street (this is considered the main entrance), and west onto Washington Street.

Festivals and Events

In keeping with South Carolina's tradition of towns hosting annual events to celebrate signature crops and products, Walterboro's **Colleton County Rice Festival** (http://thericefestival.org, free) happens every April. There's a parade, live music, a 5K run, the crowning of the year's "Rice Queen," and you just might find yourself learning something about the unique coastal lifestyle built around this ultimate cash crop of the early South.

Accommodations and Food

If you're looking for big-box lodging, the

TUSKEGEE AIRMEN IN WALTERBORO

In a state where all too often African American history is studied in the context of slavery, a refreshing change is the tale of the Tuskegee Airmen, one of the most-lauded American military units of World War II. Though named for their origins at Alabama's Tuskegee Institute, the pilots of the famed 332nd Fighter Group actually completed final training in South Carolina at Walterboro Army Airfield, where the regional airport now sits.

The U.S. military was segregated during World War II, with African Americans mostly relegated to support roles. An interesting exception was the case of the 332nd, formed in 1941 as the 99th Pursuit Squadron by an act of Congress and the only all-black flying unit in the American military at the time. For the most part flying P-47 Thunderbolts and P-51 Mustangs, the pilots of the 332nd had one of the toughest missions of the war: escorting bombers over the skies of Germany and protecting them from Luftwaffe fighters. Though initially viewed with skepticism, the Tuskegee Airmen wasted no time in proving their mettle.

In fact, it wasn't long before U.S. bomber crews—who were, needless to say, all white—specifically requested that they be escorted by the airmen, who were given the nickname "Red-tail Angels" because of the distinctive markings of their aircraft. While legend has it that the 332nd never lost a bomber, this claim has been debunked. But as Tuskegee Airman Bill Holloman said, "The Tuskegee story is about pilots who rose above adversity and discrimination and opened a door once closed to black America, not about whether their record is perfect." The 332nd's reputation for aggressiveness in air combat was so widely known that the Germans also had a nickname for them—*Schwartze Vogelmenschen*, or "Black Birdmen."

Today Walterboro honors the Airmen with a monument on the grounds of the Lowcountry Regional Airport, on U.S. 17 just northeast of town. In an easily accessible part of the airport grounds, the monument features a bronze statue and several interpretive exhibits. Another place to catch up on Tuskegee Airmen history is at the **Colleton Museum** (506 E. Washington St., 843/549-2303, www.colletonmuseum.com, Tues. noon-6 P.M., Wed.-Fri. 10 A.M.-5 P.M., Sat. 10 A.M.-noon, free), which has a permanent exhibit on the pilots and their history in the Walterboro area.

Walterboro Army Airfield's contribution to the war effort was not limited to the Tuskegee Airmen. Seven of the famed Doolittle Raiders were trained here, there was a compound for holding German prisoners of war, and it was also the site of the U.S. military's largest camouflage school.

section of Walterboro close to I-95 is chockablock with it. The quality is surprisingly good, perhaps because they tend to cater to Northerners on their way to and from Florida. A good choice is **Holiday Inn Express & Suites** (1834 Sniders Hwy., 843/538-2700, www.hiexpress.com, $85), or try the **Comfort Inn & Suites** (97 Downs Lane, 843/538-5911, www.choicehotels.com, $95).

If you'd like something with a bit more character, there are two B&Bs on Hampton Street downtown. **Old Academy Bed & Breakfast** (904 Hampton St., 843/549-3232, www.oldacademybandb.com, $80–115) has four guest rooms housed in Walterboro's first school building. They offer a full continental breakfast. Note that credit cards are not accepted. Although built recently, by local standards, the 1912 **Hampton House Bed and Breakfast** (500 Hampton St., 843/542-9498, www.hamptonhousebandb.com, $125–145) has three well-appointed guest rooms and offers a full country breakfast. By appointment only, you can see the Forde Doll and Dollhouse Collection, with over 50 dollhouses and oodles of antique dolls.

The story of food in Walterboro revolves around **◖ Duke's Barbecue** (949 Robertson Blvd., 843/549-1446, $7), one of the best-regarded barbecue spots in the Lowcountry and one of the top two joints named "Duke's" in the state (the other, by common consensus, is in Orangeburg). The pulled pork is delectable, cooked with the indigenous South Carolina mustard-based sauce. Unlike most area barbecue restaurants, some attention is devoted to the veggies, such as collard greens, green beans, and black-eyed peas with rice.

HARDEEVILLE

For most travelers, Hardeeville is known for its plethora of low-budget lodging and garish fireworks stores at the intersection of I-95 and U.S. 17. Truth be told, that's about all that's here. However, train buffs will enjoy getting a gander at the rare and excellently restored **Narrow Gauge Locomotive** near the intersection of U.S. 17 and Highway 46. Donated by the Argent Lumber Company in 1960, Engine No. 7 memorializes the role of the timber industry in the area.

If you're hungry in Hardeeville, go straight to **❰ Mi Tierrita** (U.S. 17 and I-95, 843/784-5011, $5), an excellent, authentic Mexican restaurant near the I-95–U.S. 17 confluence. It's pretty beat-up on the inside, but the food is delicious and many steps above the typical watered-down Tex-Mex you find in the Southeast. If barbecue is your thing, go on Highway 170A on the "backside" of Hardeeville in the hamlet of Levy to **The Pink Pig** (3508 S. Okatie Hwy., 843/784-3635, www.the-pink-pig.com, Tues.–Wed. and Sat. 11 A.M.–3 P.M., Thurs.–Fri. 11 A.M.–3 P.M. and 5–7 P.M., $5–15). They offer three sauces: honey mustard, spicy, and "Gullah." The place is surprisingly hip, with good music piped in and a suitably cutesy, kid-friendly decor with plenty of the eponymous rosy porcine figures.

SAVANNAH NATIONAL WILDLIFE REFUGE

Roughly equally divided between Georgia and South Carolina, the sprawling, 30,000-acre Savannah National Wildlife Refuge (912/652-4415, www.fws.gov/savannah, daily dawn–dusk, free) is a premier bird-watching and nature-observing locale in the Southeast. As with many refuges in the coastal Southeast, it's located on former plantations. The system of dikes and paddy fields once used to grow rice now helps make this an attractive stopover for migrating birds. Bird-watching is best October–April, with the winter months best for viewing migratory waterfowl. While you can kayak on your own on miles of creeks, you can also call **Swamp Girls Kayak Tours** (843/784-2249, www.swampgirls.com), who work out of nearby Hardeeville, for a guided tour. To get here, take exit 5 off I-95 onto U.S. 17. Go south to U.S. 170 and look for the Laurel Hill Wildlife Drive. Be sure to stop by the brand-new visitors center.

SAVANNAH

Rarely has a city owed so much to the vision of one person than Savannah owes to General James Edward Oglethorpe. Given the mission by King George II of England to buffer Charleston from the Spanish, this reformer had a far more sweeping vision in mind. After befriending a local Creek people, Oglethorpe laid out his settlement in a deceptively simple plan that is still studied the world over as a model of nearly perfect urban design. Many of his other progressive ideas—such as prohibiting slavery and hard liquor, to name two—soon went by the wayside. But the legacy of his original plan lives on to this day.

Savannah was built as a series of rectangular "wards," each built around a central square. As the city grew, each square took on its own characteristics, depending on who lived on the square and how they made their livelihood. It is this individuality that is so well documented in John Berendt's *Midnight in the Garden of Good and Evil.* The squares of Savannah's downtown—since 1965 a National Landmark Historic District—are also responsible for the city's walkability, another defining characteristic. Just as cars entering a square must yield to traffic already within, pedestrians are obliged to slow down and interact with the surrounding environment, both constructed and natural. You become participant and audience simultaneously, a feat made easier by the local penchant for easy conversation.

HIGHLIGHTS

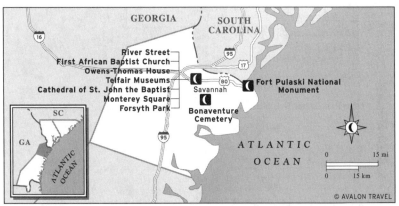

© AVALON TRAVEL

LOOK FOR **◖** TO FIND RECOMMENDED SIGHTS, ACTIVITIES, DINING, AND LODGING.

◖ River Street: Despite River Street's tourist tackiness, there's still nothing like strolling the cobblestones amid the old cotton warehouses, enjoying the cool breeze off the river, and watching the huge ships on their way to and from the bustling port (page 202).

◖ First African Baptist Church: The oldest black congregation in the United States still meets in this historic sanctuary, a key stop on the Underground Railroad (page 207).

◖ Owens-Thomas House: Possibly the country's best example of Regency architecture and definitely an example of state-of-the-art historic preservation in action, this is Savannah's single greatest historical home (page 215).

◖ Telfair Museums: Old school meets new school in this museum complex that comprises the traditional collection of the Telfair Academy of Arts and Sciences and the ultra-modern Jepson Center for the Arts, both within a stone's throw of each other (page 216).

◖ Cathedral of St. John the Baptist: This soaring Gothic Revival edifice is comple-

mented by its ornate interior and its matchless location on verdant Lafayette Square, stomping ground of the young Flannery O'Connor (page 220).

◖ Monterey Square: Perhaps Savannah's quintessential square, with some of the best examples of local architecture and world-class ironwork all around its periphery (page 222).

◖ Forsyth Park: A verdant expanse ringed with old live oaks, with chockablock memorials. The true center of downtown life, it is Savannah's backyard (page 228).

◖ Bonaventure Cemetery: This historic burial ground is the final resting place for some of Savannah's favorite citizens, including the great Johnny Mercer, and makes great use of its setting on the banks of the Wilmington River (page 231).

◖ Fort Pulaski National Monument: This well-run site, built with the help of a young Robert E. Lee, is not only historically significant, its beautiful setting makes it a great place for the entire family (page 239).

SAVANNAH

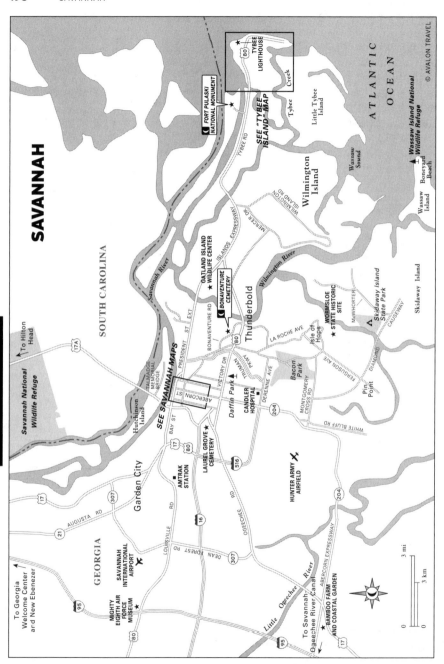

SAVANNAH

© AVALON TRAVEL

ATLANTIC OCEAN

SOUTH CAROLINA

GEORGIA

To Georgia Welcome Center and New Ebenezer

To Hilton Head

Savannah National Wildlife Refuge

Hutchinson Island

Savannah River

TALMADGE MEMORIAL BRIDGE

SEE SAVANNAH MAPS

Garden City

AMTRAK STATION

MIGHTY EIGHTH AIR FORCE MUSEUM

SAVANNAH INTERNATIONAL AIRPORT

AUGUSTA RD

LOUISVILLE RD

DEAN FOREST RD

OGEECHEE RD

To Savannah-Ogeechee River Canal

Little Ogeechee River

Ogeechee River

BAMBOO FARM AND COASTAL GARDEN

LAUREL GROVE CEMETERY

HUNTER ARMY AIRFIELD

CANDLER HOSPITAL

Daffin Park

Bacon Park

ABERCORN ST

VICTORY DR

ABERCORN EXPRESSWAY

WHITE BLUFF RD

MONTGOMERY CROSS RD

DERENNE AVE

LA ROCHE AVE

Isle of Hope

FERGUSON AVE

Pin Point

PRESIDENT ST EXT

BONAVENTURE RD

BONAVENTURE CEMETERY

OATLAND ISLAND WILDLIFE CENTER

Thunderbold

Wilmington River

ISLANDS EXPRESSWAY

MERCER DR

WILMINGTON ISLAND RD

Wilmington Island

Skidaway Island State Park

WORMSLOE STATE HISTORIC SITE

McWHORTER

CAUSEWAY

Skidaway Island

DIAMOND

Wassaw Sound

Wassaw Island

Wassaw Island National Wildlife Refuge

Boneyard Beach

TYBEE RD

SEE "TYBEE ISLAND" MAP

FORT PULASKI NATIONAL MONUMENT

Tybee Creek

Little Tybee Island

TYBEE LIGHTHOUSE

3 mi

3 km

In an increasingly homogenized society, Savannah is one of the last places left where eccentricity is celebrated and even encouraged. This outspoken, often stubborn determination to make one's own way in the world is personified by the old Georgia joke about Savannah being the capital of "the state of Chatham," a reference to the county in which it resides. In typical contrarian fashion, Savannahians take this nickname, ostensibly a pejorative, as a compliment.

Savannah is also known for being able to show you a rowdy good time, and not only during its massive, world-famous St. Patrick's Day celebration. Savannahians, like New Orleanians, will use any excuse for a party, and any excuse to drink in the full flavor of natural beauty here—whether in the heady glory of a spring day with all the flowers blooming, or the sweet release of the long-awaited autumn, brisk and bracing but not so crisp that you can't wear shorts.

While Charleston's outlying areas tend to complement the history and outlook of the Holy City itself, Savannah's outskirts are more self-contained. Despite the fact that Tybee Island is largely dependent on Savannah's economy, it has willfully kept its own fun and funky persona. More rural areas outside town, such as New Ebenezer and Midway, are reflective of a wholly different side of the state—a Georgia of country churches and tight-knit descendants of original plantation owners.

HISTORY

To understand the inferiority complex that Savannah feels with regards to Charleston, you have to remember that literally from day one, Savannah was intended to play second fiddle to its older, richer neighbor to the north. By the early 1700s, the land south of Charleston was a staging area for attacks by the Spanish and Native Americans. So in 1732, King George II granted a charter to the Trustees of Georgia, a proprietary venture that was the brainchild of a 36-year-old general and member of parliament, General James Edward Oglethorpe. On February 12, 1733, the *Anne* landed with 114 passengers along the high bluff on the south bank of the Savannah River. Oglethorpe bonded with Tomochichi, the local Creek Indian chief, and the colony prospered. (Contrary to what locals might tell you, Savannah did not get its name because it resembles a grassy savanna. The city is named for the Savannah River, which itself is named for a wandering, warring offshoot of a local Shawnee people.)

Ever the idealist, Oglethorpe had a plan for the new "classless society" in Savannah that prohibited slavery, rum, and—wait for it—lawyers! But as the settlers enviously eyed the dominance of Charleston's slave-based rice economy, the Trustees bowed to public pressure and relaxed restrictions on slavery and rum. By 1753, the crown reclaimed the charter, making Georgia America's 13th colony. Though part of the new United States in 1776, Savannah was captured by British forces in 1778, who held the city against a combined assault a year later. After the Revolution, Savannah became the first capital of Georgia, a role it had until 1786.

Despite hurricanes and yellow fever epidemics, Savannah's heyday was the antebellum period from 1800 to 1860, when for a time it outstripped Charleston as a center of commerce. By 1860, Savannah's population doubled after an influx of European immigrants, chief among them Irish workers coming to lay track on the new Central of Georgia line.

Blockaded for most of the Civil War, Savannah didn't see much action other than the fall of Fort Pulaski in April 1862, when a Union force successfully laid siege using rifled artillery, a revolutionary new technology that instantly rendered the world's masonry forts obsolete. War came to Savannah's doorstep when General William T. Sherman's March to the Sea concluded with his capture of the town in December 1864. Sherman sent

OGLETHORPE: VISIONARY ARISTOCRAT

One of the greatest products of the Enlightenment, James Edward Oglethorpe was a study in contrasts, embodying all the vitality, contradiction, and ambiguity of that turbulent age. A stern moralist yet an avowed liberal, an aristocrat with a populist streak, an abolitionist and an anti-Catholic, a man of war who sought peace—the founder of Georgia would put his own inimitable stamp on the new nation to follow, a legacy personified to this day in the city he designed.

After making a name for himself fighting the Turks, the young London native and Oxford graduate would return home only to serve a two-year prison sentence for killing a man in a brawl. The experience was a formative one for Oglethorpe, scion of a large and upwardly mobile family now forced to see how England's underbelly really lived. Upon his release, the 25-year-old Oglethorpe ran for the "family" House of Commons seat once occupied by his father and two brothers, and won. He made a name for himself as a campaigner for human rights and an opponent of slavery. Another jail-related epiphany came when Oglethorpe saw a friend die of smallpox in debtors prison. More than ever, Oglethorpe was determined to right what he saw as a colossal wrong in the draconian English justice system. His crusade took the form of establishing a sanctuary for debtors in North America.

To that end, he and his friend Lord Perceval established the Trustees, a 21-member group who lobbied King George for permission to establish such a colony. The grant from the king—who was more interested in containing the Spanish than in any humanitarian concerns—would include all land between the Altamaha and Savannah Rivers and from the headwaters of these rivers to the "south seas." Ironically, there were no debtors among Savannah's original colonists. Nonetheless, the new settlement was indeed a reflection of its founder's core values, banning rum as a bad influence (though beer and wine were allowed), prohibiting slavery, and eschewing lawyers on the theory that a gentleman should always be able to defend himself.

Nearing 40 and distracted by war with the Spanish, Oglethorpe's agenda gradually eroded in the face of opposition from settlers, who craved not only the more hedonistic lifestyle of their neighbors to the north in Charleston but the economic advantage that city enjoyed in the use of slave labor. In nearly the same hour as his greatest military victory, crushing the Spanish at the Battle of Bloody Marsh on St. Simons Island, Oglethorpe also suffered an ignominious defeat: being replaced as head of the 13th colony, which he had founded.

He went back to England, never to see the New World again. But his heart was always with the colonists. After successfully fending off a political attack and a court-martial, Oglethorpe married and commenced a healthy retirement. He supported independence for the American colonies, making a point to enthusiastically receive the new ambassador from the United States, one John Adams. The old general died on June 30, 1785, at age 88. Fittingly for this lifelong philanthropist and humanitarian, his childhood home in Godalming, Surrey, is now a nursing home.

a now-legendary telegram to President Lincoln granting him the city as a Christmas present with these words: "I beg to present you as a Christmas gift, the City of Savannah with 150 heavy guns and plenty of ammunition and also about 25,000 bales of cotton."

After a lengthy Reconstruction period, Savannah began reaching out to the outside world. From 1908 to 1911 it was a national center of road racing. In the Roaring '20s, native son Johnny Mercer rose to prominence, and the great Flannery O'Connor was born in downtown Savannah. World War II provided an economic lift, with Savannah being a major center for the building of Liberty Ships to transport soldiers and equipment overseas. But the city was still known as the "pretty woman with a dirty face," as Britain's Lady

Astor famously described it in 1946. Almost in answer to Astor's quip, city leaders in the 1950s began a misguided program to retrofit the city's infrastructure for the automobile era. This frenzy of demolition cost such civic treasures as Union Station, the City Auditorium, and the old DeSoto Hotel. Savannah's preservation movement had its seed in the fight by seven Savannah women to save the Davenport House and other buildings from similar fates.

Savannah played a pioneering, though largely unsung, role in the civil rights movement. Ralph Mark Gilbert, pastor of the historic First African Baptist Church, launched one of the first black voter registration drives in the South, which led the way for the historic integration of the police department in 1947. Gilbert's efforts were kept alive in the 1950s and 1960s by the beloved W. W. Law, a letter carrier who was head of the local chapter of the NAACP for many years. Savannah's longstanding diversity was further proved in 1970, when Greek American John P. Rousakis began his 21-year stint as mayor. During Rousakis' tenure, the first African American city alderman was elected, the movie industry discovered the area, and Atlanta was awarded the 1996 Summer Olympics, which brought several events venues to Savannah. Once-decrepit River Street and Broughton Street were revived. The opening of the Savannah College of Art and Design (SCAD) in 1979 ushered another important chapter in Savannah's renaissance.

After the publication of John Berendt's *Midnight in the Garden of Good and Evil* in 1994, nothing would ever be the same in Savannah. Old-money families cringed as idiosyncrasies and hypocrisies were laid bare in "The Book." Local merchants and politicians, however, delighted in the influx of tourists. A more recent driver of tourism to the area has been the arrival of Paula Deen, whose ubiquitous presence on the Food Channel has convinced many thousands of visitors to come eat at her world-famous, if overrated, Lady & Sons restaurant.

Savannah's first African American mayor, Floyd Adams Jr., was elected in 1995. Succeeding him was Otis Johnson, the first black Savannahian to graduate from the University of Georgia. Savannah's first female African American mayor, Edna Jackson, was elected in 2011 (the first female mayor was Susan Weiner, who served one term in the early 1990s).

PLANNING YOUR TIME

Much more than just a parade, St. Patrick's Day in Savannah—an event generally expanded to include several days before and after it—is also a time of immense crowds, with the city's usual population of about 150,000 doubling with the influx of partying visitors. Be aware that lodging on and around March 17 fills up well in advance. Unless you know someone that lives here, it's best not to just spontaneously show up in Savannah on St. Patrick's weekend.

Like Charleston, you don't need a car to have a great time and see most sights worth enjoying. A strong walker can easily traverse the length and breadth of downtown in a day, although less energetic travelers should consider a central location or use of the free downtown shuttle. To fully enjoy Savannah, however, you'll need access to a vehicle so you can go east to Tybee Island and south to various historical sights with spottier public transportation. You'll appreciate downtown all the more when you can get away and smell the salt air.

And also like Charleston, it's hard to imagine fully enjoying Savannah in a single day. Plan on two nights at an absolute minimum—not only to enjoy all the sights, but to fully soak in the local color and attitude.

ORIENTATION

It's tempting for newcomers to assume that Savannah jumps across the river into South

Carolina. But this is not the case, as Savannah emanates strictly southward from the river and never crosses the state line. (Don't be confused by the spit of land you see across the main channel of the Savannah River, the one bearing the squat Trade and Convention Center and the towering Westin Savannah Harbour hotel. That's not South Carolina, it's Hutchinson Island, Georgia, annexed by the city of Savannah for development. South Carolina begins farther north, after you cross the river's Back Channel.)

The downtown area is bounded on the east by East Broad Street and on the west by Martin Luther King Jr. Boulevard (formerly West Broad St.). For quick access to the south, take the one-way streets Price (on the east side of downtown) or Whitaker (on the west side of downtown). Conversely, if you want to make a quick trip north into downtown, three one-way streets taking you there are East Broad, Lincoln, and Drayton. Technically, Gwinnett Street is the southern boundary of the National Historic Landmark District, though in practice locals extend the boundary several blocks southward. When you're driving downtown

and come to a square, the law says traffic within the square *always* has the right of way. In other words, if you haven't yet entered the square, you must yield to any vehicles already in the square.

Many of the following neighborhood designations, like City Market and the Waterfront, are well within the National Historic Landmark District, but locals tend to think of them as separate entities, and we'll follow their lead. While largely in private hands, the Victorian District—with certification and protection of its own—contains some wonderful architecture that unfortunately is often overshadowed by the more ornate buildings in the Historic District proper. Don't miss it. The Eastside includes many areas that are technically islands, but their boundaries are so blurred by infill of the marsh and by well-constructed roads that you'll sense little difference from the mainland. To most locals, "Southside" refers to the generic strip-mall sprawl below Derenne Avenue, but for our purposes here the term also includes some outlying islands. I include them in the southern part of town because of the general direction and length of travel.

Sights

It's best to introduce yourself to the sights of Savannah by traveling from the river southward. It's no small task to navigate the nation's largest contiguous Historic District, but when in doubt it's best to follow James Oglethorpe's original plan of using the five "monumental" squares on Bull Street (Johnson, Wright, Chippewa, Madison, and Monterey) as focal points.

WATERFRONT

It's only natural to start one's adventures in Savannah where Oglethorpe's adventures themselves began: on the waterfront, now dominated by scenic and historic River Street. Once the

bustling center of Savannah's thriving cotton and naval stores export industry, the waterfront is also generally thought of as including Factor's Walk and Bay Street.

◖ River Street

It's much tamer than it was 30 years ago—when muscle cars cruised its cobblestones and a volatile mix of local teenagers, sailors on shore leave, and soldiers on liberty made things less than family-friendly after dark—but River Street still has more than enough edginess to keep things interesting. Families are safe and welcome here, but energetic pub crawling

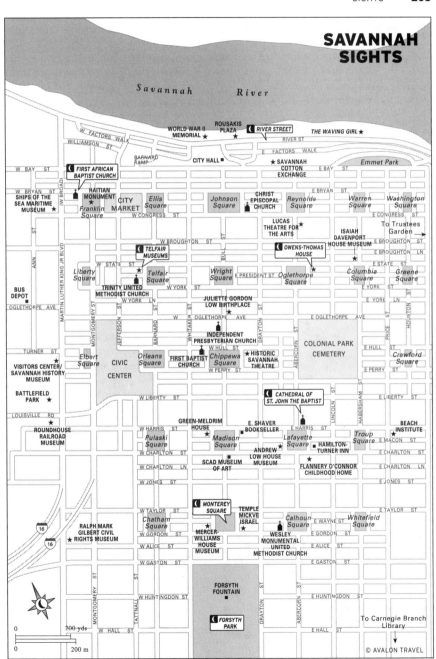

SAVANNAH SIGHTS

Savannah River

WORLD WAR II MEMORIAL ★
ROUSAKIS PLAZA
☾ RIVER STREET
THE WAVING GIRL ★

W. FACTORS WALK
WILLIAMSON ST
BARNARD RAMP
RIVER ST
E FACTORS WALK

CITY HALL ■

W BAY ST
☾ FIRST AFRICAN BAPTIST CHURCH
★ SAVANNAH COTTON EXCHANGE
E BAY ST
Emmet Park

W BRYAN ST
HAITIAN MONUMENT ★
SHIPS OF THE SEA MARITIME MUSEUM ★
CITY MARKET
Franklin Square
Ellis Square
Johnson Square
CHRIST EPISCOPAL CHURCH
Reynolds Square
E BRYAN ST
Warren Square
Washington Square

W BROAD ST
ANN ST
W CONGRESS ST
W STATE ST
BULL ST
E CONGRESS ST

LUCAS THEATRE FOR THE ARTS ★
To Trustees Garden

W BROUGHTON ST
ISAIAH DAVENPORT HOUSE MUSEUM ★
E BROUGHTON ST
E BROUGHTON LN

☾ TELFAIR MUSEUMS
☾ OWENS-THOMAS HOUSE

MARTIN LUTHER KING JR BLVD
Liberty Square
W STATE ST
Telfair Square ★
Wright Square
E PRESIDENT ST
Oglethorpe Square
E STATE ST
Columbia Square
Greene Square

BUS DEPOT ■
OGLETHORPE AVE
TRINITY UNITED METHODIST CHURCH
W YORK ST
W YORK LN
JULIETTE GORDON LOW BIRTHPLACE
E OGLETHORPE AVE
E YORK ST
E YORK LN
HOUSTON ST

TURNER ST
INDEPENDENT PRESBYTERIAN CHURCH
W HULL ST
COLONIAL PARK CEMETERY
E HULL ST
Crawford Square

VISITORS CENTER/ SAVANNAH HISTORY MUSEUM ★
Elbert Square
Orleans Square
CIVIC CENTER
FIRST BAPTIST CHURCH
Chippewa Square
★ HISTORIC SAVANNAH THEATRE
E PERRY ST

BATTLEFIELD PARK ★
W PERRY ST
W LIBERTY ST
☾ CATHEDRAL OF ST. JOHN THE BAPTIST
E LIBERTY ST

LOUISVILLE RD
ROUNDHOUSE RAILROAD MUSEUM ★
GREEN-MELDRIM HOUSE ★
Pulaski Square
Madison Square
E. SHAVER BOOKSELLER
W HARRIS ST
E HARRIS ST
Lafayette Square
Troup Square
BEACH INSTITUTE ★
E MACON ST

W CHARLTON ST
ANDREW LOW HOUSE MUSEUM
HAMILTON-TURNER INN ■
E CHARLTON ST

W CHARLTON LN
SCAD MUSEUM OF ART ■
FLANNERY O'CONNOR CHILDHOOD HOME ★
E CHARLTON LN

W JONES ST
E JONES ST

W TAYLOR ST
☾ MONTEREY SQUARE
TEMPLE MICKVE ISRAEL
E TAYLOR ST

RALPH MARK GILBERT CIVIL RIGHTS MUSEUM ★
Chatham Square
W GORDON ST
MERCER-WILLIAMS HOUSE MUSEUM ★
Calhoun Square
Whitefield Square
E WAYNE ST
E GORDON ST

W ALICE ST
WESLEY MONUMENTAL UNITED METHODIST CHURCH
E ALICE ST

W GASTON ST
E GASTON ST

MONTGOMERY ST
TATNALL ST
DRAYTON ST
ABERCORN ST

W HUNTINGDON ST
FORSYTH FOUNTAIN ■
E HUNTINGDON ST

16

☾ FORSYTH PARK

To Carnegie Branch Library

0 — 200 yds
0 — 200 m
W HALL ST
E HALL ST

© AVALON TRAVEL

SAVANNAH

remains a favorite pastime for locals and visitors alike.

If you have a car, park it somewhere else and walk. The cobblestones—actually old ballast stones from some of the innumerable ships that docked here over the years—are tough on the suspension, and much of River Street is dedicated to pedestrian traffic anyway. If you do find yourself driving here, keep in mind that the north–south "ramps" leading up and off River Street are all extensions of major downtown streets, so you can easily drive or walk up them and find yourself in the middle of bustling Bay Street and on to points beyond.

THE WAVING GIRL

Begin your walking tour of River Street on the east end, at the statue of Florence Martus, a.k.a. *The Waving Girl,* set in the emerald green expanse of little Morrell Park. Beginning at the

statue of Florence Martus, *The Waving Girl*

age of 19, Martus—who actually lived several miles downriver on Elba Island—took to greeting every passing ship with a wave of a handkerchief by day and a lantern at night, without fail for the next 40 years. Ship captains returned the greeting with a salute of their own on the ship's whistle, and word spread all over the world of the beguiling woman who waited on the balcony of that lonely house. Was she looking for a sign of a long lost love who went to sea and never returned? Was she trying to get a handsome sea captain to sweep her off her feet and take her off that little island? No one knows for sure, but the truth is probably more prosaic. Martus was a life-long spinster who lived with her brother the lighthouse keeper, and was by most accounts an eccentric, if delightful, person—which of course makes her an ideal Savannah character. After her brother died, Martus moved into a house on the Wilmington River, whiling away the hours by—you guessed it—waving at passing cars. Martus became such an enduring symbol of the personality and spirit of Savannah that a U.S. Liberty ship was named for her in 1943. She died a few months after the ship's christening at the age of 75.

ROUSAKIS PLAZA

Continue walking west to Rousakis Plaza (River Street behind City Hall), a focal point for local festivals. It's a great place to sit, feed the pigeons, and watch the huge container ships go back and forth from the Georgia Ports Authority's sprawling complex farther upriver (you can see the huge Panamax cranes in the distance). The **African American Monument** at the edge of Rousakis Plaza was erected in 2002 to controversy for its stark tableau of a dazed-looking African American family with broken shackles around their feet. Adding to the controversy was the graphic content of the inscription at the base of the 12-foot statue, written especially for the monument by famed poet Maya Angelou. It reads:

> We were stolen, sold and bought together from the African continent. We got on the slave ships together. We lay back to belly in the holds of the slave ships in each other's excrement and urine together, sometimes died together, and our lifeless bodies thrown overboard together. Today, we are standing up together, with faith and even some joy.

Nearby you can't miss the huge, vaguely cubist Hyatt Regency Savannah, another controversial local landmark. The modern architecture of the Hyatt caused quite a stir when it was first built in 1981, not only because it's so contrary to the area's historic architecture but because its superstructure effectively cuts off one end of River Street from the other. "Underneath" the Hyatt—actually still River Street—you'll find elevators to the hotel lobby, the best way to get up off the waterfront if you're not up for a walk up the cobblestones. Immediately outside the west side of the Hyatt up toward Bay Street is another exit and entry point, a steep and solid set of antebellum stairs that, despite its decidedly pre–Americans with Disabilities Act aspect, is nonetheless one of the quicker ways to leave River Street for those with strong legs and good knees.

WORLD WAR II MEMORIAL

Near the foot of the new Bohemian hotel on River Street, the newest addition to Savannah's public monuments, the World War II Memorial—fairly modernist by local standards—features a copper and bronze globe torn in half to represent the European and Pacific theaters of the war. The more than 500 local people who gave their lives in that conflict are memorialized by name.

FACTOR'S WALK

One level up from River Street, Factor's Walk has nothing to do with math, though a lot of money has been counted here. In arcane usage, a "factor" was a broker, i.e., a middleman for the sale of cotton, Savannah's chief export during most of the 1800s. Factors mostly worked in Factor's Row, the traditional phrase for the actual buildings on River Street, most all of which were used in various import-export activities before their current transformation into a mélange of shops, hotels, restaurants, and taverns. Factor's Walk is divided into Lower Factor's Walk, comprising the alleys and back entrances behind Factor's Row, and Upper Factor's Walk, the system of crosswalks at the upper levels of Factor's Row that lead directly to Bay Street.

BAY STREET

Because so few downtown streets can accommodate 18-wheelers, Bay Street unfortunately has become the default route for industrial traffic in the area on its way to and from the industrial west side of town. In front of the Hyatt Regency is a concrete bench marking the spot on which Oglethorpe pitched his first tent. But dominating Bay Street is **City Hall** (2 E. Bay St.) next door, with its gold-leaf dome. The 1907 building was designed by acclaimed architect Hyman Witcover and erected on the site of Savannah's first town hall.

The large gray Greek Revival building directly across from City Hall is the **U.S. Custom House** (1 E. Bay St.), not "customs" regardless of what the tour guides may say. Built on the spot of Georgia's first public building in 1852, the Custom House was also Georgia's first federal building and was the first local commission for renowned New York architect John Norris, who went on to design 22 other buildings in Savannah. Within its walls was held the trial of the captain and crew of the notorious slave ship *Wanderer,* which illegally plied its trade after a national ban on the importation of slaves. Local newspaper publisher and educator John

THE TWO PAULAS

It's odd that this conservative Southern city's two biggest empire-builders are women who overcome contentious divorces to get where they are today. Odder still is the fact that they both share the same first name. In any case, the empires that Paula Deen and Paula Wallace have built are two of the major reasons people enjoy Savannah today. Deen's empire centers on The Lady & Sons restaurant in City Market and her high profile on the Food Network. Wallace's empire centers on the Savannah College of Art and Design (SCAD), one of the largest art schools in the nation (and growing, now with campuses in Atlanta and Hong Kong). Their names are similar, but that's about the only similarity. These two powerhouse women and the stories of how they rose to the top could not be more different in every other way.

Deen, a native of Albany, Georgia, came to Savannah after divorcing her first husband in 1989, arriving with only $200 and her two teenage sons, Jamie and Bobby, now Food Network stars in their own right. Always ready with a self-deprecating quip, Deen still refers to herself as a former "bag lady"—the name of her first catering company—who still has a yen for shopping at Wal-Mart. Severely agoraphobic (fearing crowds), Deen gradually increased her public presence first with a job cooking at a local hotel and then with her own restaurant, Lady & Sons, initially on West Congress Street.

Her gregarious "aw, shucks" style caught the attention of producer Gordon Elliott, formerly with the seminal tabloid show *A Current Affair*. His first cooking show pilot with Deen fizzled in 1999. But soon after the 9/11 attacks, Elliott spotted an opportunity to market a good old-fashioned comfort-food show, *Paula's Home Cooking*, to the Food Network. The result was, as they say, ratings gold. Initially taped at Elliott's New York home, taping has now moved to Savannah.

Petite, soft-spoken, and often surrounded by a coterie of devoted assistants, Paula Wallace is Deen's polar opposite in temperament. She arrived in Savannah in 1979 with her then-husband Richard Rowan to establish an art school. The two 20-somethings, young children in tow, came armed with the guts to take a chance on depressed downtown real estate, the willingness to roll up their sleeves, and her parents' deep pockets. The power couple soon became the toast of the town. Then came a bitter divorce. After the smoke cleared, Paula became the clear and undisputed *presidente* of SCAD. It's hard to overstate the college's impact on Savannah. It has renovated nearly 100 historic properties and is estimated to own at least $200 million in assets, returning nearly $100 million a year into the local economy and employing over 1,000 people.

H. DeVeaux worked here after his appointment as the first African American U.S. Collector of Customs.

Directly adjacent to City Hall on the east is a small canopy sheltering two cannons, which together comprise the oldest monument in Savannah. These are the **Chatham Artillery Guns,** presented to the local militia group of the same name by President George Washington during his one and only visit to town in 1791. Today, locals use the phrase "Chatham Artillery" differently, to refer to a particularly potent local punch recipe that mixes several hard liquors.

Look directly behind the cannons and you'll see the ornate **Savannah Cotton Exchange** (100 E. Bay St.), built in 1886 to facilitate the city's huge cotton export business. Once nicknamed "King Cotton's Palace" but now a Masonic lodge, this delightful building by William Gibbons Preston is one of Savannah's many great examples of the Romanesque style. You'll become well acquainted with Preston's handiwork during your stay in Savannah— the Boston architect built many of Savannah's finest buildings. The fanciful lion figure in front—sometimes mistakenly referred to as a griffin—represents Mark the Evangelist.

However, it isn't original—the first lion was destroyed in 2009 in a bizarre traffic accident.

CITY MARKET

In local parlance, the phrase "City Market" refers not only to the refurbished warehouses that make up this tourist-friendly area of shops and restaurants in the Historic District's western portion but also its bookend squares as well—both of which had close scrapes with the bulldozer and wrecking ball before their current renaissance.

Ellis Square

Just across Bay Street on the western edge of the Historic District, Ellis Square has a history as Savannah's main open-air marketplace that goes back to 1755, when there was actually a single City Market building in the square itself. Three market buildings would come and go until the building of the fourth City Market in 1872, an ornate Romanesque affair with a 50-foot roofline. In 1954, the city, in the thrall of auto worship then sweeping the country, decided a parking garage in the square was more important than fresh food or a sense of community. So the magnificent City Market building—and Ellis Square—simply ceased to exist. Several large warehouses surrounding City Market survived, however. They carried with them the seed of real renewal, which grew with the nascent preservation movement in the 1950s and 1960s. Now a year-round hub of tourism, City Market's eclectic scene encompasses working art studios, hip bars, cute cafés, live music in the east end of the courtyard, cutting edge art galleries, gift shops, and restaurants. This is also where you pick up one of the horse-drawn carriage tours, which embark from Jefferson Street running down the middle of City Market.

The eyesore that was the Ellis Square parking garage is now gone, and the square has been literally rebuilt as a pedestrian hangout, complete with a fountain, all atop a huge underground parking garage. It cost taxpayers millions of dollars, but as any Savannahian will tell you, the return of one of their precious squares is priceless. Be sure to check out the smallish bronze of native Savannahian and Oscar-winning lyricist Johnny Mercer on the square's western edge.

Franklin Square

Just west of City Market is Franklin Square, once known simply as "Water Tank Square" because that's where the city reservoir was back in the day. Don't be alarmed by the numbers of men hanging out in the square. Scruffy heirs to an old Savannah tradition, most of them are day laborers for hire. Until recently, Franklin Square was, like Ellis Square, a victim of "progress," this time in the form of a highway going right through the middle of it. But as part of the city's effort to reclaim its history, Franklin Square was returned to its integral state in the mid-1980s.

◖ FIRST AFRICAN BAPTIST CHURCH

Without a doubt the premier historic attraction on Franklin Square—and indeed one of the most significant historic sites in Savannah—is the First African Baptist Church (23 Montgomery St., 912/233-2244, www.oldestblackchurch.org, tours Tues.–Sun. 11 A.M. and 2 P.M., $5). It's the oldest black congregation in North America, dating from 1777. The church also hosted the first African American Sunday school, begun in 1826. The church's founding pastor, George Liele, was the first black Baptist in Georgia and perhaps the first black missionary in the country. He baptized his successor, Andrew Bryan, a slave who opted to stay in Savannah and preach the Gospel instead of leaving with many other blacks after the British vacated the city. Third pastor Andrew Marshall was an ardent supporter of American independence and purchased his freedom shortly after the end of the Revolution. He served as George

SAVANNAH

COURTESY OF WWW.SAVANNAHVISIT.COM

stained glass inside First African Baptist Church

Washington's personal servant during his visit here. This founding trio is immortalized in stained-glass windows in the sanctuary.

The present building dates from 1859 and was built almost entirely by members of the congregation themselves, some of whom redirected savings intended to purchase their freedom toward the building of the church. It houses the oldest church organ in Georgia. A key staging area for the fabled Underground Railroad, First African Baptist still bears the scars of that turbulent time. In the floor of the fellowship hall—where many civil rights meetings were held, because it was safer for white citizens to go there instead of black activists going outside the church—you'll see breathing holes, drilled for use by escaped slaves hiding in a cramped crawlspace.

HAITIAN MONUMENT

This monument in the center of the square commemorates the sacrifice and service of "Les Chasseurs Volontaires de Saint-Dominigue,"

the 750 Haitian volunteers who fought for American independence and lost many of their number during the unsuccessful attempt to wrest Savannah back from the British in 1779.

HISTORIC DISTRICT
Johnson Square

Due east of City Market, Oglethorpe's very first square is named for Robert Johnson, governor of South Carolina at the time of Georgia's founding. It was here that Savannah's Liberty Pole was erected in 1774 to celebrate a new nation. And it was here that a gathering in 1861 celebrated Georgia's secession, ironically with a huge banner draped over the Greene Monument bearing the words "Don't Tread on Me"—a slogan used in the founding of the very union they sought to dissolve.

The roomy, shady square, ringed with major bank branches and insurance firms, is dominated by the **Nathanael Greene Monument** in honor of George Washington's second-in-command, who was granted nearby Mulberry

THE REBIRTH OF ELLIS SQUARE

One of the great tragedies of Savannah's 1950s love affair with "urban renewal" was the paving over of Ellis Square, site of the original City Market, replaced by a squat, drab parking garage. Savannah has finally made amends for its bad karma by bringing Ellis Square back from the grave. In the massive $22 million Ellis Square Project—also called "The Big Dig" in a nod to a similarly ambitious project in Boston—city taxpayers funded a complete facelift that boasts a new, modern landscape design, including a colorful fountain.

While not everyone in town is enamored of the new look—many local landscape architects see its self-conscious modernity as a slap in the face to Oglethorpe's original design—there's no doubt that Savannah welcomes the return of one of its most beloved squares. There's also no doubt that the city welcomes the 1,000 or so new parking spaces available in the massive Whitaker Street Garage under the new Ellis Square.

Ellis Square is not the only one to have been partially or completely destroyed, however. A small plot of worn grass on the west side of the Savannah Civic Center is all that remains of Elbert Square, eviscerated by the construction of the block-long building. And, ironically, Liberty Square was annihilated to make room for a place where some people lose their liberty—the new Chatham County Courthouse and Jail.

Grove plantation for his efforts. Marquis de Lafayette dedicated the towering obelisk during his one and only visit to Savannah in 1825. At the time it did not honor any one person. Its dedication to Greene came in 1886, followed by the reinterment of Greene's remains directly underneath the monument in 1901. (In typically maddening Savannah fashion, there is a separate square named for Greene, which has no monument to him at all.)

A much smaller but more charming and personable little monument in Johnson Square is the **William Bull Sundial** at the south side. Bull Street was named for this South Carolinian who accompanied Oglethorpe on his first journey to the new colony, helping him choose and survey the site—hence a sundial is an appropriate remembrance.

CHRIST EPISCOPAL CHURCH

The southeast corner of Johnson Square is dominated by Christ Episcopal Church (18 Abercorn St., 912/232-4131, www.christchurchsavannah.org), a.k.a. Christ Church, a historic house of worship also known as the "Mother Church of Georgia" because its congregation traces its roots to that first Anglican

service in Savannah, held the same day Oglethorpe landed. While this spot on Johnson Square was reserved for the congregation from the very beginning, this is actually the third building on the site, dating from 1838. Much of the interior is more recent than that, however, since a fire gutted the interior in 1895. In the northeast bell tower is a bell forged in 1919 by Revere and Sons of Boston.

For a special treat, walk right in to Christ Church's Compline service, held every Sunday evening at 9 P.M., and enjoy a selection of calming liturgical music sung by Christ Church's excellent Compline Choir. Colloquially known as "saying good night to God," the Compline service is free and open to those of all faiths.

Reynolds Square

Walk directly east of Johnson Square to find yourself at Reynolds Square, named for John Reynolds, the first (and exceedingly unpopular) royal governor of Georgia. First called "Lower New Square," Reynolds originally served as site of the filature, or cocoon storage warehouse, during the fledgling colony's ill-fated flirtation with the silk industry (a federal building now occupies the site). As with Johnson Square, the

SAVANNAH

monument in Reynolds Square has nothing to do with its namesake, but is instead a likeness of John Wesley dedicated in 1969 near the spot believed to have been his home. On the northeast corner of the square is the parish house of Christ Church, Wesley's congregation during his stay in Savannah.

A Reynolds Square landmark, the **Olde Pink House** (23 Abercorn St.), is not only one of Savannah's most romantic restaurants but quite a historic site as well. It's the oldest Savannah mansion from the 18th century still standing as well as the first place in Savannah where the Declaration of Independence was read aloud. Pink inside as well as out, the Georgian mansion was built in 1771 for rice planter James Habersham Jr., one of America's richest men at the time and a member of the notorious "Liberty Boys" who plotted revolution. The building's pink exterior was a matter of serendipity, resulting from its core redbrick seeping through the formerly white stucco outer covering.

At the southwest corner of Reynolds Square is the understated **Oliver Sturgis House** (27 Abercorn St.), former home of the partner with William Scarbrough in the launching of the SS *Savannah*. This is one of the few Savannah buildings to feature the stabilizing earthquake rods that are much more common in Charleston. Don't miss the dolphin downpour spouts at ground level.

LUCAS THEATRE FOR THE ARTS

The other major Savannah landmark on Reynolds Square is the Lucas Theatre for the Arts (32 Abercorn St., 912/525-5040, www.lucastheatre.com). Built in 1921 as part of Arthur Lucas's regional chain of movie houses, the Lucas also featured a stage for road shows. Ornate and stately but with cozy warmth to spare, the venue was a hit with Savannahians for four decades, until the advent of TV and residential flight from downtown led to financial disaster. In 1976, the Lucas closed after a

screening of *The Exorcist*. Several attempts to revive the venue followed, including a comedy club in the 1980s, but to no avail. When the building faced demolition in 1986, a group of citizens created a nonprofit to save it. Despite numerous starts and stops, the 14-year campaign finally paid off in a grand reopening in 2000, an event helped immeasurably by timely donations from *Midnight* star Kevin Spacey and the cast and crew of the locally shot *Forrest Gump*.

Administered by a public-private partnership between local taxpayers and the Savannah College of Art and Design, the Lucas now hosts world-class entertainment and civic events year-round. The theater's schedule stays pretty busy, so it should be easy to check out a show while you're in town. Once inside, be sure to check out the extensive gold-leaf work throughout the interior, all painstakingly done by hand.

Columbia Square

Named for the mythical patroness of America, this square features at its center not an expected portrait of that female warrior figure but the original fountain from Noble Jones's Wormsloe Plantation, placed there in 1970.

ISAIAH DAVENPORT HOUSE MUSEUM

Columbia Square is primarily known as the home of the Isaiah Davenport House Museum (324 E. State St., 912/236-8097, www.davenporthousemuseum.org, Mon.–Sat. 10 A.M.–4 P.M., Sun. 1–4 P.M., $8 adults, $5 children). The house museum is a delightful stop in and of itself because of its elegant simplicity, sweeping double staircase, and near-perfect representation of the Federalist style. But the Davenport House occupies an exalted place in Savannah history as well, because the fight to save it began the preservation movement in Savannah. In 1955 the Davenport House, then a tenement, was to be demolished for a parking lot. But Emma Adler and six other Savannah women, angered by the recent destruction of

Ellis Square, refused to let it go down quietly. Together they formed the Historic Savannah Foundation in order to raise the $22,500 needed to purchase the Davenport House. By 1963 the Davenport House—built in 1820 for his own family by master builder Isaiah Davenport—was open to the public as a museum. Another major restoration from 2000 to 2003 brought the home back to its original early-1800s state as you enjoy it today.

Most Octobers, the Davenport House hosts living history dramatizations based on Savannah's yellow fever plague of the 1820s. Despite the grim subject matter, the little playlets are usually quite entertaining.

Across the corner from the Davenport House is the Classical Revival masterpiece **Kehoe House** (123 Habersham St.), designed for local ironworks owner William Kehoe in 1892 by DeWitt Bruyn. Sadly, the proof of Kehoe's self-described "weakness for cupolas" no longer exists, the cupola having rotted away. Once a funeral home and then an inn owned briefly for a time by football legend Joe Namath, the Kehoe House is now one of Savannah's premier bed-and-breakfasts. It's unique not only in its exuberantly Victorian architecture but in its twin fireplaces and ubiquitous rococo ironwork, courtesy of the irrepressible Kehoe himself.

WARREN AND WASHINGTON SQUARES

Warren Square and its neighbor Washington Square formed the first extension of Oglethorpe's original four and still boast some of the oldest houses in the Historic District. Both squares are lovely little garden spots, ideal for a picnic in the shade. Two houses near Washington Square were restored by the late Jim Williams of *Midnight* fame: The **Hampton Lillibridge House** (507 E. St. Julian St.), which once hosted an Episcopal exorcism, and the **Charles Oddingsells House** (510 E. St. Julian St.). Now a hotel, the **Mulberry Inn** on Washington Square was once a cotton warehouse and subsequently one of the nation's first Coca-Cola bottling plants.

GREENE SQUARE

Named for Revolutionary War hero Nathanael Greene, but bearing no monument to him whatsoever, this square is of particular importance to local African American history. At the corner of Houston (pronounced "HOUSE-ton") and East State Streets is the 1810 **Cunningham House,** built for Henry Cunningham, former slave and founding pastor of the **Second African Baptist Church** (124 Houston St., 912/233-6163) on the west side of the square, in which General Sherman made his famous promise of "40 acres and a mule." In 1818, the residence at 542 East State Street was constructed for free blacks Charlotte and William Wall. The property at 513 East York Street was built for the estate of Catherine DeVeaux, part of a prominent African American family.

Old Fort

One of the lesser-known aspects of Savannah history is this well-trod neighborhood at the east end of Bay Street, once the site of groundbreaking experiments and piratical intrigue, then a diverse melting pot of Savannah citizenry.

TRUSTEES GARDEN

At the east end of Bay Street where it meets East Broad Street rises a bluff behind a masonry wall—at 40 feet off the river, still the highest point in Chatham County. This is Trustees Garden, the nation's first experimental garden. Modeled on the Chelsea Botanical Garden in London, it was intended to be the epicenter of Savannah's silk industry. Alas, the colonists had little knowledge of native soils or climate—they thought the winters would be milder—and the experiment was not as successful as hoped. Soon Trustees Garden became the site of Fort Wayne, a defensive installation overlooking the river named after General "Mad Anthony" Wayne of Revolutionary War fame, who retired to a plantation near Savannah. The Fort Wayne area—still called the "Old Fort" neighborhood by old-timers—fell from grace and became associated with the "lowest elements" of Savannah society, which in the 19th and early 20th centuries were Irish and African Americans. It also became known for its illegal activity and as the haunt of sea salts such as the ones who frequented what is now the delightfully schlocky Pirates' House restaurant. That building began life in 1753 as a seamen's inn and was later chronicled by Robert Louis Stevenson in *Treasure Island* as a rogue's gallery of pirates and nautical ne'er-do-wells.

Find the **Herb House** on East Broad Street, the older-looking clapboard structure next to the Pirates' House entrance. You're looking at what is considered the single oldest building in Georgia and one of the oldest in the United States. Constructed in 1734, it was originally the home of Trustees Garden's chief gardener.

To the rear of Trustees Garden is the 1881 Hillyer building, now the **Charles H. Morris Center,** a mixed-use performing arts and meeting space that is heavily used during the springtime Savannah Music Festival.

EMMET PARK

Just north of Reynolds Square on the north side of Bay Street you'll come to Emmet Park, first a Native American burial ground and then known as "the Strand" or "Irish Green" because of its proximity to the Irish slums of the Old Fort. In 1902 the park was named for Robert Emmet, an Irish patriot of the early 1800s, who was executed by the British for treason. Within it is the eight-foot **Celtic Cross,** erected in 1983 and carved of Irish limestone. The Celtic Cross is the center of a key ceremony for local Irish Catholics during the week prior to St. Patrick's Day.

Close by is one of Savannah's more recent

monuments, the **Vietnam War Memorial** at East Bay Street and Rossiter Lane. The reflecting pool is in the shape of Vietnam itself, and the names of all 106 Savannahians killed in the conflict are carved into an adjacent marble tablet.

Walk a little farther east and you'll find my favorite little chapter of Bay Street history, the **Beacon Range Light.** Tucked into a shady corner, few visitors bother to check out this masterfully crafted 1858 navigation aid, intended to warn approaching ships of the old wrecks sunk in the river as a defense during the Revolutionary War.

Broughton Street

Downtown's main shopping district for most of the 20th century, Broughton Street once dazzled shoppers with decorated gaslights, ornate window displays, and fine examples of terrazzo, a form of mosaic that still adorns many shop entrances. Postwar suburbs and white flight brought neglect to the area by the 1960s, and many thought Broughton was gone for good. But with the downtown renaissance brought about largely by the Savannah College of Art and Design (SCAD), Broughton was able not only to get back on its feet but to thrive as a commercial center once again.

Around the corner from the Lucas Theatre on Reynolds Square is the art moderne **Trustees Theatre** (216 E. Broughton St., 912/525-5051, www.scad.edu), a SCAD-run operation that seats 1,200 and hosts concerts, film screenings, and the school's much-anticipated spring fashion show. It began life in the postwar boom of 1946 as the Weis Theatre, another one of those ornate Southern movie houses that took full commercial advantage of being the only buildings at the time to have air conditioning. But by the end of the 1970s it followed the fate of Broughton Street, lying dormant and neglected until its purchase and renovation by SCAD in 1989.

This block of Broughton in front of Trustees

THE IRISH IN SAVANNAH

It seems Savannah's close connection to St. Patrick's Day was ordained from the beginning. The very first baby born here, Georgia Close, came into the world on March 17, 1733. Two hundred and fifty years later, Savannah holds the second-largest St. Patrick's Day celebration in the world, second only to New York City's. Three presidents have visited during the shindig—William Howard Taft, Harry Truman, and Jimmy Carter. With its fine spring weather and walkability—not to mention its liberal "to-go cup" rules allowing you to carry an adult beverage on the street—Savannah is tailor-made for a boisterous outdoor celebration. But most of all, what makes it a perfect fit is the city's large Irish-American population.

The earliest Irish in Georgia were descendants of the Calvinist Scots who "planted" Ireland's northern province of Ulster in the 1600s. Often called "crackers"—perhaps from the Gaelic *craic*, "enjoyable conversation"—these early Irish entered Georgia from upstate South Carolina and made their living trading, trapping, or soldiering. One such "cracker" was Sergeant William Jasper, mortally wounded leading the charge to retake Savannah from the British in 1779.

The main chapter in local Irish history began in the 1830s with the arrival of the first wave of Irish to build the Central of Georgia Railway. The story goes that Irish were employed on the railroad because, unlike slaves, their bodies had no commercial value and could be worked to exhaustion with impunity. A second wave of Irish immigration followed two decades later when the potato famine in the old country forced many to seek new shores.

Though the Irish were initially subject to prejudice, their willingness to work long hours for low pay soon made them irreplaceable in Savannah's economy. And as in New York, in short order the Irish became major players in politics and business. In the early days, Irish neighborhoods were clustered around East Broad Street in the Old Fort area, and on the west side near West Broad Street (now MLK Jr. Boulevard). It's no coincidence that those areas also had large African American populations. Because of their shared links of poverty and prejudice, in the early days Savannah's Irish tended to live near black neighborhoods, often socializing with them after-hours—much to the chagrin of Savannah's elite.

Ironically, given St. Patrick's Day's current close association with the Catholic faith, the first parade in Savannah was organized by Irish Protestants. Thirteen members of the local Hibernian Society—the country's oldest Irish society—took part in a private procession to Independent Presbyterian Church in 1813. The first public procession was in 1824, when the Hibernians invited all local Irishmen to parade through the streets. The first recognizably modern parade, with bands and a "grand marshal," happened in 1870.

Today's parade is a far cry from those early beginnings. Organized by a "committee" of about 700 local Irishmen—with but a tiny sprinkling of women—the three-hour procession includes marchers from all the local Irish organizations, in addition to marching bands and floats representing many local groups. Rain or shine, the assembled clans march—*amble* is perhaps a more accurate word—wearing their kelly green blazers, brandishing their walking canes and to-go cups, some pushing future committee members in strollers, fair skin gradually getting redder in the Georgia sun.

Theatre is usually blocked off to mark the gala opening of the Savannah Film Festival each fall. Searchlights crisscross the sky, limos idle in wait, and Hollywood guests strike poses for the photographers.

Across the street is SCAD's **Jen Library** (201 E. Broughton St.), a state-of-the-art facility set in the circa-1890 Levy and Maas Brothers department stores. An important piece of Broughton Street history happened farther west at its intersection with Whitaker Street. Tondee's Tavern was where the infamous "Liberty Boys" met over ale and planned Savannah's role in the American Revolution.

Only a plaque marks the site's contribution to Savannah's colonial history.

Wright Square

By now you know the drill. The big monument in Wright Square, Oglethorpe's second square, has nothing to do with James Wright, royal governor of Georgia before the Revolution, for whom it's named. Instead the monument honors **William Gordon,** former mayor and founder of the Central of Georgia Railway, which upon completion of the Savannah–Macon run was the longest railroad in the world. Gordon is in fact the only native Savannahian honored in a city square. But more importantly, Wright Square is the final resting place for the great Yamacraw chief **Tomochichi,** buried in 1737 in an elaborate state funeral at James Oglethorpe's insistence. A huge boulder of north Georgia granite honoring the chief was placed in a corner of the square in 1899 under the auspices of William Gordon's daughter-in-law. However, Tomochichi is not buried under the boulder, but rather somewhere underneath the Gordon monument. So why not rename it Tomochichi Square? Old ways die hard down here, my friend.

On the west side of the square is the **Federal Courthouse and Post Office,** built in 1898 out of Georgia marble. The building's stately facade makes an appearance in several films, including the original *Cape Fear* and *Midnight in the Garden of Good and Evil.* Across the square stands another Preston design, the **Old Chatham County Courthouse,** no longer an active judicial facility but still known as "the old courthouse." Note the yellow brick construction, quite rare for this area.

Next to the old courthouse is the historic **Evangelical Lutheran Church of the Ascension** (120 Bull St., 912/232-4151, www. elcota.org), built in the 1870s for a congregation that traced its roots to some of the first Austrian Salzburgers to come to Savannah in 1734. While most moved to adjacent

Effingham County, many stayed and thrived in town, where they were universally well-regarded for their work ethic and honest dealings.

JULIETTE GORDON LOW BIRTHPLACE

Around the corner from Wright Square at Oglethorpe and Bull is the Juliette Gordon Low Birthplace (10 E. Oglethorpe Ave., 912/233-4501, www.juliettegordonlowbirthplace.org, Mar.–Oct. Mon.–Sat. 10 A.M.–4 P.M., Sun. 11 A.M.–4 P.M., Nov.–Feb. Mon.–Tues. and Thurs.–Sat. 10 A.M.–4 P.M., Sun. 11 A.M.–4 P.M., $8 adults, $7 children, $6 Girl Scouts under age 19), declared the city's very first National Historic Landmark in 1965. The founder of the Girl Scouts of the USA lived here from her birth in 1860 until her marriage, returning home to stay until her mother's death. The house was completed in 1821 for Mayor James Moore Wayne, future Supreme Court Justice, but the current furnishings, many original, are intended to reflect the home during the 1880s.

Also called the Girl Scout National Center, the Low birthplace is probably Savannah's most festive historic site because of the heavy traffic of Girl Scout troops from across the United States. They flock here year-round to take part in programs and learn more about their organization's founder, whose family sold the house to the Girl Scouts in 1953. You don't have to be affiliated with the Girl Scouts to tour the home. Tours are given every 15 minutes, and tickets are available at the Oglethorpe Avenue entrance. Be aware the site is closed most holidays, sometimes for extended periods; be sure to check the website for details.

Oglethorpe Square

Don't look for a monument to Georgia's founder in the square named for him. That would be way too easy, so of course his monument is in Chippewa Square. Originally called "Upper New Square," Oglethorpe Square was created in 1742.

SCOUT'S HONOR: JULIETTE GORDON LOW

Known as "Daisy" to family and friends, Juliette Magill Kinzie Gordon was born to be a pioneer. Her father's family took part in the original settlement of Georgia, and her mother's kin were among the founders of Chicago. Mostly known as the founder of the Girl Scouts of the USA, Daisy was also an artist, adventurer, and healer. Born and raised in the house on Oglethorpe Avenue in Savannah known to Girl Scouts across the nation as simply "The Birthplace," she was an animal lover with an early penchant for theater, drawing, and poetry.

After school she traveled, returning home to marry wealthy cotton heir William Mackay Low, son of the builder of Savannah's exquisite Andrew Low House. A harbinger of her troubled marriage happened on her wedding day on the steps of Christ Church. A grain of rice, thrown for good luck, struck her eardrum and led to a painful infection and loss of hearing. Daisy and her husband moved to England, using the Andrew Low House as a rental property and winter residence. She maintained a home in England until her death, spending much of the year traveling in the United States and abroad.

Daisy returned to Savannah with the outbreak of the Spanish-American War in 1898. Because of the city's proximity to Cuba, one of the main theaters of the war, it became a staging area for U.S. Army troops from all over the country. For Savannah, taking such an active role was an opportunity to make amends for the alienation of the Civil War and effectively rejoin the Union again. For the first time since Sherman's March to the Sea, Savannahians proudly displayed the Stars and Stripes in an honest show of patriotism of which Daisy was a part, tending to wounded soldiers returning from Cuba. After the war, Daisy returned to England to spend the last days of her marriage, which existed in name only until her husband's death in 1905. After settling his estate, she used the proceeds to fund some traveling.

In 1911 while in England, she met another man who would change her life: Robert Baden-Powell, founder of the Boy Scouts and Girl Guides in Britain. Struck by the simplicity and usefulness of his project, she carried the seeds of a similar idea back with her to the United States. "I've got something for the girls of Savannah, and all of America, and all the world, and we're going to start it tonight," were her famous words in a phone call to a cousin after meeting Baden-Powell. So on March 12, 1912, Daisy gathered 18 girls to register the first troop of American Girl Guides, later the Girl Scouts of the USA.

Juliette "Daisy" Gordon Low died of breast cancer in her bed in the Andrew Low House on January 17, 1927. She was buried in Laurel Grove Cemetery on the city's west side. Girl Scout troops from all over the United States visit her birthplace, the Andrew Low House, and her gravesite to this day, often leaving flowers and small personal objects near her tombstone as tokens of respect and gratitude.

SAVANNAH

◀ OWENS-THOMAS HOUSE

The square's main claim to fame, the Owens-Thomas House (124 Abercorn St., 912/233-9743, www.telfair.org, Mon. noon–5 P.M., Tues.–Sat. 10 A.M.–5 P.M., Sun. 1–5 P.M., last tour 4:30 P.M., $15 adults, $5 children, $20 multi-site ticket), lies on the northeast corner. Widely known as the finest example of Regency architecture in the United States, the Owens-Thomas House was designed by brilliant young English architect William Jay. One of the first professionally trained architects in the United States, Jay was only 24 when he designed the home for cotton merchant or "factor" Richard Richardson, who lost the house in the depression of 1820 (all that remains of Richardson's tenure are three marble-top tables). The house's current name is derived from Savannah Mayor George Owens, who bought the house in 1830. It remained in his family until 1951, when his granddaughter Margaret Thomas bequeathed it to the Telfair Academy of Arts and Sciences, which currently operates the site.

Several things about the Owens-Thomas

House stand out. First, it's constructed mostly of tabby, a mixture of lime, oyster shells, and sand. Its exterior is English stucco while the front garden balustrade is a type of artificial stone called Coade stone. Perhaps most interestingly, a complex plumbing system features rain-fed cisterns, flushing toilets, sinks, bathtubs, and a shower. When built, the Owens-Thomas House in fact had the first indoor plumbing in Savannah.

While inside the house, notice the little touches like the unusual curved walls, with doors bowed to match, and the recessed skylights. While many Owens family furnishings are part of the collection, much of it is representative of American and European work from 1750 to 1830. On the south facade is a beautiful cast-iron veranda from which Revolutionary War hero Marquis de Lafayette addressed a crowd of starstruck Savannahians during his visit in 1825. The 1990s marked the most intensive phase of restoration for the home, which began with a careful renovation of the carriage house and the associated slave quarters—discovered in a surprisingly intact state, including the original "haint blue" paint. The carriage house, where all tours begin, is now the home's gift shop.

Telfair Square

One of the few Savannah squares to show consistency in nomenclature, Telfair Square was indeed named for Mary Telfair, last heir of a family that was one of the most important in Savannah history. A noted patron of the arts, Mary bequeathed the family mansion to the Georgia Historical Society upon her death in 1875 to serve as a museum. Originally called St. James Square after a similar square in London, Telfair is the last of Oglethorpe's original four squares.

◖ TELFAIR MUSEUMS

Also consistent with its name, Telfair Square indeed hosts two of the three buildings operated by the Telfair Museums (912/790-8800, www.telfair.org, $20 adults, $5 children, $12 Jepson Center and Telfair Academy, $15 Owens-Thomas House, free under age 5), an umbrella organization that relies on a combination of private and public funding and has driven much of the arts agenda in Savannah for the last 125 years. The original part of the complex and in fact the oldest public art museum in the South, the **Telfair Academy of Arts and Sciences** (121 Barnard St., Mon. noon–5 P.M., Tues.–Sat. 10 A.M.–5 P.M., Sun. 1–5 P.M.) was built in 1821 by the great William Jay for Alexander Telfair, scion of that famous Georgia family. The five statues in front are of Phidias, Raphael, Rubens, Michelangelo, and Rembrandt. Inside, the sculpture gallery and rotunda were added in 1885, the year before the building's official opening as a museum. As well as displaying Sylvia Judson Shaw's now-famous *Bird Girl* sculpture, originally in Bonaventure Cemetery (actually the third of four casts by the sculptor), the Telfair Academy features an outstanding collection of primarily 18th- and 20th-century works, most notably the largest public collection of visual art by Khalil Gibran. Major paintings include work by Childe Hassam, Frederick Frieseke, Gari Melchers, and the massive *Black Prince of Crécy* by Julian Story.

The latest and proudest addition to the Telfair brand is the striking, 64,000-square-foot **Jepson Center for the Arts** (207 W. York St., Tues.–Wed. and Fri.–Sat. 10 A.M.–5 P.M., Thurs. 10 A.M.–8 P.M., Sun.–Mon. noon–5 P.M.), whose ultramodern exterior sits catty-corner from the old Telfair. Promoting a massive, daringly designed new facility devoted to nothing but modern art was a hard sell in this traditional town, especially when renowned architect Moshe Safdie insisted on building a glassed-in flyover across a lane between two buildings. After a few delays in construction, Jepson opened its doors in 2006

A CITY OF ART

There are more art galleries per capita in Savannah than in New York City—one gallery for every 2,191 residents, to be exact. The no-brainer package experience for the visitor is the combo of the **Telfair Academy of Arts and Sciences** (121 Barnard St., 912/790-8800, www.telfair.org) and the **Jepson Center for the Arts** (207 W. York St., 912/790-8800, www.telfair.org). These two affiliated arms of the Telfair Museums run the gamut, from the Academy's impressive collection of Khalil Gibran drawings to the 2011 hanging installation of large, whimsical birds by local favorite Matt Hebermehl at the Jepson.

Naturally, Savannah College of Art & Design (SCAD) galleries (912/525-5225, www.scad.edu) are in abundance all over town, displaying the handiwork of students, faculty, alumni, and important national and regional artists. The SCAD outposts with the most consistently impressive exhibits of visiting artists—along with the occasional thesis show—are the **Pei Ling Chan Gallery** (324 MLK Jr. Blvd.), **Gutstein Gallery** (201 E. Broughton St.), and **Pinnacle Gallery** (320 E. Liberty St.). The college also runs its own museum, the **SCAD Museum of Art** (227 MLK Jr. Blvd., 912/525-7191, www.scad.edu), which recently doubled in size to accommodate a massive new wing devoted to the huge and wonderful Walter O. Evans Collection of African American Art.

While they don't get as much press, Savannah also has plenty of non-Telfair, non-SCAD galleries as well, ranging from the cutting edge to pedestrian acrylics of seagulls. An adventurous indie cooperative in town that focuses on local artists is **Kobo Gallery** (33 Barnard St., 912/201-0304, http://kobogallery.com), on Ellis Square near City Market.

Other neat locally focused spots include the fairly avant-garde **Desotorow Gallery** (2427 DeSoto Ave., 912/335-8204, www.desotorow.org); **Gallery Espresso** (234 Bull St., 912/233-5348, www.galleryespresso.com), actually a coffeehouse; and **Daedalus Gallery** (129 E. Liberty St., 912/233-2005, http://daedalus-art.com), which is run by a married couple, native Georgian William Weyman and Frenchwoman Jacqueline Carcagno, and where you'll find a nice selection of impressionist works in the French tradition, a rarity in Savannah. More serious collectors will appreciate **Kim Iocovozzi Fine Art** (539 Abercorn St., 912/234-9424), pronounced "IKE-a-vo-zee" and hosting contemporary masters and a neat collection of daguerreotypes (Kim's a guy, by the way).

An interesting, newish gallery in town, **Liquid Sands Glass Gallery** (5 W. York St., 912/232-3600, www.liquidsandsglassgallery.com), deals in intricate blown studio glass from North American artists.

and has since wowed locals and visitors alike with its cutting-edge traveling exhibits and rotating assortment of late-20th-century and 21st-century modern art. If you get hungry, you can enjoy lunch in the expansive atrium café, and, of course, there's a nice gift shop.

Paying admission to one site also gets you a one-time visit to the other two sites for a week following purchase.

TRINITY UNITED METHODIST CHURCH

Directly between the Telfair and the Jepson stands Trinity United Methodist Church (225 W. President St., 912/233-4766, www.

trinitychurch1848.org, sanctuary daily 9 A.M.–5 P.M., services Sun. 8:45 A.M. and 11 A.M.), Savannah's first Methodist church. Built in 1848 on the site of the Telfair's family garden, its masonry walls are of famous "Savannah Gray" bricks—a lighter, more porous, and elegant variety—under stucco. Virgin longleaf pine was used for most of the interior, fully restored in 1969. Call ahead for a tour.

Chippewa Square

Named for a battle in the War of 1812, Chippewa Square has a large monument not to the battle, natch, but to James Oglethorpe,

© JIM MOREKIS

statue of Gen. James Oglethorpe in Chippewa Square

clad in full soldier's regalia. Notice the general is still facing south, toward the Spanish.

Yes, the bench on the square's north side is in the same location as the one Tom Hanks occupied in *Forrest Gump,* but it's not the same bench that hosted the two-time Oscar winner's backside—that one was donated by Paramount Pictures to be displayed in the Savannah History Museum on MLK Jr. Boulevard.

From Chippewa Square look south for the huge rectangular steel-and-glass structure dominating the skyline along Liberty Street. That's the infamous **Drayton Tower,** an outstanding, nearly pure example of the internationalist architecture style nonetheless loathed by traditionalists since its construction in 1955. Until recently it served as low-cost housing for students and seniors. They've since been kicked out, as now the building is subdivided into high-end condos with retail on the ground floor.

HISTORIC SAVANNAH THEATRE

At the northeast corner is the Historic Savannah Theatre (222 Bull St., 912/233-7764, www.savannahtheatre.com), which claims to be the oldest continuously operating theater in the United States. Designed by William Jay, it opened in 1818 with a production of *The Soldier's Daughter.* In the glory days of gaslight theater in the 1800s, some of the nation's best actors, including Edwin Booth, brother to Lincoln's assassin, regularly trod the boards of its stage. Other notable visitors were Sarah Bernhardt, W. C. Fields, and Oscar Wilde. Due to a fire in 1948, little remains of Jay's original design except a small section of exterior wall. It's currently home to a semiprofessional revue company specializing in oldies shows.

INDEPENDENT PRESBYTERIAN CHURCH

Built in 1818, possibly by William Jay—scholars are unsure of the scope of his involvement—Independent Presbyterian Church (207 Bull St., 912/236-3346, www.ipcsav.org, services Sun. 11 A.M., Wed. noon) is called the "mother of Georgia Presbyterianism." A fire destroyed most of Independent Presbyterian's original structure in 1889, but the subsequent rebuilding was a very faithful rendering of the original design, based on London's St. Martin-in-the-Fields. The marble baptism font survived the fire and is still used today. Note also the huge mahogany pulpit, another original feature. The church's steeple made a cameo appearance in *Forrest Gump* as a white feather floated by.

Lowell Mason, composer of the hymn "Nearer My God to Thee," was organist at Independent Presbyterian. In 1885 President Woodrow Wilson married local parishioner Ellen Louise Axson in the manse to the rear of the church. Presiding was her grandfather, minister at the time. During the Great Awakening in 1896, almost 3,000 people jammed the sanctuary to hear famous evangelist D. L. Moody preach. Call ahead for a tour.

FIRST BAPTIST CHURCH

The nearby First Baptist Church (223 Bull St., 912/234-2671, services Sun. 11 A.M.) claims to be the oldest original church building in Savannah, with a cornerstone dating from 1830. Services were held here throughout the Civil War, with Union troops attending during the occupation. The church was renovated by renowned local architect Henrik Wallin in 1922. Call ahead for a tour.

COLONIAL CEMETERY

Just north of Chippewa Square is Oglethorpe Avenue, originally called South Broad and the southern boundary of the original colony. At Oglethorpe and Abercorn Streets is Colonial Cemetery, first active in 1750. You'd be forgiven for assuming it's the "DAR" cemetery; the Daughters of the American Revolution contributed the ornate iron entranceway in 1913, thoughtfully dedicating it to themselves instead of the cemetery itself.

Unlike the picturesque beauty of Bonaventure and Laurel Grove cemeteries, Colonial Cemetery has a morbid feel. The fact that burials stopped here in 1853 plays into that desolation, but maybe another reason is because it's the final resting ground of many of Savannah's yellow fever victims. Famous people buried here include Button Gwinnett, one of Georgia's three signers of the Declaration of Independence. The man who reluctantly killed Gwinnett in a duel, General Lachlan McIntosh, is also buried here. The original burial vault of Nathanael Greene is in the cemetery, although the Revolutionary War hero's remains were moved to Johnson Square over a century ago.

Vandalism through the years, mostly by Union troops, took a toll on the old gravestones. Many line the east wall of the cemetery, with no one alive able to remember where they originally stood.

Madison Square

Named for the nation's fourth president, Madison Square memorializes a local hero who gave his life for his city during the American Revolution. Irish immigrant Sergeant William Jasper, hero of the Battle of Fort Moultrie in Charleston three years earlier, was killed leading the American charge during the Siege of Savannah, when an allied army failed to retake the city from the British. The monument in the square honors Jasper, but he isn't buried here; his body was interred in a mass grave near the battlefield along with other colonists and soldier-immigrants killed in the one-sided battle.

The two small, suitably warlike cannons in the square have nothing to do with the Siege of Savannah. They commemorate the first two highways in Georgia, today known as Augusta Road and Ogeechee Road.

GREEN-MELDRIM HOUSE

Given the house's beauty and history, visitors will be forgiven for not immediately realizing that the Green-Meldrim House (1 W. Macon St., 912/232-1251, tours every 30 minutes Tues. and Thurs.–Fri. 10 A.M.–4 P.M., Sat. 10 A.M.–1 P.M., $7 adults, $2 children) is also the rectory of the adjacent St. John's Episcopal Church, which acquired it in 1892. Though known primarily for serving as General William T. Sherman's headquarters during his occupation of Savannah, visitors find the Green-Meldrim House a remarkably calming, serene location in and of itself, quite apart from its role as the place where Sherman formulated his ill-fated "40 acres and a mule" Field Order Number 15, giving most of the Sea Islands of Georgia and South Carolina to freed blacks. A remarkably tasteful example of Gothic Revival architecture, this 1850 design by John Norris features a beautiful external gallery of filigree ironwork. The interior is decorated with a keen and rare eye for elegant minimalism in this sometimes rococo-minded town.

Nearby, the old **Scottish Rite Temple** at Charlton and Bull Streets was designed by

SAVANNAH

© JIM MOREKIS

the Green-Meldrim House

Hyman Witcover, who also designed City Hall. A popular drugstore with a soda fountain for many years, it currently houses the Gryphon Tea Room, run by the Savannah College of Art and Design.

Directly across from that is SCAD's first building, **Poetter Hall,** known to old-timers as the Savannah Volunteer Guards Armory. With its imposing but somewhat whimsical facade right out of a Harry Potter movie, this brick and terra-cotta gem of a Romanesque Revival building was built in 1893 by William Gibbons Preston. It housed National Guard units (as well as a high school) until World War II, when the USO occupied the building during its tenant unit's service in Europe.

At the north side of Madison Square is the **Hilton Savannah DeSoto.** Imagine occupying that same space the most glorious, opulent, regal building you can think of, a paradise of brick, mortar, and buff-colored terra-cotta. That would have been the old DeSoto Hotel,

which from its opening in 1890 was known as one of the world's most beautiful hotels and the clear masterpiece in Boston architect William Gibbons Preston's already-impressive Savannah portfolio. Alas, it didn't have air-conditioning, so the Hilton chain demolished it in 1968 to build the current nondescript box.

Lafayette Square

Truly one of Savannah's favorite squares, especially on St. Patrick's Day, verdant Lafayette Square boasts a number of important sights and attractions.

C CATHEDRAL OF ST. JOHN THE BAPTIST

Spiritual home to Savannah's Irish community and the oldest Catholic church in Georgia, the Cathedral of St. John the Baptist (222. E. Harris St., 912/233-4709, www. savannahcathedral.org, daily 9 A.M.–noon and 12:30–5 P.M., mass Sun. 8 A.M., 10 A.M.,

11:30 A.M., Mon.–Sat. noon, Latin mass Sun. 1 P.M.) was initially known as Our Lady of Perpetual Help. It's the place to be for mass the morning of March 17 at 8 A.M., as the clans gather in their green jackets and white dresses to take a sip of communion wine before moving on to harder stuff in honor of St. Patrick.

Despite its overt Celtic character today, the parish was originally founded by Haitian émigrés who arrived after an uprising in their native country in the late 1700s. They were joined by other Gallic Catholics when some nobles fled from the French Revolution. The first sanctuary on the site was built in 1873, after the diocese traded a lot at Taylor and Lincoln Streets to the Sisters of Mercy in exchange for this locale. In a distressingly common event back then in Savannah, fire swept through the edifice in 1898, leaving only two spires and the external walls. In an amazing story of determination and skill, the cathedral was completely rebuilt within a year and a half. In the years since, many renovations have been undertaken, including an interior renovation following the Second Vatican Council to incorporate some of its sweeping reforms, for example, a new altar allowing the celebrant to face the congregation. The most recent renovation, from 1998 to 2000, involved the intricate removal, cleaning, and releading of more than 50 of the cathedral's stained-glass windows, a roof replacement, and an interior makeover.

When inside the magnificent interior, look for the new 9,000-pound altar and the 8,000-pound baptismal font, both made of Italian marble.

In 2003 an armed man entered the cathedral and set the pulpit and bishop's chair on fire, resulting in nearly $400,000 of damage. The pulpit you see now is an exact replica carved in Italy. The arsonist claimed he did it as a statement against organized religion.

ANDREW LOW HOUSE MUSEUM

Another major landmark on Lafayette Square is the Andrew Low House Museum (329 Abercorn St., 912/233-6854, www.andrewlowhouse.com, Mon.–Wed. and Fri.–Sat. 10 A.M.–4:30 P.M., Sun. noon–4:30 P.M., last tour 4 P.M., $8 adults, $4.50 children), once the home of Juliette "Daisy" Gordon Low, the founder of the Girl Scouts of the USA, who was married to cotton heir William "Billow" Low, Andrew Low's son. Despite their happy-go-lucky nicknames, the union of Daisy and Billow was a notably unhappy one. Still, divorce was out of the question, so the couple lived separate lives until William's death in 1905. The one good thing that came out of the marriage was the germ for the idea for the Girl Scouts, which Juliette got from England's "Girl Guides" while living there with her husband, Savannah being the couple's winter residence.

Designed by the great New York architect John Norris, the Low House is a magnificent example of the Italianate style. Check out the cast-iron balconies on the long porch, a fairly rare feature in historic Savannah homes. Antiques junkies will go nuts over the furnishings, especially the massive secretary in the parlor, one of only four of this type in existence (a sibling is in the Metropolitan Museum of Art). Author William Makepeace Thackeray ate in the dining room, now sporting full French porcelain service, and slept in an upstairs room; he also wrote at the desk by the bed. Also on the second floor you'll see the room where Robert E. Lee stayed during his visit and the bed where Juliette Gordon Low died.

FLANNERY O'CONNOR CHILDHOOD HOME

On the other corner of Lafayette Square stands the rather Spartan facade of the Flannery O'Connor Childhood Home (207 E. Charlton St., 912/233-6014, www.flanneryoconnorhome.org, Fri.–Wed. 1–4 P.M., $6 adults, $5 students, free under age 15). The Savannah-born novelist lived in this three-story townhome from her birth in 1925 until 1938 and attended church at the cathedral across the square. Once a fairly nondescript attraction for so favorite a native daughter, a recent round of renovations has returned the two main floors to the state Flannery would have known, including an extensive library. A nonprofit association sponsors O'Connor-related readings and signings. While the current backyard garden dates to 1993, it's the place where five-year-old Flannery is said to have taught a chicken to walk backward, foreshadowing the eccentric, Gothic flavor of her writing.

Across from the O'Connor house is the **Hamilton-Turner Inn** (330 Abercorn St., 912/233-1833, www.hamilton-turnerinn.com). Now a privately owned bed-and-breakfast, this 1873 Second Empire mansion is best known for the showmanship of its over-the-top Victorian appointments and its role in "The Book" as the home of Joe Odom's girlfriend "Mandy Nichols" (real name Nancy Hillis). In 1883 it was reportedly the first house in Savannah to have electricity.

Troup Square

This low-key square boasts the most modern-looking monument downtown, the **Armillary Sphere.** Essentially an elaborate sundial, the sphere is a series of astrologically themed rings with an arrow that marks the time by shadow. It is supported by six tortoises.

Troup Square is also the home of the historic **Unitarian Universalist Church of Savannah** (313 E. Harris St., 912/234-0980, www.jinglebellschurch.org, services Sun. 11 A.M.). This original home of Savannah's Unitarians, who sold the church when the Civil War came, was recently reacquired by the congregation. It is where James L. Pierpont first performed his immortal tune "Jingle Bells." When he did so, however, the church was actually on Oglethorpe Square. The entire building was moved to Troup Square in the mid-1800s.

Just east of Troup Square, near the intersection of Harris and Price Streets, is the **Beach Institute** (502 E. Harris St., 912/234-8000, www.kingtisdell.org, Tues.–Sun. noon–5 P.M., $4). Built as a school by the Freedmen's Bureau soon after the Civil War, it was named after its prime benefactor, Alfred Beach, editor of *Scientific American*. It served as an African American school through 1919. Restored by SCAD and given back to the city to serve as a museum, the Beach Institute houses the permanent Ulysses Davis collection and a rotating calendar of art events with a connection to black history.

JONES STREET

There aren't a lot of individual attractions on Jones Street, the east–west avenue between Taylor and Charlton Streets just north of Monterey Square. Rather, it's the small-scale, throwback feel of the place and its tasteful, dignified homes, including the former home of Joe Odom (16 E. Jones St.), that are the attraction. The **Eliza Thompson House** (5 W. Jones St.), now a bed-and-breakfast, was the first home on Jones Street. Cotton factor Joseph Thompson built the house for his wife, Eliza, in 1847. The carriage house is not original to the structure, having been built almost from scratch in 1980.

◀ Monterey Square

For many, this is the ultimate Savannah square. Originally named "Monterrey Square" to commemorate the local Irish Jasper Greens' participation in a victorious Mexican-American War battle in 1846, the spelling morphed into its current version somewhere along the way. But Monterey Square remains one of the most visually beautiful and serene spots in all of Savannah. At the center of the square is a monument not to the victory for which it is named but to Count Casimir Pulaski, killed while attempting to retake the city from the British, and whose remains supposedly lie under the 55-foot monument. As early as 1912, people

THE STORY OF "JINGLE BELLS"

Long after the Civil War, a North-South feud of a more harmless kind still simmers, as Boston and Savannah vie over bragging rights as to where the classic Christmas song "Jingle Bells" was written. The song's composer, James L. Pierpont, led a life at times as carefree as his song itself. Born in Boston as the son of an abolitionist Unitarian minister, Pierpont's wanderlust manifested early, when he ventured from his new wife and young children to follow the 1849 gold rush to San Francisco, coming back east after one of that city's periodic enormous fires. When his brother John was named minister of the new Unitarian congregation in Savannah in 1853–a novelty down south at the time–Pierpont followed him, becoming music director and organist, again leaving behind his wife and children in Boston. During this time Pierpont became a prolific composer of secular tunes, including polkas, ballads, and minstrel songs.

Pierpont's first wife died of tuberculosis in 1856. By August 1857 he had remarried the daughter of the mayor of Savannah. That same month, a Boston-based publisher, Oliver Ditson and Co., published his song "One Horse Open Sleigh." Two years later it was rereleased with the current title, "Jingle Bells." At neither time, however, was the song a popular hit. In 1859, with slavery tearing the country apart, the Unitarian Church in Savannah closed due to its abolitionist stance. By the outbreak of war, Pierpont's brother John had gone back up north. James Pierpont, however, opted to stay in Savannah with his second wife, Eliza Jane, going so far as to sign up with the Isle of Hope Volunteers (he served as a company clerk) of the Confederate Army.

It took action by his son Juriah in 1880 to renew the copyright to what would become one of the most famous songs of all time. Pierpont died in 1883 in Winter Haven, Florida, and by his own request was buried in Savannah's Laurel Grove Cemetery. The provenance of his now-famous song is more in doubt. In Massachusetts, they swear Pierpont wrote the song while at the home of one Mrs. Otis Waterman. In Georgia, scholars assure us a homesick Pierpont wrote the tune during a winter at a house at Oglethorpe and Whitaker Streets, long since demolished. The Savannah contingent's ace in the hole is the fact that "Jingle Bells" was first performed in public at a Thanksgiving program at the local Unitarian Universalist Church in 1857. And despite persistent claims in Massachusetts that he wrote the song there in 1850, Southern scholars point out that Pierpont was actually in California in 1850. So in this case, at least, it appears the South can claim victory over the Yankees.

In one of those delightful happenstances of serendipity, Pierpont's old church–moved to Troup Square from its original site on Oglethorpe Square–went on the market in the 1990s, and the local Unitarian Universalist congregation was able to raise enough money to buy it. It remains there to this day.

began noticing the disintegration of the monument due to substandard marble used in some key parts, but it wasn't until the 1990s that a full restoration was accomplished. The restoration company discovered that one of the monument's 34 sections had been accidentally installed upside down. So in the true spirit of preservation, they dutifully put the section back—upside down. The *Goddess of Liberty* atop the monument, however, is not original; you can see her in the Savannah History Museum. Fans of ironwork will enjoy the ornate masterpieces in wrought iron featured at many houses on the periphery of the square.

MERCER-WILLIAMS HOUSE MUSEUM

Many visitors come to see the Mercer-Williams House Museum (429 Bull St., 912/236-6352, www.mercerhouse.com, Mon.–Sat. 10:30 A.M.–4 P.M., Sun. noon–4 P.M., $12.50 adults, $8 students). While locals never begrudge the business Savannah has enjoyed since "The Book," it's a shame that this grand John Norris building is now primarily known

© JIM MOREKIS

the Mercer-Williams House Museum on Monterey Square

as a crime scene involving antiques dealer Jim Williams and his lover. Therefore it might come as no surprise that if you take a tour of the home, you might hear less about "The Book" than you may have expected. Now proudly owned by Jim Williams's sister Dorothy Kingery, an established academic in her own right, the Mercer-Williams House deliberately concentrates on the early history of the home and her brother's prodigious talent as a collector and conservator of fine art and antiques. That said, Dr. Kingery's mama didn't raise no fool, as we say down here. The house was known to generations of Savannahians as simply the Mercer House until *Midnight in the Garden of Good and Evil* took off, at which time the eponymous nod to the late Mr. Williams was added.

Built for General Hugh W. Mercer, Johnny Mercer's great-grandfather, in 1860, the war interrupted construction. General Mercer—descendant of the Revolutionary War general and George Washington's close friend Hugh

Mercer—survived the war, in which he was charged with the defense of Savannah. But he soon fell on hard times and was forced to sell the house to John Wilder, who moved in after completion in 1868. Just so you know, and despite what any tour guide might tell you, the great Johnny Mercer himself never lived in the house. Technically, no member of his family ever did either.

Tours of the home's four main rooms begin in the carriage house to the rear of the mansion. They're worth it for art aficionados even though the upstairs, Dr. Kingery's residence, is off-limits. Be forewarned that if you're coming just to see things about the book or movie, you might be disappointed.

TEMPLE MICKVE ISRAEL

Directly across Monterey Square from the Mercer House is Temple Mickve Israel (20 E. Gordon St., 912/233-1547, www.mickveisrael. org), a notable structure for many reasons: It's

Georgia's first synagogue; it's the only Gothic synagogue in the country; and it's the third-oldest Jewish congregation in North America (following those in New York and Newport, Rhode Island). Notable congregants have included Dr. Samuel Nunes Ribeiro, who helped stop an epidemic in 1733; his descendant Raphael Moses, considered the father of the peach industry in the Peach State; and current Mickve Israel Rabbi Arnold Mark Belzer, one of Savannah's most beloved community leaders. A specialist in the study of small, often-persecuted Jewish communities around the world, Belzer met Pope John Paul II in 2005 as a part of that pontiff's historic rapprochement between the Catholic Church and Judaism.

Mickve Israel offers 30–45 minute tours of the sanctuary and museum (Mon.–Fri. 10 A.M.–1 P.M. and 2–4 P.M., closed Jewish holidays).

Calhoun Square

The last of the 24 squares in Savannah's original grid, Calhoun Square is also the only square with all its original buildings intact—a rarity indeed in a city ravaged by fire so many times in its history.

Dominating the south side of the square is Savannah's first public elementary school and spiritual home of Savannah educators, the **Massie Heritage Center** (207 E. Gordon St., 912/201-5070, www.massieschool.com, Mon.–Fri. 9 A.M.–4 P.M., self-guided tour $7 adults, $3 children). In 1841, Peter Massie, a Scots planter with a populist streak, endowed the school to give poor children as good an education as the children of rich families, like Massie's own, received. Another of Savannah's masterpieces by John Norris—whose impressive oeuvre includes the Low House, the Mercer House, and the Green-Meldrim House—the central portion of the trifold building was completed in 1856 and is a great example of Greek Revival architecture. The two large wings on each side were added later by different architects. After the Civil War, the "Massie school," as it's known locally, was designated as the area's African American public school. Classes ceased in 1974, and it now operates as a living history museum, centering on the period-appointed one-room "heritage classroom." A recent million-dollar renovation includes an interactive model of Oglethorpe's urban design and several interesting exhibits on aspects of Savannah architecture and history.

Catty-corner to the Massie School is the **Wesley Monumental United Methodist Church** (429 Abercorn St., 912/232-0191, www.wesleymonumental.org, sanctuary daily 9 A.M.–5 P.M., services Sun. 8:45 A.M. and 11 A.M.). This home of Savannah's first Methodist parish was named not only for movement founder John Wesley but for his musical younger brother Charles. Built in 1875 on the model of Queen's Kirk in Amsterdam and the fourth incarnation of the parish home, this is another great example of Savannah's Gothic churches. Its acoustically wonderful sanctuary features a magnificent Noack organ, which would no doubt please the picky ears of Charles Wesley himself, author of the lyrics to "Hark! The Herald Angels Sing."

Martin Luther King Jr. Boulevard

Originally known as West Broad Street (you'll still hear old-timers refer to it that way), Martin Luther King Jr. Boulevard is the spiritual home of Savannah's African American community, though it has gone through several transformations. In the early 1800s, West Broad was a fashionable address, but during the middle of that century its north end got a bad reputation for crime and blight as thousands of Irish immigrants packed in right beside the area's poor black population.

West Broad's glory days as a center of black culture happened in the first half of the 20th century, beginning and ending with the late, great Union Station terminal. Built in 1902, the terminal was the main gateway to the city and ushered in a heyday on West Broad that saw thriving black movie theaters like the Star. Here were packed venues on the "chitlin circuit" such as The Dunbar, hosting such legends as Little Richard. The great number of African American–owned banks on the street gave it the name "the Wall Street of black America." The end came with the razing of the gorgeous Union Station in 1963 to make way for an on-ramp to I-16. The poorly planned project cut the historic boulevard in two, with several entire neighborhoods being destroyed to make way. While the hideous on-ramp remains, every now and then talk surfaces of moving it in an attempt to recreate the magic of old West Broad.

Renamed for the civil rights leader in 1990, MLK Jr. Boulevard currently is undergoing another renaissance. A city-sponsored facelift of the median and a low-interest facade loan program, begun in 1996, have beautified some formerly run-down areas near the Historic District, while an increase in businesses servicing the SCAD student population brings a vibrant, edgy hustle to the area on into the night. During his visit for the 2007 Savannah Music Festival, jazz great Wynton Marsalis dedicated a plaque to Louis Armstrong's mentor King Oliver in front of the building at 514 MLK Jr. Boulevard, where Oliver spent his last days.

RALPH MARK GILBERT CIVIL RIGHTS MUSEUM

One of the former black-owned bank buildings on MLK Jr. Boulevard is now home to the Ralph Mark Gilbert Civil Rights Museum (460 MLK Jr. Blvd., 912/231-8900, www.savcivilrights.com, Mon.–Sat. 9 A.M.–5 P.M., $8 adults, $4 children). Named for the pastor of the First African Baptist Church and a key early civil rights organizer, the building was also the local NAACP headquarters for a time. Three floors of exhibits here include photos and interactive exhibits, the highlight for historians being a fiber-optic map of nearly 100 significant civil rights sites. The first floor features a re-creation of the Azalea Room of the local Levy's department store, an early boycott diner where blacks were not allowed to eat, though they could buy goods from the store. The second floor is more for hands-on education, with classrooms, a computer room, and a video and reading room. A film chronicles mass meetings, voter registration drives, boycotts, sit-ins, kneel-ins (the integration of churches), and wade-ins (the integration of beaches).

SHIPS OF THE SEA MARITIME MUSEUM

One of Savannah's more unique museums is the quirky Ships of the Sea Maritime Museum (41 MLK Jr. Blvd., 912/232-1511, http://shipsofthesea.org, Tues.–Sun. 10 A.M.–5 P.M., $8 adults, $6 students). The stunning Greek Revival building in which it resides is known as the Scarbrough House because it was initially built in 1819 by the great William Jay for local shipping merchant William Scarbrough, owner of the SS *Savannah,* the first steamship to cross the Atlantic. After the Scarbroughs sold the property, it became the West Broad School for African Americans from Reconstruction through integration.

One of the Historic Savannah Foundation's key restoration projects in the 1970s, the museum got another major facelift in 1998, including a roof based on the original Jay design and a delightful enlargement of the mansion's garden out back. Inside, children, maritime buffs, and crafts connoisseurs can find intricate and detailed scale models of various historic vessels, such as Oglethorpe's *Anne,* the SS *Savannah,* and the NS *Savannah,* the world's first nuclear-powered surface vessel. There's even a model of the *Titanic.*

BATTLEFIELD PARK COMPLEX

Three important sites are clustered together

© JIM MOREKIS

Battlefield Park off MLK Jr. Boulevard

on MLK Jr. Boulevard under the auspices of the Coastal Heritage Society: the Savannah History Museum, the Roundhouse Railroad Museum, and the Siege of Savannah battlefield.

The **Savannah History Museum** (303 MLK Jr. Blvd., 912/651-6825, www.chsgeorgia.org, Mon.–Fri. 8:30 A.M.–5 P.M., Sat.–Sun. 9 A.M.–5 P.M., $5 adults, free for children), first stop for many a visitor to town because it's in the same restored Central of Georgia passenger shed as the visitors center, contains many interesting exhibits on local history, concentrating mostly on colonial times. Toward the rear of the museum is a room for rotating exhibits, as well as one of Johnny Mercer's two Oscars and, of course, the historic *"Forrest Gump* bench" that Tom Hanks sat on during his scenes in Chippewa Square.

The **Roundhouse Railroad Museum** (601 W. Harris St., 912/651-6823, www.chsgeorgia.org, daily 9 A.M.–5 P.M., $10 adults, $4 students) is an ongoing homage to the deep

and strangely underreported influence of the railroad industry on Savannah. Constructed in 1830 for the brand-new Central of Georgia line, the Roundhouse's design was cutting-edge for the time, the first facility to put all the railroad's key facilities in one place. Spared by Sherman, the site saw its real heyday after the Civil War. But as technology changed, so did the Roundhouse, which gradually fell further into neglect until the 1960s, when preservation-minded buffs banded together to raise enough money to save it. There's a large collection of various period locomotives and rail cars. Some of Savannah's greatest artisans have contributed their preservation skills to bring back much of the facility's muscular splendor. The real highlight of the Roundhouse is the thing in the middle that gave it its name, a huge central turntable for positioning rolling stock for repair and maintenance. Frequent demonstrations occur with an actual steam locomotive firing up and taking a turn on the turntable.

Right off MLK Jr. Boulevard is the **Battlefield Park** (dawn–dusk, free), a.k.a. the Spring Hill Redoubt, a reconstruction of the British fortifications at the Siege of Savannah with an interpretive site. Note that the redoubt is not at the actual location of the original fort; that lies underneath the nearby Sons of the Revolution marker. Eight hundred granite markers signify the battle's casualties, most of whom were buried in mass graves soon afterward. Sadly, most of the remains of these brave men were simply bulldozed up and discarded without ceremony during later construction projects.

SCAD MUSEUM OF ART

The Savannah College of Art and Design recently concluded a massive expansion of this handsome building into an old railroad facility immediately behind it, more than doubling exhibition space and adding the impressive Walter O. Evans Collection of African American Art. The SCAD Museum of Art (601 Turner Blvd., 912/525-5220, www.scad.edu, Tues.–Wed. and Fri. 10 A.M.–5 P.M., Thurs. 10 A.M.–8 P.M., Sat.–Sun. noon–5 P.M., $10, $5 students) now hosts a rotating series of exhibits, from standard painting to video installations, many of them commissioned by the school itself.

VICTORIAN DISTRICT

Boasting 50 blocks of fine Victorian and Queen Anne frame houses, Savannah's Victorian district gets nowhere near the media attention that the older, more stately homes closer to the river get. But it is truly magnificent in its own right, and nearly as expansive. The city's first suburb, built between 1870 and 1910, it runs from roughly Gwinnett Street south to Anderson Street, with Montgomery and Price Streets as eastern and western boundaries.

In addition to the glories of Forsyth Park, some key areas for connoisseurs of truly grand Victorian architecture are the residential blocks of East Hall Street between Lincoln and Price

Streets—one of the few street sections in town with the original paving. Some other nice examples are in the 1900–2000 blocks of Bull Street near the large Bull Street Public Library, including the famous "Gingerbread House" at 1917 Bull Street, now a private bridal design studio.

◖ Forsyth Park

A favorite with locals and visitors alike, the vast, lush expanse of Forsyth Park is a center of local life, abuzz with activity and events year-round. The park owes its existence to William B. Hodgson, who donated its core 10 acres to the city for use as a park. Deeply influenced by the then-trendy design of green-space areas in France, Forsyth Park's landscape design by William Bischoff dates to 1851. Named for Georgia Governor John Forsyth, the park covers 30 acres, and its perimeter is about a mile.

Near the center of the park is the "fort," actually a revitalized version of an old dummy fort used for military drills in the early 20th century. Now managed by the nearby Mansion on Forsyth hotel, it's a good place to stop in and get a snack or use the public restroom.

The park is a center of activities all year long, from free festivals to concerts to Ultimate Frisbee games to the constant circuit around the periphery of walkers, joggers, dog owners, and bicyclists. The only time you shouldn't venture into the park is after midnight; otherwise, enjoy.

A WALKING TOUR OF FORSYTH PARK

Here's a walking tour of Savannah's backyard, the one-of-a-kind Forsyth Park, beginning at the north end at Gaston and Bull Streets: As you approach the park, don't miss the ornate ironwork on the west side of Bull street marking the **Armstrong House,** designed by Henrik Wallin. Featured in the 1962 film *Cape Fear* as well as 1997's *Midnight in the Garden of Good and Evil,* this Italianate mansion was once home to Armstrong Junior College before its move to the south side. When he's not practicing law in this building, Sonny Seiler, one of the characters in "The Book," still raises the University of Georgia's signature bulldog mascots. Directly across Bull Street is another site of *Midnight* fame, the Oglethorpe Club, one of the many brick and terra-cotta designs by local architect Alfred Eichberg.

It's easy to miss, but as you enter the park's north side, you encounter the **Marine Memorial,** erected in 1947 to honor the 24 Chatham County Marines killed in World War II. Subsequently, the names of Marines killed in Korea and Vietnam were added. Look west at the corner of Whitaker and Gaston Streets; that's **Hodgson Hall,** home of the Georgia Historical Society. This 1876 building was commissioned by Margaret Telfair to honor her late husband, William Hodgson, chief benefactor of the park the house overlooks. The Georgia Historical Society (912/651-2125, www.georgiahistory.com) administers a treasure of books, documents, maps, photos, and prints that has been a boon to writers and researchers since it was chartered by the state legislature in 1839.

Looking east at the corner of Drayton and Gaston Streets, you'll see the old **Poor House and Hospital,** in use until 1854, when it was converted to serve as the headquarters for the Medical College of Georgia. During the Civil War, General Sherman used the hospital to treat Federal soldiers. From 1930 to 1980 the building was the site of Candler Hospital. Behind Candler Hospital's cast-iron fence, you can soak in the venerable beauty of Savannah's most famous tree, the 300-year-old **Candler Oak.** During Sherman's occupation, wounded Confederate prisoners were treated within a barricade around the oak. The tree is on the National Register of Historic Trees and was the maiden preservation project of the Savannah Tree Foundation, which secured the country's first-ever conservation easement on a single tree.

Walking south into the park proper, you can't miss the world-famous **Forsyth Fountain,** an iconic Savannah sight if there ever was one. Cast in iron on a French model, the fountain was dedicated in 1858. Its water is typically dyed green a few days before St. Patrick's Day. Interestingly, two other versions of this fountain exist—one in Poughkeepsie, New York, and the other in, of all places, the central plaza in Cusco, Peru. Various acts of vandalism and natural disaster took its toll on the fountain until a major restoration in 1988 brought it to its present level of beauty.

Continuing south, you'll encounter two low buildings in the center of the park. The one on the east side is the so-called "Dummy Fort," circa 1909, formerly a training ground for local militia. Now it's the **Forsyth Park Café** (daily 7 A.M.–dusk, open later on festival evenings) managed by the hotel Mansion on Forsyth Park just across Drayton Street. To the west is the charming **Fragrant Garden for the Blind.** One of those precious little Savannah gems that is too often overlooked in favor of other attractions, the Fragrant Garden was initially sponsored by the local Garden Club and based on others of its type throughout the United States.

The tall monument dominating Forsyth Park's central mall area is the **Confederate Memorial,** which recently received a major facelift. Dedicated in 1875, it wasn't finished in its final form until several years later. A New York sculptor carved the Confederate soldier atop the monument. A copy of it is in Poughkeepsie, New York, as a memorial to the Federal dead—with the "CSA" on the soldier's rucksack changed to "USA." The Bartow and McLaws monuments surrounding the Confederate Memorial were originally in Chippewa Square.

We'll close the walking tour with my favorite Forsyth Park landmark, at the extreme southern end. It's the Memorial to Georgia Veterans of the Spanish-American War, more commonly known as *The Hiker* because of the

SAVANNAH

subject's almost casual demeanor and confident stride. Savannah was a major staging area for that conflict, and many troops were bivouacked in the park. Sculpted in 1902 by Alice Ruggles Kitson, more than 50 replicas of *The Hiker* were made and put up all over the United States; because the same bronze formula was used for all 50 of them, the statues are used by scientists today to gauge the effects of acid rain across the nation.

Carnegie Branch Library

Looking like Frank Lloyd Wright parachuted one of his buildings into Victorian Savannah, the Carnegie Branch Library (537 E. Henry St., 912/652-3600, Mon. 10 A.M.–8 P.M., Tues.–Thurs. 10 A.M.–6 P.M., Fri. 2–6 P.M., Sat. 10 A.M.–6 P.M.) is the only example of prairie architecture in town, designed by Savannah architect Julian de Bruyn Kops and built, as the name implies, with funding from tycoon-philanthropist Andrew Carnegie in 1914. But more importantly, the Carnegie Library was for decades the only public library for African Americans in Savannah. One of its patrons was a young Clarence Thomas, who would of course grow up to be a U.S. Supreme Court justice.

EASTSIDE
Old Fort Jackson

The oldest standing brick fort in Georgia, Old Fort Jackson (Fort Jackson Rd., 912/232-3945, http://chsgeorgia.org, daily 9 A.M.–5 P.M., $6, free under age 7), named for Georgia Governor James Jackson, is also one of eight remaining examples of the so-called Second System of American forts built prior to the War of 1812. Its main claim to fame is its supporting role in the saga of the CSS *Georgia,* a Confederate ironclad now resting under 40 feet of water directly in front of the fort. Built with $115,000 in funds raised by the Ladies Gunboat Society, the *Georgia*—wrapped in an armor girdle of railroad ties—proved too heavy for its engine. So

it was simply anchored in the channel opposite Fort Jackson as a floating battery. With General Sherman's arrival in 1864, Confederate forces evacuating to South Carolina scuttled the vessel where it lay to keep it out of Yankee hands.

Maritime archaeology on the *Georgia* continues apace, with dive teams bringing up cannons, ammunition, and other artifacts. Unlike Charleston's CSS *Hunley* submarine, no lives were lost in the *Georgia* incident, therefore there are no concerns about disrupting a grave site. Every now and then, talk surfaces of raising the ironclad—both for research and because the port views it as an impediment to dredging the channel even deeper—but most experts say it's unlikely to survive the stress.

Operated by the nonprofit Coastal Heritage Society, Fort Jackson is in an excellent state of preservation and provides loads of information for history buffs as well as for kids, who will enjoy climbing the parapets and running on the large parade ground (this area was once a rice field). Inside the fort's casemates underneath the ramparts you'll find well-organized exhibits on the fort's construction and history. Most visitors especially love the daily cannon firings during the summer. If you're really lucky, you'll be around when Fort Jackson fires a salute to passing military vessels on the river—the only historic fort in the United States that does so.

To get to Fort Jackson, take President Street Extension (Islands Expressway) east out of downtown. The entrance is several miles down on the left.

Oatland Island Wildlife Center

The closest thing Savannah has to a zoo is the vast, multipurpose Oatland Island Wildlife Center (711 Sandtown Rd., 912/898-3980, www.oatlandisland.org, daily 10 A.M.–5 P.M., $5 adults, $3 children). Set on a former Centers for Disease Control site, it has undergone an extensive environmental cleanup and is now owned by the local school system, although

memorial to "Gracie" in Bonaventure Cemetery

© JIM MOREKIS

supported purely by donations. Families by the hundreds come here for a number of special Saturdays throughout the year, including an old-fashioned cane-grinding in November and a day of sheep-shearing in April.

The main attractions here are the critters, located at various points along a meandering two-mile nature trail through the woods and along the marsh. All animals at Oatland are there because they're somehow unable to return to the wild. Highlights include a tight-knit pack of Eastern wolves, a pair of bison, cougars (once indigenous to the region), some really cute foxes, and an extensive raptor aviary. Kids will love the petting zoo of farm animals, some of which are free to roam the grounds at will.

The massive central building was designed by noted local architect Henrik Wallin as a retirement home for railroad conductors. Inside, check out the display of a huge set of whalebones, the remains of a 50-foot-long endangered fin whale that washed ashore on Tybee Island in 1989.

To get here from downtown, take President Street Extension (Islands Expressway) about five miles. Begin looking for the Oatland Island sign on the right. You'll go through part of a residential neighborhood until you take a bend to the right; Oatland's gate is then on the left. To get here from Bonaventure Cemetery, go straight out the gate on Bonaventure Road and take a right on Pennsylvania Avenue. As you dead-end on Islands Expressway, take a right and look for the entrance farther along on the right.

◖ Bonaventure Cemetery

On the banks of the Wilmington River just east of town lies one of Savannah's most unique sights, Bonaventure Cemetery (330 Bonaventure Rd., 912/651-6843, daily 8 A.M.–5 P.M.). John Muir, who went on to found the Sierra Club, wrote of Bonaventure's Spanish moss–bedecked beauty in his 1867 book *A Thousand-mile Walk to the Gulf,* marveling at the screaming bald eagles that then frequented the area. The bald eagles are long gone, but, like Muir, Savannahians to this day reserve a special place in their hearts for Bonaventure. While its pedigree as Savannah's premier public cemetery goes back 100 years, it was used as a burial ground as early as 1794. In the years since, this achingly poignant vista of live oaks and azaleas has been the final resting place of such local and national luminaries as Johnny Mercer, Conrad Aiken, Wormsloe Historic Site founder Noble Jones, and, of course, the Trosdal plot, former home of the famous *Bird Girl* statue (the original is now in the Telfair Academy of Arts and Sciences). Fittingly, the late, great Jack Leigh, who took the *Bird Girl* photo for the cover of *Midnight in the Garden of Good and Evil,* is interred here as well.

Go to Section K to see the Greek cemetery, a veritable stone chronicle of that local community's history from the late 1800s. Section

SAVANNAH

K also holds many memorials to Spanish-American War veterans, commemorated by a special cross. Close by is the Jewish section, established by congregants of Temple Mickve Israel, with many evocative inscriptions on the tombs of the many Holocaust survivors buried here. Closer to the river is an interesting plot set aside for railroad conductors. While strolling through Bonaventure, you might see some burial sites lined with reddish-brown tiles, their tops studded with half circles. Mistakenly known as "slave tiles," these are actually a rare type of Victorian garden tile that has nothing whatsoever to do with slaves.

Several local tour companies offer options that include a visit to Bonaventure. If you're doing a self-guided tour, go by the small visitors center at the entrance and pick up one of the free guides to the cemetery, assembled by the local volunteer Bonaventure Historical Society. By all means, do the tourist thing and pay your respects at Johnny Mercer's final resting place, and go visit beautiful little "Gracie" in Section E, Lot 99. But I also suggest doing as the locals do: Bring a picnic lunch and a blanket and set yourself beside the breezy banks of the Wilmington River, taking in all the lazy beauty and evocative bygone history surrounding you.

To get here from downtown, take President Street Extension east and take a right on Pennsylvania Avenue, then a left on Bonaventure Road. Alternately, go east on Victory Drive (U.S. 80) and take a left on Whatley Road in the town of Thunderbolt. Veer left onto Bonaventure Road. The cemetery is one mile ahead on the right.

Thunderbolt

Take a left out of Bonaventure Cemetery and continue on Bonaventure Road to find yourself in the little fishing village of Thunderbolt, almost as old as Savannah itself. According to Oglethorpe, the town was named after "a rock which was here shattered by a thunderbolt,

causing a spring to gush from the ground, which continued ever afterward to emit the odor of brimstone."

Just off Victory Drive is the **Thunderbolt Museum** (Victory Dr. and Mechanics Ave., 912/351-0836, http://thunderboltmuseum.org, Wed.–Thurs. 9:30 A.M.–2:30 P.M., Sat. 1–5 P.M., free), housed in the humble former town hall. Cross Victory Drive onto River Road and notice how the road is built around the live oak tree in the middle of it. Most of the nice views of the river have been obscured by high-rise condos, but there's a cute public fishing pier.

Continue on River Road and you'll soon be at the entrance to **Savannah State University** (3219 College St., 912/356-2186, www.savstate.edu). This historically black university began life in 1890 as the Georgia State Industrial College for Colored Youth. Famous graduates include NFL great Shannon Sharpe. The main landmark is the newly restored Hill Hall, a 1901 building featured in the film *The General's Daughter*.

Daffin Park

A century spent in Forsyth Park's more genteel shadow doesn't diminish the importance of Daffin Park (1500 E. Victory Dr.) as Savannah's second major green space. Designed by John Nolen in 1907 and named for a former local parks commissioner, Daffin not only hosts a large variety of local athletes on its fields and courts, it's also home to Historic Grayson Stadium on the park's east end. Recently given a serious face-lift, Grayson Stadium hosts the minor league Savannah Sand Gnats. One of the great old ballparks of America, this venue dates from 1941 and has hosted greats such as Babe Ruth, Jackie Robinson, and Mickey Mantle.

Most picturesque for the visitor, however, is the massive fountain set in the middle of the expansive central pond on the park's west side. Originally built in the shape of the continental United States, the pond was the backdrop

JOHNNY MERCER'S BLACK MAGIC

Visitors might be forgiven for thinking Paula Deen is Savannah's most famous native, but the Food Network star, born 200 miles away in Albany, Georgia, technically cannot claim that title. The great Johnny Mercer is not only without a doubt Savannah's most noteworthy progeny, he is also one of the greatest lyricists music has ever known. He grew up in south-side Savannah on a small river then called the Back River but since renamed Moon River in honor of his best-known song. Armed with an innate talent for rhythm and a curious ear for dialogue—both qualities honed by his frequent boyhood contact with Savannah African American culture and musicians during the Jazz Age—Mercer moved away from Savannah to New York when he was only 19 to try his hand in Tin Pan Alley, then the world center of popular music.

There he met the woman who would be his wife, Ginger Meehan (real name Elizabeth Meltzer). This Brooklyn Jewish chorus girl—once Bing Crosby's lover—would be both muse and foil for Mercer in the decades to follow. Mutual infidelity and a partying lifestyle combined for a stormy marriage, yet both remained together until Mercer's death from a brain tumor in 1976 (Ginger died in 1994). In a few years he was an established success in New York. By 1935, however, the show business center of gravity was moving toward Hollywood, and Mercer—ahead of his time as usual—sensed the shift early and moved to the West Coast to write musicals for RKO. The advent of high-quality microphones was tailor-made for Mercer's nuanced lyrics. During his long and productive Hollywood career in the 1930s and 1940s, he wrote such classics as "Jeepers Creepers," "That Old Black Magic," "Come Rain or Come Shine," "Skylark," and "Ac-Cent-Tchu-Ate the Positive."

Mercer embarked on an affair with the young Judy Garland in 1941, a dalliance which he later said inspired the song "I Remember You." While the advent of rock and roll in the postwar era signaled the decline of Mercer's career, he wrote what is arguably his greatest song, "Moon River," in 1961. The song, debuted by Audrey Hepburn in the film *Breakfast at Tiffany's*, won an Academy Award for Best Original Song. In addition to "Moon River," Mercer won three other Oscars, for "On the Atchinson, Topeka and Santa Fe" (1946), "In the Cool, Cool, Cool of the Evening" (1951), and "Days of Wine and Roses" (1962).

Today you can pay your respects to Mercer in three places: his boyhood home (509 E. Gwinnett St., look for the historical marker in front of this private residence); the bronze sculpture of Mercer in the newly revitalized Ellis Square near City Market, erected in 2009 in honor of the centennial of his birth; and, of course, at his gravesite in beautiful Bonaventure Cemetery. And regardless of what anyone tells you, neither Johnny Mercer nor any member of his family ever lived in the Mercer-Williams House on Monterey Square, of *Midnight in the Garden of Good and Evil* fame. Although it was built for his great-grandfather, the home was sold to someone else before it was completed.

SAVANNAH

for a presidential visit by Franklin D. Roosevelt in 1933 that included a speech to an African American crowd. On the far west end of Daffin Park along Waters Avenue is a marker commemorating the site of the Grandstand for the Great Savannah Races of 1911.

WESTSIDE
Laurel Grove Cemetery

Its natural vista isn't as alluring as Bonaventure's, but Laurel Grove Cemetery boasts its own exquisitely carved memorials and a distinctly Victorian type of surreal beauty that not even Bonaventure can match. In keeping with the racial apartheid of Savannah's early days, there are actually two cemeteries: **Laurel Grove North** (802 W. Anderson St., daily 8 A.M.–5 P.M.) for whites, and **Laurel Grove South** (2101 Kollock St., daily 8 A.M.–5 P.M.) for blacks. Both are well worth visiting.

By far the most high-profile site in the North Cemetery is that of Juliette Gordon Low, founder of the Girl Scouts of the USA. Other historically significant sites there include the graves of 8th Air Force founder Frank O. Hunter, Central of Georgia Railway founder William Gordon, and "Jingle Bells" composer James Pierpont. But it's the graves of the anonymous and near-anonymous that are the most poignant sights. The various sections for infants, known as "babylands," cannot fail to move. "Mr. Bones," a former Savannah Police dog, is the only animal buried at Laurel Grove. There's an entire site reserved for victims of the great yellow fever epidemic. And don't blink or you'll miss the small rock pile, or cairn, near Governor James Jackson's tomb, the origin and purpose of which remains a mystery. Make sure to view the otherworldly display of Victorian statuary, originally from the grand Greenwich Plantation, which burned in the early 20th century. As with Bonaventure, throughout Laurel Grove you'll find examples of so-called "slave tiles," actually Victorian garden tiles, lining gravesites.

Laurel Grove South features the graves of Savannah's early black Baptist ministers, such as Andrew Bryan and Andrew Cox Marshall. Some of the most evocative sites are those of African Americans who obtained their freedom and built prosperous lives for themselves and their families. The vast majority of local firefighters in the 1800s were African Americans, and their simple graves are among the most touching, such as the headstone for one known simply as "August," who died fighting a fire.

To get to Laurel Grove North, take MLK Jr. Boulevard to Anderson Street and turn west. To get to Laurel Grove South, take Victory Drive (U.S. 80) west to Ogeechee Road. Take a right onto Ogeechee, then a right onto West 36th Street. Continue on to Kollock Street.

Mighty Eighth Air Force Museum

Military and aviation buffs mustn't miss the Mighty Eighth Air Force Museum (175 Bourne Ave., 912/748-8888, www.mightyeighth.org, daily 9 A.M.–5 P.M., $10 adults, $6 children and active duty military) in Pooler, Georgia, right off I-95. The 8th Air Force was born at Hunter Field in Savannah as the 8th Bomber Command in 1942, becoming the 8th Air Force in 1944; it is now based in Louisiana.

A moving testament to the men and machines who conducted those strategic bombing campaigns over Europe in World War II, the museum also features later 8th Air Force history such as the Korean War, the Linebacker II bombing campaigns over North Vietnam, and the Persian Gulf. Inside you'll find not only airplanes like the P-51 Mustang and the German ME-109, there's also a restored B-17 bomber, the newest jewel of the collection. Outside are several more aircraft, including a MiG-17, an F-4 Phantom, and a B-47 Stratojet bomber like the one that dropped the fabled "Tybee Bomb" in 1958. The nearby Chapel of the Fallen Eagles is a fully functioning sanctuary to honor the more than 26,000 members of the Mighty Eighth that died during World War II.

To get to the Mighty Eighth Museum from downtown, take I-16 west until it intersects I-95. Take I-95 north, take exit 102, and follow the signs.

Savannah-Ogeechee River Canal

A relic of the pre-railroad days, the Savannah-Ogeechee River Canal (681 Ft. Argyle Rd., 912/748-8068, www.savannahogeecheecanal. com, daily 9 A.M.–5 P.M., $2 adults, $1 students) is a 17-mile barge route joining the two rivers. Finished in 1830, it saw three decades of prosperous trade in cotton, rice, bricks, guano, naval stores, and agriculture before the coming of the railroads finished it off. You can walk some of its length today near the Ogeechee River terminus, admiring the impressive engineering of its multiple locks to stabilize the water level. Back in the day, the canal would continue through four lift locks as it traversed 16 miles before reaching the Savannah River. Naturalists will enjoy the built-in nature trail that walking along the canal provides. Be sure to check out the unique sand hills on a nearby trail, a vestige of a bygone geological era when this area was an offshore sandbar. Kids will enjoy the impromptu menagerie of gopher turtles near the site's entrance. Do bring mosquito repellent, although often there's a community spray can at the front door of the little visitor center–museum where you pay your fee.

To get here, get on I-95 south and take exit 94. The canal is a little over two miles west.

Bamboo Farm and Coastal Garden

A joint project of the University of Georgia and Chatham County, the Bamboo Farm and Coastal Garden (2 Canebrake Rd., 912/921-5460, www.bamboo.caes.uga.edu, Mon.–Fri. 8 A.M.–5 P.M., Sat. 10 A.M.–5 P.M., Sun. noon–5 P.M., free) is an education and demonstration center featuring a wide array of native species in addition to the eponymous Asian wonder weed, which has its roots in a private collection dating from the late 1800s. Many of the mature trees were planted in the 1930s. They also periodically hold you-pick-'em harvest days for berries. To get here, take exit 94 off of I-95 and take Highway 204 east toward Savannah. Turn right on East Gateway Boulevard, then left on Canebrake Road. Enter at the Canebrake gate.

SOUTHSIDE
Wormsloe State Historic Site

The one-of-a-kind Wormsloe State Historic Site (7601 Skidaway Rd., 912/353-3023, www.gastateparks.org/info/wormsloe, Tues.–Sun. 9 A.M.–5 P.M., $6 adults, $3.50 children) was first settled by Noble Jones, who landed with Oglethorpe on the *Anne* and fought beside him

Wormsloe State Historic Site

in the War of Jenkins' Ear. One of the great renaissance men of history, this soldier was also an accomplished carpenter, surveyor, forester, botanist, and physician. Wormsloe became famous for its bountiful gardens, so much so that the famed naturalist William Bartram mentioned them in his diary after a visit in 1765 with father John Bartram. After his death, Noble Jones was originally buried in the family plot on the waterfront, but now his remains are at Bonaventure Cemetery. Jones's descendants donated 822 acres to The Nature Conservancy, which transferred the property to the state. The house, dating from 1828, and 65.5 acres of land are still owned by his family, and no, you can't visit them.

The stunning entrance canopy of 400 live oaks, Spanish moss dripping down the entire length, is one of those iconic images of Savannah that will stay with you forever. A small interpretive museum, a one-mile nature walk, and occasional living history demonstrations make this a great site for the entire family. Walk all the way to the Jones Narrows to see the ruins of the original 1739 fortification, one of the oldest and finest examples of tabby construction in the United States. No doubt the area's abundance of Native American shell middens, where early inhabitants discarded their oyster shells, came in handy for its construction. You can see one nearby.

To get to Wormsloe, take Victory Drive (U.S. 80) to Skidaway Road. Go south on Skidaway Road for about 10 miles and follow the signs; you'll see the grand entrance on the right.

Isle of Hope

A charming, friendly seaside community and National Historic District, Isle of Hope is one of a dwindling number of places where parents still let their kids ride around all day on bikes, calling them in at dinnertime. It doesn't boast many shops or restaurants—indeed, the marina is the only real business—but the row of

waterfront cottages on Bluff Drive should not be missed. You might recognize some of them from movies such as *Forrest Gump* and *Glory*. Built from 1880 to 1920, they reflect Isle of Hope's reputation as a healing area and serene Wilmington River getaway from Savannah's capitalist hustle.

To get to Isle of Hope, take Victory Drive (U.S. 80) east and take a right on Skidaway Road. Continue south on Skidaway Road and take a left on Laroche Avenue. Continue until you hit Bluff Drive.

Pin Point

Off Whitfield Avenue (Diamond Causeway) on the route to Skidaway Island is tiny **Pin Point, Georgia,** a predominantly African American township better known as the boyhood home of Supreme Court Justice Clarence Thomas. Pin Point traces its roots to a community of former slaves on Ossabaw Island. Displaced by a hurricane, they settled at this idyllic site overlooking the Moon River, itself a former plantation. Many new residents made their living by shucking oysters at the Varn Oyster Company, the central shed of which still remains and forms the basis of the new **Pin Point Heritage Museum** (9924 Pin Point Ave., www.pinpointheritagemuseum.com). The museum tells the story of the Pin Point community through exhibits, a film, and demonstrations of some of the maritime activities at the Varn Oyster Company through the decades, such as crabbing, canning, shucking and shrimp net making.

Skidaway Island

Though locals primarily know Skidaway Island as the site of The Landings, the first gated community in Savannah, Skidaway Island is notable for two beautiful and educational nature-oriented sites. The first, the **University of Georgia Marine Educational Center and Aquarium** (30 Ocean Science Circle, 912/598-3474, www.uga.edu/aquarium, Mon.–Fri. 9 A.M.–4 P.M.,

PIN POINT ON THE MOON RIVER

On Ossabaw Island off the Georgia coast, former slaves had settled into freedom as subsistence farmers after the Civil War. But when a massive hurricane devastated the island in 1893, many moved to the mainland, finding themselves south of Savannah along what would later be known as Moon River, at a place called Pin Point. While many continued farming on the long, skinny lots particular to the area, plenty of them gained employment at local packing factories on the marsh-front, where crabs and oysters were packed and sold. By far the largest and longest-lived of those factories was A. S. Varn & Son, which during its heyday employed nearly 100 Pin Point residents—about half of the adult population. There they shucked oysters and picked crabs for five cents a pound and tended to the various machinery of a seafood factory operation, down to sewing the crab nets (itself a vanishing art).

Because so many local people worked at the same place, Pin Point developed an extraordinarily strong community bond, one that was instrumental in forging the life and career of future Supreme Court Justice Clarence Thomas, who was born at Pin Point in 1948. Until he was seven, Thomas lived in a tiny house there with his parents, one without plumbing and insulated with newspapers in the old Southern vernacular tradition. After a house fire, Thomas moved to Savannah with his grandparents, attending a Catholic school where he was for a time the only African American student. He often studied at the Carnegie Library on Henry Street, then the only library where blacks were allowed. Savannah's more active intellectual and social life no doubt influenced his choice of career, and his grandfather, a successful businessman, was his greatest role model. But Thomas's heart was always in Pin Point.

While times have certainly changed here—paved roads finally came in the 1970s, and most of the old shotgun shacks have been replaced with mobile homes—Pin Point remains a small, closely-knit community of about 300 people, with most property still owned by descendants of the freedmen who bought it after Reconstruction. (Pin Point hasn't been immune to big-city problems, however, including a high-profile drug bust in the 1990s that claimed none other than Thomas's nephew.) The Varn factory remained the economic heart of Pin Point until it shut down in 1985, a victim of changing economic and environmental fortunes. Today, the old factory forms the heart of an ambitious new project, the Pin Point Heritage Museum (www.pinpointheritagemuseum.com), which conveys the spirit and history of that community, including its most famous native son, through a series of exhibits and demonstrations.

Sat. 10 A.M.–5 P.M., $6 adults, $3 children, cash only) shares a scenic 700-acre campus on the scenic Skidaway River with the research-oriented **Skidaway Institute of Oceanography,** also University of Georgia (UGA) affiliated. It hosts scientists and grad students from around the nation, often on trips on research vessel, the RV *Sea Dawg*. The main attraction of the Marine Center is the small but well-done and recently upgraded aquarium featuring 14 tanks with 200 live animals. Don't expect Sea World here; remember you're essentially on a college campus and the emphasis is on education, not flash. There's also a range of natural history exhibits.

The second site of interest to visitors is **Skidaway Island State Park** (52 Diamond Causeway, 912/598-2300, www.gastateparks.org/info/skidaway, daily 7 A.M.–10 P.M., parking $2). Yeah, you can camp here ($25–28), but the awesome nature trails leading out to the marsh—featuring an ancient Native American shell midden and an old whiskey still—are worth a trip just on their own, especially when combined with the Marine Education Center Aquarium. To get here, take Victory Drive (U.S. 80) until you get to Waters Avenue and continue south as it turns into Whitefield Avenue and then the Diamond Causeway. The park is on your left after the drawbridge. An alternate route from downtown is to take the Truman Parkway all the way to its dead end at Whitefield Avenue; take a left and continue as it turns into Diamond Causeway into Skidaway.

TYBEE ISLAND

Its name means "salt" in the old Euchee tongue, indicative of the island's chief export in those days. And Tybee Island—"Tybee" to locals— is indeed one of the essential seasonings of life

in Savannah. First incorporated as Ocean City and then Savannah Beach, the island has since reclaimed its original name. Eighteen miles from Savannah, in truth Tybee is part and parcel of the city's social and cultural fabric. Many of the island's 3,000 full-time residents, known for their boozy bonhomie and quirky personal style, commute to work in the city. And those living "in town" often reciprocate by visiting Tybee to dine in its few but excellent restaurants, drink in its casual and crazy

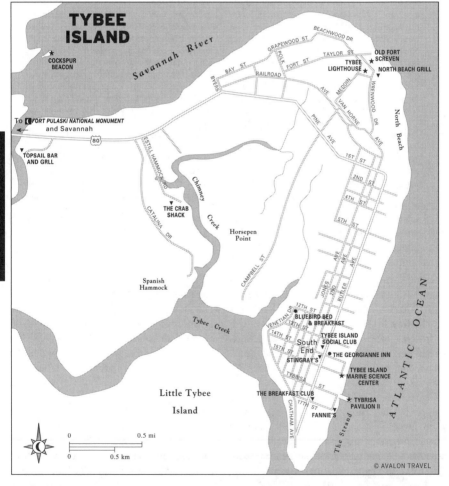

© JIM MOREKIS

Fort Pulaski, on the way to Tybee Island

SAVANNAH

watering holes, and frolic on its wide, beautiful beaches lined with rare sea oats waving in the Atlantic breeze.

(Fort Pulaski National Monument

There's one must-see before you get to Tybee Island proper. On Cockspur Island you'll find Fort Pulaski National Monument (U.S. 80 E., 912/786-5787, www.nps.gov/fopu, fort Sept.– May daily 9 A.M.–5 P.M., June–Aug. daily 9 A.M.–6:30 P.M., visitors center Sept.–May daily 9 A.M.–5 P.M., June–Aug. daily 9 A.M.– 6:45 P.M., $5 pp, free under age 16). Not only a delight for any history buff, the fort's also a fantastic place to take the kids. They can climb on the parapets, earthworks, and cannons, and burn off calories on the great nature trail nearby. Along the way they'll no doubt learn a few things as well.

HISTORY

Synchronicity and irony practically scream from every brick. Perhaps prophetically named for Count Casimir Pulaski, who died leading an ill-fated charge on the British in 1779, Fort Pulaski is also symbolic of a catastrophic defeat, this one in 1862 when Union forces using new rifled cannons reduced much of it to rubble in 30 hours. Robert E. Lee—yes, *that* Robert E. Lee—helped build the fort while a lieutenant with the U.S. Army Corps of Engineers. And the Union general who destroyed the fort, Quincy A. Gillmore, was in the Corps of Engineers himself, helping to oversee its construction.

Fort Pulaski's construction was part of a broader initiative by President James Madison in the wake of the disastrous War of 1812, which dramatically revealed the shortcoming of U.S. coastal defense. Two hundred new forts were planned, but by the beginning of the Civil War only 30 were complete. Based on state-of-the-art European design forged in the cauldron of the Napoleonic Wars, Fort Pulaski's thick masonry construction used 25 million bricks, many of them of the famous "Savannah Gray" variety handmade at the nearby Hermitage Plantation. At its unveiling, Fort Pulaski was considered to be invincible—indeed, perhaps the finest fortress ever made.

When Georgia seceded from the Union in January 1861, a small force of 134 Confederates immediately took control of two Savannah area fortifications, Fort Pulaski and Fort Jackson. However, in early 1862 a Union sea-land force under General Quincy Gillmore came to covertly lay the groundwork for a siege of Fort Pulaski to ensure the success of Lincoln's naval blockade. (Besides being one of the North's most brilliant officers, Gillmore had a built-in advantage: Like Robert E. Lee, he also helped build the fort before the war.) The siege would rely on several batteries secretly set up across the Savannah River. Some of the Union guns utilized new rifled chamber technology, which dramatically increased the muzzle velocity and penetrating power of their shells. The Union barrage began at 8:15 A.M. on April 10, 1862, and Fort Pulaski's walls immediately began to crumble under the withering Union fire. At least one shell struck a powder magazine, igniting an enormous explosion. After a mere 30 hours, Confederate general Charles Olmstead surrendered the "invincible" fortress.

But it was not only Fort Pulaski that was rendered obsolete—it was the whole concept of masonry fortification. From that point forward, military forts would rely on earthwork rather than brick to withstand artillery bombardment. In fact, the section of earthworks you see as you enter Fort Pulaski, the "demilune," was added after the Civil War—an ironic nod to the fort's own premature demise.

Fort Pulaski's new commander, General David Hunter, immediately issued an order freeing all local slaves and guaranteeing them a wage working at the fort. As the war dragged on over the next three years, a community of escaped slaves gradually grew on Cockspur Island, aided mostly by a former slave named March Haynes who ferried runaways from Savannah under cover of darkness. The fort was occupied mostly by troops of the 48th New York Volunteers, who sometimes relieved the boredom of garrison duty by playing the brand-new game of baseball on the fort's vast, grassy parade ground. One of the first photographs of a baseball game was taken at Fort Pulaski in 1863.

VISITING THE FORT

By all means, visit the visitors center, a few hundred yards from the fort itself—but the palpable pleasure starts when you cross the drawbridge over the moat and see a cannon pointed at you from a narrow gun port. Enter the inside of the fort and take in just how big it is—Union occupiers regularly played baseball on the huge, grassy parade ground. Take a walk around the perimeter, underneath the ramparts. This is where the soldiers lived and worked, and you'll see re-creations of officer's quarters, meeting areas, sick rooms, and prisoners' bunks among the cannons, where Confederate prisoners of war were held after the fort's surrender. Cannon firings happen most Saturdays.

And now for the pièce de résistance: Take the steep corkscrew staircase up to the ramparts themselves and take in the jaw-dropping view of the lush marsh, the Savannah River and Tybee Island spreading out in the distance. Stop and sit near one of the several remaining cannons and contemplate what went on here a century and a half ago. (Warning: There's no railing of any kind on the inboard side of the ramparts. Keep the kids well back from the edge, because it's a lethal fall to the fort interior.) Afterward, take a stroll all the way around the walls and see the power of those Yankee guns. Though much of the devastation was soon repaired, some sections of the wall remain in their damaged state. You can even pick out a few cannonballs still stuck in the masonry, like blueberries in a pie.

Save some time and energy for the extensive palmetto-lined nature trail through the sandy upland of Cockspur Island on which the fort is located. There are informative markers, a picnic area, and, as a bonus, there's a coastal defense facility from the Spanish-American War, Battery Hambright.

Cockspur Beacon

Continue east on U.S. 80, passing over Lazaretto Creek, named for the quarantine or "lazaretto" built in the late 1700s to make sure newcomers, mostly slaves, were free of disease. As you cross, look to your left over the river's wide south channel. On a tiny oyster shell islet, find the little Cockspur Beacon lighthouse, in use from 1848 to 1909, when major shipping was routed through the deeper north channel of the river. The site is now preserved by the National Park Service, and is accessible only by boat or kayak. You have to time your arrival with the right tide; Check with a local rental place for advice.

Tybee Lighthouse

Reaching Tybee proper on U.S. 80, you'll soon arrive at the intersection with North Campbell Avenue. This is the entrance to the less-populated, more historically significant north end of the island, once almost entirely taken up by Fort Screven, a coastal defense fortification of the early 1900s. Take a left onto North Campbell Avenue then left again on Van Horne Street. Take an immediate right onto Meddin Drive. Continue until you see a lighthouse on the left and a parking lot on the right.

Rebuilt several times in its history, the Tybee Island Light Station and Museum (30 Meddin Ave., 912/786-5801, www.tybeelighthouse. org, Wed.–Mon. 9 A.M.–5 P.M., last ticket sold 4:30 P.M., $8 adults, $6 children) traces

its construction to the first year of the colony, based on a design by the multitalented Noble Jones. At its completion in 1736, it was the tallest structure in the United States. One of a handful of working 18th-century lighthouses today, the facility has been restored to its 1916– 1964 incarnation, featuring a nine-foot-tall first order Fresnel lens installed in 1867.

The entrance fee gives you admission to the lighthouse, the lighthouse museum, and the nearby Tybee Island Museum. All the outbuildings on the lighthouse grounds are original, including the residence of current lighthouse keeper and Tybee Island Historical Society Director Cullen Chambers, which is also the oldest building on the island. If you've got the legs and the lungs, definitely take all 178 steps up to the top of the lighthouse for a stunning view of Tybee, the Atlantic, and Hilton Head Island.

Old Fort Screven

All around the area of the north end around the lighthouse complex you'll see low-lying concrete bunkers. These are remains of Fort Screven's coastal defense batteries, and many are in private hands. Battery Garland is open to tours, and also houses the **Tybee Island Museum** (30 Meddin Ave., 912/786-5801, Wed.–Mon. 9 A.M.–5:30 P.M., last ticket sold 4:30 P.M., $8 adults, $6 children, includes admission to lighthouse and lighthouse museum), a charming, almost whimsical little collection of exhibits from various eras of local history.

On nearby Van Horne Avenue is a key part of Fort Screven, the **Tybee Post Theater** (912/323-7727, www.tybeeposttheater.org). Once a site for Army entertainment such as movies, concerts, and theatrical productions, the Post Theater is currently undergoing extensive renovation. It occasionally hosts events; check the website for details.

Continue on Van Horne around the delightful Jaycee Park to the row of ornate mansions with expansive porches facing the Atlantic. This

THE TYBEE BOMB

On a dark February night in 1958 at the height of the Cold War, a USAF B-47 Stratojet bomber based at Homestead, Florida, made a simulated nuclear bombing run somewhere over southeast Georgia. A Charleston-based F-86 fighter on a mock intercept came too close, clipping the big bomber's wing. Before bringing down the wounded B-47 at Savannah's Hunter Airfield—then a Strategic Air Command base—Commander Howard Richardson decided he first had to jettison his lethal cargo: a 7,000-pound Mark 15 hydrogen bomb, serial number 47782. We know for sure that he jettisoned it over water; Richardson, who won the Distinguished Flying Cross for his efforts that night, said so himself. What no one knows is exactly where. And thus began the legend of "the Tybee bomb." Go in any Tybee watering hole and ask 10 people where they think it is and you'll get 10 different answers. Some say it's in the north side of Wassaw Sound, some say the south. Some say it's in the shallows, some in deep water. Many locals who work in shrimping, crabbing, and fishing have claimed at various times to have ripped their nets on the bomb. Or on something...Speculation ran wild, with some locals fearing a nuclear explosion, radioactive contamination, or even that a team of scuba-diving terrorists would secretly retrieve the ancient weapon.

Former Army colonel and present-day raconteur and soldier of fortune Derek Duke took it as his personal mission to find the bomb. He says the Air Force could easily find it but won't do so either because they don't want to go to the expense of finding it or they don't want to admit they lost a thermonuclear weapon for half a century. Duke claims to have found a radiation-emitting object off Little Tybee Island during a search in 2004.

Commander Richardson, now retired and living in Jackson, Mississippi, says the point is moot because the bomb wasn't armed when he jettisoned it. Environmentalists say that doesn't matter, because the enriched uranium the Air Force admits was in the bomb is toxic whether or not there's the risk of a nuclear detonation. People who work in the fishing industry on Tybee say the fact that the bomb also had 400 pounds of high explosive "nuclear trigger" is reason enough to get it out of these waterways, which hosted the 1996 Olympic yachting competition. And what of the owners of the Tybee Bomb, the Air Force? In 2000, they sent a team to Savannah to find the bomb, concluding it was buried somewhere off the coast in 5-15 feet of mud. In 2005, in another attempt to find the weapon—and also to shut down the rampant conspiracy theories, most of them propagated by Duke—they sent another team of experts down to look one last time. Their verdict: The bomb's still lost. That won't stop local speculation about its whereabouts, however. Who can resist a real-life cloak-and-dagger story? Certainly few people around here.

Postscript: No one was injured that night in 1958, except for some frostbite the F-86 pilot suffered as a result of ejecting from his damaged plane. In an interesting bit of synchronicity, the fighter pilot, Clarence Wilson, and the B-47 commander, Howard Richardson, grew up miles away from each other in Winston County, Mississippi.

---

is **Officer's Row,** former home of Fort Screven's commanding officers and now a mix of private residences, vacation rentals, and B&Bs.

South End

Next, scoot out Van Horne Street to Butler Avenue and take a left. This is Tybee's main drag, the beach fully public and accessible from any of the numbered side streets on the left. Go all the way down to **Tybrisa Street** (formerly 16th St.) to get a flavor of old Tybee. Here's where you'll find the old five-and-dimes like T. S. Chu's, still a staple of local life, and little diners, ice cream spots, and taverns. The new pride of the island is the large, long pier structure called the **Tybrisa Pavilion II,** built in 1996 in an attempt to recreate the lost glory of the Tybrisa Pavilion, social and spiritual center of the island's gregarious resort days. Built in 1891 by the Central of Georgia Railway, the Tybrisa hosted name entertainers and big bands on its expansive dance floor. Sadly, fire destroyed it in 1967, an enormous blow to area morale.

Literally at the foot of the Pavilion you'll find the little **Tybee Island Marine Science Center** (1510 Strand Ave., 912/786-5917, www.tybeemarinescience.org, daily 10 A.M.–5 P.M., $4 adults, $3 children), with nine aquariums and a touch tank featuring native species. Here is the nerve center for the Tybee Island Sea Turtle Project, an ongoing effort to document and preserve the local comings and goings of the island's most beloved inhabitant and unofficial mascot, the endangered sea turtle.

TOURS

Savannah's tourist boom has resulted in a similar explosion of well over 50 separate tour services, ranging from simple guided trolley journeys to horse-drawn carriage rides to specialty tours to ecotourism adventures. There's even an MP3-player walking tour. Fair warning: Although local tour guides technically must pass a competency test demonstrating their knowledge of Savannah history, in practice whatever they learned is often thrown out the window in favor of whatever sounds good to them at the time. I've heard the craziest, most untrue things said from passing trolleys and horse carriages. By all means go on a tour, but do so with the knowledge that much of what you're likely to hear won't be true at all.

Here's a listing of the key categories with the most notable offerings in each. Don't forget to tip your guide if you were satisfied with the tour.

Trolley Tours

The vehicle of choice for the bulk of the masses visiting Savannah, trolley tours allow you to sit back and enjoy the views in reasonable comfort. As in other cities, the guides provide commentary while attempting, with various degrees of success, to navigate the cramped downtown traffic environment. The main trolley companies in town are **Old Savannah Tours** (912/234-8128, www.oldsavannahtours.com, basic on-off tour $25 adults, $11 children), **Old Town Trolleys** (800/213-2474, www.trolleytours.com, basic on-off tour $23 adults, $10 children), **Oglethorpe Trolley Tours** (912/233-8380, www.oglethorpe-tours.com, basic on-off tour $22.50 adults, $10 children), and **Gray Line Tours** (912/234-8687, www.graylineofsavannah.com, basic on-off tour $15). All embark from the Savannah Visitors Center on Martin Luther King Jr. Boulevard about every 20–30 minutes on the same schedule, daily 9 A.M.–4:30 P.M.

Frankly there's not much difference between them, as they all offer a very similar range of services for similar prices, with most offering pickup at your downtown hotel. While the common "on-off privileges" allow trolley riders to disembark for a while and pick up another of the same company's trolleys at marked stops, be aware there's no guarantee the next trolley will have enough room to take you on board. Or the one after that.

Specialty Tours

Besides the standard narrated Historic District tours, all the above companies also offer a number of spin-off tours. Samples include the Pirate's House Dinner & Ghost Tour, Belles of Savannah, the Evening Haunted Trolley, and multiple Paula Deen tours.

The copious ghost tours, offered by all the companies, can be fun for the casual visitor who wants entertainment rather than actual history. Students of the paranormal are likely to be disappointed by the cartoonish, Halloween aspect of some of the tours. A standout in the ghost field is the **Hearse Ghost Tours** (912/695-1578, www.hearseghosttours.com), a unique company that also operates tours in New Orleans and St. Augustine, Florida. Up to eight guests at a time ride around in the open

SAVANNAH

top of a converted hearse, painted all black, of course, and get a 90-minute, suitably over-the-top narration from the driver-guide. It's still pretty cheesy, but a hip kind of cheesy. For those who take their paranormal activity *very* seriously, there's Shannon Scott's **Sixth Sense Savannah Ghost Tour** (866/666-3323, www.sixthsensesavannah.com, $20, midnight tour $38.50), an uncensored, straightforward look at Savannah's poltergeist population.

Longtime tour guide and raconteur Greg Proffit and his staff offer fun walking "pub crawls," **Savannah Tours by Foot** (912/238-3843, www.savannahtours.com), wherein the point is to meet your guide at some local tavern, ramble around, learn a little bit, and imbibe a lot, though not necessarily in that order. The adult tour is the "Creepy Crawl" ($18) whereas the tour suitable for kids and Girl Scouts is the "Creepy Stroll" ($10 adults, $5 Girl Scouts). You may not want to believe everything you hear, but you're sure to have a lot of fun. The tours book up early, so make arrangements in advance.

To learn about Savannah's history of filmmaking and to enjoy the best of local cuisine, try a **Savannah Movie Tour** (912/234-3440, www.savannahmovietours.net, $25 adults, $15 children), taking you to various film locations in town, and a newer **Savannah Foody Tour** (912/234-3440, www.savannahmovietours.net, $48) featuring 6–9 local eateries.

Storyteller and author Ted Eldridge leads **A Walk Through Savannah Tours** (912/921-4455, www.awalkthroughsavannah.bravehost.com, $15 adults, $5 6–12, free under age 6) and offers all kinds of specialty walking tours, such as a garden tour, a ghost tour, a historic churches tour, and of course a *Midnight in the Garden of Good and Evil* tour. For a more enlightened take than you'll usually get on a local tour, contact licensed guide **Orlando Montoya** (912/308-2952, $20) for a personalized walking tour. His regular job is as a journalist with Georgia Public Radio, so expect a higher level of taste and information with this journey. Another offbeat tour option is **Savannah's Uncommon Walk** (912/358-0700, www.sellersandhiggins.com, $20), a two-hour exploration of little-known Savannah leaving at 9:30 A.M. and 1:30 P.M. daily from Chippewa Square.

To see downtown Savannah by bicycle—quite a refreshing experience—try **Savannah Bike Tours** (41 Habersham St., 912/704-4043, www.savannahbiketours.com, $15 adults, $10 under age 12), two-hour trips through all 19 squares and Forsyth Park with your "rolling concierge." They leave daily at 9:30 A.M., 12:30 P.M., and 4 P.M. Rent bikes from them or ride your own.

The unique **Negro Heritage Trail Tour** (912/234-8000, $19 adults, $10 children) takes you on a 90-minute air-conditioned bus tour of over 30 of Savannah's key African American history sites. Pick up the Negro Heritage Tour at the Visitors Center downtown (301 MLK Jr. Blvd.) Tuesday–Saturday at 10 A.M. and noon.

Carriage Tours

Ah, yes—what could be more romantic and more traditional than enjoying downtown Savannah the way it was originally intended to be traveled, by horse-drawn carriage? Indeed, this is one of the most fun ways to see the city, for couples as well as for those with horse-enamored children. Yes, the horses sometimes look tired, but the tour operators generally take great care to keep the horses hydrated and out of the worst of the heat. There are three main purveyors of equine tourism in town: **Carriage Tours of Savannah** (912/236-6756, www.carriagetoursofsavannah.com, pickup in City Market), **Historic Savannah Carriage Tours** (888/837-1011, www.savannahcarriage.com, pickup at the Hampton Inn), and **Plantation Carriage Company** (912/201-0001, pickup in City Market). As with the trolleys, the length of the basic tour and the price is about the same for all—45–60 minutes, about $20 adults and

$10 children. All offer specialty tours as well, from ghost tours to evening romantic rides with champagne. Some will pick you up at your hotel.

Water Tours

The heavy industrial buildup on the Savannah River means that the main river tours, all departing from the docks in front of the Hyatt Regency hotel, tend to be disappointing in their unrelenting views of cranes, docks, storage tanks, and smokestacks. Still, for those into that kind of thing, narrated trips up and down the river on the *Georgia Queen* and the *Savannah River Queen* are offered by **Savannah Riverboat Cruises** (912/232-6404, www.savannahriverboat.com, $19 adults, $10 ages 4–12).

If you've just *got* to get out on the river for a short time, by far the best bargain is to take one of the two little **Savannah Belles** (daily 7:30 A.M.–10:30 P.M., free) water ferries, which shuttle passengers from River Street to Hutchinson Island and back every 15–20 minutes. Pick up either the *Juliette Gordon Low* or the *Susie King Taylor* on River Street in front of City Hall or at the Waving Girl landing a few blocks east.

Ecotours

The 35-year-old nonprofit **Wilderness Southeast** (912/897-5108, www.wildernesssoutheast.org, $10–35) offers guided trips, including paddles to historic Mulberry Grove, birding trips, and beach explorations. Regularly scheduled "Walks on the Wild Side" run the gamut from "Alligators to Anhingas" to the "Urban Forest" to "Explore the Night Sky" to the "Blackwater River Float." Custom tours are also available.

The most highly-regarded local canoe and kayak tour operator and rental house is **Savannah Canoe & Kayak** (912/341-9502, www.savannahcanoeandkayak.com), run by the husband-wife team of Nigel and Krstin Law. They offer several kayak trips, including a short jaunt to Little Tybee Island. On U.S. 80 just as you get on Tybee is another quality tour service, **Sea Kayak Georgia** (1102 U.S. 80, 888/529-2542, www.seakayakgeorgia.com, half-day tour $55). Run by locals Marsha Henson and Ronnie Kemp, Sea Kayak offers many different types of kayak tours. Run by Captain Mike Neal, an experienced local boatman and conservationist, **Moon River Kayak Tours** (912/898-1800, www.moonriverkayak.com, $50) focuses on 2.5-hour tours of the Skidaway Narrows and scenic Moon River, departing from the public boat ramp at the foot of the bridge to Skidaway Island. No kayaking experience required.

Entertainment and Events

If you like to have a good time, you're in the right place. Savannah is known for its heavy year-round schedule of festivals, many of them outdoors, as well as its copious variety of watering holes hosting a diverse range of local residents and adventurous visitors.

NIGHTLIFE

Savannah is a hard-drinking town, and not just on St. Patrick's Day. Visitors expecting a Bible Belt atmosphere are sometimes surprised—often, it must be said, pleasantly so—at Savannah's high tolerance for intoxication and its associated behavior patterns. A few years ago a city councilman decided he'd had a few too many and simply got a ride home from an on-duty cop. The ability to legally walk downtown streets with beer, wine, or a cocktail in hand also contributes to the overall joie de vivre.

A party here is never far away any night of

the week, so it makes sense to begin this section with a close, loving look at the bars, pubs, and taverns that are the heart of Savannah's social scene and really make it tick. Bars close in Savannah at 3 A.M., a full hour later than in Charleston. One catch: Due to Georgia's notorious blue laws, establishments that serve alcohol that do not derive at least 50 percent of their revenue from food may not open on Sundays. A city-wide indoor smoking ban is in effect and you may not smoke cigarettes in any bar in Savannah.

Bars and Pubs

Uncharacteristically, Savannah now sports several good hotel bars, and chief among them is no doubt **Rocks on the Roof** (102 W. Bay St., 912/721-3800, daily 11 A.M.–3 P.M.) atop the Bohemian Hotel Savannah on the waterfront. In good weather the exterior walls are opened up to reveal a large wraparound seating area with stunning views of downtown on one side and of the Savannah River on the other. The crowd is a fun mix of locals and visitors.

Savannah's best dive—and I mean that in the nicest way—is **Pinkie Masters** (318 Drayton St., 912/238-0447, Mon.–Fri. 4 P.M.–3 A.M., Sat. 5 P.M.–3 A.M.). Named for a legendary local political kingmaker, Pinkie's is a favorite not only with students, artists, and professors but also with lawyers, journalists, and grizzled war vets. This is where Jimmy Carter, ironically a teetotaler, stood on the bar and announced his candidacy for Georgia governor. The service is very informal; bartenders often finish their shift and simply take their place on a barstool with the customers. Think of **Hang Fire** (27 Whitaker St., 912/443-9956, Mon.–Sat. 5 P.M.–3 A.M.) as Pinkie's, the new generation. Only a few years old, this Whitaker Street haunt, occupying the site of downtown's last strip bar, is already one of the most popular bars in town and, like Pinkie's, caters to a wide range of people who seem to get along in

more or less perfect harmony. Trivia nights on Tuesdays are a hoot.

One of the hottest hangouts downtown is **The Distillery** (416 W. Liberty St., 912/236-1772, www.distillerysavannah.com), located in, yes, a former distillery. As such, the atmosphere isn't exactly dark and romantic—it's sort of one big open room—but the excellent location at the corner of MLK Jr. Boulevard and Liberty Street, the long vintage bar, and the great selection of beers on tap combine to make this a happening spot. The real hipsters hang out in ironic fashion drinking PBRs at the **American Legion Bar** (1108 Bull St., 912/233-9277, http://alpost135.com), located in, yes, an actual American Legion post. While the Legionnaires themselves are a straight-laced patriotic bunch, the patrons of "the Legion," as the bar is colloquially known, tend toward the counterculture. The drinks are some of the cheapest in town. Fun historical fact: The building housing the Legion was the birthplace of the U.S. 8th Air Force during World War II.

The main landmark on the west end of River Street is the famous (or infamous, depending on which side of "The Troubles" you're on) **Kevin Barry's Irish Pub** (117 W. River St., 912/233-9626, www.kevinbarrys.com, daily 11 A.M.–3 A.M.), one of Savannah's most beloved establishments. KB's keeps alive the spirit of Irish independence. It's open seven days a week, with evenings seeing performances by a number of Irish troubadours, all veterans of the East Coast trad circuit. An eclectic mix of travelers, local Irish, military, and sailors keeps this place always interesting and alive. While no one in their right mind goes to an Irish pub for the food, Kevin Barry's offers a good, solid range of typical fare, including serviceable corned beef and cabbage. Check out the view of the river from the second-floor "Hall of Heroes," featuring tons of military memorabilia and 9/11 tributes.

Don't get too excited about the "rooftop

THE TO-GO CUP TRADITION

Arguably the single most civilized trait of Savannah, and certainly one of the things that most sets it apart, is the glorious old tradition of the "to-go cup." True to its history of hard-partying and general open-mindedness, Savannah, like New Orleans, legally allows you to walk the streets downtown with an open container of your favorite adult beverage. Of course, you have to be 21 and over, and the cup must be Styrofoam or plastic, never glass or metal, and no more than 16 ounces. While there are boundaries to where to-go cups are legal, in practice this includes almost all areas of the Historic District frequented by visitors. The quick and easy rule of thumb is, keep your to-go cups north of Jones Street.

Every other election year, some local politician tries to get the church folk all riled up and proposes doing away with to-go cups in the interest of public safety, and he or she is inevitably shouted down by the outcry from the tourism-conscious Chamber of Commerce and from patriotic Savannahians defending their way of life. Every downtown watering hole has stacks of cups at the bar for patrons to use. You can either ask the bartender for a to-go cup—alternately a "go cup"—or just reach out and grab one yourself. Don't be shy; it's the Savannah way.

dining" advertised at **Churchill's Pub & Restaurant** (13–17 W. Bay St., 912/232-8501, www.thebritishpub.com, Mon.–Fri. 5 P.M.–3 A.M., Sat. 10 A.M.–3 A.M., kitchen until 10 P.M. Sun.–Thurs., 11 P.M. Fri.–Sat.), unless you enjoy looking at the sides of other buildings. The fish-and-chips here are among the best in town. The "other" English pub in town, **Six Pence Pub** (245 Bull St., 912/233-3151, daily 11:30 A.M.–midnight), is centrally located off Chippewa Square downtown, and though more popular with visitors than with

locals, it is still a good place to stop in for a pint on a rainy day. Look for the big red London telephone booth out front.

The only brewpub in Savannah, **Moon River Brewing Company** (21 W. Bay St., 912/447-0943, www.moonriverbrewing. com, Mon.–Thurs. 11 A.M.–11 P.M., Fri.–Sat. 11 A.M.–midnight, Sun. 11 A.M.–10 P.M.) directly across from the Hyatt Regency, offers half a dozen handcrafted beers—from a pale ale to a stout and all points between.

Live Music and Karaoke

Despite its high-volume offerings, the hard-core and heavy metal club **The Jinx** (127 W. Congress St., 912/236-2281, www.thejinx. net, Mon.–Sat. 4 P.M.–3 A.M.) is a friendly watering hole and probably the closest thing Savannah has to a full-on Athens, Georgia, music club. Shows start *very* late here, never before 11 P.M. and often later than that. If you're here for the show, bring earplugs. The other live rock club of note in Savannah is **Live Wire Music Hall** (307 W. River St., 912/233-1192, www.livewiremusichall.com, Mon.–Thurs. 4 P.M.–3 A.M., Fri.–Sat. 11 A.M.–3 A.M.). The music is on the ground floor, while the second floor has a bar and a few pool tables.

Savannah's undisputed karaoke champion is **McDonough's** (21 E. McDonough St., 912/233-6136, www.mcdonoughsofsavannah.com, Mon.–Sat. 8 P.M.–3 A.M., Sun. 8 P.M.–2 A.M.), an advantage compounded by the fact that a lot more goes on here than karaoke. The kitchen at McDonough's is quite capable, and many locals swear you can get the best burger in town. Despite the sports bar atmosphere, the emphasis here is on the karaoke, which ramps up every night at 9:30 P.M., and a very competent group of regulars never fails to entertain. The crowd here is surprisingly diverse, racially and socioeconomically mixed, featuring lawyers and students, rural folks and Rangers in equal numbers.

SAVANNAH

SAVANNAH

Gay and Lesbian

Any examination of gay and lesbian nightlife in Savannah must, of course, begin with **Club One Jefferson** (1 Jefferson St., 912/232-0200, www.clubone-online.com) of *Midnight in the Garden of Good and Evil* fame, with its famous drag shows, including the notorious Lady Chablis, upstairs in the cabaret, and its rockin' 1,000-square-foot dance floor downstairs. Cabaret showtimes are Thursday–Saturday 10:30 P.M. and 12:30 A.M., Sunday 10:30 P.M., and Monday 11:30 P.M. Call for Lady Chablis's showtimes. As with all local gay nightclubs, straights are more than welcome.

A friendly, kitschy little tavern at the far west end of River Street near the Jefferson Street ramp, **Chuck's Bar** (301 W. River St., 912/232-1005, www.myspace.com/chucks_bar, Mon.–Wed. 8 P.M.–3 A.M., Thurs.–Sat. 7 P.M.–3 A.M.) is a great place to relax and see some interesting local characters. Karaoke at Chuck's is especially a hoot, and they keep the Christmas lights up all year.

PERFORMING ARTS
Theater

While live theater isn't what it used to be in Savannah, the multiuse venue **Muse Arts Warehouse** (703D Louisville Rd., 912/713-1137, www.musesavannah.org) hosts a variety of community-based plays and performances within a well-restored historic train depot. Get there by taking Liberty Street west from downtown, where it turns into Louisville Road.

The semipro troupe at the **Historic Savannah Theatre** (222 Bull St., 912/233-7764, www.savannahtheatre.com) performs a busy rotating schedule of oldies revues (a typical title: *Return to the '50s*), which make up for their lack of originality with the tightness and energy of their talented young cast of regulars.

There are few things to recommend Savannah's south side to the visitor, but one of them is the **Armstrong Atlantic State**

University Masquers (11935 Abercorn St., 912/927-5381, www.finearts.armstrong.edu), the second-oldest college theater group in the country (only Harvard's Hasty Pudding Theatricals is older). Now marking their 75th anniversary, the Masquers boast a newly restored performance space at the Jenkins Theatre, and might surprise you with the high quality of their performances despite being a student program. Parking is never a problem.

Music and Dance

The Savannah Symphony is no more, a victim of the same economic challenges facing orchestras in small-to-midsize cities all over the United States. But carrying on their proud tradition—and using many of the same musicians—is the **Savannah Philharmonic** (800/514-3849, www.thesavannahphil.org), a professional troupe that performs concertos and sonatas at various venues around town and is always worth checking out.

A prime dance company in town is **Savannah Danse Theatre** (912/897-2100, www.savannahdansetheatre.org), known chiefly for its complete *Nutcracker* performance each December at the Lucas Theatre, with live accompaniment by a full symphony orchestra hired specially for the occasion—quite a rarity in a city this size.

CINEMA

The closest multiplex to downtown is the **Victory Square Stadium 9** (1901 E. Victory Dr., 912/355-5000, www.trademarkcinemas.com), which also hosts the screenings of **The Reel Savannah Group** (reelsavanah@hotmail.com, www.reelsavannah.org), a nonprofit that brings in foreign independent releases one Sunday a month. The historic **Lucas Theatre for the Arts** (32 Abercorn St., 912/525-5040, www.lucastheatre.com) downtown is a great place to see a movie, and the Savannah Film Society hosts screenings there throughout the year. Check the website for scheduling. The **Sentient Bean Coffeehouse** (13 E. Park Ave., 912/232-4447, www.sentientbean.com) hosts counterculture and political documentaries and kitsch classics.

FESTIVALS AND EVENTS

Savannah's calendar fairly bursts with festivals, many outdoors. Dates shift from year to year, so it's best to consult the listed websites for details.

January

Floats and bands take part in the **Martin Luther King Jr. Day Parade** downtown to commemorate the civil rights leader and Georgia native. The bulk of the route is on historic MLK Jr. Boulevard, formerly West Broad Street.

February

Definitely not to be confused with St. Patrick's Day, the **Savannah Irish Festival** (912/232-3448, www.savannahirish.org) focuses on Celtic music. A regular performer and Savannah's most popular "Irishman at large" is folk singer Harry O'Donoghue, a native of Ireland who regularly plays at Kevin Barry's Irish Pub on River Street and hosts his own Celtic music show, "The Green Island," on local public radio 91.1 FM Saturday evenings.

Hosted by the historically black Savannah State University at various venues around town, the month-long **Black Heritage Festival** (912/691-6847) is tied into Black History Month and boasts name entertainers like the Alvin Ailey Dance Theatre (performing free!). This event also usually features plenty of historical lectures devoted to the very interesting and rich history of African Americans in Savannah.

Also in February is the **Savannah Book Festival** (www.savannahbookfestival.org), modeled after a similar event in Washington DC and featuring many local and regional authors at various venues.

March

One of the most anticipated events for house-proud Savannahians, the **Tour of Homes and Gardens** (912/234-8054, www.savannahtourofhomes.org) offers guests the opportunity to visit six beautiful sites off the usual tourist-trod path. This is a great way to expand your understanding of local architecture and hospitality beyond the usual house museums.

More than just a day, the citywide **St. Patrick's Day** (www.savannahsaintpatricksday.com) celebration generally lasts at least half a week and temporarily triples the population. The nearly three-hour parade—the second-biggest in the United States—always begins at 10 A.M. on St. Patrick's Day (unless that falls on a Sunday, in which case it's generally on the previous Saturday) and includes an interesting mix of marching bands, wacky floats, and sauntering local Irishmen in kelly green jackets. The appeal of the event comes not only from the festive atmosphere and generally beautiful spring weather but from Savannah's unique law allowing partiers to walk the streets with a plastic cup filled with the adult beverage of their choice. Because of this, however, there is inevitably going to be overimbibing, which Savannahians generally think of as "local character." Your best course of action is to simply put on a "Kiss Me I'm Irish" button, sample a beverage yourself, and live and let live if possible. While the parade itself is very family-friendly, afterward hardcore partiers generally head en masse to River Street, which is blocked off for the occasion and definitely not where you want to take small children. If you want to hear traditional Celtic music on St. Patrick's Day in Savannah, River Street also isn't the place to go, with the exception of Kevin Barry's on the west end. Outdoor entertainment on River Street during the celebration is generally a lame assortment of cover bands. For authentic Irish music on St. Paddy's Day, wander around the pubs on the periphery of City Market.

CINEMA IN SAVANNAH

The first high-profile film made in Savannah was 1962's *Cape Fear,* starring Gregory Peck and Robert Mitchum (who was arrested and briefly jailed years before for public indecency while wandering in a drunken state through Savannah). But 1975's *Gator,* directed by and starring Burt Reynolds, really put the city on the Hollywood map, due in no small part to the then-mega star power of Reynolds himself, whose filmmaking mission was, in his words, to "say some nice things about the South."

In short order, parts of the landmark 1970s TV miniseries *Roots* were filmed in and around Savannah, as were part of the follow-up *Roots: The Next Generation.*

Film aficionados fondly remember the 1980 TV movie *The Ordeal of Dr. Mudd,* starring Dennis Weaver. In addition to the infamous story from "The Book" where Jim Williams unfurls a swastika banner to ruin a shot on Monterey Square, there are other reasons to remember the film. *Dr. Mudd* also expertly uses interiors of Fort Pulaski to tell this largely sympathetic account of the physician accused of aiding Abraham Lincoln's assassin John Wilkes Booth. In a chilling bit of synchronicity, Booth's brother Edwin, the most famous actor in the United States during the 1800s, played in Savannah often.

A key chapter in local filmography came with the filming of 1989's *Glory.* River Street was the set for parade scenes, and as Colonel Shaw, Matthew Broderick delivered his address to the troops a block west of Mrs. Wilkes' Boarding House. The railroad roundhouse off MLK Jr. Boulevard stood in for a Massachusetts training ground.

Another brush with Hollywood came with the filming of 1994's *Forrest Gump* in and around Savannah. Look for Tom Hanks on a bench in Chippewa Square—and note how the traffic runs the wrong direction around the square! The bench itself now resides in the Savannah History Museum on MLK Jr. Boulevard. The steeple in the shot of the floating white feather is of nearby Independent Presbyterian Church.

Ben Affleck and Sandra Bullock filmed many scenes of 1999's *Forces of Nature* on Tybee Island and in Savannah (yours truly's house is in the final scene for about two seconds). Longtime Hollywood producer and Savannah native Stratton Leopold, who also owns Leopold's Ice Cream on Broughton Street, helped Savannah land 1999's *The General's Daughter* starring John Travolta (look for the grand exterior of the main building at Oatland Island). Trotting out a serviceable Southern accent for a Brit, Kenneth Branagh came to town to play a disgruntled Savannah lawyer in Robert Altman's *Gingerbread Man.*

Though quite a few downtown art students had no idea what the fuss was about, Robert Redford still turned female heads when he came to town to direct 2000's *The Legend of Bagger Vance,* with Will Smith as the eponymous caddie. In the film, watch for the facsimile of a Depression-era storefront specially built around City Market. Redford returned to Savannah in late 2009 to film *The Conspirator,* another locally shot film about the Lincoln assassination. (Savannah stands in for Washington DC.) Cate Blanchett and Katie Holmes starred in 2000's *The Gift,* one of the few movies to take full advantage of the beauty of Bonaventure Cemetery.

Ironically, considering the impact of "The Book" on Savannah, Clint Eastwood's *Midnight in the Garden of Good and Evil* (1997) is arguably the worst movie ever filmed here. Eastwood's famously laissez-faire attitude toward filmmaking—reportedly there were no rehearsals before cameras rolled—did not work well, perhaps because Savannah's already a pretty darn laissez-faire kind of place to begin with.

But the biggest stir of them all came in summer 2009, when Disney star Miley Cyrus of *Hannah Montana* fame came to Tybee Island to film *The Last Song.*

Savannah's answer to Charleston's Spoleto, the three-week **Savannah Music Festival** (912/234-3378, www.savannahmusicfestival. org) is held at various historical venues around town and begins right after St. Patrick's Day. Past festivals have featured Wynton Marsalis, the Beaux Arts Trio, and Diane Reeves. The jazz portion is locked down tight, thanks to the efforts of festival director Rob Gibson, a Georgia native who cut his teeth as the founding director of Jazz at Lincoln Center. The classical side is equally impressive, helmed by one of the world's great young violinists, Daniel Hope, acting as associate director. Other genres are featured in abundance as well, including gospel, bluegrass, zydeco, world music, and the always-popular American Traditions vocal competition. The most economical way to enjoy the Music Festival is to purchase tickets online before December of the previous year at a 10 percent discount. However, if you just want to take in a few events, individual tickets are available at a tiered pricing system that allows everyone to enjoy this popular event. You can buy tickets to individual events in town at the walk-up box office beside the Trustees Theatre on Broughton Street.

April

Short for "North of Gaston Street," the **NOGS Tour of Hidden Gardens** (912/961-4805, www.gcofsavnogstour.org, $30) is available two days in April and focuses on Savannah's amazing selection of private gardens selected for excellence of design, historical interest, and beauty.

Everyone loves the annual free **Sidewalk Arts Festival** (912/525-5865, www.scad.edu) presented by the Savannah College of Art and Design in Forsyth Park. Contestants claim a rectangular section of sidewalk on which to display their chalk art talent. There's a noncontest section with chalk provided.

May

The SCAD-sponsored **Sand Arts Festival** (www.scad.edu) on Tybee Island's North Beach centers on a competition of sand castle design, sand sculpture, sand relief, and wind sculpture. You might be amazed at the level of artistry lavished on the sometimes-wondrous creations only for them to wash away with the tide.

If you don't want to get wet, don't show up at the **Tybee Beach Bum Parade,** an uproarious event held the weekend prior to Memorial Day weekend. With a distinctly boozy overtone, this unique 20-year-old event features homemade floats filled with partiers who squirt the assembled crowds with various water pistols. The crowds, of course, pack their own heat and squirt back.

July

Two key events happen around **Fourth of July,** primarily the large fireworks show on River Street, always on July 4, and also an impressive fireworks display from the Tybee Pier and Pavilion, which is sometimes on a different night. A nice bonus of the Tybee event is that sometimes you can look out over the Atlantic and see a similar fireworks display on nearby Hilton Head Island, South Carolina, a few minutes away by boat (but nearly an hour by car).

September

The second-largest gay and lesbian event in Georgia (only Atlanta's version is larger), the **Savannah Pride Festival** (www.savannahpride.org, various venues, free) happens every September. Crowds get pretty big for this festive, fun event, which usually features lots of dance acts and political booths.

Though the quality of the acts has been overshadowed lately by the Savannah Music Festival in the spring, the **Savannah Jazz Festival** (www.savannahjazzfestival.org) has two key things going for it: It's free, and it's outside in the glorious green expanse of Forsyth Park. Generally spread out over several nights, the volunteer-run festival draws a good crowd regardless of the lineup, and concessions are available.

October

The Savannah Symphony Orchestra is now defunct, but area musicians unite to play a free evening at **Picnic in the Park** (www.savannahga.gov), a concert in Forsyth Park that draws thousands of noshers. Arrive early to check out the ostentatious, whimsical picnic displays, which compete for prizes. Then set out your blanket, pop open a bottle of wine, and enjoy the sweet sounds.

The combined aroma of beer, sauerkraut, and sausage that you smell coming from the waterfront is the annual **Oktoberfest on the River** (www.riverstreetsavannah.com), which has evolved to be Savannah's second-largest celebration (behind only St. Patrick's Day). Live entertainment of varying quality is featured, though the attraction, of course, is the aforementioned beer and German food. A highlight is the Saturday morning "Weiner Dog races" involving, you guessed it, competing dachshunds.

If pickin' and grinnin' is your thing, don't miss the low-key but always entertaining **Savannah Folk Music Festival** (www.savannahfolk.org). The main event of the weekend is held on a Sunday night in the historic Grayson Stadium in Daffin Park, but a popular Old-Time Country Dance is usually held the previous Saturday. Members of the Savannah Folk Music Society will help you learn how to do the dance, so don't be shy!

It's a fairly new festival, but the **Tybee Island Pirate Festival** (http://tybeepiratefest.com) is a fun and typically rollicking Tybee event in October featuring, well, everybody dressing up like pirates, saying "Arr" a lot, eating, drinking, and listening to cover bands. It may not sound like much, and it's really not, but it's typically very well-attended.

Sponsored by St. Paul's Greek Orthodox Church, the popular **Savannah Greek Festival** (www.stpaulsgreekorthodox.org) features food, music, and Greek souvenirs. The weekend event is held across the street from the church at the parish center—in the gym, to be exact, right on the basketball court. Despite the pedestrian location, the food is authentic and delicious, and the atmosphere convivial and friendly.

Despite its generic-sounding name, the **Fall Festival** (www.bamboo.caes.uga.edu) is actually quite interesting, given its location in the unique Bamboo Farm and Coastal Garden. A joint project of the University of Georgia and Chatham County, the Bamboo Farm features a wide array of native species, all lovingly tended. The festival features tours, displays, arts and crafts, food, and lots of kids' activities. The event is free, but parking is $1. To get here, take exit I-95 exit 94 and take Highway 204 east toward Savannah. Turn right on East Gateway Boulevard, then left on Canebrake Road. Enter at the Canebrake gate.

Hosted by the Savannah College of Art and Design, the weeklong **Savannah Film Festival** (www.scad.edu) beginning in late October is rapidly growing not only in size but in prestige. Lots of older, more established Hollywood names appear as honored guests for the evening events, while buzz-worthy up-and-coming actors, directors, producers, writers, and animators give excellent workshops during the day. Many of these usually jaded showbiz types really let their hair down for this festival, because, as you'll see, Savannah is the real star. The best way to enjoy this excellent event is to buy a pass, which enables you to walk from event to event. Most importantly, the passes gain you admission to what many locals consider the best part of the festival: the after-parties, where you'll often find yourself face to face with some famous star or director. But whatever you do, don't ask for an autograph. The thing at these parties is to be cool—and if you can't *be* cool, at least act that way.

One of Savannah's most unique events is late October's **"Shalom Y'all" Jewish Food Festival** (912/233-1547, www.mickveisrael. org), held in Forsyth Park and sponsored by the historic Temple Mickve Israel. Latkes, matzo, and other nibbles are all featured along with entertainment.

November

Generally kicking off the month is the popular **Telfair Art Fair** (www.telfair.org), a multiday annual art show and sale under a huge tent in Telfair Square between its two museums, the Telfair Academy and the Jepson Center. Browse or buy; either way it's a culturally enlightening good time.

The name says it all: The **Savannah Seafood Festival** (www.riverstreetsavannah.com) on River Street offers mouthwatering fare from a variety of local vendors, plus live entertainment.

December

Arts and crafts and holiday entertainment highlight the **Christmas on the River and Lighted Parade** (www.riverstreetsavannah. com), which happens on River Street.

Another beloved local tour, the annual **Holiday Tour of Homes** (912/236-8362, www.dnaholidaytour.net), sponsored by the Downtown Neighborhood Association, is a great way to get up close with a half-dozen or so of some of Savannah's best private homes, all dolled up in their finest for the holidays. There's an afternoon tour and a candlelight tour by trolley.

Shopping

Downtown Savannah's main shopping district is Broughton Street, which is included here along with several other key shopping areas of note.

BROUGHTON STREET

The historic center of downtown shopping has recently seen a major renaissance and is once again home to the most vibrant shopping scene in Savannah, just like it was in the 1940s and 1950s. While several chain stores have made inroads onto the avenue, here are some of the most notable independent shops.

Art Supply

A great art town needs a great art supply store, and in Savannah that would be **Primary Art Supply** (14 E. Broughton St., 912/233-7624, http://primaryartsupply.com, Mon.–Fri. 8 A.M.–8 P.M., Sat.–Sun. 10 A.M.–6 P.M.), which has two full floors of equipment and tools for the serious artist—priced to be affordable for students. But

casual shoppers will enjoy it as well for its collection of hip magazines and offbeat gift items.

Clothes and Fashion

Perhaps Broughton's most beloved old shop is **Globe Shoe Co.** (17 E. Broughton St., 912/232-8161), a Savannah institution and a real throwback to a time of personalized retail service. They have no website and no Facebook page—they're all about simple one-to-one service, like in the old days. Easily one of the coolest women's stores in town is **Go Fish** (106 W. Broughton St., 912/231-0609, www.gofishretail.com). This regional franchised operation provides for a lot of independence on the part of the owners; Debbie and Lloyd Ryysylainen offer a sharply curated range of upscale-looking clothes and shoes at reasonable prices. **Gaucho** is another popular choice for women, with a strong emphasis on accessories, jewelry, and shoes. There are two

© JIM MOREKIS

The Paris Market & Brocante is one of Broughton's coolest stores.

locations: 18 East Broughton Street (912/234-7414, Mon.–Sat. 10 A.M.–6 P.M.) and the original location at 250 Bull Street (912/232-7414, Mon.–Sat. 10 A.M.–6 P.M., Sun. 1–5 P.M.). **Copper Penny** (22 W. Broughton St., 912/629-6800, www.shopcopperpenny. com) is easily the premier women's shoe showcase on the historic avenue. Vintage shoppers will enjoy **Civvies** (22 E. Broughton St., 912/236-1551), a second-floor shop with a nice selection of previously owned clothing.

Home Goods

While Savannah is an Anglophile's dream, Francophiles will enjoy **The Paris Market & Brocante** (36 W. Broughton St., 912/232-1500, www.theparismarket.com, Mon.–Sat. 10 A.M.–6 P.M., Sun. 11 A.M.–4 P.M.) on a beautifully restored corner of Broughton Street. Home and garden goods, bed and bath accoutrements, and a great selection of antique and vintage items combine for a rather opulent

shopping experience. Plus there's an old-school Euro café inside where you can enjoy a coffee, tea, or hot chocolate.

Those looking for great home decorating ideas with inspiration from both global and Southern aesthetics, traditional as well as sleekly modern, should check out **24e Furnishings at Broughton** (24 E. Broughton St., 912/233-2274, www.twentyfoure.com, Mon.–Thurs. 10 A.M.–6 P.M., Fri.–Sat. 10 A.M.–7 P.M., Sun. noon–5 P.M.), located in an excellent restored 1921 storefront. Be sure to check out the expansive second-floor showroom.

One of the more unique Savannah retail shops is the **Savannah Bee Company** (104 W. Broughton St., 912/233-7873, www.savannahbee.com, Mon.–Sat. 10 A.M.–7 P.M., Sun. 11 A.M.–5 P.M.), which, as the name implies, carries an extensive line of honey-based merchandise, from foot lotion to lip balm. All the honey comes from area hives owned by company founder and owner Ted Dennard. The company now has a sizeable national presence since being picked up for the Williams-Sonoma catalogue 10 years ago. The flagship Broughton location provides plenty of sampling opportunities at the little café area and even boasts a small theater space for instructional films.

Outdoor Outfitters

Outdoors lovers should make themselves acquainted with **Half Moon Outfitters** (15 E. Broughton St., 912/201-9313, www.halfmoonoutfitters.com, Mon.–Sat. 10 A.M.–7 P.M., Sun. noon–6 P.M.), a full-service camping, hiking, skiing, and kayaking store. Half Moon is part of a regional chain that also has two locations in Charleston.

WATERFRONT

Amid the T-shirt shops, candy stores, and tchotchke places, Savannah's waterfront area does have a handful of quality shopping options.

Antiques

One of the coolest antiques shops in town is **Jere's Antiques** (9 N. Jefferson St., 912/236-2815, www.jeresantiques.com, Mon.–Sat. 9:30 A.M.–5 P.M.). It's in a huge historic warehouse on Factor's Walk and has a concentration on fine European pieces.

Clothes

Clothe your inner biker at **Harley-Davidson** (503 E. River St., 912/231-8000, Mon.–Sat. 10 A.M.–6 P.M., Sun. noon–6 P.M.).

CITY MARKET

A borderline tourist trap, City Market strongly tends toward more touristy, less unique items. Here are a couple of exceptions: The whimsical **A. T. Hun Gallery** (302 W. St. Julian St., 912/233-2060, www.athun.com, Mon.–Thurs. 10 A.M.–6 P.M., Fri.–Sat. 10 A.M.–10 P.M., Sun. 11 A.M.–5 P.M.) is one of the first true art galleries in town and features a variety of adventurous art

from local and regional favorites. **Kobo Gallery** (33 Barnard St., 912/201-0304, http://kobogallery.com, Mon.–Sat. 10:30 A.M.–5:30 P.M., Sun. 11 A.M.–5 P.M.) is Savannah's newest local artist cooperative and offers a nice range of adventurous artwork in a variety of media.

DOWNTOWN DESIGN DISTRICT

Focusing on upscale art and home goods, this small but chic shopping area runs for three blocks on Whitaker Street downtown beginning at Charlton Lane and ending at the Mercer-Williams House on Monterey Square.

Antiques

Arcanum Antiques and Interiors (422 Whitaker St., 912/236-6000, Mon.–Sat. 10 A.M.–5 P.M.) deals in a tasteful range of vintage items with a chic twist. For a more European take, try **The Corner Door** (417 Whitaker St., 912/238-5869, Tues.–Sat. 10 A.M.–5 P.M.). Perhaps the most eclectic antiques shop in the Downtown Design District is **Peridot Antiques and Interiors** (400 Whitaker St., 912/596-1117).

Clothes

Custard Boutique (414 Whitaker St., 912/232-4733) has a cute, fairly cutting-edge selection of women's clothes. **Mint Boutique** (413 Whitaker St., 912/341-8961, Mon.–Fri. 10 A.M.–6 P.M.) right next door brings a similarly modern style to this often very conservative town.

Home Goods

An eclectic European-style home goods store popular with locals and visitors alike is **One Fish Two Fish** (401 Whitaker St., 912/484-4600, Mon.–Sat. 10 A.M.–5 P.M., Sun. noon–5 P.M.). Owner Jennifer Beaufait Grayson, a St. Simons Island native, came to town a decade ago to set up shop in this delightfully restored old dairy building on the corner of Whitaker and Jones and has been getting rave reviews since. **Madame Chrysanthemum** (101 W. Taylor St., 912/238-3355) is technically a florist, and a fine one at that, but they also deal with fun home items and gift ideas.

BOOKS

The fact that **E. Shaver Bookseller** (326 Bull St., 912/234-7257, Mon.–Sat. 9 A.M.–6 P.M.) is one of the few locally owned independent bookstores left in town should not diminish the fact that it is also one of the best bookstores in town. Esther Shaver and her friendly, well-read staff can help you around the rambling old interior of their ground-level store and its generous stock of regionally themed books. Don't miss the rare map room, with some gems from the 17th and 18th centuries.

Specializing in "gently used" books in good condition, **The Book Lady** (6 E. Liberty St., 912/233-3628, Mon.–Sat. 10 A.M.–5:30 P.M.) on Liberty Street features many rare first editions. Enjoy a gourmet coffee while you browse the stacks. The beautiful Monterey Square location and a mention in *Midnight in the Garden of Good and Evil* combine to make **V&J Duncan** (12 E. Taylor St., 912/232-0338, www.vjduncan.com, Mon.–Sat. 10:30 A.M.–4:30 P.M.) a Savannah "must-shop." Owner John Duncan and his wife Virginia ("Ginger" to friends) have collected an impressive array of prints, books, and maps over the past quarter-century, and are themselves a treasure trove of information.

OTHER UNIQUE STORES

Not only a valuable outlet for SCAD students and faculty to sell their artistic wares, **shopSCAD** (340 Bull St., 912/525-5180, www.shopscadonline.com, Mon.–Wed. 9 A.M.–5:30 P.M., Thurs.–Fri. 9 A.M.–8 P.M., Sat. 10 A.M.–8 P.M., Sun. noon–5 P.M.) is also one of Savannah's most unique boutiques. You never really know what you'll find, but whatever it is, it will be one-of-a-kind. The jewelry in particular is always cutting-edge in design

and high-quality in craftsmanship. The designer T-shirts are a hoot too.

Possibly the most beloved antiques store in town is **Alex Raskin Antiques** (441 Bull St., 912/232-8205, Mon.–Sat. 10 A.M.–5 P.M.) in Monterey Square, catty-corner from the Mercer-Williams House. Set in the historic Hardee mansion, a visit is worth it just to explore the home. But the goods Alex lovingly curates are among the best and most tasteful in the region.

A delightful little slice of Manhattan's Fashion District on Liberty Street, **Fabrika Fine Fabrics** (2 E. Liberty St., 912/236-1122, www.fabrikafinefabrics.com) has provided high-quality supplies for local luminaries such as former *Project Runway* contestant April Johnston. Run by two SCAD grads, the hip space is is jammed with high-quality, buzz-worthy bolts of fabric, oodles of beads, and lots of sewing paraphernalia. They offer custom sewing and sewing lessons.

And in this town so enamored of all things Irish, a great little locally owned shop is **Saints and Shamrocks** (309 Bull St., 912/233-8858, www.saintsandshamrocks.org, Mon.–Sat. 9:30 A.M.–5:30 P.M., Sun. 11 A.M.–4 P.M.). Pick up your St. Patrick's–themed gear and gifts to celebrate Savannah's highest holiday along with high-quality Irish imports

Set in a stunningly restored multi-level Victorian within a block of Forsyth Park, the globally conscious **Folklorico** (440 Bull St., 912/232-9300, Mon.–Sat. 10 A.M.–5 P.M., Sun. 1–5 P.M.) brings in a fascinating and diverse collection of sustainably made jewelry, gifts, and home goods from around the world, focusing on Central and South America and Asia.

MALLS

The mall closest to downtown—though not that close, at about 10 miles south—is **Oglethorpe Mall** (7804 Abercorn St., 912/354-7038, www.oglethorpemall.com, Mon.–Sat.

10 A.M.–9 P.M., Sun. noon–6 P.M.). Its anchor stores are Sears, Belk, J. C. Penney, and Macy's.

Much farther out on the south side is the **Savannah Mall** (14045 Abercorn St., 912/927-7467, www.savannahmall.com, Mon.–Sat. 10 A.M.–9 P.M., Sun. noon–6 P.M.). Its anchor stores are Dillard's, Target, and Bass Pro Shops Outdoor World.

GROCERIES AND MARKETS

Savannah's first and still premier health-food market, **Brighter Day Natural Foods** (1102 Bull St., 912/236-4703, www.brighterday-foods.com, Mon.–Sat. 10 A.M.–7 P.M., Sun. 12:30–5:30 P.M.) has been the labor of love of Janie and Peter Brodhead for 30 years, all of them in the same location at the southern tip of Forsyth Park. Boasting organic groceries, regional produce, a sandwich and smoothie bar in the back, and an extensive vitamin, supplement, and herb section, Brighter Day is an oasis in Savannah's sea of chain supermarkets.

Fairly new but already thriving, the **Forsyth Park Farmers Market** (www.forsythfarmers-market.org, Sat. 9 A.M.–1 P.M.) happens in the south end of scenic and wooded Forsyth Park. You'll find very fresh fruit and produce from a variety of fun and friendly regional farmers. If you have access to a real kitchen while you're in town, you might be glad to know there's usually a very good selection of organic, sustainably grown meat and poultry products as well—not always a given at farmers markets.

If you need some good quality groceries downtown—especially after-hours—try **Parker's Market** (222 E. Drayton St., 912/231-1001, daily 24 hours). In addition to a pretty wide array of gourmet-style victuals inside, there are gas pumps outside to fuel your vehicle.

A local tradition for 20 years, **Keller's Flea Market** (5901 Ogeechee Rd., I-95 exit 94, 912/927-4848, www.ilovefleas.com, Sat.–Sun. 8 A.M.–6 P.M., free) packs in about 10,000 shoppers over the course of a typical weekend, offering a range of bargains in antiques, home goods, produce, and general kitsch. There are concessions on-site.

A short ways into south-side Savannah is a **Fresh Market** (5525 Abercorn St., 912/354-6075, Mon.–Sat. 9 A.M.–9 P.M., Sun. 11 A.M.–8 P.M.). There's one 24-hour full-service supermarket in downtown Savannah, **Kroger** (311 E. Gwinnett St., 912/231-2260, daily 24 hours).

Sports and Recreation

Savannah more than makes up for its sad organized sports scene with copious outdoor options that take full advantage of its temperate climate and the natural beauty of its marshy environment next to the Atlantic Ocean.

ON THE WATER
Kayaking and Canoeing

Maybe the single best kayak or canoe adventure in Savannah is the run across the Back River from Tybee to **Little Tybee Island,** an undeveloped State Heritage Site that despite its name is actually twice as big as Tybee, albeit mostly marsh. Many kayakers opt to camp on the island. You can even follow the shoreline out into the Atlantic, but be aware that wave action can get intense offshore. Begin the paddle at the public boat ramp on the Back River. To get here, take Butler Avenue all the way to 18th Street and take a right, then another quick right onto Chatham Avenue. The parking lot for the landing is a short way up Chatham Avenue on your left. Warning: Do not attempt to swim to Little Tybee no matter how strong a swimmer you think you are—the currents are exceptionally vicious. Also, do not be tempted to walk far out onto the Back River beach at low tide. The tide comes in very quickly and often strands people on the sandbar.

Lazaretto Creek, on the western edge of the island, is a great place to explore Tybee and environs. From here you can meander several miles through the marsh, or go the other way and actually head into a channel of the Savannah River. If you're into ocean kayaking, you can even head into the Atlantic from here. Put in at the Lazaretto Creek landing, at the foot of the Lazaretto Creek bridge on the south side of U.S. 80 on the way to Tybee Island. This is a peaceful, pretty paddle for novice and experienced kayakers alike. You can also put in at the nearby Tybee Marina (4 Old Tybee Rd., 912/786-5554, www.tybeeislandmarina.com), also on Lazaretto Creek.

One of the great overall natural experiences in the area is the massive **Savannah National Wildlife Refuge** (912/652-4415, www.fws.gov/savannah, daily dawn–dusk, free). This 30,000-acre reserve—half in Georgia, half in South Carolina—is on the Atlantic Flyway, so you'll be able to see birdlife in abundance, in addition to alligators and manatee. Earthen dikes crisscrossing the refuge are vestigial remnants of paddy fields from plantation days. You can kayak on your own, but many opt to take guided tours offered by **Wilderness Southeast** (912/897-5108, www.wilderness-southeast.org, two-hour trips from $37.50 for two people), **Sea Kayak Georgia** (888/529-2542, www.seakayakgeorgia.com, $55 pp), and **Swamp Girls Kayak Tours** (843/784-2249, www.swampgirls.com, $45). To get here, take U.S. 17 north over the big Talmadge Bridge, over the Savannah River into South Carolina. Turn left on Highway 170 south and look for the entrance to Laurel Hill Wildlife Drive on the left.

Another pleasant kayaking route is the **Skidaway Narrows.** Begin this paddle at the public boat ramp, which you find by taking Waters Avenue all the way until it turns to Whitefield Avenue and then Diamond Causeway. Continue all the way over the Moon River to a drawbridge; park at the foot of the bridge. Once in the water, paddle northeast. Look for the osprey nests on top of the navigational markers in the narrows as you approach Skidaway Island State Park. Continuing on, you'll find scenic Isle of Hope high on a bluff to your left, with nearly guaranteed dolphin sightings around marker 62.

Farther out of town but worth the trip for any kayaker is the beautiful blackwater **Ebenezer Creek,** near the tiny township of New Ebenezer in Effingham County. Cypress trees lining this nationally designated Wild and Scenic River hang overhead, and wildlife abounds on this peaceful paddle. Look for old wooden sluice gates, vestiges of the area's rice plantation past. To get here, take exit 109 off I-95. Go north on Highway 21 to Rincon, Georgia, then east on Highway 275 (Ebenezer Rd.). Put in at the Ebenezer Landing ($5).

The best guided water tour in the area is Capt. Rene Heidt's **Sundial Nature Tours** (912/786-9470, www.sundialcharters.com). Rene is an expert in local marine life and offers a variety of tours, including dolphin watches, fossil hunts, and trips to various barrier islands. Rates start at about $160 for two people. A great one-stop shop for local kayaking information, tours, and equipment is **Savannah Canoe & Kayak** (414 Bonaventure Rd., 912/341-9502, www.savannahcanoeandkayak.com), run by the husband-wife team of Nigel and Kristin Law. To rent an ocean-worthy kayak on Lazaretto Creek, stop by **North Island Surf and Kayak** (1C Old Hwy. 80, 912/786-4000, www.northislandkayak.com, Mon.–Fri. 10 A.M.–5 P.M., Sat.–Sun. 9 A.M.–6 P.M., $45), located at Tybee Marina. Reservations are recommended.

Fishing

Savannah is a saltwater angler's paradise, rich in trout, flounder, and king and Spanish mackerel.

Offshore there's a fair amount of deep-sea action, including large grouper, white and blue marlin, wahoo, snapper, sea bass, and big amberjack near some of the many offshore wrecks.

Perhaps the best-known local angler is Captain Judy Helmey, a.k.a. "Miss Judy." In addition to her frequent and entertaining newspaper columns, she runs a variety of well-regarded charters out of **Miss Judy Charters** (912/897-2478, www.missjudycharters.com). Four-hour trips start at $500. To get there, go west on U.S. 80, take a right onto Bryan Woods Road, a left onto Johnny Mercer Boulevard, a right onto Wilmington Island Way, and a right down the dirt lane at her sign. Another highly regarded local fishing charter is the Tybee-based **Amick's Deep Sea Fishing** (912/897-6759, www.amicksdeepseafishing.com). Captain Steve Amick and crew run offshore charters daily starting at $120 pp. Go east on U.S. 80 and turn right just past the Lazaretto Creek Bridge. Another charter service is offered from **Lazaretto Creek Marina** (1 U.S. 80, 912/786-5848, www.tybeedolphins.com). Half- and full-day inshore and offshore fishing charters are available, starting at $250 for four hours. Go east on U.S. 80 and turn right just past the Lazaretto Creek Bridge. Turn right at the dead end.

Shallow-water fly fishers might want to contact **Savannah Fly Fishing Charters** (56 Sassafras Trail, 912/308-3700, www.savannahfly.com). Captain Scott Wagner takes half- and full-day charters both day and night from Savannah all the way down to St. Simons Island. Half-day rate starts at $300. Book early.

Diving

Diving is a challenge off the Georgia coast because of the silty nature of the water and its mercurial currents. Though not particularly friendly to the novice, plenty of great offshore opportunities abound around the many artificial reefs created by the Georgia Department of Natural Resources (www.coastalgadnr.org).

Certainly no underwater adventure in the area would be complete without a dive at **Gray's Reef National Marine Sanctuary** (912/598-2345, www.graysreef.noaa.gov). Administered by the National Oceanic and Atmospheric Administration, this fully protected marine sanctuary 17 miles offshore is in deep enough water to provide divers good visibility of its live-bottom habitat. Not a classic living coral reef but rather one built by sedimentary deposits, Gray's Reef's provides a look at a truly unique ecosystem. Some key dive charter operators that can take you to Gray's Reef are Captain Walter Rhame's **Mako Dive Charter** (600 Priest Landing Dr., 912/604-6256), which leaves from the Landings Harbor Marina; **Georgia Offshore** (1191 Lake Dr., Midway, 912/658-3884); and **Fantasia Scuba** (3 E. Montgomery Cross Rd., 912/921-8933). The best all-around dive shop in town is **Diving Locker and Ski Chalet** (74 W. Montgomery Cross Rd., 912/927-6603, www.divinglocker-skichalet.com, Mon.–Fri. 10 A.M.–6 P.M., Sat. 10 A.M.–5 P.M.) on the south side.

Surfing and Boarding

Other than some action around the pier, the surfing is poor on Tybee Island, with its broad shelf, tepid wave action, and lethal rip currents. But board surfers and kite boarders have a lot of fun on the south end of Tybee beginning at about 17th Street. The craziest surf is past the rock jetty, but be advised that the rip currents are especially treacherous there.

The best—and pretty much only—surf shop in town is **High Tides Surf Shop** (405 U.S. 80, 912/786-6556, www.hightidesurfshop.com). You can get a good local surf report and forecasts at their website.

ON THE LAND
Golf

There are a couple of strong public courses in Savannah that are also very good bargains. Chief among these has to be the

© JIM MOREKIS

the McQueen Island Trail is more commonly known as the "Rails to Trails."

Henderson Golf Club (1 Al Henderson Blvd., 912/920-4653, www.hendersongolfclub.com), an excellent municipal course with very reasonable green fees (Mon.–Fri. $28, Sat.–Sun. $33) that include a half-cart. Another local favorite and unbeatable bargain is the circa-1926 **Bacon Park Golf Course** (Shorty Cooper Dr., 912/354-2625, www.baconparkgolf.com, green fees about $20), comprising three nine-hole courses with a choice of three 18-hole combinations and some very small, fast greens. A relatively new course but not one you'd call a bargain is the **Club at Savannah Harbor** (2 Resort Dr., 912/201-2007, www.theclubatsavannahharbor.com, green fees $135, $70 for twilight) across the Savannah River on Hutchinson Island, adjacent to the Westin Savannah Harbor Resort. Home to the Liberty Mutual Legends of Golf Tournament each spring, the Club's tee times are 7:30 A.M.–3 P.M., with half-light play 2–5 P.M. The **Wilmington Island Club** (501 Wilmington Island Rd., 912/897-1612, green fees about $70) has arguably the quickest greens in town and is unarguably the most beautiful local course, set close by the Wilmington River amid lots of mature pines and live oaks.

Tennis

The closest public courts to the downtown area are at the south end of **Forsyth Park** (912/351-3850), which features four free lighted courts. They are unsupervised, and as you might expect, they get serious use. Farther south in **Daffin Park** (1001 E. Victory Dr., 912/351-3850), there are six clay courts and three lighted hard courts ($3). On the south side, **Bacon Park** (6262 Skidaway Rd., 912/351-3850) has 16 lighted hard courts ($3). If you get the tennis jones on Tybee, there are two free courts at **Tybee Island Memorial Park** (Butler Ave. and 4th St., 912/786-4573, www.cityoftybee.org).

Hiking

Though hiking in Savannah and the Lowcountry is largely a 2-D experience given the flatness of the terrain, there are plenty of good nature trails from which to observe the area's rich flora and fauna up close. My favorite trails are at **Skidaway Island State Park** (52 Diamond Causeway, 912/598-2300, www.gastateparks.org, daily 7 A.M.–10 P.M., parking $2 per vehicle per day). The three-mile Big Ferry Trail is the best overall experience, taking you out to a wooden viewing tower from which you can see the vast expanse of the Skidaway Narrows. A detour takes you past a Native American shell midden, Confederate earthworks, and even a rusty old still—a nod to Skidaway Island's former notoriety as a bootlegger's sanctuary. The shorter but still fun Sandpiper Trail is wheelchair-accessible.

An interesting, if hardly challenging, trail is the **McQueen Island Trail,** more commonly known as "Rails to Trails." This paved, palm-lined walking trail along the Savannah River was built on the old bed of the Savannah-to-Tybee railroad, which operated during Tybee's heyday as a major East Coast vacation spot in the 1930s and 1940s. To get here, cross the long, low, Bull River Bridge and take an immediate left into the small parking area, being very mindful of fast-moving inbound traffic on U.S. 80.

Biking

Most biking activity centers on Tybee Island, with the **McQueen Island Trail** being a popular and simple ride. Many locals like to load up their bikes and go to **Fort Pulaski** (912/786-5787, www.nps.gov, fort daily 8:30 A.M.–5:15 P.M., visitors center daily 9 A.M.–5 P.M., closed Christmas Day, $2 pp, free under age 16). From the grounds you can ride all over scenic and historic Cockspur Island.

Plenty of folks ride their bikes downtown, and it is particularly enriching and fun to pedal around the squares. Legally, however, you're not allowed to ride through the squares; you're supposed to stay on the street around them. And always yield to traffic already within the square as you enter. For a guided two-hour tour of downtown, try **Savannah Bike Tours** (41 Habersham St., 912/704-4043, www.savannahbiketours.com, $15 adults, $10 under age 12), leaving every day at 9:30 A.M., 12:30 P.M., and 4 P.M.

Bird-Watching

Birding in the Savannah area is excellent at two spots on the **Colonial Coast Birding Trail** (http://georgiawildlife.dnr.state.ga.us). The main site is **Skidaway Island State Park** (52 Diamond Causeway, 912/598-2300, www.gastateparks.org, daily 7 A.M.–10 P.M., parking $2 per vehicle per day). Spring and fall bring a lot of the usual warbler action, while spring and summer feature nesting osprey and painted bunting, always a delight. The other trail spot is Tybee Island's **North Beach** area (parking $5 per day, meters available). You'll see a wide variety of shorebirds and gulls, as well as piping plover, northern gannets, and purple sandpipers (winter).

Wading birds in particular are in wide abundance at the **Savannah National Wildlife Refuge** (912/652-4415, www.fws.gov/savannah, daily dawn–dusk, free). The views are excellent all along the Lauren Hill wildlife drive, which takes you through the heart of the old paddy fields that crisscrossed the entire area. To get here, take U.S. 17 north over the big Talmadge Bridge, over the Savannah River into South Carolina. Turn left on Highway 170 south and look for the entrance to Laurel Hill Wildlife Drive on the left.

SPECTATOR SPORTS

Topping the list of local spectator sports is the **Savannah Sand Gnats** (912/351-9150, www.sandgnats.com, season Apr.–Sept.) baseball franchise, currently a single-A affiliate of the

SAVANNAH BASEBALL

Savannah has a long and important history with the national pastime. In fact, the first known photograph of a baseball game was taken in Fort Pulaski, of Union occupation troops at play on the parade ground.

A pivotal figure in baseball history also has a crucial association with Savannah. Long before gaining notoriety for his role on the infamous Chicago "Black Sox" that threw the 1919 World Series, baseball legend Shoeless Joe Jackson was a stalwart on the South Atlantic or "Sally" League circuit. Playing for the Savannah Indians in 1909, Joe played ball predominantly at Bolton Street Park, off what's now Henry Street. After retirement Joe returned to town, began a thriving dry-cleaning business, and lived with his wife at 143 Abercorn Street and then on East 39th Street.

Another early great who played in Savannah was Georgia native Ty Cobb, who visited in 1905 with an Augusta team. He's remembered, typically enough, for getting into a fistfight with a teammate who voiced his displeasure at Cobb eating popcorn in the outfield and muffing an easy catch.

Savannah got a proper ballpark in 1926, named Municipal Stadium. After a hurricane destroyed it in 1940, rebuilding began but abruptly stopped when Pearl Harbor was attacked the next year and all the laborers rushed off to enlist. So abruptly did they drop their tools, in fact, that to this day behind third base you can still clearly see the jagged line indicating where construction halted.

The great Babe Ruth played in the stadium once in 1935 in his final year as a major leaguer, as his Boston Braves beat the South Georgia Teachers College (now Georgia Southern University) 15-1 in an exhibition game. Ruth, of course, hit a home run.

Mickey Mantle and the defending world champion New York Yankees played the Cincinnati Reds in a 1959 exhibition game in Savannah. The switch-hitting slugger hit two of his trademark mammoth home run shots during the game—both left-handed and each over 500 feet, according to witnesses.

Atlanta Braves great Hank Aaron, then a skinny second baseman with a Jacksonville club, played in Grayson's first game with both black and white players in 1953. Jackie Robinson stole home base in an exhibition game.

But in a way, all these names pale in comparison to one Savannah player whose influence can be felt to this day, not only in sports but in the business world at large: Curt Flood, who gave the world free agency. Flood, who played for the Savannah Redlegs in 1957, refused to report to the Phillies after the Cardinals traded him in 1969. Flood sued Major League Baseball the next year, saying the so-called "reserve clause" allowing the trade violated antitrust laws. While Flood would lose the lawsuit in the U.S. Supreme Court, the narrowly worded decision left the way open for collective bargaining and today's massive free agent salaries.

The Savannah Braves, a double-A team, began a successful run in 1971 (including a 12-game winning season by pitcher and controversial *Ball Four* writer Jim Bouton), followed in 1984 by the Savannah Cardinals.

The current single-A team, the Savannah Sand Gnats, had their name chosen by a poll of daily newspaper readers. While their level of play rarely conjures mental images of Shoeless Joe or the Babe, Grayson Stadium itself has just been given an impressive new facelift courtesy of the city, with a new scoreboard and upgraded seating. By far the Sand Gnats' most famous face so far has been Cy Young Award-winning pitcher Éric Gagné, who pitched his very first professional game with the local club.

New York Mets. The attraction here is not the level of play but the venue itself: Grayson Stadium (1401 E. Victory Dr.) in Daffin Park in the city's midtown area, a historic venue that has hosted such greats as Babe Ruth, Jackie Robinson, and Mickey Mantle over the years. There's not a bad seat in the house, so your best bet by far is to just buy a $7 general admission ticket. The games never sell out, so there's no need to stress. Entertainment runs the usual gamut of minor league shenanigans, including frequent fireworks displays after the games.

For sports action that's a good bit more hard-hitting and comes with a certain hipster kitsch quotient, check out the bruising bouts of the women of the **Savannah Derby Devils** (www. savannahderby.com), who bring the Roller Derby thunder against other regional teams. They skate downtown at the Savannah Civic Center (301 W. Oglethorpe Ave., 912/651-6556), and the matches are usually quite well attended.

Accommodations

The hotel scene in Savannah, once notorious for its absurdly high price-to-service ratio, has improved a great deal in the past couple of years. Perhaps ironically, several stylish new downtown hotels opened concurrently with the recent economic downturn. Their appearance means increased competition, and therefore marginally lower prices, across the board. Savannah's many historic bed-and-breakfasts are competitive with the hotels on price, and often outperform them on service and ambience. If you don't need a swimming pool and don't mind climbing some stairs every now and then, a B&B is usually your best bet. And the breakfasts, of course, are great too.

CITY MARKET
$150-300
A Days Inn property, the **Inn at Ellis Square** (201 W. Bay St., 912/236-4440, www.in-natellissquare.com, $189) is smack-dab be-tween City Market and Bay Street—in other words, the heart of the tourist action. Set in the renovated 1851 Guckenheimer Building, the inn is one of the better-appointed chain ho-tels in town.

Over $300
Providing a suitably modernist decor to go with its somewhat atypical architecture for Savannah, the new **⟨ AVIA Savannah** (14 Barnard St., 912/233-2116, www.aviahotels. com, $320) overlooks restored Ellis Square and abuts City Market with its shopping, restaurants, and nightlife. Named one of the top new U.S. hotels by *Condé Nast Traveler* magazine, the AVIA's guest rooms and suites feature top-of-the-line linens, extra-large and well-equipped baths, in-room snack bars, and technological features such as MP3 docking stations, free Wi-Fi, and, of course, the ubiq-uitous flat-screen TV. Customer service is a particular strong suit. Just off the lobby is a very hip lounge–wine bar that attracts locals as well as hotel guests. Keep in mind things can get a little noisy in this area at night on weekends.

WATERFRONT
$150-300
A cut above the Holiday Inn chain, with which it is affiliated, the **⟨ Mulberry Inn** (601 E. Bay St., 912/238-1200, www.holidayinn.com, $189) is a longtime favorite with travelers to Savannah, with a charming central courtyard and with peaceful little Washington Square on the back of the building. Don't miss the genu-ine English teatime, complete with jazz piano accompaniment, observed in the lobby each af-ternoon at 4 P.M. (as if there's another English teatime). Another nifty touch is a dedicated parking garage—an amenity only someone who has spent half an hour looking for a park-ing space in downtown Savannah will truly appreciate. Parking is free for Holiday Inn "pri-ority members" (you can sign up for member-ship at check-in). The building formerly housed one of the first Coca-Cola bottling plants in the

SAVANNAH

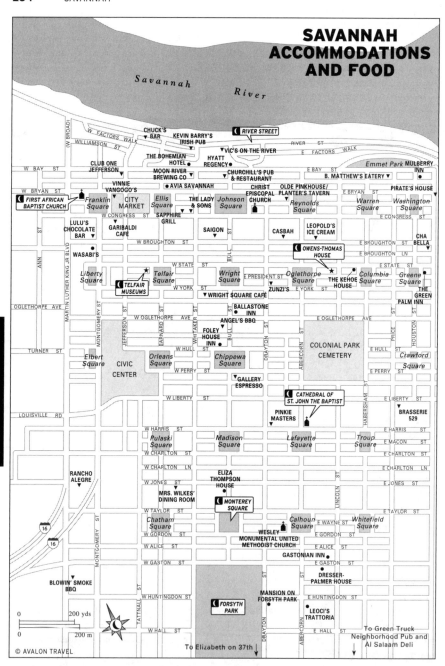

SAVANNAH ACCOMMODATIONS AND FOOD

Savannah River

CHUCK'S BAR
KEVIN BARRY'S IRISH PUB
RIVER STREET
VIC'S ON THE RIVER
THE BOHEMIAN HOTEL
HYATT REGENCY
CHURCHILL'S PUB & RESTAURANT
MOON RIVER BREWING CO
AVIA SAVANNAH
CLUB ONE JEFFERSON
B. MATTHEW'S EATERY
EMMET PARK
MULBERRY INN
VINNIE VANGOGO'S
CHRIST EPISCOPAL CHURCH
OLDE PINKHOUSE/PLANTER'S TAVERN
PIRATE'S HOUSE
FIRST AFRICAN BAPTIST CHURCH
Franklin Square
CITY MARKET
Ellis Square
THE LADY & SONS
Johnson Square
Reynolds Square
Warren Square
Washington Square
SAPPHIRE GRILL
LULU'S CHOCOLATE BAR
GARIBALDI CAFÉ
SAIGON
CASBAH
LEOPOLD'S ICE CREAM
CHA BELLA
WASABI'S
OWENS-THOMAS HOUSE
Liberty Square
Telfair Square
Wright Square
Oglethorpe Square
Columbia Square
Greene Square
THE GREEN PALM INN
TELFAIR MUSEUMS
ZUNZI'S
THE KEHOE HOUSE
WRIGHT SQUARE CAFE
BALLASTONE INN
ANGEL'S BBQ
FOLEY HOUSE INN
COLONIAL PARK CEMETERY
Elbert Square
CIVIC CENTER
Orleans Square
Chippewa Square
Crawford Square
GALLERY ESPRESSO
CATHEDRAL OF ST. JOHN THE BAPTIST
PINKIE MASTERS
BRASSERIE 529
Pulaski Square
Madison Square
Lafayette Square
Troup Square
RANCHO ALEGRE
ELIZA THOMPSON HOUSE
MRS. WILKES' DINING ROOM
MONTEREY SQUARE
Chatham Square
Calhoun Square
Whitefield Square
WESLEY MONUMENTAL UNITED METHODIST CHURCH
GASTONIAN INN
BLOWIN' SMOKE BBQ
DRESSER-PALMER HOUSE
MANSION ON FORSYTH PARK
FORSYTH PARK
LEOCI'S TRATTORIA

To Green Truck Neighborhood Pub and Al Salaam Deli

0 — 200 yds
0 — 200 m

© AVALON TRAVEL

To Elizabeth on 37th

The Bohemian is one of Savannah's favorite new hotels.

United States; look for the historical photos all around the building.

Although it's new, **◖ The Bohemian Hotel** (102 W. Bay St., 912/721-3800, www.bohemianhotelsavannah.com, $279–350) is already gaining a reputation as one of Savannah's premier hotels, both for the casual visitor as well as visiting celebrities. Located between busy River Street and bustling City Market, this isn't the place for peace and quiet, but its combination of boutique-style retro-hip decor and happening rooftop bar scene (swank and quite popular with local scenesters) make it a great place to go for a fun stay that's as much Manhattan as Savannah. Valet parking is available, which you will come to appreciate.

Over $300

For years critics have called it an insult to architecture and to history. That said, one of the few name-brand hotels in Savannah worth the price and providing a consistent level of service is one of its original chain hotels, the **◖ Hyatt Regency Savannah** (2 E. Bay St., 912/238-1234, www.savannah.hyatt.com, $379). It is more than three decades old, but a competent renovation means that the Hyatt—a sort of exercise in cubism straddling an entire block of River Street—has avoided the neglect of many older chain properties downtown. While the price may seem daunting, consider the location: literally smack-dab on top of River Street, mere blocks from the bulk of the important attractions downtown and some of its best restaurants. Three sides of the hotel offer views of the bustling Savannah waterfront, with its massive ships coming in from all over the world.

HISTORIC DISTRICT
$150-300

Easily the best bed-and-breakfast for the price in Savannah is **The Green Palm Inn** (546 E. President St., 912/447-8901, www.greenpalminn.com, $159–189), a folksy and romantic little Victorian number with some neat gingerbread exterior stylings and four cute guest rooms, each named after a species of palm tree. It's situated on the very easternmost edge of the Historic District—hence it's reasonable rates—but let's face it, being right next to charming little Greene Square is far from the worst place you could be. Delightful innkeeper Diane McCray provides a very good and generous breakfast plus a pretty much constant dessert bar.

One of Savannah's original historic B&Bs, the **◖ Eliza Thompson House** (5 W. Jones St., 912/236-3620, www.elizathompsonhouse.com, $180–225) is a bit out of the bustle on serene, beautiful Jones Street but still close enough to get involved whenever you feel the urge. You can enjoy the various culinary offerings—breakfast, wine and cheese, nighttime munchies—either in the parlor or on the patio overlooking the house's classic Savannah garden. One of the half-dozen lodging properties owned by the locally based HLC group, the Eliza Thompson House hews to their generally high standard of service.

The circa-1896 **◖ Foley House Inn** (14 W. Hull St., 912/232-6622, www.foleyinn. com, $199–375) is a four-diamond B&B with some rooms available at a three-diamond price. Its 19 individualized, Victorian-decor guest rooms, in two town houses, range from the smaller Newport overlooking the "grotto courtyard" to the four-poster, bay-windowed Essex room, complete with a fireplace and a whirlpool bath. The location on Chippewa Square is pretty much perfect: well off the busy east–west thoroughfares but in the heart of Savannah's active theater district and within walking distance of anywhere.

One of Savannah's favorite bed-and-break-fasts, **The Kehoe House** (123 Habersham St., 912/232-1020, www.kehoehouse.com, $215–315) is a great choice for its charm and attention to guests. Its historic location, on quiet little Columbia Square catty-corner to the Isaiah Davenport House, is within walking distance to all the downtown action, but far enough from the bustle to get some peace out on one of the rocking chairs on the veranda.

Once a bordello, the 1838 mansion that is home to the 16-room **Ballastone Inn** (14 E. Oglethorpe Ave., 912/236-1484, www.ballastone.com, $235–355) is one of Savannah's favorite inns. Highlights include an afternoon tea service and one of the better full breakfasts in town. Note that some guest rooms are at what Savannah calls the "garden level," meaning sunken basement–level rooms with what amounts to a worm's-eye view.

VICTORIAN DISTRICT
$150-300

A short walk from Forsyth Park, the **Dresser-Palmer House** (211 E. Gaston St., 912/238-3294, www.dresserpalmerhouse.com, $189–319) features 15 guest rooms in two wings but still manages to make things feel pretty cozy. Garden-level rooms go for a song (under $200).

The 1868 **◖ Gastonian Inn** (220 E. Gaston St., 912/232-2869, www.gastonian.com, $245–455) got a major renovation in 2005 and remains a favorite choice for travelers to Savannah, mostly for its 17 sumptuously decorated guest rooms and suites, all with working fireplaces, and the always outstanding full breakfast. They pile on the epicurean delights with teatime, evening nightcaps, and complimentary wine. This is one of the six properties owned by the local firm HLC, which seems to have consistently higher standards than most out-of-town chains.

Over $300

How ironic that a hotel built in a former mortuary would be one of the few Savannah hotels not to have a resident ghost story. But that's the case with **Mansion on Forsyth Park** (700 Drayton St., 912/238-5158, www.mansiononforsythpark.com, $339–419), which dominates an entire block alongside Forsyth Park, including partially within the high-Victorian former Fox & Weeks Mortuary building. Its sumptuous guest rooms, equipped with big beds, big baths, and big-screen TVs, scream "boutique hotel," as does the swank little bar and the alfresco patio area. The Mansion's Addams Family decor of thick velvet and vaguely dadaist artwork isn't for everyone, but still, it certainly beats seagulls and pink flamingos.

TYBEE ISLAND

Most of the hotels on the main drag, Butler Avenue, are what we describe in the South as "rode hard and put away wet," meaning that they see a lot of wear and tear from eager vacationers. For that reason it's difficult for me to recommend any of them in good conscience. Also be aware that any place on Butler Avenue, even the substandard places, charges a premium during the high season (Mar.–Oct.). For long-term stays, weekly rentals are the name of the game. Though not cheap—expect to pay roughly $1,000 per week in the summer—they provide a higher level of accommodations than some hotels on the island. For weekly rentals, try **Oceanfront Cottage Rentals** (800/786-5889, www.oceanfrontcottage.com), **Tybee Island Rentals** (912/786-4034, www.tybeeislandrentals.com), or **Tybee Vacation Rentals** (866/359-0297, www.tybeevacationrentals.com).

Here are a few other places that are a cut above. One of Tybee's most worthwhile lodging experiences for the money, the single-suite 🄲 **Bluebird Bed and Breakfast** (1206 Venetian Dr., 912/786-0786, www.tybeebandb.com, $125) is tucked away on Horsepen Creek and the Back River, away from the general beach-town hubbub—but that's what makes it all the more romantic, in a whimsical sort of way. Its spacious and charming interior comprises a master bedroom, a large kitchen-den area, and a delightful breakfast nook overlooking the marsh. There's even a resident dock if you want to put in your kayak or canoe. There is a two-night minimum on weekends.

Available for daily or weekly rentals, the delightful and well-appointed upstairs apartment of **The Octopus Lair** (1206 2nd Ave., 912/660-7164, $125) is tucked away on the south side of the island, equidistant from both the beach and the more active areas. There's even a propane grill on the porch so you can cook out. Another good B&B-style experience can be found at **The Georgianne Inn** (1312 Butler Ave., 912/786-8710, $125–235), a short walk off the beach.

CAMPING

The best overall campground in town is at the well-managed and rarely crowded **Skidaway Island State Park** (52 Diamond Causeway, 912/598-2300, www.gastateparks.org, parking $2 per vehicle per day, tent and RV sites $24, group camping $35). There are 88 sites with 30-amp electric hookups. A two-night minimum stay is required on weekends and a three-night minimum for Memorial Day, Labor Day, Independence Day, and Thanksgiving. Despite these restrictions and the comparatively high rates, the natural beauty of the park and its easy access to some great nature trails make it worth the price.

There's one campground on Tybee Island, the **River's End Campground and RV Park** (915 Polk St., 912/786-5518, www.cityoftybee.org, water and electric sites $34, 50-amp full hookup sites $45) on the north side. Owned by the city of Tybee Island, River's End offers 100 full-service sites plus some primitive tent sites. During Tybee's sometimes-chilly off-season (Nov.–Mar.), you can relax and get warm inside the common "River Room." There's also a swimming pool and laundry facilities.

Totally wilderness camping can be done on state-owned Little Tybee, accessible across the Back River by boat only; there are no facilities. The best camping and wilderness resource locally is **Half Moon Outfitters** (15 E. Broughton St., 912/201-9393, www.halfmoonoutfitters.com).

SAVANNAH

Food

Although Charleston's cuisine scene is clearly a cut or two above Savannah's, the Georgia city is still a foodie's paradise, with a big-city selection of cuisine concocted by a cast of executive chefs who despite their many personal idiosyncrasies tend to go with what works rather than experimenting for the sake of experimentation. Here's a breakdown of the most notable offerings, by area and by type of cuisine. You'll note there's rarely a separate *Seafood* section listed; that's because seafood is an intrinsic part of most restaurant fare in Savannah, whether through regular menu offerings or through specials.

CITY MARKET
Classic Southern

Every year, thousands of visitors come to Savannah for the privilege of waiting for hours outside in all weather, the line stretching a full city block, for a chance to eat at **The Lady & Sons** (102 W. Congress St., 912/233-2600, www.ladyandsons.com, lunch Mon.–Sat. 11 A.M.–3 P.M., dinner Mon.–Sat. from 5 P.M., buffet Sun. 11 A.M.–5 P.M., $17–25) and sample some of local celebrity Paula Deen's "home" cooking—actually a fairly typical Southern buffet with some decent fried chicken, collard greens, and mac-and-cheese. For the privilege, you must begin waiting in line as early as 9:30 A.M. for lunch and as early as 3:30 P.M. for dinner in order to be assigned a dining time. You almost assuredly will never see Paula, who has precious little to do with the restaurant these days. Eating at this Savannah landmark provides a story that visitors will be able to tell friends and family for the rest of their lives, and far be it from me to look down on them for doing so. That being said: If it were me, I'd take that four hours spent waiting in line and instead go to one of Savannah's many other excellent eating establishments, leaving

lots of time for an afternoon beer or coffee or dessert, and leaving yet more time to see one of Savannah's many interesting and beautiful sights. A chef friend of mine puts it best: When food sits out under a heat lamp too long, it all tastes the same anyway.

Italian

One would never call Savannah a great pizza town, but the best pizza here is ⬤ **Vinnie VanGoGo's** (317 W. Bryan St., 912/233-6394, www.vinnievangogos.com, Mon.–Thurs. 4–11:30 P.M., Fri. 4 P.M.–1 A.M., Sat. noon–1 A.M., Sun. noon–11:30 P.M., $3–13, cash only) at the west end of City Market on Franklin Square. Featuring some of the best local characters both in the dining area and behind the counter, Vinnie's is a classic Savannah hangout, due in no small part to its excellent beer selection and late hours on weekends. Their pizza is a thin-crust Neapolitan style—although the menu claims it to be New York style—with a delightful tangy sauce and fresh cheese. Individual slices are huge, so don't feel obliged to order a whole pie. Personally I opt for Italian sausage and extra cheese to offset the richness of the sauce. Calzones are also massive and well stuffed. The waiting list for a table can get pretty long, but take heart: Vinnie's offers free delivery throughout downtown, delivered by bicycle courier. Remember, cash only.

Many Savannahians recall a time when the charmingly old-school **Garibaldi Café** (315 W. Congress St., 912/232-7118, daily 5–10 P.M., $11–33) was the only fine-dining restaurant downtown, and it's still great. More like a spot you'd find in Little Italy than Savannah, Garibaldi features the over-the-top decor typical of the genre, from Roman busts to massive brocade curtains and the huge chandelier in the "Grand Ballroom." But longtime master chef Gerald Green's food is still the draw, a dependable northern Italian menu known for its well-made veal dishes, its raw bar offerings, and the signature dish, the popular crispy scored flounder with apricot glaze.

New Southern

Accomplishing the difficult task of being achingly hip while also offering some of the best food in town, **Sapphire Grill** (110 W. Congress St., 912/443-9962, www.sapphiregrill.com, Fri.–Sat. 5:30–11:30 P.M., Sun.–Thurs. 6–10:30 P.M., $25–40) comes closer than any other Savannah restaurant to replicating a high-class trendy Manhattan eatery—at prices to match. With its bare stone walls, lean ambience, and romantically dark interior, you'd be tempted to think it's all sizzle and no steak. But executive chef Chris Nason, former exec at Charleston's Anson Restaurant, has a way with coastal cuisine, relying on the freshest local seafood. His classic meat dishes like lamb, filet mignon, and veal are equally skillful. The lobster bisque is a must-have, and the benne-encrusted local black grouper is always a good choice.

Coffee, Tea, and Sweets

Combine a hip bar with outrageously tasty dessert items and you get **Lulu's Chocolate Bar** (42 MLK Jr. Blvd., 912/238-2012, www.luluschocolatebar.net). While the whole family is welcome before 10 P.M. to enjoy chocolate chip cheesecake and the like, after that it's strictly 21-and-over. The late crowd is younger and trendier and comes mostly for the unique specialty martinis, including the pineapple upside-down martini.

WATERFRONT
Breakfast

If you're downtown and need something more than your hotel breakfast—and you will!—go to **B. Matthew's Eatery** (325 E. Bay St., 912/233-1319, www.bmatthewseatery.com, Mon.–Thurs. 8 A.M.–9 P.M., Fri.–Sat. 8 A.M.–10 P.M., brunch Sun. 9 A.M.–3 P.M., $15), widely considered the best breakfast in the entire Historic District. The omelets—most under $10—are uniformly wonderful, and the sausage & bacon excellent and most ungreasy. There is a range of more healthy selections as well, and you can actually get a decent bowl of oatmeal—but I suggest something more decadent. Sunday brunch is incredible, as you might imagine. And they don't just do breakfast—lunch sandwiches and salads are of similarly high quality, and dinner entrées (from $17) include killer osso buco, lamb, and seafood.

Classic Southern

Locals rarely eat at the Savannah institution called the **Pirate's House** (20 E. Broad St., 912/233-5757, www.thepirateshouse.com, lunch daily 11 A.M.–4 P.M., dinner Sun.–Thurs. 4–9:30 P.M., Fri.–Sat. 4–10 P.M., $17–26), known primarily for its delightfully kitschy pre–Jack Sparrow pirate decor and its dependably pedestrian food. Still, the history here is undeniable: One of the country's oldest buildings, built in 1753, the Pirate's House hosted many a salty sea dog—though perhaps few actual pirates—in its day as a seamen's inn. And any place that rates a shout-out in Robert Louis Stevenson's *Treasure Island* has to be worth a visit. The rambling interior of the old house, each of the 15 dining rooms with its own different nautical flavor, just adds to the general air of jaunty buccaneer insouciance. "The Captain's Room" is allegedly where shipmasters would shanghai unwary men to complete their chronically shorthanded crews. Supposedly, a tunnel from there goes all the way to the river, the better to transport the drugged kidnapping victims. The "Southern Buffet" (daily 11 A.M.–3 P.M.) features the Pirate House's signature honey pecan fried chicken.

Very few restaurants on River Street rise

above tourist schlock, but a clear standout is **Vic's on the River** (16 E. River St., 912/721-1000, www.vicsontheriver.com, Sun.–Thurs. 11 A.M.–10 P.M., Fri.–Sat. 11 A.M.–11 P.M., $22–40). Hewing more to Charleston-style fine dining than most Savannah restaurants—with dishes like wild Georgia shrimp, stone-ground grits, and blue crab cakes with a three-pepper relish—Vic's combines a romantic old Savannah atmosphere with an adventurous take on Lowcountry cuisine. Note the entrance to the dining room is not on River Street but on the Bay Street level on Upper Factor's Walk.

HISTORIC DISTRICT
Asian
Part of the renovation of the Martin Luther King Jr. Boulevard corridor, the relatively new **Wasabi's** (113 MLK Jr. Blvd., 912/233-8899, daily 11 A.M.–10:30 P.M., $8–20) is making a name for itself with its sushi in a town with several very good sushi restaurants already. The à la carte tempura is also especially tasty, and the Sapporo on draft is a real plus. There's an early-bird sushi boat for two ($30) offered 4–6:30 P.M.

With an unprepossessing interior but an excellent, inexpensive Vietnamese-Thai hybrid menu, **Saigon** (4 W. Broughton St., 912/232-5288, $7) is a good place to stop in for a quick tasty lunch while shopping.

Barbecue
Purists may scoff at its attractive interior and awesome bottled beer selection, but the barbecue is rockin' at **Blowin' Smoke BBQ** (514 MLK Jr. Blvd., 912/231-2385, www.blowin-smokebbq.com, Sun.–Thurs. 11 A.M.–9 P.M., Fri.–Sat. 11 A.M.–10 P.M., $7–12). It isn't necessarily the most authentic, but it's the most fun, with a large outdoor courtyard in addition to the roomy interior. The service is good, the selection on tap quite vast, and the barbecue portions are vast and tasty, with a delicious sauce

that avoids the overly sweet nature of many regional sauces.

Another great local barbecue joint tucked away in a lane is **Angel's BBQ** (21 W. Oglethorpe Lane, 912/495-0902, www.angels-bbq.com, Tues. 11:30 A.M.–3 P.M., Wed.–Sat. 11:30 A.M.–6 P.M., $5–9), which was featured on a recent episode of Travel Channel's *Man v. Food*. Get there by finding Independent Presbyterian Church at the northwest corner of Chippewa Square and walking down the lane next to the church. Angel's offers a particularly Memphis-style take on barbecue, but you might try the unique house specialty, the barbecued bologna. Don't miss the peanuts-and-greens on the side. Vegetarians can opt for the "Faux-Q," barbecue-flavored tofu.

Classic Southern
The meteoric rise of Paula Deen and her Lady & Sons restaurant has only made local epicures even more exuberant in their praise for ◖ **Mrs. Wilkes' Dining Room** (107 W. Jones St., 912/232-5997, www.mrswilkes.com, Mon.–Fri. 11 A.M.–2 P.M., $13), Savannah's original comfort-food mecca. President Obama's impromptu lunchtime visit with the local mayor in 2010 has further raised the restaurant's already legendary profile. The delightful Sema Wilkes herself has passed on, but nothing has changed—not the communal dining room, the cheerful service, the care taken with take-out customers, and, most of all, not the food—a succulent mélange of the South's greatest hits, including the best fried chicken in town, snap beans, black-eyed peas, and collard greens. While each day boasts a different set menu, almost all of the classics are on the table at each meal.

Once the home of General James Habersham and the first place the Declaration of Independence was read aloud in Savannah, the ◖ **Olde Pink House** (23 Abercorn St., 912/232-4286, Sun.–Thurs. 5:30–10:30 P.M., Fri.–Sat. 5:30–11 P.M., $15–30) is still a hub

© JIM MOREKIS

Angel's BBQ is hard to find, but well worth the effort.

of activity in Savannah, as visitors and locals alike frequent the classic interior of the dining room and the downstairs Planter's Tavern. Regularly voted "Most Romantic Restaurant in Savannah"—but make no mistake, they pack you in pretty tight here—the Pink House is known for its savvy (and often sassy) service and the uniquely regional flair it adds to traditional dishes, with liberal doses of pecans, vidalia onions, shrimp, and crab. The she-crab soup and lamb chops in particular are crowd-pleasers, and the scored crispy flounder stacks up to similar versions of this dish at several other spots in town. Reservations are recommended.

Some writers would be tempted to put **Cha Bella** (102 E. Broad St., 912/790-7888, www. cha-bella.com, Tues.–Sun. 5:30–10 P.M., $17–35) in the *New Southern* category, but I prefer to think that this restaurant's forte—savory dishes using only the freshest locally grown organic ingredients—makes it a classic throwback to the way food was always intended to

be. This new spot is getting a large local following eager to enjoy its concise menu from chefs Vikram Bhonsle and Amie Linton, featuring fresh salads like grilled eggplant and plum tomatoes topped with local artisanal goat cheese, and entrées like the Georgia white shrimp risotto. The patio bar is a favorite hangout for downtown's hip movers and shakers.

Cuban

Rancho Alegre (402 MLK Jr. Blvd., 912/292-1656, $8–20), at the fringe of the Historic District, brings authentic Cuban cuisine downtown. Try the tamale with roasted pork on the side, or perhaps the *chicharrones de pollo*. If you have a large party, call ahead so Chef Juan Manuel Rodriguez can prepare his signature seafood paella. In any case, save room for dark, delicious Cuban coffee.

French

The only honest-to-goodness French restaurant

in town is the fairly new **🎬 Brasserie 529** (529 E. Liberty St., 912/238-0045, Tues.–Sat. 11 A.M.–3 P.M. and 5–10 P.M., from $20). The interior is freshly renovated in contemporary bistro style (although the lighting is slightly too bright for my taste). The food is splendid and authentically French in both flavor and cost. Everything on the frequently rotating menu is guaranteed to please, but house specialties include the côtes de boeuf (a bone-in rib eye for two), the rabbit stew, and the steak frites, featuring a hanger steak and the best french fries you'll ever enjoy. My favorite dish, however, is the Fish Normande, a succulently cooked piece of halibut that is the best whitefish entrée I've eaten anywhere. The wine list is good and refreshingly pared down. As mundane as this sounds after all that buildup, the fact that Brasserie 529 has a dedicated parking lot is another huge plus given the general dearth of parking spaces in downtown Savannah.

Italian

For sure, the hot Italian place in town is **Leoci's Trattoria** (606 Abercorn St., 912/335-7027, www.leocis.com, daily 11 A.M.–10 P.M., $10–20), named for its skillful and personable young executive chef, Roberto Leoci. His compact but diverse menu offers delights such as a crispy delicious pizza, excellent paninis, and a wild-mushroom risotto. The room is small and intimate, and the restaurant is quite popular, so a wait is not unusual.

Moroccan

Savannah's single most unique dining experience happens at **Casbah** (118 E. Broughton St., 912/234-6168, daily 5:30–10:30 P.M., $10–20). This Moroccan restaurant features nightly belly dancing shows, with the dancers doing their thing from table to table to prerecorded (and loud) music beginning at 6:30 or 7 P.M., with continuing shows through the evening. Beware—sometimes they grab a guest

for a quick "lesson." But don't let the over-the-top floor show or the "market" of authentic but overpriced Moroccan goods take away from the incredible food. Served in communal Moroccan style, these dishes hew to the deceptively simple cuisine of North Africa, with an emphasis on expertly grilled and seasoned meats and saffron rice. The lamb kabobs are to die for—best I've had anywhere.

South African

Look for the long lunchtime line outside the tiny storefront that is **Zunzi's** (108 E. York St., 912/443-9555, Mon.–Sat. 11 A.M.–6 P.M., $5–10). This takeout joint is one of Savannah's favorite lunch spots, the labor of love of South African expatriates Gabby and Johnny DeBeer. Try the exquisite South African–style sausage.

Coffee, Tea, and Sweets

He helped produce *Mission Impossible III* and

Leopold's Ice Cream is in the heart of the theater district.

© JIM MOREKIS

other Hollywood movies, but Savannah native Stratton Leopold's other claim to fame is running the 100-year-old family business at **Leopold's Ice Cream** (212 E. Broughton St., 912/234-4442, www.leopoldsicecream. com, Sun.–Thurs. 11 A.M.–10 P.M., Fri.–Sat. 11 A.M.–11 P.M.). Now in a new location but with the same delicious family ice cream recipe, Leopold's also offers soup and sandwiches to go with its delicious sweet treats. Memorabilia from Stratton's various movies is all around the shop, which stays open after every evening performance at the Lucas Theatre around the corner. You can occasionally find Stratton himself behind the counter doling out scoops.

A coffeehouse before coffeehouses were cool, Savannah's original java joint **Gallery Espresso** (234 Bull St., 912/233-5348, www. galleryespresso.com, Mon.–Fri. 7:30 A.M.– 10 P.M., Sat.–Sun. 8 A.M.–11 P.M.) currently occupies a prime corner lot on beautiful Chippewa Square. Of course, there's the requisite free Wi-Fi, and while you sip and surf you can also enjoy the regular rotating modern art exhibits by well-known local artists, all curated by owner Jessica Barnhill.

For a more upscale take on sweets, check out the chocolate goodies at **Wright Square Cafe** (21 W. York St., 912/238-1150). While they do offer tasty wraps and sandwiches, let's not kid ourselves; the draw here is the outrageous assortment of high-quality European-style brownies, cookies, cakes, and other sweet treats.

VICTORIAN DISTRICT

This pretty, quiet, but up-and-coming area—occasionally referred to by the somewhat precious new term SoFo, for South of Forsyth—spans Forsyth Park south to Victory Drive (U.S. 80).

Burgers

Cozy **Green Truck Neighborhood Pub** (2430 Habersham St., 912/234-5885, http:// greentruckpub.com, Tues.–Sat. 11 A.M.– 11 P.M., $10) earns its raves on the basis of delicious regionally sourced meat and produce offered at reasonable prices. (The large selection of craft beers on tap is a big draw too). The marquee item is the signature five-ounce grass-fed burger. A basic burger is $7, but several other, increasingly more dressed-up versions are offered, none over $12.50. Burgers are also offered with chicken or veggie patties. Salads here are also particularly awesome, all with the added option of burger, chicken, or veggie patty to any salad for $4.50 extra. It's a small room that often has a big line, and they don't take reservations, so be prepared.

Middle Eastern

For a falafel fix, travel well off the beaten path to **Al Salaam Deli** (2311 Habersham St., 912/447-0400, daily 9 A.M.–9 P.M., $5–10). The signature falafel at this humble little storefront is big-city quality, and the gyros are almost as good. While it's not in the most elegant of neighborhoods, Al Salaam—run by a family of Jordanian expatriates—has a devoted local following, and deservedly so. In a nod to the cosmopolitan background of the owner and his cuisine, the walls are decorated with *National Geographic* magazine covers.

New Southern

Before there was Paula Deen, there was Elizabeth Terry, Savannah's first well-known high-profile chef and founder of this most elegant of all Savannah restaurants, **Elizabeth on 37th** (105 E. 37th St., 912/236-5547, daily 6–10 P.M., from $25). Terry has since sold the place to two of her former waiters, Greg and Gary Butch, but this restaurant has, for the most part, continued to maintain her high standards. In a beautifully restored Victorian mansion just outside the Historic District, with its own lovingly tended herb garden and emphasis on local suppliers, Elizabeth on 37th

Elizabeth on 37th is still Savannah's best restaurant.

continues to be—a quarter-century after its founding—where many Savannahians go when the evening calls for something really memorable. Executive chef Kelly Yambor uses eclectic, seasonally shifting ingredients that blend the South with the south of France. Along with generally attentive service, it makes for a wonderfully old-school fine dining experience. Reservations are recommended.

A fairly new darling of local foodies is the aptly named **Local 11 Ten** (1110 Bull St., 912/790-9000, www.local11ten.com, Tues.–Thurs. 6–10 P.M., Fri.–Sat. 6–10:30 P.M., $22–39), just off the south end of Forsyth Park. Its wide-open dining room has a great view of the streetscape along with adventurous cuisine and a cute bar—each are proven big attractions. Try the hanger steak with a side of vidalia onion rings.

Coffee, Tea, and Sweets

The coffee at **The Sentient Bean** (13 E. Park Ave., 912/232-4447, www.sentientbean.com, daily 7:30 A.M.–10 P.M.) is all fair-trade and organic, and the all-vegetarian fare is a major upgrade above the usual coffeehouse offering. But "The Bean" is more than a coffeehouse—it's a community. Probably the best indie film venue in town, the Bean regularly hosts screenings of cutting-edge left-of-center documentary and kitsch films, as well as rotating art exhibits. When there's no movie, there's usually some low-key live entertainment or spoken word open mike action.

Primarily known for its sublime sweet treats, **Back in the Day Bakery** (2403 Bull St., 912/495-9292, www.backinthedaybakery.com, Tues.–Fri. 9 A.M.–5 P.M., Sat. 8 A.M.–3 P.M., $7) in the Starland Design District at the southern edge of the Victorian District also offers a small but delightfully tasty (and tasteful) range of lunch soups, salads, and sandwiches (11 A.M.–2 P.M.) Lunch highlights are the baguette with camembert, roasted red peppers, and lettuce; and the *caprese,* the classic tomato, mozzarella, and basil trifecta on a perfect *ciabatta*. But whatever you do, save room for dessert, which runs the full sugar spectrum: red velvet cupcakes, lemon bars, macaroons, carrot cake, Cosmopolitan Cake, Nana's Pudding, and my favorite, Omar's Mystic Espresso Cheesecake.

Hard to define easily, and perhaps successful precisely because of that, **Form** (1801 Habersham St., 912/236-7642, www.form-cwg.com, Mon.–Fri. 10 A.M.–7 P.M., Sat. 11 A.M.–6 P.M.) is part winery, part bakery, and part foodie gathering place. Form is the kind of place you can pick up an amazing made-from-scratch cheesecake and get advice on which bottle of wine might go with said cheesecake. They also host a variety of special events, from dinners and wine tastings to guest chef demos.

For a quick coffee or a panini, stop by the **Forsyth Park Café** (621 Drayton St., 912/233-7848, daily 7 A.M.–dusk, open later on festival evenings) located in what was once the circa-1920 "dummy fort."

EASTSIDE
Classic Southern

Located just across the Wilmington River from the fishing village of Thunderbolt, ◖**Desposito's** (187 Old Tybee Rd., 912/897-9963, www.despositosseafood.com, Tues.–Fri. 5–10 P.M., Sat. noon–10 P.M., $15–25) is a big hit with locals and visitors alike, although it's not in all the guidebooks. The focus here is on crab, shrimp, and oysters, and lots of them, all caught wild in local waters and served humbly on tables covered with newspapers.

Mexican

There aren't too many authentic Mexican places in Savannah, and frankly the situation has become worse with the recent passage of immigration legislation in Georgia that has caused an exodus from area Hispanic communities. A survivor is the family-operated

La Xalapena (2308 Skidaway Rd., 912/234-8076, www.la-xalapena.com, Mon.–Thurs. 10 A.M.–9 P.M., Fri.–Sat. 10 A.M.–10 P.M., Sun. 10 A.M.–8 P.M., $10), which is still patronized by many local Mexican Americans. Note that this restaurant is not to be confused with a lesser but more heavily marketed local chain called Jalapeno's. The menu is strong on tamales, empanadas, and pork-skin gorditas, everything much lighter and more agile in flavor than the usual fatty stuff that passes for Mexican elsewhere. The only drawback is that they have no liquor license, so you won't be able to enjoy a margarita or cerveza.

SOUTHSIDE
Asian

Opposite Oglethorpe Mall across busy Abercorn is **Chiriya's** (7805 Abercorn St., 912/303-0555, Mon.–Sat. 11 A.M.–3 P.M. and 5–10 P.M., Sun. 5–10 P.M., $15–20), an excellent Thai place with some Hawaiian touches sprinkled into the mix. The kitchen will gladly spice up your food to your personal comfort level.

It's not pretty and it's not fancy, but hands-down the best Vietnamese cuisine in town is at ◖ **Saigon Flavors** (6604 Waters Ave., 912/352-4182, daily 11 A.M.–9 P.M., $6–9), a humble little place in a nondescript storefront. The food is anything but nondescript—excellent, authentic, inexpensive, and tasty. I usually get the pork and noodles dish with a side order of delicious fried spring rolls, but any of their shrimp dishes are great too.

Southwestern

Should you find yourself shopping at Oglethorpe Mall on Savannah's ugly paved-over south side, take a quick jaunt across Abercorn to **Moe's Southwestern Grill** (7801 Abercorn St., 912/303-6688, daily 11 A.M.–10 P.M., $5–10) in the Chatham Plaza shopping center. This regional franchise offers made-to-order Southwestern fare—or a Southeastern version of it, anyway—in a boisterous atmosphere. Local vegetarians and vegans love this spot, since you tell the counter staff exactly what you want in your burrito and you can always substitute tofu for any meat.

WHITEMARSH ISLAND

Pronounced "WIT-marsh," this overwhelmingly residential area is on the way from the city of Savannah to Tybee Island's beaches. It's notable for the presence of two outstanding barbecue joints, right across U.S. 80 from each other.

Barbecue

Though relatively new, ⟨ **Wiley's Championship BBQ** (4700 U.S. 80 E., 912/201-3259, www.wileyschampionshipbbq.com, lunch Mon.–Sat. 11 A.M.–3 P.M., dinner Wed.–Thurs. 5–8 P.M., Fri.–Sat. 5–9 P.M., $8–25) has what is already widely considered the best pulled pork in Savannah. In addition—and unusually for this area—they smoke a mean brisket too. Save room for the great sides, such as mac-and-cheese and sweet-potato casserole.

Papa's Bar-B-Q (4700 U.S. 80, 912/897-0236, www.papasbar-b-que.com, Mon.–Wed. 11 A.M.–9 P.M., Thurs.–Sat. 11 A.M.–10 P.M., Sun. noon–9 P.M., $6–15) has a very wide-ranging menu in addition to its signature pulled pork sandwiches, including shrimp, tilapia, and flounder cooked in a variety of ways, and cold plates that include chef, shrimp, and chicken salads. Their house barbecue sauce is very smooth and a clear cut above the generally poor-quality sauce in this area.

TYBEE ISLAND
Breakfast and Brunch

Considered the best breakfast in the Savannah area for 30 years and counting, ⟨ **The Breakfast Club** (1500 Butler Ave., 912/786-5984, http://tybeeisland.com/breakfast-club, daily 6:30 A.M.–1 P.M., $5–15), with its brisk

diner atmosphere and hearty Polish sausage–filled omelets, is like a little bit of Chicago in the South. Lines start early for a chance to enjoy such house specialties as Helen's Solidarity, the Athena Omelet, and the Chicago Bear Burger, but don't worry—you'll inevitably strike up a conversation with someone interesting while you wait.

Casual Dining

One of Tybee's most cherished restaurants is on the north end in the shadow of the Tybee Lighthouse. Like a little slice of Jamaica near the dunes, the laid-back ⟨ **North Beach Grill** (33 Meddin Ave., 912/786-4442, lunch and dinner daily, $8–17) deals in tasty Caribbean fare such as its signature jerk chicken, fish sandwiches, and, of course, delicious fried plantain, all overseen by chef-owner "Big George" Spriggs. Frequent live music adds to the island vibe.

If you're hanging out near the Pier, you can't miss the three-story pink building with the open decks and the words "Time to Eat" in six-foot letters across the top of the facade. That's not the name of the restaurant—it's actually **Fannie's on the Beach** (1613 Strand Ave., 912/786-6109, www.fanniesonthebeach.com, Mon.–Thurs. 11 A.M.–10 P.M., Fri.–Sun. 11 A.M.–11 P.M., brunch Sun. noon–3 P.M., $8–24) a great-for-all-ages restaurant and bar with a menu that's a cut above the usual tavern fare. Sunday brunches noon–3 P.M. are a local favorite.

For a leisurely and tasty dinner, try **Tybee Island Social Club** (1311 Butler Ave., 912/472-4044, http://tybeeislandsocialclub.com, Tues. 5–9:30 P.M., Wed.–Fri. noon–9:30 P.M., Sat.–Sun. 11:30 A.M.–10 P.M., brunch Sun. 11:30 A.M.–2 P.M., $15). Their menu is somewhat unusual for this seafood-heavy island: Primarily an assortment of gourmet-ish tacos, including fish, duck, and lime- and tequila-marinated steak, all under $10 each. The beer and wine list is accomplished, and the live entertainment usually very good—which is fortunate, since the service here can be on the slow side.

Known far and wide for its sublime pizza on Tybee is **Huc-a-Poo's Bites & Booze** (1213 E. Hwy 80, 912/786-5900, http://hucapoos. com, daily 11:00 A.M.–11 P.M., $10). Individual slices run about four bucks and can easily feed two. Out of the tourist ruckus and tucked away within a small shopping center just as you arrive onto Tybee proper, Huc-a-Poo's also has a lively bar scene.

Seafood

Set in a large former fishing camp overlooking Chimney Creek, **The Crab Shack** (40 Estill Hammock Rd., 912/786-9857, www.thecrab-shack.com, Mon.–Thurs. 11:30 A.M.–10 P.M., Fri.–Sun. 11:30 A.M.–11 P.M., $6–30) is a favorite local seafood place and also something of an attraction in itself. Don't expect gourmet fare or quiet seaside dining; the emphasis is on mounds of fresh, tasty seafood, heavy on the raw-bar action, all in a casual and boisterous outdoor atmosphere. Getting there is a little tricky: Take U.S. 80 to Tybee, cross the bridge over Lazaretto Creek, and begin looking for Estill Hammock Road to Chimney Creek on the right. Take Estill Hammock Road and veer right. After that, it's hard to miss.

For a typically rough and rowdy Tybee experience alongside locals and visitors alike, there's always **Stingray's** (1403 Butler Ave., 912/786-0209, http://stingraysontybee.com, Sun.–Thurs. 11 A.M.–9 P.M., Fri.–Sat. 11 A.M.–11 P.M., $20), located in a quaint but usually crowded semi-historic seafood shack on the main drag. This is the sort of place that has live entertainment and often a live remote from a local radio station, all for your drinking and dining pleasure. They even got some national exposure when Miley Cyrus played and sang onstage here briefly while she was in town filming the otherwise forgettable *The Last Song*. That said, people rave about the seafood entrées, chief among them the crispy scored flounder and the fresh local blue crab.

Information and Services

VISITORS CENTERS

The main clearinghouse for visitor information is the downtown **Savannah Visitors Center** (301 MLK Jr. Blvd., 912/944-0455, Mon.–Fri. 8:30 A.M.–5 P.M., Sat.–Sun. and holidays 9 A.M.–5 P.M.). The newly revitalized Ellis Square features a small visitors kiosk (Mon.–Fri. 8 A.M.–6 P.M.), at the northwest corner of the square, with public restrooms and elevators to the underground parking garage beneath the square.

Other visitors centers in the area include the **River Street Hospitality Center** (1 River St., 912/651-6662, daily 10 A.M.–10 P.M.), the **Tybee Island Visitor Center** (S. Campbell Ave. and U.S. 80, 912/786-5444, daily 9 A.M.–5:30 P.M.), and the **Savannah Airport Visitor Center** (464 Airways Ave., 912/964-1109, daily 10 A.M.–6 P.M.).

Visit Savannah (101 E. Bay St., 877/SAVANNAH—877/728-2662, www.savannahvisit.com), the local convention and visitors bureau, maintains a list of lodgings on its website.

HOSPITALS

Savannah has two very good hospital systems. Centrally located near midtown, **Memorial Health University Hospital** (4700 Waters Ave., 912/350-8000, www.memorialhealth.com) is the region's only Level-I Trauma Center and is one of the best in the nation. The St. Joseph's–Candler Hospital System (www.sjchs.org) has two units, **St. Joseph's Hospital** (11705 Mercy Blvd., 912/819-4100) on the extreme south side and **Candler Hospital** (5401 Paulsen St., 912/819-6000), closer to midtown.

SAVANNAH

POLICE

The city and county police forces recently merged to form the **Savannah-Chatham County Metropolitan Police Department.** For nonemergencies, call 912/651-6675; for emergencies, call 911.

MEDIA
Newspapers

The daily newspaper of record is the *Savannah Morning News* (912/525-0796, www.savannahnow.com). It puts out an entertainment insert, called "Do," on Thursdays. The free weekly newspaper in town is *Connect Savannah* (912/721-4350, www.connectsavannah.com), hitting stands each Wednesday. Look to it for culture and music coverage as well as an alternative take on local politics and issues.

Two glossy magazines compete: the hipper *The South* magazine (912/236-5501, www.thesouthmag.com) and the more establishment *Savannah* magazine (912/652-0293, www.savannahmagazine.com).

Radio and Television

The National Public Radio affiliate is the Georgia Public Broadcasting station WSVH (91.1 FM). Savannah State University offers jazz, reggae, and Latin music on WHCJ (90.3 FM). Georgia Public Broadcasting is on WVAN. The local NBC affiliate is WSAV, the CBS affiliate is WTOC, the ABC affiliate is WJCL, and the Fox affiliate is WTGS.

LIBRARIES

The **Live Oak Public Library** (www.liveoakpl.org) is the umbrella organization for the libraries of Chatham, Effingham, and Liberty Counties. By far the largest branch is south of downtown Savannah, the **Bull Street Branch** (222 Bull St., 912/652-3600, Mon.–Tues. 9 A.M.–8 P.M., Wed.–Fri. 9 A.M.–6 P.M., Sun. 2–6 P.M., closed Sat.). Farthest downtown and tucked away on Upper Factor's Walk is the charming little **Ola Wyeth Branch** (4 E. Bay St., 912/232-5488, Mon.–Fri. noon–3 P.M.). In midtown Savannah is the historic **Carnegie Branch** (537 E. Henry St., 912/231-9921, Mon. 10 A.M.–8 P.M., Tues.–Thurs. 10 A.M.–6 P.M., Fri. 2–6 P.M., Sat. 10 A.M.–6 P.M.).

The **Georgia Historical Society** (501 Whitaker St., 912/651-2128, www.georgiahistory.com, Tues.–Sat. 10 A.M.–5 P.M.) has an extensive collection of clippings, photos, maps, and other archived material at its headquarters at the corner of Forsyth Park in Hodgson Hall. Their website has been extensively revamped and is now one of the Southeast's best online resources for Georgia history information.

The **Jen Library** (201 E. Broughton St., 912/525-4700, www.scad.edu, Mon.–Fri. 7:30 A.M.–1 A.M., Sat. 10 A.M.–1 A.M., Sun. 11 A.M.–1 A.M., shorter hours during school breaks), run by the Savannah College of Art and Design, features 3,000 Internet connections in its cavernous 85,000-square-foot space. Its main claim to fame is the remarkable variety of art periodicals to which it subscribes, nearly 1,000 at last count. It was built for the school's 7,000-plus art students, but the public can enter and use it as well with photo ID (you just can't check anything out).

POST OFFICES

There are two post offices of note for most visitors to Savannah. The largest with the longest hours is the **Main Branch** (2 N. Fahm St., Mon.–Fri. 8 A.M.–5:30 P.M., Sat. 9 A.M.–1 P.M.). It's off Bay Street just past the western edge of the Historic District. A smaller but more convenient branch downtown is the **Telfair Square Station** (118 Barnard St., Mon.–Fri. 8 A.M.–5 P.M.).

GAY AND LESBIAN RESOURCES

Visitors often find Savannah to be surprisingly cosmopolitan and diverse for a Deep South city, and nowhere is this truer than in its sizeable and influential gay and lesbian community. In line with typical Southern protocol, the community is largely apolitical and more concerned with integration than provocation. But they're still very much aware of their growing impact on the local economy and are major players in art and commerce.

The **Savannah Pride Festival** is held every September at various venues in town. Top-flight dance-oriented musical acts perform, restaurants show off their creativity, and activists staff information booths. The chief resource for local gay and lesbian information and concerns is the First City Network, whose main website (www.firstcitynetwork.org) features many useful links, though many might find its MySpace page (www.myspace.com/firstcitynetwork) useful as well. Another great Internet networking resource is Gay Savannah (www.gaysavannah.com). For specifically gay-friendly accommodations, try the **Under the Rainbow Inn** (104–106 W. 38th St., 912/790-1005, www.under-the-rainbow.com, $109–155), a great B&B in the historic Thomas Square district, a former streetcar suburb of Savannah.

Getting There and Around

BY AIR

Savannah is served by the fairly new and efficient **Savannah/Hilton Head International Airport** (SAV, 400 Airways Ave., 912/964-0514, www.savannahairport.com) directly off I-95 at exit 104. The airport is about 20 minutes from downtown Savannah and an hour from Hilton Head Island. Airlines with routes to SAV include American Eagle (www.aa.com), Continental (www.continental.com), Delta (www.delta.com), United Express (www.ual.com), and US Airways (www.usairways.com).

Taxi stands provide taxi transportation to Savannah at the following regulated fares and conditions: The cost is $2 for the first one-sixth of a mile and $0.32 per sixth of a mile thereafter, not to exceed $3.60 for the first mile and $1.92 per mile thereafter. Waiting charge is $21 per hour. No charge for baggage. The maximum fare for destinations in the Historic District is $25.

BY CAR

Savannah is the eastern terminus of I-16, and that interstate is the most common entrance to the city. However, most travelers get to I-16 via I-95, taking the exit for downtown Savannah (Historic District). Once on I-16, the most common entry points into Savannah proper are via the Gwinnett Street exit, which puts you near the southern edge of the Historic District near Forsyth Park, or more commonly, the Montgomery Street exit farther into the heart of downtown.

Paralleling I-95 is the old coastal highway, now U.S. 17, which goes through Savannah. U.S. 80 is Victory Drive for most of its length through town; after you pass through Thunderbolt on your way to the islands area, however, including Tybee, it reverts to U.S. 80.

BY TRAIN

Savannah is on the New York–Miami *Silver Service* of Amtrak (2611 Seaboard Coastline Dr., 912/234-2611, www.amtrak.com). To get to the station on the west side of town, take I-16 west and then I-516 north. Immediately take the Gwinnett Street–Railroad Station exit and follow the Amtrak signs.

BY BUS

Chatham Area Transit (www.catchacat.org, Mon.–Sat. 5:30 A.M.–11:30 P.M., Sun. 7 A.M.–9 P.M., $1.25, includes one transfer, free for children under 41 inches tall, exact change only), Savannah's publicly supported bus system, is quite thorough and efficient considering Savannah's relatively small size. Plenty of routes crisscross the entire area.

Of primary interest to visitors is the free **Dot Express Shuttle** (daily 7 A.M.–9 P.M.), which travels a continuous circuit route through the Historic District with 11 stops at hotels, historic sites, and the Savannah Visitors Center. The Shuttle is wheelchair-accessible.

If you're on River Street, a neat experience is to jump on the free **River Street Trolley** (www. catchacat.org, Thurs.–Sun.). This restored historical trolley moves on the old trolley lines on River Street, and while it only goes a short distance, serving six stops, it's certainly fun.

BY RENTAL CAR

The majority of rental car facilities are at the Savannah/Hilton Head International Airport, including **Avis** (800/831-2847), **Budget** (800/527-0700), **Dollar** (912/964-9001), **Enterprise** (800/736-8222), **Hertz** (800/654-3131), **National** (800/227-7368), and **Thrifty** (800/367-2277). Rental locations away from the airport are **Avis** (7810 Abercorn St., 912/354-4718), **Budget** (7070 Abercorn St., 912/355-0805), **Enterprise** (3028 Skidaway Rd., 912/352-1424; 9505 Abercorn St., 912/925-0060; 11506-A Abercorn Expressway, 912/920-1093; 7510 White Bluff Rd., 912/355-6622).

BY TAXI

Taxi services in Georgia tend to be less regulated than in other states, but service is plentiful in Savannah and is generally reasonable. The chief local provider is **Yellow Cab** (866/319-9646, www.savannahyellowcab.com). For wheelchair accessibility, request cab number 14. Other providers include **Adam Cab** (912/927-7466), **Magikal Taxi Service** (912/897-8294), and **Sunshine Cab** (912/272-0971). If you like some local flavor to go with your cab ride, call **Concierge Taxi Services** (912/604-8466), the one-man show of local author Robert S. Mickles. He's very friendly and always has a great Savannah story to tell.

If you're not in a big hurry, it's always fun to take a **Savannah Pedicab** (912/232-7900, www.savannahpedicab.com) for quick trips around downtown. Your friendly driver will pedal one or two passengers anywhere within the Historic District for a reasonable price.

PARKING

Parking is at a premium in downtown Savannah. The city's Parking Services Department is extremely vigilant about parking violations. Traditional coin-operated meter parking is available throughout the city, but more and more the city is going to self-pay kiosks where you purchase a stamped receipt to display inside your car's dashboard. Bottom line: Be sure to pay for all parking weekdays 8:30 A.M.–5 P.M. No matter what the printed information on the meter tells you, there is *no* enforcement of parking meters at all on weekends or any day after 5 P.M. That information has been on the meters for years and almost seems intended to bilk visitors. That said, know that parking illegally and parking in sweep zones will get you ticketed or towed any time of day. Tybee Island is even stricter about parking regulations than Savannah. If the meter says to feed it until 8 P.M. on the weekend, feed the meter until 8 P.M. on the weekend.

The city operates several parking garages at various rates and hours: the **Bryan Street Garage** (100 E. Bryan St., daily 24 hours, rates Mon.–Fri. 7 A.M.–6 P.M. $1 per hour, Mon.–Fri. 6 P.M.–7 A.M. $2 flat rate, Sat.–Sun. $3 flat rate), the **Robinson Garage** (132 Montgomery St., daily 24 hours, rates Mon.–Fri. 7 A.M.–6 P.M. $1 per hour, Mon.–Fri. 6 P.M.–7 A.M. $2 flat rate, Sat.–Sun. $3 flat rate), the **State Street Garage** (100 E. State

St., open Sun.–Fri. 5 A.M.–1 A.M., Sat. 5 A.M.–Sun. 5 A.M., rates Mon.–Fri. 5 A.M.–6 P.M. $1 per hour, Mon.–Fri. 6 P.M.–1 A.M. $2 flat rate, Sat.–Sun. $3 flat rate), the **Liberty Street Garage** (401 W. Liberty St., open Mon.–Fri. 5 A.M.–1 A.M., Sat. 5 A.M.–Sun. 5 A.M., rates Mon.–Fri. 5 A.M.–6 P.M. $1 per hour, Mon.–Fri. 6 P.M.–1 A.M. $2 flat rate, Sat.–Sun. $1 flat rate), and the new **Whitaker Street Garage** (daily 24 hours, $2 per hour) underneath revitalized Ellis Square. Special events sometimes incur rates of $5–20.

Outside Savannah

As is the case with Charleston, Savannah's outlying areas still bear the indelible marks of the plantation era. The marsh still retains traces of the old paddy fields, and the economics of the area still retain a similar sense of class and racial stratification. While history is no less prominent, it is more subtle in these largely semirural areas, and the tourist infrastructure is much less well-developed than Savannah proper. This area contains some of the most impoverished communities in Georgia, so keep in mind that the locals may have more on their minds than

the historic Midway Church

keeping you entertained—though certainly at no point will their Southern manners fail them. And also keep in mind that you are traveling in one of the most unique ecosystems in the country, and natural beauty is never far away.

MIDWAY AND LIBERTY COUNTY

Locals will tell you that Midway is named because it's equidistant from the Savannah and Altamaha Rivers on Oglethorpe's old "river road," which it certainly is, but others say the small but very historic town is actually named after the Medway River in England. In any case, we know that in seeking to pacify the local Creek people, the Council of Georgia in 1752 granted a group of Massachusetts Puritans then residing in Dorchester, South Carolina, a 32,000-acre land grant as incentive to move south. After moving into Georgia and establishing New Dorchester, they soon founded a nearby settlement that would later take on the modern spelling of Midway. Midway's citizens were very aggressive early on in the cause for American independence, which is why the area's three original parishes were combined and named Liberty County in 1777—the only Georgia county named for a concept rather than a person. Two of Georgia's three signers of the Declaration of Independence, Lyman Hall and Button Gwinnett, resided primarily in Midway, and both attended the historic Midway Church. A key part of Liberty County history is no more: The once-thriving

THE DEAD TOWN OF SUNBURY

If you spend much time in Liberty County, you'll probably hear someone mention that a certain place or person is "over near Sunbury." Such is the lasting legacy of this long-gone piece of Georgia history on the Midway River that locals still refer to it in the present tense, though the old town itself is no more.

Founded soon after Midway in 1758, by 1761 Sunbury rivaled Savannah as Georgia's main commercial port, with a thriving trade in lumber, rice, indigo, corn, and, unfortunately, slaves. At one time, one writer recalls, seven square-rigged vessels called on the port in a single day. At various times, all three of Georgia's signers of the Declaration of Independence—Button Gwinnett, Lyman Hall, and George Walton—had connections to Sunbury.

The beginning of the end came with those heady days of revolution, however, when Sun-bury was the scene of much fighting between colonists and the British army in 1776-1779. A British siege in 1778 culminated in this immortal reply from the colonial commander, Colonel John McIntosh, to a redcoat demand for surrender: "Come and take it." By the beginning of 1779, a separate British assault did indeed "take it," adding to the increasingly violent pillage of the surrounding area. After U.S. independence, Sunbury remained the Liberty County seat until 1797, but it was never the same, beset by decay, hurricanes, and yellow fever outbreaks. (Fort Morris, however, would defend the area against the British one more time, in the War of 1812, as Fort Defiance.) By 1848, nothing of the town remained but the old cemetery, which you can find a short drive from the Fort Morris State Historic Site; ask a park employee for directions.

seaport of Sunbury, which formerly challenged Savannah for economic supremacy in the region, no longer exists.

The main highways in Midway are I-95, U.S. 17, and U.S. 84, also called Oglethorpe Highway, which becomes Highway 38 (Islands Hwy.) east of I-95.

Sights

Tourism in this area has been made much more user-friendly by the liberal addition of signage for the "Liberty Trail," a collection of key attractions. When in doubt, follow the signs.

In Midway proper is the charming **Midway Museum** (U.S. 17, 912/884-5837, Tues.–Sat. 10 A.M.–4 P.M., Sun. 2–4 P.M., $3) and the adjacent **Midway Church,** sometimes called the Midway meetinghouse. The museum contains a variety of artifacts, most from the 18th and 19th centuries, and an extensive genealogy collection. The Midway Church, built in 1756, was burned during the Revolution but rebuilt in 1792. Both Button Gwinnett and Lyman

Hall attended services here, and during the Civil War some of Sherman's cavalry set up camp. The cemetery across the street is wonderfully poignant and is the final resting place of two Revolutionary War generals; Union cavalry kept horses within its walls. The museum, church, and cemetery are easy to find: take exit 76 from I-95 South, and take a right on U.S. 84 (Oglethorpe Highway). Turn right on U.S. 17, and they're just ahead on the right.

Farther west off Islands Highway is **Seabrook Village** (660 Trade Hill Rd., 912/884-7008, Tues.–Sat. 10 A.M.–4 P.M., $3), a unique living-history museum chronicling the everyday life of Liberty County's African Americans, with a direct link to Sherman's famous "40 acres and a mule" Field Order No. 15. There are eight restored vernacular buildings on the 100-acre site, including the simple but sublime one-room Seabrook School.

Youmans Pond (daily, free) is a prime stop for migratory fowl. Its main claim to fame is that it was visited in 1773 by the great naturalist

William Bartram on one of his treks across the Southeast. Youmans Pond has changed little since then, with its tree-studded pond and oodles of owls, ospreys, herons, egrets, wood storks, and many more. To get here, take I-95 south from Savannah to exit 76. Take a left onto Highway 38 (Islands Hwy.) and then a left onto Camp Viking Road. About one mile ahead, take a right onto Lake Pamona Drive. About 0.75 miles ahead, look for the pond on the right. It's unmarked, but there's a wooden boardwalk.

Less easy to find is **LeConte-Woodmanston Botanical Garden** (912/884-6500, www.hist. armstrong.edu/publichist/LeConte/leconte-home.htm, Feb. 15–Dec. 17 Tues.–Sat. 9 A.M.–5 P.M., call first to verify hours and road conditions, $2). Part of William Bartram's historic nature trail, this was the home of Dr. Louis LeConte, renowned 19th-century botanist, and his sons John LeConte, first president of the University of California, Berkeley; and Joseph LeConte, who founded the Sierra Club with John Muir. The highlight here is the rare tidally influenced freshwater wetland, featuring the blackwater Bulltown Swamp. This visit is best done in a 4WD vehicle. From Savannah, take I-95 south to exit 76. Turn right on U.S. 84, then left on U.S. 17. Turn right on Barrington Ferry Road until the pavement ends at Sandy Run Road. Continue until you see the historic markers. Turn left onto the dirt road, then drive another mile.

Dorchester Academy and Museum (8787 E. Oglethorpe Hwy., 912/884-2347, www.dorchesteracademy.com, Tues.–Fri. 11 A.M.–2 P.M., Sat. 2–4 P.M., free) was built as a boarding and day school for freed African Americans after the Civil War. Liberty County was one of the earliest integrated school districts in Georgia, and Martin Luther King Jr. came to Dorchester in 1962 to plan the march on Birmingham. In 1997 an extensive renovation brought the multiple-building facility to its current state. The museum is small but features an interesting display of memorabilia. Take exit 76 off I-95 and go west on U.S. 84, about two miles past the intersection with U.S. 17.

Built to defend the once-proud port of Sunbury, **Fort Morris State Historic Site** (2559 Ft. Morris Rd., 912/884-5999, www. gastateparks.org/info/ftmorris, Tues.–Sat. 9 A.M.–5 P.M., Sun. 2–5:30 P.M., $3) was reconstructed during the War of 1812 and was an encampment during the Civil War. It was here that Colonel John McIntosh gave his famous reply to the British demand for his surrender: "Come and take it." The museum has displays of military and everyday life of the era. Reenactments and cannon firings are highlights. There's a visitors center and a nature trail. To get here, take exit 76 off I-95 south. Go east on Islands Highway and take a left on Fort Morris Road; the site is two miles down.

A little way south of Midway on the Liberty Trail in tiny Riceboro is **Geechee Kunda** (622 Ways Temple Rd., Riceboro, 912/884-4440, www.geecheekunda.net), a combination museum–outreach center dedicated to explaining and exploring the culture of Sea Island African Americans on the Georgia coast. (Don't be confused: *Geechee* is the Georgia word for the Gullah people. Both groups share similar folkways and history, and the terms are virtually interchangeable.) There are artifacts from slavery and Reconstruction, including authentic Geechee-Gullah relics.

Liberty County is also home to part of the sprawling Fort Stewart army installation, home of the U.S. Army "Rock of the Marne" 3rd Infantry Division. The only thing open to the public is the **Fort Stewart Museum** (Bldg. T904, 2022 Frank Cochran Dr., Fort Stewart, 912/767-7885, Tues.–Sat. 10 A.M.–4 P.M., free), which chronicles the division's activity in World War II, Vietnam, Korea, Desert Storm, and Iraq. All visitors must stop at the main gate and provide proof of registration, insurance,

SAVANNAH

© JIM MOREKIS

reenactors at Fort Morris State Historic Site

and a driver's license to receive a visitor's pass. To get here, take exit 87 off I-95 south. Take a left on U.S. 17, then veer right onto Highway 196 west. Turn right at U.S. 84. Turn right onto General Stewart Way, and follow directions to the main gate.

Accommodations and Food

While industry is coming quickly to Liberty County, it's still a small self-contained community with not much in the way of tourist amenities (many would say that is part of its charm). A great choice for a stay is **C Dunham Farms** (5836 Islands Hwy., Midway, 912/880-4500, www.dunhamfarms.com). The B&B ($165–205) is in the converted 1940s Palmyra Barn, and the self-catered circa-1840 Palmyra Cottage ($300) nearby is right on the river, with plenty of kayaking and hiking opportunities. Your hosts, Laura and Meredith Devendorf, couldn't be more charming or informed about the area, and the breakfasts are absurdly rich

and filling in that hearty and deeply comforting Southern tradition.

Restaurants of note include the **Sunbury Crab Company** (541 Brigantine Dunmore Rd., Midway, 912/884-8640, lunch Sat.–Sun., dinner Wed.–Sun., $10–30), providing, you guessed it, great crab cakes in a casual atmosphere on the Midway River. Get here by taking Highway 38 east of Midway and then a left onto Fort Morris Road. Many locals eat at least once a week at **Holton's Seafood** (13711 E. Oglethorpe Hwy., Midway, 912/884-9151, daily lunch and dinner, $7–17), an unpretentious and fairly typical family-run fried seafood place just off I-95 at the Midway exit.

RICHMOND HILL AND BRYAN COUNTY

Known as the "town that Henry Ford built," Richmond Hill is a growing bedroom community of Savannah in adjacent Bryan County. Sherman's March to the Sea ended here with much destruction, so little history before that time is left. Most of what remains is due to Ford's philanthropic influence, still felt in many place names around the area, including the main drag, Highway 144, known as Ford Avenue. After the auto magnate and his wife Clara made the area, then called Ways Station, a summer home, they were struck by the area's incredible poverty and determined to help improve living conditions, building hospitals, schools, churches, and homes. The Fords eventually acquired over 85,000 acres in Bryan County, including the former Richmond plantation. What is now known as Ford Plantation—currently a private luxury resort—was built in the 1930s and centered on the main house, once the central building of the famous Hermitage Plantation on the Savannah River, purchased and moved by Ford south to Bryan County.

Sights

The little **Richmond Hill Historical Society and Museum** (Ford Ave. and Timber Trail Rd., Richmond Hill, 912/756-3697, daily 10 A.M.–4 P.M., donation) is housed in a former kindergarten built by Henry Ford.

Perhaps the main attraction here, especially for Civil War buffs, is **Fort McAllister State Historic Site** (3894 Ft. McAllister Rd., Richmond Hill, 912/727-2339, www.gastateparks.org/info/ftmcallister, daily 7 A.M.–10 P.M., $5 adults, $3.50 children). Unlike the masonry forts of Savannah, Fort McAllister is an all-earthwork fortification on the Ogeechee River, the site of a short but savage assault by Sherman's troops in December 1864 in which 5,000 Union soldiers quickly overwhelmed the skeleton garrison of 230 Confederate defenders. After the war, the site fell into disrepair until Henry Ford funded and spearheaded restoration in the 1930s, as he did with so many historic sites in Bryan County. The fort, which features many reenactments throughout the

year, has a well-run new **Civil War Museum** (Mon.–Sat. 9 A.M.–5 P.M., Sun. 2–5 P.M.). An adjacent recreational site features a beautiful oak-lined picnic ground, a nature trail, and the nearby 65-site Savage Island Campground. To get here from I-95, take exit 90 and go 10 miles east on Highway 144.

Practicalities

There's no end to the chain food offerings here, but one of the better restaurants in town is **The Upper Crust** (1702 U.S. 17, 912/756-6990, lunch Mon.–Sat., dinner Mon.–Sun., $7–12), a casual American place with great pizza in addition to soups, salads, and hot sandwiches. Another popular place, also on U.S 17, is **Steamers Restaurant & Raw Bar** (4040 U.S. 17, 912/756-3979, daily 5–10 P.M., $10–20), home of some good Lowcountry boil.

To get to Richmond Hill, drive south of Savannah on I-95 and take exit 90. Most lodgings in the area are clustered off I-95 at exit 87 (exit 90 also takes you to Richmond Hill). Keep in mind the two most important thoroughfares are the north–south U.S. 17 and the east–west Highway 144, also known as Ford Avenue.

NEW EBENEZER

Few people visit New Ebenezer today, west of Savannah in Effingham County. Truth is, there's not much there anymore except for one old church. But oh, what a church. The **Jerusalem Evangelical Lutheran Church** (2966 Ebenezer Rd., Rincon, 912/754-3915, www.effga.com/jerusalem) hosts the oldest continuous congregation in the United States. Built of local clay brick in 1769, its walls are 21 inches thick. Some original panes of glass remain, and its European bells are still rung before each service (Sun. 11 A.M.). Several surrounding structures are also heirs to New Ebenezer's Salzburg legacy. Around the corner from the church is a much newer spiritually themed site, the **New Ebenezer Retreat**

and Conference Center (2887 Ebenezer Rd., Rincon, 912/754-9242, www.newebenezer. org). Built in 1977, the Retreat provides acres of calm surroundings, lodging, and meals in an ecumenical Christian setting.

Scenic blackwater **Ebenezer Creek** is best experienced by putting in at the private Ebenezer Landing ($5). To get to New Ebenezer, take exit 109 off I-95. Go north on Highway 21 to Rincon, Georgia, then east on Highway 275 (Ebenezer Rd.). The New Ebenezer Retreat and Conference Center offers a range of very reasonably priced lodgings, most including meals, in a beautiful setting. The extremely fast-growing town of Rincon, through which you will most likely drive on your way to New Ebenezer, offers an assortment of the usual chain food and lodging establishments.

WASSAW ISLAND NATIONAL WILDLIFE REFUGE

Totally unique in that it's the only Georgia barrier island never cleared for agriculture or development, the 10,000-acre Wassaw Island National Wildlife Refuge (www.fws.gov/wassaw) is accessible only by boat. There are striking driftwood-strewn beaches, and the interior of the island has some beautiful old-growth stands of longleaf pine and live oak. Wassaw is a veritable paradise for nature lovers and birdwatchers, with migratory activity in the spring and fall, waterfowl in abundance in the summer, and manatee and loggerhead turtle activity (about 10 percent of Georgia's transient loggerhead population makes use of Wassaw for nesting). There are also about 20 miles of trails and a decaying Spanish-American War–era battery, Fort Morgan, on the north end. National Wildlife Refuge Week is celebrated in October.

Because of its comparatively young status—it was formed only about 1,600 years ago—Wassaw Island also has some unique geographical features. You can still make out the parallel ridge features, vestiges of successive ancient shorelines. A central ridge forms the backbone of the island, reaching an amazing (for this area) elevation of 45 feet above sea level at the south end. Native Americans first settled the island, whose name comes from an ancient word for sassafras, which was found in abundance here. During the Civil War, both Confederate and Union troops occupied the island successively. In 1866 the wealthy New England businessman George Parsons bought the island, which stayed in that family's hands until it was sold to the Nature Conservancy in 1969 for $1 million. The Conservancy in turn sold Wassaw to the U.S. government for $1 to be managed as a wildlife refuge.

It's easiest to get to Wassaw Island from Savannah. Charters and scheduled trips are available from **Captain Walt's Charters** (Thunderbolt Marina, 3124 River Dr., 912/507-3811, www.waltsadventure.com/charters), the **Bull River Marina** (8005 E. U.S. 80, 912/897-7300), **Delegal Marina** (1 Marina Dr., 912/598-0023), **Captain Joe Dobbs** (Delegal Marina, 1 Marina Dr., 912/598-0090, www. captjdobbs.com), and **Isle of Hope Marina** (50 Bluff Dr., 912/354-8187, www.isleofhopemarina.com). Most docking is either at the beaches on the north and south ends or in Wassaw Creek, where the U.S. Fish and Wildlife Service dock is also located (temporary mooring only). There's no camping allowed on Wassaw Island; it's for day use only.

OSSABAW ISLAND

Owned and operated by Georgia as a heritage and wildlife preserve, the island was a gift to the state in 1978 from Eleanor Torrey-West and family, who still retain some property on the island. All public use of the island is managed by the **Ossabaw Island Foundation** (www.ossabawisland.org).

The 12,000-acre island is much older than

NEW EBENEZER AND THE SALZBURGERS

Perhaps the most unsung chapter in Europe's great spiritual diaspora of the 1700s, the Salzburgers of New Ebenezer—a thrifty, peaceful, and hard-working people—were Georgia's first religious refugees and perhaps the most progressive as well. The year after Oglethorpe's arrival, a contingent of devout Lutherans from Salzburg in present-day Austria arrived after being expelled from their home country for their beliefs. Oglethorpe, mindful of Georgia's mission to provide sanctuary for persecuted Protestants and also wishing for a military buffer to the west, eagerly welcomed them. Given land about 25 miles west of Savannah, the Salzburgers named their first settlement Ebenezer ("stone of help" in Hebrew). Disease prompted them to move the site to better land nearer to the river and call it—in pragmatic Germanic style—New Ebenezer, and so it remains to this day.

Because they continued to speak German instead of English, the upriver colony maintained its isolation. Still, the Salzburgers were among Oglethorpe's most ardent and loyal supporters. Their pastor and de facto political leader, Johann Martin Boltzius, seeking to build an enlightened agrarian utopia of small farmers, was an outspoken foe of slavery and the exploitative plantation system of agriculture. His system largely worked: The fragile silk industry thrived in New Ebenezer while it had failed miserably in Savannah, and the nation's first rice mill was built here. However, don't get the idea that the Salzburgers were all work and no play. They enjoyed their beer, so

much so that Oglethorpe was forced to send regular shipments, rationalizing that "cheap beer is the only means to keep rum out."

For 10 years, Georgia hosted another progressive Lutheran sect, the Moravians, whom John Wesley called the only genuine Christians he'd ever met. Despite their professed pacifism, however, they had to leave New Ebenezer because they didn't get along with the Salzburgers, and their communal living arrangements led to internal discord.

The Trustees' turnover of Georgia back to the crown in 1750 signaled the final victory of pro-slavery forces—so much so that even Pastor Boltzius acquired a couple of slaves as domestic servants. New Ebenezer's influence began a decline that rapidly accelerated when British forces pillaged much of the town in the Revolution, even burning pews and Bibles. Fifty years later, nothing at all remained except the old Jerusalem Church, now the Jerusalem Evangelical Lutheran Church. Built in 1769, it still stands today and hosts regular worship services. Right around the corner is the New Ebenezer Retreat, nestled along the banks of the Savannah River, providing an ecumenical meeting and natural healing space for those of all faiths.

Although New Ebenezer is often called a "ghost town," this is a misnomer. Extensive archaeological work continues in the area, and the Georgia Salzburger Society works hard to maintain several historic buildings and keep the legacy alive through special events.

SAVANNAH

Wassaw Island to its north and so has traces of human habitation back to 2000 B.C. The island's name comes from an old Muskogean word referring to yaupon holly, found in abundance on the island and used by Native Americans in purification rituals to induce vomiting. Wading birds and predators such as bald eagles make their homes on the island, as do feral horses and a transient population of loggerhead turtles, who lay eggs in the dunes during the summer. There are several tabby

ruins on the island, along with many miles of walking trails. Unlike the much-younger Wassaw, Ossabaw Island was not only timbered extensively but hosted several rice and cotton plantations, particularly on the north end. The first property transfer in Georgia involved Ossabaw, St. Catherine's, and Sapelo Islands, which were ceded to the Yamacraws in exchange for the English getting the coastal region. The Yamacraws then granted those islands to Mary Musgrove, who began the modern era on the island by planting and introducing livestock.

Descendants of the island's slaves moved to the Savannah area after the Civil War, founding the community of Pin Point. Similarly to Jekyll Island to the south, Ossabaw was a hunting preserve for wealthy families in the Roaring '20s. Even today, hunting is an important activity on the island, with lotteries choosing who gets a chance to pursue its overly large populations of deer and wild hogs, the latter of which are descended from pigs brought by the Spanish.

Now reserved exclusively for educational and scientific purposes, the island is accessible only by boat. Georgia law ensures public access to all beaches up to the high-tide mark—which simply means that the public can ride out to Ossabaw and go on the beach for day use, but any travel to the interior is restricted and you must have permission first. Contact the Ossabaw Island Foundation (info@ossabawisland.org) for information. Day trips can be arranged with charter operators at the marinas in Savannah.

THE GOLDEN ISLES

More than any other area in the region, the Georgia coast retains a timeless mystique evocative of a time before the coming of Europeans, even before humankind itself. Often called the Golden Isles because of the play of the afternoon sun on the vistas of marsh grass, its other nickname, "the Debatable Land," is a nod to its centuries-long role as a constantly shifting battleground of European powers.

On the map it looks relatively short, but Georgia's coastline is the longest contiguous salt marsh environment in the world—a third of the country's remaining salt marsh. Abundant with wildlife, vibrant with exotic, earthy aromas, constantly refreshed by a steady, salty sea breeze, it's a place with no real match anywhere else. Filled with rich sediments from rivers upstream and replenished with nutrients from the twice-daily ocean tide, Georgia's marshes from the mainland to the barrier islands are an amazing engine of natural production. Producing more food energy than any estuary on the East Coast, each acre of marsh produces about 20 tons of biomass—four times more productive than an acre of corn.

Ancient Native Americans held the area in special regard, intoxicated not only by the easy sustenance it offered but its spiritual solace. Their shell middens, many still in existence, are not only a sign of well-fed people but those thankful for nature's bounty. Avaricious for gold as they were, the Spanish also admired

© JIM MOREKIS

HIGHLIGHTS

◖ **Jekyll Island Historic District:** Relax and soak in the salty breeze at this onetime playground of the country's richest people (page 304).

◖ **The Village:** The center of social life on St. Simons Island has shops, restaurants, a pier, and a beachside playground (page 313).

◖ **Fort Frederica National Monument:** An excellently preserved tabby fortress from the first days of English settlement in Georgia (page 314).

◖ **Harris Neck National Wildlife Refuge:** This former wartime airfield is now one of the East Coast's best birding locations (page 322).

◖ **Cumberland Island National Seashore:** Wild horses—such as the ones that live here—might not be able to drag you off this evocative, undeveloped island paradise (page 331).

◖ **Okefenokee National Wildlife Refuge:** More than just a swamp, the Okefenokee is a natural wonderland that takes you back into the mists of prehistory (page 334).

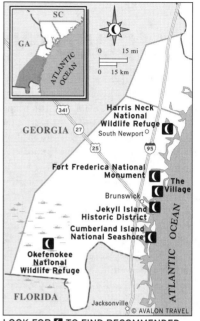

LOOK FOR ◖ TO FIND RECOMMENDED SIGHTS, ACTIVITIES, DINING, AND LODGING.

the almost monastic enchantment of Georgia's coast, choosing it as the site of their first colony in North America. Their subsequent chain of Roman Catholic missions are now long gone but certainly testified to their own quest here. While the American tycoons who used these barrier islands as personal playgrounds had avarice of their own, we must give credit where it's due: Their self-interest kept these places largely untouched by the kind of development that has plagued many of South Carolina's barrier islands to the north. Though isolated even today, the Golden Isles played an irreplaceable role in the defense of the young United States.

It was here that massive live oaks were forested and used in the construction of the bulked-up superfast frigates of the fledgling U.S. Navy. The USS *Constitution* got its nickname, "Old Ironsides," from the strength of these pieces of Georgia oak, so resilient as to literally repel British cannonballs during the War of 1812. Although the South Carolina Sea Islands are generally seen as the center of Gullah culture, the African American communities of the Golden Isles, Georgia's Sea Islands, also boast a long and fascinating history of survival, resourcefulness, and proud cultural integrity carried on to this day.

THE GOLDEN ISLES

HISTORY

For over 5,000 years, the Golden Isles of what would become Georgia were an abundant food and game source for Native Americans. In those days, long before erosion and channel dredging had taken their toll, each barrier island was an easy canoe ride away from the next one—a sort of early Intracoastal Waterway—and there was bounty for everyone. But all that changed in 1526 when the Golden Isles became the site of the first European settlement in what is now the continental United States, the fabled San Miguel de Gualdape, founded nearly a century before the first English settlements in Virginia. Historians remain unsure where expedition leader Lucas de Ayllón actually set up camp with his 600 colonists and slaves, but recent research breakthroughs have put it somewhere around St. Catherine's Sound. San Miguel disintegrated within a couple of months, but it set the stage for a lengthy Spanish presence on the Georgia coast that culminated in the mission period (1580–1684). Working with the coastal chiefdoms of Guale and Mocama, almost all of Georgia's barrier islands and many interior spots hosted Catholic missions, each with an accompanying contingent of Spanish regulars. The missions began retreating with the English incursion into the American Southeast in the 1600s, and the coast was largely free of European presence until an early English outpost, Fort King George near modern-day Darien, Georgia, was established decades later in 1721. Isolated and hard to provision, the small fort was abandoned seven years later.

The next English project was Fort Frederica on St. Simons Island, commissioned by General James Edward Oglethorpe following his establishment of Savannah to the north. Oglethorpe's settlement of Brunswick and Jekyll Island came soon afterward. With the final vanquishing of the Spanish at the Battle of Bloody Marsh near Fort Frederica, the Georgia coast quickly emulated the profitable rice-based plantation culture of the South Carolina Lowcountry, and indeed many notable Carolina planters expanded their holdings with marshland on the Georgia coast.

During the Civil War the southern reaches of Sherman's March to the Sea came down as far as Darien, a once-vital trading port that was burned to the ground by Union troops. With slavery gone and the plantation system in disarray, the coast's African American population was largely left to its own devices. Although the famous "40 acres and a mule" land and wealth redistribution plan for freed slaves was not to see fruition, the black population of Georgia's Sea Islands, like that of South Carolina's, developed an inward-looking culture that persists to this day. The generic term for this culture is Gullah, but in Georgia you'll also hear it referred to as Geechee, local dialect for the nearby Ogeechee River.

As with much of the South after the Civil War, business carried on much as before, with the area becoming a center for lumber, the turpentine trade, and an increasing emphasis on fishing and shrimping. But by the start of the 20th century, the Golden Isles had become firmly established as a playground for the rich, who hunted and dined on the sumptuous grounds of exclusive retreats such as the Jekyll Island Club.

As it did elsewhere, World War II brought new economic growth in the form of military bases, even as German U-boats ranged off the coast. Today the federal presence is most notable in the massive Trident submarine base at Kings Bay toward the Florida border.

PLANNING YOUR TIME

Generally speaking, the peak season in this area is March–Labor Day. With the exception of some resort accommodations on St. Simons Island, Little St. Simons Island, and Sea Island, lodging is generally far more affordable than up the coast in either Savannah or Charleston.

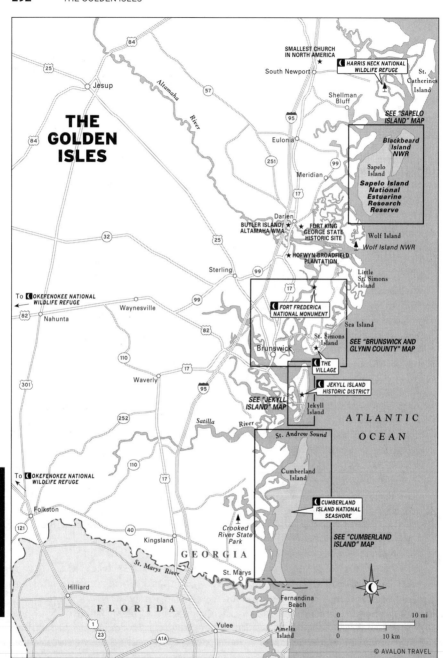

THE
GOLDEN
ISLES

SMALLEST CHURCH
IN NORTH AMERICA ★

HARRIS NECK NATIONAL
WILDLIFE REFUGE

St.
Catherines
Island

South Newport

SEE "SAPELO
ISLAND" MAP

Shellman
Bluff

Eulonia

*Blackbeard
Island
NWR*

Meridian

Sapelo
Island

*Sapelo Island
National
Estuarine
Research
Reserve*

Darien

**BUTLER ISLAND/
ALTAMAHA WMA** ★

★ **FORT KING
GEORGE STATE
HISTORIC SITE**

Wolf Island

Wolf Island NWR

★ **HOFWYN-BROADFIELD
PLANTATION**

Little
St. Simons
Island

Sterling

To OKEFENOKEE NATIONAL
WILDLIFE REFUGE

Waynesville

★ **FORT FREDERICA
NATIONAL MONUMENT**

Sea Island

Nahunta

St. Simons
Island

SEE "BRUNSWICK AND
GLYNN COUNTY" MAP

Brunswick

★
**THE
VILLAGE**

Waverly

JEKYLL ISLAND
HISTORIC DISTRICT

SEE "JEKYLL
ISLAND" MAP

Jekyll
Island

ATLANTIC

Satilla   River

St. Andrew Sound

OCEAN

To OKEFENOKEE NATIONAL
WILDLIFE REFUGE

Cumberland
Island

CUMBERLAND
ISLAND NATIONAL
SEASHORE

Folkston

*Crooked
River State
Park*

SEE "CUMBERLAND
ISLAND" MAP

Kingsland

GEORGIA

Hilliard

St. Marys River

St. Marys

FLORIDA

Fernandina
Beach

Yulee

Amelia
Island

Jesup

Altamaha   River

0   10 mi

0   10 km

© AVALON TRAVEL

Many travelers take I-95 south from Savannah to the Golden Isles, but U.S. 17 roughly parallels the interstate—in some cases so closely that drivers on both roads can see each other—and is a far more scenic and enriching drive for those with a little extra time to spend. Indeed, U.S. 17 is an intrinsic part of the life and lore of the region, and you are likely to spend a fair amount of time on it regardless.

Geographically, Brunswick is similar to Charleston in that it lies on a peninsula laid out roughly north–south. And like Charleston, it's separated from the Atlantic by barrier islands, in Brunswick's case St. Simons Island and Jekyll Island. Once you get within city limits, however, Brunswick has more in common with Savannah due to its Oglethorpe-designed grid layout. Brunswick itself can easily be fully experienced in a single afternoon. But really—as its nickname "Gateway to the Golden Isles" indicates—Brunswick's main role is as an economic and governmental center for Glynn County, to which Jekyll Island and St. Simons Island, the real attractions in this area, belong.

Both Jekyll Island and St. Simons Island are well worth visiting, and have their own separate pleasures—Jekyll more contemplative, St. Simons more upscale. Give an entire day to Jekyll so you can take full advantage of its relaxing, open feel. A half-day can suffice for St. Simons because most of its attractions are clustered in the Village area near the pier, and there's little beach recreation to speak of.

Getting to the undeveloped barrier islands, Sapelo and Cumberland, takes planning in advance because there is no bridge to either. Both require a ferry booking and hence a more substantial commitment of time. There are no real stores and few facilities on these islands, so pack along whatever you think you'll need, including be food, water, medicine, suntan lotion, insect repellent, and so on. Sapelo Island is limited to day use unless you have prior reservations, with the town of Darien in McIntosh County as the gateway. The same is true for Cumberland Island National Seashore, with the town of St. Marys in Camden County as the gateway.

Brunswick and Glynn County

Consider Brunswick sort of a junior Savannah, sharing with that city twice its size to the north a heavily English flavor, great manners, a city plan with squares courtesy of General James Oglethorpe, a thriving but environmentally intrusive seaport, and a busy shrimping fleet. While Brunswick never became the dominant commercial center, à la Savannah, that it was envisioned to be, it has followed the Savannah model in modern times, both in terms of downtown revitalization and an increasing emphasis on port activity. Sadly, unlike Savannah, Brunswick has not seen fit to preserve the integrity of its six existing squares, all but one of which (Hanover Square) have been bisected by streets or built on.

The first real English-speaking settler in the area, Mark Carr, began cultivating land near Brunswick in 1738, but the city wasn't laid out until 1771, in a grid design similar to Savannah's. Originally comprising nearly 400 acres, Brunswick was named for Braunschweig, the seat of the House of Hanover in Germany and also for the Duke of Brunswick, a brother of King George III. The Brunswick area hosted a number of profitable plantations and a burgeoning lumber industry, but a series of financial panics in the late 1830s hit particularly hard. When the Civil War started, most white citizens fled to nearby Waynesville, Georgia, and wharves and key buildings were burned to keep them out of Union hands. Brunswick saw

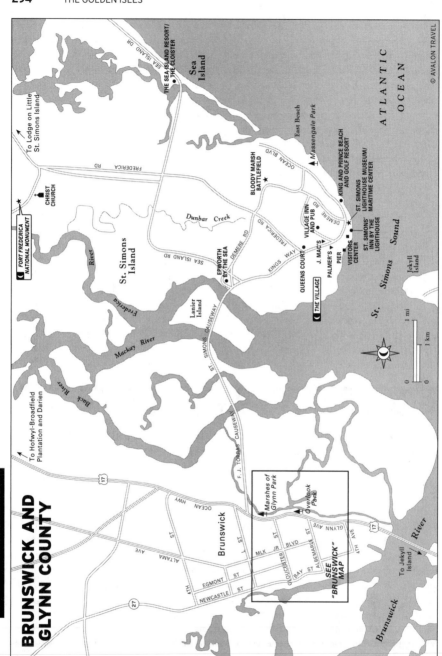

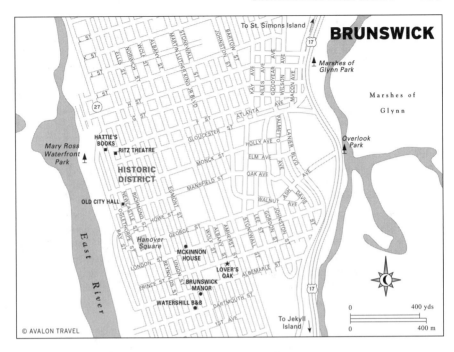

a boom in population during World War II as a home of wartime industry such as the J. A. Jones Construction Company, which in a two-year span built 99 massive Liberty ships and at its peak employed 16,000 workers (they managed to build seven ships in a single month in 1944).

Since the war, the shrimping industry has played a big role in Brunswick's economy, so much so that it calls itself the "Shrimp Capital of the World." But lately the local shrimping industry is in steep decline, both from depleted coastal stocks and increased competition from Asian shrimp farms. Hit hard by the recent economic downturn, Brunswick has seen better days. Despite an admirable effort at downtown revitalization centering on Newcastle Street, most visitors to the area seem content to employ Brunswick, as its nickname implies, as a "Gateway to the Golden Isles" rather than as a destination in itself.

SIGHTS
Brunswick Historic District

Technically, Brunswick has an "Old Town" district on the National Register of Historic Places as well as an adjacent district called "Historic Brunswick" centering on the storefronts of Newcastle Street. Since it's all pretty close together, we'll consider it all one nice package. Unlike Savannah, which renamed many of its streets in a fit of patriotism after the American Revolution, Brunswick's streets bear their original Anglophilic names, like Gloucester, Albemarle, and Norwich. You'd be forgiven for thinking that Brunswick's Union Street is a post–Civil War statement of national unity, but the name actually commemorates the union of Scotland and England in 1707. Most of the visitor-friendly activity centers on **Newcastle Street,** where you'll find the bulk of the galleries, shops, and restored buildings. Adjacent in the more historic areas are some nice residential homes.

The new pride of downtown is **Old City Hall** (1212 Newcastle St.), an amazing circa-1889 Richardsonian Romanesque edifice designed by noted regional architect Alfred Eichberg, who also planned many similarly imposing buildings in Savannah. City Hall reopened in 2004 after extensive renovations, bringing back to life its great vintage fireplaces and refitting its original gaslight fixtures.

Another active restored building is the charming **Ritz Theatre** (1530 Newcastle St., 912/262-6934, www.goldenislearts.org), built in 1898 to house the Grand Opera House and the offices of the Brunswick and Birmingham Railroad. This ornate three-story Victorian transitioned with the times, becoming a vaudeville venue, then a movie house. Under the management of the Golden Isles Arts and Humanities Association since 1989, the Ritz now hosts performances, studios, an art gallery, and classes.

Mary Ross Waterfront Park

This downtown gathering place at Bay and Gloucester Streets also has economic importance as a center of local economic activity—it's here where Brunswick's shrimp fleet is moored and the town's large port facilities begin. Unfortunately, nearby is a huge factory, dispensing its unpleasant odor over the waterfront 24-7. In 1989 the park was dedicated to Mary Ross, member of a longtime Brunswick shrimping family and author of the popular Georgia history book *The Debatable Land.* While the book is still a great read, sadly Ms. Ross was wrong when she wrote that the tabby ruins in the area were of Spanish origin. Devastated by the discovery that they actually dated from later and were of English construction, she vowed never to publish another word again.

At the entrance to the park is a well-done model of a Liberty ship, like the thousands that were built in Brunswick during World War II.

Lover's Oak

At the intersection of Prince and Albany Streets, you'll find the Lover's Oak, a nearly 1,000-year-old tree. Local lore tells us that it has been a secret meeting place for young lovers for centuries (though one does wonder how much of a secret it actually could have been). It's about 13 feet in diameter and has 10 sprawling limbs.

Marshes of Glynn

Amid the light industrial sprawl of this area of the Golden Isles Parkway is the interesting little **Overlook Park,** just south of the visitors center on U.S. 17—a good, if loud, place for a picnic. From the park's picnic grounds or overlook you can see the fabled Marshes of Glynn, which inspired Georgia poet Sidney Lanier to write his famous poem of the same title under the **Lanier Oak,** located a little farther up the road in the median.

Hofwyl-Broadfield Plantation

South Carolina doesn't own the patent on well-preserved old rice plantations, as the Hofwyl-Broadfield Plantation (5556 U.S. 17, 912/264-7333, www.gastateparks.org, Thurs.–Sat. 9 A.M.–5 P.M., last main house tour 4:45 P.M., $5), a short drive north of Brunswick, proves. With its old paddy fields along the gorgeous and relatively undeveloped Altamaha River estuary, the plantation's main home is an antebellum wonder, with an expansive porch and a nice house museum inside, with silver, a model of a rice plantation, and a slide show. There's also a nice nature trail.

William Brailsford of Charleston finished the plantation in 1807, which soon passed into the hands of the Troup family, who expanded the holdings to over 7,000 acres. Rice finally became financially unfeasible in the early 20th century, and the plantation turned to dairy farming, a pursuit that lasted until World War II. Ophelia Troup Dent would finally will the site to the state of Georgia in 1973.

Lanier Oak, near the fabled Marshes of Glynn

The best way to get here is by taking U.S. 17 north of Brunswick until you see the signs; the plantation entrance is on the east side of the road.

ENTERTAINMENT AND EVENTS

The **Golden Isles Arts and Humanities Association** (1530 Newcastle St., 912/262-6934, www.goldenislesarts.org) is an umbrella organization for many arts activities in the Brunswick, Jekyll, and St. Simons area. They also manage the historic **Ritz Theatre** (1530 Newcastle St., 912/262-6934) in downtown Brunswick, which offers a yearly performance season that's worth checking out if you have a free weekend night.

Nightlife

Brunswick is a conservative place with little bar scene to speak of. But a few miles offshore is quite a different story when the **Emerald Princess Dinner and Casino Cruises** (Gisco Point, 912/265-3558, www. emeraldprincesscasino.com, Mon.–Thurs. 7 p.m.–midnight, Fri.–Sat. 11 a.m.–4 p.m. and 7 p.m.–1 a.m., Sun. 1–6 p.m., $10) is operating. This is the classic gambling and party boat experience, with the action starting when the *Emerald Princess* slips into international waters and out of domestic gambling regulations. Ten bucks for the cruise gets you a light dinner. Drinks and chips, of course, are on you. No one under age 21 is allowed, and minimum and maximum bets vary by table. Reservations are required. To get to the dock, take U.S. 17 over the massive Sidney Lanier Bridge. Take a left onto the Jekyll Island Causeway and then an immediate left onto Gisco Point Drive. Follow signs into the parking lot.

Performing Arts

Based in St. Simons Island, the **Coastal Symphony of Georgia** (912/634-2006, www. coastalsymphonyofgeorgia.org), under the baton of Vernon Humbert, plays concerts in

THE GOLDEN ISLES

IN THE FOOTSTEPS OF BARTRAM

The West has its stirring tale of Lewis and Clark, but the Southeast has its own fascinating—if somewhat less dramatic—tale of discovery, in the odyssey of William Bartram. In March 1733, the 36-year-old Bartram—son of royal botanist John Bartram and definitely a chip off the old block—arrived in Savannah to begin what would become a four-year journey through eight Southern states and colonies. As Lewis and Clark would do in the following century, Bartram not only exhaustively documented his encounters with nature and with Native Americans, he made discoveries whose impact has stayed with us to this day.

Young "Willie," born near Philadelphia in 1739, had a talent for drawing and for plants, which, of course, thrilled his father, who wrote to a friend that "Botany and drawing is his darling delight." A failure at business, Bartram was happy to settle on a traveling lifestyle that mixed both his loves: art and flora. After accompanying his father on several early trips, Bartram set out on his own at the request of an old friend of his father's in England, Dr. John Fothergill, who paid Bartram 50 pounds per year plus expenses to send back specimens and drawings.

Though Bartram's quest would eventually move farther inland and encompass much of the modern American South, most of the first year was spent in coastal Georgia. After arriving in Savannah he moved southward, roughly paralleling modern U.S. 17, to the now-dead town of Sunbury, through Midway, and on to Darien, where he stayed at the plantation of Lachlan McIntosh on the great Altamaha River, which inspired Bartram to pen some of his most beautiful writing. Bartram also journeyed to Sapelo Island, Brunswick, St. Marys, and even into the great Okefenokee Swamp. Using Savannah and Charleston as bases, Bartram mostly traveled alone, either by horse, by boat, or on foot. Word of his trip preceded him, and he was usually greeted warmly by local traders and Indian chiefs (except for one encounter with a hostile Native American near the St. Marys River). In many places, he was the first European seen since De Soto and the Spanish. His epic journey ended in late 1776, when Bartram gazed on his beloved Altamaha for the last time. Heading north and crossing the Savannah River south of Ebenezer, he proceeded to Charleston and from there to his hometown of Philadelphia—where he would remain for the rest of his days.

At its publication, his 1791 chronicle, *Travels Through North and South Carolina, Georgia, East and West Florida,* was hailed as "the most astounding verbal artifact of the early republic." In that unassuming yet timeless work, Bartram cemented his reputation as the country's first native-born naturalist and practically invented the modern travelogue. Thanks to the establishment of the William Bartram Trail in 1976, you can walk in his footsteps—or close to them, anyway, since historians are not sure of his route. The trail uses a rather liberal interpretation, including memorials, trails, and gardens, but many specific "heritage sites" in coastal Georgia have their own markers, as follows:

- River and Barnard Streets in Savannah to mark his disembarkation and the beginning of his trek

- LeConte-Woodmanston Plantation in Liberty County (Barrington Ferry Rd. south of Sandy Run Rd. near Riceboro)

- 1.5 miles south of the South Newport River off U.S. 17

- St. Simon's Island on Frederica Road near the Fort Frederica entrance

- Off Highway 275 at Old Ebenezer Cemetery in Effingham County

Among the indigenous species Bartram was the first to record are:

- Fraser magnolia

- Gopher tortoise

- Florida sandhill crane

- Flame azalea

- Oakleaf hydrangea

the historic Ritz Theatre in downtown Brunswick

© JIM MOREKIS

Brunswick during its season at different venues. Check the website for details. **Art Downtown** (209 Gloucester St., 912/262-0628, www.art-downtowngallery209.com) hosts locally written shows performed by the Brunswick Actors Theatre in its black box space and showcases local visual artists in its attached Gallery 209. The **Brunswick Community Concert Association** (912/638-5616, www.brunswickcommunityconcert.org, $25 adults, $10 students) brings an eclectic variety of high-quality national and regional vocal acts to various venues. The **C.A.P.E. Theater** (916 Albany St., 912/996-7740, www.capetheater.org), short for Craft, Appreciation, Performance, and Education, is a community group that performs a mix of classics and musicals at various venues. No reservations are necessary unless you're attending a dinner theater show, which is about $30 adults, $15 students. The town's main dance group is **Invisions Dance**

Company, which performs out of **Studio South** (1307 Grant St., 912/265-3255, www.studio-southga.com).

Festivals and Events

Each Mother's Day at noon, parishioners of the local St. Francis Xavier Church hold the **Our Lady of Fatima Processional and Blessing of the Fleet** (www.brunswick.net), begun in 1938 by the local Portuguese fishing community. After the procession, at about 3 P.M. at Mary Ross Waterfront Park, comes the actual blessing of the shrimp-boat fleet.

Foodies will enjoy the **Brunswick Stewbilee** ($9 adults, $4 children), held on the second Saturday in October 11:30 A.M.–3 P.M. Pro and amateur chefs match skills in creating the local signature dish and vying for the title of "Brunswick Stewmaster." There are also car shows, contests, displays, and much live music.

SHOPPING

Right in the heart of the bustle on Newcastle is a good indie bookstore, **Hattie's Books** (1531 Newcastle St., 912/554-8677, www.hatties-books.net, Mon.–Fri. 10 A.M.–5:30 P.M., Sat. 10 A.M.–4 P.M.). Not only do they have a good selection of local and regional authors, you can also get a good cup of coffee.

Like Beaufort, South Carolina, Brunswick has made the art gallery a central component of its downtown revitalization, with nearly all of them on Newcastle Street. Near Hattie's you'll find the eclectic **Kazuma Gallery** (1523 Newcastle St., 912/279-0023, Mon.–Fri. 10 A.M.–5:30 P.M., Sat. 10 A.M.–2 P.M.) as well as the **Ritz Theatre** (1530 Newcastle St., 912/262-6934, Tues.–Fri. 9 A.M.–5 P.M., Sat. 10 A.M.–2 P.M.), which has its own art gallery inside. Farther down is **The Gallery on Newcastle Street** (1626 Newcastle St., 912/554-0056, Thurs.–Sat. 11 A.M.–5 P.M.), showcasing the original oils of owner Janet Powers.

THE GOLDEN ISLES

SPORTS AND RECREATION
Hiking, Biking, and Bird-Watching

As one of the Colonial Coast Birding Trail sites, **Hofwyl-Broadfield Plantation** (5556 U.S. 17, 912/264-7333, www.gastateparks.org, Tues.– Sat. 9 A.M.–5 P.M., Sun. 2–5:30 P.M.) offers a great nature trail along the marsh. Clapper rails, marsh wrens, and a wide variety of warblers come through the site regularly.

Birders and hikers will also enjoy the **Earth Day Nature Trail** (1 Conservation Way, 912/264-7218), a self-guided, fully accessible walk where you can see such comparative rarities as the magnificent wood stork and other indigenous and migratory waterfowl. There are observation towers and binoculars available for checkout. To get here, take U.S. 17 south through Brunswick. Just north of the big Sidney Lanier Bridge, turn left on Conservation Way; you'll see signage and come to a parking lot.

Just across the Brunswick River from town is **Blythe Island Regional Park** (6616 Blythe Island Hwy., 912/261-3805), a 1,100-acre public park with a campground, picnic area, and boat landing. The views are great, and it's big enough to do some decent biking and hiking. The best way to get here is to get back on I-95 and head south.

Another scenic park with a campground is **Altamaha Park of Glynn County** (1605 Altamaha Park Rd., 912/264-2342), northwest of Brunswick off U.S. 341, with 30 campsites and a boat ramp.

Kayaking and Boating

Most recreational adventurers in the area prefer to launch from St. Simons Island. The key public landing in Brunswick, however, is **Brunswick Landing Marina** (2429 Newcastle St., 912/262-9264). You can also put in at the public boat ramps at **Blythe Island Regional Park,** which is on the Brunswick River, or the **Altamaha Park of Glynn County** (1605 Altamaha Park Rd., 912/264-2342), on the Altamaha River slightly north.

For expert guided tours at a reasonable price, check out **South East Adventures** (1200 Glynn Ave./U.S. 17, 912/265-5292, www.southeastadventure.com), which has a dock right on the fabled "Marshes of Glynn."

ACCOMMODATIONS

In addition to the usual variety of chain hotels—most of which you should stay far away from—there are some nice places to stay in Brunswick, if you want to make it a base of operations, at very reasonable prices. In the heart of Old Town in a gorgeous Victorian is the **❰ McKinnon House** (1001 Egmont St., 912/261-9100, www.mckinnonhousebandb. com, $125), which had a cameo role in the 1974 film *Conrack.* Today, this bed-and-breakfast is Jo Miller's labor of love, a three-suite affair with some plush interiors and an exterior that is one of Brunswick's most photographed spots. Surprisingly affordable for its elegance, the **WatersHill Bed & Breakfast** (728 Union St., 912/264-4262, www.watershill.com, $100) serves a full breakfast and offers a choice of five themed suites, such as the French country Elliot Wynell Room or the large Mariana Mahlaney room way up in the restored attic. Another good B&B is the **Brunswick Manor** (825 Egmont St., 912/265-6889, www.brunswickmanor.com, $130), offering four suites in a classic Victorian and a tasty meal each day.

The most unique lodging in the area is the **❰ Hostel in the Forest** (Hwy. 82, 912/264-9738, www.foresthostel.com, $25, cash only), essentially a group of geodesic domes and whimsical tree houses a little way off the highway. Formed over 30 years ago as an International Youth Hostel, the place initially gives off a hippie vibe, with an evening communal meal (included in the rates) and a near-total ban on cell phones. But don't expect a wild time: No pets are allowed, the hostel discourages young children, and quiet time is strictly enforced at 11 P.M. It's an adventurous, peaceful, and very inexpensive place to stay, but be warned that there is no heating or cooling. To reach the hostel, take I-95 exit 29 and go west for two miles. Make a U-turn at the intersection at mile marker 11. Continue east on Highway 82 for 0.5 miles. Look for a dirt road on the right with a gate and signage.

FOOD

Brunswick is notorious for its paucity of dining options, more so since the economic downturn claimed a few of the more notable names. The most famous restaurant in the Brunswick area is at the humble but renowned **Georgia Pig** (2712 U.S. 17 S., 912/264-6664, Mon.–Thurs. 11 A.M.–7 P.M., Fri.–Sat. 11 A.M.–9 P.M., Sun. 11 A.M.–8 P.M., $6–10). Go over the South Brunswick River on I-95 and take exit 29 onto U.S. 17 to find this roadside classic. It serves a good pulled-pork sandwich in the tomato-based sauce common to the region.

INFORMATION AND SERVICES

The **Brunswick-Golden Isles Visitor Center** (2000 Glynn Ave., 912/264-5337, daily 9 A.M.–5 P.M.) is at the intersection of U.S. 17 and the Torras Causeway to St. Simons Island. It features the famous pot in which the first batch of Brunswick stew was cooked over the bridge on St. Simons. A downtown **information station** is in the Ritz Theatre (1530 Newcastle St., 912/262-6934, Tues.–Fri. 9 A.M.–5 P.M., Sat. 10 A.M.–2 P.M.).

The newspaper of record in town is the **Brunswick News** (www.thebrunswicknews.com). The main **post office** (805 Gloucester St., 912/280-1250) is in downtown Brunswick.

GETTING THERE AND AROUND

Brunswick is directly off I-95. Take exit 38 to the Golden Isles Parkway, and take a right on U.S. 17. The quickest way to the historic district is to make a right onto Gloucester Street. Plans and funding for a city-wide public transit system are pending, but currently Brunswick has no public transportation.

Jekyll Island

Few places in the United States have as paradoxical a story as Jekyll Island. Once the playground of the world's richest people—whose indulgence allowed it to escape the overdevelopment that plagues nearby St. Simons—Jekyll then became a dedicated vacation area for Georgians of modest means, by order of the state legislature. Today, it's somewhere in the middle—a great place for a relaxing nature-oriented vacation with some of the perks of luxury owing to its Gilded Age pedigree.

HISTORY

In prehistoric times, Jekyll was mainly a seasonal getaway for Native Americans. Indigenous people visited the area during the winter to enjoy its temperate weather and abundant shellfish. The Spanish also knew it well, calling it Isla de Las Ballenas (Island of the Whales) for the annual gathering of calving right whale families directly off the coast every winter—a mystical event that happens to this day. After securing safe access to the island from the Creeks in 1733, Georgia's founder, General James Oglethorpe, gave the island its modern name, after his friend Sir Joseph Jekyll. The first English settler was Major William Horton in 1735, recipient of a land grant from the general, and the tabby ruins of one of Horton's homes remain today. A Frenchman, Christophe Du Bignon, purchased the island in 1800 and remained a leading figure. A mysterious event

THE GOLDEN ISLES

BRUNSWICK STEW

Of course, Virginians being Virginians, they'll insist that the distinctive Southern dish known as Brunswick stew was named for Brunswick County, Virginia, in 1828, where a political rally featured stew made from squirrel meat. But all real Southern foodies know the dish is named for Brunswick, Georgia. Hey, there's a plaque to prove it in downtown Brunswick—although it says the first pot was cooked on July 2, 1898, on St. Simons Island, not in Brunswick at all. However, I think we can all agree that "Brunswick stew" rolls off the tongue much more easily than "St. Simons stew."

In any case, it seems likely that what we now know as Brunswick stew is based on an old colonial recipe, adapted from Native Americans, that relied on the meat of small game—originally squirrel or rabbit but nowadays mostly chicken or pork—along with vegetables like corn, onions, and okra simmered over an open fire. Today, this tangy, thick, tomato-based delight is a typical accompaniment to barbecue along the Lowcountry and Georgia coasts, as well as a freestanding entrée on its own. Done traditionally and correctly, a proper pot of Brunswick stew is an involved kitchen project taking most of a day, but it's worth it. Here's a typical recipe from Glynn County, home of the famous Brunswick Stewbilee festival held the second Saturday of October:

SAUCE
Melt ¼ cup butter over low heat, then add:
1¾ cups ketchup
¼ cup yellow mustard
¼ cup white vinegar

Blend until smooth, then add:
½ tablespoon chopped garlic
1 teaspoon ground black pepper
½ teaspoon crushed red pepper
½ ounce Liquid Smoke
1 ounce Worcestershire sauce
1 ounce hot sauce
½ tablespoon fresh lemon juice

Blend until smooth, then add:
¼ cup dark brown sugar
Stir constantly and simmer for 10 minutes, being careful not to boil. Set aside.

STEW
Melt ¼ pound butter in a two-gallon pot, then add:
3 cups diced small potatoes
1 cup diced small onion
2 14½-ounce cans chicken broth
1 pound baked chicken
8-10 ounces smoked pork

Bring to a boil, stirring until potatoes are nearly done, then add:
1 8½-ounce can early peas
2 14½-ounce cans stewed tomatoes
1 16-ounce can baby lima beans
¼ cup Liquid Smoke
1 14½-ounce can creamed corn

Stir in sauce. Simmer slowly for two hours. Makes one gallon of Brunswick stew.

© JIM MOREKIS

The first Brunswick stew was cooked in this pot.

happened in 1858, when Jekyll Island was the final port of entry for the infamous voyage of *The Wanderer,* the last American slave ship. After intercepting the ship and its contraband manifest of 409 African slaves—the importation of slaves having been banned in 1807—its owners and crew were put on trial in Savannah.

As a home away from home for the country's richest industrialists—including J. P. Morgan, William Rockefeller, and William Vanderbilt—in the late 1800s and early 1900s, Jekyll Island was the unlikely seat of some of the most crucial events in modern American history. It was at the Jekyll Island Club that the Federal Reserve banking system was set up, in a secret convocation of investors and tycoons, in 1910. Five years later, AT&T President Theodore Vail, on the grounds of the club, would listen in on the first transcontinental phone call.

Jekyll's unspoiled beauty prompted the state legislature in 1947 to purchase the island and—ironically, considering the island's former history—declare it a totally accessible "playground" for Georgians of low to middle income (a causeway wasn't completed until the mid-1950s). This stated public mission is why prices on the island—currently administered on behalf of the state by the Jekyll Island Authority—have stayed so low and development has been so well managed. Every so often a controversial redevelopment plan is proposed, with the potential to introduce high-dollar resort-style development to parts of Jekyll for the first time since the days of J. P. Morgan and company. Residents and conservationists alike continue to work together to protect this magical barrier island known as "Georgia's Jewel."

ORIENTATION

You'll have to stop at the entrance gate and pay a $5 "parking fee" to gain access to this state-owned island. A friendly attendant will give you a map and newsletter, and from there you're free to enjoy the whole island at your leisure.

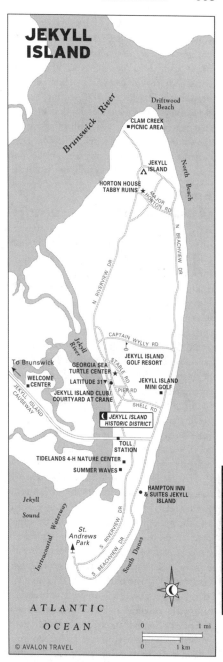

As you dead-end into Beachview Drive, you're faced with a decision to turn either left or right. Most scenic and social activity is to the north, a left turn. For more peaceful beach-oriented activity with few services, turn right and head south. One historical reason for the lesser development at the south end is due to the fact that segregation laws were still in effect after the state's purchase of Jekyll in 1947. African American facilities were centered on the south end, while white activities were in the north.

SIGHTS
◖ Jekyll Island Historic District

A living link to one of the most glamorous eras of American history, the Jekyll Island Historic District is also one of the largest ongoing restoration projects in the southeastern United States. A visit to this 240-acre riverfront area is like stepping back in time to the Gilded Age, with croquet grounds, manicured gardens, and even ferry boats with names like the *Rockefeller* and the *J. P. Morgan*. The Historic District essentially comprises the buildings and grounds of the old **Jekyll Island Club,** not only a full-service resort complex—consisting of the main building and several amazing "cottages" that are mansions themselves—but a sort of living history exhibit chronicling that time when Jekyll was a gathering place for the world's richest and most influential people.

The Queen Anne–style main clubhouse, with its iconic turret, dates from 1886. Within a couple of years the club had already outgrown it, and the millionaires began building the ornate cottages on the grounds surrounding it. The Chicora cottage is gone, demolished after the supposedly accidental gunfire death of Edwin Gould in 1917, with only a hole in the ground remaining, but most of the others have been fully restored as lodgings. In 2000 a renovation took place for the most magnificent outbuilding, the 24-bedroom Crane Cottage, a Mediterranean villa that also hosts a fine restaurant. The most

recent renovation was the 2010 reopening of the Indian Mound Cottage, once William Rockefeller's vacation getaway, to tours.

The **Jekyll Island Museum** (100 Stable Rd., 912/635-4036, www.jekyllisland.com, daily 9 A.M.–5 P.M., free), in the Historic District at the old club stables, houses some good history exhibits. The museum also provides a number of guided themed tours (daily 11 A.M., 1 P.M., and 3 P.M., $16 adults, $8 ages 6–12) focusing on the Historic District, including the popular "Passport to the Century" (which includes entrance to two restored cottages) and "In the Service of Others" (focusing on the support staff of the golden age of the Jekyll Island Club). You can also purchase a guidebook for self-guided tours of the Historic District.

Georgia Sea Turtle Center

Within the grounds of the Historic District in a whimsically renovated historic 1903 building is the Georgia Sea Turtle Center (214 Stable Rd., 912/635-4444, www.georgiaseaturtle-center.org, Mon. 10 A.M.–2 P.M., Tues.–Sun. 9 A.M.–5 P.M., $6 adults, $4 children), which features interactive exhibits on these important marine creatures, for whom Jekyll Island is a major nesting ground. Don't miss the attached rehabilitation building, where you can see the Center's turtles in various states of treatment and rehabilitation before being released into the wild. Children and adults alike will enjoy this unique opportunity to see these creatures up close and learn about the latest efforts to protect them.

Helping to raise awareness about the need to protect the nesting areas of the big loggerheads that lay eggs on Jekyll each summer, the Sea Turtle Center also guides nighttime tours (early June–Aug. daily 8:30 P.M. and 9:30 P.M.) on the beach in order to explain about the animals and their habitat and hopefully to see some loggerheads in action. These tours fill up fast, so make reservations in advance.

JEKYLL ISLAND'S MILLIONAIRE'S CLUB

After the Civil War, as the Industrial Revolution gathered momentum seemingly everywhere but Georgia's Golden Isles, a couple of men decided to do something to break the foggy miasma of Reconstruction that had settled into the area and make some money in the process. In the late 1870s, John Eugene DuBignon and his brother-in-law Newton Finney came up with a plan to combine DuBignon's long family ties to Jekyll with Finney's extensive Wall Street connections in order to turn Jekyll into an exclusive winter hunting club. Their targeted clientele was a no-brainer: the newly minted American mega-tycoons of the Industrial Age. Finney found 53 such elite millionaires willing to pony up to become charter members of the venture, dubbed the Jekyll Island Club. Among them were William Vanderbilt, J.P. Morgan, and Joseph Pulitzer. As part of the original business model, in 1886 Finney purchased the island from DuBignon for $125,000.

With the formal opening two years later began Jekyll Island's half-century as a premier playground for the country's richest citizens, centered on the Victorian winter homes, called "cottages," built by each member and preserved today in the Historic District. While it was formed as a hunt club, the Jekyll Island Club welcomed the millionaires' families. In the 1920s, the focus began shifting to golf, and you can still play a portion of the historic course at the club today. By 1900 the club's membership represented one-sixth of the world's wealth. And the word *exclusive* has never been more appropriate: Nonmembers were not allowed to enjoy the facilities, regardless of social stature. Winston Churchill and even President McKinley were refused admission.

As the mega-rich are wont to do even today, these influential men often mixed business with pleasure. In 1910, secret meetings of the so-called "First Name Club" led to the development of the Aldrich Plan, which laid the groundwork for the modern Federal Reserve System.

Under assumed names, Senator Nelson Aldrich, Assistant Treasury Secretary A. Piatt Andrew, Banker's Trust vice president Benjamin Strong, National City Bank president Frank Vanderlip, investment banker Paul Warburg, and J.P. Morgan partner Henry P. Davison came into the Club with the cover story of participating in a duck hunt. After they arrived by train at Brunswick, the stationmaster told them the cat was out of the bag and a gaggle of reporters had already gathered. But Davison took the stationmaster aside, saying, "Come out, old man, I will tell you a story." Returning a few minutes later, Davison told his colleagues, "That's all right. They won't give us away." What Davison's "story" was remains a mystery, but it must have been a pretty compelling one.

A few years later, AT&T president Theodore Vail, nursing a broken leg at his Mound Cottage on Jekyll, participated in the first transcontinental telephone call on January 25, 1915, among New York City, San Francisco, and the special line strung down the coast from New York and across Jekyll Sound to the club grounds. Also on the line were the telephone's inventor, Alexander Graham Bell, his assistant Thomas Watson, the mayors of New York and San Francisco, and President Woodrow Wilson.

The millionaires continued to frolic on Jekyll through the Great Depression, but worsening international economic conditions reduced membership, even though the cost of membership was lowered in 1933. The outbreak of World War II and the resulting drain of labor into the armed forces put a further cramp in the club's workings, and it finally closed for good in 1942. By the time prowling German U-boats began appearing off the Georgia coast, prompting island-wide blackouts, the Jekyll Island Club era already seemed like ancient history. The state would acquire the island after the war in 1947, turning the once-exclusive playground of millionaires into a playground for all the people.

© JIM MOREKIS

Jekyll Island's Driftwood Beach

Driftwood Beach

Barrier islands like Jekyll are in a constant state of southward flux as currents erode the north end and push sand down the beach to the south end. Hence the creation of Driftwood Beach, as the soil erodes from under the large trees, causing them to fall and settle into the sand. In addition to a naturalist's wonderland, it's also a starkly beautiful and strangely romantic spot. The newsletter you get as you enter the island has a map with Driftwood Beach on it, but here's a tip: Drive north on Beachview Drive until you see a pullover on your right immediately after the Villas by the Sea (there's no signage). Park and take the short trail through the maritime forest, and you'll find yourself right there among the fallen trees and sand.

Horton House Tabby Ruins

Round the curve and go south on Riverview Drive, and you'll see the large frame of a two-story house on the left (east) side of the road. That is the ruins of the old Horton House, built by Jekyll's original English-speaking setter, William Horton. Horton's house has survived two wars, a couple of hurricanes, and a clumsy restoration in 1898 to its current state of preservation at the hands of the Jekyll Island Authority and various federal, state, and local partners. His first house, also made of tabby, was burned by the Spanish during their retreat after losing the Battle of Bloody Marsh on nearby St. Simons Island. But the intrepid major rebuilt on the same spot in 1742, continuing to farm barley and indigo plants on the surrounding grounds as well as hosting Georgia's first brewery, the ruins of which are nearby.

Frenchman Christophe Poulain du Bignon would live in the Horton House for a while after purchasing the island in the 1790s. Across the street from the house is the poignant little **Du Bignon Cemetery,** around which winds a nicely done pedestrian and bike path overlooking one of the most beautiful areas of marsh you'll see in all the Golden Isles.

ENTERTAINMENT AND EVENTS

There's no real nightlife to speak of on Jekyll, it being intended for quiet, affordable daytime relaxation. The focus instead is on several annual events held at the **Jekyll Island Convention Center** (1 N. Beachview Dr., 912/635-3400), which has undergone a massive restoration to bring it in line with modern convention standards.

In the beginning of the new year comes one of the area's most beloved and well-attended events, the **Jekyll Island Bluegrass Festival** (www.aandabluegrass.com). Many of the genre's biggest traditional names come to play at this casual multiday gathering. The focus here is on the music, not the trappings, so come prepared to enjoy wall-to-wall bluegrass played by the best in the business. Keep in mind that during this weekend the island is awash in RVs from all over the country, so if you're camping, you'd better make reservations.

In September as the harvest comes in off the boats, the **Wild Georgia Shrimp and Grits Festival** (www.jekyllisland.com, free admission), seeks to promote the value of the Georgia shrimping industry by focusing on how good the little critters taste in various regional recipes.

SPORTS AND RECREATION
Hiking and Biking

Quite simply, Jekyll Island is a paradise for bicyclists and walkers, with a very well-developed and very safe system of paths, totaling about 20 miles, running the entire circumference of the island, going by all major sights, including the Jekyll Island Club in the Historic District. In addition, walkers and bicyclists can enjoy much of the seven miles of beachfront at low tide.

Rent your bikes at **Jekyll Island Miniature Golf** (100 James Rd., 912/635-2648, daily 9 A.M.–8 P.M., $5.25 per hour, $11.50 per day).

Take a left when you dead-end after the entrance gate, then another left.

Bird-Watching

The **Clam Creek Picnic Area** on the island's north end is on the Colonial Coast Birding Trail, and without even trying you will see a wide variety of wading birds and shorebirds. Shell collectors will also have a blast, as will those with a horticultural bent, who will marvel at the variety of species presented in the various ecosystems on the island, from beach to marsh hammock to maritime forest.

Golf and Tennis

True to Jekyll Island's intended role as a playground for Georgians of low to medium income, its golf and tennis facilities—all centrally located at the middle of the island—are quite reasonably priced. The **Jekyll Island Golf Resort** (322 Captain Wylly Rd., 912/635-2368, www.jekyllisland.com, green fees $40–60) comprises the largest public golf resort in Georgia. A total of 63 holes on four courses—Pine Lakes, Indian Mound, Oleander, and Ocean Dunes (nine holes)—await. Check the website for "golf passport" packages that include local lodging.

The adjacent **Jekyll Island Tennis Center** (400 Captain Wylly Rd., 912/635-3154, www.gate.net/~jitc, $25 per hour) boasts 13 courts, seven of them lighted, as well as a pro shop (daily 9 A.M.–6 P.M.).

If a different kind of golf is your thing, try **Jekyll Island Miniature Golf** (100 James Rd., 912/635-2648, Sun.–Thurs. 9 A.M.–8 P.M., Fri.–Sat. 9 A.M.–10 P.M., $6).

Fishing

Continuing north on Beachview Drive at the very top of the island is the well-done **Clam Creek Picnic Area** (daily dawn–dusk, free). This facility on the Colonial Coast Birding Trail has a spacious fishing pier over the Jekyll

River and a trailhead through the woods and out onto the beach. About a 20-minute walk on the sand gets you to Driftwood Beach from the other side.

A good local fishing charter company is Captain Vernon Reynolds's **Coastal Expeditions** (3202 E. 3rd St., 912/265-0392, www.coastalcharterfishing.com), departing from the Jekyll Harbor Marina. Half-day and full-day trips are available; call for rates.

Kayaking and Boating

Most kayaking activity in the area centers on St. Simons across the sound. But **Tidelands 4-H Nature Center** (100 Riverview Dr., 912/635-5032, www.tidelands4h.org) offers a variety of Jekyll-oriented guided kayak tours and also rents kayaks and canoes March–October.

Water Parks

Summer Waves (210 S. Riverview Dr., 912/635-2074, www.jekyllisland.com, Memorial Day–Labor Day, $20 adults, $16 children under 48 inches tall) is just what the doctor ordered for kids with a surplus of energy. The 11-acre facility has a separate section for toddlers to splash around in, with the requisite more daring rides for hard-charging preteens. Hours vary, so call ahead.

Horseback Riding and Tours

Victoria's Carriages and Trail (100 Stable Rd., 912/635-9500, Mon.–Sat. 11 A.M.–4 P.M.) offers numerous options, both on horseback as well as in a horse-drawn carriage, including carriage tours of the island (Mon.–Sat. every hour 11 A.M.–4 P.M., $15 adults, $7 children). There's a 6–8 P.M. night ride ($38 per couple). Horseback rides include a one-hour beach ride ($55) that leaves at 11 A.M., 1 P.M., and 3 P.M. and a sunset ride (6:30 P.M., $65) that lasts a little over an hour. Victoria's is at the entrance to the Clam Creek Picnic Area on the north

end of the island directly across the street from the Jekyll Island campground.

The **Tidelands 4-H Center** (912/635-5032) gives 1.5–2-hour Marsh Walks (Mon. 9 A.M., $5 adults, $3 children) leaving from Clam Creek Picnic Area, and Beach Walks ($5 adults, $3 children) leaving Wednesdays at 9 A.M. from the St. Andrews Picnic area and Fridays at 9 A.M. from South Dunes Picnic Area.

Captain Vernon Reynolds's **Coastal Expeditions** (3202 E. 3rd St., 912/265-0392, www.coastalcharterfishing.com, $24 adults, $10 children) provides dolphin tours March–May Tuesday–Saturday at 1:30 P.M., and three trips daily June–August.

ACCOMMODATIONS
Under $150

While most bargain lodging on Jekyll is sadly subpar, the old **Days Inn** (60 S. Beachview Dr., 912/635-9800, www.daysinnjekyll.com, $100) has seen a remodeling lately and is the best choice if budget is a concern (and you don't want to camp, that is). It has a good location on the south side of the island with nice ocean views.

$150-300

Any discussion of lodging on Jekyll Island begins with the legendary ◖ **Jekyll Island Club** (371 Riverview Dr., 800/535-9547, www.jekyllclub.com, $199–490), which is reasonably priced considering its history, postcard-perfect setting, and delightful guest rooms. Some of its 157 guest rooms in the club and annex areas are available for under $200, and even the finest, the Presidential Suite, tops out at under $500 in high season (Mar.–Oct.). There are 60 guest rooms are in the main club building, and several outlying cottages, chief among them the Crane, Cherokee, and Sans Souci Cottages, are also available. All rates include use of the big outdoor pool overlooking the river, and a neat amenity is a choice of meal plans for an extra daily fee.

Despite its auspicious beginnings, the club

© JIM MOREKIS

Jekyll Island Campground is a great place to spend the night.

has not been a total success story. The state tried to run it as a resort in the 1950s and 1960s but gave up in 1971. With Historic Landmark District status coming in 1978, restoration wasn't far behind, and the club was first run as a Radisson. Now operated by Landmark, the club is one of the "Historic Hotels of America" as ranked by the National Trust for Historic Preservation. Keep in mind that not all the fixtures are original and the present interior design scheme was done with an eye to current commercial taste (those crusty old millionaires would never have gone for pastels).

The first hotel built on the island in 35 years, the brand-new **◖ Hampton Inn & Suites Jekyll Island** (200 S. Beachview Dr., 912/635-3733, www.hamptoninn.com, $180–210) was built according to an exacting set of conservation guidelines, conserving much of the original tree canopy and various low-impact design and building techniques. Quite simply, it's one of the best ecofriendly hotel designs I've experienced.

An elevated wooden walkway to the beach preserves as much of the natural dune-scape as possible, though keep in mind that the tradeoff is that you can't see the ocean from the hotel. The beach isn't far away, and the walk-in saltwater pool is particularly enjoyable and relaxing.

Camping

One of the niftiest campgrounds in the entire area is the **Jekyll Island Campground** (197 Riverview Dr., 912/635-3021, tent sites $25, RV sites $32). It's a friendly place with an excellent location at the north end of the island—a short drive or bike ride from just about anywhere and directly across the street from the Clam Creek Picnic Area, with easy beach access. There are more than 200 sites, from tent to full-service pull-through RV sites. There's a two-night minimum on weekends and a three-night minimum on holiday and special event weekends; reservations are recommended.

FOOD

Cuisine offerings are few and far between on Jekyll. I'd suggest you patronize one of the three dining facilities at the **Jekyll Island Club** (371 Riverview Dr.), which are all open to non-guests. They're not only delicious but pretty reasonable as well, considering the swank setting. My favorite is the ◖**Courtyard at Crane** (912/635-2400, lunch Sun.–Fri. 11 A.M.–4 P.M., Sat. 11 A.M.–2 P.M., dinner Sun.–Thurs. 5:30–9 P.M., $27–38). In the circa-1917, beautifully restored Crane Cottage, one of the old tycoon villas, the Courtyard offers romantic evening dining (call for reservations) as well as tasty and stylish lunch dining in the alfresco courtyard area or inside. The lunch menu—a great deal for the quality—is Mediterranean heavy, with wraps, sandwiches, and soups. The dinner menu moves more toward wine-country casual chic, with a lot of pork, veal, and beef dishes to go with the requisite fresh seafood. As a plus, the coffee is great—not at all a given in Southern restaurants. Casual dress is OK.

For a real and figurative taste of history, make a reservation at the **Grand Dining Room** (912/635-2400, breakfast Mon.–Sat. 7–11 A.M., Sun. 7–10 A.M., lunch Mon.–Sat. 11:30 A.M.–2 P.M., brunch Sun. 10:45 A.M.–2 P.M., dinner daily 6–10 P.M., dinner $26–35), the club's full-service restaurant. Focusing on continental cuisine—ordered either à la carte or as a prix fixe "sunset dinner"—the Dining Room features a pianist each evening and for Sunday brunch. Jackets or collared shirts are required for men.

For a tasty breakfast, lunch, or dinner on the go or at odd hours, check out **Café Solterra** (912/635-2600, daily 7 A.M.–10 P.M.), great for deli-type food and equipped with Starbucks coffee. There are two places for seaside dining and cocktails at the historic Jekyll Island Club Wharf. **Latitude 31** (1 Pier Rd., 912/635-3800, www.crossoverjekyll.com, Tues.–Sun. 5:30–10 P.M., $15–25, no reservations) is an upscale seafood-oriented fine-dining place, while the attached **Rah Bar** (Tues.–Sat. 11 A.M.–close, Sun. 1 P.M.–close, depending on weather) serves up oysters and shellfish in a very casual setting; try the Lowcountry boil or the crab legs.

INFORMATION AND SERVICES

The **Jekyll Island Visitor Center** (901 Downing Musgrove Causeway, 912/635-3636, daily 9 A.M.–5 P.M.) is on the long causeway along the marsh before you get to the island. Set in a charming little cottage it shares with the Georgia State Patrol, the Center has a nice gift shop and loads of brochures on the entire Golden Isles region. Don't hesitate to ask questions of the person taking your $5 entrance fee when you get to the island itself.

The **U.S. Postal Service** keeps an outpost at 18 South Beachview Drive (912/635-2625).

GETTING THERE AND AROUND

Jekyll Island is immediately south of Brunswick. Take I-95 exit 38 to the Golden Isles Parkway. Take a right onto U.S. 17 and keep going until you cross the huge Sidney Lanier Bridge over the Brunswick River. Take an immediate left at the foot of the bridge onto the Downing Musgrove Causeway (Jekyll Island Rd.). This long, scenic route over the beautiful marshes eventually takes you directly onto Jekyll, where you'll have to pay a $5 per vehicle fee to get onto the island. Once on the island, most sites are on the north end (a left as you reach the dead-end at Beachview Dr.). The main circuit route around the island is Beachview Drive, which suitably enough changes into Riverview Drive as it rounds the bend to landward at the north end.

Many visitors choose to bicycle around the island once they're here, which is certainly the best way to experience both the sights and the beach itself at low tide.

St. Simons Island

Despite a certain reputation for aloof affluence, the truth is that St. Simons Island is also very visitor-friendly, and there's more to do here than meets the eye. Think of St. Simons—with a year-round population of about 13,000—as a smaller, less-hurried Hilton Head and you've got the right idea. For those looking for island-style relaxation with no high-rise cookie-cutter development—but still all the modern amenities and luxuries—St. Simons fits the bill perfectly. A major difference from Hilton Head is that St. Simons respects much of its history, and a lot of it is still left to enjoy, particularly the expansive and archaeologically significant Fort Frederica National Monument.

HISTORY

St. Simons Island and its much smaller, symbiotic neighbor Sea Island (originally Long Island) were well known to Native Americans as a hunting and fishing ground. Eventually the Spanish would have two missions on St. Simons, one at the south end and one at the north end, as well as a town for nonconverted native peoples called San Simon, which would eventually give the island its modern name. A lasting European influence didn't come until 1736 with General James Oglethorpe's construction of Fort Frederica. The fort and surrounding town was a key base of operations for the British struggle to evict the Spanish from Georgia—which culminated in the decisive Battle of Bloody Marsh south of the fort—but fell into decline after the Spanish threat subsided.

In the years after American independence, St. Simons woke up from its slumber as acre after acre of virgin live oak was felled to make the massive timbers of new warships for the U.S. Navy, including the USS *Constitution*. In their place was planted a new crop—cotton. The island's antebellum plantations boomed to world-class heights of profit and prestige when the superior strain of the crop known as Sea Island Cotton came in the 1820s.

On St. Simons in 1803, one of the most poignant chapters in the dark history of American slavery was written. In one of the first documented slave uprisings in North America, a group of slaves from the Igbo region of West Africa escaped custody and took over the ship that was transporting them to St. Simons from Savannah. But rather than do any further violence, immediately upon reaching shore on the west side of St. Simons, the slaves essentially committed mass suicide by walking into the swampy waters nearby, which forever after would be known as Ebo Landing (a corruption of the original Igbo).

The Civil War came to St. Simons in late 1861 with a Union blockade and invasion, leading Confederate troops to dynamite the lighthouse. Initially St. Simons was a sanctuary for freed slaves from the island's 14 plantations, and by late 1862 over 500 former slaves lived on St. Simons, including Susie King Taylor, who began a school for African American children. But in November of that year all former slaves were dispersed to Hilton Head and Fernandina, Florida. St. Simons was chosen as one of the implementation sites of General William Sherman's Special Field Order No. 15, the famous "40 acres and a mule" order giving the Sea Islands of South Carolina and Georgia to freed slaves. However, Sherman's order was quickly rescinded by President Andrew Johnson.

The next landmark development for St. Simons didn't come until the building of the first causeway in 1924, which led directly to the island's resort development by the mega-rich industrialist Howard Coffin of Hudson Motors fame, who also owned nearby Sapelo Island to the north. By 1928, Coffin had completed the

GOLDEN ISLES ON THE PAGE

And now from the Vast of the
Lord will the waters of sleep

Roll in on the souls of men,

But who will reveal to our waking ken

The forms that swim and
the shapes that creep

Under the waters of sleep?

And I would I could know what swim-
meth below when the tide comes in

On the length and the breath of the
marvelous marshes of Glynn.

Sidney Lanier

Many authors have been inspired by their time in the Golden Isles, whether to pen flights of poetic fancy, page-turning novels, or politically oriented chronicles. Here are a few of the most notable names:

· **Sidney Lanier:** Born in Macon, Georgia, Lanier was a renowned linguist, mathematician, and legal scholar. Fighting as a Confederate during the Civil War, he was captured while commanding a blockade runner and taken to a POW camp in Maryland, where he came down with tuberculosis. After the war, he stayed at his brother-in-law's house in Brunswick to recuperate, and it was during that time that he took up poetry, writing the famous "Marshes of Glynn," quoted above.

· **Eugenia Price:** Although not originally from St. Simons, Price remains the best-known local cultural figure, setting her *St. Simons Trilogy* here. After relocating to the island in 1965, she stayed here until her death in 1996. She's buried in the Christ Church cemetery on Frederica Road.

· **Tina McElroy Ansa:** Probably the most notable literary figure currently living on St. Simons Island is award-winning African American author Tina McElroy Ansa. Few of her books deal with the Golden Isles region, but they all deal with life in the South, and Ansa is an ardent devotee of St. Simons and its relaxed, friendly ways.

· **Fanny Kemble:** In 1834, this renowned English actress married Georgia plantation heir Pierce Butler, who would become one of the largest slave owners in the United States. Horrified by the treatment of Butler's slaves at Butler Island, just south of Darien, Georgia, Kemble penned one of the earliest antislavery chronicles, *Journal of a Residence on a Georgian Plantation in 1838-1839*. Kemble's disagreement with her husband over slavery hastened their divorce in 1849.

Sea Island Golf Club on the grounds of the old Retreat Plantation on the south end of St. Simons Island. He would move on to develop the famous Cloisters resort on Long Island (later Sea Island) itself.

ORIENTATION

Because it's only a short drive from downtown Brunswick on the Torras Causeway, St. Simons has much less of a remote feel than most other Georgia barrier islands and is much more densely populated than any other Georgia island except for Tybee. Most visitor-oriented activity on this 12-mile-long, heavily residential island about the size of Manhattan is clustered at the south end, where St. Simons Sound meets the Atlantic. The main reasons to travel north on the island are to golf or visit the historic site of Fort Frederica on the landward side.

The main roads to remember are Kings Way, which turns into Ocean Boulevard as it nears the active south end of the island, called

"The Village"; Demere ("DEM-er-ee") Road, which loops west to east around the little island airport and then south, joining up with Ocean Boulevard down near the lighthouse; Frederica Road, the dominant north–south artery; and Mallory Street, which runs north–south through the Village area and dead-ends at the pier on St. Simons Sound. (You'll notice that Mallory Street is sometimes spelled "Mallery," which is actually the correct spelling of the avenue's namesake: Mallery King, child of Thomas King, owner of the historic Retreat Plantation.)

SIGHTS
◀ The Village

Think of "The Village" at the extreme south end of St. Simons as a mix of Tybee's downscale accessibility and Hilton Head's upscale exclusivity. This compact, bustling area only a few blocks long offers not only boutique shops and stylish cafés but vintage stores and busking musicians. While visitors and residents here tend toward the affluent, they also tend not to be as flashy about it as in some other locales. You'll find the vast majority of quality eating spots here, along with most quality lodging. It's fun to meander down Mallory Drive, casually shopping or noshing, and then make your way out onto the short but fun **St. Simons Pier** to enjoy the breeze and occasional spray coming off the sound. The long, low, sprawling building immediately to the north overlooking the expanse of Massengale Park is the old Casino building, now used for local government offices and community meetings.

St. Simons Lighthouse Museum

Unlike many East Coast lighthouses, which tend to be in hard-to-reach places, anyone can walk right up to the St. Simons Lighthouse Museum (101 12th St., 912/638-4666,

The Village is the center of activity on St. Simons Island.

© JIM MOREKIS

THE GOLDEN ISLES

www.saintsimonslighthouse.org, Mon.–Sat. 10 A.M.–5 P.M., Sun. 1:30–5 P.M., $6 adults, $3 children). Once inside, you can enjoy the museum's exhibit and take the 129 steps up to the top of the 104-foot beacon—which is, unusually, still active—for a gorgeous view of the island and the ocean beyond. The museum offers a "Family of Four" package admission ($25) for two adults and two children as well as a combo ticket to the nearby Maritime Center ($10 adults, $5 children).

The first lighthouse on the spot came about after planter John Couper sold this land, known as Couper's Point, to the government in 1804 for $1. This original beacon was destroyed by retreating Confederate troops in 1862 to hinder Union navigation on the coast. Traces of its foundations are near the current facility. The current lighthouse dates from 1872, built by Irishman Charles Cluskey, who was responsible for a lot of Greek Revival architecture up and down the Georgia coast. Attached to the lighthouse is the oldest brick structure in Glynn County, the 1872 lighthouse keeper's cottage, now the museum and gift shop run by the Coastal Georgia Historical Society.

Maritime Center

A short walk from the lighthouse and also administered by the Coastal Georgia Historical Society, the Maritime Center (4201 1st St., 912/638-4666, www.saintsimonslighthouse.org, Mon.–Sat. 10 A.M.–5 P.M., Sun. 1:30–5 P.M., $6 adults, $3 children) is at the historic East Beach Coast Guard Station. Authorized by President Franklin Roosevelt in 1933 and completed in 1937 by the Works Progress Administration, the East Beach Station took part in military action in World War II, an episode chronicled in exhibits at the Maritime Center. On April 8, 1942, the German U-boat U-123 torpedoed and sank two cargo ships off the coast of St. Simons Island. The Coast Guardsmen of East Beach station mounted a full rescue effort, saving many crewmen of the merchant ships, including one ship's canine mascot. The Coast Guard's tenure on East Beach ended after a 1993 fire burned down their boathouse. Two years later the station was decommissioned, and the Coasties moved to a new station in Brunswick.

The Maritime Center offers a "Family of Four" package admission ($25) for two adults and two children as well as a combo ticket to the St. Simons Lighthouse ($10 adults, $5 children).

◖ Fort Frederica National Monument

The expansive and well-researched Fort Frederica National Monument (Frederica Rd., 912/638-3639, www.nps.gov/fofr, daily 9 A.M.–5 P.M., $3 adults, free under age 15) lies on the landward side of the island. Established by General James Oglethorpe in 1736 to protect Georgia's southern flank from the Spanish, the fort (as well as the village that sprang up around it, in which the Wesley brothers preached for a short time) was named for Frederick Louis, the Prince of Wales. The feminine suffix -a was added to distinguish it from the older Fort Frederick in South Carolina.

You don't just get to see a military fort here (actually the remains of the old powder magazine; most of the fort itself eroded into the river long ago); this is an entire colonial town site a mile in circumference, originally modeled after a typical English village. A self-guided walking tour through the beautiful grounds—the oak trees here have the longest, most luxurious Spanish moss I've ever seen—shows foundations of building sites that have been uncovered, including taverns, shops, and the private homes of influential citizens. Closer to the river is the large tabby structure of the garrison barracks.

As for the actual fort itself, from its location astride a bend in the Frederica River you

Fort Frederica on St. Simons Island

can instantly see why this was such a strategic location, guarding the approach to the great Altamaha River. The Frederica garrison took part in the unsuccessful attack on St. Augustine, Florida, in 1740 and was also the force that sallied out of the fort and southward to repulse the Spanish at Bloody Marsh two years later.

Take in the accompanying exhibits in the visitors center, including a 23-minute film shown every half-hour 9 A.M.–4 P.M., which is actually quite good. A park ranger also gives informative talks throughout the day, and there are occasional reenactments by uniformed colonial "soldiers."

Bloody Marsh Battlefield

There's not a lot to see at the site of the Battle of Bloody Marsh (Frederica Rd., 912/638-3639, www.nps.gov/fofr, daily 8 A.M.–4 P.M., free), but—as with the similarly stirring site of Custer's Last Stand at the Little Bighorn—your

imagination fills in the gaps, giving it perhaps more emotional impact than other, more substantial historic sites.

Essentially just a few interpretive signs overlooking a beautiful piece of salt marsh, the site is believed to be near the place where British soldiers from nearby Fort Frederica ambushed a force of Spanish regulars on their way to besiege the fort. Frederica's garrison, the 42nd Regiment of Foot, was augmented by a company of tough Scottish Highlanders from Darien, Georgia, who legend says attacked to the tune of bagpipes. The battle wasn't actually that bloody—some accounts say the Spanish lost only seven men—but the stout British presence convinced the Spanish to leave St. Simons a few days later, never again to project their once-potent military power that far north in the New World.

While the Battle of Bloody Marsh site is part of the National Park Service's Fort Frederica site, it's not at the same location. Get to the

© JIM MOREKIS

battlefield from the fort by taking Frederica Road south, and then a left (east) on Demere Road. The site is on your left as Demere Road veers right, in the 1800 block.

Christ Church

Just down the road from Fort Frederica is historic Christ Church (6329 Frederica Rd., 912/638-8683, www.christchurchfrederica. org, daily 2–5 P.M.). The first sanctuary dates from 1820, but the original congregation at the now-defunct town of Frederica held services under the oaks at the site as early as 1736. The founder of Methodism, John Wesley, and his brother Charles both ministered to island residents during 1736–1737.

The original church was rendered unusable by Union occupation during the Civil War. A handsome new church, the one you see today, was funded and built in 1883 by a local mill owner, Anson Dodge, as a memorial to his first wife. But Christ Church's claim to fame in modern culture is as the setting of local novelist Eugenia Price's *The Beloved Invader,* the first work in her Georgia trilogy. The late Price, who died in 1996, is buried in the church cemetery.

Tours

St. Simons Island Trolley Tours (912/638-8954, www.stsimonstours.com, daily 11 A.M., $22 adults, $10 age 4–12, free under age 4) offers just that, a ride around the island in comparative comfort, leaving from the pier.

ENTERTAINMENT AND EVENTS
Nightlife

St. Simons is far from Charleston's or Savannah's league when it comes to partying, but there is a fairly active nightlife scene, with a strong dose of island casual. Unlike some areas this far south on the Georgia coast, there's usually a sizeable contingent of young people out looking for a good time. The island's premier

club, **Rafters Blues and Raw Bar** (315½ Mallory St., 912/634-9755, www.raftersblues. com, Mon.–Sat. 4:30 P.M.–2 A.M.), known simply as "Rafters," brings in live music most every Thursday–Saturday night, focusing on the best acts on the regional rock circuit.

My favorite spot on St. Simons for a drink or an espresso—or a panini for that matter—is **Palm Coast Coffee, Cafe, and Pub** (316 Mallory St., 912/634-7517, www.palmcoastssi. com, daily 8 A.M.–10 P.M.). This handy little spot, combining a hip, relaxing coffeehouse with a hearty menu of brunchy items, is in the heart of the village. The kicker, though, is the cute little bar the size of a large walk-in closet right off the side of the main room—a little bit of Key West on St Simons. Mondays are open mike nights.

Inside the Village Inn is the popular nightspot the **Village Pub** (500 Mallory St., 912/634-6056, www.villageinnandpub.com, Mon.–Sat. 5 P.M.–midnight, Sun. 5–10 P.M.). Slightly more upscale than most watering holes on the island, this is the best place for a quality martini or other premium cocktail.

Performing Arts

Because of its close proximity to Brunswick, a short drive over the bridge, St. Simons has a symbiotic relationship with that larger city in areas of art and culture. Each summer, beginning Memorial Day weekend and continuing into September, there are several Jazz in the Park concerts by regional artists. The shows are usually Sunday 7–9 P.M. on the lawn of the St. Simons Lighthouse, and the beautiful setting and calming breeze is a delight. Admission is charged; bring a chair or blanket if you like.

Cinema

The island has its own multiplex, the **Island Cinemas 7** (44 Cinema Lane, 912/634-9100, www.georgiatheatrecompany.com).

SHOPPING

Most shopping on St. Simons is centered in the Village and is a typical beach town mix of hardware and tackle, casual clothing, and souvenir stores. A funky highlight is **Beachview Books** (215 Mallory St., 912/638-7282, Mon.–Sat. 10:30 A.M.–5:30 P.M., Sun. 11:30 A.M.–3 P.M.), a rambling used bookstore with lots of regional and local goodies, including books by the late great local author Eugenia Price. Probably the best antiques shop in this part of town is **Village Mews** (504 Beachview Dr., 912/634-1235, Mon.–Sat. 10 A.M.–5 P.M.).

The closest thing to a mall is farther north on St. Simons at **Redfern Village,** with some cute indie stores like **Beach Cottage Linens** (912/634-2000, Mon.–Fri. 10 A.M.–5:30 P.M., Sat. 10 A.M.–5 P.M.), **Thomas P. Dent Clothiers** (912/638-3118, Mon.–Sat. 9:30 A.M.–6 P.M.), and the craftsy **Rarebbits and Pieces** (912/638-2866, Mon.–Sat. 10 A.M.–5:30 P.M.). Redfern Village is on Frederica Road, one traffic light past the corner of Frederica Road and Demere Road.

SPORTS AND RECREATION
Beaches

Keep going from the pier past the lighthouse to find **Massengale Park** (daily dawn–dusk), with a playground, picnic tables, and restrooms right off the beach on the Atlantic side. The beach itself on St. Simons is underwhelming compared to some in these parts, but nonetheless it's easily accessible from the pier area and good for a romantic stroll if it's not high tide. There's a great playground, Neptune Park, right next to the pier overlooking the waterfront.

Kayaking and Boating

With its relatively sheltered landward side nestled in the marsh and an abundance of wildlife, St. Simons Island is an outstanding kayaking site, attracting connoisseurs from all over. A good spot to put in on the Frederica River is the **Golden Isles Marina** (206 Marina Dr.,

912/634-1128, www.gimarina.com), which is actually on little Lanier Island on the Torras Causeway right before you enter St. Simons proper. For a real adventure, put in at the ramp at the end of South Harrington Street off Frederica Road, which will take you out Village Creek on the seaward side of the island.

Undoubtedly the best kayaking outfitter and tour operator in this part of the Golden Isles is **SouthEast Adventure Outfitters** (313 Mallory St., 912/638-6732, www.southeastadventure.com, daily 10 A.M.–6 P.M.), which also has a location in nearby Brunswick. Michael Gowen and company offer an extensive range of guided tours all over the St. Simons marsh and sound area as well as trips to undeveloped Little St. Simons Island to the north. Prices vary, so call or go to the website for information.

Hiking and Biking

Like Jekyll Island, St. Simons is a great place for bicyclists. Bike paths go all over the island, and a special kick is riding on the beach almost the whole length of the island (but only at high tide). There are plenty of bike rental spots, with rates generally $15–20 per day depending on the season. The best place to rent bikes is **Monkey Wrench Bicycles** (1700 Frederica Rd., 912/634-5551). You can rent another kind of pedal-power at **Wheel Fun Rentals** (532 Ocean Blvd., 912/634-0606), which deals in four-seat pedaled carts with steering wheels.

Golf and Tennis

A popular place for both sports is the **Sea Palms Golf and Tennis Resort** (5445 Frederica Rd., 800/841-6268, www.seapalms.com, green fees $70–80) in the middle of the island, with three nine-hole public courses and three clay courts. The **Sea Island Golf Club** (100 Retreat Rd., 800/732-4752, www.seaisland.com, green fees $185–260) on the old Retreat Plantation as you first come onto the island has two award-winning 18-hole courses, the Seaside and the Plantation. Another public course is the 18-hole **Hampton Club** (100 Tabbystone Rd., 912/634-0255, www.hamptonclub.com, green fees $95) on the north side of the island, part of the King and Prince Beach and Golf Resort.

ACCOMMODATIONS
Under $150

A charming and reasonable place a stone's throw from the Village is ❰ **Queens Court** (437 Kings Way, 912/638-8459, $85–135), a traditional roadside motel from the late 1940s, with modern upgrades that include a nice outdoor pool in the central courtyard area. Despite its convenient location, you'll feel fairly secluded.

One of the most interesting lodgings in the Lowcountry and Georgia coast is **Epworth by the Sea** (100 Arthur J. Moore Dr., 912/638-8688, www.epworthbythesea.org, $90–100). This Methodist retreat in the center of the island boasts an entire complex of freestanding motels and lodges on its grounds, in various styles and configurations. Cafeteria-style meetings are the order of the day, and there are plenty of recreational activities on-site, including tennis, volleyball, baseball, football, soccer, and basketball. They also rent bikes, which is always a great way to get around St. Simons. Everyone loves the **Lovely Lane Chapel,** a picturesque sanctuary that is a favorite spot for weddings and holds services Sunday at 8:45 A.M. (casual dress OK). Researchers can utilize the resources of the **Arthur J. Moore Methodist Museum and Library** (Tues.–Sat. 9 A.M.–4 P.M.).

You couldn't ask for a better location than the **St. Simons' Inn by the Lighthouse** (609 Beachview Dr., 912/638-1101, www.saintsimonsinn.com, $120–300), which is indeed in the shadow of the historic lighthouse and right next to the hopping Village area. A so-called "condo-hotel," each of the standard and deluxe

suites at the Inn are individually owned by off-site owners—however, each guest gets full maid service and a complimentary breakfast.

$150-300

The best-known lodging on St. Simons Island is the ❰ **King and Prince Beach and Golf Resort** (201 Arnold Rd., 800/342-0212, $249–320). Originally opened as a dance club in 1935, the King and Prince brings a swank old-school glamour similar to the Jekyll Island Club (though less imposing). And like the Jekyll Island Club, the King and Prince is also designated as one of the Historic Hotels of America. Its nearly 200 guest rooms are spread over a complex that includes several buildings, including the historic main building, beach villas, and freestanding guesthouses. Some standard rooms can go for under $200 even in the spring high season. Winter rates for all guest rooms are appreciably lower and represent a great bargain. For a dining spot overlooking the sea, try the **Blue Dolphin** (lunch daily 11 A.M.–4 P.M., dinner daily 5–10 P.M., $15–30). The Resort's Hampton Club provides golf for guests and the public.

An interesting B&B on the island that's also within walking distance of most of the action on the south end is the 28-room **Village Inn & Pub** (500 Mallory St., 912/634-6056, www.villageinnandpub.com, $160–245), nestled among shady palm trees and live oaks. The pub, a popular local hangout in a renovated 1930 cottage, is a nice plus.

Over $300

Affiliated with the Sea Island Resort, the **Lodge at Sea Island** (100 Retreat Ave., 912/638-3611, $650–2,500) is actually on the south end of St. Simons Island on the old Retreat Plantation. Its 40 grand guest rooms and suites all have great views of the Atlantic Ocean, the associated Plantation Course links, or both. Full butler service makes this an especially pampered and aristocratic stay.

FOOD

While the ambience at St. Simons has an upscale feel, don't feel like you have to dress up to get a bite to eat—the emphasis is on relaxation and having a good time.

Breakfast and Brunch

⟨C Palmer's Village Cafe (223 Mallory St., 912/634-5515, www.palmersvillagecafe.com, Tues.–Sun. 7:30 A.M.–2 P.M., $10–15), formerly called Dressner's, is right in the middle of the Village's bustle. It's one of the island's most popular places but still with enough seats so you usually don't have to wait. Sandwiches and burgers are great, but breakfast all day is the real attraction and includes lovingly crafted omelets, hearty pancakes, and a "build your own biscuit" menu.

Named for the birthday that the original three co-owners share, **Fourth of May Deli** (444 Ocean Blvd., 912/638-5444, breakfast daily 7 A.M.–1 P.M., lunch daily 11 A.M.–9 P.M., $8–20) is a popular breakfast and lunch place in the Village. Breakfast focuses on specialties like eggs benedict and huevos rancheros, along with some fantastic breakfast burritos, a comparative rarity in the South.

Seafood

Despite its somewhat unappetizing name, **Mullet Bay** (512 Ocean Blvd., 912/634-9977, daily 11:30 A.M.–10 P.M., $7–18) in the Village is a favorite good old-fashioned Southern seafood place, the kind where you get a big fried platter with two sides and hushpuppies. A popular seafood place right in the action in the Village is **Barbara Jean's** (214 Mallory St., 912/634-6500, www.barbarajeans.com, Sun.–Thurs. 11 A.M.–9 P.M., Fri.–Sat. 11 A.M.–10 P.M., $7–20), which also has a great variety of imaginative veggie dishes to go along with its formidable seafood menu, including some excellent she-crab soup and crab cakes. They also have plenty of good landlubber treats for those not inclined to the marine critters.

Fine Dining

⟨C J. Mac's Island Restaurant (407 Mallory St., 912/634-0403, www.jmacsislandrestaurant.com, Tues.–Sat. 6–9 P.M., $20–30) is the Village's high-end restaurant, one that wouldn't be out of place in downtown Charleston or Savannah. Owner J. Mac Mason and head chef Connor Rankin conspire to bring a fresh take on Southern and seafood classics, with adventurous entrées like seared "Creamsicle" marlin with jumbo asparagus and sweet corn puree-seared filet with gorgonzola and herb gratin.

Inside the King and Prince Resort, you'll find the old-school glory of the **Blue Dolphin** (201 Arnold Rd., 800/342-0212, lunch daily 11 A.M.–4 P.M., dinner daily 5–10 P.M., $15–30), redolent of the *Great Gatsby* era. The Blue Dolphin claims to be the only oceanfront dining on the island, and the views are certainly magnificent.

INFORMATION AND SERVICES

The **St. Simons Visitors Center** (530-B Beachview Dr., 912/638-9014, www.bgivb.com, daily 9 A.M.–5 P.M.) is in the St. Simons Casino Building near Neptune Park and the Village. The main newspaper in St. Simons is the *Brunswick News* (www.thebrunswicknews.com). The **U.S. Postal Service** (800/275-8777) has an office at 620 Beachview Drive.

GETTING THERE AND AROUND

Get to St. Simons through the gateway city of Brunswick. Take I-95 exit 38 for Golden Isles, which will take you to the Golden Isles Parkway. Take a right onto U.S. 17 and look for the intersection with the Torras Causeway, a toll-free road that takes you the short distance onto St. Simons.

Immediately as you cross the Frederica River onto the island, look for a quick right onto Kings Way to take you directly to the Village area. You can also take a quick left onto Demere Road to reach Frederica Road and the more northerly portion of the island, where you'll find Fort Frederica and Christ Church.

LITTLE ST. SIMONS ISLAND

This 10,000-acre privately owned island, accessible only by water, is almost totally undeveloped—thanks to its salt-stressed trees, which discouraged timbering—and boasts seven miles of beautiful beaches. All activity centers on the circa-1917 **[Lodge on Little St. Simons Island** (1000 Hampton Point Dr., 888/733-5774, www.littlestsimonsisland.com, from $625), named by *Condé Nast Traveler* as the top U.S. mainland resort in 2007. Within it lies the famed Hunting Lodge, where meals and cocktails are served. With 15 ultra-plush guest rooms and suites in an assortment of historic buildings, all set amid gorgeous natural beauty—there are five full-time naturalists on staff—the Lodge is a reminder of what St. Simons proper used to look like. The guest count is limited to 30 people.

Getting There and Around

Unless you enlist the aid of a local kayaking charter company, you have to be a guest of the Lodge to have access to Little St. Simons. The ferry, a 15-minute ride, leaves from a landing at the northern end of St. Simons at the end of Lawrence Road. Guests have full use of bicycles

once on the island and can also request shuttle transportation just about anywhere.

SEA ISLAND

The only way to enjoy Sea Island—basically a tiny appendage of St. Simons facing the Atlantic Ocean—is to be a guest at **[The Sea Island Resort** (888/732-4752, www.seaisland.com, from $700). And guests visiting now are truly lucky; the legendary facility, routinely ranked as one of the best resorts on the planet, completed extensive renovations in 2008. Unfortunately, the economic downturn sent the institution into bankruptcy as of this writing; they do plan to stay in business, however. The rooms at the Resort's premier lodging institution, **The Cloister,** nearly defy description—enveloped in Old World luxury, they also boast 21st-century technology. And the service at The Cloister is equally world-class, featuring 24-hour butler service in the European tradition. There are hundreds of cottages for rental on Sea Island as well, all of which grant temporary membership in the Sea Island Club and full use of its many amenities and services.

Getting There and Around

Get to Sea Island by taking Torras Causeway onto the island and then making a left onto Sea Island Causeway, which takes you all the way to the gate marking the only land entrance to Sea Island.

Darien and McIntosh County

It doesn't get near the attention or the number of visitors as Savannah to the north or the St. Simons–Jekyll area to the south, but the small fishing and shrimping village of Darien in McIntosh County has an interesting historic pedigree of its own. It is centrally located near some of the best treasures the Georgia coast has to offer, including the Harris Neck National Wildlife Refuge, the beautiful Altamaha River, and the sea island of Sapelo, and it also boasts what many believe to be the best traditional seafood restaurants in the state.

HISTORY

Unlike Anglophilic Savannah to the north, the Darien area has had a distinctly Scottish flavor from the beginning. In 1736, Scottish Highlanders established a settlement at the mouth of the Altamaha River at the bequest of General James Oglethorpe, who wanted the tough Scots protecting his southern border against the Spanish. The colony was at the site of an earlier English effort, the abandoned Fort King George, but they came up with a new name, Darien, honoring the failed 1697 settlement in Panama. Leading them was John McIntosh Mohr, who would go on to father several sons who would become famous in their own right and eventually lend his surname to the county. The Scots brought a singularly populist sentiment to the New World. When Georgia planters lobbied to legalize slavery, which was outlawed by Oglethorpe, the Scots of Darien signed a petition against them in 1739—believed to be the first organized protest of slavery in America. The Darien settlers were also known for keeping more cordial relations with the Native Americans than the area's English settlements. Of course, they were a frugal bunch too.

Darien's heyday was unquestionably in that antebellum period, when for a brief time the town was the world's largest exporter of cotton, floated downriver on barges and shipped out through the port of Darien. The Bank of Darien was the largest bank south of Philadelphia in the early 1800s. A prosperous rice culture grew up around the Altamaha estuary as well, relying on the tidal flow of the area's acres and acres of marsh. Almost nothing from this period remains, however, because on June 11, 1863, a force of mostly African American Union troops under the command of Colonel Robert G. Shaw (portrayed in the movie *Glory*) burned Darien to the ground, with all its homes and warehouses going up in smoke.

After the Civil War, lumber became the new cash crop, and Darien once again became a thriving seaport and mill headquarters. The late 1800s saw a new reliance on shrimping and oystering, industries that survive to this day. A different kind of industry prospered in the years after World War II. In those pre–interstate highway days, U.S. 17 was the main route south to booming Florida. McIntosh County got a bad reputation for "clip joints," which would fleece gullible travelers with a variety of illegal schemes. This period is recounted in the best-seller *Praying for Sheetrock* by Melissa Fay Greene.

SIGHTS
Smallest Church in North America

While several other churches claim that title, in any case fans of the devout and of roadside kitsch alike will enjoy the tiny and charming little **Memory Park Christ Chapel** (U.S. 17, daily 24 hours). Built in 1949 by local grocer Agnes Harper, the church—which contains a pulpit and chairs for a dozen people—was intended as a round-the-clock travelers' sanctuary

© JIM MOREKIS

Memory Park Christ Chapel, the "Smallest Church in North America"

on what was then the main coastal road, U.S. 17. Upon her death, Harper simply willed the church to Jesus Christ. The stained-glass windows are imported from England, and there's a guestbook so you can leave any note of appreciation. Get there by taking I-95 exit 67 and going south a short way on U.S. 17; the church is on the east side of the road.

◖ Harris Neck National Wildlife Refuge

Literally a stone's throw away from the "Smallest Church" is the turnoff east onto the seven-mile Harris Neck Road leading to the Harris Neck National Wildlife Refuge (912/832-4608, www.fws.gov/harrisneck, daily dawn–dusk, free). In addition to being one of the single best sites in the South from which to view wading birds and waterfowl in their natural habitat, Harris Neck also has something of a poignant backstory. For generations after the Civil War, an African American community descended from the area's original slaves quietly struggled to eke out a living by fishing and farming. But their land was taken by the federal government in World War II to build a U.S. Army Air Force base, primarily to train pilots on the P-40 Tomahawk fighter, the same plane used by the famed Flying Tigers. After the war, the base was decommissioned and given to McIntosh County as a municipal airport. But the notoriously corrupt local government so mismanaged the facility that the feds once again took it over, eventually transferring it to the forerunner of the U.S. Fish and Wildlife Service.

Now a nearly 3,000-acre nationally protected refuge, Harris Neck gets about 50,000 visitors a year to experience its mix of marsh, woods, and grassland ecosystems and for its nearly matchless bird-watching. Its former life as a military base has the plus of leaving behind a decent system of roads, many of them based on old runways. Most visitors use the four-mile

© JIM MOREKIS

Harris Neck National Wildlife Refuge

"wildlife drive" to travel through the refuge, stopping occasionally for hiking or bird-watching. In the summer, look for egrets, herons, and wood storks nesting in rookeries. In the winter, waterfowl like mallards and teal flock to the brackish and freshwater pools. You can see painted buntings late April–late September.

Kayaks and canoes can put in at the public boat ramp on the Barbour River. Near the landing is an old African American cemetery, publicly accessible, with some charming handmade tombstones that evoke the post–Civil War era of Harris Neck before the displacement of local citizens to build the airfield.

To get here, take I-95 exit 67 and go south on U.S. 17 about one mile, then east on Harris Neck Road (Hwy. 131) for seven miles to the entrance gate on the left.

Shellman Bluff

Just northeast of Darien is the old oystering community of Shellman Bluff. It's notable not only for the stunning views from the high bluff but for fresh seafood. Go to **Shellman's Fish Camp** (912/832-4331) to put in for a kayak or canoe ride. Save room for some food; there are some great seafood places here.

To get to Shellman Bluff, take I-95 exit 67 for South Newport and get on U.S. 17 south. There are two easy ways to get to Shellman Bluff from U.S. 17: East on Minton Road and then left onto Shellman Bluff Road, or east on Pine Harbor Road followed by an immediate left onto Shellman Bluff Road. In either case, take Shellman Bluff Road until it dead-ends, then a right onto Sutherland Bluff Drive.

Darien Waterfront Park

Right where U.S. 17 crosses the Darien River, find the **Darien Welcome Center** (U.S. 17 and Fort King George Dr., 912/437-6684, daily 9 A.M.–5 P.M.). From there it's a short walk down some steps to the newly refurbished little Darien Waterfront Park. This

THE GOLDEN ISLES

small but charming area on a beautiful bend of the Darien River—a tributary of the mighty Altamaha River just to the south—features some old tabby warehouse ruins, some of the only remnants of Darien's glory days as a major seaport and old enough to have century-old live oaks growing around them. To the east are the picturesque docks where the town shrimp-boat fleet docks.

McIntosh Old Jail Art Center

Within Darien proper is the **McIntosh Old Jail Art Center and Welcome Center** (404 North Way, 912/437-7711, www.visitdarien.com, Tues.–Sat. 10 A.M.–4 P.M.), which also hosts several small art galleries and the McIntosh County History Museum.

Vernon Square

Right around the corner from the Welcome Center on Washington Street is Vernon Square, a charming little nook of live oaks and Spanish moss that was the social center of Darien in the town's antebellum heyday. The **Darien Methodist Church** on the square was built in 1843, damaged during the Civil War, then rebuilt in 1884 using materials from the first church. The nearby **St. Andrews Episcopal Church,** built in 1878, was once the site of the powerful Bank of Darien. Nearby is the affiliated and equally historic **St. Cyprian's Episcopal Church** (Fort King George Rd. and Rittenouse St.) built by an African American congregation and one of the largest tabby structures still in use anywhere.

Fort King George State Historic Site

The oldest English settlement in what would become Georgia, Fort King George State Historic Site (1600 Wayne St., 912/437-4770, www.gastateparks.org/fortkinggeorge, Tues.–Sun. 9 A.M.–5 P.M., $5 adults, $2.50 children) for a short time protected the Carolinas from attack, with its establishment in 1721 to its abandonment in 1727. Walking onto the site, with its restored 40-foot-tall cypress blockhouse fort, instantly reveals why this place was so important: It guards a key bend in the wide Altamaha River, vital to any attempt to establish transportation and trade in the area. In addition to chronicling the ill-fated English occupation of the area—plagued by insects, sickness, danger, and boredom—the site also has exhibits about other aspects of local history, including the Guale Indians, the Spanish missionary presence, and the era of the great sawmills. Nature lovers will enjoy the site as well, as it offers gorgeous vistas of the marsh. Fort King George holds regular reenactments, living history demonstrations, and cannon firings; go to the website for details.

To get here, take U.S. 17 to the Darien River Bridge, and then go east on Fort King George Drive. There's a bike route to the fort if you want to park in town.

Butler Island

South of Darien is the Altamaha River, Georgia's largest and only undammed river as well as one of the country's great estuarine habitats, with the second-largest watershed on the East Coast. It's a paradise for outdoors enthusiasts, one that amazed and delighted famed naturalist William Bartram on his journey here in the late 1700s. Over 30,000 ducks visit each year mid-October–mid-April on this key stop on the Colonial Coast Birding Trail.

A great way to enjoy the river ecosystem is at the **Altamaha Waterfowl Management Area** (912/262-3173, http://georgiawildlife.dnr.state.ga.us). This was the site of Butler Island Plantation, one of the largest and most successful tidewater plantations in the antebellum era. (The 75-foot brick chimney just off U.S. 17 is part of an old rice mill belonging to the plantation.) In 1834, planter Pierce Butler II married English actress Fanny Kemble, who would go on to write one of the earliest antislavery chronicles, *Journal of a Residence on a Georgian Plantation in 1838–39,* about what she saw during her short stay at Butler Island. Just past the chimney is a large plantation house, which now houses offices of the Nature Conservancy. There's a picnic ground nearby. The dominance of the plantation culture in this area is proved by the dikes and gates throughout the marsh, still plainly visible from the road. Many are still used by the Georgia Department of Natural Resources to maintain bird habitat. Birds you can see throughout the area include endangered wood storks, painted bunting, white ibis, all types of ducks, and even bald eagles.

Some of the best hiking and birding in the area is just south of the chimney on U.S. 17. Park on the east side of the road at an old dairy barn, and from there you'll find the trailhead for a four-mile round-trip hike on the Billy Cullen Memorial Trail, which offers great bird-watching opportunities and interpretive signage. On the other side of U.S. 17 is the entrance to the Ansley Hodges Memorial, where a 0.25-mile hike takes you to an observation tower. Be aware that hunting goes on near this area on some Saturdays during the year.

Kayaks and canoes can easily put in at the state-run landing at **Champney River Park** right where U.S. 17 crosses the Champney River. There are a variety of fish camps up and down this entire riverine system, providing fairly easy launching and recovery.

TOURS

Altamaha Coastal Tours (229 Ft. King George Rd., 912/437-6010, www.altamaha.com) is your best bet to take a guided kayak tour (from $50) or rent a kayak (from $20 per day) to explore the beautiful Altamaha River, Georgia's longest.

ACCOMMODATIONS

If you want to stay in McIntosh County, I strongly recommend booking one of the five charming guest rooms at ◖ **Open Gates Bed and Breakfast** (301 Franklin St., Darien, 912/437-6985, www.opengatesbnb.com, $125–140). This lovingly restored and reasonably priced inn is on historic and relaxing Vernon Square in downtown Darien. Owners Kelly and Jeff Spratt are not only attentive innkeepers who rustle up a mean breakfast, they're also biologists who can hook you up with the best nature-oriented experiences and tours on this part of the coast.

FOOD

McIntosh County is a powerhouse in the food department, and as you might expect, fresh and delicious seafood in a casual atmosphere is the order of the day here. One of my favorite restaurants—indeed, one of my favorite experiences, period—is ◖ **The Old School Diner** (1080 Jesse Grant Rd. NE, Townsend, 912/832-2136, http://oldschooldiner.com, Wed.–Fri. 5:30–9:30 P.M., Sat.–Sun. noon–9:30 P.M., $15–30, cash only), located in a whimsical semirural compound seven miles off U.S. 17 just off Harris Neck Road on the way to the wildlife refuge. Run by the gregarious comfort-food culinary genius Jerome Brown, the restaurant is a reflection of the man himself—warm, inviting, eccentric, and full of life. The interior almost defies description, but here goes: Imagine a series of rambling, dimly-lit rooms with no identifiable decor, every wall and surface covered with memorabilia, kitsch, and endless photographs of diners (yes, one of them will be you—the servers take your picture at the end of the meal). However, it's Chef Jerome's food that has people driving here from literally all over Georgia (last time I was here I met someone who had driven in from Augusta, about three hours away): succulent fresh seafood in the coastal Georgia tradition—delicately fried and imbued with the subtle, inviting flavors of soul food. Not a seafood fan? His ribs are also some of the best anywhere.

THE GOLDEN ISLES

Old School's prices aren't so old school, but keep in mind that the portions are huge, rich, and filling. And besides, no one comes all the way out here to scrimp and save—this is an experience you'll never forget. Reservations are recommended, and remember, it's cash only. They take no plastic of any kind, and there are no ATMs nearby.

Even farther off the main roads than the Old School Diner, the community of Shellman Bluff is also well worth the drive. Find **C Hunter's Café** (Shellman Bluff, 912/832-5771, lunch Mon.–Fri. 11 A.M.–2 P.M., dinner Mon.–Fri. 5–10 P.M., Sat.–Sun. 7 A.M.–10 P.M., $10–20) and get anything that floats your boat—it's all fresh and local. Wild Georgia shrimp are a particular specialty, as is the hearty cream-based crab stew. Take a right off Shellman Bluff Road onto Sutherland Bluff Drive, then a left onto New Shellman Road. Take a right onto the unpaved River Road and you can't miss it. Another Shellman Bluff favorite is **C Speed's Kitchen** (Shellman Bluff, 912/832-4763, Thurs.–Sat. 5 P.M.–close, Sun. noon–close, $10–20), where people move anything but fast and the fried fish and crab-stuffed flounder are out of this world. Take a right off of Shellman Bluff Road onto Sutherland Bluff Drive. Take a right onto Speed's Kitchen Road.

On the Darien waterfront, you'll find **Skipper's Fish Camp** (85 Screven St., Darien, 912/437-3579, www.skippersfishcamp.com, daily 11 A.M.–9 P.M., $15–25), which, as is typical for this area, also hosts a marina. Try the fried wild Georgia Shrimp, fresh from local waters. South of Darien just off U.S. 17 on the Altamaha River, try **Mudcat Charlie's** (250 Ricefield Way, 912/261-0055, daily 8 A.M.–2 P.M., $10–20), where fresh seafood is served in a friendly and very casual atmosphere, yes, right in the middle of a busy fish camp.

INFORMATION AND SERVICES

The **Darien Welcome Center** (1111 Magnolia Bluff Way, www.visitdarien.com, Mon.–Sat.

10 A.M.–8 P.M., Sun. 11 A.M.–6 P.M.) is located within the Preferred Outlets mall just off I-95 at exit 49.

The closest hospital is the Brunswick campus of **Southeast Georgia Health System** (2415 Parkwood Dr., Brunswick, 912/466-7000, http://sghs.org).

GETTING THERE AND AROUND

U.S. 17 goes directly through Darien. The closest I-95 exit is exit 49. Once you get off U.S. 17, Darien is a pretty bike-friendly place; you can park the car downtown and ride your bike east on Fort King George Drive to visit Fort King George.

SAPELO ISLAND

Another of those amazing, undeveloped Georgia barrier islands that can only be reached by boat, Sapelo also shares with some of those islands a link to the Gilded Age.

History

The Spanish established a Franciscan mission on the north end of the island in the 1500s. Sapelo didn't become fully integrated into the Lowcountry plantation culture until its purchase by Thomas Spalding in the early 1800s. After the Civil War, many of the nearly 500 former slaves on the island remained, with a partnership of freedmen buying land as early as 1871.

Hudson Motors mogul Howard Coffin bought all of Sapelo, except for the African American communities, in 1912, building a palatial home and introducing a modern infrastructure. Among Coffin's visitors were two presidents, Calvin Coolidge and Herbert Hoover, and aviator Charles Lindbergh. Coffin hit hard times in the Great Depression and in 1934 sold Sapelo to tobacco heir R. J. Reynolds, who consolidated the island's African Americans into the single Hog Hammock community. By the mid-1970s the Reynolds family

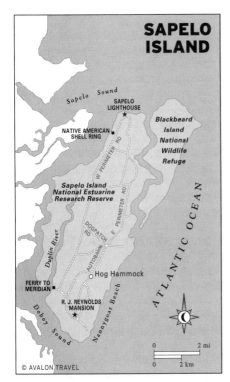

SAPELO ISLAND

Sapelo Sound

SAPELO LIGHTHOUSE

NATIVE AMERICAN SHELL RING

W. PERIMETER RD

Blackbeard Island National Wildlife Refuge

Sapelo Island National Estuarine Research Reserve

E. PERIMETER RD

ATLANTIC OCEAN

DOGPATCH RD

Duplin River

AUTOGRAPH RD

Hog Hammock

FERRY TO MERIDIAN

R. J. REYNOLDS MANSION

Nannygoat Beach

Doboy Sound

0   2 mi

0   2 km

© AVALON TRAVEL

had sold the island to the state, again with the exception of the 430 acres of Hog Hammock, at the time with slightly more than 100 residents. Today most of the island is administered for marine research purposes under the designation of **Sapelo Island National Estuarine Research Reserve** (www.sapelonerr.org).

Sights

Once on the island, you can take guided tours under the auspices of the Georgia Department of Natural Resources. Wednesday 8:30 A.M.–12:30 P.M. is a tour of the **R. J. Reynolds Mansion** (www.reynoldsonsapelo.com) on the south end along with the rest of the island, including Hog Hammock and the Long Tabby ruins. Saturday 9 A.M.–1 P.M. is a tour of the historic **Sapelo Lighthouse** on the north end along with the rest of the island. June–Labor

Day there's an extra lighthouse-island tour Friday 8:30 A.M.–12:30 P.M. March–October on the last Tuesday of the month they do an extra-long day trip, 8:30 A.M.–3 P.M. Tours cost $10 adults, $6 children, free under age 6. Call 912/437-3224 for reservations. You can also arrange private tours.

Another key sight on Sapelo is a 4,500-year-old **Native American shell ring** on the north end, one of the oldest and best preserved anywhere. Beach-lovers will especially enjoy the unspoiled strands on Sapelo, including the famous **Nannygoat Beach.**

Accommodations

While it's theoretically possible to stay overnight at the **R. J. Reynolds Mansion** (www.reynoldsonsapelo.com), it is limited to groups of at least 16 people. Realistically, to stay overnight on Sapelo you need a reservation with one of the locally owned guesthouses. One recommendation is Cornelia Bailey's six-room **The Wallow** (912/485-2206, call for rates) in historic Hog Hammock. The Baileys also run a small campground, **Comyam's Campground** (912/485-2206, $10 pp). Another option is **The Weekender** (912/485-2277, call for rates).

Getting There

Visitors to Sapelo must embark on the ferry at the **Sapelo Island Visitors Center** (912/437-3224, www.sapelonerr.org, Tues.–Fri. 7:30 A.M.–5:30 P.M., Sat. 8 A.M.–5:30 P.M., Sun. 1:30–5 P.M., $10 adults, $6 ages 6–18) in little Meridian, Georgia, on Highway 99 north of Darien. The visitors center actually has a nice nature hike of its own as well as an auditorium where you can see an informative video. From here it's a half-hour trip to Sapelo over the Doboy Sound. Keep in mind you must call in advance for reservations before showing up at the visitors center. April–October it's recommended to call at least a week in advance.

THE GOLDEN ISLES

ST. CATHERINE'S ISLAND

The interior of this beautiful island off the coast of Midway, Georgia, is off-limits to the public, but you can visit the beach up to the high-water mark by boat, enjoy its beautiful unspoiled beaches, and spy on local wildlife. While that's about all you can do, it's important to know a little of the interesting background of this island. Owned and administered by the St. Catherine's Island Foundation, it's unusual in that it has a 25-foot-high bluff on the northern end, an extraordinarily high geographic feature for a barrier island in this part of the world.

Once central to the Spanish missionary effort on the Georgia coast, St. Catherine's was found to be home to over 400 graves of Christianized Native Americans (a large shell ring also exists on the island). Declaration of Independence signer Button Gwinnett made a home here for a while until his death from a gunshot wound suffered in a duel in Savannah in 1777. After General Sherman's famous "40 acres and a mule" order, a freed slave named Tunis Campbell was governor of the island, living in Gwinnett's home. But when the order was rescinded, all former slaves had to leave for the mainland. In 1986, American Museum of Natural History archaeologist David Hurst Thomas began extensive research on Spanish artifacts left behind from the Santa Catalina de Guale mission, including foundations of living quarters, a kitchen, and a church—possibly the first church in what is now the United States. Today, however, the island, a National Historic Landmark, is better known as host to a New York Zoological Society project to recover injured or sick animals of endangered species and nurse them back to health for a possible return to the wild.

The closest marinas for the trip to the island's peaceful beaches are Shellman Fish Camp (1058 River Rd. NE, Townsend, 912/832-4331) in McIntosh County and Halfmoon Marina (171 Azalea Rd., Midway, 912/884-5819) in Liberty County.

BLACKBEARD ISLAND

While no one is positive if the namesake of Blackbeard Island actually landed here, the legends tell us he used it as a layover—even leaving some treasure here. Now federally administered as **Blackbeard Island National Wildlife Refuge** (912/652-4415, www.fws.gov/blackbeardisland), the island is accessible to the public by boat and gets about 10,000 visitors a year. Plenty of hiking trails exist, and the birdwatching is fantastic. It's also a major nesting ground for the endangered loggerhead turtle. Cycling is permitted, but overnight camping is not. For charters to Blackbeard, I recommend **SouthEast Adventures** (313 Mallory St., St. Simons, 912/638-6732) on St. Simons Island.

Cumberland Island and St. Marys

Actually two islands—Great Cumberland and Little Cumberland—Cumberland Island National Seashore is the largest and one of the oldest of Georgia's barrier islands, and also one of its most remote and least developed. Currently administered by the National Park Service, it's accessible only by ferry or private boat. Most visitors to Cumberland get here from the gateway town of St. Marys, Georgia, a nifty little fishing village that has so far managed to defy the increasing residential sprawl coming to the area.

ST. MARYS

Much like Brunswick to the north, the fishing town of St. Marys plays mostly a gateway role, in this case to the Cumberland Island National Seashore. That being said, it's a very friendly

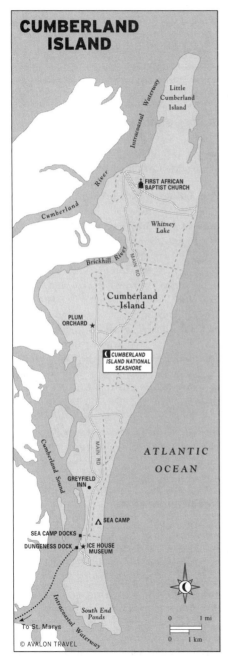

CUMBERLAND ISLAND

Little Cumberland Island

Intracoastal Waterway

FIRST AFRICAN BAPTIST CHURCH

Cumberland River

Whitney Lake

Brickhill River

MAIN RD

Cumberland Island

PLUM ORCHARD

CUMBERLAND ISLAND NATIONAL SEASHORE

MAIN RD

ATLANTIC OCEAN

Cumberland Sound

GREYFIELD INN

SEA CAMP

SEA CAMP DOCKS

DUNGENESS DOCK

ICE HOUSE MUSEUM

South End Ponds

Intracoastal Waterway

To St. Marys

© AVALON TRAVEL

0   1 mi

0   1 km

little waterfront community with undeniable charms of its own and a historic pedigree going back to the very beginnings of the nation.

History

As early as 1767, once the Spanish threat subsided, plans were made to establish a town, then known as Buttermilk Bluff, in the area near the Florida border. But it wasn't until 20 years later that a meeting was held on Cumberland Island to close the deal with Jacob Weed to purchase the tract—acquired by confiscation from two loyalist landowners—for the grand sum of $38. The first influx of immigration to the area came as French Canadian refugees from Acadia (who would become known as Cajuns in Louisiana) came to St. Marys after being deported by the British. Another group of French speakers came, fleeing Toussaint Louverture's slave rebellion in Haiti.

During the colonial period, St. Marys was the southernmost U.S. city and enjoyed not only importance as a seaport but was militarily important as well. Ironically, this strategic importance came into play more during the conflict with Great Britain than with anything to do with the Spanish. In 1812 a British force took over Cumberland Island and St. Marys, with a contingent embarking up the river to track down the customs collection. However, in a bloody skirmish they were ambushed by American troops firing from the riverbanks. They vowed to avenge their loss by burning every building between the St. Marys and the Altamaha Rivers, but the ensuing peace treaty ending the War of 1812 brought a ceasefire.

Unlike towns such as Darien, which was put to the torch by Union troops, St. Marys was saved from destruction in the Civil War. The lumber industry boomed after that conflict as well as the local fishing and shrimping industries. A hotel was built in 1916 (and hosted Marjorie Kinnan Rawlings, author of *The Yearlings*), but tourists didn't discover the area

THE GOLDEN ISLES

until the 1970s. It was also then that the U.S. Navy built the huge nuclear submarine base at Kings Bay, currently the area's largest employer with almost 10,000 employees. Development has increased in the area, with suburban sprawl beginning to cover the area like mushrooms after a heavy rain. Indeed, there's so much growth in the St. Marys–Camden County area that it's increasingly considered an outpost of the huge Jacksonville, Florida, metropolitan area to the south.

Orientation

As in Brunswick, the waterfront faces opposite the ocean and is instead oriented west, toward a river, in this case the St. Marys River. Most activity in downtown St. Marys happens up and down Osborne Street, which perhaps not coincidentally is also how you get to the **Cumberland Island Visitor Center** (113 St. Marys St., 912/882-4335, daily 8 A.M.–4:30 P.M.) and from there board the *Cumberland Queen* for the trip to the island.

Sights

Tying the past to the present, it's only fitting that the home of the Kings Bay Submarine Base (which is not open to the public) has a museum dedicated to the "Silent Service." The **St. Marys Submarine Museum** (102 St. Marys St., 912/882-2782, www.stmaryssubmuseum.com, Tues.–Sat. 10 A.M.–4 P.M., Sun. 1–5 P.M., $5 adults, $3 children) on the riverfront has a variety of exhibits honoring the contribution of American submariners. There's a neat interactive exhibit where you can look through the genuine sub periscope that sticks out of the roof of the museum.

The most notable historic home in St. Marys is the **Orange Hall House Museum** (311 Osborne St., 912/576-3644, www.orangehall.org, Tues.–Sat. 9 A.M.–4 P.M., Sun. 1–4 P.M., $3 adults, $1 children). This beautiful Greek Revival home, circa 1830, survived the Civil

War and was the center of town social life during the Roaring '20s, when it was owned by a succession of socialites from up north. The home is gorgeous inside and out, particularly during the holidays when it gets the full decorative treatment.

Events and Recreation

As a nod to its Cajun history, St. Marys hosts a heck of a **Mardi Gras Festival** each February, closing down six blocks of the riverfront for a parade. There's also live entertainment, vendors, and a costume ball.

For outdoor recreation near St. Marys, go to **Crooked River State Park** (6222 Charlie Smith Sr. Hwy., 912/882-5256, www.gastateparks.org, office Fri.–Wed. 8 A.M.–10 P.M., Thurs. 8 A.M.–5 P.M.), which is not only a great place to put in for kayaking trips, including jaunts to Cumberland Island, but also has a wide range of lodging options as well. A key stop on the Colonial Coast Birding Trail, Crooked River features its own nature center and is near a historic site just upriver, the tabby ruins of the McIntosh Sugar Works—actually a lumber mill from the early 1800s. The easiest way to get here is to take I-95 exit 3 and go about eight miles east. To rent kayaks or book kayak and ecotours, try **Up the Creek Xpeditions** (111 Osborne St., 912/882-0911, www.upthecreekx.com), which can take you all around the area, including out to Cumberland Island.

Accommodations

Don't even think about staying at a chain hotel when you're in St. Marys. Stay at one of these cute historic inns for a song. The most notable lodging for historic as well as economic value is the 18-room **Riverview Hotel** (105 Osborne St., 912/882-3242, www.riverviewhotelstmarys.com, under $100). The waterfront locale, like many old hotels in this area, has a great retro feel. It was built in the 1920s and has hosted such notables as author Marjorie

Rawlings, John Rockefeller, poet Sidney Lanier, and Andrew Carnegie. **[** **Emma's Bed and Breakfast** (300 West Conyers St., 912/882-4199, www.emmasbedandbreakfast. com, under $200) is situated on four beautiful acres in downtown St. Marys in a grand Southern-style mansion with all the trappings and hospitality you'd expect. You can also hang out on the stunning veranda at the historic **[** **Goodbread House** (209 Osborne St., 912/882-7490, www.goodbreadhouse.com, under $200), which offers rates below $100 in the off-season. The 1870 house features sumptuous interiors, including a classic dining room in which awesome breakfasts are served.

More outdoorsy visitors can stay at cottage, tent, or RV sites at **Crooked River State Park** (6222 Charlie Smith Sr. Hwy., 912/882-5256, www.gastateparks.org). There are 62 tent and RV sites (about $22) and 11 cottages ($85–110) as well as primitive camping ($25).

Food

St. Marys cannot compete in culinary sophistication with Charleston or Savannah, but it does have some of the freshest seafood around. One of the best places to eat seafood on the waterfront in St. Marys is at **Lang's Marina Restaurant** (307 W. St. Marys St., 912/882-4432, lunch Tues.–Fri. 11 A.M.–2 P.M., dinner Wed.–Sat. 5–9 P.M., $15–20). The other premier seafood place is **Trolley's** (109 W. St. Marys St., 912/882-1525, Sun.–Thurs. 11 A.M.–9 P.M., Fri.–Sat. 11 A.M.–10 P.M., $15–20).

Information and Services

The **St. Marys Convention and Visitors Bureau** (406 Osborne St., 912/882-4000, www.st-maryswelcome.com) is a good source of information not only for the town but for Cumberland Island, but keep in mind that this is not actually where you catch the ferry to the island.

Getting There and Around

Take I-95 exit 3 for Kingsland–St. Marys Road (Hwy. 40). This becomes Osborne Road, the main drag of St. Marys, as it gets closer to town. The road by the waterfront is St. Marys Street.

[CUMBERLAND ISLAND NATIONAL SEASHORE

Not only one of the richest estuarine environments in the world, Cumberland Island National Seashore (912/882-4335, www.nps. gov/cuis) is quite simply one of the most beautiful and romantic places on the planet, as everyone learned when the "it" couple of their day, John F. Kennedy Jr. and Carolyn Bessette, were wed on the island in 1996. With more than 16 miles of gorgeous beach and an area of over 17,000 acres, there's no shortage of beauty either, and the island's already remote feel is further enhanced by the efforts that have been taken to protect it from development.

Cumberland is far from pristine: It has been used for timbering and cotton, is dotted with evocative abandoned ruins, and hosts a band of beautiful but voracious wild horses. But it is still a remarkable island paradise in a world where those kinds of locations are getting harder and harder to find.

History

Like modern-day Americans, the Timucuan Indians also revered this site, visiting it often for shellfish and for sassafras, a medicinal herb common on the island. Cumberland's size and great natural harbor made it a perfect base for Spanish friars, who established the first missionary on the island, San Pedro Mocama, in 1587. In fact, the first Christian martyr in Georgia was created on Cumberland, when Father Pedro Martinez was killed by the Indians.

As part of his effort to push the Spanish back into Florida for good, General James Oglethorpe established Fort William at the south end of Cumberland—the remains of which are now underwater—and a hunting lodge named Dungeness, an island place-name that persists today. While land grants were made in the 1760s, they saw little follow-through, and by the time of naturalist William Bartram's visit in 1774, Cumberland Island was almost uninhabited. But inevitably, the Lowcountry planters' culture made its way down to Cumberland, which was soon the site of 15 thriving plantations and small farms. After the Revolution, the heirs of one of its heroes, General Nathanael Greene, established Dungeness Plantation in 1802, its central building a now-gone tabby structure right on top of an ancient shell mound.

Actual military action wouldn't come to Cumberland until the War of 1812, when the British came in force and occupied the island for two months, using Dungeness as their headquarters. In the process they freed 1,500 slaves, who would then emigrate to various British colonies. In 1818, Revolutionary War hero General "Light-Horse" Harry Lee—father of Robert E. Lee—arrived on Cumberland's shore, in failing health and determined to see the home of his old friend General Greene one last time. He died a month later and was buried here, his son returning later to erect a gravestone. Light-Horse Harry remained on Cumberland until 1913, when his remains were taken to Lexington, Virginia, to be beside those of his son. His gravestone on Cumberland remains to this day.

The Civil War—and another freeing of slaves—came again in the 1860s, when Union troops occupied the island. At war's end Cumberland was set aside as a home for freed African Americans—part of the famous and ill-fated "40 acres and a mule" proposal—but politics intervened: Most of Cumberland's slaves were rounded up and taken to Amelia Island, Florida, although some settled at the north end (the "Settlement" area today).

As elsewhere on the Georgia coast, the Industrial Revolution came to Cumberland in the form of a vacation getaway for a mega-tycoon, in this case Thomas Carnegie, industrialist and brother of the better-known Andrew Carnegie of Carnegie Library fame. Carnegie built a new, even grander Dungeness, which suffered the same fate as its predecessor in a 1959 fire.

Cumberland Island narrowly avoided becoming the next Hilton Head—literally—in 1969 when Hilton Head developer Charles Fraser bought the northern tip of the island and began bulldozing a runway. The dwindling but still influential Carnegies joined with the Georgia Conservancy to broker an agreement that resulted in dubbing Cumberland a National Seashore in 1972, saving it from further development. A $7.5 million gift from the Mellon Foundation enabled the purchase of Fraser's tract and the eventual incorporation of the island within the National Park system.

Sights

The ferry typically stops at two docks a short distance from each other, the Sea Camp dock and the Dungeness dock. At 4 P.M., Rangers offer a "Dockside" interpretive program at the Sea Camp. A short way farther north at the Dungeness Dock, Rangers offer a "Dungeness Footsteps Tour" at 10 A.M. and 12:45 P.M., concentrating on the historic sites at the southern end of the island. Also at the Dungeness dock is the little **Ice House Museum** (912/882-4336, daily 9 A.M.–5 P.M., free) containing a range of exhibits on the island's history from Native American times to the present day.

Down near the docks are also where you'll find the stirring, almost spooky **Dungeness Ruins** and the nearby grave marker of Light-Horse Harry Lee. Controversy continues to this day as to the cause of the 1866 fire that destroyed the old Dungeness home. Some say it was those freed slaves on the north end who lit the blaze, but others say it was the plantation's final owner, Robert Stafford, who did it out of spite after his former slaves refused to work for him after the war.

WILD HORSES OF CUMBERLAND

Cumberland Island's famous wild horses are not actually direct descendants of the first horses brought to the island by Spanish and English settlers, although certainly feral horses have ranged the island for most of recorded history. The current population of 250 or so is actually descended from horses brought to the island by the Carnegie family in the 1920s.

Gorgeous and evocative though these magnificent animals are, they have a big appetite for vegetation and are frankly not the best thing for this sensitive barrier island ecosystem. But their beauty and visceral impact on the visitor is undeniable, which means the horses are likely to stay as long as nature will have them. And yes, these really are *wild* horses, meaning you shouldn't feed them even if they approach you for food, and you certainly won't be riding them.

Sports and Recreation

There are more than 50 miles of trails all over Cumberland, about 17 miles of nearly isolated beach to comb, and acres of maritime forest to explore—the latter an artifact of Cumberland's unusually old age for a barrier island. Upon arrival, you might want to rent a bicycle at the **Sea Camp docks** (no reservations, arrange rentals on the ferry, adult bikes $16 per day, youth bikes $10, $20 overnight).

Shell-and-sharks-teeth collectors might want to explore south of Dungeness Beach as well as between the docks. Unlike some parks, you are allowed to take shells and fossils off the island.

Wildlife enthusiasts will be in heaven. More than 300 species of birds have been recorded on the island, which is also a favorite nesting ground for female loggerhead turtles in the late summer. Of course, the most iconic image of Cumberland Island is its famous **wild horses,** a free-roaming band of feral equines who traverse the island year-round, grazing as they please.

Moving north on the Main Road (Grand Ave.) you come to **Greyfield Inn** (904/261-6408, www.greyfieldinn.com). Because it is a privately owned hotel, don't trespass through the grounds. A good way farther north, just off the main road, you'll find the restored, rambling 20-room mansion **Plum Orchard,** another Carnegie legacy. Guided tours of Plum Orchard are available on the second and fourth Sunday of the month ($6 plus ferry fare); reserve a space at 912/882-4335.

At the very north end of the island, accessible only by foot or by bicycle, is the former freedmen's community simply known as **The Settlement,** featuring a small cemetery and the now-famous **First African Baptist Church** (daily dawn–dusk)—a 1937 version of the 1893 original—a humble and rustic one-room church made of whitewashed logs in which the 1996 Kennedy-Bessette marriage took place.

Accommodations

The only "civilized" lodging on Cumberland is the 13-room **◖ Greyfield Inn** (Grand Ave., 904/261-6408, www.greyfieldinn.com, $475), ranked by the American Inn Association as one of the country's "Ten Most Romantic Inns." Opened in 1962 as a hotel, the Greyfield was originally built in 1900 as the home of the Carnegies. The room rates includes meals, transportation, tours, and bicycle usage.

Many visitors opt to camp on Cumberland (reservations 877/860-6787, limit of seven nights, $4) in one of three basic ways: at the **Sea Camp,** which has restrooms and shower facilities and allows fires; the remote **Stafford Beach,** a good hike from the docks and with no facilities; and pure wilderness camping farther north at **Hickory Hill, Yankee Paradise,** and **Brickman Bluff,** all of which are a several-mile hike away, do not permit fires, and have no facilities of any kind. Reservations are required for camping. All trash must be packed out on departure, as there are no refuse facilities on the island. Responsible alcohol consumption is limited to those 21 and over.

Getting There and Around

The most vital information about Cumberland is how to get ashore in the first place. Most visitors do this by purchasing a ticket on the *Cumberland Queen* at the **Cumberland Island Visitor Center** (113 St. Marys St., St. Marys, 912/882-4335, daily 8 A.M.–4:30 P.M., $20 adults, $18 seniors, $12 under age 13) on the waterfront at St. Marys. The ferry ride is 45 minutes each way. You can call for reservations Monday–Friday 10 A.M.–4 P.M. The ferry does not transport pets, bicycles, kayaks, or cars. However, you can rent bicycles at the Sea Camp docks once you're there. Every visitor to Cumberland over age 16 must pay a $4 entry fee, including campers.

March 1–November 30, the ferry leaves St. Marys at 9 A.M. and 11:45 A.M., returning from Cumberland at 10:15 A.M. and 4:45 P.M. March 1–September 30 Wednesday–Saturday, there's an additional 2:45 P.M. departure from Cumberland back to St. Marys. December 1–February 28 the ferry operates only Thursday–Monday.

One of the quirks of Cumberland, resulting from the unusual way in which it passed into federal hands, is the existence of some private property on which you mustn't trespass, except where trails specifically allow it. Also, unlike the general public, these private landowners are allowed to use vehicles. For these reasons, it's best to make sure you have a map of the island, which you can get before you board the ferry at St. Marys. There are no real stores and very few facilities on Cumberland. *Bring whatever you think you'll need,* whether it be food, water, medicine, suntan lotion, insect repellent, or otherwise.

The Okefenokee Swamp

Scientists often refer to Okefenokee as an "analogue," an accurate representation of a totally different epoch in the earth's history. In this case it's the Carboniferous Period, about 350 million years ago, when the living plants were lush and green and the dead plants simmered in a slow-decaying peat that would one day end up as the oil that powers our civilization. But for the casual visitor, Okefenokee might also be simply a wonderful place to get almost completely away from human influence and witness firsthand some of the country's most interesting wildlife in its natural habitat. Despite the enormous wildfires of the spring of 2007 and the summer of 2011—some of the largest the Southeast has seen in half a century, so large they were visible from space—the swamp has bounced back, for the most part, and is once again hosting visitors to experience its timeless beauty.

◖ OKEFENOKEE NATIONAL WILDLIFE REFUGE

It's nearly the size of Rhode Island and just a short drive off I-95, but the massive and endlessly fascinating Okefenokee National Wildlife Refuge (912/496-7836, www.fws.gov/okefenokee, Mar.–Oct. daily dawn–7:30 P.M., Nov.–Feb. daily dawn–5:30 P.M., $5 per vehicle) is one of the lesser-visited national public lands. Is it that very name "swamp" that keeps people away, with its connotations of fetid misery and lurking danger? Or simply its location, out of sight and out of mind in south Georgia? In any case, while it long ago entered the collective subconscious as a metaphor for the most

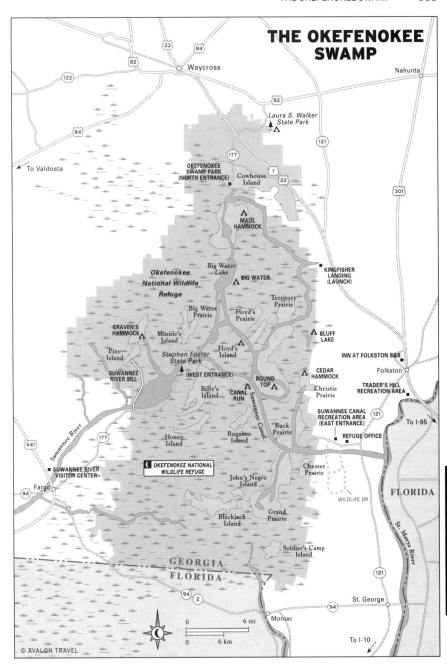

THE OKEFENOKEE SWAMP

Waycross

Nahunta

To Valdosta

Laura S. Walker State Park

OKEFENOKEE SWAMP PARK (NORTH ENTRANCE)

Cowhouse Island

MAUL HAMMOCK

Okefenokee National Wildlife Refuge

Big Water Lake

BIG WATER

KINGFISHER LANDING (LAUNCH)

Territory Prairie

Big Water Prairie

Floyd's Prairie

CRAVEN'S HAMMOCK

Minnie's Island

BLUFF LAKE

Pine Island

Stephen Foster State Park

Floyd's Island

INN AT FOLKSTON B&B

Folkston

SUWANNEE RIVER SILL

(WEST ENTRANCE)

CEDAR HAMMOCK

Christie Prairie

TRADER'S HILL RECREATION AREA

ROUND TOP

Billy's Island

CANAL RUN

Suwannee Canal

SUWANNEE CANAL RECREATION AREA (EAST ENTRANCE)

Buck Prairie

To I-95

Honey Island

Bugaboo Island

REFUGE OFFICE

Suwannee River

SUWANNEE RIVER VISITOR CENTER

OKEFENOKEE NATIONAL WILDLIFE REFUGE

Chesser Prairie

FLORIDA

Fargo

John's Negro Island

WILDLIFE DR

Blackjack Island

Grand Prairie

St. Marys River

GEORGIA
FLORIDA

Soldier's Camp Island

St. George

0   6 mi

0   6 km

Moniac

To I-10

© AVALON TRAVEL

untamed, darkly dangerous aspects of the American South—as well as the place where Pogo the Possum lived—the Okefenokee remains one of the most intriguing natural areas on the planet. The nearby old rail town of Folkston is the gateway to the swamp for most visitors off I-95, which is to say most of them. In true Georgia fashion, the town is insular but friendly, slow but sincere.

History

The Okefenokee Swamp was created by an accident of geology. About 250,000 years ago, the Atlantic Ocean washed ashore about 70 miles farther inland from where it does today. Over time, a massive barrier island formed off this primeval Georgia coastline, running from what is now Jesup, Georgia, south to Starke, Florida. When the ocean level dropped during the Pleistocene Era, this sandy island became a topographical feature known today as the Trail Ridge, its height effectively creating a basin to its west. Approximately 90 percent of the Okefenokee's water comes from rainfall into that basin, which drains slowly via the Suwannee and St. Marys Rivers. Ordinarily, what the summer heat evaporates from the Okefenokee is more than replenished by rain, unless there's a severe drought like the one that caused the recent wildfires. But even the fires can't hold the swamp back. In fact, the Okefenokee is a fire ecosystem, meaning some plant species, like the cypress, depend on heat generated by wildfires to open their seed cones and perpetuate their lifecycle. Indeed, because of the particularly combustible nature of the peat that forms most of the swamp, fire is never far away—sometimes it's right under your feet! Portions of the massive Honey Prairie Fire of 2011 in the swamp's southwestern area, caused by a lightning strike, still smolder to this day under the surface. Because of constant rejuvenation by water and fire, biologists estimate that the oldest portion of this supposedly "ancient" swamp is actually no older than 7,000 years—the faintest blink of an eye in geological terms. Unlike Florida's Everglades, which are actually a single large and very slow-moving river—the Okefenokee is a true swamp.

Native Americans used the swamp as a hunting ground and gave us its current name, which means "Land of the Trembling Earth," a reference to the floating peat islands, called "houses," that dominate the landscape. The Spanish arrived about 1600, calling the swamp Laguna de Oconi (Lake Oconi) and establishing at least two missions in the area near two Timucuan villages. During the Seminole Wars of the 1830s, the Timucua took refuge within the swamp for a time before continuing south into Florida. While trade had occurred on the outskirts for nearly a century before, it wasn't until the 1850s that the first non-native settlers set up camp inside the swamp itself.

It's a common mistake to call the Okefenokee "pristine," because like much of the heavily timbered and farmed southeastern coast, it is anything but. The swamp's ancient cypress stands and primordial longleaf pine forests were heavily harvested in the early 20th century. About 200 miles of old rail bed through the swamp remain as a silent testament to the scope of that logging operation. But the pace of logging gradually slowed to a stop as the cost of the operation became prohibitive. In 1918 the Okefenokee Society, the first organized attempt to protect the habitat, was formed in nearby Waycross, Georgia. In 1937, President Franklin Roosevelt brought the area within the federal wildlife refuge system.

In recent years, large deposits of titanium prompted several mining interests, including DuPont, to exercise rights in the area, to great outcry from conservationists who worried that the intrusive 24-hour mining operations would destroy the swamp's habitat. A series of transactions involving the state and conservation trusts, however, have so far resulted in halting those mining efforts.

Sights

Contrary to the popular image of a nasty, dank swamp, the Okefenokee is anything but a monoculture. It features a wide variety of ecosystems, including peat bogs, sand hills, and black gum and bay forests. Perhaps most surprising is the wide open vista of the swamp's many prairies or extended grasslands, 22 in all, which besides being stirring to the eye are also great places to see birds. So you see, not all of the Okefenokee is wet. There is water aplenty here, though, with over 60 named lakes and 120 miles of boating trails. And as you kayak or canoe on one of the water trails or on the old **Suwannee Canal** from the logging era, you'll notice the water is all very dark. This blackwater is not due to dirt or silt but to natural tannic acid released into the water from the decaying vegetation that gave the swamp its name. While I don't recommend that you drink the water, it's actually very clean despite its color.

As you'd expect on a national wildlife refuge, the Okefenokee hosts a huge variety of animal life—more than 400 species of vertebrates, including over 200 varieties of birds and more than 60 types of reptiles. Birders get a special treat in late November–early December when sandhill cranes come south to winter in the swamp. In January their colonies are at their peak, and the swamp echoes with their loud cries. Other common bird species you'll see are herons, egrets, and endangered wood storks and red-cockaded woodpeckers. The white ibis has seen a big spike in population in the refuge recently, as has the bald eagle. A great way to see the sandhill cranes and other birds of the Okefenokee is to hike the 0.75-mile boardwalk out to the 50-foot **Chesser Island Observation Tower** on the eastern end of the swamp. Get here by driving or biking the eight-mile round-trip **Wildlife Drive,** which also takes you by the old **Chesser Homestead,** the remnants of one of the oldest settlements in the swamp. You can also hike out to Chesser; indeed, there are many miles of hiking trails through the upland areas of the swamp near the East Entrance.

Probably the first creature one thinks of when one thinks of a swamp is the alligator. Certainly Okefenokee has plenty of them, and no one who has heard the roar of a male alligator break the quiet of the night will ever forget the experience. Most of the time, though, alligators are quite shy, and spotting them is an acquired skill. They often look like floating logs. Conversely, in warm weather you might see them out in the open sunning themselves. While no one can remember an incident of a gator attacking a human in the refuge, whatever you do, don't feed alligators in the wild. As a Fish and Wildlife ranger in Okefenokee once told me: "If a gator attacks a human, at some point in the past someone has fed that gator. Gators get used to being fed. Unfortunately, they can't tell the difference between the person and the food." Believe it or not, the alligator is not even the top predator in the Okefenokee; that title belongs to the black bear. Biologists estimate that as many as 90 percent of alligator eggs laid in the refuge are eaten by the local black bear population. And as with the gators, don't feed the bears.

Recreation and Accommodations

For most visitors, the best way to enjoy the Okefenokee is to book a guided tour through **Okefenokee Adventures** (866/843-7926, www.okefenokeeadventures.com), the designated concessionaire of the refuge. They offer a 90-minute guided boat tour ($18 adults, $11 children) that leaves each hour, and a 2.5-hour reservation-only sunset tour ($25 adults, $17 children) that takes you to see the gorgeous sunset over Chesser Prairie. Extended or custom tours, including multiday wilderness excursions, are also available. They also rent bikes, canoes, and camping gear, and even run a decent little café where you can either sit down and have a meal or take it to go out on the trail.

If fire and water levels permit, it's possible to stay the night in the swamp, canoeing to one of the primitive camping "islands" in the middle of the refuge. You need to make reservations up to two months in advance, however, by calling **U.S. Fish and Wildlife** (912/496-3331, Mon.–Fri. 7–10 A.M.). A nonrefundable fee of $10 pp (which also covers your entrance fee) must be received 16 days before you arrive (mailing address: Okefenokee National Wildlife Refuge, Route 2, Box 3330, Folkston, GA 31537). Campfires are allowed only at Canal Run and Floyds Island. A camp stove is required for cooking at all other shelters. (Keep in mind that in times of extreme drought or fire threat, boat trips may not be allowed. Always check the website for the latest announcements.)

Privately owned canoes and boats with motors under 10 hp may put in with no launch fee, but you must sign in and out. No ATVs are allowed on the refuge, and bicycles are allowed only on designated bike trails. Keep in mind that some hunting goes on in the refuge at designated times. Pets must be leashed at all times.

At the **Stephen Foster State Park** (17515 Hwy. 177, 912/637-5274, fall–winter daily 7 A.M.–7 P.M., spring–summer daily 6:30 A.M.–8:30 P.M.), a.k.a. the **West Entrance,** near Fargo, Georgia, there are 66 tent sites ($24) and nine cottages ($100). Several miles away, the state has recently opened the **Suwannee River Visitor Center** (912/637-5274, www.gastateparks.org, Wed.–Sun. 9 A.M.–5 P.M.), a "green" building featuring an orientation video and exhibits.

Getting There and Around

For anyone using this guide as a travel resource, the best way to access the Okefenokee—and the one I recommend—is the **East Entrance** (912/496-7836, www.fws.gov/okefenokee, Mar.–Oct. daily dawn–7:30 P.M., Nov.–Feb. daily dawn–5:30 P.M., $5 per vehicle), otherwise known as the **Suwannee Canal Recreation Area.** This is the main U.S. Fish and Wildlife Service entrance and the most convenient way to hike, rent boating and camping gear, and observe nature. The **Richard S. Bolt Visitor Center** (912/496-7836) has some cool nature exhibits and a surround-sound orientation video. Get to the East Entrance by taking I-95 exit 3 for Kingsland onto Highway 40 west. Go through Kingsland and into Folkston until it dead-ends. Take a right, then an immediate left onto Main Street. At the third light, make a left onto Okefenokee Drive (Hwy. 121) south.

Families with kids may want to drive a bit farther and hit the **North Entrance** at the privately run **Okefenokee Swamp Park** (U.S. 1, 912/283-0583, www.okeswamp.com, daily 9 A.M.–5:30 P.M., $12 adults, $11 ages 3–11) near Waycross, Georgia. (Fans of the old *Pogo* will recall Waycross from the comic strip; and yes, there's a real "Fort Mudge" nearby.) Here you will find a more touristy vibe, with a reconstructed pioneer village, serpentarium, and animals in captivity. From here you can take various guided tours for an additional fee. There's camping at the nearby but unaffiliated **Laura S. Walker State Park** (5653 Laura Walker Rd., 800/864-7275, www.gastateparks.org). Be aware the state park is not in the swamp and isn't very swampy. Get to the North Entrance by taking I-95 exit 29 and going west on U.S. 82 about 45 miles to Highway 177 (Laura Walker Rd.). Go south through Laura S. Walker State Park; the Swamp Park is several miles farther.

If you really want that cypress-festooned, classic swamp look, take the long way around the Okefenokee to **Stephen Foster State Park** (17515 Hwy. 177, 912/637-5274, fall–winter daily 7 A.M.–7 P.M., spring–summer daily 6:30 A.M.–8:30 P.M.), a.k.a. the **West Entrance,** near Fargo, Georgia. Guided tours are available. Get to Stephen Foster State Park by taking I-95 exit 3 and following the signs to Folkston. Get on Highway 121 south to St. George, and then go west on Highway 94.

FOLKSTON

The chief attraction in Folkston, the little town right outside the refuge's East Entrance, is the excellent ◖ **Inn at Folkston Bed and Breakfast** (509 W. Main St., 888/509-6246, www.innatfolkston.com, $120–170). There is nothing like coming back to its cozy Victorian charms after a long day out in the swamp. The four-room inn boasts an absolutely outstanding breakfast, an extensive reading library, and a whirlpool tub.

A five-minute drive from the Inn is another Folkston claim to fame, the viewing depot for the **Folkston Funnel** (912/496-2536, www.folkston.com), a veritable train watcher's paradise. This is the spot where the big CSX double-track rail line—following the top of the ancient Trail Ridge—hosts 60 or more trains a day. Railroad buffs from all over the South congregate here, anticipating the next train by listening to their scanners. The first Saturday each April brings buffs together for the all-day Folkston RailWatch.

BACKGROUND

The Land

GEOGRAPHY

The area covered by this guide falls within the **Coastal Plain** region of the southeastern United States, which contains some of the most unique ecosystems in North America. It's a place where water is never far away and features large in the daily lives, economy, and folkways of the region's people.

The ancient geography of the region determines the nature of the coast today, still in a profound state of flux from a variety of factors. Although it's hundreds of miles away, the Appalachian Mountain chain has a major influence on the southeastern coast. It's in Appalachia where so much of the coast's freshwater—in the form of rain—comes together and flows southeast—in the form of rivers—to the Atlantic Ocean. Moving east, the next level down from the Appalachians is the **Piedmont** region (in South Carolina often called simply the Upstate). The Piedmont is a hilly area, the eroded remains of an ancient mountain chain. At the Piedmont's eastern edge is the **fall line**, so named because it's where rivers make a drop toward the sea, generally becoming navigable. Around the fall line zone in the **Upper Coastal**

© JIM MOREKIS

Plain you can sometimes spot **sand hills,** usually only a few feet in elevation, generally thought to be the vestigial remains of primordial sand dunes and offshore sandbars. Well beyond the fall line and sometimes nearly invisible sand hills lies the **Lower Coastal Plain,** gradually built up over a 150-million-year span by sedimentary runoff from the Appalachian Mountains, then as high or even higher than the modern-day Himalayas. The Coastal Plain was sea bottom for much of the earth's history, and in some eroded areas you can see dramatic proof of this in prehistoric shells, shark's teeth, and fossilized whale bones and oyster beds, often many miles inland. Sea level has fluctuated wildly with climate and geological changes through the eons. At various times over the last 50 million years, the Coastal Plain has submerged, surfaced, and submerged again. At the height of the last major ice age, when global sea levels were very low, the east coast of North America extended out nearly 100 miles farther than the present shoreline. (We now call this former coastal region the **continental shelf.**) The Coastal Plain has been roughly in its current form for about the last 15,000 years.

Rivers

Visitors from drier climates are sometimes shocked to see how huge the rivers can get in coastal Georgia and South Carolina, wide and voluminous as they saunter to the sea, their seemingly slow speed belying the massive power they contain. Georgia and South Carolina's big **alluvial,** or sediment-bearing, rivers originate in the region of the Appalachian mountain chain. The headwaters of the Savannah River, for example, are near Tallulah Gorge in extreme north Georgia. Some rivers form out of the confluence of smaller rivers, such as Georgia's mighty Altamaha River, actually the child of the Ocmulgee and Oconee Rivers in the middle of the state. Others, like the Ashley and Cooper Rivers in South Carolina, originate much closer to the coast in the Piedmont.

The **blackwater river** is a particularly interesting Southern phenomenon, duplicated only in South America and one example each in New York and Michigan. While alluvial rivers generally originate in highlands and carry with them a large amount of sediment, blackwater rivers originate in low-lying areas and move slowly toward the sea, carrying with them very little sediment. Rather, their dark tea color comes from the tannic acid of decaying vegetation all along their banks, washed out by the slow, inexorable movement of the river toward the sea. While I don't necessarily recommend drinking it, despite its dirty color, blackwater is for the most part remarkably clean and hygienic. Blackwater courses featured prominently in this guide are the Edisto River (the longest blackwater river in the world), Ebenezer Creek near Savannah, and Georgia's Suwannee River, which originates in the Okefenokee Swamp and empties in the Gulf of Mexico. Georgia's Altamaha River is a hybrid of sorts because it is partially fed by the blackwater Ohoopee River.

The Intracoastal Waterway

You'll often see its acronym, ICW, on signs—and sadly you'll probably hear the locals mispronounce it "intercoastal"—but the casual visitor might actually find the Intracoastal Waterway difficult to spot. Relying on a natural network of interconnected estuaries and channels, combined with artificial **cuts,** the ICW often blends in rather subtly with the already extensive network of creeks and rivers in the area.

Mandated by Congress in 1919 and maintained by the U.S. Army Corps of Engineers, the Atlantic portion of the ICW runs from Key West, Florida, to Boston and carries recreational and barge traffic away from the perils of offshore currents and weather. Even if they don't use it specifically, kayakers and boaters often find themselves on it at some point during their nautical adventures.

Estuaries

Most biologists will tell you that the Coastal Plain is where things get interesting. The place where a river interfaces with the ocean is called an estuary, and it's perhaps the most interesting place of all. Estuaries are heavily tidal in nature (indeed, the word derives from *aestus,* Latin for "tide"), and feature brackish water and heavy silt content. This portion of the U.S. coast typically has about a 6–8-foot tidal range, and the coastal ecosystem depends on this steady ebb and flow for life. At high tide, shellfish open and feed. At low tide, they literally clam up, keeping saltwater inside their shells until the next tide comes. Water birds and small mammals feed on shellfish and other animals at low tide, when their prey is exposed. High tide brings an influx of fish and nutrients from the sea, in turn drawing predators like dolphins, who often come into tidal creeks to feed. In the region covered by this guide, key estuaries from north to south are: Cape Romain, Charleston Harbor, the ACE (Ashepoo, Combahee, Edisto) Basin, Beaufort River, May River, Calibogue Sound, Savannah River, Wilmington River, Midway River, Altamaha River, and the Brunswick River.

Salt Marsh

All this water action in both directions—freshwater coming from inland, saltwater encroaching from the Atlantic—results in the phenomenon of the salt marsh, the single most recognizable and iconic geographic feature of the Georgia and South Carolina coast, also known simply as "wetlands." (Freshwater marshes are rarer, Florida's Everglades being perhaps the premier example.) Far more than just a transitional zone between land and water, marsh is also nature's nursery. Plant and animal life in marshes tends not only to be diverse but

encompasses multitudes. You may not see its denizens easily, but on close inspection you'll find the marsh absolutely teeming with creatures. Visually, the main identifying feature of a salt marsh is its distinctive, reedlike marsh grasses, adapted to survive in brackish water. Like estuaries, marshes and all life in them are heavily influenced by the tides, which bring in nutrients.

The marsh has also played a key role in human history as well, for it was here that the massive rice and indigo plantations grew their signature crops, aided by the natural ebb and flow of the tides. While most marsh you see will look quite undisturbed, very little of it could be called pristine. In the heyday of the rice plantations, much of the coastal salt marsh was crisscrossed by the canal-and-dike system of the paddy fields. You can still see evidence almost everywhere in this area if you look hard enough (the best time to look is right after takeoff or before landing in an airplane, since many approaches to regional airports take you over wetlands). Anytime you see a low, straight ridge running through a marsh, that's likely the eroded, overgrown remnant of an old paddy field dike. Kayakers occasionally find old wooden sluice gates on their paddles.

In the Lowcountry, you'll often hear the term **pluff mud.** This refers to the area's distinctive variety of soft, dark mud in the salt marsh, which often has an equally distinctive odor that locals love but some visitors have a hard time getting used to. Extraordinarily rich in nutrients, pluff mud helped make rice such a successful crop in the marshes of the Lowcountry.

In addition to their huge role as wildlife incubators and sanctuaries, wetlands are also one of the most important natural protectors of the health of the coastal region. They serve as natural filters, cleansing runoff from the land of toxins and pollutants before it hits the ocean. They also help humans by serving as natural hurricane barriers, their porous nature helping to ease the brunt of the damaging storm surge.

Beaches and Barrier Islands

The beautiful, broad beaches of Georgia and South Carolina are almost all situated on barrier islands, long islands parallel to the shoreline and separated from the mainland by a sheltered body of water. Because they're formed by the deposit of sediment by offshore currents, they change shape over the years, with the general pattern of deposit going from north to south (meaning the northern end will begin eroding first). Most of the barrier islands are geologically quite young, only having formed within the last 25,000 years or so. Natural erosion by currents and by storms, combined with the accelerating effects of dredging for local port activity, has quickened the decline of many barrier islands. Many beaches in the area are subject to a mitigation of erosion called **beach renourishment,** which generally involves redistributing dredged material closely offshore so that it will wash up on and around the beach.

As the name indicates, barrier islands are another of nature's safeguards against hurricane damage. Historically, the barrier islands have borne the vast bulk of the damage done by hurricanes in the region. Tybee Island near Savannah was completely under water in the hurricane of 1898. More recently, Sullivan's Island near Charleston was submerged by 1989's Hurricane Hugo. Like the marshes, barrier islands also help protect the mainland by absorbing the brunt of the storm's wind and surging water.

Though barrier islands are ephemeral by nature, they have played an important role in the area's geography from the beginning of time. In fact, nearly every major settlement on the Georgia coast today—including Savannah, Darien, and Brunswick—is built on the vestiges of massive barrier islands that once guarded a primordial shoreline many miles inland from the present one. By far the largest of these ancient barrier islands, now on dry land, is the fabled **Trail Ridge,** which runs from Jesup, Georgia, to Starke, Florida. The Trail Ridge's height all along its distance made it a favorite route first for Native Americans and then for railroads, which still run along its crest today. The Trail Ridge is such a dominant geographical feature even today that it's actually responsible for the formation of the Okefenokee Swamp. The Ridge effectively acts as a levee on the swamp's eastern side, preventing its drainage to the sea.

CLIMATE

One word comes to mind when one thinks about Southern climate: *hot.* That's the first word that occurs to Southerners as well, but virtually every survey of why residents are attracted to the area puts the climate at the top of the list. Go figure. How hot is hot? The average high for July, the region's hottest month, in Savannah is about 92°F, in Charleston about 89°F. While that's nothing compared to Tucson or Death Valley, coupled with the region's notoriously high **humidity** it can have an altogether miserable effect. Heat aside, there's no doubt that one of the most difficult things for an outsider to adjust to in the South is the humidity. The average annual humidity in Charleston and Savannah is about 55 percent in the afternoons and a whopping 85 percent in the mornings. The most humid months are August and September. There is no real antidote to humidity—other than air conditioning, that is—although many film crews and other outside workers swear by the use of Sea Breeze astringent. If you and your traveling companions can deal with the strong minty odor, dampen a hand towel with the astringent, drape it across the back of your neck, and go about your business. Don't assume that because it's humid you shouldn't drink fluids. Just as in any hot climate, you should drink lots of water if you're going to be out in the Southern heat.

August and September are by far the wettest months in terms of rainfall, with averages well over six inches for each of those months. July is also quite wet, coming in at over five inches on average.

Winters here are pretty mild but can seem much colder than they actually are because of the dampness in the air. The coldest month is January, with a high of about 58°F for the month and 42°F the average low. You're highly unlikely to encounter snow in the area, and if you do, it will likely be only skimpy flurries that a resident of the Great Lakes region wouldn't even notice as snow. But don't let this lull you into a false sense of security. If such a tiny flurry were to hit, be aware that most people down here have no clue how to drive in rough weather and will not be prepared for even such a small amount of snowfall. Visitors from snow country are often surprised, sometimes bordering on shock, by how completely a Southern city will shut down when that once-in-a-decade few tenths of an inch of snow finally hits.

Hurricanes

The major weather phenomenon of concern for residents and visitors alike is the mighty hurricane. These massive storms, with counterclockwise-rotating bands of clouds and winds pushing 200 mph, are an ever-present danger to the southeast coast June–November each year. While the South Carolina coast has had its share of hurricane strikes, historically the Georgia coast has been relatively safe, if not immune, from major hurricane activity. In fact, as of this writing the last major storm to hit the Georgia coast directly was in 1898. Meteorologists chalk this up to the Georgia coast's relatively sheltered, concave position relative to the rest of the southeastern coastline, as well as prevailing pressure and wind patterns that tend to deflect the oncoming storms. In any case, as most everyone is aware of now from the horrific, well-documented damage from such killer storms as Hugo, Andrew, and Katrina, hurricanes are not to be trifled with. Old-fashioned drunken "hurricane parties" are a thing of the past for the most part, the images of cataclysmic destruction everyone has seen on TV having long since eliminated any lingering romanticism about riding out the storm.

Tornadoes—especially those that come in the "back door" through the Gulf of Mexico and overland to the Georgia or Carolina coast—are a very present danger with hurricanes. As hurricanes die out over land, they can spawn literally dozens of tornadoes, which in many cases prove more destructive than the hurricanes that spawned them.

Local TV, websites, and print media can be counted on to give more than ample warning in the event a hurricane is approaching the area during your visit. Whatever you do, do not discount the warnings; it's not worth it. If the locals are preparing to leave, you should too. Typically when a storm is likely to hit the area, there will first be a suggested evacuation. But if authorities determine there's an overwhelming likelihood of imminent hurricane damage, they will issue a **mandatory evacuation order.** What this means in practice is that if you do choose to stay behind, you cannot count on any type of emergency services or help whatsoever.

Generally speaking, the most lethal element of a hurricane is not the wind but the **storm surge,** the wall of ocean water that the winds drive before them onto the coast. During 1989's Hurricane Hugo, Charleston's Battery was inundated with a storm surge of over 12 feet, with an amazing 20 feet reported farther north at Cape Romain.

In the wake of such devastation, local governments have dramatically improved their once tepid disaster-response plans. For example, the large red traffic barriers you see stowed in their ready positions at many exits along I-16 in Georgia are a direct result of the chaos of the botched evacuation during Hurricane Floyd in 1999. Learning from that lesson, Georgia officials decided to make all four lanes of I-16 westbound in the event of a major evacuation, and those red barriers are there today to reroute traffic should they ever be needed.

ENVIRONMENTAL ISSUES

The coast of Georgia and South Carolina is currently experiencing a double whammy, environmentally speaking: Not only are its distinctive wetlands extraordinarily sensitive to human interference, this is one of the most rapidly developing parts of the country. New and often poorly planned subdivisions and resort communities are popping up all over the place. Vastly increased port activity is also taking a devastating toll on the salt marsh and surrounding barrier islands. Combine all that with the South's often skeptical attitude toward environmental activism and you have a recipe for potential ecological disaster.

Thankfully, there are some bright spots. More and more communities are seeing the value of responsible planning and not greenlighting every new development sight unseen. Land trusts and other conservation organizations are growing in size, number, funding, and influence. The large number of marine biologists in these areas at various research and educational institutions means there's a wealth of education and talent available in advising local governments and citizens on how best to conserve the area's natural beauty.

Here's a closer look at some of the most urgent environmental issues facing the region today:

Marsh Dieback

The dominant species of marsh grass, *Spartina alterniflora* (pronounced Spar-TINE-uh) and *Juncus roemerianus,* thrive in the typically brackish water of the coastal marsh estuaries, their structural presence helping to stem erosion of banks and dunes. While drought and blight have taken their toll on the grass, increased coastal development and continued channel deepening have also led to a steady creep of ocean saltwater farther and farther into remaining marsh stands.

Effects of Dredging

Port activity is economically vital—and becoming more so—to the coastal cities of Charleston, Savannah, and Brunswick. The downside of such large-scale industrial dredging is threefold:

- 1. The deeper the channel, the farther upstream salty ocean water pushes. This destroys freshwater and brackish habitats such as the salt marsh.
- 2. Deepening the channel increases both the volume and the velocity of the river, quickening erosion of the riverbanks.
- 3. Too much dredging risks the intrusion of ocean saltwater into underground freshwater aquifers that provide drinking water to millions of people in the area.

Currently the debate over harbor deepening has hit home in both Charleston and Savannah, two of the country's busiest ports. As of this writing the states of South Carolina and Georgia are both pursuing deepening at each city's port, much to the consternation of local environmentalists.

The Paper Industry

Early in the 20th century, the Southeast's abundance of cheap undeveloped land and plentiful free water led to the establishment of massive pine tree farms to feed coastal pulp and paper mills. Chances are, if you used a paper grocery bag recently, it was made in a paper mill in the South. But in addition to making a whole lot of paper bags and providing lots of employment for residents through the decades, the paper industry also gave the area lots of air and water pollution, stressed local water supplies (it takes a lot of freshwater to make paper from trees), and took away natural species diversity from the area by devoting so much acreage to a single crop, pine trees.

Currently the domestic paper industry is reeling from competition from cheaper Asian lumber stocks and paper mills. As a result, an interesting—and not altogether welcome—phenomenon has been the wholesale entry of Southeastern paper companies into the real estate business. Discovering that they can make a whole lot more money selling or developing tree farms for residential lots than making paper bags, pulp and paper companies are helping to drive overdevelopment in the region by encouraging development on their land rather than infill development closer to urban areas. So, in the long run, the demise of the paper industry in the South may not prove to be the net advantage to the environment that was anticipated.

Aquifers

Unlike parts of the western United States, where individuals can enforce private property rights to water, the South has generally held that the region's water is a publicly held resource. The upside of this is that everybody has equal claim to drinking water without regard to status or income or how long they've lived here. The downside is that industry also has the same free claim to the water that citizens do—and they use a heck of a lot more of it.

Currently most of the Georgia and South Carolina coasts get their water from aquifers, which are basically huge underground caverns made of limestone. Receiving **groundwater** drip by drip, century after century, from rainfall farther inland, the aquifers essentially act as massive sterile warehouses for freshwater, accessible through wells. The aquifers have human benefit only if their water remains fresh. Once saltwater from the ocean begins intruding into an aquifer, it doesn't take much to render all of it unfit for human consumption—forever. What keeps that freshwater fresh is natural water pressure, keeping the ocean at bay. But nearly a century ago, paper mills began pumping millions and millions of gallons of water out of coastal aquifers. Combined with the dramatic rise in coastal residential development and a continuing push to deepen existing shipping channels, the natural water pressure of the aquifers has decreased, leading to measurable saltwater intrusion at several points under the coast.

Currently, local and state governments in both states are increasing their reliance on **surface water** (treated water from rivers and creeks) to relieve the strain on the underground aquifer system. But it's too soon to tell if that has contained the threat from saltwater intrusion.

Air Pollution

Despite growing awareness of the issue, air pollution is still a big problem in the coastal region. Paper mills still operate, putting out their distinctive rotten-eggs odor, and auto emissions standards are notoriously lax in both Georgia and South Carolina. The biggest culprit, though, are coal-powered electric plants, which are the norm throughout the region and which continue to pour large amounts of toxins into the atmosphere.

Flora and Fauna

FLORA

Undoubtedly the most iconic plant life of the coastal region is the **Southern live oak** (*Quercus virginiana*) the official state tree of Georgia. Named because of its evergreen nature, a live oak is technically any of a number of evergreens in the *Quercus* genus, many of which reside on the Georgia and South Carolina coast, but in local practice almost always refers to the Southern live oak. Capable of living over 1,000 years and possessing wood of legendary resilience, the Southern live oak is one of nature's most magnificent creations. The timber value of live oaks has been well known since the earliest days of the American shipbuilding industry—when the oak dominated the entire coast inland of the marsh—but their value as a canopy tree has finally been widely recognized by local and state governments.

Fittingly, the other iconic plant life of the coastal region grows on the branches of the live oak. Contrary to popular opinion, **Spanish moss** (*Tillandsia usneoides*) is neither Spanish nor moss. It's an air plant, a wholly indigenous cousin to the pineapple. Also contrary to folklore, Spanish moss is not a parasite nor does it harbor parasites while living on an oak tree—although it can after it has already fallen to the ground. Also growing on the bark of a live oak, especially right after a rain shower, is the **resurrection fern** (*Polypodium polypodioides*), which can stay dormant for amazingly long periods of time, only to spring back to life with the introduction of a little water. You can find live oak, Spanish moss, and resurrection fern anywhere in the **maritime forest** ecosystem of coastal Georgia and South Carolina, a zone generally behind the **interdune meadows,** which is right behind the beach zone.

The oak may be Georgia's state tree, but far and away its most important commercial tree is the pine, used for paper, lumber, and turpentine. Rarely seen in the wild today due to tree farming, which has covered most of southern Georgia, the dominant species is now the **slash pine** (*Pinus elliottii*), often seen in long rows on either side of rural highways. Before the introduction of large-scale monoculture tree farming, however, a rich variety of native pines flourished in the **upland forest** inland from the maritime forest, including **longleaf** (*Pinus palustris*) and **loblolly** (*Pinus taeda*) pines.

Right up there with live oaks and Spanish moss in terms of instant recognition would have to be the colorful, ubiquitous **azalea,** a flowering shrub of the *Rhododendron* genus. Over 10,000 varieties have been cultivated through the centuries, with quite a wide range of them on display during blooming season, March–April, on the Georgia and South Carolina coast (slightly earlier farther south, slightly later farther north). The area's other great floral display comes from the **camellia** (*Camellia japonica*), a large, cold-hardy evergreen shrub that generally blooms in late winter (Jan.–Mar.). An import from Asia, the southeastern coast's camellias are close cousins to *Camellia sinensis,* also an import and the plant from which tea is made. Other colorful ornamentals of the area include the ancient and beautiful **Southern magnolia** (*Magnolia grandiflora*), a native plant with distinctive large white flowers that evolved before the advent of bees; and the **flowering dogwood** (*Cornus florida*), which, despite its very hard wood—great for daggers, hence its original name "dagwood"—is actually quite fragile. An ornamental imported from Asia that has now become quite obnoxious in its aggressive invasiveness is the **mimosa** (*Albizia julibrissin*), which blooms March–August.

An indigenous bush with an interesting history is the **yaupon holly** (*Ilex vomitoria*), from

© SOPHIA MOREKIS

azaleas in full bloom

which coastal Native Americans made the famous "black drink." (Indeed, Ossabaw Island, Georgia, gets its name from a Native American phrase meaning "yaupon holly bushes place.") This bitter, caffeinated tea not only gave Native Americans a buzz that helped them in spiritual quests, it was used for ritual purification and cleansing because it induces copious vomiting and loosens the bowels. However, holly tea in moderate amounts will have no noticeable effect other than a little caffeine boost, and the drink is still quaffed today in some rural areas of the coast.

Moving into watery areas, you'll find the remarkable **bald cypress** (*Taxodium distichum*), a flood-resistant conifer recognizable by its tufted top, its great height (up to 130 feet), and its distinctive "knees," parts of the root that project above the waterline and which are believed to help stabilize the tree in lowland areas. Much prized for its beautiful pest-resistant wood, great stands of ancient cypress once

dominated the marsh along the coast; sadly, overharvesting and destruction of wetlands has made the magnificent sight of this ancient, dignified species much less common. The acres of **smooth cordgrass** for which the Golden Isles are named are plants of the *Spartina alterniflora* species. (A cultivated cousin, *Spartina anglica,* is considered invasive.) Besides its simple natural beauty, *Spartina* is also a key food source for marsh denizens. Playing a key environmental role on the coast are **sea oats** (*Uniola paniculata*). This wispy, fast-growing perennial grass anchors sand dunes and hence is a protected species on the Georgia coast (it's a misdemeanor to pick them).

South Carolina isn't called the "Palmetto State" for nothing. Palm varieties are not as common up here as in Florida, but you'll definitely encounter several types along the Georgia and South Carolina coast. The **cabbage palm** (*Sabal palmetto*), for which South Carolina is named, is the largest variety, up to 50–60 feet tall. Its "heart of palm" is an edible delicacy, which coastal Native Americans boiled in bear fat as porridge. In dunes and sand hills you'll find clumps of the low-lying **saw palmetto** (*Serenoa repens*). The **bush palmetto** (*Sabal minor*) has distinctive fan-shaped branches. The common **Spanish bayonet** (*Yucca aloifolia*) looks like a palm, but it's actually a member of the agave family.

FAUNA
On the Land

Perhaps the most iconic land animal—or semi-land animal, anyway—of the Georgia and South Carolina coast is the legendary **American alligator** (*Alligator mississippiensis*), the only species of crocodilian native to the area. Contrary to their fierce reputation, locals know these massive reptiles, 6–12 feet long as adults, to be quite shy. If you come in the colder months, you won't see them at all, since alligators require an outdoor temperature over 70°F to become active and feed (indeed, the appearance of alligators was once a well-known symbol of spring in the area). Often all you'll see is a couple of eyebrow ridges sticking out of the water, and a gator lying still in a shallow creek can easily be mistaken for a floating log. But should you see one or more gators basking in the sun—a favorite activity on warm days for these cold-blooded creatures—it's best to admire them from afar. A mother alligator, in particular, will destroy anything that comes near her nest. Despite the alligator's short, stubby legs, they run amazingly fast on land—faster than you, in fact.

If you're driving on a country road at night, be on the lookout for **white-tailed deer** (*Odocoileus virginianus*), which, besides being quite beautiful, also pose a serious road hazard. Because coastal development has dramatically reduced the habitat—and therefore the numbers—of their natural predators, deer are very plentiful throughout the area, and as you read this they are hard at work devouring vast tracts of valuable vegetation. No one wants to hurt poor little Bambi, but the truth is that area hunters perform a valuable service by culling the local deer population, which is in no danger of extinction anytime soon.

The coast hosts fairly large populations of playful **river otters** (*Lontra canadensis*). Not to be confused with the larger sea otters of the West Coast, these fast-swimming members of the weasel family inhabit inland waterways and marshy areas, with dominant males sometimes ranging as much as 50 miles within a single waterway. While you're unlikely to encounter an otter, if you're camping, you might easily run into the **raccoon** (*Procyon lotor*), an exceedingly intelligent and crafty relative of the bear, sharing that larger animal's resourcefulness in stealing your food. Though nocturnal, raccoons will feed whenever food is available. Rabies is prevalent in the raccoon population, and you should always, always keep your distance.

Another common campsite nuisance, the **opossum** (*Didelphis virginiana*) is a shy, primitive creature that is much more easily discouraged. North America's only marsupial, an opossum's usual "defense" against predators is to play dead. That said, however, they have an immunity to snake venom and often feed on the reptiles, even the most poisonous ones.

While you're highly unlikely to actually see a **red fox** (*Vulpes vulpes*), you might very well see their distinctive footprints in the mud of a marsh at low tide. These nocturnal hunters, a nonnative species introduced by European settlers, range the coast seeking mice, squirrels, and rabbits.

Once fairly common in Georgia and South Carolina, the **black bear** (*Ursus americanus*) has suffered from hunting and habitat destruction. Of the regions in this guide, the Okefenokee Swamp area is the only place in which you'll be close to one.

In the Water

Without a doubt the most magnificent denizen—if only part-time—of the southeastern coast is the **North American right whale** (*Eubalaena glacialis*), which can approach 60 feet in length. Each year December–March the mothers give birth to their calves and nurse them in the warm waters off the Georgia coast in an eons-old ritual. (In the summers they like to hang around the rich fishing grounds off the New England coast, although biologists still can't account for their whereabouts at other times of the year.) Their numbers were so abundant in past centuries that the Spanish name for Jekyll Island, Georgia, was Isla de las Ballenas (Island of the Whales). Whaling and encounters with ship propellers have taken their toll, and numbers of this endangered species are dwindling fast now, with less than 500 estimated left in the world.

Another of humankind's aquatic cousins, the **Atlantic bottle-nosed dolphin** (*Tursiops*

© JIM MOREKIS

Waterfowl abound in the coastal region.

truncatus) is a well-known and frequent visitor to the coast, coming far upstream into creeks and rivers to feed. Children, adults, and experienced sailors alike all delight in encounters with the mammals, sociable creatures who travel in family units. When not occupied with feeding or mating activities—both of which can get surprisingly rowdy—dolphins show great curiosity about human visitors to their habitat. They will gather near boats, surfacing often with the distinctive chuffing sound of air coming from their blowholes. Occasionally they'll even lift their heads out of the water to have a look at you; consider yourself lucky indeed to have such a close encounter. Don't be fooled by their cuteness, however. Dolphins live life with gusto and aren't scared of much. They're voracious eaters of fish, amorous and energetic lovers, and will take on an encroaching shark in a heartbeat.

Another beloved part-time marine creature of the barrier islands of the Georgia and South Carolina coast is the **loggerhead turtle** (*Caretta caretta*). Though the species prefers to stay well offshore the rest of the year, females weighing up to 300 pounds come out of the sea each May–July to dig a shallow hole in the dunes and lay over 100 leathery eggs, returning to the ocean and leaving the eggs to hatch on their own after two months. Interestingly, the mothers prefer to nest at the same spot on the same island year after year. After hatching, the baby turtles then make a dramatic, extremely dangerous (and extremely slow) trek to the safety of the waves, at the mercy of various predators. A series of dedicated research and conservation efforts, like the Caretta Project based on Wassaw Island, Georgia, are working hard to protect the loggerheads' traditional nursery grounds to ensure survival of this fascinating, loveable, and threatened species.

Of course, the coastal waters and rivers are chockablock with fish. The most abundant and sought-after recreational species in the area is the **spotted sea trout** (*Cynoscion nebulosus*), followed by the **red drum** (*Sciaenops ocellatus*). Local anglers also pursue many varieties of **bass, bream, sheepshead,** and **crappie.** It may sound strange to some accustomed to considering it a "trash" fish, but many types of **catfish** are not only plentiful here but are a common and well-regarded food source. Many species of **flounder** inhabit the silty bottoms of estuaries all along the coast. Farther offshore are game and sport fish like **marlin, swordfish, shark, grouper,** and **tuna.**

Each March, anglers jockey for position on coastal rivers for the yearly running of the **American shad** (*Alosa sapidissima*) upstream to spawn. This large (up to eight pounds) catfish-like species is a regional delicacy as a seasonal entrée as well as for its tasty roe. There's a catch limit of eight shad per person per season. One of the more interesting fish species in the area is the endangered **shortnose sturgeon** (*Acipenser brevirostrum*). A fantastically ancient species that has evolved little in hundreds of millions of years, this small freshwater fish is known to exist in the Altamaha, Savannah, and Ogeechee Rivers of Georgia and the estuaries of the ACE Basin in South Carolina. Traveling upriver to spawn in the winter, the sturgeons remain around the mouths of waterways the rest of the year, venturing near the ocean only sparingly.

Crustaceans and shellfish have been a key food staple in the area for thousands of years, with the massive shell middens of the coast being testament to Native Americans' healthy appetite for them. The beds of the local variant, the **eastern oyster** (*Crassostrea virginica*), aren't what they used to be due to overharvesting, water pollution, and disruption of habitat. In truth, these days most local restaurants import the little filter-feeders from the Gulf of Mexico. Oysters spawn May–August, hence the old folk wisdom about eating oysters only in months with the letter *r* so as not to disrupt the breeding cycle.

Each year April–January, shrimp boats up and down the southeastern coast trawl for **shrimp,** most commercially viable in two local species, the white shrimp (*Litopenaeus setiferus*), and the brown shrimp (*Farfantepenaeus aztecus*). Shrimp are the most popular seafood item in the United States and account for bringing hundreds of millions of dollars in revenue into the coastal economy. While consumption won't slow down anytime soon, the Georgia and South Carolina shrimping industries are facing serious threats, both from species decline due to pollution and overfishing as well as from competition from shrimp farms and the Asian shrimp industry.

Another important commercial crop is the **blue crab** (*Callinectes sapidus*), the species used in such Lowcountry delicacies as crab cakes. You'll often see floating markers bobbing up and down in rivers throughout the region. These signal the presence directly below of a crab trap, often of an amateur crabber. A true

living link to primordial times, the alien-looking **horseshoe crab** (*Limulus polyphemus*) is frequently found on beaches of the coast during the spring mating season (it lives in deeper water the rest of the year). More closely related to scorpions and spiders than crabs, the horseshoe has evolved hardly a lick in hundreds of millions of years. Any trip to a local salt marsh at low tide will likely uncover hundreds of **fiddler crabs** (*Uca pugilator* and *Uca pugnax*), so-named for the way the males wave their single enlarged claws in the air to attract mates. (Their other, smaller claw is the one they actually eat with.) The fiddlers make distinctive burrows in the pluff mud for sanctuary during high tide, recognizable by the little balls of sediment at the entrances (the crabs spit out the balls after sifting through the sand for food).

One charming beach inhabitant, the **sand dollar** (*Mellita quinquiesperforata*), has seen its numbers decline drastically due to being entirely too charming for its own good. Beachcombers are now asked to enjoy these flat little cousins to the sea urchin in their natural habitat and to refrain from taking them home. Besides, they start to smell bad when they dry out. The **sea nettle** (*Chrysaora quinquecirrha*), a less-than-charming beach inhabitant, is a jellyfish that stings thousands of people on the coast each year (although only for those with severe allergies are the stings potentially life-threatening). Stinging their prey before transporting it into their waiting mouths, the jellyfish also sting when disturbed or frightened. Most often, people are stung by stepping on the bodies of jellyfish washed up on the sand. If you're stung by a jellyfish, don't panic. You'll probably experience a stinging rash for about half an hour. Locals say applying a little baking soda or vinegar helps cut the sting. (Some also swear fresh urine will do the trick, and I pass that tip along to you purely in the interest of thoroughness.)

In the Air

When enjoying the marshlands of the coast, consider yourself fortunate to see an endangered **wood stork** (*Mycteria americana*), although their numbers are on the increase. The only storks to breed in North America, these graceful long-lived birds (routinely living over 10 years) are usually seen on a low flight path across the marsh, although at some birding spots beginning in late summer you can find them at a **roost,** sometimes numbering over 100 birds. Resting at high tide, they fan out over the marsh to feed at low tide on foot. Old-timers sometimes call them "Spanish buzzards" or simply "the preacher." Often confused with the wood stork is the gorgeous **white ibis** (*Eudocimus albus*), distinguishable by its orange bill and black wingtips. Like the wood stork, the ibis is a communal bird that roosts in colonies. Other similar-looking coastal denizens are the white-feathered **great egret** (*Ardea alba*) and **snowy egret** (*Egretta thula*), the former distinguishable by its yellow bill and the latter by its black bill and the tuft of plumes on the back of its head. Egrets are in the same family as herons. The most magnificent is the **great blue heron** (*Ardea herodias*). Despite their imposing height—up to four feet tall—these waders are shy. Often you hear them rather than see them, a loud shriek of alarm that echoes over the marsh. So how to tell the difference between all these wading birds at a glance? It's actually easiest when they're in flight. Egrets and herons fly with their necks tucked in, while storks and ibis fly with their necks extended.

Dozens of species of shorebirds comb the beaches, including **sandpipers, plovers,** and the wonderful and rare **American oystercatcher** (*Haematopus palliatus*), instantly recognizable for its prancing walk, dark brown back, stark white underside, and long bright-orange bill. **Gulls** and **terns** also hang out wherever there's water. They can frequently be seen swarming around incoming shrimp boats, attracted by the catch of little crustaceans.

The chief raptor of the salt marsh is the fish-eating **osprey** (*Pandion haliaetus*). These large grayish birds of prey are similar to eagles but are adapted to a maritime environment, with a reversible outer toe on each talon (the better for catching wriggly fish) and closable nostrils so they can dive into the water after prey. Very common all along the coast, they like to build big nests on top of buoys and channel markers in addition to trees. The **bald eagle** (*Haliaeetus leucocephalus*) is making a comeback in the area thanks to increased federal regulation and better education of trigger-happy locals. Apparently not as all-American as their bumper stickers might sometimes indicate, local farmers would often regard the national symbol as more of a nuisance and fire away anytime they saw one. Of course, as we all should have learned in school, the bald eagle is not actually bald but has a head adorned with white feathers. Like the osprey, they prefer fish, but unlike the osprey will settle for rodents and rabbits.

Inland among the pines you'll find the most common area woodpecker, the huge **pileated woodpecker** (*Dryocopus pileatus*) with its huge crest. Less common is the smaller, more subtly marked **red-cockaded woodpecker** (*Picoides borealis*). Once common in the vast primordial pine forests of the southeast, the species is now endangered, its last real refuge being the big tracts of relatively undisturbed land on military bases.

Insects

Down here they say that God invented bugs to keep the Yankees from completely taking over the South. And insects are probably the most unpleasant fact of life in the southeastern coastal region. The list of annoying indigenous insects must begin with the infamous **sand**

gnat (*Culicoides furens*). This tiny and persistent nuisance, a member of the midge family, lacks the precision of the mosquito with its long proboscis. No, the sand gnat is more torture master than surgeon, brutally gouging and digging away its victim's skin until it hits a source of blood. Most prevalent in the spring and fall, the sand gnat is drawn to its prey by the carbon dioxide trail of its breath. While long sleeves and long pants are one way to keep gnats at bay, the only real antidote to the sand gnat's assault—other than never breathing—is the Avon skin care product Skin So Soft, which has taken on a new and wholly unplanned life as the South's favorite antignat lotion. In calmer moments, grow to appreciate the great contribution sand gnats make to the salt marsh ecosystem—as food for birds and bats.

Running a close second to the sand gnat are the over three dozen species of highly aggressive **mosquito,** which breeds anywhere a few drops of water lie stagnant. Not surprisingly, massive populations blossom in the rainiest months, in late spring and late summer, feeding in the morning and late afternoon. Like the gnat, the mosquito—the biters are always female—homes in on its victim by trailing the plume of carbon dioxide exhaled in the breath. More than just a biting nuisance, mosquitoes are now carrying West Nile disease to the Lowcountry and Georgia coast, signaling a possibly dire threat to public health. Local governments in the region pour millions of dollars of taxpayer money into massive pesticide spraying programs from helicopters, planes, and trucks. While that certainly helps stem the tide, it by no means eliminates the mosquito population. Alas, Skin So Soft has little effect on the mosquito. Try over-the-counter sprays, anything smelling of citronella, and wearing long sleeves and long pants when weather permits.

But undoubtedly the most viscerally loathed of all pests on the Lowcountry and Georgia coasts is the so-called "palmetto bug," or **American cockroach** (*Periplaneta americana*). These black, shiny, and sometimes grotesquely massive insects—up to two inches long—are living fossils, virtually unchanged over hundreds of millions of years. And perfectly adapted as they are to life in and among wet, decaying vegetation, they're unlikely to change a bit in 100 million more years. While they spend most of their time crawling around, usually under rotting leaves and tree bark, the American cockroach can indeed fly—sort of. There are few more hilarious sights than a room full of people frantically trying to dodge a palmetto bug that has just clumsily launched itself off a high point on the wall. Because the cockroach doesn't know any better than you do where it's going, it can be a particularly bracing event—though the insect does not bite and poses few real health hazards. Popular regional use of the term *palmetto bug* undoubtedly has its roots in a desire for polite Southern society to avoid using the ugly word *roach* and its connotations of filth and unclean environments. But the colloquialism actually has a basis in reality. Contrary to what anyone tells you, the natural habitat of the American cockroach—unlike its kitchen-dwelling, much-smaller cousin the German cockroach—is outdoors, often up in trees. They only come inside human dwellings when it's especially hot, especially cold, or especially dry outside. Like you, the palmetto bug is easily driven indoors by extreme temperatures and by thirst. Other than visiting the Southeast during the winter, when the roaches go dormant, there's no convenient antidote for their presence. The best way to keep them out of your life is to stay away from decaying vegetation and keep doors and windows closed on especially hot nights.

History

BEFORE THE EUROPEANS

Based on artifacts found throughout the state, anthropologists know the first humans arrived to the coasts of South Carolina and Georgia at least 13,000 years ago, at the tail end of the last ice age. During this **Paleo-Indian Period,** sea levels were over 200 feet lower than present levels, and large mammals such as woolly mammoths, horses, and camels were hunted for food and skins. However, rapidly increasing temperatures, rising sea levels, and efficient hunting techniques combined to quickly kill off these large mammals, relics of the Pleistocene Era, ushering in the **Archaic Period.** Still hunter-gatherers, Archaic Period Indians began turning to small game such as deer, bears, and turkeys, supplemented with fruit and nuts. The latter part of the Archaic era saw more habitation on the coasts, with an increasing reliance on fish and shellfish. It's during this time that the great **shell middens** of the Georgia and South Carolina coasts trace their origins. Basically serving as trash heaps for discarded oyster shells, as the middens grew in size they also took on a ceremonial status, often being used as sites for important rituals and meetings. Such sites are often called **shell rings,** and the largest yet found was over nine feet high and 300 feet in diameter.

The introduction of agriculture and improved pottery techniques about 3,000 years ago led to the **Woodland Period** of Native American settlement. Extended clan groups were much less migratory, establishing year-round communities of up to 50 people, who began the practice of clearing land to grow crops. The ancient shell middens of their ancestors were not abandoned, however, and were

Ancient shell middens are legacies of Native Americans.

© JIM MOREKIS

continually added onto. Native Americans had been cremating or burying their dead for years, a practice which eventually gave rise to the construction of the first **mounds** during the Woodland Period. Essentially built-up earthworks sometimes marked with spiritual symbols, often in the form of animal shapes, mounds not only contained the remains of the deceased but items like pottery to accompany the deceased into the afterlife.

Increased agriculture led to increased population, and with that population growth came competition over resources and a more formal notion of warfare. This period, about A.D. 800–1600, is termed the **Mississippian Period.** It was the Mississippians who would be the first Native Americans in what's now the continental United States to encounter European explorers and settlers after Columbus. The Native Americans who would later be called **Creek Indians** were the direct descendants of the Mississippians in lineage, language, and lifestyle. Native American social structure north of Mexico reached its apex with the Mississippians, who were not only prodigious mound builders but constructed elaborate wooden villages and evolved a top-down class system. The defensive palisades surrounding some of the villages attest to the increasingly martial nature of the groups and their chieftains, or *micos*. Described by later European accounts as a tall, proud people, the Mississippians often wore elaborate body art and, like the indigenous inhabitants of Central and South America, used the practice of **head shaping,** whereby an infant's skull was deliberately deformed into an elongated shape by tying the baby's head to a board for about a year. The influence and mystique of the *micos* were so powerful to the Mississippians that the tribes and the areas they controlled were simply named after the chiefs themselves. What the earliest European visitors thought were Indian place names—for example, Guale in coastal Georgia, in the vicinity of modern-day St. Catherine's Island—were actually the names of the dominant *micos* in those areas. By about A.D. 1400, however, change came to the Mississippian culture for reasons that are still not completely understood. In some areas, large chiefdoms began splintering into smaller subgroups in an intriguing echo of the medieval feudal system going on concurrently in Europe. In other areas, however, the rise of a handful of über-*micos* subsumed smaller communities under their influence. In either case, the result was the same: The landscape of the Southeast became less peopled as many of the old villages, built around huge central mounds, were abandoned. As tensions and paranoia among the chiefdoms increased, the contested land between them became more and more dangerous for the poorly armed or poorly connected. Indeed, at the time of the Europeans' arrival, much of the coastal area was more thinly inhabited than it had been for many decades.

THE SPANISH ARRIVE

The first known contact by Europeans on the southeastern coast came in 1521, roughly concurrent with Cortés's conquest of Mexico. A party of Spanish slavers ventured into what's now Port Royal Sound, South Carolina, from Santo Domingo in the Caribbean. Naming the area Santa Elena, they kidnapped a few Indian slaves and left, ranging as far north as the Cape Fear River in present-day North Carolina.

The first serious exploration of the coast came in 1526, when Lucas Vázquez de Ayllón and about 600 colonists made landfall at Winyah Bay in South Carolina, near present-day Georgetown. They didn't stay long, however, immediately moving down the coast and trying to set down roots in the St. Catherine's Sound area of modern-day Liberty County, Georgia. That colony—called San Miguel de Gualdape—was the first European colony in North America (the continent's oldest continuously occupied settlement, St. Augustine, Florida, wasn't founded until 1565). The colony also brought with it the seed of a future nation's dissolution: slaves from Africa. While San Miguel lasted only six weeks due to political tension and a slave uprising, artifacts from its brief life have been discovered in the area.

Hernando de Soto's ill-fated trek of 1539–1543 from Florida through Georgia to Alabama (where De Soto died of a fever) did not find the gold he anticipated, nor did it enter the coastal region covered in this guide. But De Soto's legacy was indeed soon felt there and throughout the Southeast in the form of various diseases for which the Mississippian people had no immunity whatsoever: smallpox, typhus, influenza, measles, yellow fever, whooping cough, diphtheria, tuberculosis, and bubonic plague. While the cruelties of the Spanish certainly took their toll, far more damaging were these deadly diseases to a population totally unprepared for them. Within a few years, the Mississippian people—already in a state of internal decline—were losing huge percentages of their population to disease, echoing what had already happened on a massive scale to the indigenous people of the Caribbean after Christopher Columbus's expeditions. As the viruses they introduced ran rampant, the Europeans themselves stayed away for a couple of decades after the ignominious end of De Soto's fruitless quest. During that quarter-century, the once-proud Mississippian culture continued to disintegrate, dwindling into a shadow of its former greatness. In all, disease would claim the lives of at least 80 percent of all indigenous inhabitants of the western hemisphere.

THE FRENCH MISADVENTURE

The next European presence on the Georgia and South Carolina coast was another ill-fated attempt, the establishment of Charlesfort in 1562 by French Huguenots under Jean Ribault on present-day Parris Island, South Carolina. Part of a covert effort by the Protestant French Admiral Coligny to send Huguenot colonists around the globe, Ribault's crew of 150 first explored the mouth of the St. Johns River near present-day Jacksonville, Florida, before heading north.

After establishing Charlesfort, Ribault returned to France for supplies. In his absence, religious war had broken out in his home country. Ribault sought sanctuary in England but was clapped in irons anyway. Meanwhile, most of Charlesfort's colonists grew so demoralized they joined another French expedition led by René Laudonnière at Fort Caroline on the St. Johns River. The remaining 27 built a ship to sail from Charlesfort back to France; 20 of them survived the journey, which was cut short in the English Channel when they had to be rescued.

Ribault himself was dispatched to reinforce Fort Caroline, but was headed off by a contingent from the new Spanish settlement at St. Augustine. The fate of the French presence on the southeast coast was sealed when not only did the Spanish take Fort Caroline but a storm destroyed Ribault's reinforcing fleet. Ribault and all survivors were killed as soon as they came ashore. To keep the French away for good and cement Spain's hold on this northernmost part of their province of La Florida, the Spanish built the fort of Santa Elena directly on top of Charlesfort. Both layers are currently being excavated and studied today.

THE MISSION ERA

With Spanish dominance of the region ensured for the near future, the lengthy mission era began. It's rarely mentioned as a key part of U.S. history, but the Spanish missionary presence on the Georgia coast was longer and more comprehensive than its much more widely known counterpart in California. St. Augustine's governor Pedro Menéndez de Avilés—sharing "biscuits with honey" on the beach at St. Catherine's Island with a local *mico*—negotiated for the right to establish a system of Jesuit missions in two coastal chiefdoms: the Mocama on and around Cumberland Island, and the Guale (pronounced "wallie") to the north. Those early missions, the first north of Mexico, were largely unsuccessful. But a renewed, organized effort by the Franciscan Order came to fruition during the 1580s. Starting with Santa Catalina de Guale on St. Catherine's Island, missions were established all along the Georgia coast.

The looming invasion threat to St. Augustine from English adventurer and privateer Sir Francis Drake was a harbinger of trouble to come, as was a Guale uprising in 1597. The Spanish consolidated their positions near St. Augustine, and Santa Elena was abandoned. As Spanish power waned, in 1629 Charles I of England laid formal claim to what is now the Carolinas, Georgia, and much of Florida, but made no effort to colonize the area. Largely left to their own devices and facing an indigenous population dying from disease, the missions in the Georgia interior nonetheless carried on. A devastating Indian raid in 1661 on a mission at the mouth of the Altamaha River, possibly aided by the English, persuaded the Spanish to pull the mission effort to the barrier islands. But even as late as 1667, right before the founding of Charles Towne far to the north, there were 70 missions still extant in the old Guale kingdom.

Pirate raids and slave uprisings finished off the Georgia missions for good by 1684. By 1706 the Spanish mission effort in the southeast had fully retreated to St. Augustine. In an interesting postscript, 89 Native Americans—the only surviving descendants of Spain's Georgia missions—evacuated to Cuba with the final Spanish exodus from Florida in 1763.

ENTER THE ENGLISH

With the native populations in steep decline due to disease and a wholesale retrenchment by European powers, a sort of vacuum came to the southeastern coast. Into the vacuum came the first English-speaking settlers of South Carolina. The first attempt was an expedition by a Barbadian colonist, William Hilton, in 1663. While he didn't establish a new colony, he did leave his name on the most notable geographic feature he saw—Hilton Head Island.

In 1665 King Charles II gave a charter to eight **Lords Proprietors** to establish a colony, generously to be named Carolina after the monarch himself. (One of the Proprietors, Lord Ashley Cooper, would see not one but both rivers in the Charleston area named after him.) Remarkably, none of the Proprietors ever set foot in the colony they established for their own profit. Before their colony was even established, the Proprietors themselves set the stage for the vast human disaster that would eventually befall it. They encouraged slavery by promising that each colonist would receive 20 acres of land for every black male slave and 10 acres for every black female slave brought to the colony within the first year.

In 1666 explorer Robert Sandford officially claimed Carolina for the king. The Proprietors then sent out a fleet of three ships from England, only one of which, the *Carolina,* would make it the whole way. After stops in the thriving English colonies of Barbados and Bermuda, the ship landed in Port Royal. They were greeted without violence, but the fact that the local indigenous people spoke Spanish led the colonists to conclude that perhaps the site was too close for comfort to Spain's sphere of influence. A Kiawah chief, eager for allies against the fierce, slave-trading Westo people, invited the colonists north to settle instead. So the colonists—148 of them, including three African slaves—moved 80 miles up the coast and in 1670 pitched camp on the Ashley River at a place they dubbed Albemarle Point after one of their lost ships. Living within the palisades of the camp—you can visit it today at the Charlestowne Landing State Historic Site just

HENRY WOODWARD, COLONIAL INDIANA JONES

He's virtually unsung in the history books, and there are no movies made about him, but Dr. Henry Woodward, the first English settler in South Carolina, lived a life that is the stuff of novels and screenplays. Educated in medicine in London, Woodward first tried his hand in the colony of Barbados. But Barbados, crowded and run by an elite, was no place for a young man with a sense of adventure but no contacts in the sugar industry. Still in his teens, Woodward left Barbados in Captain Robert Sandford's 1664 expedition to Carolina. Landing in the Cape Fear region, Sandford's cohort made its way down to Port Royal Sound to contact the Cusabo Indians. In 1666, in what is perhaps the New World's first "cultural-exchange program," Woodward volunteered to stay behind while the rest of the expedition returned to England with a Native American named Shadoo.

Woodward learned the local language and established political relations with surrounding Native Americans, actions for which the Lords Proprietors granted him temporary "formall possession of the whole Country to hold as Tennant att Will." The Spanish had different plans, however. They came and kidnapped the young Englishman, taking him to what turned out to be a very permissive state of house arrest at the Spanish stronghold of St. Augustine in Florida. Surprising the Spanish with his request—in Latin, no less—to convert to Catholicism, Woodward was popular and well-treated. An excellent student of the Catechism, Woodward became a favorite of the Spanish governor and was even promoted to official surgeon. During that time, he studied Spanish government, commerce, and culture, with the same diligence with which he studied the Indians a year earlier. In 1668, Woodward was "rescued" by English privateers—pirates, really—under the command of Robert Searle, who'd come to sack St. Augustine. Woodward's sojourn with the pirates would last two years, during which he was kept on board as ship's surgeon. Was the pirate raid a coincidence? Or, as some scholars

suggest, was Woodward really one of history's greatest spies? We will probably never know.

Incredibly, the plot thickens. In another coincidence, in 1670 Woodward was rescued when the pirates shipwrecked on the Caribbean island of Nevis. His rescuers were none other than the settlers on their way to found Charles Towne. On landfall, Woodward asserted his previous experience in the area to direct the colonists away from Port Royal to an area of less Spanish influence. That same year he began a series of expeditions to contact Native Americans in the Carolina interior—the first non-Spanish European to set foot in the area. Using economic espionage gained from the Spanish, Woodward's goal was to jumpstart the trade in deerskins that would be the bulwark of the Charles Towne colony. Woodward's unlikely 1674 alliance with the aggressive Westo people was instrumental in this burgeoning trade. As if all this weren't enough, in 1680 Woodward, now with property of his own on Johns Island, would introduce local farmers to a certain strange crop recently imported from Madagascar: rice.

Woodward made enemies, however, of settlers who were envious of his growing affluence and suspicious of his friendship with the Westo. His outspoken disgust with the spread of Indian slavery brought a charge against him of undermining the interests of the crown. But Woodward, by now a celebrity of sorts, returned to England to plead his case directly to the Lords Proprietors. They not only pardoned him but made him their official Indian agent—with a 20 percent share of the profits. Woodward would never again see the land of his birth. He returned to the American colonies to trek inland, making alliances with groups of Creek Indians in Spanish-held territory. Hounded by Spanish troops, Woodward fell ill of a fever somewhere in the Savannah River valley. He made it to Charleston and safety but never fully recovered and died around 1690—after living the kind of life you usually only see in the movies.

outside Charleston—the colonists farmed 10-acre plots outside the walls.

The Native Americans of the area were of the large and influential Cusabo people of the Creek Nation, sometimes even today known as the **Settlement Indians.** Subgroups of the Cusabo whose names live on today in South Carolina geography were the Kiawah, Edisto, Wando, Stono, and Ashepoo. A few years later some colonists from Barbados, which was beginning to suffer the effects of overpopulation, joined the Carolinians. The Barbadian influence, with an emphasis on large-scale slave labor and a caste system, would have an indelible imprint on the colony. Indeed, within a generation a majority of settlers in the new colony would be African slaves. By 1680, however, Albemarle Point was feeling growing pains as well, and the Proprietors ordered the site moved to Oyster Point at the confluence of the Ashley and Cooper Rivers (the present-day Battery). Within a year Albemarle Point was abandoned, and the walls of Charles Towne were built a few hundred yards up from Oyster Point on the banks of the Cooper River.

The original Anglican settlers were quickly joined by various **Dissenters,** among them French Huguenots, Quakers, Congregationalists, and Jews. A group of Scottish Presbyterians established the short-lived Stuart Town near Port Royal in 1684. Recognizing this diversity, the colony in 1697 granted religious liberty to all "except Papists," meaning Catholics. The Anglicans attempted a crackdown on Dissenters in 1704, but two years later Queen Anne stepped in and ensured religious freedom for all Carolinians (again with the exception of Catholics, who wouldn't be a factor in the colony until after the American Revolution).

THE YAMASEE WAR

Within 20 years the English presence had expanded throughout the Lowcountry to include Port Royal and Beaufort. Charles Towne became a thriving commercial center, dealing in deerskins with traders in the interior and with foreign concerns from England to South America. Its success was not without a backlash, as the local **Yamasee** people became increasingly disgruntled at the settlers' growing monopolies on deerskin and the slave trade. Slavery was a sad and common fact of life from the earliest days of European settlement in the region. Indians were the most frequent early victims, with not only white settlers taking slaves from among the Native Americans, but the Native American groups themselves conducting slaving raids on each other, often selling hostages to colonists.

As rumors of war spread, on Good Friday, 1715, a delegation of six white Carolinians went to the Yamasee village of Pocataligo to address some of the Native Americans' grievances in the hopes of forestalling violence. Their effort was in vain, however, as warriors murdered four of them in their sleep, the remaining two escaping to sound the alarm. The treacherous attack signaled the beginning of the two-year Yamasee War, which would claim the lives of nearly 10 percent of the colony's population and an unknown number of Native Americans—making it one of the bloodiest conflicts in American history. Energized and ready for war, the Yamasee attacked Charles Towne itself and killed almost all white traders in the interior, effectively ending commerce in the area. As Charles Towne began to swell with refugees from the hinterland, water and supplies ran low, and the colony was in peril for its very existence.

After an initially poor performance by the Carolina militia, a professional army—including armed African slaves—was raised. Well trained and well led, the new army more than held its own despite being outnumbered. A key alliance with local Cherokees was all the advantage the colonists needed to turn the tide. While the Cherokee never received the overt military backing from the settlers that they sought, they did garner enough supplies and influence to convince their Creek rivals, the Yamasee, to begin the peace process. The war-weary settlers, eager to get back to life and to business, were eager to negotiate with them, offering goods as a sign of their earnest intent. By 1717 the Yamasee threat had subsided and trade in the region began flourishing anew.

No sooner had the Yamasee War ended, however, that a new threat emerged: the dreaded pirate Edward Teach, a.k.a. Blackbeard. Entering Charleston harbor in May 1718 with his flagship *Queen Anne's Revenge* and three other vessels, he promptly plundered five ships and began a full-scale blockade of the entire settlement. He took a number of prominent citizens hostage before finally departing northward.

SLAVERY

For the colonists, the Blackbeard episode was the final straw. Already disgusted by the lack of support from the Lords Proprietors during the Yamasee War, the humiliation of the pirate blockade was too much to take. To almost universal agreement in the colony, the settlers threw off the rule of the Proprietors and lobbied in 1719 to become a crown colony, an effort that came to final fruition in 1729.

While this outward-looking and energetic Charleston was originally built on the backs of merchants, with the introduction of the rice and indigo crops in the early 1700s it would increasingly be built on the backs of slaves. For all the wealth gained through the planting of rice and cotton seeds, another seed was sown by the Lowcountry plantation culture. The area's total dependence on slave labor would soon lead to a disastrous war, a conflict signaled for decades to those smart enough to read the signs. By now Charleston and Savannah were firmly established as the key American ports for the importation of African slaves, with about 40 percent of the trade centered in Charleston alone. As a result,

the black population of the coast outnumbered the white population by more than three to one, and much more than that in some areas. The fear of violent slave uprisings had great influence over not only politics but day-to-day affairs.

These fears were eventually realized in the great **Stono Rebellion** on September 9, 1739. Twenty African American slaves led by an Angolan known only as Jemmy met near the Stono River near Charleston. Marching with a banner that read "Liberty," they seized guns with the plan of marching all the way to Spanish Florida and sanctuary in the wilderness. On the way they burned seven plantations and killed 20 more whites. A militia eventually caught up with them, killing 44 escaped slaves and losing 20 of their own. The prisoners were decapitated and had their heads spiked on every milepost between the spot of that final battle and Charleston. Inspired by the rebellion, at least two other uprisings would take place over the next two years in South Carolina and Georgia. The result was not only a 10-year moratorium on slave importation into Charleston but a severe crackdown on the education of slaves—a move that would have damaging implications for generations to come.

OGLETHORPE'S VISION

In 1729, Carolina was divided into north and south. In 1731, a colony to be known as Georgia, after the new English king, was carved out of the southern part of the Carolina land grant. A young general, aristocrat, and humanitarian named James Edward Oglethorpe gathered together a group of Trustees—similar to Carolina's Lords Proprietors—to take advantage. While Oglethorpe would go on to found Georgia, his wasn't the first English presence. A garrison built Fort King George in modern-day Darien, Georgia, in 1721. A cypress blockhouse surrounded by palisaded earthworks, the fort defended the southern reaches of England's claim for seven years before being abandoned in 1728.

PIRATES OF THE ATLANTIC

Pirates, along with their close cousins, slavers, were among the earliest explorers of the Atlantic seaboard of North America, and other than Native American chiefs, were the only real authority in the area for decades. The creeks and barrier islands of the Georgia and Carolina coast provided important, hard-to-find sanctuaries off the regular pirate circuit down in the booty-laden Spanish Caribbean.

For most of us, pirate stories and movies are a form of escapism, in which the most unlikely scenarios happen with ease. But a real-life pirate story from the earliest days of the Charleston seems almost too unbelievable, even for Hollywood. The encounter was at the hands of the infamous Edward Teach, a.k.a. Blackbeard. A tall, terrifying bully of a man, the legendary pirate also had a flair for the dramatic, as all proper pirates should. Given to twisting flaming wads of cloth into his beard when he attacked his prey, Blackbeard was also quite eccentric, as his Charleston escapade shows. In May 1718, Blackbeard, driven north from his usual hunting grounds in the Bahamas by a concerted effort of the British Navy, approached Charleston harbor in his flagship *Queen Anne's Revenge*, accompanied by three smaller vessels. He immediately seized several ships and kidnapped several leading citizens, including Councilman Samuel Wragg and his four-year-old son. He sent one captive ashore with the message that unless his demand was met, the heads of Wragg and son would soon be delivered to the colonial governor's doorstep. Blackbeard's demand? A chest of medicine. For what purpose, we still aren't sure, but apparently it really was all he wanted. The medicines were delivered in short order, and Blackbeard released his hostages and sailed north to Ocracoke Island, North Carolina, to enjoy a royal pardon he'd just received.

One of the pirates serving under Blackbeard during the Charleston escapade was Stede Bon-net, quite a contrasting figure in his debonair nature and posh finery. When Charleston's Colonel William Rhett—his house at 54 Hasell Street is still standing, the city's oldest—got wind that Bonnet and crew were still a-pirating off Cape Fear, North Carolina, he set out with a fleet to bring him to justice. And that he did, bringing pirate and crew back to Charleston for a trial that almost didn't happen after Bonnet escaped from custody dressed as a woman (he was captured on Sullivan's Island). The dashing Bonnet actually garnered quite a bit of public sympathy—especially when he begged not to be hanged—but it wasn't enough to forestall the grim fate of the pirate and his crew: public execution at White Point, the bodies left to dangle as a warning to other buccaneers.

Another coastal menace, Richard Worley, was also hanged in Charleston. He was supposedly buried in a marshy creek downtown, where Meeting and Water Streets intersect today. Though Savannah is home to the famous Pirate's House restaurant and got a major shout-out in Robert Louis Stevenson's *Treasure Island*, actual pirate history there is hard to nail down. There seems little doubt that a host of ne'er-do-wells made their way onto the rowdy Savannah waterfront, but the port's location nearly 20 miles upriver would have made it less-than-ideal territory for a true buccaneer, who always needed a fast getaway handy.

As for Blackbeard, his retirement plans were interrupted by a contingent of Virginians who tracked him down and killed him near Ocracoke. However, his legend lives to this day on Blackbeard Island, Georgia, a gorgeous, undeveloped barrier island that has changed little since the days when Teach himself allegedly stopped over between pirate raids. The legends even say he left some treasure there, but don't try to look for it—Blackbeard Island is now a National Wildlife Refuge.

On February 12, 1733, after stops in Beaufort and Charleston, the ship *Anne* with its 114 passengers made its way to the highest bluff on the Savannah River. The area was controlled by the peaceful Yamacraw people, who had been encouraged by the powers-that-be in Charleston to settle on this vacant land 12 miles up the river to serve as a buffer for the Spanish. Led by an elderly chief, or *mico,* named Tomochichi, the Yamacraw enjoyed the area's natural bounty of shellfish, fruit, nuts, and small game. A deft politician, Oglethorpe struck up a treaty and eventually a genuine friendship with Tomochichi. To the Yamacraw, Oglethorpe was a rare bird—a white man who behaved with honor and was true to his word. The Native Americans reciprocated by helping the settlers and pledging fealty to the crown. Oglethorpe reported to the Trustees that Tomochichi personally requested "that we would Love and Protect their little Families." In negotiations with local tribes using Mary Musgrove, a Creek-English settler in the area, as translator, the persuasive Oglethorpe convinced the coastal Creek to cede to the crown all Georgia land to the Altamaha River "which our Nation hath not occasion for to use" in exchange for goods. The Native Americans also reserved the Georgia Sea Islands of Sapelo, Ossabaw, and St. Catherine's. Oglethorpe's impact was felt farther down the Georgia coast, as St. Simons Island, Jekyll Island, Darien, and Brunswick were settled in rapid succession, and with them the entrenchment of the plantation system and slave labor.

While the Trustees' utopian vision was largely economic in nature, like Carolina the Georgia colony also emphasized religious freedom. While to modern ears Charleston's antipathy toward "papists" and Oglethorpe's original ban of Catholics from Georgia might seem incompatible with this goal, the reason was a coldly pragmatic one for the time: England's two main global rivals, France and Spain, were both staunchly Catholic countries.

SPAIN VANQUISHED

Things heated up on the coast in 1739 with the so-called War of Jenkins' Ear, which despite its seemingly trivial beginnings over the humiliation of a British captain by Spanish privateers was actually a proxy struggle emblematic of changes in the European balance of power. A year later Oglethorpe cobbled together a force of settlers, Indian allies, and Carolinians to reduce the Spanish fortress at St. Augustine,

Florida. The siege failed, and Oglethorpe retreated to St. Simons Island to await the inevitable counterattack. In 1742, a Spanish force invaded the island but was eventually turned back for good at the **Battle of Bloody Marsh.** That clash marked the end of Spanish overtures on England's colonies in what is now the United States.

Though Oglethorpe returned to England a national hero, things fell apart in Savannah. The settlers became envious of the success of Charleston's slave-based rice economy and began wondering aloud why they couldn't also make use of free labor. With Oglethorpe otherwise occupied in England, the Trustees of Georgia—distant in more ways than just geographically from the new colony—bowed to public pressure and relaxed the restrictions on slavery and rum. By 1753 the Trustees voted to return their charter to the crown, officially making Georgia the 13th and final colony of England in America. With first the French and then the Spanish effectively shut off from the American East Coast, the stage was set for an internal battle between England and its burgeoning colonies across the Atlantic.

REVOLUTION AND INDEPENDENCE

The population of the colonies swelled in the mid-1700s, not only from an influx of slaves but a corresponding flood of European immigrants. The interior began filling up with Germans, Swiss, Scottish, and Irish settlers. Their subsequent demands for political representation led to tension between them and the coastal inhabitants, typically depicted through the years as an Upcountry versus Lowcountry competition. It is a persistent but inaccurate myth that the affluent elite on the southeastern coast were reluctant to break ties with England. While the Lowcountry's cultural and economic ties to England were certainly strong, the **Stamp Act** and the **Townshend Acts** combined to turn public sentiment against the mother country here as elsewhere in the colonies.

South Carolinian planters like Christopher Gadsden, Henry Laurens, John Rutledge, and Arthur Middleton were early leaders in the movement for independence. Planters in what would be called Liberty County, Georgia, also strongly agitated for the cause. War broke out between the colonists and the British in New England, and soon made its way southward. The British failed to take Charleston—the fourth-largest city in the colonies—in June 1776, an episode which gave South Carolina its "Palmetto State" moniker when Redcoat cannonballs bounced off the palm tree–lined walls of Fort Moultrie. The British under General Sir Henry Clinton successfully took the city in 1780, however, occupying it until 1782.

The British, under General Archibald Campbell, took Savannah in 1778. Royal Governor Sir James Wright returned from exile to Georgia to reclaim it for the crown, the only one of the colonies to be subsumed again into the British Empire. A polyglot force of colonists, Haitians, and Hessians attacked the British fortifications on the west side of Savannah in 1779 but were repulsed with heavy losses. Although the area's two major cities were captured, the war raged on throughout the surrounding area. Indeed, throughout the Lowcountry, fighting was as vicious as anything yet seen on the North American continent. With over 130 known military engagements occurring here, South Carolina sacrificed more men during the war than any other colony—including Massachusetts, "Cradle of the Revolution."

The struggle became a guerrilla war of colonists versus the British as well as a civil war between patriots and loyalists, or **Tories.** Committing what would today undoubtedly be called war crimes, the British routinely burned homes, churches, and fields and massacred civilians. Using Daufuskie Island as a base, British soldiers staged raids on Hilton Head plantations. In response, patriots of the Lowcountry bred a group of deadly guerrilla soldiers under legendary leaders such as Francis Marion, "the Swamp Fox," and Thomas Sumter, "the Gamecock," who attacked the British in daring hit-and-run raids staged from swamps and marshes. A covert group of patriots called the **Sons of Liberty** met clandestinely throughout the Lowcountry, plotting revolution over pints of ale. Sometimes their efforts transcended talk, however, and atrocities were committed against area loyalists.

In all, four South Carolinians signed the Declaration of Independence (Thomas Heyward Jr., Thomas Lynch Jr., Arthur Middleton, and Edward Rutledge), as did three Georgians (Button Gwinnett, Lyman Hall, and George Walton).

HIGH COTTON

True to form, the new nation wasted no time in asserting its economic strength. Rice planters from Georgetown north of Charleston on down to the Altamaha River in Georgia built on their already impressive wealth, becoming the new nation's richest men by far—with fortunes built on the backs of the slaves working in their fields.

In 1786, a new crop was introduced that would only enhance the financial clout of the coastal region: cotton. A former loyalist colonel, Roger Kelsal, sent some seed from the West Indies to his friend James Spaulding, owner of a plantation on St. Simons Island, Georgia. This crop, soon to be known as **Sea Island cotton** and considered the best in the world, would supplant rice as the crop of choice for coastal plantations. At the height of the Southern cotton boom in the early 1800s, a single Sea Island cotton harvest on a single plantation might go for $100,000—in 1820 dollars. While Charleston was still by far the largest, most powerful, and most influential city on the

NATHANAEL GREENE AND MULBERRY GROVE

Like John Wesley, Nathanael Greene's time in Savannah was short and mostly unfortunate. Unlike Wesley, however, Greene never got a chance to leave and start anew. One of the American Revolution's greatest heroes, Greene rose from the rank of private in the Continental Army to become George Washington's right-hand man. Ironically, this skillful soldier was born into a family of pacifist Quakers in Rhode Island in 1742. As a brigadier general in the Rhode Island militia, Greene's innate military prowess caught Washington's eye during the siege of Boston, whereupon the future president gave Greene command of the entire southern theater of the fight for independence. While Greene never attempted the suicidal aim of taking on Lord Cornwallis's large and well-trained Southern contingent of British veterans, his guerrilla tactics did force the English contingent to divide and hence weaken itself. It was Greene who sent General "Mad Anthony" Wayne in 1782 to finally free Savannah from the British, who had resisted an earlier attempt to retake the city in 1779. Perhaps in a nod to his Quaker roots, Greene insisted that no revenge be taken on Savannah's Loyalists, instead welcoming them into the new nation as partners. As a reward for his service, Washington granted Greene a large estate on the banks of the Savannah River known as Mulberry Grove, primarily known to history as the place where Eli Whitney would later invent the cotton gin while serving as tutor to the Greene children. (Wayne was awarded nearby Richmond Plantation.)

Mulberry Grove was less productive for Greene himself, however, who as a lifelong abolitionist refused to use slave labor on the plantation, and hence paid a steep financial price. The 44-year-old Greene spent less than a year at Mulberry Grove, mostly worrying about finances, when he caught sunstroke on a particularly brutal June day in 1786 and died shortly thereafter.

And there's where the real mystery begins. At some point Greene's remains were said to have been lost after a family vault in Colonial Cemetery was vandalized by Union troops. Almost a century passed until in 1900 the Society of the Cincinnati of Rhode Island appointed a search committee to find and properly inter the general's long-lost remains. The remains were indeed found—right in the vault in Colonial Cemetery where they were supposed to have been, which you can see to this day. However, they were underneath someone else: After removing the coffin of one Robert Scott, excavators found "a mass of rotten wood and human bones mixed with sand," along with a rusty coffin plate reading:

Nathanael Greene,
Obit June 19, 1786
Age, 41 Years

So it was that in 1902, Greene's remains were finally put to rest under his monument in Johnson Square—dedicated to him by the Marquis de Lafayette 76 years earlier in 1825.

Sadly, all buildings at Mulberry Grove were razed by Sherman's troops in 1864, with only a few brick stairs and portions of foundation remaining. The area—visited not once but twice by George Washington after his friend's untimely death—entered industrial use in 1975 and is currently occupied by the Georgia Ports Authority. No full-scale archaeological dig has ever been done at the site, although the nonprofit Mulberry Grove Foundation (www.mulberrygrove.org) is working toward that as well as a plan to make part of the 2,200 acre parcel a wildlife preserve.

Greene's widow, Catherine, would go on to remarry and build another mostly vanished plantation, the famed Dungeness on Cumberland Island.

southeastern coast of the United States, at the peak of the cotton craze Savannah was actually doing more business—a fact that grated to no end on the Holy City's elite. Unlike Charleston, where the planters themselves dominated city life, in Savannah it was cotton brokers called **factors** who were the city's leading class. During this time most of the grand homes of downtown Savannah's Historic District were built. This boom period, fueled largely by cotton exports, was perhaps most iconically represented by the historic sailing of the SS *Savannah* from Savannah to Liverpool in 29 days, the first transatlantic voyage by a steamship.

During the prosperous antebellum period, the economy of Charleston, Savannah, and surrounding areas was completely dependent on slave labor, but the cities themselves boasted large numbers of African Americans who were active in business and agriculture. For example, the vending stalls at the City Markets of both Charleston and Savannah were predominantly staffed by African American workers, some of them free. Despite the undeniable lack of equality, the racial apartheid typical of Reconstruction and the later Jim Crow era was generally not in evidence at this time. Working-class blacks and whites alike often frequented the same watering holes and lived in mixed neighborhoods, much to the consternation of the elite. Many churches of the coast had regular biracial attendance during this period. In fact, a case could be made that the area's churches are more segregated now than they were before the Civil War.

SECESSION

Much of the lead-in to the Civil War focused on whether slavery would be allowed in the newest U.S. territories in the West, but there's no doubt that all figurative roads eventually led to South Carolina. During Andrew Jackson's presidency in the 1820s, his vice president, South Carolina's John C. Calhoun, became a thorn in Jackson's side with his aggressive advocacy for **nullification.** In a nutshell, Calhoun said that if a state decided the federal government wasn't treating it fairly—in this case with regard to tariffs that were hurting the cotton trade in the Palmetto State—it could simply nullify the federal law, superseding it with law of its own.

As the abolition movement gained steam and tensions over slavery rose, South Carolina congressman Preston Brooks took things to the next level. On May 22, 1856, he beat fellow senator Charles Sumner of Massachusetts nearly to death with his walking cane on the Senate floor. Sumner had just given a speech criticizing pro-slavery forces—including a relative of Brooks—and called slavery "a harlot." (In a show of support, South Carolinians sent Brooks dozens of new canes to replace the one he broke over Sumner's head.)

In 1860, the national convention of the Democratic Party, then the dominant force in U.S. politics, was held in—where else?—Charleston. Rancor over slavery and state's rights was so high that they couldn't agree on a single candidate to run to replace President James Buchanan. Reconvening in Maryland, the party split along sectional lines, with the Northern wing backing Stephen A. Douglas. The Southern wing, fervently desiring secession, deliberately chose its own candidate, John Breckenridge, in order to split the Democratic vote and throw the election to Republican Abraham Lincoln, an outspoken opponent of the expansion of slavery. During that so-called **Secession Winter** before Lincoln took office, seven states seceded from the union, first among them the Palmetto State, followed by Mississippi, Florida, Alabama, Georgia, Louisiana, and Texas.

CIVIL WAR

Five days after South Carolina's secession on December 21, 1860, U.S. Army Major Robert Anderson moved his garrison from Fort Moultrie in Charleston harbor to nearby Fort Sumter. Over the next few months and into the spring, Anderson would ignore many calls to surrender, and Confederate forces would prevent any Union resupply or reinforcement. The stalemate was broken and the Confederates finally got their *casus belli* when a Union

ROBERT E. LEE AND SAVANNAH

That spot of spots! That place of places!! That city of cities!!!

Robert E. Lee on Savannah,
in a letter to John Mackay

Before reluctantly surrendering his commission to serve the Confederacy, Robert E. Lee was a bright young up-and-comer with the U.S. Army Corps of Engineers. As a 22-year-old lieutenant, the multitalented Virginian spent a year and a half in and around Savannah overseeing the construction of Fort Pulaski, named for the brave Polish count who lost his life in 1779's Siege of Savannah. On Lee's arrival in Savannah, construction was on hiatus due to the stifling summer heat. The handsome and dashing young man made the most of his time off, making significant inroads into Savannah high society downtown. He was heartily welcomed into the home of his old West Point roommate John Mackay, whose three daughters adored him. The same was true of the two Minis daughters who lived nearby and also frequently had the young lieutenant over (and all this while Lee was conducting a long-distance courtship with his future wife back home in Virginia).

Construction on Cockspur Island began in 1829 under Major Samuel Babcock, whose health problems soon forced Lee to take over. Most of Lee's work focused on draining and diking the marshy island and its blue clay soil, and much of his handiwork remains functional today. After Lee was reassigned in 1831, Lieutenant Joseph Mansfield completed construction of the fort in 1847. A mix of slave labor and paid artisans lived in a sprawling construction camp, but only brick structures remain, the wooden ones not surviving a series of hurricanes in subsequent years.

Long after the war, Robert E. Lee paid a final visit to Savannah at age 63, accompanied by his daughter Agnes, to see his old comrade-in-arms General Joseph E. Johnston, who lived at 105 East Oglethorpe Avenue. During his stay in town, Lee slept at the Andrew Low house (Andrew's wife, Mary, was Jack Mackay's niece). Lee died six months later.

Fort Pulaski is currently administered by the National Park Service, which maintains an excellent website (www.nps.gov) detailing the rich history and fascinating archaeology of this, one of Savannah's great must-see sights.

---

supply ship successfully ran the blockade and docked at Fort Sumter. Shortly before dawn on April 12, 1861, Confederate batteries around Charleston—ironically none of which were at the famous Battery itself—opened fire on Fort Sumter for 34 straight hours, until Anderson surrendered on April 13.

In a classic example of why you should always be careful what you wish for, the secessionists had been too clever by half in pushing for Lincoln. Far from prodding the North to sue for peace, the fall of Fort Sumter instead caused the remaining states in the Union to rally around the previously unpopular tall man from Illinois. Lincoln's skillful management of the Fort Sumter standoff meant that from then on out, the South would bear history's blame

for initiating the conflict that would claim over half a million American lives.

After Fort Sumter, the remaining four states of the Confederacy—Arkansas, Tennessee, North Carolina, and Virginia—seceded. The Old Dominion was the real prize for the secessionists, as Virginia had the South's only ironworks and by far the largest manufacturing base.

In November 1861, a massive Union invasion armada landed in Port Royal Sound in South Carolina, effectively taking the entire Lowcountry out of the war. Hilton Head was a Union encampment, and Beaufort became a major hospital center for the U.S. Army. The coast of Georgia was also blockaded, with Union forces using new rifled cannons in 1862 to quickly reduce Fort Pulaski at the mouth of the Savannah River. Charleston, however, did host two battles in the conflict. The **Battle of Secessionville** came in June 1862, when a Union force attempting to take Charleston was repulsed on James Island with heavy casualties. The next battle, an unsuccessful Union landing on Morris Island in July 1863, was immortalized by the movie *Glory*. The 54th Massachusetts Regiment, an African American unit with white commanders, performed so gallantly in its failed assault on the Confederate Battery Wagner that it inspired the North and was cited by abolitionists as further proof that African Americans should be given freedom and full citizenship rights. Another invasion attempt on Charleston would not come, but it was besieged and bombarded for nearly two years (devastation made even worse by a massive fire, unrelated to the shelling, that destroyed much of the city in 1861). Otherwise, the coast grew quiet. From Charleston to Brunswick, white Southerners evacuated the coastal cities and plantations for the hinterland, leaving behind only slaves to fend for themselves. In many coastal areas, African Americans and Union garrison troops settled into an awkward but peaceful coexistence. Many islands under Union control, such as Cockspur Island, where Fort Pulaski sat, became endpoints in the Underground Railroad.

In Savannah, General William Sherman concluded his **March to the Sea** in Savannah in 1864, famously giving the city to Lincoln as a Christmas present. While staunch Confederates, city fathers were wise enough to know what would happen to their accumulated wealth and fine homes should they be foolhardy enough to resist Sherman's army of war-hardened veterans, most of them farm boys from the Midwest with a pronounced distaste for the "peculiar institution" of slavery. The only military uncertainty left was in how badly Charleston, the "cradle of secession," would suffer for its sins. Historians and local

wags have long debated why Sherman spared Charleston, the hated epicenter of the Civil War. Did he fall in love with the city during his brief posting there as a young lieutenant? Did he literally fall in love there, with one of its legendarily beautiful and delicate local belles? We may never know for sure, but it's likely that the Lowcountry's marshy, mucky terrain simply made it too difficult to move large numbers of men and supplies. So Sherman turned his terrifying battle-hardened army inland toward the state capital, Columbia, which would not be so lucky. Most of Charleston's once-great plantation homes were also put to the torch.

For the African American population of Charleston and Savannah, however, it was not a time of sadness but the great Day of Jubilee. Soon after the Confederate surrender, black Charlestonians held one of the largest parades the city has ever seen, with one of the floats being a coffin bearing the sign, "Slavery is dead."

As for the place where it all began, a plucky Confederate garrison remained underground at Fort Sumter throughout the war, as the walls above them were literally pounded into dust by the long Union siege. The garrison quietly left the fort under cover of night on February 17, 1865. Major Robert Anderson, who surrendered the fort at war's beginning, returned to Sumter in April 1865 to raise the same flag he'd lowered exactly four years earlier. Three thousand African Americans attended the ceremonies. Later that same night, Abraham Lincoln was assassinated in Washington DC.

RECONSTRUCTION

A case could be made that slavery need not have led the United States into Civil War. The U.S. government had banned the importation of slaves long before, in 1808. The great powers of Europe would soon ban slavery altogether (Spain in 1811, France in 1826, and Britain in 1833). Visiting foreign dignitaries in the mid-1800s were often shocked to find the practice in full swing in the American South. Even Brazil, the world center of slavery, where four out of every 10 slaves taken from Africa were brought (less than 5 percent came to the United States), would ban slavery in 1888. Still, the die was cast, the war was fought, and everyone had to deal with the aftermath.

For a brief time, Sherman's benevolent dictatorship on the coast held promise for an orderly postwar future. In 1865 he issued his sweeping "40 acres and a mule" order seeking dramatic economic restitution for coastal Georgia's free blacks. Politics reared its ugly head in the wake of Lincoln's assassination, however, and the order was rescinded, ushering in the chaotic Reconstruction era, echoes of which linger to this day.

Even as the trade in cotton and naval stores resumed to even greater heights than before, urban life and racial tension became more and more problematic. Urban populations swelled as freed blacks from all over the depressed countryside rushed into the cities. As one of them, his name lost to history, famously said: "Freedom was freer in Charleston." It was at this time that the foundation for Jim Crow and its false promise of "separate but equal" was laid. Racial in origin, the Jim Crow laws also displayed a clear socioeconomic bias as well; it was during Reconstruction that the practice evolved in some areas of wealthy whites walking on one side of the streets and poor whites and all blacks walking on the other side.

RECONCILIATION

The opening of the exclusive Jekyll Island Club in 1886 marked the coming of the effects of the Industrial Revolution to the Deep South and the rejuvenation of regional economies. In Savannah, the Telfair Academy of Arts and Sciences, the South's first art museum, opened that same year. The cotton trade built back up to antebellum levels, and the South was on the long road to recovery.

The Spanish-American War of 1898 was a major turning point for the South, the first time since the Civil War that Americans were joined in patriotic unity. The southeastern coast felt this in particular, as it was a staging area for the invasion of Cuba. President McKinley addressed the troops bivouacked in Savannah's Daffin Park, and Charlestonians cheered the exploits of their namesake heavy cruiser the USS *Charleston,* which played a key role in forcing the Spanish surrender of Guam.

Charleston would elect its first Irish American mayor, John Grace, in 1911, who would serve until 1923 (with a break 1915–1919). Although it wouldn't open until 1929, the first Cooper River Bridge joining Charleston with Mount Pleasant was the child of the Grace administration, credited today for modernizing the Holy City's infrastructure.

The arrival of the tiny but devastating boll weevil all but wiped out the cotton trade on the coast after the turn of the century, forcing the economy to diversify. Naval stores and lumbering were the order of the day at the advent of World War I, the combined patriotic effort for which did wonders in repairing the wounds of the Civil War, still vivid in many local memories. A major legacy of World War I that still greatly influences life in the Lowcountry is the Marine Corps Recruiting Depot Parris Island, which began life as a small Marine camp in 1919.

RENAISSANCE AND DEPRESSION

In the Roaring '20s, that boom period following World War I, both Charleston and Savannah entered the world stage and made some of their most significant cultural contributions to American life. It was also the era of Prohibition. Savannah, particularly Tybee Island, became notorious as a major import center for illegal rum from the Bahamas. As elsewhere in the country, Prohibition ironically brought out a new appreciation for the arts and just plain having fun. The "Charleston" dance, originated on the streets of the Holy City and popularized in New York, would sweep the world. The Jenkins Orphanage Band, often credited with the dance, traveled the world, even playing at President Taft's inauguration. In the visual arts, the "Charleston Renaissance" took off, specifically intended to introduce the Holy City to a wider audience. Key work included the Asian-influenced work of self-taught painter Alice Ravenel Huger Smith and the etchings of Elizabeth O'Neill Verner. Edward Hopper was a visitor to Charleston during that time and produced several noted watercolors. The Gibbes Art Gallery, now the Gibbes Museum of Art, opened in 1905. Recognizing the cultural importance of the city and its history, in 1920 socialite Susan Pringle Frost and other concerned Charlestonians formed the Preservation Society of Charleston, the oldest community-based historic preservation organization in the country.

In 1924, lauded Charleston author DuBose Heyward wrote the locally set novel *Porgy*. With Heyward's cooperation, the book would soon be turned into the first American opera, *Porgy and Bess,* by George Gershwin, who labored over the composition in a cottage on Folly Beach. Ironically, *Porgy and Bess,* which premiered with an African American cast in New York in 1935, wouldn't be performed in its actual setting until 1970 because of segregation laws. In Savannah, the Roaring '20s coincided with the rise of Johnny Mercer, who began his theater career locally in the Town Theater Group. In 1925, Flannery O'Connor was born in Savannah, and the quirky, Gothic nature of the city would mark her later writing indelibly.

The Depression hit the South hard, but since wages and industry were already behind the national average, the economic damage wasn't as bad as elsewhere in the country. As elsewhere in the South, public works programs in President Franklin D. Roosevelt's New Deal helped not only to keep locals employed but contributed greatly to the cultural and archaeological record of the area. The Public Works of Art Project stimulated the visual arts, especially in Charleston, while the Georgia Writers Project published what is still one of the seminal oral histories of the Gullah or Geechee culture, *Drums and Shadows.* The Works Progress Administration renovated the old Dock Street Theatre in Charleston, and theatrical productions once again graced that historic stage. The Civilian Conservation Corps built much of the modern state park system in the area.

WORLD WAR II AND THE POSTWAR BOOM

With the attack on Pearl Harbor and the coming of World War II, life on the Georgia and South Carolina coast would never be the same. Military funding and facilities swarmed into the area, and populations and long-depressed living standards rose as a result. In many outlying Sea Islands of Georgia and South Carolina, electricity came for the first time. The Charleston Navy Yard became the city's largest employer, and the city's population soared as workers swarmed in. The "Mighty Eighth" Air Force was founded and based in Savannah, and Camp Stewart, later Fort Stewart, was built in nearby Hinesville. In shipyards in Savannah and Brunswick, hundreds of Liberty ships were built to transport cargo to the citizens and allied armies of Europe.

The postwar U.S. infatuation with the automobile—and its troublesome child, the suburb—brought exponential growth to the great cities of the coast. The first bridge to Hilton Head Island was built in 1956, leading to the first of many resort developments, Sea Pines, in 1961. With rising coastal populations came pressure to demolish more and more fine old buildings to put parking lots and high-rises in their place. A backlash grew among the cities' elites, aghast at the destruction of so much history.

The immediate postwar era brought about the formation of both the Historic Charleston Foundation and the Historic Savannah Foundation, which began the financially and politically difficult work of protecting historic districts from the wrecking ball. They weren't always successful, but the work of these organizations—mostly older women from the upper crust—laid the foundation for the successful coastal tourist industry to come, as well as preserving important American history for the ages.

CIVIL RIGHTS

The ugly racial violence that plagued much of the country during the civil rights era rarely visited the Georgia and South Carolina coast. Whether due to the laid-back ambience or the fact that African Americans were simply too numerous there to be denied, cities like Charleston and Savannah experienced little real unrest during that time.

Contrary to popular opinion, the civil rights era wasn't just a blip in the 1960s. The gains of that decade were the fruits of efforts begun decades earlier. Many of the efforts involved efforts to expand black suffrage. Though African Americans had secured the nominal right to vote years before, primary contests were not under the jurisdiction of federal law. As a result, Democratic Party primary elections—the de facto general elections because of that party's total dominance in the South at the time—were effectively closed to African American voters. Savannah was at the forefront, and Ralph Mark Gilbert, pastor of the historic First African Baptist Church, launched one of the first black voter registration drives in the South. In Charleston, the Democratic primary was opened to African Americans for the first time in 1947. In 1955, a successful black realtor, J. Arthur Brown, became head of the Charleston chapter of the NAACP and membership soared, bringing an increase in activism. In 1960, the Charleston Municipal Golf Course voluntarily integrated to avoid a court battle. Lunch counter sit-ins happened all over Charleston, successfully challenging the remaining segregation laws, all of which were eventually overturned.

Martin Luther King Jr. visited South Carolina in the late 1960s, speaking in Charleston in 1967 and helping reestablish the Penn Center on St. Helena Island as not only a cultural center but a center of political activism as well. The hundred-day strike of hospital workers at the Medical University of South Carolina in 1969—right after King's assassination—got national attention and was the culmination of Charleston's struggle for civil rights. By the end of the 1960s, the city councils of Charleston and Savannah had elected their first black aldermen, and the next phase in local history began.

A COAST REBORN

The decade of the 1970s brought the seeds of the future success of the South Carolina and Georgia coasts. In Charleston, the historic tenure of Mayor Joe Riley began, and in Savannah came the election of a similarly influential and long-serving mayor, John P. Rousakis. The Irish American and the Greek American would break precedents and forge key alliances in both municipalities, reviving not only the local economies but the age-old rivalry between the two cities.

Beginning with downtown's Charleston Place, Riley embarked on a series of high-profile public works projects to reinvigorate the then-moribund Charleston historic area. King Street would soon follow. In the years 1970–1976, tourism in the Holy City would increase by 60 percent. The resort industry, already established on Hilton Head, would hit Kiawah Island, Seabrook Island, and Isle of Palms with a vengeance. In Savannah, Rousakis renovated the then-seedy riverfront district, making it the centerpiece of the city's burgeoning tourist trade. The Savannah College of Art and Design (SCAD) opened in 1979 and began the process of renovating dozens of the city's historic buildings, a process that continues today.

The coast's combination of beautiful scenery and cheap labor proved irresistible to the movie and TV industry, which would begin filming many series and films in the area in the 1970s and continuing to this day. Beaufort, South Carolina, in particular would emerge from its stately slumber as the star of several popular films, including *The Great Santini* and *The Big Chill.*

Charleston received its first major challenge since the Civil War in 1989 when Hurricane Hugo—originally headed directly for Savannah—changed course at the last minute and slammed into the South Carolina coast just north of Charleston. The Holy City, including many of its most historic locations, was massively damaged, with hardly a tree left standing. In a testament to the toughness just beneath Charleston's genteel veneer, the city not only rebounded but came back stronger. In perhaps typically mercantile fashion, Charlestonians used the devastation of Hugo as a reason to introduce a new round of residential construction to the entire area, particularly the surrounding islands.

The economic boom of the 1990s was particularly good to Charleston and Savannah, whose ports saw a huge dividend from increasing globalization. Also in the 1990s came the *Midnight in the Garden of Good and Evil* phenomenon, which would put Savannah—already on the upswing—on the tourist map for good. Although not a Savannah native, the iconic Paula Deen has brought a new national focus on the city through her presence on the Food Channel and through her local restaurant, The Lady & Sons.

Today Savannah's tourism business is healthier than ever, and Charleston is perennially ranked as one of the top U.S. cities both for visitors as well as for residents. Attracted by the coastal region, artists, writers, and entrepreneurs continue to flock, increasing the economic and social diversity of the area and taking it to new heights of livability.

Government and Economy

GOVERNMENT

Charleston is run by the **strong mayor** form of municipal government, which means that the elected mayor, in Charleston's case currently Joe Riley, has extensive powers, including the ability to veto a measure approved by the city council. In practice this means that a mayor, for better or worse, is able to stamp the city with his or her own vision—Riley's influence can be seen in everything from the chichi Charleston Place to new low-income housing developments.

Savannah, however, is run by the **council-manager** form of municipal government, in which the mayor is but one vote of many on the city council. Day-to-day operations are in the hands of an appointed city manager who answers to the council. In practice this means a generally more professional and objective approach to the nuts-and-bolts of government but an often-frustrating lack of accountability at the top.

Because of both states' strong rural roots, county governments are also very important, but becoming less so as urbanization continues and more areas consider city and county consolidation. In particular, county governments in Georgia hold great sway, in large part because there are so many of them. Visitors to the Peach State are often amazed by how small the counties are, and how many there are—159 in total. In practice this means that county governments hold a greater proportion of political power than in states where the counties are much larger in land area, like South Carolina.

Political Parties

For many decades, the South was dominated by the Democratic Party. Originally the party of slavery, segregation, and Jim Crow, the Democratic Party began attracting Southern African American voters in the 1930s with the election of Franklin D. Roosevelt. The allegiance of black voters was further cemented in the Truman, Kennedy, and Johnson administrations. The region would remain solidly Democratic until a backlash against the civil rights movement of the 1960s drove many white Southerners, ironically enough, into the party of Lincoln. This added racial element, so confounding to Americans from other parts of the country, remains just as potent today. The default mode in the South is that white voters are massively Republican, and black voters massively Democratic. Since South Carolina is 69 percent white and Georgia 67 percent white, doing the math translates to an overwhelming Republican dominance.

However, the coastal areas covered in this guide, with their large, predominantly Democratic African American populations, function somewhat separately from this realignment. For instance, in 2008 both South Carolina and Georgia gave over 50 percent of their total vote to John McCain for president. But in Charleston County, Barack Obama received 54 percent of the vote. In Chatham County, Georgia, where Savannah is located, Obama won nearly 60 percent of the vote.

But don't make the mistake of assuming that local African Americans are particularly liberal because of their voting habits. Deeply religious and traditional in background and upbringing, African Americans in the area covered by this guide are among the most socially conservative people in the region, even if their choice of political party does not always reflect that.

Intrastate Relations

A few years back a sociologist proposed, partially tongue-in-cheek, that since the coastal regions of the Southeast have more in common with each other than with residents of other parts of their own states, the borders should be realigned to reflect this demographic, cultural, and historic affiliation. Anyone who has spent time in the inland areas of South Carolina and Georgia will immediately recognize the basic truth in this proposal, however unlikely it is to actually happen. The simple, easily observable fact is that Charleston, Beaufort, Savannah, and Brunswick have far more in common with each other than Charleston has with, say, Spartanburg, South Carolina, or Savannah has with Macon, Georgia. I don't know what you would name the state that resulted from the union of the coastal cities and towns, but I do know that the food would be awesome.

Georgia's largest city and capital is Atlanta, which is even farther removed—both physically and metaphysically—from Savannah than Columbia is from Charleston. Indeed, Savannah and Chatham County are considered so different from the rest of Georgia that old-timers still call Savannah the capital of the "State of Chatham."

ECONOMY

The coastal areas of South Carolina and Georgia are currently experiencing profound changes in economy and business. The rice crop moved offshore in the late 1800s, and the center of the cotton trade moved to the Gulf states in the early 1900s. That left timber as the main cash crop all up and down the coast, specifically huge pine tree farms to feed the pulp and paper business. For most of the 20th century, the largest employers along the coast were massive, sulfur-smelling paper mills, which had as big an effect on the local environment as on its economy. But even that is changing as Asian competition is driving paper companies to sell off their tracts for real estate development—not necessarily a more welcome scenario.

Since World War II, the U.S. Department of Defense has been a major employer and economic driver in the entire South, and the Georgia and South Carolina coast is no exception. Of the services, the U.S. Navy (which includes the Marines) is the dominant military presence in coastal South Carolina, employing over 16,000 military and civilian workers. Coastal Georgia tends to be more Army-dominated. Despite the closing of the Charleston Naval Yard in the mid-1990s, the grounds now host the East Coast headquarters of the Space and Naval Warfare Systems Center (SPAWAR), which provides high-tech engineering solutions for the Navy. Charleston also retains a large military presence in the Charleston Air Force Base near North Charleston, which hosts two airlift wings and employs about 6,000. Farther down the coast, Beaufort is home to the Naval Hospital Beaufort and the Marine Corps Air Station Beaufort and its six squadrons of FA-18 Hornets. On nearby Parris Island is the legendary Marine Corps Recruit Depot Parris Island, which puts all new Marine recruits from east of the Mississippi River through rigorous basic training. In the middle of south-side Savannah sits Hunter Army Airfield, host to a battalion of U.S. Army Rangers. In nearby and largely rural Liberty County, Georgia, is the sprawling Fort Stewart, home base of the 3rd Infantry Division. Near the Florida border in St. Marys is the Naval Submarine Base Kings Bay, home port of eight Trident subs. These defense facilities combine to bring billions of dollars into the local economy in payroll alone, not to mention the ancillary spending (home-buying, renting, etc.) that goes with it. However, the defense dollar has a downside: When large numbers of troops are deployed on repeat tours of duty, local economies suffer along with the troops' families.

Of course, tourism is also an important factor in the local economies of the area, particularly in seasonal resort-oriented areas like Hilton Head, Kiawah, and Seabrook Islands. Though they have very diversified economies, Charleston and Savannah both rely on tourist dollars as well. The Holy City in particular has a well-honed tourist infrastructure, bringing at least $5 billion a year into the local economy. Savannah's tourism industry, though growing very rapidly, is still behind Charleston's at less than $2 billion a year.

Some of the biggest economic news of modern times has been the exponential growth of local seaports. Of course, the entire coast from Charleston to Brunswick has been dependent on maritime trade since its settlement. But from the 1990s on, the quickened pace of globalization has brought enormous investment, volume, and expansion to area port facilities. Both the Charleston and Savannah ports experienced record volume in 2006–2007. After years of trying, the port of Savannah finally caught up with Charleston in 2007 to become not only the fastest-growing American port but the fourth-busiest in the country. In 2011, Savannah was the second busiest U.S. export port.

Indeed, despite all other trends, manufacturing and industry remain the largest sectors of the economy in both Charleston and Savannah—due in no small part to the fact that both South Carolina and Georgia are "right to work" states with exceedingly low unionization rates. Increasingly, however, higher education is more and more important to local economies and will only continue to be so. For their size, Charleston and Savannah have impressive institutions of learning, almost all of which are growing in enrollment and endowment. In Charleston, the Medical University of South Carolina is not only the city's largest employer but is growing in importance as a key national bioscience research center. In the liberal arts, the College of Charleston is known for excellence, especially its nationally renowned music program. The American College of the Building Arts works to educate new generations of artisans, with some classes held at the Old City Jail downtown. Clemson University also has a strong agricultural research presence in Charleston. The University of South Carolina Beaufort, on a beautiful campus near the historic downtown, is not only increasing its enrollment as the state's newest four-year facility but has even opened a satellite campus in little Bluffton.

Savannah's higher education scene is best known for the Savannah College of Art and Design, a private institution that is one of the nation's largest art schools and the downtown area's main restorer of old buildings. But another local institution worth mentioning is the rapidly growing Armstrong Atlantic State University, possibly the best education buy in the country. In addition, the University of Georgia maintains a strong marine research presence in Savannah at the Skidaway Institute of Oceanography, and the Georgia Institute of Technology has a satellite campus in Savannah's new high-tech corridor near the airport and I-95.

People and Culture

Contrary to how the region is portrayed in the media, the coast from Charleston down to the Georgia-Florida border is hardly exclusive to natives with thick, flowery accents who still obsess over the Civil War and eat grits three meals a day. As you will quickly discover, the entire coastal area is heavily populated with transplants from other parts of the country, and in some areas you can actually go quite a long time without hearing even one of those Scarlett O'Hara accents. Some of this is due to the region's increasing attractiveness to professionals and artists, drawn by the temperate climate, natural beauty, and business-friendly environment. Part of it is due to its increasing attractiveness to retirees, most of them from the frigid Northeast. Indeed, in some places, chief among them Hilton Head, the most common accent is a New York or New Jersey one, and a Southern accent is rare.

In any case, don't make the common mistake of assuming you're coming to a place where footwear is optional and electricity is a recent development (though it's true that many of the islands didn't get electricity until the 1950s and 1960s). Because so much new construction has gone on in the South in the last quarter-century or so, you might find some aspects of the infrastructure—specifically the roads and the electrical utilities—actually superior to where you came from.

POPULATION

For demographic purposes, Charleston is part of the Charleston–North Charleston Metropolitan Statistical Area (MSA), which includes Berkeley, Dorchester, and Charleston Counties. In the 2010 census, it comprised about 664,000 people. The city of Charleston proper has a population of about 120,000. The Hilton Head/Beaufort MSA includes Beaufort and Jasper Counties and comprised about 180,000 people in the 2010 census. The town of Hilton Head had about 37,000 residents in 2010, and Beaufort had about 13,000. The Savannah MSA, which includes Chatham, Bryan, and Effingham Counties, numbered about 347,000 people in the 2010 census. The city of Savannah itself has a population of about 136,000. The Brunswick MSA includes Brantley, Glynn, and McIntosh Counties and has about 100,000 people.

VOODOO AND HOODOO

The spiritual system we know as voodoo—the word is a corruption of various West African spellings—came to the western hemisphere with the importation of slaves. Contrary to popular belief, voodoo isn't a mere collection of primitive superstitions but is a clearly defined religion in its own right and is still the dominant religion of millions of West Africans.

Like many ancient belief systems, voodoo is based on the veneration of ancestors and the possibility of continued communication with them, and it's perhaps this characteristic that is responsible for so much misunderstanding. For example, up until fairly recently the African American Gullah and Geechee populations of the South Carolina and Georgia Sea Islands still had a common belief that the older slaves who were born in Africa could actually fly in spirit form back to the continent of their birth and back again.

While voodoo has always been unfairly sensationalized—the most notable recent example being the "voodoo priestess" Minerva in *Midnight in the Garden of Good and Evil*—it's not necessarily as malevolent in actual practice as in the overactive imaginations of writers and directors. For example, the stereotypical practice of sticking pins in dolls to bring pain to a living person actually has its roots in European and Native American folklore. But sensationalism sells, so you'll sometimes find such items being hawked to the gullible as "voodoo dolls."

Much of what the layperson thinks is voodoo is actually hoodoo, a body of folklore—not a religion—indigenous to the American South. Hoodoo combines elements of voodoo (communicating with the dead) and fundamentalist Christianity (extensive scriptural references). In the United States, most African American voodoo tradition was long ago subsumed within Protestant Christianity, but the Gullah populations of the Sea Islands of South Carolina and Georgia still keep alive the old ways. In the Gullah and Geechee areas of the Georgia and Carolina Sea Islands, the word *conjure* is generally the preferred terminology for this hybrid belief system, which has good sides and bad sides and borrows liberally from African lore and Christian folkways.

The old Southern practice of painting shutters and doors blue to ward off evil comes from hoodoo, where the belief in ghosts, or "haints," is largely a byproduct of poorly understood Christianity (Mediterranean countries also use blue to keep evil at bay, and the word *haint* is of Scots-Irish origin). If you keep your eyes attuned, you can still see this particular shade of "haint blue" on rural and vernacular structures throughout the Lowcountry. (Were you to enter one of these homes, you would almost certainly find a horseshoe tacked over the front door as well.)

Another element of hoodoo that you can still encounter today is the role of the "root doctor," an expert at folk remedies who blends together various indigenous herbs and plants in order to produce a desired effect or result. In *Midnight in the Garden of Good and Evil,* this role belongs to the fabled Dr. Buzzard, who teaches Minerva everything she knows about "conjure work." However, a root doctor is not to be confused with a "gifted reader," a fortune-teller born with the talent to tell the future. From the no-doubt embellished account in John Berendt's *Midnight,* scholars would put the late Minerva squarely into the category of root doctor or "conjurer" rather than the undeniably more compelling "voodoo priestess."

Racial Makeup

Its legacy as the center of the U.S. slave trade and plantation culture means that the Charleston-Savannah region has a large African American population. The Charleston MSA is about 31 percent African American, and the Savannah MSA about 35 percent. In the cities proper, the black population is higher, about 35 percent in Charleston's case and nearly 60 percent in Savannah's.

The Hispanic population, as elsewhere in the United States, is growing rapidly, but statistics can be misleading. Though Hispanics are growing at a triple-digit clip in the region, they still remain under 3 percent of each state's population. Bilingual signage is becoming more common but is still quite rare.

RELIGION

The area from Charleston to Savannah is unusual in the Deep South for its wide variety of religious faiths. While South Carolina and Georgia remain overwhelmingly Protestant—at least three-quarters of all Christians in both states are members of some Protestant denomination, chief among them Southern Baptist and Methodist—Charleston and Savannah's cosmopolitan, polyglot histories have made them real melting pots of faith. Both cities were originally dominated by the Episcopal Church (known as the Anglican Church in other countries), but from early on they were also havens for those of other faiths. Various types of Protestant offshoots soon arrived, including the French Huguenots and Congregationalists in Charleston and the Scottish Presbyterians and German Salzburger Lutherans in the Savannah area. The seeds of Methodism and the "Great Awakening" were planted along the coast from Savannah up to Charleston.

Owing to vestigial prejudice from the European realpolitik of the founding era, the Roman Catholic presence on the coast was late in arriving, but once it came it was there to stay. Savannah, in particular, has quite a large Roman Catholic population by Southern standards, mostly due to the influx of Irish in the mid-1800s.

But most unusually of all for the Deep South, Charleston and Savannah not only have large Jewish populations but ones that have been key participants in the cities from the very first days of settlement. Sephardic Jews of primarily Portuguese descent were among the first settlers of both Charleston and Savannah, and they kept up an energetic trade between the two cities for centuries afterward, continuing to the present day.

MANNERS

The prevalence and importance of good manners is the main thing to keep in mind about the South. While it's tempting for folks from more outwardly assertive parts of the world to take this as a sign of weakness, that would be a major mistake. Southerners use manners, courtesy, and chivalry as a system of social interaction with one goal above all: to maintain the established order during times of stress. A relic from a time of extreme class stratification, etiquette and chivalry are ways to make sure that the elites are never threatened—and, on the other hand, that even those on the lowest rungs of society are afforded at least a basic amount of dignity. But as a practical matter, it's also true that Southerners of all classes, races, and backgrounds rely on the observation of manners as a way to sum up people quickly. To any Southerner, regardless of class or race, your use or neglect of basic manners and proper respect indicates how seriously they should take you—not in a socioeconomic sense, but in the big picture overall.

The typical Southern sense of humor—equal parts irony, self-deprecation, and good-natured teasing—is part of the code. Southerners are loath to criticize another individual directly, so often they'll instead take the opportunity to make an ironic joke. Self-deprecating humor is also much more common in the South than in other areas of the country. Because of this, conversely you're also expected to be able to take a joke yourself without being too sensitive.

Another key element in Southern manners is the discussion of money—or rather, the non-discussion. Unlike some parts of the United States, in the South it's considered the height of rudeness to ask someone what their salary is or how much they paid for their house. Not that the subject is entirely taboo—far from it; you just have to know the code. For example, rather than brag about how much or how little they paid for their home, a Southern head of

SEPHARDIC JEWS IN THE SOUTH

Visitors are sometimes surprised to discover that two of the oldest cities in the Anglo-Saxon Protestant South have rich and early histories of an active Jewish presence—specifically, **Sephardic Jews** (those with a Spanish or Portuguese background). Contrary to modern trends, Jews and Muslims on the Iberian Peninsula got along quite well while the Islamic Moors of North Africa dominated the area. But after Ferdinand and Isabella's completion of the Reconquista in that pivotal year of 1492—also the date of Columbus's famous voyage—the Jews of Spain went from being respected citizens to persecuted pariahs nearly overnight. Five years later, Portugal followed suit, expelling all Jews on pain of death unless they became "New Christians," or *conversos*. A sizeable proportion of *conversos*, however, were actually so-called crypto-Jews, who publicly practiced Roman Catholicism while secretly remaining devout Jews. Many synagogues of Sephardic origin today have their floors covered in sand to remember that dark time when Jewish congregations practiced their faith in basements covered with sand to muffle the sounds of their feet.

The diaspora of the Sephardic Jews, ironically, contributed greatly to the health of the global Jewish community, as skilled tradesmen, doctors, and men of letters spread out to Spanish, Portuguese, English, and Dutch colonies where the Inquisition had little sway. It was primarily from the ranks of this Sephardic diaspora that the Jewish settlers of the Lowcountry and Georgia coast came.

The first Jewish presence in Charleston was recorded in 1695, with Jews voting in local elections as early as 1702. Stimulated by the busy port, the Charleston Jewish community quickly grew with the addition of **Ashkenazi,** or Eastern European, Jews in the late 1700s. By 1820, Charleston boasted the biggest Jewish population in the United States. Savannah wasn't the first colonial town to host Jewish settlers, but the group of 42 Sephardic Jews that arrived five months after Oglethorpe's landing in 1733 was by far the largest contingent to travel to North America up to that time. All but eight of this core group were Spanish and Portuguese Jews who emigrated to London after spending years as crypto-Jews in their home countries. Accepted without question by Oglethorpe, the Jews of Savannah quickly rose in power and influence. In fact, the first white male child born in Georgia was a Jewish boy, Philip "Uri" Minis.

In one of the great tales of the American melting pot, the assimilation of the Jews into Southern society was so complete that the Secretary of State of the Confederate States of America, Judah Benjamin, was a practicing Jew of Sephardic origin. This assimilation also had a flip side, however, in that the Sephardic Jews were generally just as enthusiastic about owning slaves as any other white citizens of the area. In 1830 about 83 percent of Jewish households in Charleston had slaves, compared to an almost-identical percentage of 87 percent of white Christian Charlestonians.

The center of Jewish culture in Charleston is **Kahal Kadosh Beth Elohim Reform Temple** (90 Hasell St., 843/723-1090, www.kkbe.org, service Sat. 11 A.M., tours Mon.-Fri. 10 A.M.-noon, Sun. 10 A.M.-4 P.M.), birthplace of Reform Judaism in the United States and the oldest continuously active synagogue in the nation. In Savannah, the key Judaic attraction is **Temple Mickve Israel** (20 E. Gordon St., 912/233-1547, www.mickveisrael.org), the only Gothic synagogue in the country and the third-oldest Jewish congregation in North America.

household will instead take you on a guided tour of the grounds. Along the way they'll make sure to detail: (a) all the work that was done; (b) how grueling and unexpected it all was; and (c) how hard it was to get the contractors to show up. Depending on the circumstances, in the first segment, (a), you were just told either that the head of the house is made of money and has a lot more of it to spend on renovating than you do, or that they are a brilliant negotiator who got the house for a song. In part (b) you were told that you are not messing around

WALTER EDGAR'S JOURNAL

He's originally from Alabama, but you could call University of South Carolina (USC) professor Walter Edgar the modern voice of the Palmetto State. From the rich diversity of barbecue to the inner workings of the poultry business and the charms of beach music, Edgar covers the gamut of South Carolina culture and experience on his popular weekly radio show *Walter Edgar's Journal,* airing on South Carolina public radio stations throughout the state.

Currently director of the USC Institute of Southern Studies, the Vietnam vet and certified barbecue contest judge explains the show like this: "On the *Journal* we look at current events in a broader perspective, trying to provide context that is often missing in the mainstream media." More specifically, Edgar devotes each one-hour show to a single guest, usually a South Carolinian—by birth or by choice—with a unique perspective on some aspect of state culture, business, arts, or folkways. By the time the interview ends, you not only have a much deeper understanding of the topic of the show but of the interviewee as well. And because of Edgar's unique way of tying strands of his own vast knowledge and experience into every interview, you also leave with a deeper understanding of South Carolina itself.

In these days of media saturation, a public radio show might sound like a rather insignificant perch from which to influence an entire state. But remember that South Carolina is a small close-knit place, a state of Main Street towns rather than impersonal metro areas. During any given show, many listeners in Edgar's audience will know his guests on a personal basis. And by the end of the show, the rest of the listeners will feel as if they do.

Listen to "Walter Edgar's Journal" each Friday at noon on South Carolina public radio, with a repeat each Sunday at 8 P.M. Hear podcasts of previous editions at www.scetv.org.

with a lazy deadbeat here, but with someone who knows how to take care of themselves and can handle adversity with aplomb. And with part (c) you were told that the head of the house knows the best contractors in town and can pay enough for them to actually show up, and if you play your cards right, they might pass on their phone numbers to you with a personal recommendation. See? Breaking the code is easy once you get the hang of it.

Etiquette

As we've seen, it's rude here to inquire about personal finances, along with the usual no-go areas of religion and politics. Here are some other specific etiquette tips:

- **Basics:** Be liberal with "please" and "thank you," or conversely, "no thank you" if you want to decline a request or offering.

- **Eye contact:** With the exception of very elderly African Americans, eye contact is not only accepted in the South, it's encouraged. In fact, to avoid eye contact in the South means you're likely a shady character.

- **Handshake:** Men should always shake hands with a *very* firm, confident grip and appropriate eye contact. It's OK for women to offer a handshake in professional circles, but otherwise not required.

- **Chivalry:** When men open doors for women here—and they will—it is not thought of as a patronizing gesture but as a sign of respect. Accept graciously and walk through the door.

- **The elderly:** Senior citizens—or really anyone obviously older than you—should be called "sir" or "ma'am." Again, this is not a patronizing gesture in the South but is considered a sign of respect. Also, in any situation where you're dealing with someone in the service industry, addressing them as "sir" or "ma'am" regardless of their age will get you far.

- **Bodily contact:** Interestingly, though public displays of affection by romantic couples are generally frowned upon here, Southerners are otherwise pretty touchy-feely once they get to know you. Full-on body hugs are rare, but Southerners who are well acquainted often say hello or goodbye with a small hug.

• **Driving:** With the exception of the interstate perimeter highways around the larger cities, drivers in the South are generally less aggressive than in other regions. Cutting sharply in front of someone in traffic is taken as a personal offense. If you need to cut in front of someone, poke the nose of your car a little bit in that direction and wait for a car to slow down and wave you in front. Don't forget to wave back as a thank-you. Similarly, using a car horn can also be taken as a personal affront, so use your horn sparingly, if at all. In rural areas, don't be surprised to see the driver of an oncoming car offer a little wave. This is an old custom, sadly dying out. Just give a little wave back; they're trying to be friendly.

THE GUN CULTURE

One of the most misunderstood aspects of the South is the value the region places on the personal possession of firearms. No doubt, the 2nd Amendment to the U.S. Constitution ("A well regulated Militia, being necessary to the security of a free State, the right of the people to keep and bear Arms, shall not be infringed") is well known here and fiercely protected, at the governmental and at the grassroots levels. But while guns are indeed more casually accepted in everyday life in the South, the reason for this has less to do with personal safety than with the rural background of the region and its long history of hunting. If you're traveling U.S. 17, for example, from Charleston to I-95, and you see a pickup truck with a gun rack in the back containing one or more rifles or shotguns, this is not intended to be menacing or intimidating. Chances are the driver is a hunter, nothing more.

State laws do tend to be significantly more accommodating of gun owners here than in much of the rest of the country. It is legal to carry a concealed handgun in South Carolina and Georgia with the proper permit, and you need no permit at all to possess a weapon for self-defense. However, there are regulations regarding how a handgun must be conveyed in automobiles. Both states now have so-called "stand your ground" laws, whereby if you're in imminent lethal danger, you do not have to first try to run away before resorting to deadly force to defend yourself.

ESSENTIALS

Getting There and Around

AIR

The most centrally located airport for the region covered in this guide is **Savannah/Hilton Head International Airport** (SAV, 400 Airways Ave., 912/964-0514, www.savannahairport. com), directly off I-95 at exit 104, about 20 minutes from downtown Savannah, 30 minutes from Hilton Head Island, and less than two hours from Charleston. Airlines with routes to SAV include AirTran (www.airtran.com), American Eagle (www.aa.com), Continental (www.continental.com), Delta (www.delta. com), United Express (www.ual.com), and US Airways (www.airways.com).

A bit less convenient to the rest of the region because of its location well north of town is **Charleston International Airport** (CHS, 5500 International Blvd., 843/767-1100, www.chs-airport.com), served by AirTran (www.airtran.com), American Airlines (www.aa.com), Continental Airlines (www.continental.com), Delta (www.delta.com), United Airlines (www.ual.com), and US Airways (www.usairways.com).

Many travelers to the region are using

© JIM MOREKIS

Jacksonville International Airport (JAX, 2400 Yankee Clipper Dr., 904/741-4902, www.jia.com), about 20 miles north of Jacksonville, Florida. While it's a two-hour drive from Savannah, this airport's proximity to the attractions south of Savannah makes it attractive for some visitors, who can often find a good deal on airfare that makes it worth their while to make the drive.

CAR

The main interstate highway arteries into the region are the heavily traveled north–south I-95, the east–west I-26 to Charleston from Columbia, South Carolina, and the east–west I-16 to Savannah from Macon, Georgia. A common landmark road through the entire area covered by this guide is U.S. 17, which used to be known as the Coastal Highway and which currently goes by a number of local incarnations as it winds its way down the coast, roughly paralleling I-95. Charleston has a "perimeter" interstate, I-526 (the Mark Clark Expressway), while Savannah has a much smaller version, I-516 (Lynes Parkway).

Rental Car

You don't have to have a car to enjoy Charleston and Savannah, but to really explore the areas surrounding those cities you'll need your own vehicle. Renting a car is easy and fairly inexpensive, as long as you play by the rules, which are simple. You need either a valid U.S. driver's license from any state or a valid International Driving Permit from your home country, and you must be at least 25 years old.

If you do not either purchase insurance coverage from the rental company or already have insurance coverage through the credit card you rent the car with, you will be 100 percent responsible for any damage caused to the car during your rental period. While purchasing insurance at the time of rental is by no means mandatory, it might be worth the extra expense just to have that peace of mind.

Some rental car locations are in cities proper, but the vast majority of outlets are in airports, so plan accordingly. The airport locations have the bonus of generally holding longer hours than their in-town counterparts.

TRAIN

Passenger rail service in the car-dominated United States is far behind other developed nations, both in quantity and quality. Charleston and Savannah are both served by the New York–Miami *Silver Service* route of the national rail system, Amtrak (www.amtrak.com), which is pretty good, if erratic at times—although it certainly pales in comparison with European rail transit. Both cities' Amtrak stations are in light industrial parts of town, nowhere near the major tourist centers. Charleston's station is at 4565 Gaynor Street (843/744-8263), while Savannah's is at 2611 Seaboard Coastline Drive (912/234-2611).

BOAT

One of the coolest things about the Charleston and Savannah area is the prevalence of the Intracoastal Waterway, a combined artificial and natural sheltered seaway from Miami to Maine. Many boaters enjoy touring the coast by simply meandering up or down the Intracoastal, putting in at marinas along the way. There's a website for Intracoastal information at wwww.cruiseguides.com and a good resource of area marinas at www.marinamate.com.

Recreation

BEACHES

Some of the best beaches in the United States are in the region covered by this guide. While the upscale amenities aren't always there and they aren't very surfer-friendly, the area's beaches are outstanding for anyone looking for a relaxing, scenic getaway.

By law, beaches in the United States are fully accessible to the public up to the high-tide mark during daylight hours, even if the beach fronts private property and even if the only means of public access is by boat. While certain seaside resorts have over the years attempted to make the dunes in front of their property exclusive to guests, this is actually illegal, although it can be hard to enforce. On federally run National Wildlife Refuges, access is limited to daytime hours, sunrise to sunset.

It is a misdemeanor to disturb the **sea oats,** those wispy, waving, wheat-like plants among the dunes. Their root system is vital to keeping the beach intact. Also, never disturb a turtle nesting area, whether it is marked or not.

South Carolina

The barrier islands of the Palmetto State have seen more private development than their Georgia counterparts. Some Carolina islands, like Kiawah, Fripp, and Seabrook, are not even accessible unless you are a guest at their affiliated resorts, which, of course, means that the only way to visit the beaches there if you're not a guest is by boat, which I really don't advise. Charleston-area beaches include **Folly Beach, Sullivan's Island,** and **Isle of Palms.** Folly Beach has a county recreation area with parking at **Folly Beach County Park.** Isle of Palms has a county recreation area with parking at **Isle of Palms County Park.**

Moving down the coast, some delightful beaches are at **Edisto Island** and **Hunting Island,** which both feature state parks with lodging. **Hilton Head Island** has about 12 miles of beautiful family-friendly beaches, and while most of the island is devoted to private golf resorts, the beaches remain accessible to the general public at four convenient points with parking: **Driessen Beach Park, Coligny Beach Park, Alder Lane Beach Access,** and **Burkes Beach Road.**

Georgia

The main beach in Georgia is outside Savannah at **Tybee Island,** with full accessibility from end to end. The beach on the north end is smaller and quieter, while the south end is wider, windier, and more populated. There are public parking lots, but you can park at metered spots near the beach as well.

Farther south, a very good beach is at **Jekyll Island,** a largely undeveloped barrier island owned by the state. There are three picnic areas with parking: **Clam Creek, South Dunes,** and **St. Andrew.** Nearby **St. Simons Island** does have a beach area, but it is comparatively narrow and small. Adjacent **Sea Island** is accessible only if you're a guest of the Sea Island Club.

The rest of Georgia's barrier islands are only accessible by ferry, charter, or private boat. Many outfitters will take you on a tour to barrier islands such as Wassaw or Sapelo; don't be shy about inquiring. The most gorgeous beach of all is at **Cumberland Island National Seashore.**

Surfing

By far the most popular surfing area in the region is the **Washout** at Charleston's Folly Beach. The key surf shop on Folly is **McKevlin's.** For Folly surf conditions, go to www.mckevlins.com or www.surfline.com. The only other surfing of note in the area is on the south end of **Tybee Island** near the Pier and

Pavilion. The key surf shop on Tybee is **High Tide Surf Shop.** For a surf report go to www.hightidesurfshop.com.

ON THE WATER
Kayaking and Canoeing

Some key kayaking and canoeing areas in the Charleston area are **Cape Romain National Wildlife Refuge, Shem Creek, Isle of Palms, Charleston Harbor,** and the **Stono River.** The best outfitter and tour operator in the area is **Coastal Expeditions.** Farther south in the Lowcountry are the Ashepoo, Combahee, and Edisto blackwater rivers, which combine to form the **ACE Basin.** Next is **Port Royal Sound** near Beaufort; a good outfitter and tour operator in this area is **Carolina Heritage Outfitters.** The Hilton Head/Bluffton area have good kayaking opportunities at Hilton Head's **Calibogue Creek** and Bluffton's **May River.** The best outfitter and tour operator here is **Outside Hilton Head.**

The Savannah area has rich kayaking and canoeing at Tybee Island, Skidaway Island, and the blackwater Ebenezer Creek. The best local outfitter and tour operator in this area is **Savannah Canoe and Kayak.** Farther south, down the Georgia coast, the richest kayaking and canoeing area is in the **Altamaha River** estuary, a hybrid blackwater-alluvial river. Good kayaking can be found in the St. Simons Island area. The best outfitter and tour operator in the area is **SouthEast Adventures.** Kayaking to Cumberland Island is a special experience; contact **Up the Creek Xpeditions** in St. Marys.

Fishing and Boating

Because of the large number of islands and wide area of salt marsh, life on the water is largely inseparable from life on the land in the Lowcountry and Georgia coast. Fishing and boating are very common pursuits here, with species of fish including spotted sea trout, channel bass, flounder, grouper, mackerel, sailfish, whiting, shark, amberjack, and tarpon. Farther inshore you'll find largemouth bass, bream, catfish, and crappie, among many more. While entire books can be and are devoted to each, here is an overview.

It's easy to fish on piers, lakes, and streams, but if you're over age 16, you have to get a nonresident fishing license from the state. These are inexpensive and available in hardware stores, marinas, and tackle shops anywhere. In Georgia, a regular license is $9, a one-day license $3.50. A separate license is required for trout fishing. Go to http://georgiawildlife.dnr.state.ga.us for more information or to purchase a license online. In South Carolina, a nonresident seven-day license is $11. Go to www.dnr.sc.gov for more information or to purchase a license online.

The most popular places for casual anglers are the various public piers throughout the area. There are public fishing piers at Folly Beach, Hunting Island, Tybee Island, St. Simons Island, and Jekyll Island. Two nice little public docks are at the North Charleston Riverfront Park on the grounds of the old Charleston Navy Yard, and the Bluffton public landing on the May River. Many anglers cast from abandoned bridges, unless signage dictates otherwise. Fishing charters and marinas are ample throughout the region, for both inshore and offshore trips.

ON THE LAND
Golf and Tennis

The first golf club in the country was formed in Charleston, and that area has more than its share of fine courses. As far as quality is concerned, consensus pick for best course in South Carolina is definitely the Pete Dye–designed Ocean Course at the **Kiawah Island Golf Resort,** which is open to guests of the club. Coming in second would almost certainly be **Harbour Town** on Sea Pines Plantation in Hilton Head. Not coincidentally, both courses host PGA events.

In Georgia, the Ocean Forest Course at the **Sea Island Club** on Sea Island is a gem—though you must be a guest at the Club to play—as is the affiliated Seaside Course. For value, go in the off-season, in the colder months, when prices are lowest. Not all courses close, and most are in great shape because of the reduced traffic.

The premier tennis facility in the Charleston area is the new **Family Circle Cup Tennis Center** on Daniel Island, home of the eponymous women's event and some great public courts. Other key tennis facilities are at the **King and Prince** on St. Simons and **Jekyll Island Tennis Center.**

Hiking and Biking

Due to the flat nature of the Lowcountry and Georgia coast, hiking and biking here is not very strenuous. However, the great natural beauty and prevalence of a rich range of plant and animal life make hiking and biking very rewarding experiences. Probably the best trails can be found at state parks in the region, such as **Edisto Island State Park, Hunting Island State Park,** and **Skidaway Island State Park.** Many National Wildlife Refuges (NWRs) in the area also feature excellent trails, such as **Pinckney Island NWR, Harris Neck NWR,** and **Cape Romain NWR.**

There are a couple of "rails to trails" projects that might appeal: the **James Island Trail** outside Charleston and the **McQueen Island Trail** on the way to Tybee Island outside Savannah. Some areas are almost defined by the plethora of bike and pedestrian trails running nearly their entire length and breadth, such as Jekyll Island and Hilton Head Island.

Wide beaches, very conducive to biking on the sand, are one of the great pleasures of this area. Most bikes you rent in the area will have fat enough tires to do the job correctly. The best beach rides are on Sullivan's Island, Hilton Head Island, Jekyll Island, St. Simons Island, Cumberland Island, and Tybee Island.

Tips for Travelers

TRAVELING WITH CHILDREN

The Lowcountry and Georgia coast are very kid-friendly, with the possible exception of some B&Bs that are clearly not designed for younger children. If you have any doubts about this, feel free to inquire. Otherwise, there are no special precautions unique to this area. There are no zoos per se in the area, but animal lovers of all ages will enjoy **Charles Towne Landing** in Charleston and **Oatland Island Wildlife Center** in Savannah. Better still, take the kids on nature outings to the amazing National Wildlife Refuges in the area.

WOMEN TRAVELING ALONE

Women should take the same precautions they would take anywhere else. Many women traveling to this region have to adjust to the prevalence of traditional chivalry. In the South, if a man opens a door for you, it's considered a sign of respect, not condescension. Another adjustment is the possible assumption that two or three women who go to a bar or tavern together might be there to invite male companionship. This misunderstanding can happen anywhere, but in some parts of the South it might be slightly more prevalent. Being aware of it is the best defense; otherwise no other steps need to be taken.

ACCESS FOR TRAVELERS WITH DISABILITIES

While the vast majority of attractions and accommodations make every effort to comply with federal law regarding those with disabilities, as they're obliged to do, the very historic nature of this region means that some structures simply cannot be retrofitted for maximum accessibility. This is something you'll need to find out on a case-by-case basis, so call ahead. The sites administered by the National Park Service in this guide (Charles Pinckney National Historic Site, Fort Sumter, Fort Moultrie, Fort Pulaski, Fort Frederica, and Cumberland Island National Seashore) are as wheelchair-accessible as possible.

Some special shuttles are available. In Charleston, call the "Tel-A-Ride" service (843/724-7420). A couple of cab companies in town to check out are **Express Cab Company** (843/577-8816) and **Flag A Cab** (842/554-1231). In Savannah, Chatham Area Transit (www.catchacat.org) runs a Teleride service (912/354-6900). For the visually impaired, in Charleston there's the **Association for the Blind** (1071 Morrison Dr., 843/723-6915, www.afb.org) and in Savannah the **Savannah Association for the Blind** (214 Drayton St., 912/236-4473). Hearing disadvantaged individuals can get assistance in Charleston at the Charleston Speech and Hearing Center (843/552-1212).

GAY AND LESBIAN TRAVELERS

Don't believe all the negative propaganda about the South. The truth is that the metropolitan areas of Charleston, Beaufort, and Savannah are tolerant, and gay and lesbian travelers shouldn't expect anything untoward to happen. Outside the metro areas, locals are less welcoming to gay men and lesbian women, although overt hostility is rare. The best approach is to simply observe dominant Southern mores for anyone, gay or straight. In a nutshell, that means keep public displays of affection and politics to a minimum. Southerners in general have a low opinion of anyone who flagrantly espouses a viewpoint too obviously or loudly.

SENIOR TRAVELERS

Both because of the large proportion of retirees in the region and because of Southerners' traditional respect for the elderly, the area is quite friendly to senior citizens. Many accommodations and attractions offer a slight senior discount, which can add up over the course of a trip. Always inquire before making a reservation, however, as checkout time is too late.

TRAVELING WITH PETS

While the United States is very pet-friendly, that friendliness rarely extends to restaurants and other indoor locations. More and more accommodations are allowing pet owners to bring pets, often for an added fee, but inquire before you arrive. In any case, keep your dog on a leash at all times. Some beaches in the area permit dog-walking at certain times of the year, but as a general rule, keep dogs off of beaches unless you see signage saying otherwise.

Health and Safety

CRIME

While crime rates are indeed above national averages in many of the areas covered in this guide, especially in inner city areas, incidents of crime in the more heavily trafficked tourist areas are no more common than anywhere else. In fact, these areas might be safer because of the amount of foot traffic and police attention.

By far the most common crime against visitors here is simple theft, primarily from cars. (Pickpocketing, thankfully, is rare in the United States.) Always lock your car doors. Conversely, only leave them unlocked if you're absolutely comfortable living without whatever's inside at the time. As a general rule, I try to lock valuables—such as CDs, a recent purchase, or my wife's purse—in the trunk. (Just make sure the "valet" button, allowing the trunk to be opened from the driver's area, is disabled.)

Should someone corner you and demand your wallet or purse, just give it to them. Unfortunately, the old advice to scream as loud as you can is no longer the deterrent it once was, and in fact may hasten aggressive action by the robber.

If you are the victim of a crime, *always call the police.* Law enforcement wants more information, not less, and at very least you'll have an incident report in case you need to make an insurance claim for lost or stolen property.

Remember that in the United States, as elsewhere, no good can come from a heated argument with a police officer. The place to prove a police officer wrong is in a court of law, perhaps with an attorney by your side, not at the scene.

For emergencies, always call 911.

AUTO ACCIDENTS

If you're in an auto accident, you're bound by law to wait for police to respond. Failure to do so can result in a "leaving the scene of an accident" charge, or worse. In the old days, cars in accidents had to be left exactly where they came to rest until police gave permission to move or tow them. However, South Carolina and Georgia have recently loosened regulations so that if a car is blocking traffic as a result of an accident, the driver is allowed to move it enough to allow traffic to flow again. That is, if the car can be moved safely. If not, you're not required to move it out of the way.

Since it's illegal to drive in these states without auto insurance, I'll assume you have some. And because you're insured, the best course of action in a minor accident, where injuries are unlikely, is to patiently wait for the police and give them your side of the story. In my experience, police react negatively to people who are too quick to start making accusations against other people. After that, let the insurance companies deal with it; that's what they're there for. If you suspect any injuries, call 911 immediately.

ILLEGAL DRUGS

Marijuana, heroin, methamphetamine, and cocaine and all its derivatives are illegal in the United States with only a very few select exceptions, none of which apply to the areas covered by this guide. The use of ecstasy and similar mood-elevators is also illegal. The penalties for illegal drug possession and use in South Carolina and Georgia are quite severe.

ALCOHOL

The drinking age in the United States is 21. Most restaurants that serve alcoholic beverages allow those under 21 inside. Generally speaking, if only those over 21 are allowed inside, you will be greeted at the door by someone asking to see identification. These people are often poorly trained and anything other than a state driver's license may confuse them, so be forewarned.

Drunk driving is a problem on the highways of the United States, and South Carolina and Georgia are no exceptions. Always drive defensively, especially late at night, and obey all posted speed limits and road signs—and never assume the other driver will do the same. You may never drive with an open alcoholic beverage in the car, even if it belongs to a passenger.

As far as retail purchase goes, in South Carolina you may only buy beer and wine, not hard liquor, on Sundays. In most parts of Georgia, no alcoholic beverages are sold at the retail level on Sundays, other than in restaurants that also sell food.

MEDICAL SERVICES

Unlike most developed nations, the United States has no comprehensive national health care system (although there are programs for the elderly and the poor). Indeed, the mere proposal of it seems quite polarizing. Visitors from other countries who need nonemergency medical attention are best served by going to freestanding medical clinics. The level of care is typically very good, but unfortunately you'll be paying out of pocket for the service. For emergencies, however, do not hesitate to go to the closest hospital emergency room, where the level of care is generally also quite good, especially for trauma. Worry about payment later; emergency rooms in the United States are required to take true emergency cases whether or not the patient can pay for services. Call 911 for ambulance service.

Pharmaceuticals

Unlike many other nations, antibiotics are available in the United States only on a prescription basis and are not available over the counter. Most cold, flu, and allergy remedies are available over the counter. While homeopathic remedies are gaining popularity in the United States, they are nowhere near as prevalent as in Europe.

Drugs with the active ingredient ephedrine are available in the United States without a prescription, but their purchase is tightly regulated to cut down on the use of these products to make the illegal drug methamphetamine.

STAYING HEALTHY
Vaccinations

As of this writing, there are no vaccination requirements to enter the United States. Contact your embassy before coming to confirm this before arrival, however. In the autumn, at the beginning of flu season, preventive influenza vaccinations, simply called "flu shots," often become available at easily accessible locations like clinics, health departments, and even supermarkets.

Humidity, Heat, and Sun

There is only one way to fight the South's high heat and humidity, and that's to drink lots of fluids. A surprising number of people each year refuse to take this advice and find themselves in various states of dehydration, some of which can land you in a hospital. Remember: If you're thirsty, you're already suffering from dehydration. The thing to do is keep drinking fluids *before* you're thirsty as a preventative action rather than a reaction.

Always use sunscreen, even on a cloudy day. If you do get a sunburn, get a pain-relief product with aloe vera as an active ingredient. On extraordinarily sunny and hot summer days, don't even go outside between the hours of 10 A.M. and 2 P.M.

HAZARDS
Insects

Because of the recent increase in the mosquito-borne West Nile virus, the most important step to take in staying healthy in the Lowcountry and Georgia coast—especially if you have small children—is to keep mosquito bites to a minimum. Do this with a combination of mosquito repellent and long sleeves and long pants, if possible. Not every mosquito bite will give you the virus; in fact, chances are quite slim that one will. But don't take the chance if you don't have to.

The second major step in avoiding insect nastiness is to steer clear of **fire ants,** whose large gray or brown-dirt nests are quite common in this area. They attack instantly and in great numbers, with little or no provocation. They don't just bite; they inject you with poison from their stingers. In short, fire ants are not to be trifled with. While the only real remedy is the preventative one of never coming in contact with them, should you find yourself being bitten by fire ants, the first thing to do is to stay calm. Take off your shoes and socks and get as many of the ants off you as you can. Unless you've had a truly large number of bites—in which case you should seek medical help immediately— the best thing to do next is wash the area to get any venom off, and then disinfect with alcohol if you have any handy. Then a topical treatment such as calamine lotion or hydrocortisone is advised. A fire ant bite will leave a red pustule that lasts about a week. Try your best not to scratch it so that it won't get infected.

Outdoor activity, especially in woodsy, undeveloped areas, may bring you in contact with another unpleasant indigenous creature, the tiny but obnoxious **chigger,** sometimes called the redbug. The bite of a chigger can't be felt, but the enzymes it leaves behind can lead to a very itchy little red spot. Contrary to folklore, putting fingernail polish on the itchy bite will not "suffocate" the chigger, because by this point the chigger itself is long gone. All you can do is get some topical itch or pain relief and go on with your life. The itching will eventually subside.

Threats in the Water

While enjoying area beaches, a lot of visitors become inordinately worried about **shark attacks.** Every couple of summers there's a lot of hysteria about this, but the truth is that you're much more likely to slip and fall in a bathroom than you are even to come close to being bitten by a shark in these shallow Atlantic waters.

A far more common fate for area swimmers is to get stung by a **jellyfish,** or sea nettle. They can sting you in the water, but most often beachcombers are stung by stepping on beached jellyfish stranded on the sand by the tide. If you get stung, don't panic; wash the area with saltwater, not freshwater, and apply vinegar or baking soda. A product called Jellyfish Squish is also available and seems to work well.

Lightning

The southeastern United States is home to vicious, fast-moving thunderstorms, often with an amazing amount of electrical activity. Death by lightning strike occurs often in this region and is something that should be taken quite seriously. The general rule of thumb is that if you're in the water, whether at the beach or in a swimming pool, and hear thunder, get out of the water immediately until the storm passes. If you're on dry land and see lightning flash a distance away, that's your cue to seek safety indoors. Whatever you do, do not play sports outside when lightning threatens.

Information and Services

VISITOR INFORMATION
Charleston

The main visitors center is the **Charleston Visitor Reception and Transportation Center** (375 Meeting St., 800/774-0006, www.charlestoncvb.com, Mon.–Fri. 8:30 A.M.–5 P.M.). Outlying visitors centers are the **Mt. Pleasant-Isle of Palms Visitor Center** (Johnnie Dodds Blvd., 843/853-8000, 9 A.M.–5:30 P.M.), and the **North Charleston Visitor Center** (4975-B Centre Pointe Dr., 843/853-8000, Mon.–Sat. 10 A.M.–5 P.M.).

Beaufort and the Lowcountry

The Beaufort **Visitors Information Center** is within the Beaufort Arsenal building (713 Craven St., 843/986-5400, www.beaufortsc.org, daily 9 A.M.–5:30 P.M.). In Hilton Head, get information, book a room, or secure a tee time just as you come onto the island at the **Hilton Head Island Chamber of Commerce Welcome Center** (100 William Hilton Pkwy., 843/785-3673, www.hiltonheadisland.org, daily 9 A.M.–6 P.M.), in the same building as the Coastal Discovery Museum. You'll find Bluffton's visitors center in the **Heyward House Historic Center** (70 Boundary St., 843/757-6293, www.heywardhouse.org, Mon.–Fri. 10 A.M.–3 P.M., Sat. 11 A.M.–2 P.M.).

Savannah

The main place for visitor information in Savannah is the downtown **Savannah Visitors Center** (301 MLK Jr. Blvd., 912/944-0455, Mon.–Fri. 8:30 A.M.–5 P.M., Sat.–Sun. and holidays 9 A.M.–5 P.M.). The **Savannah Convention and Visitors Bureau** (101 E. Bay St., 877/728-2662, www.savcvb.com, Mon.–Fri. 8:30 A.M.–5 P.M.) keeps an up-to-date list of lodgings at its website. Other visitors centers in the area include the **River Street Hospitality Center** (1 River St., 912/651-6662, daily 10 A.M.–10 P.M.), the **Tybee Island Visitor Center** (S. Campbell Ave. and U.S. 80, 912/786-5444, daily 9 A.M.–5:30 P.M.) and the **Savannah Airport Visitor Center** (464 Airways Ave., 912/964-1109, daily 10 A.M.–6 P.M.).

The Golden Isles

The **Brunswick-Golden Isles Visitor Center** (2000 Glynn Ave., 912/264-5337, daily 9 A.M.–5 P.M.) is at the intersection of U.S. 17 and the Torras Causeway to St. Simons Island. A downtown information station is in Old City Hall, at the corner of Mansfield and Newcastle Streets (912/262-6934, daily 8 A.M.–5 P.M.).

The **Jekyll Island Visitor Center** (901 Downing Musgrove Causeway, 912/635-3636, daily 9 A.M.–5 P.M.) is before you get to the island, on the long causeway along the marsh. The **St. Simons Visitor Center** (530-B Beachview Dr., 912/638-9014, www.bgivb.com, daily 9 A.M.–5 P.M.) is in the St. Simons Casino Building near Neptune Park and the Village.

The **Darien Welcome Center** is at the corner of U.S. 17 and Fort King George Drive (912/437-6684, Mon.–Sat. 9 A.M.–5 P.M.). The **Sapelo Island Visitors Center** (912/437-3224, www.sapelonerr.org, Tues.–Fri. 7:30 A.M.–5:30 P.M., Sat. 8 A.M.–5:30 P.M., Sun. 1:30–5 P.M.) is actually not on Sapelo but at the dock where you take the ferry, in Meridian, Georgia, on Highway 99 from Darien.

The **St. Marys Visitor Center** is located at 406 Osborne Street (912/882-4000, www.stmaryswelcome.com, Mon.–Sat. 9 A.M.–5 P.M., Sun. noon–5 P.M.). **Cumberland Island Visitors Center** is at 113 St. Marys Street (912/882-4336, daily 8 A.M.–6 P.M.).

There are several entrances to the Okefenokee Swamp, with the closest thing to a visitors center being at the U.S. Fish and Wildlife Service's **Richard S. Bolt Visitor Center** (912/496-7836, daily 9 A.M.–5 P.M.) at the eastern entrance near Folkston, Georgia.

MONEY

Automated Teller Machines (ATMs) are available in all urban areas covered in this guide. Be aware that if the ATM is not owned by your bank, not only will that ATM likely charge you a service fee, but your bank may charge you one as well. While ATMs have made traveler's checks less essential, traveler's checks do have the important advantage of accessibility, as some rural and less-developed areas covered in this guide have few or no ATMs. You can purchase traveler's checks at just about any bank.

Establishments in the United States only accept the national currency, the U.S. dollar. To exchange foreign money, go to any bank.

Generally, establishments that accept credit cards will feature stickers on the front entrance with the logo of the particular cards they accept, although this is not a legal requirement. The use of debit cards has dramatically increased in the United States. Most retail establishments and many fast-food chains are now accepting them. Make sure you get a receipt whenever you use a credit card or a debit card.

MEDIA AND COMMUNICATIONS
Newspapers

The closest thing to a national newspaper in the United States is *USA Today,* which you will find at diverse locations from airports to gas stations. The national paper of record is the *New York Times,* which is available in larger urban areas but only rarely in outlying areas.

In Charleston, the paper of record is the *Post and Courier* (www.charleston.net). Its entertainment insert, "Preview," comes out on Thursdays. The free alternative weekly is

the decade-old *Charleston City Paper* (www.charlestoncitypaper.com), which comes out on Wednesdays and is the best place to find local music and arts listings. A particularly well-done and lively metro glossy is *Charleston* magazine (www.charlestonmag.com), which comes out once a month.

In Beaufort, the daily newspaper of record is the *Beaufort Gazette* (www.beaufortgazette.com). An alternative weekly focusing mostly on the arts is *Lowcountry Weekly* (www.lcweekly.com). Hilton Head's paper of record is the *Island Packet* (www.islandpacket.com). A good Bluffton publication is *Bluffton Today* (www.blufftontoday.com).

In Savannah, the daily newspaper of record is the *Savannah Morning News* (912/525-0796, www.savannahnow.com). It puts out an entertainment insert on Thursdays called "Do." The independent free weekly newspaper in town is *Connect Savannah* (912/721-4350, www.connectsavannah.com), hitting stands each Wednesday.

The main paper in the much more sparsely populated Golden Isles region is the *Brunswick News* (www.thebrunswicknews.com), but many people read the newspaper of record of nearby Jacksonville, Florida, the *Florida Times-Union* (www.jacksonville.com).

Internet Access

Visitors from Europe and Asia are likely to be disappointed at the quality of Internet access in the United States, particularly the area covered in this guide. Fiber-optic lines are still a rarity, and while many hotels and B&Bs now offer in-room Internet access—some charge, some don't, make sure to ask ahead—the quality and speed of the connection might prove poor. Wireless (Wi-Fi) networks are also less than impressive, but that situation continues to improve on a daily basis in coffeehouses, hotels, and airports. Unfortunately, many hotspots in private establishments charge fees. Charleston does have a municipal free Wi-Fi network, however. While Savannah does not yet have a citywide Wi-Fi network, you can get a list of free Savannah Wi-Fi hotspots at www.thecreativecoast.org/datainfo/hotspots.

Phones

Generally speaking, the United States is behind Europe and much of Asia in terms of cell phone technology. Unlike Europe, where "pay as you go" refills are easy to find, most American cell phone users pay for monthly plans through a handful of providers. Still, you should have no problem with cell phone coverage in urban areas.

Where it gets much less dependable is in rural areas and on beaches. Bottom line: don't depend on having cell service everywhere you go.

As with a regular landline, any time you face an emergency, call 911 on your cell phone.

All phone numbers in the United States are seven digits preceded by a three-digit area code. You may have to dial "1" before a phone number if it's a long-distance call, even within the same area code. The area code for the part of South Carolina covered in this guide is 843. The area code for the part of Georgia covered in this guide is 912.

RESOURCES

Suggested Reading

NONFICTION
Georgia

Calonius, Erik. *The Wanderer: Last American Slave Ship and the Conspiracy That Set Its Sails.* New York: St. Martin's Press, 2006. A page-turning tale of the last illegal slave shipment to land in the United States, on Jekyll Island, Georgia.

Fraser, Walter J. Jr. *Savannah in the Old South.* Athens, GA: University of Georgia Press, 2005. An insightful and balanced history of Georgia's first city, from founding through Reconstruction.

Georgia Writers Project. *Drums and Shadows: Survival Studies Among the Georgia Coastal Negroes.* Athens, GA: University of Georgia Press, 1986. Arising from a government-funded research project during the Depression, this still ranks as one of the best oral histories ever assembled, using firsthand accounts from African American residents of Georgia's Sea Islands to paint a picture of a lifestyle gone by.

Greene, Melissa Fay. *Praying for Sheetrock.* New York: Ballantine, 1992. In this modern classic, Greene explores the racism and corruption endemic in McIntosh County, Georgia, during the era of the civil rights movement.

Kemble, Fanny. *Journal of a Residence on a Georgian Plantation in 1838–1839.* Athens, GA: University of Georgia Press, 1984. A famed English actress's groundbreaking anti-slavery account of her stay on a rice plantation in McIntosh County, Georgia.

Morgan, Philip, ed. *African American Life in the Georgia Lowcountry: The Atlantic World and the Gullah Geechee.* Athens, GA: University of Georgia Press, 2010. The best book I've come by on the history and folkways of Georgia's Gullah or Geechee people. Balanced, scholarly, yet still readable in the extreme.

Seabrook, Charles. *Cumberland Island: Strong Women, Wild Horses.* Winston-Salem, NC: John F. Blair, 2002. An even-handed journalistic look inside the tension between environmentalists and the residents of Cumberland Island.

Wood, Betty, ed. *Mary Telfair to Mary Few: Selected Letters, 1802–1844.* Athens, GA: University of Georgia Press, 2007. The revealing, chatty letters of a great arts patron and member of a major Savannah slave-owning family, to her best friend who left the city and moved North because of her abolitionist leanings. We know that Mary Few replied, but her letters remain undiscovered.

South Carolina

Fraser Jr., Walter J. *Charleston! Charleston! The History of a Southern City.* Columbia, SC: University of South Carolina Press, 1991. Another typically well-written and balanced tome by this important regional historian.

Gessler, Diana Hollingsworth. *Very Charleston: A Celebration of History, Culture, and Lowcountry Charm.* Chapel Hill, NC: Algonquin Books, 2003. A quick, visually appealing insider's perspective with some wonderfully whimsical cartoon-style illustrations.

Klein, Maury. *Days of Defiance: Sumter, Secession, and the Coming of the Civil War.* New York: Vintage, 1999. A gripping and vivid account of the lead-up to war, with Charleston as the focal point.

Rogers, George C. Jr. *Charleston in the Age of the Pinckneys.* Columbia, SC: University of South Carolina Press, 1980. This 1969 history is a classic of the genre.

Rosen, Robert. *A Short History of Charleston.* Columbia, SC: University of South Carolina Press, 1997. Quite simply the most concise, readable, and entertaining history of the Holy City I've found.

Woodward, C. Vann, ed. *Mary Chesnut's Civil War.* New Haven, CT: Yale University Press, 1981. The Pulitzer Prize–winning classic compilation of the sardonic and quietly heartbreaking letters of Charleston's Mary Chesnut during the Civil War.

General Background

Aberjhani and Sandra West. *Encyclopedia of the Harlem Renaissance.* New York: Checkmark Books, 2003. A brilliantly researched account of the great African American diaspora out of the South that eventually gave birth to the Charleston dance craze of the 1920s.

Lewis, Lloyd. *Sherman: Fighting Prophet.* Lincoln, NE: University of Nebraska Press, 1993. Though first published in 1932, this remains the most thorough, insightful, and well-written biography of General William Sherman in existence.

Robinson, Sally Ann. *Gullah Home Cooking the Daufuskie Island Way.* Chapel Hill, NC: University of North Carolina Press, 2007. Subtitled "Smokin' Joe Butter Beans, Ol' 'Fuskie Fried Crab Rice, Sticky-Bush Blackberry Dumpling, and Other Sea Island Favorites," this cookbook by a native Daufuskie Islander features a foreword by Pat Conroy.

Stehling, Robert. *Hominy Grill Recipes.* Charleston, SC: Big Cartel, 2009. This humble, hand-illustrated, self-published little tome features 23 great recipes from one of Charleston's most respected Southern cooking joints, Hominy Grill on Rutledge Avenue. At only $12.95, one of the best cookbooks for the value you'll find.

FICTION

Berendt, John. *Midnight in the Garden of Good and Evil.* New York: Vintage, 1999. Well, not exactly fiction, but far from completely true, nonetheless this modern classic definitely reads like a novel while remaining one of the unique and readable travelogues of recent times.

Conroy, Pat. *The Lords of Discipline.* New York: Bantam, 1985. For all practical purposes set at the Citadel, this novel takes you behind the scenes of the notoriously insular Charleston military college.

Conroy, Pat. *The Water is Wide.* New York: Bantam, 1987. Immortal account of Conroy's time teaching African American children in a two-room schoolhouse on "Yamacraw" (actually Daufuskie) Island.

Hervey, Harry. *The Damned Don't Cry*. Marietta, GA: Cherokee Publishing, 2003. The original *Midnight*, this bawdy 1939 potboiler takes you into the streets, shanties, drawing rooms, and boudoirs of real Savannahians during the Depression.

O'Connor, Flannery. *Flannery O'Connor: Collected Works*. New York: Library of America, 1988. For a look into Savannah's conflicted, paradoxical soul, read anything by this native-born writer, so grounded in tradition yet so ahead of her time even to this day. This volume includes selected letters, an especially valuable (and entertaining) insight.

Internet Resources

RECREATION

South Carolina Department of Natural Resources
www.dnr.sc.gov
More than just a compendium of license and fee information—though there's certainly plenty of that—this site features a lot of practical advice on how best to enjoy South Carolina's great outdoors, whether you're an angler, a kayaker, a bird-watcher, a hiker, or a biker.

Georgia Department of Natural Resources
www.gadnr.org
Ditto for this site, which has lots of great information on the wildlife and geology of Georgia's beautiful and largely undeveloped barrier islands.

Savannah Bicycle Campaign
www.bicyclecampaign.org
The clearinghouse for routes and rides by Savannah's most dedicated cyclists.

Georgia State Parks
www.gastateparks.org
Vital historical and visitor information for Georgia's underrated network of historical state park sites along the coast, including camping reservations.

South Carolina State Parks
www.southcarolinaparks.com
Ditto for this site all about South Carolina's state parks.

Dozier's Waterway Guide
www.waterwayguide.com
A serious boater's guide to stops on the Intracoastal Waterway, with a lot of solid navigational information.

NATURE AND ENVIRONMENT

Go Green Charleston
www.gogreencharleston.org
The latest environmental and sustainable living news in Charleston, with a lot of practical and fun visitor information and links.

Ocean Science
http://oceanscience.wordpress.com
A blog by the staff of Savannah's Skidaway Institute of Oceanography, focusing on barrier island ecology and the maritime environment.

CUISINE AND ENTERTAINMENT

Savannah Foodie
www.savannahfoodie.com
An insider's look at the Savannah restaurant scene, with an emphasis on breaking news.

Charleston City Paper blogs
http://ccpblogs.com
The collected staff blogs of the Charleston City Paper, dealing with the latest foodie news in town and entertainment options.

HISTORY AND BACKGROUND
South Carolina Information Highway
www.sciway.net
An eclectic cornucopia of interesting South Carolina history and assorted background facts, which makes for an interesting Internet portal into all things Palmetto State.

New Georgia Encyclopedia
www.georgiaencyclopedia.org
A mother lode of concise, neutral, and well-written information on the natural and human history of Georgia from prehistory to the present.

Charleston Wiki Project
www.charlestonwiki.org
A Wikipedia just for Charleston, with a residents' point of view.

TOURISM INFORMATION
Charleston Convention and Visitors Bureau
www.charlestoncvb.com
This very professional and user-friendly tourism site is perhaps the best and most practical Internet portal for visitors to Charleston.

Index

List of Maps

www.moon.com

DESTINATIONS | ACTIVITIES | BLOGS | MAPS | BOOKS

MOON.COM is ready to help plan your next trip! Filled with fresh trip ideas and strategies, author interviews, informative travel blogs, a detailed map library, and descriptions of all the Moon guidebooks, Moon.com is all you need to get out and explore the world—or even places in your own backyard. While at Moon.com, sign up for our monthly e-newsletter for updates on new releases, travel tips, and expert advice from our on-the-go Moon authors. As always, when you travel with Moon, expect an experience that is uncommon and truly unique.

KEEP UP WITH MOON ON FACEBOOK AND TWITTER
JOIN THE MOON PHOTO GROUP ON FLICKR

MAP SYMBOLS

▭▭▭ Expressway	🅒 Highlight	✗ Airfield	⚲ Golf Course
▭▭▭ Primary Road	○ City/Town	✈ Airport	🅿 Parking Area
▭▭▭ Secondary Road	◉ State Capital	▲ Mountain	⬗ Archaeological Site
▭▭▭ Unpaved Road	⊛ National Capital	✛ Unique Natural Feature	⸸ Church
------- Trail	★ Point of Interest		
·········· Ferry	• Accommodation	🆈 Waterfall	🅖 Gas Station
⬤—⬤ Railroad	▼ Restaurant/Bar	▲ Park	◌ Glacier
▭▭▭ Pedestrian Walkway	■ Other Location	🅣 Trailhead	Mangrove
‖‖‖‖ Stairs	Λ Campground	🎿 Skiing Area	Reef
			Swamp

CONVERSION TABLES

°C = (°F - 32) / 1.8
°F = (°C x 1.8) + 32
1 inch = 2.54 centimeters (cm)
1 foot = 0.304 meters (m)
1 yard = 0.914 meters
1 mile = 1.6093 kilometers (km)
1 km = 0.6214 miles
1 fathom = 1.8288 m
1 chain = 20.1168 m
1 furlong = 201.168 m
1 acre = 0.4047 hectares
1 sq km = 100 hectares
1 sq mile = 2.59 square km
1 ounce = 28.35 grams
1 pound = 0.4536 kilograms
1 short ton = 0.90718 metric ton
1 short ton = 2,000 pounds
1 long ton = 1.016 metric tons
1 long ton = 2,240 pounds
1 metric ton = 1,000 kilograms
1 quart = 0.94635 liters
1 US gallon = 3.7854 liters
1 Imperial gallon = 4.5459 liters
1 nautical mile = 1.852 km

°FAHRENHEIT | °CELSIUS

WATER BOILS — 100°C / 212°F
WATER FREEZES — 0°C / 32°F

INCH 0 1 2 3 4

CM 0 1 2 3 4 5 6 7 8 9 10

MOON CHARLESTON & SAVANNAH

Avalon Travel
a member of the Perseus Books Group
1700 Fourth Street
Berkeley, CA 94710, USA
www.moon.com

Editor and Series Manager: Kathryn Ettinger
Copy Editor: Christopher Church
Graphics Coordinator: Tabitha Lahr
Production Coordinator: Lucie Ericksen
Cover Designer: Tabitha Lahr
Map Editor: Kat Bennett
Cartographers: June Thammasnong,
   Chris Henrick
Indexer: Greg Jewett

ISBN-13: 978-1-61238-344-6
ISSN: 1539-1027

Printing History
1st Edition – 2002
5th Edition – September 2012
5 4 3 2 1

Front cover photo: Drayton Hall, Charleston © Walter
   Bibikow/Getty Images

Title page photo: the grand live oaks of Wormsloe
   State Historic Site, Savannah © Jim Morekis
Interior color photos: page 4: © daveallenphoto/123rf.
   com; page 5: © dndavis/123rf.com; pages 6 (inset),
   7 top-left, top-right, and bottom-right, 10-13, 14
   right, 15-19, 21-24 : © Jim Morekis; pages 6 bottom,
   14 left: © Sophia Morekis; page 7 bottom-left: ©
   isame/123rf.com; page 8: © dndavis/123rf.com; page
   20: © William Manning/123rf.com

Printed in Canada by Friesens

KEEPING CURRENT

If you have a favorite gem you'd like to see included in the next edition, or see anything
that needs updating, clarification, or correction, please drop us a line. Send your com-
ments via email to feedback@moon.com, or use the address above.